"PHP and MySQL are two of today's most popular web development technologies, and this book shows readers why. Building a site without them is now as unthinkable as doing web design without CSS. This book is a great introduction and is laugh-out-loud funny. It's the book I wish I had learned from."

— **Harvey Quamen, Associate Professor of English and Humanities Computing, University of Alberta**

"Everything we've come to accept about the drudgery of technical learning has been abandoned and in its place an unusually fun method for learning is created. I have full confidence that the Head First series will revolutionize the technical publishing industry, and that these new methods will be the eventual standard. I bet my tech-phobic grandmother could pick up PHP and MySQL techniques after a single reading. She'd probably even have a good time doing it!"

— **Will Harris, Database Administrator, Powered By Geek**

"Reading Head First PHP & MySQL is like taking a class from the 'cool' teacher. It makes you look forward to learning."

— **Stephanie Liese, Web Developer**

"Using images and humor the book is easy to digest and yet delivers real technical know-how."

— **Jereme Allen, Web Developer**

"After a challenging, high-speed read-through and lots of quirky "Do This" projects, such as "My dog was abducted by aliens" and the "Mismatch Dating Agency," I can't wait to add some real PHP power to my web sites."

— **David Briggs, Software Engineer and Technical Author**

Praise for *Head First* HTML with CSS & XHTML

"Eric and Elisabeth Freeman clearly know their stuff. As the Internet becomes more complex, inspired construction of web pages becomes increasingly critical. Elegant design is at the core of every chapter here, each concept conveyed with equal doses of pragmatism and wit."

> **— Ken Goldstein, Executive Vice President & Managing Director, Disney Online**

"The Web would be a much better place if every HTML author started off by reading this book."

> **— L. David Baron, Technical Lead, Layout & CSS, Mozilla Corporation,**
> *http://dbaron.org/*

"I've been writing HTML and CSS for ten years now, and what used to be a long trial and error learning process has now been reduced neatly into an engaging paperback. HTML used to be something you could just hack away at until things looked okay on screen, but with the advent of web standards and the movement towards accessibility, sloppy coding practice is not acceptable anymore... from a business standpoint or a social responsibility standpoint. *Head First HTML with CSS & XHTML* teaches you how to do things right from the beginning without making the whole process seem overwhelming. HTML, when properly explained, is no more complicated than plain English, and the Freemans do an excellent job of keeping every concept at eye-level."

> **— Mike Davidson, President & CEO, Newsvine, Inc.**

"Oh, great. You made an XHTML book simple enough a CEO can understand it. What will you do next? Accounting simple enough my developer can understand it? Next thing you know we'll be collaborating as a team or something."

> **—Janice Fraser, CEO, Adaptive Path**

"This book has humor, and charm, but most importantly, it has heart. I know that sounds ridiculous to say about a technical book, but I really sense that at its core, this book (or at least its authors) really care that the reader learn the material. This comes across in the style, the language, and the techniques. Learning – real understanding and comprehension – on the part of the reader is clearly top most in the minds of the Freemans. And thank you, thank you, thank you, for the book's strong, and sensible advocacy of standards compliance. It's great to see an entry level book, that I think will be widely read and studied, campaign so eloquently and persuasively on behalf of the value of standards compliance in web page code. I even found in here a few great arguments I had not thought of – ones I can remember and use when I am asked – as I still am – 'what's the deal with compliance and why should we care?' I'll have more ammo now! I also liked that the book sprinkles in some basics about the mechanics of actually getting a web page live - FTP, web server basics, file structures, etc."

> **—Robert Neer, Director of Product Development, Movies.com**

"So practical and useful, and so well explained. This book does a great job of introducing a complete newbie to JavaScript, and it's another testament to Head First's teaching style. Out of the other JavaScript books, *Head First JavaScript* is great for learning, compared to other reference books the size of a phone book."

> — **Alex Lee, Student, University of Houston**

"An excellent choice for the beginning JavaScript developer."

> — **Fletcher Moore, Web Developer & Designer, Georgia Institute of Technology**

"Yet another great book in the classic 'Head First' style."

> — **TW Scannell**

"JavaScript has long been the client-side engine that drives pages on the Web, but it has also long been misunderstood and misused. With *Head First JavaScript*, Michael Morrison gives a straightforward and easy-to-understand introduction of this language, removing any misunderstanding that ever existed and showing how to most effectively use it to enhance your web pages."

> — **Anthony T. Holdener III, Web applications developer, and the author of *Ajax: The Definitive Guide*.**

"A web page has three parts—content (HTML), appearance (CSS), and behaviour (JavaScript). *Head First HTML* introduced the first two, and this book uses the same fun but practical approach to introduce JavaScript. The fun way in which this book introduces JavaScript and the many ways in which it reinforces the information so that you will not forget it makes this a perfect book for beginners to use to start them on the road to making their web pages interactive."

> — **Stephen Chapman, Owner Felgall Pty Ltd., JavaScript editor, *about.com***

"This is the book I've been looking for to recommend to my readers. It is simple enough for complete beginners but includes enough depth to be useful to more advanced users. And it makes the process of learning fun. This might just be the only JavaScript book you ever need."

> —**Julie L Baumler, JavaScript Editor, *BellaOnline.com***

Other related books from O'Reilly

Learning PHP & MySQL

Web Database Applications with PHP and MySQL

Programming PHP

Learning MySQL

PHP in a Nutshell

PHP Cookbook™

PHP Hacks™

MySQL in a Nutshell

MySQL Cookbook™

Other books in O'Reilly's *Head First* series

Head First Java™

Head First Object-Oriented Analysis and Design (OOA&D)

Head First HTML with CSS and XHTML

Head First Design Patterns

Head First Servlets and JSP

Head First EJB

Head First PMP

Head First SQL

Head First Software Development

Head First JavaScript

Head First Ajax

Head First Physics

Head First Statistics

Head First Rails

Head First Web Design

Head First Algebra

Head First PHP & MySQL

Wouldn't it be dreamy if there was a PHP & MySQL book that made databases and server-side web programming feel like a match made in heaven? It's probably just a fantasy...

Lynn Beighley
Michael Morrison

O'REILLY®

Beijing • Cambridge • Köln • Sebastopol • Tokyo

Head First PHP & MySQL

by Lynn Beighley and Michael Morrison

Printed in the United States of America.

Published by O'Reilly Media, Inc., 1005 Gravenstein Highway North, Sebastopol, CA 95472.

O'Reilly Media books may be purchased for educational, business, or sales promotional use. Online editions are also available for most titles (*safari.oreilly.com*). For more information, contact our corporate/institutional sales department: (800) 998-9938 or *corporate@oreilly.com*.

Series Creators:	Kathy Sierra, Bert Bates
Series Editor:	Brett D. McLaughlin
Editor:	Sanders Kleinfeld
Design Editor:	Louise Barr
Cover Designers:	Louise Barr, Steve Fehler
Production Editor:	Brittany Smith
Proofreader:	Colleen Gorman
Indexer:	Julie Hawks
Page Viewers:	Julien and Drew

Printing History:

December 2008: First Edition.

Michael's nephew Julien generously lent his Superman powers to help get this book finished.

Drew is, at this very moment, installing a new kitchen in Lynn's new old house.

No hardwood floors, UFOs, Elvis look-alikes, or virtual guitars were harmed in the making of this book. But a few broken hearts were mended thanks to some careful mismatching!

ISBN: 978-0-596-00630-3

[M] [2011-08-26]

For my parents, who frequently use web applications and are always there for me.

 - Lynn Beighley

To Rasmus Lerdorf, who single-handedly sparked the language that would eventually become PHP as we know it now. Enduring proof that it really only takes one person to lead us all down a new, more enlightened path.

 - Michael Morrison

Author(s) of Head First PHP & MySQL

Lynn Beighley

Michael Morrison

Lynn Beighley is a fiction writer stuck in a technical book writer's body. Upon discovering that technical book writing actually paid real money, she learned to accept and enjoy it. After going back to school to get a Masters in Computer Science, she worked for the acronyms NRL and LANL. Then she discovered Flash, and wrote her first bestseller. A victim of bad timing, she moved to Silicon Valley just before the great crash. She spent several years working for Yahoo! and writing other books and training courses. Finally giving in to her creative writing bent, she moved to the New York area to get an MFA in Creative Writing. Her Head First-style thesis was delivered to a packed room of professors and fellow students. It was extremely well received, and she finished her degree, finished *Head First SQL*, and just finished *Head First PHP & MySQL*. Whew!

Lynn loves traveling, writing, and making up elaborate background stories about complete strangers. She's a little scared of UFOs.

Michael Morrison has been an enthusiastic contributor to the online world ever since he ran a BBS on his Commodore 64 way back when being a nerd was far less cool than it is these days. A few thousand baud later, he still marvels at how far we've come, and how fast. Michael doesn't run a BBS anymore, but he's still very much involved in the modern equivalents and the tools we use to build them. He spends most of his "official" time writing about web-related technologies, having authored or co-authored over fifty books ranging from mobile game programming to XML. He entered the Head First foray with *Head First JavaScript*, and hasn't looked back.

Michael is also the founder of Stalefish Labs (www.stalefishlabs.com), an entertainment company specializing in games, toys, and interactive media. And he's been known to actually spend time offline (gasp!) skateboarding, playing ice hockey, and hanging out next to his koi pond with his wife, Masheed. He even sleeps every once in a while.

Table of Contents (Summary)

Table of Contents (the real thing)

Intro

Your brain on PHP & MySQL.

Here *you* are trying to *learn* something, while here your *brain* is doing you a favor by making sure the learning doesn't *stick*. Your brain's thinking, "Better leave room for more important things, like which wild animals to avoid and whether underwater yoga is a bad idea." So how *do* you trick your brain into thinking that your life depends on knowing PHP and MySQL?

add life to your static pages

It's Alive

You've been creating great web pages with HTML, and a sprinkling of CSS. But you've noticed that visitors to your site can't do much other than passively look at the content on the pages. The communication's one-way, and you'd like to change that. In fact, you'd really like to know what your audience is thinking. But you need to be able to allow users to enter information into a web form so that you can find out what's on their minds. And you need to be able to process the information and have it delivered to you. It sounds as if you're going to need more than HTML to take your site to the next level.

Have you seen him?

connecting to MySQL

How it fits together

2

Knowing how things fit together before you start building is a good idea. You've created your first PHP script, and it's working well. But getting your form results in an email isn't good enough anymore. You need a way to save the results of your form, so you can keep them as long as you need them and retrieve them when you want them. A MySQL database can store your data for safe keeping. But you need to hook up your PHP script to the MySQL database to make it happen.

The new report form is great, but now I'm getting too many emails. I can't drink enough caffeine to go through them all when I first receive them.

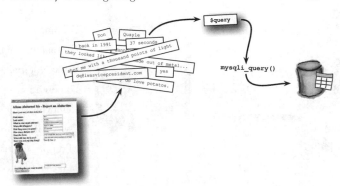

3

create and populate a database
Creating your own data

You don't always have the data you need.

Sometimes you have to create the data before you can use it. And sometimes you have to create tables to hold that data. And sometimes you have to create the database that holds the data that you need to create before you can use it. Confused? You won't be. Get ready to learn how to create databases and tables of your very own. And if that isn't enough, along the way, you'll build your very first PHP & MySQL application.

4

realistic and practical applications
Your Application on the Web

Sometimes you have to be realistic and rethink your plans.

Or plan more carefully in the first place. When your application's out there on the Web, you may discover that you haven't planned well enough. Things that you thought would work aren't good enough in the real world. This chapter takes a look at some real-world problems that can occur as you move your application from testing to a live site. Along the way, we'll show you more important PHP and SQL code.

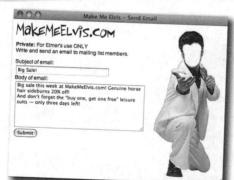

5

working with data stored in files

When a database just isn't enough

Don't believe the hype...about databases, that is. Sure, they work wonders for storing all kinds of data involving text, but what about binary data? You know, stuff like JPEG images and PDF documents. Does it really make sense to store all those pictures of your rare guitar pick collection in a database table? Usually not. That kind of data is typically stored in files, and we'll leave it in files. But it's entirely possible to have your virtual cake and eat it too—this chapter reveals that you can use files and databases together to build PHP applications that are awash in binary data.

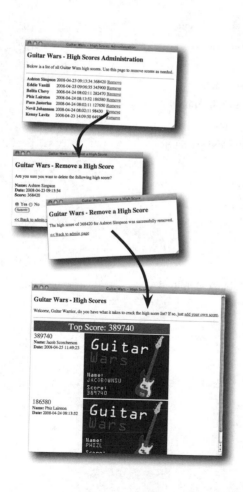

6

securing your application

Assume they're all out to get you

Your parents were right: don't talk to strangers. Or at least don't trust them. If nothing else, don't give them the keys to your application data, assuming they'll do the right thing. It's a cruel world out there, and you can't count on everyone to be trustworthy. In fact, as a web application developer you have to be part cynic, part conspiracy theorist. Yes, people are generally bad and they're definitely out to get you! OK, maybe that's a little extreme, but it's very important to take security seriously and design your applications so that they're protected against anyone who might choose to do harm.

building personalized web apps

Remember me?

No one likes to be forgotten, especially users of web applications. If an application has any sense of "membership," meaning that users somehow interact with the application in a personal way, then the application needs to remember the users. You'd hate to have to reintroduce yourself to your family every time you walk through the door at home. You don't have to because they have this wonderful thing called memory. But web applications don't remember people automatically - it's up to a savvy web developer to use the tools at their disposal (PHP and MySQL, maybe?) to build personalized web apps that can actually remember users.

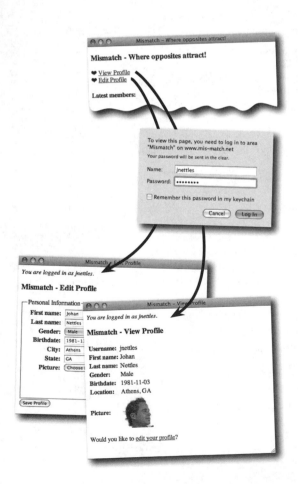

eliminate duplicate code

Sharing is caring

7 1/2

Umbrellas aren't the only thing that can be shared. In any web application you're bound to run into situations where *the same code is duplicated* in more than one place. Not only is this wasteful, but it leads to **maintenance headaches** since you will inevitably have to make changes, and these changes will have to be carried out in multiple places. The solution is to **eliminate duplicate code by sharing it**. In other words, you stick the duplicate code in one place, and then just reference that single copy wherever you need it. Eliminating duplicate code results in applications that are **more efficient**, **easier to maintain**, and ultimately **more robust**.

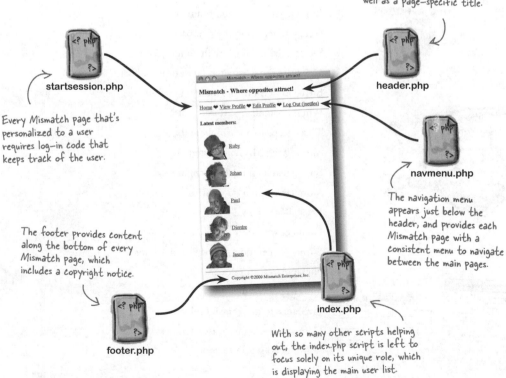

The header appears at the top of every Mismatch page, and displays the application title as well as a page-specific title.

header.php

startsession.php

Every Mismatch page that's personalized to a user requires log-in code that keeps track of the user.

navmenu.php

The navigation menu appears just below the header, and provides each Mismatch page with a consistent menu to navigate between the main pages.

The footer provides content along the bottom of every Mismatch page, which includes a copyright notice.

footer.php

index.php

With so many other scripts helping out, the index.php script is left to focus solely on its unique role, which is displaying the main user list.

control your data, control your world

Harvesting data

8

There's nothing like a good fall data harvest. An abundance of information ready to be *examined*, *sorted*, *compared*, *combined*, and generally made to do whatever it is your killer web app needs it to do. Fulfilling? Yes. But like real harvesting, **taking control of data in a MySQL database** requires some hard work and a fair amount of expertise. Web users demand more than tired old wilted data that's dull and unengaging. They want data that enriches...data that fulfills...data that's relevant. So what are you waiting for? Fire up your MySQL tractor and get to work!

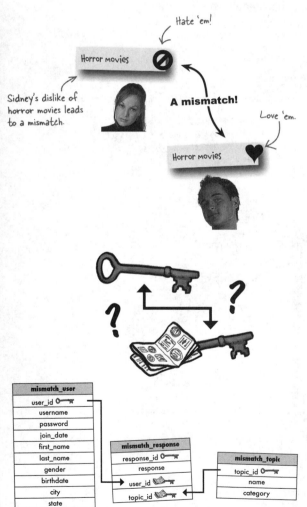

Hate 'em!

Horror movies

Sidney's dislike of horror movies leads to a mismatch.

A mismatch!

Love 'em.

Horror movies

string and custom functions

Better living through functions

Functions take your applications to a whole new level.

You've already been using PHP's built-in functions to accomplish things. Now it's time to take a look at a few more really useful **built-in functions**. And then you'll learn to build your very own **custom functions** to take you farther than you ever imagined it was possible to go. Well, maybe not to the point of raising laser sharks, but custom functions will streamline your code and make it reusable.

9

10

regular expressions
Rules for replacement

String functions are kind of lovable. But at the same time, they're limited. Sure, they can tell the length of your string, truncate it, change certain characters to other certain characters. But sometimes you need to break free and tackle more complex text manipulations. This is where **regular expressions** can help. They can **precisely modify strings** based on a **set of rules** rather than a single criterion.

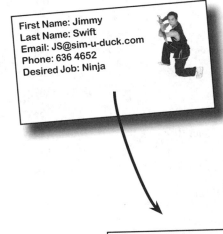

First Name: Jimmy
Last Name: Swift
Email: JS@sim-u-duck.com
Phone: 636 4652
Desired Job: Ninja

First Name: Jimmy
Last Name: Swift
Email: JS@sim-u-duck.com
Phone: (555) 636 4652
Desired Job: Ninja

I got an error and then entered my entire phone number. And then I got a ninja job!

visualizing your data...and more!

Drawing dynamic graphics

11

Sure, we all know the power of a good query and a bunch of juicy results. But query results don't always speak for themselves. Sometimes it's helpful to cast data in a different light, a more visual light. PHP makes it possible to provide a **graphical representation of database data**: *pie charts*, *bar charts*, *Venn diagrams*, *Rorschach art*, you name it. Anything to help users get a grip on the data flowing through your application is game. But not all worthwhile graphics in PHP applications originate in your database. For example, did you know it's possible to **thwart form-filling spam bots with dynamically generated images**?

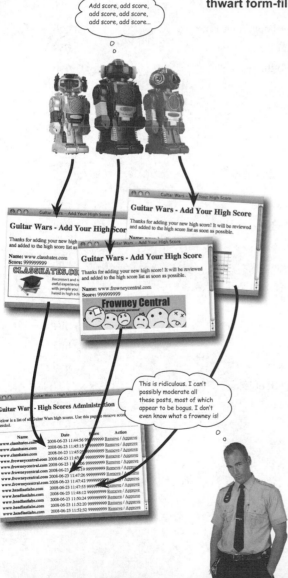

12

syndication and web services

Interfacing to the world

It's a big world out there, and one that your web application can't afford to ignore. Perhaps more importantly, you'd rather the world not ignore your web application. One excellent way to tune the world in to your web application is to make its data available for syndication, which means users can subscribe to your site's content instead of having to visit your web site directly to find new info. Not only that, your application can interface to other applications through web services and take advantage of other people's data to provide a richer experience.

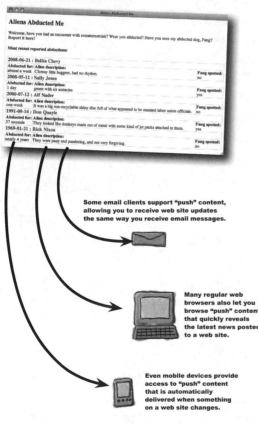

Some email clients support "push" content, allowing you to receive web site updates the same way you receive email messages.

Many regular web browsers also let you browse "push" content that quickly reveals the latest news posted to a web site.

Even mobile devices provide access to "push" content that is automatically delivered when something on a web site changes.

leftovers

The Top Ten Topics (we didn't cover)

Even after all that, there's a bit more. There are just a few more things we think you need to know. We wouldn't feel right about ignoring them, even though they only need a brief mention. So before you put the book down, take a read through these short but important PHP and MySQL tidbits. Besides, once you're done here, all that's left are a couple short appendices... and the index... and maybe some ads... and then you're really done. We promise!

set up a development environment
A place to play

You need a place to practice your newfound PHP and MySQL skills without making your data vulnerable on the web. It's always a good idea to have a safe place to develop your PHP application before unleashing it on the world (wide web). This appendix contains instructions for installing a web server, MySQL, and PHP to give you a safe place to work and practice.

Server computer

extend your php
Get even more

Yes, you can program with PHP and MySQL and create great web applications. But you know there must be more to it. And there is. This short appendix will show you how to install the mysqli extension and GD graphics library extension. Then we'll mention a few more extensions to PHP you might want to get. Because sometimes it's okay to want more.

You should see php_gd2.dll and php_mysqli.dll

Grab the version of mysqli to match your version of PHP.

how to use this book

Intro

In this section we answer the burning question: "So why DID they put that in a PHP & MySQL book?"

Who is this book for?

If you can answer "yes" to all of these:

(1) Are you a web designer with HTML or XHTML experience and a desire to take your web pages to the next level?

(2) Do you want to go beyond simple HTML pages to **learn**, **understand**, and **remember** how to **use PHP and MySQL to build web applications?**

(3) Do you prefer **stimulating dinner party conversation** to **dry**, **dull**, **academic lectures**?

this book is for you.

Who should probably back away from this book?

If you can answer "yes" to any of these:

(1) **Are you completely unfamiliar with basic programming concepts like variables and loops?**

(But even if you've never programmed before, you'll probably be able to get the key concepts you need from this book.)

(2) Are you a kick-butt PHP web developer looking for a *reference* book?

(3) Are you **afraid to try something different**? Would you rather have a root canal than mix stripes with plaid? Do you believe that a technical book can't be serious if it creates an alien abduction database?

this book is not for you.

[Note from marketing: this book is for anyone with a credit card.]

"How can *this* be a serious PHP and MySQL book?"

"What's with all the graphics?"

"Can I actually *learn* it this way?"

We know what your *brain* is thinking

Your brain craves novelty. It's always searching, scanning, *waiting* for something unusual. It was built that way, and it helps you stay alive.

So what does your brain do with all the routine, ordinary, normal things you encounter? Everything it *can* to stop them from interfering with the brain's *real* job—recording things that *matter*. It doesn't bother saving the boring things; they never make it past the "this is obviously not important" filter.

How does your brain *know* what's important? Suppose you're out for a day hike and a tiger jumps in front of you, what happens inside your head and body?

Neurons fire. Emotions crank up. *Chemicals surge.*

And that's how your brain knows...

This must be important! Don't forget it!

But imagine you're at home, or in a library. It's a safe, warm, tiger-free zone. You're studying. Getting ready for an exam. Or trying to learn some tough technical topic your boss thinks will take a week, ten days at the most.

Just one problem. Your brain's trying to do you a big favor. It's trying to make sure that this *obviously* non-important content doesn't clutter up scarce resources. Resources that are better spent storing the really *big* things. Like tigers. Like the danger of fire. Like how to quickly hide the browser window with the YouTube video of space alien footage when your boss shows up.

And there's no simple way to tell your brain, "Hey brain, thank you very much, but no matter how dull this book is, and how little I'm registering on the emotional Richter scale right now, I really *do* want you to keep this stuff around."

Your brain thinks THIS is important.

Great. Only 750 more dull, dry, boring pages.

Your brain thinks THIS isn't worth saving.

UFO footage on YouTube is obviously more interesting to your brain than some computer book.

UFO Spotted Near Eiffel Tower!

We think of a "Head First" reader as a <u>learner</u>.

So what does it take to *learn* something? First, you have to *get* it, then make sure you don't *forget* it. It's not about pushing facts into your head. Based on the latest research in cognitive science, neurobiology, and educational psychology, *learning* takes a lot more than text on a page. We know what turns your brain on.

Some of the Head First learning principles:

`user_id = 1`

Make it visual. Images are far more memorable than words alone, and make learning much more effective (up to 89% improvement in recall and transfer studies). It also makes things more understandable. **Put the words within or near the graphics** they relate to, rather than on the bottom or on another page, and learners will be up to *twice* as likely to solve problems related to the content.

Use a conversational and personalized style. In recent studies, students performed up to 40% better on post-learning tests if the content spoke directly to the reader, using a first-person, conversational style rather than taking a formal tone. Tell stories instead of lecturing. Use casual language. Don't take yourself too seriously. Which would *you* pay more attention to: a stimulating dinner party companion, or a lecture?

Get the learner to think more deeply. In other words, unless you actively flex your neurons, nothing much happens in your head. A reader has to be motivated, engaged, curious, and inspired to solve problems, draw conclusions, and generate new knowledge. And for that, you need challenges, exercises, and thought-provoking questions, and activities that involve both sides of the brain and multiple senses.

Get—and keep—the reader's attention. We've all had the "I really want to learn this but I can't stay awake past page one" experience. Your brain pays attention to things that are out of the ordinary, interesting, strange, eye-catching, unexpected. Learning a new, tough, technical topic doesn't have to be boring. Your brain will learn much more quickly if it's not.

Touch their emotions. We now know that your ability to remember something is largely dependent on its emotional content. You remember what you care about. You remember when you *feel* something. No, we're not talking heart-wrenching stories about a boy and his dog. We're talking emotions like surprise, curiosity, fun, "what the...?", and the feeling of "I Rule!" that comes when you solve a puzzle, learn something everybody else thinks is hard, or realize you know something that "I'm more technical than thou" Bob from engineering *doesn't*.

> Error!
> Pass-phrase unknown.

Small correction. We actually do have a heart-wrenching story about a boy and his dog — the dog was abducted by aliens, and you'll be helping the boy find him!

Metacognition: thinking about thinking

If you really want to learn, and you want to learn more quickly and more deeply, pay attention to how you pay attention. Think about how you think. Learn how you learn.

I wonder how I can trick my brain into remembering this stuff...

Most of us did not take courses on metacognition or learning theory when we were growing up. We were *expected* to learn, but rarely *taught* to learn.

But we assume that if you're holding this book, you really want to learn how to build database-driven web sites with PHP and MySQL. And you probably don't want to spend a lot of time. If you want to use what you read in this book, you need to *remember* what you read. And for that, you've got to *understand* it. To get the most from this book, or *any* book or learning experience, take responsibility for your brain. Your brain on *this* content.

The trick is to get your brain to see the new material you're learning as Really Important. Crucial to your well-being. As important as a tiger. Otherwise, you're in for a constant battle, with your brain doing its best to keep the new content from sticking.

So just how *DO* you get your brain to treat PHP & MySQL like it was a hungry tiger?

There's the slow, tedious way, or the faster, more effective way. The slow way is about sheer repetition. You obviously know that you *are* able to learn and remember even the dullest of topics if you keep pounding the same thing into your brain. With enough repetition, your brain says, "This doesn't *feel* important to him, but he keeps looking at the same thing *over* and *over* and *over*, so I suppose it must be."

Neuron, schmeuron. Some of us are here to rock!

The faster way is to do **anything that increases brain activity,** especially different *types* of brain activity. The things on the previous page are a big part of the solution, and they're all things that have been proven to help your brain work in your favor. For example, studies show that putting words *within* the pictures they describe (as opposed to somewhere else in the page, like a caption or in the body text) causes your brain to try to makes sense of how the words and picture relate, and this causes more neurons to fire. More neurons firing = more chances for your brain to *get* that this is something worth paying attention to, and possibly recording.

A conversational style helps because people tend to pay more attention when they perceive that they're in a conversation, since they're expected to follow along and hold up their end. The amazing thing is, your brain doesn't necessarily *care* that the "conversation" is between you and a book! On the other hand, if the writing style is formal and dry, your brain perceives it the same way you experience being lectured to while sitting in a roomful of passive attendees. No need to stay awake.

But pictures and conversational style are just the beginning…

Here's what WE did:

We used **pictures**, because your brain is tuned for visuals, not text. As far as your brain's concerned, a picture really *is* worth a thousand words. And when text and pictures work together, we embedded the text *in* the pictures because your brain works more effectively when the text is *within* the thing the text refers to, as opposed to in a caption or buried in the text somewhere.

A mismatch!

We used **redundancy**, saying the same thing in *different* ways and with different media types, and *multiple senses*, to increase the chance that the content gets coded into more than one area of your brain.

We used concepts and pictures in **unexpected** ways because your brain is tuned for novelty, and we used pictures and ideas with at least *some* **emotional** *content*, because your brain is tuned to pay attention to the biochemistry of emotions. That which causes you to *feel* something is more likely to be remembered, even if that feeling is nothing more than a little **humor**, **surprise**, or **interest.**

We used a personalized, **conversational style**, because your brain is tuned to pay more attention when it believes you're in a conversation than if it thinks you're passively listening to a presentation. Your brain does this even when you're *reading*.

We included more than 80 **activities**, because your brain is tuned to learn and remember more when you **do** things than when you *read* about things. And we made the exercises challenging-yet-do-able, because that's what most people prefer.

We used **multiple learning styles**, because *you* might prefer step-by-step procedures, while someone else wants to understand the big picture first, and someone else just wants to see an example. But regardless of your own learning preference, *everyone* benefits from seeing the same content represented in multiple ways.

Try this!

We include content for **both sides of your brain**, because the more of your brain you engage, the more likely you are to learn and remember, and the longer you can stay focused. Since working one side of the brain often means giving the other side a chance to rest, you can be more productive at learning for a longer period of time.

Test Drive

And we included **stories** and exercises that present **more than one point of view,** because your brain is tuned to learn more deeply when it's forced to make evaluations and judgments.

We included **challenges**, with exercises, and by asking **questions** that don't always have a straight answer, because your brain is tuned to learn and remember when it has to *work* at something. Think about it—you can't get your *body* in shape just by *watching* people at the gym. But we did our best to make sure that when you're working hard, it's on the *right* things. That **you're not spending one extra dendrite** processing a hard-to-understand example, or parsing difficult, jargon-laden, or overly terse text.

DON'T TRUST THIS SMILE!

We used **people**. In stories, examples, pictures, etc., because, well, because *you're* a person. And your brain pays more attention to *people* than it does to *things*.

Here's what YOU can do to bend your brain into submission

So, we did our part. The rest is up to you. These tips are a starting point; listen to your brain and figure out what works for you and what doesn't. Try new things.

Cut this out and stick it on your refrigerator.

---

① Slow down. The more you understand, the less you have to memorize.

Don't just *read*. Stop and think. When the book asks you a question, don't just skip to the answer. Imagine that someone really *is* asking the question. The more deeply you force your brain to think, the better chance you have of learning and remembering.

② Do the exercises. Write your own notes.

We put them in, but if we did them for you, that would be like having someone else do your workouts for you. And don't just *look* at the exercises. **Use a pencil.** There's plenty of evidence that physical activity *while* learning can increase the learning.

③ Read the "There are No Dumb Questions"

That means all of them. They're not optional sidebars—*they're part of the core content!* Don't skip them.

④ Make this the last thing you read before bed. Or at least the last challenging thing.

Part of the learning (especially the transfer to long-term memory) happens *after* you put the book down. Your brain needs time on its own, to do more processing. If you put in something new during that processing time, some of what you just learned will be lost.

⑤ Drink water. Lots of it.

Your brain works best in a nice bath of fluid. Dehydration (which can happen before you ever feel thirsty) decreases cognitive function.

⑥ Talk about it. Out loud.

Speaking activates a different part of the brain. If you're trying to understand something, or increase your chance of remembering it later, say it out loud. Better still, try to explain it out loud to someone else. You'll learn more quickly, and you might uncover ideas you hadn't known were there when you were reading about it.

⑦ Listen to your brain.

Pay attention to whether your brain is getting overloaded. If you find yourself starting to skim the surface or forget what you just read, it's time for a break. Once you go past a certain point, you won't learn faster by trying to shove more in, and you might even hurt the process.

⑧ Feel something.

Your brain needs to know that this *matters*. Get involved with the stories. Make up your own captions for the photos. Groaning over a bad joke is *still* better than feeling nothing at all.

⑨ Write a lot of code!

There's only one way to learn to program: **writing a lot of code**. And that's what you're going to do throughout this book. Coding is a skill, and the only way to get good at it is to practice. We're going to give you a lot of practice: every chapter has exercises that pose problems for you to solve. Don't just skip over them—a lot of the learning happens when you solve the exercises. We included a solution to each exercise—don't be afraid to **peek at the solution** if you get stuck! (It's easy to get snagged on something small.) But try to solve the problem before you look at the solution. And definitely get it working before you move on to the next part of the book.

PHP and MySQL let you build real-world web applications - don't forget to upload them and try them out on a real web server.

Read Me

This is a learning experience, not a reference book. We deliberately stripped out everything that might get in the way of learning whatever it is we're working on at that point in the book. And the first time through, you need to begin at the beginning, because the book makes assumptions about what you've already seen and learned.

We begin by teaching simple programming concepts and database connection basics, then more complicated PHP functions and MySQL statements, and finally more complex application concepts.

While it's important to create applications that allow users to add data to and retrieve data from your web application, before you can do that you need to understand the syntax of both PHP and MySQL. So we begin by giving you PHP and MySQL statements that you can actually try yourself. That way you can immediately do something with PHP and MySQL, and you will begin to get excited about them. Then, a bit later in the book, we show you good application and database design practices. By then you'll have a solid grasp of the syntax you need, and can focus on *learning the concepts*.

We don't cover every PHP and MySQL statement, function, or keyword.

While we could have put every single PHP and MySQL statement, function, and keyword in this book, we thought you'd prefer to have a reasonably liftable book that would teach you the most important statements, functions, and keywords. We give you the ones you need to know, the ones you'll use 95 percent of the time. And when you're done with this book, you'll have the confidence to go look up that function you need to finish off that kick-ass application you just wrote.

We support PHP 5 and MySQL 5.0. ←

You can actually use PHP 4 with this book by making a few modifications to the code. Check them out in #1 of Appendix i.

Because so many people still use PHP 4 or 5, we avoid any PHP 4, 5, or 6 specific code wherever possible. We suggest you use PHP 5 or 6 and MySQL 5 or 6 while learning the concepts in this book. In developing this book, we focused on PHP 5 and MySQL 5, while making sure our code was compatible with later versions.

You need a web server that supports PHP.

PHP has to be run through a web server to work correctly. You need Apache or some other web server installed on your local machine or a machine to which you have some access so that you can run MySQL commands on the data. Check out Appendixes ii and iii for instructions on how to install and extend PHP and MySQL.

We use MySQL.

While there's Standard SQL language, in this book we focus on the particular syntax of MySQL. With only a few syntax changes, the code in this book should work with Oracle, MS SQL Server, PostgreSQL, DB2, and quite a few more Relational Database Management Systems (RDBMSs) out there. You'll need to look up the particular PHP functions and syntax if you want to connect to these other RDBMSs. If we covered every variation in syntax for every command in the book, this book would have many more pages. We like trees, so we're focusing on MySQL.

The activities are NOT optional.

The exercises and activities are not add-ons; they're part of the core content of the book. Some of them are to help with memory, some are for understanding, and some will help you apply what you've learned. ***Don't skip the exercises.*** The crossword puzzles are the only thing you don't *have* to do, but they're good for giving your brain a chance to think about the words and terms you've been learning in a different context.

The redundancy is intentional and important.

One distinct difference in a Head First book is that we want you to *really* get it. And we want you to finish the book remembering what you've learned. Most reference books don't have retention and recall as a goal, but this book is about *learning*, so you'll see some of the same concepts come up more than once.

The examples are as lean as possible.

Our readers tell us that it's frustrating to wade through 200 lines of an example looking for the two lines they need to understand. Most examples in this book are shown within the smallest possible context, so that the part you're trying to learn is clear and simple. Don't expect all of the examples to be ultra robust, or always complete—they are written specifically for learning, and aren't necessarily fully-functional.

Several of the examples are full-blown web applications that do some pretty powerful things.

We've placed all of the example code and applications on the Web so you can copy and paste parts of them into your text editor or MySQL Terminal, or upload them as-is to your own web server for testing. You'll find it all at
http://www.headfirstlabs.com/books/hfphp/

The Brain Power exercises don't have answers.

For some of them, there is no right answer, and for others, part of the learning experience of the Brain Power activities is for you to decide if and when your answers are right. In some of the Brain Power exercises, you will find hints to point you in the right direction.

The technical review team

Jereme Allen  David Briggs  Will Harris  Stephanie Liese  Steve Milano

Harvey Quamen  Chris Shiflett

Technical Reviewers:

Jereme Allen is a senior level web developer with experience utilizing state of the art technologies to create web applications. He has nine plus years of experience utilizing PHP, MySQL, as well as various other frameworks, operating systems, programming languages and development software.

David Briggs is a technical author and software localization engineer living in Birmingham, England. When he's not being finicky about how to guide users through a particularly tricky piece of software, he likes nothing better than to get out in the local park with his wife, Paulette, and Cleo, the family dog.

Will Harris spends his days running an IT department that provides services to 11 companies on 4 continents, and he is the Vice President of the Las Vegas PASS (Professional Association for SQL Server) chapter. At night, he hops into a phone booth and puts on his web 2.0 suit, helping the designers and developers at Powered By Geek ensure that their data platforms are flexible, portable, maintainable, and FAST, using MySQL and Rails. He also enjoys spending time with his wife, Heather, his beautiful children, Mara and Ellie, and his dog, Swiper.

Stephanie Liese is a technical trainer and web developer in Sacramento, California. When she isn't extolling the virtues of standards compliant code or debugging a CSS layout, you will find her sweating it out in a hot yoga class.

If **Steve Milano** isn't slinging code for The Day Job™ or playing punk rock with his band, Onion Flavored Rings, in some unventilated basement, he's probably at home with his laptop, neglecting feline companion, Ralph, and human companion, Bianca.

Harvey Quamen gave up a computer programming career to join the jet-setting, paparazzi-filled, high profile world of academia. He's currently an Associate Professor of English and Humanities Computing at the University of Alberta, where he teaches courses on cyberculture, 20th-century literature, and web development—including PHP and MySQL.

Chris Shiflett is the Chief Technology Officer of OmniTI, where he leads the web application security practice and guides web development initiatives. Chris is a thought leader in the PHP and web application security communities—a widely-read blogger at shiflett.org, a popular speaker at industry conferences worldwide, and the founder of the PHP Security Consortium. His books include *Essential PHP Security* (O'Reilly) and *HTTP Developer's Handbook* (Sams).

Acknowledgments

Brett McLaughlin

Our editors:

Many thanks go to **Brett McLaughlin** for the awesome storyboarding session that got us on the right track, and his ruthless commitment to cognitive learning.

The book would not exist if not for the heroic effort, patience, and persistence of **Sanders Kleinfeld**. He always managed to catch the balls, or was it cats, we were juggling when we inevitably dropped one (or three!), and we appreciate it. We hope he gets a chance to put his feet up for a couple of days before taking on another project as difficult as this one.

The O'Reilly team:

Lou Barr

Thanks to **Lou Barr** for her phenomenal design skill, making this book such a visual treat.

Thanks also to **Brittany Smith** for all her hard work at the last minute, and to **Caitrin McCullough** for getting the example web sites up and running. And to **Laurie Petrycki** for having faith that we could write another great Head First book.

Sanders Kleinfeld

And more:

Finally, a big thanks goes out to **Elvis Wilson** for putting together the alien YouTube videos for Chapter 12. Excellent job! Especially seeing as how he's merely a simple caveman art director.

Safari® Books Online

 When you see a Safari® icon on the cover of your favorite technology book that means the book is available online through the O'Reilly Network Safari Bookshelf.

Safari offers a solution that's better than e-books. It's a virtual library that lets you easily search thousands of top tech books, cut and paste code samples, download chapters, and find quick answers when you need the most accurate, current information. Try it for free at `http://safari.oreilly.com`.

1 add life to your static pages

It's Alive

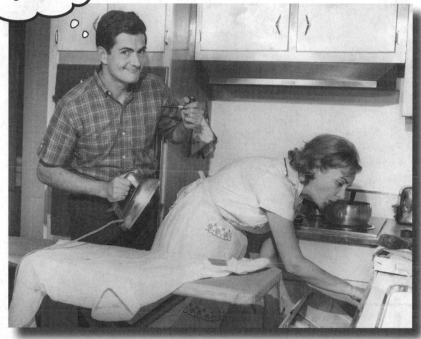

Just let her tell me
I'm boring now...

You've been creating great web pages with HTML, and a sprinkling of CSS. But you've noticed that visitors to your site can't do much other than passively look at the content on the pages. The communication's one-way, and you'd like to change that. In fact, you'd really like to *know what your audience is thinking*. But you need to be able to allow users to **enter information into a web form** so that you can find out what's on their minds. And you need to be able to **process the information** and **have it delivered to you**. It sounds as if you're going to need more than HTML to take your site to the next level.

HTML is static and boring

HTML's great for creating web pages, that much we already know. But what about when you need web pages that actually **do** something? Suppose you need to search a database or send an email... what then? HTML falls short because it's a pretty lifeless language, designed for displaying information that never changes.

Hello?

HTML is great if you just want to share a picture of your pet... but not so great if you want to interact with visitors to your site.

These people are looking for interaction!

The HTML code in these pages is determined when the web developer creates the pages.

Static HTML pages are only changed when a web developer edits a .html file and uploads it to their web server.

Web server

Client web browser

The web server is limited to serving up one static HTML page after another.

The web server's a big part of the problem with lifeless HTML since it serves as nothing more than a boring delivery mechanism. A browser requests a page, the server responds with HTML, end of story. To turn web sites into interactive web **applications**, the web server has to take on a new, more dynamic role... a role made possible by **PHP**.

With pure HTML, web pages, the server simply serves up static HTML that can only display content.

PHP brings web pages to life

With a little help from the server!

PHP allows you to manipulate web page content *on the server* just before a page is delivered to the client browser. It works like this: A PHP script runs on the server and can alter or generate HTML code at will. An HTML web page is still delivered to the browser, which doesn't know or care that PHP is involved in tweaking the HTML on the server.

With PHP in the mix, the web server is able to <u>dynamically</u> generate <u>HTML</u> web pages on the fly.

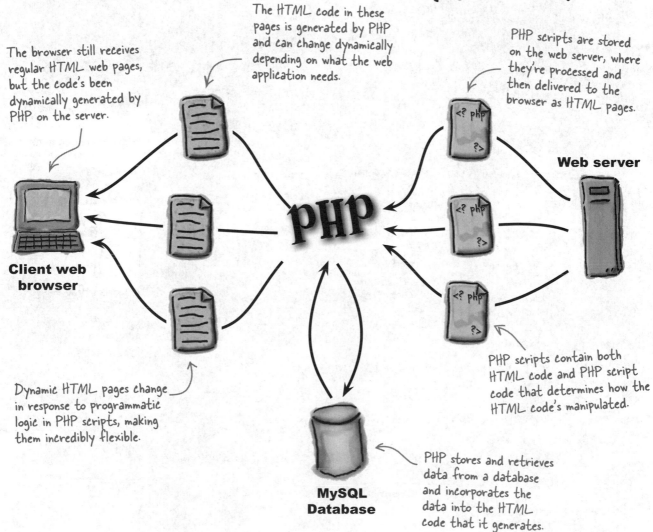

The HTML code in these pages is generated by PHP and can change dynamically depending on what the web application needs.

The browser still receives regular HTML web pages, but the code's been dynamically generated by PHP on the server.

PHP scripts are stored on the web server, where they're processed and then delivered to the browser as HTML pages.

Web server

Client web browser

Dynamic HTML pages change in response to programmatic logic in PHP scripts, making them incredibly flexible.

PHP scripts contain both HTML code and PHP script code that determines how the HTML code's manipulated.

MySQL Database

PHP stores and retrieves data from a database and incorporates the data into the HTML code that it generates.

Dogs in space

Meet Owen. Owen's lost his dog, Fang. But finding his dog isn't just a matter of searching the neighborhood. You see, Fang was abducted by aliens, which expands Owen's search to the entire galaxy. Owen knows some HTML and CSS, and he thinks a custom web site may help solve his problem by allowing other people to share their own alien abduction experiences.

But to get information from others, Owen's going to need a web form that's capable of receiving user input, lots of it, and notifying him about it. Not a problem—HTML has plenty of tags for whipping together web forms.

Have you seen him?

Details are sketchy, but we do know that Fang was whisked into the sky in a beam of light.

Owen knows some HTML and CSS and thinks he might be able to use the web to help track down his dog, Fang.

A form helps Owen get the whole story

Owen's new web site, AliensAbductedMe.com, aims to connect Owen with alien abductees who might be able to shed some light on Fang's disappearance. Owen knows he needs an HTML form to solicit abduction stories from visitors and that it must find out if they've run into Fang during their interstellar journeys. But he needs your help getting it up and running. Here's what he has in mind for the form.

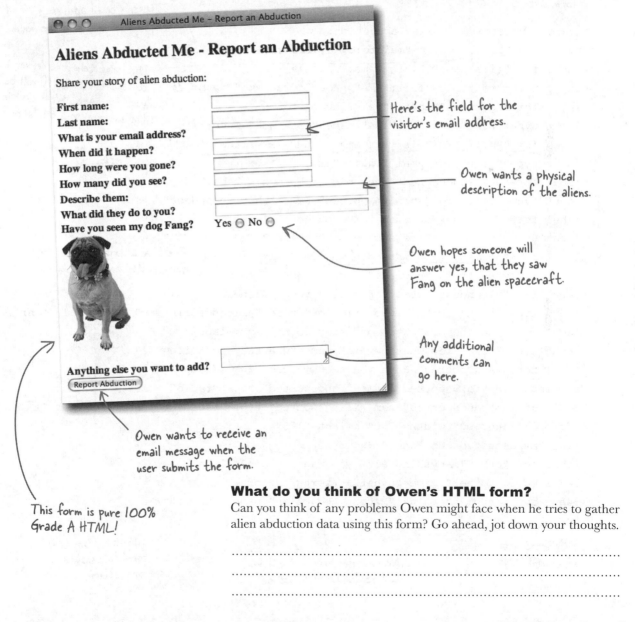

Here's the field for the visitor's email address.

Owen wants a physical description of the aliens.

Owen hopes someone will answer yes, that they saw Fang on the alien spacecraft.

Any additional comments can go here.

Owen wants to receive an email message when the user submits the form.

This form is pure 100% Grade A HTML!

What do you think of Owen's HTML form?

Can you think of any problems Owen might face when he tries to gather alien abduction data using this form? Go ahead, jot down your thoughts.

....

....

....

Forms are made of HTML

Owen's Report an Abduction form is built entirely out of HTML tags and attributes. There are text fields for most of the questions, radio buttons to find out if his visitor saw Fang, and a text area for additional comments. And the form is set up to deliver form data to Owen's email address.

If you need a refresher on creating HTML forms, check out Chapter 14 of Head First HTML with CSS & XHTML.

"mailto" is a protocol that allows form data to be delivered via email.

Owen will get the contents of this form sent to him at this email address — change Owen's email address to yours to test out the form.

```
<p>Share your story of alien abduction:</p>
<form method="post" action="mailto:owen@aliensabductedme.com">
  <label for="firstname">First name:</label>
  <input type="text" id="firstname" name="firstname" /><br />
  <label for="lastname">Last name:</label>
  <input type="text" id="lastname" name="lastname" /><br />
  <label for="email">What is your email address?</label>
  <input type="text" id="email" name="email" /><br />
  <label for="whenithappened">When did it happen?</label>
  <input type="text" id="whenithappened" name="whenithappened" /><br />
  <label for="howlong">How long were you gone?</label>
  <input type="text" id="howlong" name="howlong" /><br />
  <label for="howmany">How many did you see?</label>
  <input type="text" id="howmany" name="howmany" /><br />
  <label for="aliendescription">Describe them:</label>
  <input type="text" id="aliendescription" name="aliendescription" size="32" /><br />
  <label for="whattheydid">What did they do to you?</label>
  <input type="text" id="whattheydid" name="whattheydid" size="32" /><br />
  <label for="fangspotted">Have you seen my dog Fang?</label>
  Yes <input id="fangspotted" name="fangspotted" type="radio" value="yes" />
  No <input id="fangspotted" name="fangspotted" type="radio" value="no" /><br />
  <img src="fang.jpg" width="100" height="175"
    alt="My abducted dog Fang." /><br />
  <label for="other">Anything else you want to add?</label>
  <textarea id="other" name="other"></textarea><br />
  <input type="submit" value="Report Abduction" name="submit" />
</form>
```

This value tells the server how to send the data. It will be "post" or "get". We'll explain the difference a bit later.

Input tags tell the form to expect information.

The type attribute tells the form action to expect text.

The form is bracketed with open and close <form> tags.

No surprises here — the form is pure, 100% HTML code!

The submit button tells the form to execute the form action.

Test Drive

Try out the Report an Abduction form.

Download the code for the Report an Abduction web page from the Head First Labs web site at **www.headfirstlabs.com/books/hfphp**. It's in the **chapter01** folder. The folder contains Owen's web form in **report.html**, as well as a style sheet (**style.css**) and an image of Fang (**fang.jpg**).

Open the report.html page in a text editor and change Owen's email address to yours. Then open the page in a web browser, enter some alien abduction information in the form, and click the Report Abduction button.

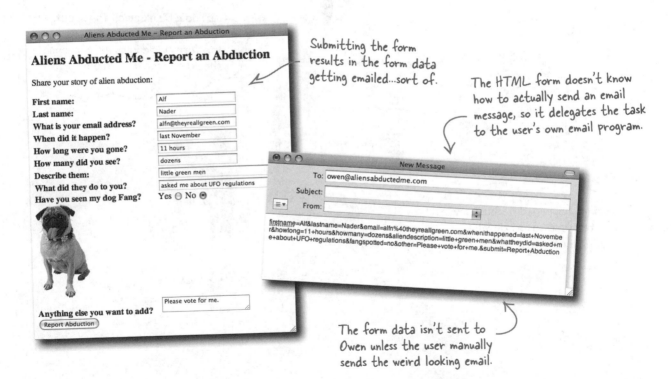

Submitting the form results in the form data getting emailed...sort of.

The HTML form doesn't know how to actually send an email message, so it delegates the task to the user's own email program.

The form data isn't sent to Owen unless the user manually sends the weird looking email.

So, what do you think? Did you receive the form data as an email message in your Inbox?

The HTML form has problems

Owen's Report an Abduction form is up and running, but he doesn't get much information from users. Is Fang's abduction really such an isolated incident... or is something wrong with his form? Let's see what the users have to say about it.

When I click the button, it opens my email program, Outlook, and doesn't have anything I just spent 15 minutes typing in the form!

I saw something like this in the Subject field: ?When=&Where=. I'm confused.

I had a blank email to fill out. All my carefully typed answers from the form were ignored. Someone should abduct this stupid form!

Nothing happened because my web browser has no **default email client**... whatever that is.

Somehow Owen's form is extracting more frustration than information from visitors to his site.

What's going on here? Do you have any ideas about how to fix the form?

> The form looks OK. Does the problem have something to do with that mailto part?

Yes. The HTML form code is fine, but `mailto` isn't a good way to deliver form data.

Owen's form is perfectly fine until the user clicks the Report Abduction button. At that point you rely on `mailto` to package up the form data in an email. But this email doesn't get sent automatically—it's created in the default email program on the user's computer instead. And the real kicker... the user has to **send the email themselves** in order for the data to get sent to you! So you have no control over the email delivery, meaning that it may or may not successfully make the trip from your web form through their browser to their email client and back to you as an email message. Not good.

You need a way to take control of the delivery of the web form. More specifically, you need PHP to package the form data into an email message, and then make sure it gets sent. This involves shifting your attention from the **client** (HTML, `mailto`, etc.) to the **server** (PHP).

The form's wonderful until you click Report Abduction — then all bets are off!

Aliens Abducted Me - Report an Abduction

Share your story of alien abduction:

First name:
Last name:
What is your email address?
When did it happen?
How long were you gone?
How many did you see?
Describe them:
What did they do to you?
Have you seen my dog Fang?   Yes ○ No ○

Anything else you want to add?
Report Abduction

HTML acts on the CLIENT

Owen's form is written in pure HTML with a `mailto` form action that attempts to send the form data via email. Although the `report.html` web page comes from a web server, it's filled out and processed entirely on the user's web browser.

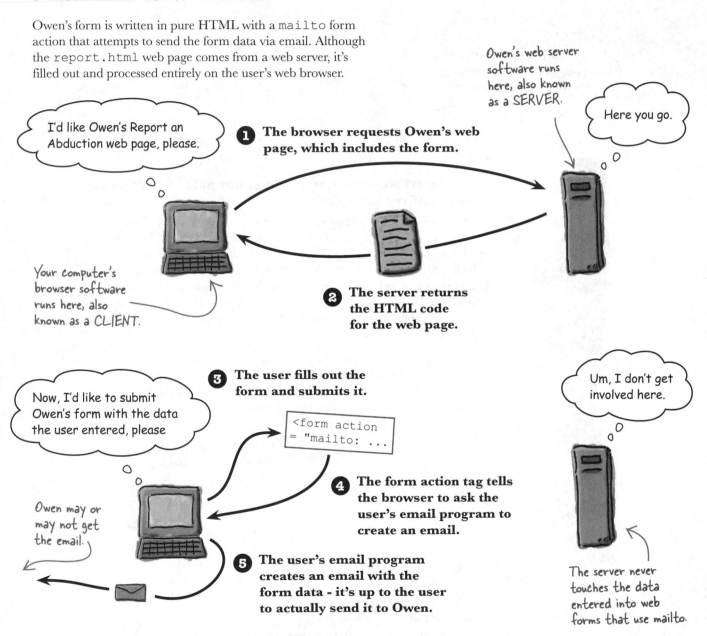

Owen's web server software runs here, also known as a SERVER.

Here you go.

I'd like Owen's Report an Abduction web page, please.

1 **The browser requests Owen's web page, which includes the form.**

Your computer's browser software runs here, also known as a CLIENT.

2 **The server returns the HTML code for the web page.**

3 **The user fills out the form and submits it.**

Now, I'd like to submit Owen's form with the data the user entered, please

Um, I don't get involved here.

```
<form action
= "mailto: ...
```

4 **The form action tag tells the browser to ask the user's email program to create an email.**

Owen may or may not get the email.

5 **The user's email program creates an email with the form data - it's up to the user to actually send it to Owen.**

The server never touches the data entered into web forms that use mailto.

The server's role here is limited to just **delivering** the web page to the browser. When the user submits the form, the browser (client!) is left to its own devices to work out how to get the form data sent via email. The client isn't equipped to deliver form data—that's a job for the server.

PHP acts on the SERVER

PHP lets you take control of the data a user types into the form by emailing it to you **transparently**. The user types his abduction story into the form, hits the Report Abduction button, and he's done! The PHP code creates the email message, sends it to you, and then generates a web page confirmation for the user.

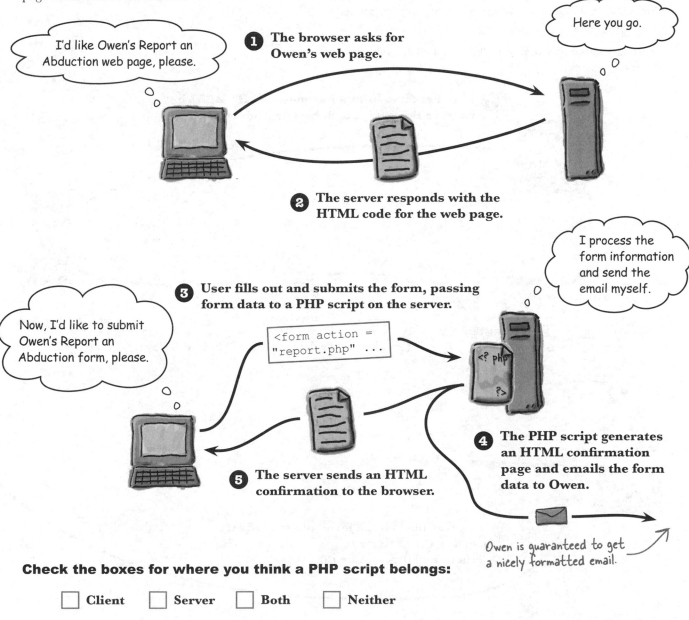

Check the boxes for where you think a PHP script belongs:

☐ **Client**　　☐ **Server**　　☐ **Both**　　☐ **Neither**

PHP scripts run on the <u>server</u>

PHP code runs on the server and is stored in PHP **scripts** that usually have a `.php` file extension. PHP scripts often look a lot like normal HTML web pages because they can contain both HTML code and CSS code. In fact, when the server runs a PHP script the end result is always pure HTML and CSS. So every PHP script ultimately gets turned into HTML and CSS once it's finished running on the server.

Let's take a closer look at how a PHP script changes the flow of Owen's web form.

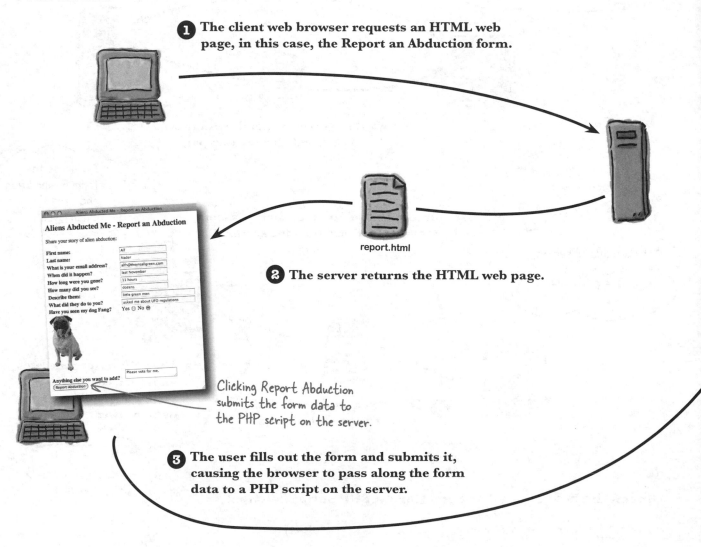

1 The client web browser requests an HTML web page, in this case, the Report an Abduction form.

report.html

2 The server returns the HTML web page.

Clicking Report Abduction submits the form data to the PHP script on the server.

3 The user fills out the form and submits it, causing the browser to pass along the form data to a PHP script on the server.

PHP is a server-side programming language – it runs on a web server.

5 The server returns a pure HTML web page that was generated by the PHP script.

The PHP script runs on the server!

Although the page name shows up with a .php name in the browser, it's pure HTML at this point.

report.php

6 The browser displays the confirmation web page.

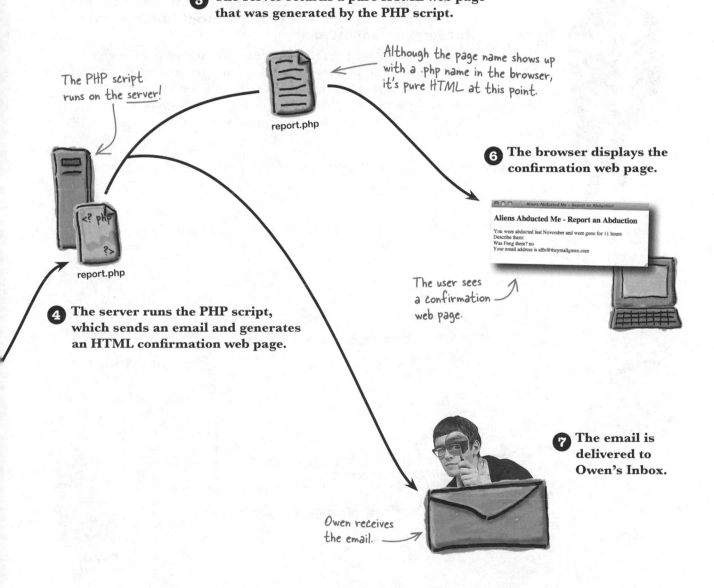

Aliens Abducted Me – Report an Abduction

Aliens Abducted Me - Report an Abduction

You were abducted last November and were gone for 11 hours
Describe them:
Was Fang there? no
Your email address is alfn@theyreallgreen.com

The user sees a confirmation web page.

report.php

4 The server runs the PHP script, which sends an email and generates an HTML confirmation web page.

7 The email is delivered to Owen's Inbox.

Owen receives the email.

Okay. But what actually causes a PHP script to get run on the server?

A form element's action attribute is what connects a form to a PHP script, causing the script to run when the form is submitted.

Forms are created using the HTML <form> tag, and every <form> tag has an action attribute. Whatever filename you set the action attribute to is used by the web server to process the form when it is submitted. So if Owen's PHP script is named report.php, then the <form> tag that connects it to the form looks like this:

<form action = "report.php" method = "post">

This is the filename of your PHP script.

When the user clicks the Report Abduction button in the form, the form action causes the report.php script to be run **on the server** to process the form data.

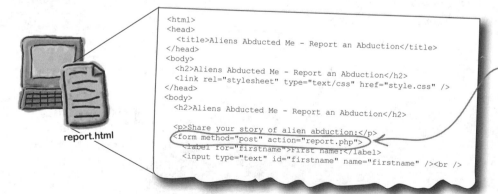

```html
<html>
<head>
  <title>Aliens Abducted Me - Report an Abduction</title>
</head>
<body>
  <h2>Aliens Abducted Me - Report an Abduction</h2>
  <link rel="stylesheet" type="text/css" href="style.css" />
</head>
<body>
  <h2>Aliens Abducted Me - Report an Abduction</h2>

  <p>Share your story of alien abduction:</p>
<form method="post" action="report.php">
    <label for="firstname">First name:</label>
    <input type="text" id="firstname" name="firstname" /><br />
```

report.html

The action attribute of the <form> tag is what causes the PHP script to run on the server when the form is submitted.

report.php

there are no
Dumb Questions

Q: What does PHP stand for?

A: PHP is an acronym that originally stood for **P**ersonal **H**ome **P**ages. Somewhere along the way the acronym was changed to mean **P**HP: **H**ypertext **P**rocessor. The latter is considered a recursive acronym because it references itself—the acronym (PHP) is inside the acronym. Clever? Confusing? You decide!

Q: Even though my web browser shows that a web page has a name that ends in `.php`, it's still pure HTML? How is that?

A: It's possible because the page **originates** as PHP code on the server but is **transformed** into HTML code before making its way to the browser. So the server runs the PHP code and converts it into HTML code before sending it along to the browser for viewing. This means that even though a .php file contains PHP code, the browser never sees it—it only sees the HTML code that results from running the PHP code on the server.

Q: But don't all web pages originate on the server, even pure HTML pages in `.html` files?

A: Yes. All of the files for a web site are stored on the server—`.html`, `.css`, `.php`, etc. But they aren't all **processed** by the server. HTML and CSS files, as well as image files, are sent directly to the client browser without worrying about what's actually inside them. PHP files are different because they contain code that's processed and **run** on the web server. It's not the PHP code that's sent to the browser, it's the **results** of running the PHP code that are sent, and these results are pure HTML and CSS.

Use PHP to access the form data

So Owen needs a PHP script that can get the alien abduction form information to him more reliably than the `mailto` technique. Let's create it. Don't worry about understanding everything yet—we'll get to that:

> It's perfectly normal for a PHP script to include regular HTML tags and attributes.

PHP scripts often start out looking a lot like HTML web pages.

```
<html>

<head>

   <title>Aliens Abducted Me - Report an Abduction</title>

</head>

<body>

   <h2>Aliens Abducted Me - Report an Abduction</h2>
```

> This entire block of script code is PHP...the rest of the script is normal HTML.

Ah, here's where things get interesting — this is the beginning of the actual PHP code.

```php
<?php
   $when_it_happened = $_POST['whenithappened'];

   $how_long = $_POST['howlong'];

   $alien_description = $_POST['description'];

   $fang_spotted = $_POST['fangspotted'];

   $email = $_POST['email'];


   echo 'Thanks for submitting the form.<br />';
   echo 'You were abducted ' . $when_it_happened;
   echo ' and were gone for ' . $how_long . '<br />';
   echo 'Describe them: ' . $alien_description . '<br />';
   echo 'Was Fang there? ' . $fang_spotted . '<br />';
   echo 'Your email address is ' . $email;
?>
```

> This chunk of PHP code grabs the form data so that it can be displayed as part of a confirmation page.

> Here we use PHP to generate HTML code from the form data.

```
</body>

</html>
```

> Just like a normal web page, this PHP script finishes up by closing out open HTML tags.

TEST DRIVE

Change Owen's form to use a PHP script to process the form data.

Create a new text file called **report.php**, and enter all of the code on the facing page. This is the script that will process Owen's web form.

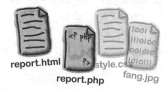

report.html   report.php   style.css   fang.jpg

The PHP script isn't connected to the form yet, so open the report.html page in a text editor and change the form action to report.php instead of mailto.

```
<form action = "report.php" method = "post">
```

Open the report.html page in a web browser, enter some alien abduction information in the form, and click Report Abduction.

> Depending on your browser, you may see a web page with some weird text in it, or possibly just the PHP source code for the report.php script.

Aliens Abducted Me - Report an Abduction

Share your story of alien abduction:

First name: Alf
Last name: Nader
What is your email address?   alfn@theyreallgreen.com
When did it happen?   last November
How long were you gone?   11 hours
How many did you see?   dozens
Describe them: little green men
What did they do to you?   asked me about UFO regulation
Have you seen my dog Fang?   Yes ◯ No ◉

Anything else you want to add?   Please vote for me.

[Report Abduction]

Aliens Abducted Me - Report an Abduction

You were abducted ' . $when_it_happened; echo ' and were gone for ' . $show_long; echo ' Describe them: ' . $alien_description; echo ' Was Fang there? ' . $fang_spotted; echo ' Your email address is ' . $email; ?>

```
report.php
Transitional//EN"
    "http://www.w3.org/TR/xhtml1/DTD/xhtml1-
transitional.dtd">
<html xmlns="http://www.w3.org/1999/xhtml" xml:lang="en"
lang="en">
<head>
    <meta http-equiv="Content-Type" content="text/html;
charset=utf-8"/>
    <title>Aliens Abducted Me - Report an Abduction</title>
</head>
<body>
    <h2>Aliens Abducted Me - Report an Abduction</h2>
```

Do you think this is how the PHP script is supposed to work? Write down why or why not, and what you think is going on.

....
....
....

PHP scripts must live on a server!

Unless you happen to have a web server running on your local computer, the report.php script can't run when you submit the Report an Abduction form. Remember, PHP is a programming language, and it needs an environment to run in. This environment is a web server with PHP support. PHP scripts and web pages that rely on the scripts **must be placed on a real web server**, as opposed to just opening a script directly from a local file system.

If you do have a web server installed locally and it has PHP support, then you can test out PHP scripts directly on your local computer.

Unlike HTML web pages, which can be opened locally in a web browser, PHP scripts must always be "opened" through a URL from a web server.

Web browsers know nothing about PHP and, therefore, have no ability to run PHP scripts.

This PHP script is just a bunch of meaningless code to the web browser.

The web server understands this PHP code and runs the script!

Web servers with PHP support are equipped to run PHP scripts and turn them into HTML web pages that browsers can understand.

A quick way to tell if a web page is being delivered by a web server is to look for the URL starting with "http:". Web pages opened as local files always start with "file:".

PHP scripts must be run <u>on a web server</u> or they won't work.

Get your PHP scripts to the server

It's perfectly fine to create and edit PHP scripts on your local computer. But you need to put the files on a web server to run them. PHP files are often placed alongside HTML files on a web server. There's nothing magical about putting PHP scripts on a web server—just upload them to a place where your web pages can access them. Uploading files to a web server requires the help of a utility, such as an FTP (File Transfer Protocol) utility.

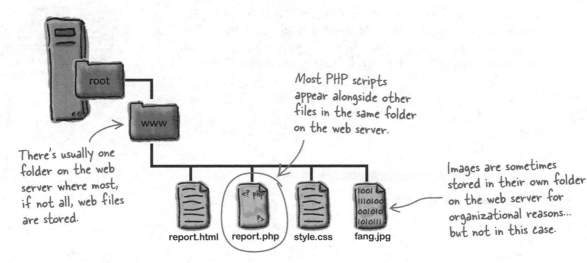

Most PHP scripts appear alongside other files in the same folder on the web server.

There's usually one folder on the web server where most, if not all, web files are stored.

Images are sometimes stored in their own folder on the web server for organizational reasons... but not in this case.

Uploading your PHP scripts to a web server isn't enough—that web server must also have PHP installed on it. Some web servers include PHP by default, some don't.

there are no Dumb Questions

Q: How do I know if my web server has PHP installed?

A: You could ask your web administrator or web hosting company, or you could just perform a little test yourself. Create a text file called `test.php` and enter the following code into it:

```php
<?php
  phpinfo();
?>
```

This code asks PHP to display information about itself.

Now upload `test.php` to your web server, and then enter its URL into a web browser. If PHP is installed on your server, you'll see lots of detailed information about PHP, including its version. Bingo!

If you don't have PHP installed on your web server, check out Appendix ii.

You'll find instructions here for getting PHP up and running on your web server.

Remember to delete phpinfo() script when you're done, so no one else can see it.

TEST DRIVE

Upload the Report an Abduction files to a web server, and try out the form...again.

Upload `report.html`, `report.php`, `style.css`, and `fang.jpg` to a web server that has PHP installed. Enter the URL of the `report.html` page into your browser, fill out the form with alien abduction information, and click the Report Abduction button.

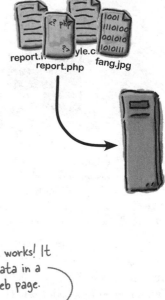

report.h... yle.c...
report.php   fang.jpg

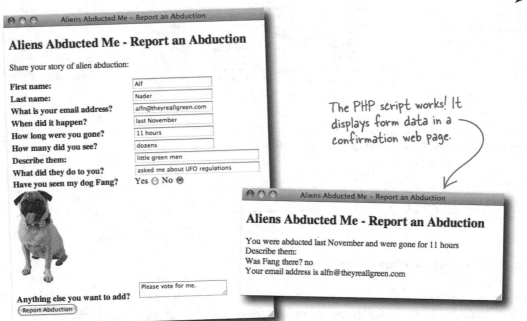

Aliens Abducted Me – Report an Abduction

Aliens Abducted Me - Report an Abduction

Share your story of alien abduction:

First name:	Alf
Last name:	Nader
What is your email address?	alfn@theyreallgreen.com
When did it happen?	last November
How long were you gone?	11 hours
How many did you see?	dozens
Describe them:	little green men
What did they do to you?	asked me about UFO regulations
Have you seen my dog Fang?	Yes ○ No ⊙

The PHP script works! It displays form data in a confirmation web page.

Aliens Abducted Me – Report an Abduction

Aliens Abducted Me - Report an Abduction

You were abducted last November and were gone for 11 hours
Describe them:
Was Fang there? no
Your email address is alfn@theyreallgreen.com

Anything else you want to add? Please vote for me.

[Report Abduction]

Cool. Now you just need to add some PHP code to take care of emailing the form data.

That's right. The `report.php` script's still missing code to email the alien abduction data to Owen.

But that's not a problem because PHP offers a function, a pre-built chunk of reusable code, that you can use to send email messages. You just need to figure out what the email message needs to say and then use PHP to create and send it.

Time out! We don't even know how the original report.php script works, and now we're charging ahead into sending emails. This is like majorly overwhelming...hello!?

It's true. Doing more with PHP requires <u>knowing</u> <u>more</u> about PHP.

So in order to add email functionality to Owen's `report.php` script, you're going to have to dig a little deeper into PHP and get a solid handle on how the script works up to this point.

The server turns PHP into HTML

A big part of understanding how a PHP script works is getting a handle on what happens to the script when it runs on the server. Most PHP scripts contain both PHP code and HTML code, and the PHP's run and turned into HTML before the server passes the whole thing off as HTML to the client web browser. In Owen's `report.php` script, PHP code generates most of the HTML content in the body of the confirmation page. The HTML code surrounding it is delivered unchanged.

This HTML code is passed along unchanged to the browser.

```html
<html>
<head>
  <title>Aliens Abducted Me - Report an Abduction</title>
</head>
<body>
  <h2>Aliens Abducted Me - Report an Abduction</h2>
```

This PHP code is run by the server and generates HTML code containing data that was entered into the form.

```php
<?php
  $when_it_happened = $_POST['whenithappened'];
  $how_long = $_POST['howlong'];
  $alien_description = $_POST['aliendescription'];
  $fang_spotted = $_POST['fangspotted'];
  $email = $_POST['email'];

  echo 'Thanks for submitting the form.<br />';
  echo 'You were abducted ' . $when_it_happened;
  echo ' and were gone for ' . $how_long . '<br />';
  echo 'Describe them: ' . $alien_description . '<br />';
  echo 'Was Fang there? ' . $fang_spotted . '<br />';
  echo 'Your email address is ' . $email;
?>
```

```html
</body>
</html>
```

More static HTML code, which the server passes along to the browser with no changes.

report.php

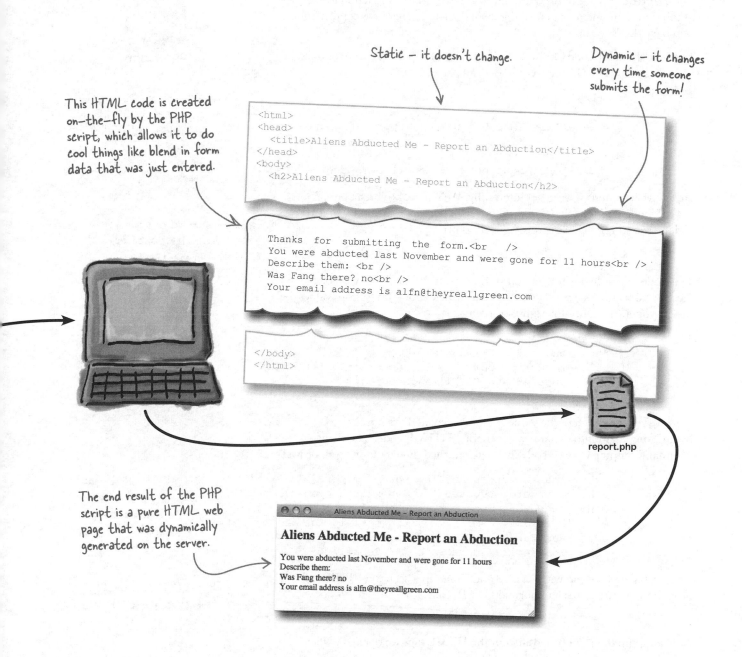

Static – it doesn't change.

Dynamic – it changes every time someone submits the form!

This HTML code is created on-the-fly by the PHP script, which allows it to do cool things like blend in form data that was just entered.

```
<html>
<head>
  <title>Aliens Abducted Me - Report an Abduction</title>
</head>
<body>
  <h2>Aliens Abducted Me - Report an Abduction</h2>


  Thanks  for  submitting  the  form.<br    />
  You were abducted last November and were gone for 11 hours<br />
  Describe them: <br />
  Was Fang there? no<br />
  Your email address is alfn@theyreallgreen.com


</body>
</html>
```

report.php

The end result of the PHP script is a pure HTML web page that was dynamically generated on the server.

Aliens Abducted Me – Report an Abduction

Aliens Abducted Me - Report an Abduction

You were abducted last November and were gone for 11 hours
Describe them:
Was Fang there? no
Your email address is alfn@theyreallgreen.com

Deconstructing Owen's PHP script

report.php

The `report.php` script is triggered by the Report an Abduction form, and its job (at the moment) is to take the form data and generate a confirmation web page. Let's see how.

The first chunk of code is pure HTML. It just sets up the page we're building, including a few HTML tags required of all pages.

```
<html>
<head>
   <title>Aliens Abducted Me - Report an Abduction</title>
</head>
<body>
   <h2>Aliens Abducted Me - Report an Abduction</h2>
```

Yes, this HTML code is pretty minimal — ideally you'd have a DOCTYPE, `<meta>` tag, etc., but we're keeping things simple here.

Here's where things start to get interesting. We're ready to break out of HTML code and into PHP code. The `<?php` tag opens a section of PHP code—everything following this tag is pure PHP.

```
<?php
```

From here on, we're dealing with PHP code...at least until we get to the closing `?>` tag.

This code grabs the form data and stores it away in individual variables so that we can easily access it later. PHP **variables** allow you to store values, be they numbers, text, or other kinds of data.

```
$when_it_happened = $_POST['whenithappened'];
$how_long = $_POST['howlong'];
$alien_description = $_POST['description'];
$fang_spotted = $_POST['fangspotted'];
$email = $_POST['email'];
```

Each line of PHP code assigns the data from a form field to a new variable.

Now we're talking! Here the variables we just created are put to work by inserting them into dynamically generated HTML code. The `echo` command outputs HTML code that gets returned directly to the web browser.

```
echo 'Thanks for submitting the form.<br />';
echo 'You were abducted ' . $when_it_happened;
echo ' and were gone for ' . $how_long . '<br />';
echo 'Describe them: ' . $alien_description . '<br />';
echo 'Was Fang there? ' . $fang_spotted . '<br />';
echo 'Your email address is ' . $email;
```

This PHP code blends variables into HTML code that's output to the browser.

The `?>` tag matches up with `<?php` and closes up a section of PHP code. From here on, we're back to normal HTML code.

```
?>
```

This ends the PHP code — after this we're back to normal HTML.

Now wrap up the page by closing out the HTML tags we opened earlier.

```
</body>
</html>
```

Don't forget, we're generating an HTML web page, so wrap up the HTML code.

A few PHP rules to ~~live~~ by

code

Owen's `report.php` script reveals a few fundamental rules of the PHP language that apply to all PHP scripts. Let's take a look at them.

☑ **PHP code is always enclosed by <?php and ?>.**

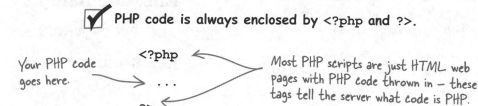

Your PHP code goes here.

```
<?php
...
?>
```

Most PHP scripts are just HTML web pages with PHP code thrown in — these tags tell the server what code is PHP.

☑ **Every PHP statement must end with a semicolon (;).**

```
echo 'Thanks for submitting the form.<br />';
```

If your code ever breaks, check to make sure you haven't forgotten a semicolon. It happens more often than you'd think.

The semicolon lets PHP know that this is the end of a statement.

☑ **If there is any PHP code in a web page, it's a good idea to name the file on the web server with .php, not .html.**

report.php

This isn't a deal breaker, but it's a good idea to name PHP scripts with a .php file extension.

☑ **PHP variable names must begin with a dollar sign ($).**

```
$email = $_POST['email'];
```

The dollar sign clearly identifies a PHP variable, which stores information within a PHP script.

Given the variables used in the report.php script, do you see any other PHP rules pertaining to variables? Write 'em down!

....

....

....

Finding the perfect variable name

In addition to starting with a $, PHP variable names are also case-sensitive. But that's not all—there are other important rules governing how you name variables. Some of these rules are syntax rules, meaning your code will break if you ignore them, while other rules are just good ideas passed down from wise old PHP coders.

Let's start with the official rules that will absolutely cause problems if you ignore them when naming variables. Follow these rules to create **legal** variable names.

> ## A variable is a __container__ that you can store data in, and every variable has a unique name.

☑ The first character must be a dollar sign ($). ← *Got it!*

☑ A variable name must be at least __one__ character in length.

Not counting the $ character, which is required of every variable name.

☑ The first character after the dollar sign can be a letter or an underscore (_), and characters after that can be a letter, an underscore, or a number.

☑ Spaces and special characters other than _ and $ are not allowed in any part of a variable name.

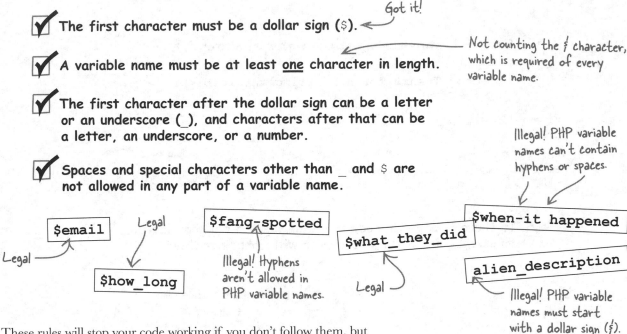

Legal `$email`

Legal `$how_long`

`$fang-spotted`

Illegal! Hyphens aren't allowed in PHP variable names.

`$what_they_did`

Legal

Illegal! PHP variable names can't contain hyphens or spaces.

`$when-it happened`

`alien_description`

Illegal! PHP variable names must start with a dollar sign ($).

These rules will stop your code working if you don't follow them, but there are a couple more rules that are good to follow as more of a coding convention. These rules help make PHP code a little more consistent and easier to read.

☑ Use all lowercase for variable names.

☑ Separate words in a multi-word variable name with underscores.

These last two rules won't break your code if you ignore them, and you'll certainly run across PHP code that doesn't adhere to them yet works just fine. This is because they are just a stylistic convention—but they will serve you well as you begin creating and naming variables of your own.

> ## PHP variable names must __begin__ with a dollar sign, and __cannot__ contain spaces. $

there are no
Dumb Questions

Q: **Does it matter whether I put PHP commands in uppercase or lowercase?**

A: Yes and no. For the most part, PHP isn't case-sensitive, so you can get away with mixing the case of most commands. That means you can use `echo`, `ECHO`, or `EchO` when echoing content. However, as a matter of convention, it's a very good idea to be consistent with case in your scripts. Most PHP coders prefer lowercase for the vast majority of PHP code, which is why you'll see `echo` used throughout the example code in the book.

Q: **So even if it's a bad coding convention, I can mix and match the case of PHP code?**

A: No, not entirely. The huge exception to the case insensitivity of PHP is variable names, which apply to data storage locations that you create. So let's take the `$email` variable used in the Report an Abduction script as an example. This variable name is case-sensitive, so you can't refer to it as `$EMAIL` or `$eMail`. All variable names in PHP are case-sensitive like this, so it's important to name variables carefully and then reference them consistently in your code. More on variable names in just a moment.

Q: **Is it really OK to put both PHP and HTML code in the same file?**

A: Absolutely. In fact, in many cases it's absolutely necessary to do so.

Q: **Why would I want to do that?**

A: Because the whole idea behind a web server is to serve up HTML web pages to browsers. PHP doesn't change that fact. What PHP allows you to do is change the HTML content on the fly with things like today's date, data pulled from a database, or even calculated values such as the order total in a shopping cart. So PHP allows you to manipulate the HTML that goes into web pages, as opposed to them just being created statically at design time. It's very common to have HTML code for a page with PHP code sprinkled throughout to plug in important data or otherwise alter the HTML programmatically.

Q: **Does PHP code embedded in an HTML file have to be on its own line, or can I embed it in an HTML line, like as part of an HTML tag attribute?**

A: Other than needing to place your PHP code within the `<?php` and `?>` tags, there are no restrictions in how you embed it in HTML code. In fact, it's often necessary to wedge a piece of PHP code into the middle of HTML code, like when you're setting the attribute of an HTML tag. This is a perfectly legitimate usage of PHP.

Q: **I've seen PHP code that's enclosed by `<?` as the start tag instead of `<?php`. Is that right?**

A: Not really. Technically speaking, it's legal, but it isn't recommended. A server setting must be enabled for the short open tag (`<?`) to work. The usual `<?php` tag always works, so it's better to use that and know that your code will just work.

Q: **If a web server always returns pure HTML code to a client browser, why do URLs show the PHP script name, like webpage.php?**

A: Remember that every web page is the result of a two-sided communication involving a request from the client browser and a response from the web server. The URL is the basis of the request, while the content returned from the server is the response. PHP scripts are requested just like normal HTML web pages through URLs entered into the browser or linked from other pages, or as form actions. That explains why the URL for a PHP "page" shows the name of the PHP script.

The other half of the equation is the response from the server, which is the resulting code that's generated by the PHP script. Since most PHP scripts generate HTML code, it makes sense that the code is HTML and not PHP. So it's no accident that a URL references a .php file on a server, which causes PHP code to be executed on the server, ultimately resulting in pure HTML content being returned to the browser.

Q: **Can PHP variables store any other kinds of data?**

A: Absolutely. You can use variables to store Boolean (true/false) data. And numeric data can be either integer or floating-point (decimal). There are also arrays, which store a collection of data, as well as objects, which associate a collection of data with code that is used to manipulate the data. Arrays are covered a little later in this chapter, while objects are tackled in Chapter 12. There is also a special data type called `NULL`, which represents no value. For example, a variable that hasn't been assigned a value is considered `NULL`.

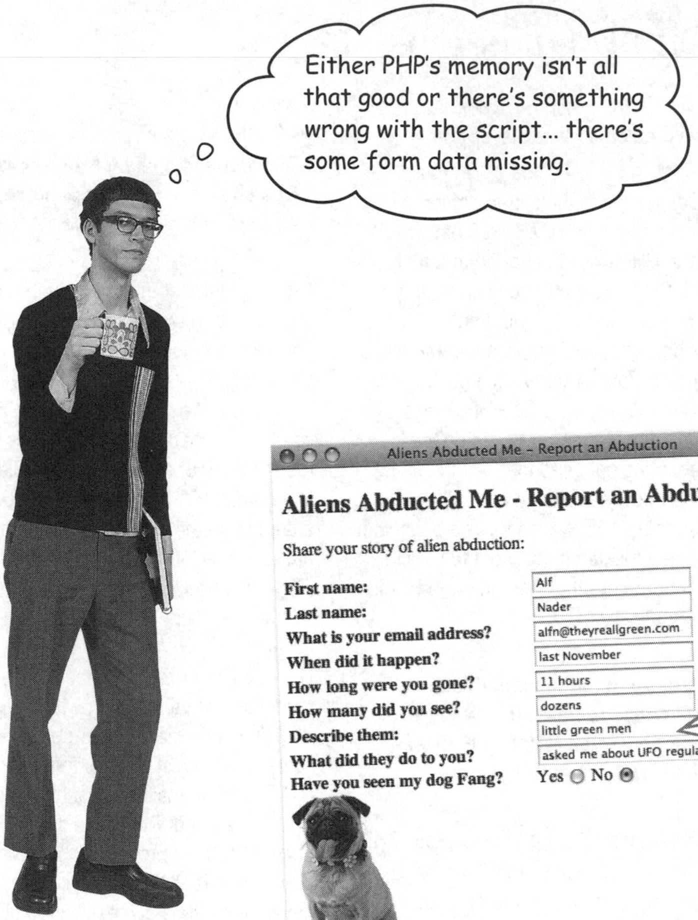

Either PHP's memory isn't all that good or there's something wrong with the script... there's some form data missing.

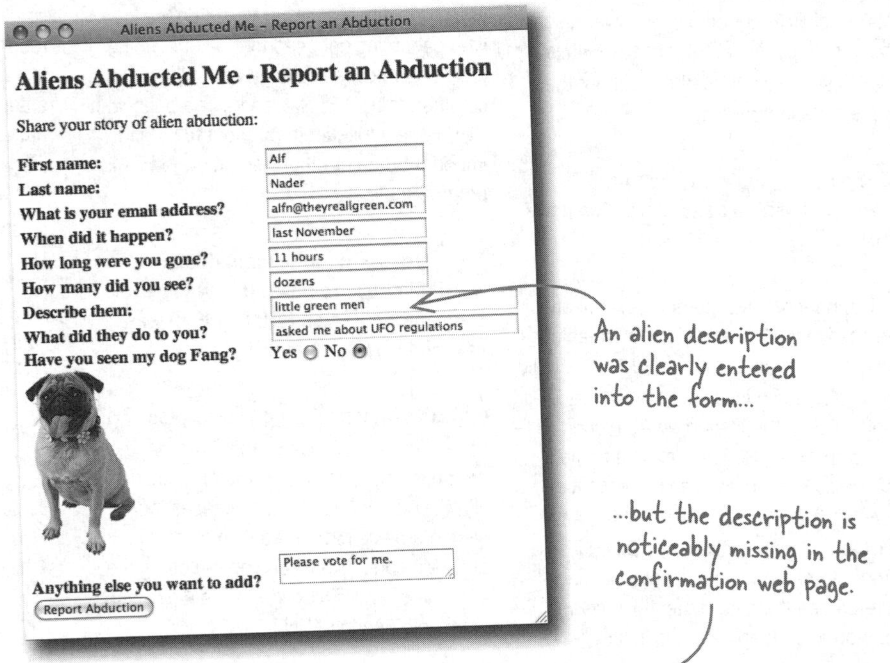

Aliens Abducted Me – Report an Abduction
Aliens Abducted Me - Report an Abduction
Share your story of alien abduction:
First name: Alf
Last name: Nader
What is your email address? alfn@theyreallgreen.com
When did it happen? last November
How long were you gone? 11 hours
How many did you see? dozens
Describe them: little green men
What did they do to you? asked me about UFO regulations
Have you seen my dog Fang? Yes No
Anything else you want to add? Please vote for me.
Report Abduction
An alien description was clearly entered into the form...
...but the description is noticeably missing in the confirmation web page.

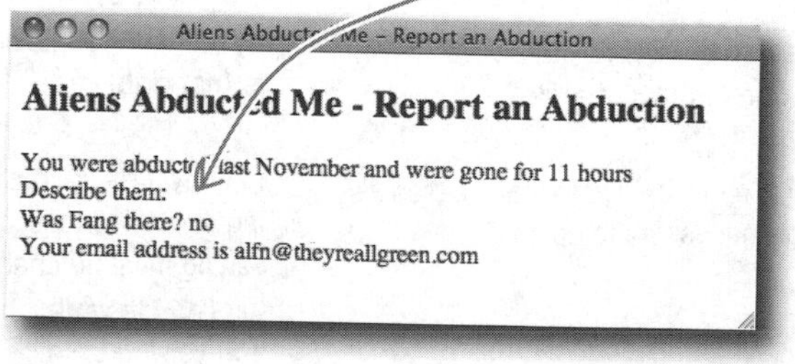

Aliens Abducted Me – Report an Abduction
Aliens Abducted Me - Report an Abduction
You were abducted last November and were gone for 11 hours
Describe them:
Was Fang there? no
Your email address is alfn@theyreallgreen.com

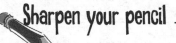

Sharpen your pencil

There's a problem with the alien description form data in Owen's report.php script. Circle the lines of code that you think relate to the problem, and write down what they do. Any idea what's wrong?

```html
<html>

<head>

  <title>Aliens Abducted Me - Report an Abduction</title>

</head>

<body>

  <h2>Aliens Abducted Me - Report an Abduction</h2>


<?php

  $when_it_happened = $_POST['whenithappened'];

  $how_long = $_POST['howlong'];

  $alien_description = $_POST['description'];

  $fang_spotted = $_POST['fangspotted'];

  $email = $_POST['email'];


  echo 'Thanks for submitting the form.<br />';

  echo 'You were abducted ' . $when_it_happened;

  echo ' and were gone for ' . $how_long . '<br />';

  echo 'Describe them: ' . $alien_description . '<br />';

  echo 'Was Fang there? ' . $fang_spotted . '<br />';

  echo 'Your email address is ' . $email;

?>


</body>

</html>
```

report.php

Sharpen your pencil
Solution

There's a problem with the alien description form data in Owen's report.php script. Circle the lines of code that you think relate to the problem, and write down what they do. Any idea what's wrong?

This line of code grabs the alien description from the HTML form field and stores it in a PHP variable named $alien_description.

This code combines the alien description with some other text and HTML code, and outputs all of it to the browser.

```
<html>

<head>

  <title>Aliens Abducted Me - Report an Abduction</title>

</head>

<body>

  <h2>Aliens Abducted Me - Report an Abduction</h2>


<?php

  $when_it_happened = $_POST['whenithappened'];

  $how_long = $_POST['howlong'];

  $alien_description = $_POST['description'];

  $fang_spotted = $_POST['fangspotted'];

  $email = $_POST['email'];


  echo 'Thanks for submitting the form.<br />';

  echo 'You were abducted ' . $when_it_happened;

  echo ' and were gone for ' . $how_long . '<br />';

  echo 'Describe them: ' . $alien_description . '<br />';

  echo 'Was Fang there? ' . $fang_spotted . '<br />';

  echo 'Your email address is ' . $email;

?>


</body>

</html>
```

For some reason the $alien_description variable appears to be empty...not good.

report.php

Variables are for storing script data

PHP variables are storage containers that store information kinda like how a cup stores a beverage. Since the `$alien_description` variable is empty, we know that the form data is never making its way into it. So the `$alien_description` variable remains empty despite our attempt to **assign** data to it.

We're looking for a cup that overfloweth with an alien description!

$alien_description

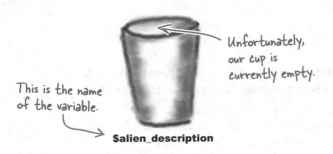

Unfortunately, our cup is currently empty.

This is the name of the variable.

$alien_description

One way to fix the script would be to just assign the exact string we're expecting to the `$alien_description` variable, like this:

```
$alien_description = 'little green men';
```

The equal sign tells PHP to assign the value on the right to the variable on the left.

Pieces of text in PHP, also known as strings, must always be enclosed by quotes, either single quotes or double quotes.

This code works in that it most definitely stores the text `'little green men'` in the `$alien_description` variable. But we solved one problem by creating another one—this code causes the alien description to always be the same regardless of what the user enters into the form.

BRAIN POWER

Somehow the assignment of alien description form data to the `$alien_description` variable is coming up empty.

```
$alien_description = $_POST['description'];
```

What do you think this code is doing wrong?

The problem obviously has something to do with that $_POST thingy. But I have no idea what it is.

The problem does have to do with $_POST, which is a mechanism used to pass along form data to a script.

The dollar sign at the beginning of $_POST is a clue... $_POST is a storage container! More specifically, $_POST is a **collection** of storage locations used to hold data from a web form. In Owen's case, it holds all the data that gets sent to our report.php script when someone fills out the form and clicks the Report Abduction button. So in order to access the form data and do anything with it, we have to go through $_POST. Remember this code?

```
$when_it_happened = $_POST['whenithappened'];

$how_long = $_POST['howlong'];

$alien_description = $_POST['description'];

$fang_spotted = $_POST['fangspotted'];

$email = $_POST['email'];
```

The piece of form data holding the duration of the abduction is assigned to the variable $how_long.

Same deal here, except the email form data is being grabbed and stored away in the $email variable.

So the data in each field of the Report an Abduction form is accessed using $_POST. But what exactly is $_POST... a variable?

$_POST is a special variable that holds form data

$_POST is a special variable that is known as a **superglobal** because it is built into PHP and is available throughout an entire script. $_POST already exists when your script runs—you don't create it like you do other PHP variables.

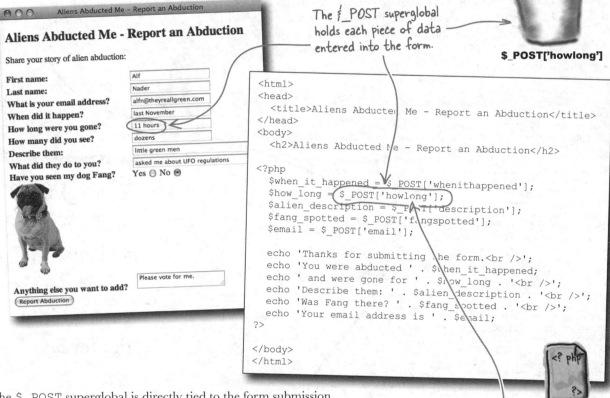

The $_POST superglobal holds each piece of data entered into the form.

$_POST['howlong']

```html
<html>
<head>
  <title>Aliens Abducted Me - Report an Abduction</title>
</head>
<body>
  <h2>Aliens Abducted Me - Report an Abduction</h2>

<?php
  $when_it_happened = $_POST['whenithappened'];
  $how_long = $_POST['howlong'];
  $alien_description = $_POST['description'];
  $fang_spotted = $_POST['fangspotted'];
  $email = $_POST['email'];

  echo 'Thanks for submitting the form.<br />';
  echo 'You were abducted ' . $when_it_happened;
  echo ' and were gone for ' . $how_long . '<br />';
  echo 'Describe them: ' . $alien_description . '<br />';
  echo 'Was Fang there? ' . $fang_spotted . '<br />';
  echo 'Your email address is ' . $email;
?>

</body>
</html>
```

report.php

The name "howlong" comes from the name attribute of the <input> tag for this form field.

The $_POST superglobal is directly tied to the form submission method used by the HTML form. If the method's set to post, then all of the form data gets packaged into the $_POST superglobal, where each piece of data can be plucked out and used as needed.

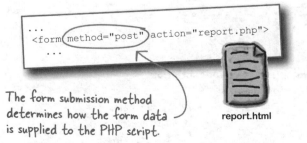

```html
...
<form method="post" action="report.php">
  ...
```

report.html

The form submission method determines how the form data is supplied to the PHP script.

BRAIN POWER

How do you think the $_POST superglobal works? How can it store multiple values from all those text boxes on Owen's form?

$_POST transports form data to your script

$_POST is a special kind of PHP storage container known as an **array**, which stores a collection of variables under a single name. When someone submits Owen's form, the data they've typed into the form fields is stored in the $_POST array, whose job is to pass the data along to the script.

Each element in the $_POST array corresponds to a piece of data entered into a form field. To access the data for a specific form field, you use the name of the field with $_POST. So the duration of an abduction is stored in $_POST['howlong']. The HTML code for Owen's form reveals how form names relate to data stored in $_POST.

```
<p>Share your story of alien abduction:</p>
<form method="post" action="report.php">
  <label for="firstname">First name:</label>
  <input type="text" id="firstname" name="firstname" /><br />
  <label for="lastname">Last name:</label>
  <input type="text" id="lastname" name="lastname" /><br />
  <label for="email">What is your email address?</label>
  <input type="text" id="email" name="email" /><br />
  <label for="whenithappened">When did it happen?</label>
  <input type="text" id="whenithappened" name="whenithappened" /><br />
  <label for="howlong">How long were you gone?</label>
  <input type="text" id="howlong" name="howlong" /><br />
  <label for="howmany">How many did you see?</label>
  <input type="text" id="howmany" name="howmany" /><br />
  <label for="aliendescription">Describe them:</label>
  <input type="text" id="aliendescription" name="aliendescription" size="32" /><br />
  <label for="whattheydid">What did they do to you?</label>
  <input type="text" id="whattheydid" name="whattheydid" size="32" /><br />
  <label for="fangspotted">Have you seen my dog Fang?</label>
  Yes <input id="fangspotted" name="fangspotted" type="radio" value="yes" />
  No <input id="fangspotted" name="fangspotted" type="radio" value="no" /><br />
  <img src="fang.jpg" width="100" height="175"
    alt="My abducted dog Fang." /><br />
  <label for="other">Anything else you want to add?</label>
  <textarea name="other"></textarea><br />
  <input type="submit" value="Report Abduction" name="submit" />
</form>
```

The $_POST array is filled with the values the user entered into the form.

The name of the form field determines how it is accessed within the $_POST array.

'firstname'   'email'   'howlong'   'aliendescription'
   'lastname'   'whenithappened'   'howmany'

$_POST

All of the form data is accessible through the $_POST array.

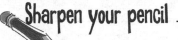

Sharpen your pencil

Scratch through the code in `report.php` that is causing the alien description to come up blank, and then write down how to fix it. Hint: Use the HTML form code on the facing page to help isolate the problem.

```html
<html>

<head>

  <title>Aliens Abducted Me - Report an Abduction</title>

</head>

<body>

  <h2>Aliens Abducted Me - Report an Abduction</h2>


<?php

  $when_it_happened = $_POST['whenithappened'];

  $how_long = $_POST['howlong'];

  $alien_description = $_POST['description'];

  $fang_spotted = $_POST['fangspotted'];

  $email = $_POST['email'];


  echo 'Thanks for submitting the form.<br />';

  echo 'You were abducted ' . $when_it_happened;

  echo ' and were gone for ' . $how_long . '<br />';

  echo 'Describe them: ' . $alien_description . '<br />';

  echo 'Was Fang there? ' . $fang_spotted . '<br />';

  echo 'Your email address is ' . $email;

?>


</body>

</html>
```

Remember, earlier we isolated the problem down to these two lines of code.

report.php

Sharpen your pencil
Solution

Scratch through the code in `report.php` that is causing the alien description to come up blank, and then write down how to fix it. Hint: Use the HTML form code on the facing page to help isolate the problem.

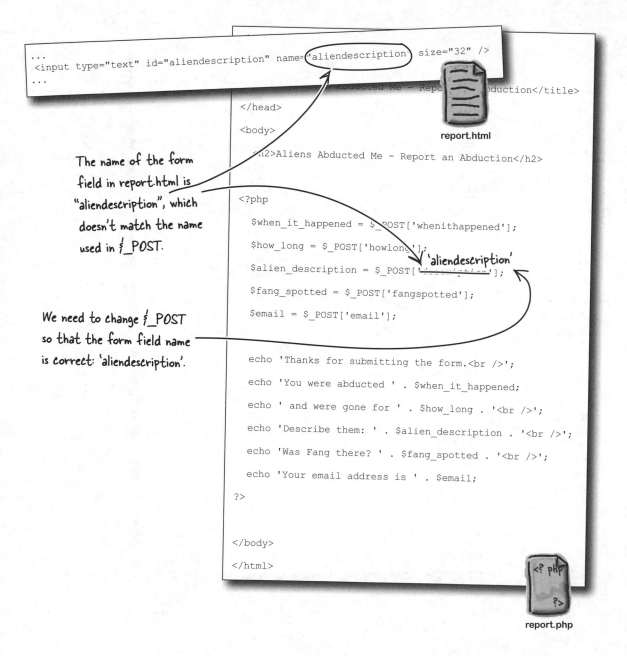

```
...
<input type="text" id="aliendescription" name="aliendescription" size="32" />
...
```

```
                                    ...Abducted Me - Report ...bduction</title>
  </head>

  <body>
    ...2>Aliens Abducted Me - Report an Abduction</h2>

    <?php
      $when_it_happened = $_POST['whenithappened'];

      $how_long = $_POST['howlong'];
                                              'aliendescription'
      $alien_description = $_POST['_____'];

      $fang_spotted = $_POST['fangspotted'];

      $email = $_POST['email'];


      echo 'Thanks for submitting the form.<br />';
      echo 'You were abducted ' . $when_it_happened;
      echo ' and were gone for ' . $how_long . '<br />';
      echo 'Describe them: ' . $alien_description . '<br />';
      echo 'Was Fang there? ' . $fang_spotted . '<br />';
      echo 'Your email address is ' . $email;
    ?>


  </body>

  </html>
```

report.html

The name of the form field in report.html is "aliendescription", which doesn't match the name used in $_POST.

We need to change $_POST so that the form field name is correct: 'aliendescription'.

report.php

Test Drive

Fix the script and test it out.

Change the broken line of code in `report.php`, and then upload it to your web server. Open the `report.html` page in your browser, fill out the form with alien abduction information, and click the Report Abduction button to submit it to the newly repaired script.

The confirmation page now correctly shows the form data for the alien description!

Awesome. But you know, we're *still* missing some form data...

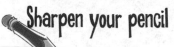

Sharpen your pencil

There's some data entered into Owen's Report an Abduction form that we aren't currently using. Remember, this data contains vital information about an alien abduction that could lead Owen back to his lost dog, Fang. So we need to grab all of the abduction data and store it away in PHP variables.

> The report.php script currently ignores five different pieces of form data. Shocking!

Aliens Abducted Me - Report an Abduction

Share your story of alien abduction:

First name: Alf
Last name: Nader
What is your email address? alfn@theyreallgreen.com
When did it happen? last November
How long were you gone? 11 hours
How many did you see? dozens
Describe them: little green men
What did they do to you? asked me about UFO regulations
Have you seen my dog Fang? Yes ○ No ●

Anything else you want to add? Please vote for me.
Report Abduction

```
...
<form method="post" action="report.php">
  <label for="firstname">First name:</label>
  <input type="text" id="firstname" name="firstname" /><br />
  <label for="lastname">Last name:</label>
  <input type="text" id="lastname" name="lastname" /><br />
  <label for="email">What is your email address?</label>
  <input type="text" id="email" name="email" /><br />
  <label for="whenithappened">When did it happen?</label>
  <input type="text" id="whenithappened" name="whenithappened" /><b
  <label for="howlong">How long were you gone?</label>
  <input type="text" id="howlong" name="howlong" /><br />
  <label for="howmany">How many did you see?</label>
  <input type="text" id="howmany" name="howmany" /><br />
  <label for="aliendescription">Describe them:</label>
  <input type="text" id="aliendescription" name="aliendescription" size="32" /><br />
  <label for="whattheydid">What did they do to you?</label>
  <input type="text" id="whattheydid" name="whattheydid" size="32" /><br />
  <label for="fangspotted">Have you seen my dog Fang?</label>
  Yes <input id="fangspotted" name="fangspotted" type="radio" value="yes" />
  No <input id="fangspotted" name="fangspotted" type="radio" value="no" /><br />
  <img src="fang.jpg" width="100" height="175"
     alt="My abducted dog Fang." /><br />
  <label for="other">Anything else you want to add?</label>
  <textarea id="other" name="other"></textarea><br />
  <input type="submit" value="Report Abduction" name="submit" />
</form>
</body>
</html>
```

report.html

> The <input> tag for each form field holds the key to accessing form data from PHP.

Write PHP code to create four new variables that store the missing form data: $name, $how_many, $what_they_did, and $other. Hint: Create the $name variable so that it stores the user's **full name**.

....

....

....

....

Your work is not quite done. The confirmation web page generated by the PHP script needs to use those new variables to display more information about the alien abduction.

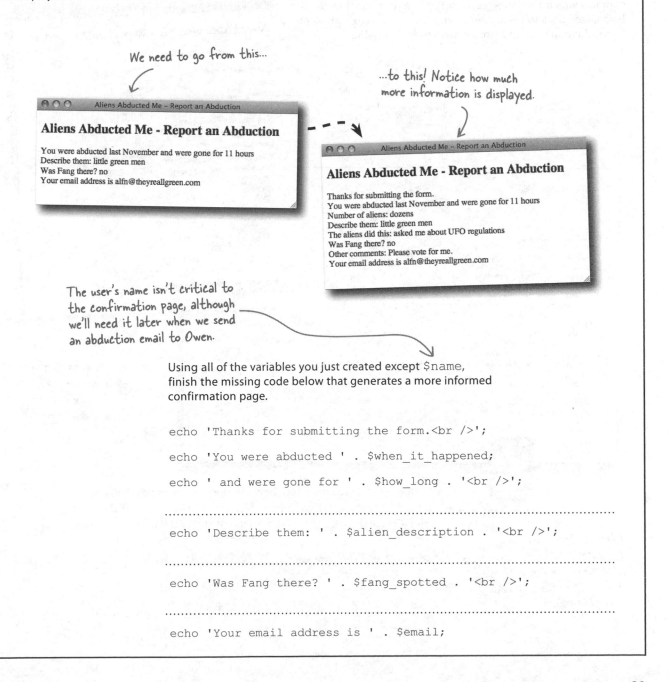

We need to go from this...

...to this! Notice how much more information is displayed.

Aliens Abducted Me - Report an Abduction

You were abducted last November and were gone for 11 hours
Describe them: little green men
Was Fang there? no
Your email address is alfn@theyreallgreen.com

Aliens Abducted Me - Report an Abduction

Thanks for submitting the form.
You were abducted last November and were gone for 11 hours
Number of aliens: dozens
Describe them: little green men
The aliens did this: asked me about UFO regulations
Was Fang there? no
Other comments: Please vote for me.
Your email address is alfn@theyreallgreen.com

The user's name isn't critical to the confirmation page, although we'll need it later when we send an abduction email to Owen.

Using all of the variables you just created except $name, finish the missing code below that generates a more informed confirmation page.

```php
echo 'Thanks for submitting the form.<br />';

echo 'You were abducted ' . $when_it_happened;

echo ' and were gone for ' . $how_long . '<br />';

.......................................................................

echo 'Describe them: ' . $alien_description . '<br />';

.......................................................................

echo 'Was Fang there? ' . $fang_spotted . '<br />';

.......................................................................

echo 'Your email address is ' . $email;
```

Sharpen your pencil
Solution

There's some data entered into Owen's Report an Abduction form that we aren't currently using. Remember, this data contains vital information about an alien abduction that could lead Owen back to his lost dog, Fang. So we need to grab all of the abduction data and store it away in PHP variables.

> The report.php script currently ignores five different pieces of form data. Shocking!

Aliens Abducted Me - Report an Abduction

Share your story of alien abduction:

First name:
Last name:
What is your email address?
When did it happen?
How long were you gone?
How many did you see?
Describe them:
What did they do to you?
Have you seen my dog Fang?

Alf
Nader
alfn@theyreallgreen.com
last November
11 hours
dozens
little green men
asked me about UFO regulations
Yes ○ No ⊙

Anything else you want to add?
Please vote for me.

Report Abduction

```
...
<form method="post" action="report.php">
  <label for="firstname">First name:</label>
  <input type="text" id="firstname" name="firstname" /><br />
  <label for="lastname">Last name:</label>
  <input type="text" id="lastname" name="lastname" /><br />
  <label for="email">What is your email address?</label>
  <input type="text" id="email" name="email" /><br />
  <label for="whenithappened">When did it happen?</label>
  <input type="text" id="whenithappened" name="whenithappened" /><br
  <label for="howlong">How long were you gone?</label>
  <input type="text" id="howlong" name="howlong" /><br />
  <label for="howmany">How many did you see?</label>
  <input type="text" id="howmany" name="howmany" /><br />
  <label for="aliendescription">Describe them:</label>
  <input type="text" id="aliendescription" name="aliendescription" size="32" /><br />
  <label for="whattheydid">What did they do to you?</label>
  <input type="text" id="whattheydid" name="whattheydid" size="32" /><br />
  <label for="fangspotted">Have you seen my dog Fang?</label>
  Yes <input id="fangspotted" name="fangspotted" type="radio" value="yes" />
  No <input id="fangspotted" name="fangspotted" type="radio" value="no" /><br />
  <img src="fang.jpg" width="100" height="175"
    alt="My abducted dog Fang." /><br />
  <label for="other">Anything else you want to add?</label>
  <textarea id="other" name="other"></textarea><br />
  <input type="submit" value="Report Abduction" name="submit" />
</form>
</body>
</html>
```

> The <input> tag for each form field holds the key to accessing form data from PHP.

report.html

> This space separates the first and last names.

Write PHP code to create four new variables that store the missing form data: `$name`, `$how_many`, `$what_they_did`, and `$other`. Hint: Create the `$name` variable so that it stores the user's **full name**.

> The period allows you to stick multiple strings of text together as one — a process known as concatenation.

```
$name = $_POST['firstname'] . ' ' . $_POST['lastname'];
$how_many = $_POST['howmany'];
$what_they_did = $_POST['whattheydid'];
$other = $_POST['other'];
```

Your work is not quite done. The confirmation web page generated by the PHP script needs to use those new variables to display more information about the alien abduction.

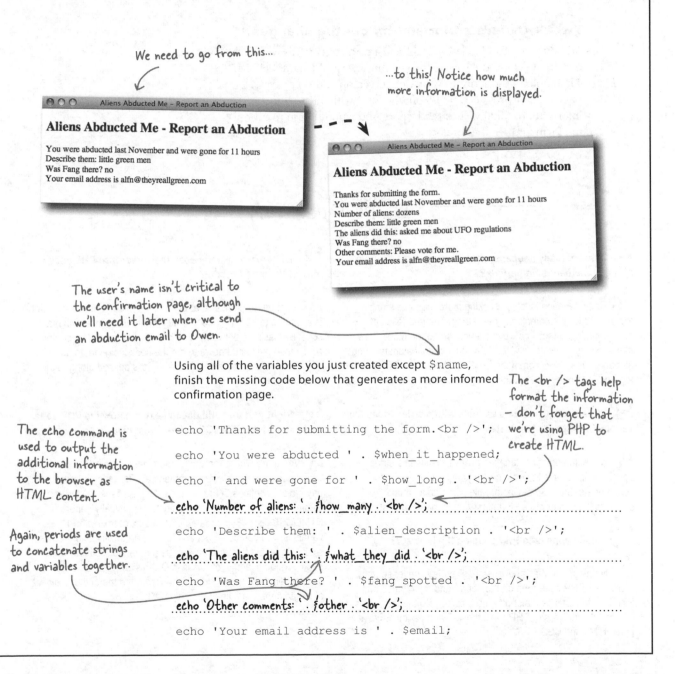

We need to go from this...

...to this! Notice how much more information is displayed.

Aliens Abducted Me - Report an Abduction

You were abducted last November and were gone for 11 hours
Describe them: little green men
Was Fang there? no
Your email address is alfn@theyreallgreen.com

Aliens Abducted Me - Report an Abduction

Thanks for submitting the form.
You were abducted last November and were gone for 11 hours
Number of aliens: dozens
Describe them: little green men
The aliens did this: asked me about UFO regulations
Was Fang there? no
Other comments: Please vote for me.
Your email address is alfn@theyreallgreen.com

The user's name isn't critical to the confirmation page, although we'll need it later when we send an abduction email to Owen.

Using all of the variables you just created except `$name`, finish the missing code below that generates a more informed confirmation page.

The `<br />` tags help format the information – don't forget that we're using PHP to create HTML.

The echo command is used to output the additional information to the browser as HTML content.

Again, periods are used to concatenate strings and variables together.

```php
echo 'Thanks for submitting the form.<br />';
echo 'You were abducted ' . $when_it_happened;
echo ' and were gone for ' . $how_long . '<br />';
echo 'Number of aliens: ' . $how_many . '<br />';
echo 'Describe them: ' . $alien_description . '<br />';
echo 'The aliens did this: ' . $what_they_did . '<br />';
echo 'Was Fang there? ' . $fang_spotted . '<br />';
echo 'Other comments: ' . $other . '<br />';
echo 'Your email address is ' . $email;
```

Test Drive

Tweak Owen's script and try out the changes.

Add the code for the new variables to `report.php`, as well as the code that echoes the variables to the browser as formatted HTML. Then upload the script to your web server, open the `report.html` page in your browser, and fill out the form with alien abduction information. Finally, click the Report Abduction button to submit the form and see the results.

there are no Dumb Questions

Q: What actually happens when I concatenate multiple strings together using periods?

A: Concatenation involves sticking more than one string together to form a completely new string. The end result of concatenating strings is always a single string, no matter how many strings you started with. So when you concatenate strings as part of an `echo` command, PHP combines the strings together into one first, and then echoes that string to the browser.

Q: When I concatenate a variable with a string, does the variable have to contain text?

A: No. Although concatenation always results in a string, variables don't have to contain strings in order for you to concatenate them. So say a variable contains a number, PHP converts the number to a string first and then concatenates it.

Q: What happens to PHP code on the browser?

A: Nothing. And that's because PHP code is never seen by a browser. PHP code runs on the server and gets turned into HTML code that's sent along to the browser. So the browser is completely unaware of PHP's existence—web pages arrive as pure HTML and CSS.

Q: OK, so how exactly does the server turn PHP code into HTML and CSS code?

A: First off, remember that by default the code in a PHP script is assumed to be HTML code. You identify PHP code within a script by placing it between `<?php` and `?>` tags. The server sees those tags and knows to run the code inside them as PHP, and all of the code outside of those tags is passed along to the browser as HTML.

Q: Right. But that still doesn't explain how the PHP code gets turned into HTML/CSS code. What gives?

A: Ah, that's where the `echo` command enters the picture. You can think of the `echo` command as outputting information beyond the confines of the `<?php` and `?>` tags. So the `echo` command is the key to PHP's ability to dynamically generate HTML/CSS code. By concatenating strings of text with PHP variables, you can construct HTML code on-the-fly, and then use `echo` to output it to the browser as part of the resulting web page. A good example of this is in Owen's `report.php` script when the `<br />` tag is tacked on to the end of a piece of text to generate a line break in HTML.

The confirmation web page is helpful to the user but it's no good to me. I still need the form data sent to me in an email.

The PHP script still needs to email the form data to Owen.

As it stands, the `report.php` script is grabbing the data from the Report an Abduction form and generating an HTML confirmation page for the user. But it's not yet solving the original problem of emailing a message to Owen when the form is submitted. He just wants to receive a simple text email message that looks something like this:

Similar to the confirmation web page, this email message consists of static text combined with form data.

> Alf Nader was abducted last November and was gone for 11 hours.
>
> Number of aliens: dozens
>
> Alien description: little green men
>
> What they did: asked me about UFO regulations
>
> Fang spotted: no
>
> Other comments: Please vote for me.

This email message can be generated from PHP code by putting together a string that combines static text such as `"Other comments:"` with form field data stored in variables.

Write down how you'd put together an email message string from static text and PHP variables.

....

....

Creating the email message body with PHP

You've already seen how a period can be used in PHP code to concatenate multiple strings of text together into a single string. Now you need to use concatenation again to build an email message string with variables sprinkled in among static text.

Variables and static text are concatenated into a single email message string using periods.

Most text editors will automatically wrap the code to the next line even if you don't put in your own line break (return).

```
$msg = $name . ' was abducted ' . $when_it_happened . ' and was gone for ' . $how_long . '.' .
'Number of aliens:' . $how_many . 'Alien description: ' . $alien_description . 'What they did: ' .
$what_they_did . 'Fang spotted: ' . $fang_spotted . 'Other comments:' . $other;
```

Remember, each variable holds a string of text that was pulled from the Report an Abduction form.

One problem with building such a large string is that it requires a huge line of PHP code that's difficult to read and understand. You can break the PHP code across multiple lines to make it easier to follow. Just make sure to separate the code in spots where the spacing doesn't matter, like **between** two concatenated strings, not in the middle of a string. Then put a semicolon at the end of the last line of the code to finish the PHP statement.

This is really just one big line of code divided across multiple lines.

```
$msg = $name . ' was abducted ' . $when_it_happened . ' and was gone for ' . $how_long . '.' .
   'Number of aliens: ' . $how_many .
   'Alien description: ' . $alien_description .
   'What they did: ' . $what_they_did .
   'Fang spotted: ' . $fang_spotted .
   'Other comments: ' . $other;
```

The line of code is carefully extended by not breaking it in the middle of a string.

You still have to finish the entire statement with a semicolon.

When a line of PHP code is deliberately extended across multiple lines, it's customary to indent the lines after the first one to help you see which lines belong together in your code.

A long line of PHP code can be spanned across multiple lines as long as you're careful about how you break up the code.

> That PHP code sure is pretty. But with no formatting, won't the email message be all jumbled together?

Yes. Just because the PHP code is organized nicely doesn't mean its output will automatically look good.

Organizing PHP code so that **you** can better understand it is completely different than formatting the output of PHP code that users will see. You'll normally use HTML tags to format the output of PHP code since in most cases PHP is used to dynamically generate a web page. But not in this case.

Here we're generating an email message, which is plain text, not HTML. We need to deal with the fact that the message currently looks like this:

> Alf Nader was abducted last November and was gone for 11 hours. Number of aliens: dozensAlien description: little green menWhat they did: asked me about UFO regulationsFang spotted: noOther comments: Please vote for me.

Ouch! This is NOT what Owen had in mind for his Abduction Report email messages.

there are no Dumb Questions

Q: Is there a way to use HTML formatting in emails you send from a PHP script?

A: There is. But it requires an additional step that involves setting the content type header for the message. Headers and content types are a bit beyond the scope of this discussion, which is why we're sticking with pure text email messages for Owen's email responses. You'll learn more about headers in Chapter 6, so you'll definitely gain the knowledge to revisit HTML emails later.

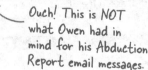

BRAIN POWER

How would you reformat the plain text email message so that it is easier to read?

Even plain text can be formatted... a little

Since Owen's sending email messages as plain text with no HTML formatting, he can't just stick in `<br />` tags to add line breaks where the content's running together. But he *can* use newline characters, which are **escaped** as `\n`. So wherever `\n` appears in the email text, a newline will be inserted, causing any content after it to start on the next line. Here's the new email message code with newlines added:

Escape characters in PHP start with a backslash (\).

> `\n` is used to place newline characters throughout the email message.

```php
$msg = $name . ' was abducted ' . $when_it_happened . ' and was gone for ' . $how_long . '.\n' .

  'Number of aliens: ' . $how_many . '\n' .

  'Alien description: ' . $alien_description . '\n' .

  'What they did: ' . $what_they_did . '\n' .

  'Fang spotted: ' . $fang_spotted . '\n' .

  'Other comments: ' . $other;
```

> Alf Nader was abducted last November and was gone for 11 hours. \nNumber of aliens: dozens\nAlien description: little green men \nWhat they did: asked me about UFO regulations\nFang spotted: no\nOther comments: Please vote for me.

> Newlines sound like a great idea... too bad that code doesn't work.

> The \n is appearing as normal text instead of a newline character...not good.

there are no Dumb Questions

Q: What exactly is an escape character?

A: An escape character is a character that's either difficult to type or would otherwise cause confusion in PHP code. You may be familiar with escape characters from HTML, where they're coded a little differently, like `&#169;` or `&copy;` for the copyright symbol. PHP has a very small set of escape characters that are helpful for escaping things that might be confused with the PHP language itself, such as single quotes (`\'`), double quotes (`\"`), and of course, newlines (`\n`).

Newlines need double-quoted strings

The problem with Owen's code is that PHP handles strings differently depending on whether they're enclosed by single or double quotes. More specifically, newline characters (\n) can only be escaped in double-quoted strings. So the Abduction Report email message must be constructed using double-quoted strings in order for the newlines to work.

But there's more to the single vs. double quote story than that. Single-quoted strings are considered raw text, whereas PHP processes double-quoted strings looking for variables. When a variable is encountered within a double-quoted string, PHP inserts its value into the string as if the strings had been concatenated. So not only is a double-quoted string necessary to make the newlines work in the email message, but it also allows us to simplify the code by sticking the variables directly in the string.

Concatenation is no longer necessary since variables can be referenced directly within a double-quoted string.

```
$msg = "$name was abducted $when_it_happened and was gone for $how_long.\n" .

  "Number of aliens: $how_many\n" .

  "Alien description: $alien_description\n" .

  "What they did: $what_they_did\n" .

  "Fang spotted: $fang_spotted\n" .

  "Other comments: $other";
```

Newline characters are now interpreted properly thanks to the double-quoted string.

But we still need to break the message into multiple concatenated strings so that the code's easier to read across multiple lines.

There's no need for a newline at the very end since this is the last line of the email message.

there are no Dumb Questions

Q: If double-quoted strings are so cool, why have we used mostly single-quoted strings up until now?

A: Well, keep in mind that single-quoted strings are not processed by PHP in any way, which makes them ideal for strings that are pure text with no embedded variables. So we'll continue to use single-quoted strings throughout the book unless there is a compelling reason to use a double-quoted string instead. The most important thing about using single vs. double quotes around strings is to try and be as consistent as possible.

Q: What happens if I need to use a single quote (apostrophe) within a single-quoted string, as in `'He's lost!'`?

A: This is where escape characters come in handy. To use a single quote inside of a single-quoted string, just escape it as `\'`, like this: `'He\'s lost!'`. The same applies to a double quote inside of a double-quoted string—use `\"`. You don't have to escape quotes when they don't conflict, such as a single quote inside of a double-quoted string: `"He's lost!"`.

Q: So single-quoted strings support `\'` but not `\n`. How do I know what escape characters I can use within single quotes?

A: Single-quoted strings only allow the `\'` and `\\` escape characters—all other escape characters can only be used in double-quoted strings.

Assemble an email message for Owen

With the body of the email message generated as a string, you can move on to assembling the rest of Owen's email. An email message is more than just a message body—there are several different parts. Although some are optional, the following pieces of information are used in pretty much all emails:

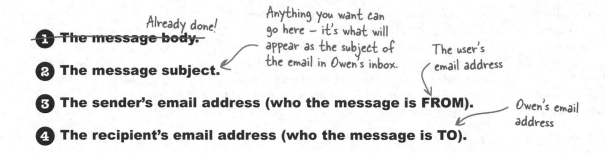

Already done!

Anything you want can go here – it's what will appear as the subject of the email in Owen's inbox.

The user's email address

Owen's email address

1 ~~The message body.~~

2 **The message subject.**

3 **The sender's email address (who the message is FROM).**

4 **The recipient's email address (who the message is TO).**

This is the kind of email message Owen hopes to receive upon someone submitting an alien abduction report.

This is the user's email address, which is already stored away in the $email variable.

This can be a static string.

This is Owen's email address, which can also be a static string.

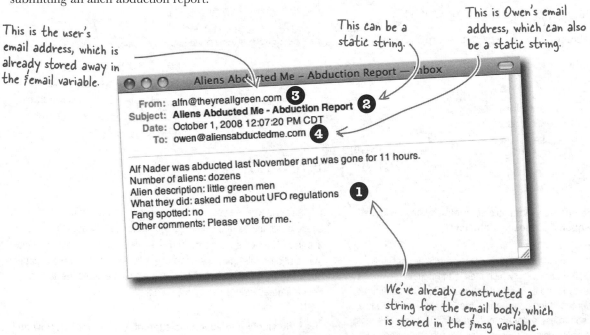

We've already constructed a string for the email body, which is stored in the $msg variable.

This sample email message reveals that most of the content is in the body of a message, which you've already finished. All that's left is coming up with a message subject, "from" and "to" email addresses... and of course, somehow using PHP to actually send the message!

Variables store the email pieces and parts

We already have the message body stored in $msg, but we're still missing the message subject and "from" and "to" email addresses. The subject and the "to" email address can just be set as static text in new variables, while the "from" email address is already stored away in the $email variable thanks to the form-handling code we wrote earlier in the chapter.

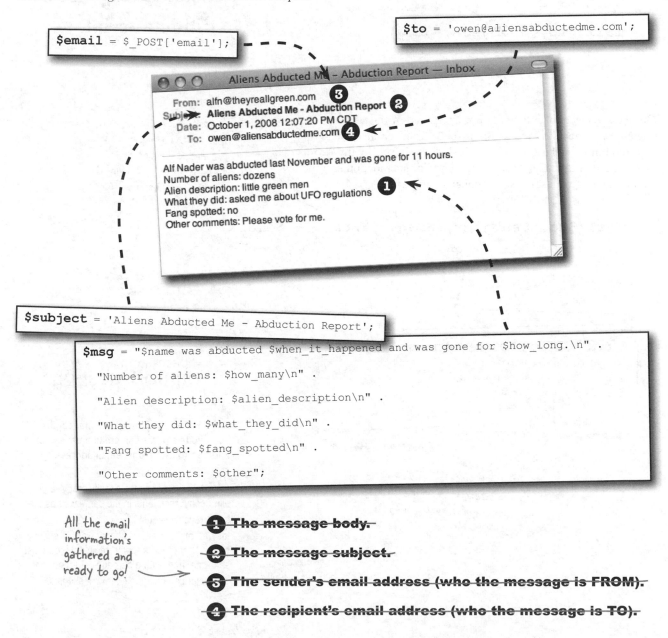

```
$email = $_POST['email'];
```

```
$to = 'owen@aliensabductedme.com';
```

From: alfn@theyreallgreen.com ❸
Subject: **Aliens Abducted Me - Abduction Report** ❷
Date: October 1, 2008 12:07:20 PM CDT
To: owen@aliensabductedme.com ❹

Alf Nader was abducted last November and was gone for 11 hours.
Number of aliens: dozens
Alien description: little green men
What they did: asked me about UFO regulations ❶
Fang spotted: no
Other comments: Please vote for me.

```
$subject = 'Aliens Abducted Me - Abduction Report';
```

```
$msg = "$name was abducted $when_it_happened and was gone for $how_long.\n" .

    "Number of aliens: $how_many\n" .

    "Alien description: $alien_description\n" .

    "What they did: $what_they_did\n" .

    "Fang spotted: $fang_spotted\n" .

    "Other comments: $other";
```

All the email information's gathered and ready to go! →

❶ ~~The message body.~~

❷ ~~The message subject.~~

❸ ~~The sender's email address (who the message is FROM).~~

❹ ~~The recipient's email address (who the message is TO).~~

Sending an email message with PHP

So you're ready to write the PHP code to actually *send* the email message to Owen. This requires PHP's built-in `mail()` function, which sends a message based on information you provide it.

> **The PHP mail() function sends an email message from within a script.**

The "to" email address

The subject of the message

```
mail($to, $subject, $msg);
```

The body of the message

These three pieces of information are required by the `mail()` function, so you always need to provide them. The "from" email address isn't required but it's still a good idea to include it. To specify the "from" field when calling the `mail()` function, an additional function argument's required, along with some string concatenation.

The text 'From:' must be prepended to the email address when specifying the address of the email <u>sender</u>.

```
mail($to, $subject, $msg, 'From:' . $email);
```

The period's handy yet again for concatenating 'From:' with Owen's email address.

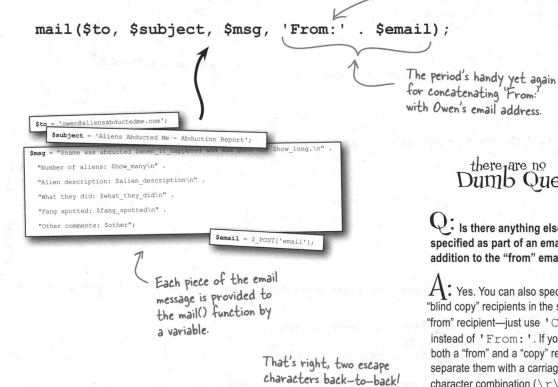

```
$to = 'owen@aliensabductedme.com';
$subject = 'Aliens Abducted Me - Abduction Report';
$msg = "$name was abducted $when_it_happened and was gone $how_long.\n" .
    "Number of aliens: $how_many\n" .
    "Alien description: $alien_description\n" .
    "What they did: $what_they_did\n" .
    "Fang spotted: $fang_spotted\n" .
    "Other comments: $other";
$email = $_POST['email'];
```

Each piece of the email message is provided to the mail() function by a variable.

That's right, two escape characters back-to-back!

there are no Dumb Questions

Q: Is there anything else that can be specified as part of an email message in addition to the "from" email address?

A: Yes. You can also specify "copy" and "blind copy" recipients in the same way as the "from" recipient—just use `'Cc:'` or `'Bcc:'` instead of `'From:'`. If you want to specify both a "from" and a "copy" recipient, you must separate them with a carriage-return newline character combination (`\r\n`), like this:

```
"From:" . $from . "\r\nCc:" . $cc
```

We have to use double quotes here since we're using the \r and \n escape characters.

So how do we actually **use** the mail() function?

Just add the code that calls `mail()` to your script.

The line of code that calls the `mail()` function is all you need to send the email message. Make sure this code appears in the script **after** the code that creates the email variables, and you're good to go. Here's the complete code for Owen's `report.php` script, including the call to the `mail()` function.

```html
<html>
<head>
  <title>Aliens Abducted Me - Report an Abduction</title>
</head>
<body>
  <h2>Aliens Abducted Me - Report an Abduction</h2>

<?php
  $name = $_POST['firstname'] . ' ' . $_POST['lastname'];
  $when_it_happened = $_POST['whenithappened'];
  $how_long = $_POST['howlong'];
  $how_many = $_POST['howmany'];
  $alien_description = $_POST['aliendescription'];
  $what_they_did = $_POST['whattheydid'];
  $fang_spotted = $_POST['fangspotted'];
  $email = $_POST['email'];
  $other = $_POST['other'];

  $to = 'owen@aliensabductedme.com';
  $subject = 'Aliens Abducted Me - Abduction Report';
  $msg = "$name was abducted $when_it_happened and was gone for $how_long.\n" .
    "Number of aliens: $how_many\n" .
    "Alien description: $alien_description\n" .
    "What they did: $what_they_did\n" .
    "Fang spotted: $fang_spotted\n" .
    "Other comments: $other";
  mail($to, $subject, $msg, 'From:' . $email);

  echo 'Thanks for submitting the form.<br />';
  echo 'You were abducted ' . $when_it_happened;
  echo ' and were gone for ' . $how_long . '<br />';
  echo 'Number of aliens: ' . $how_many . '<br />';
  echo 'Describe them: ' . $alien_description . '<br />';
  echo 'The aliens did this: ' . $what_they_did . '<br />';
  echo 'Was Fang there? ' . $fang_spotted . '<br />';
  echo 'Other comments: ' . $other . '<br />';
  echo 'Your email address is ' . $email;
?>

</body>
</html>
```

Grab all the form data from the $_POST array and stick it in individual variables.

Make sure to change this email address to your own to test out the script.

Send the email message.

Assemble the different pieces of the email message to be sent to Owen.

Generate an HTML web page on the fly that confirms the successful form submission.

report.php

TEST DRIVE

Finish up Owen's script and then try it out.

Add the three new email variables ($to, $subject, and $msg) to the
report.php script, as well as the call to the mail() function. Make
sure the $to variable is set to **your** email address, not Owen's! Upload
the script to your web server, open it in your browser, and fill out the
form with alien abduction information. Click the Report Abduction
button to submit the form. Wait a few seconds and then go check your
email Inbox for the message.

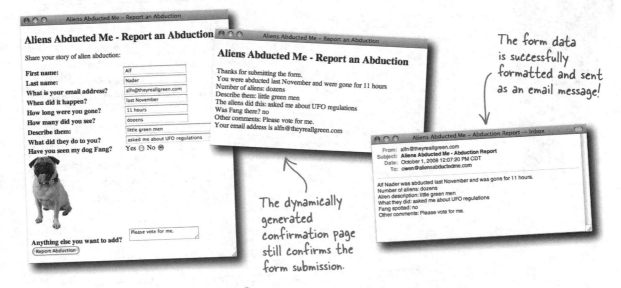

The form data
is successfully
formatted and sent
as an email message!

The dynamically
generated
confirmation page
still confirms the
form submission.

Watch it!

You may need to configure PHP on your web server so it knows how to send email.

If the mail() *function doesn't work for you,
the problem may be that email support isn't
properly configured for your PHP installation. Check out*
www.php.net/mail *for details on how to configure
email features on your web server.*

Owen starts getting emails

Owen is thrilled that he's reliably receiving alien abduction information from a web form directly to his email Inbox. Now he doesn't have to worry if he hears that someone saw his dog because he'll have email addresses from everyone who contacts him. And even better, he'll be able to look through the responses at his leisure.

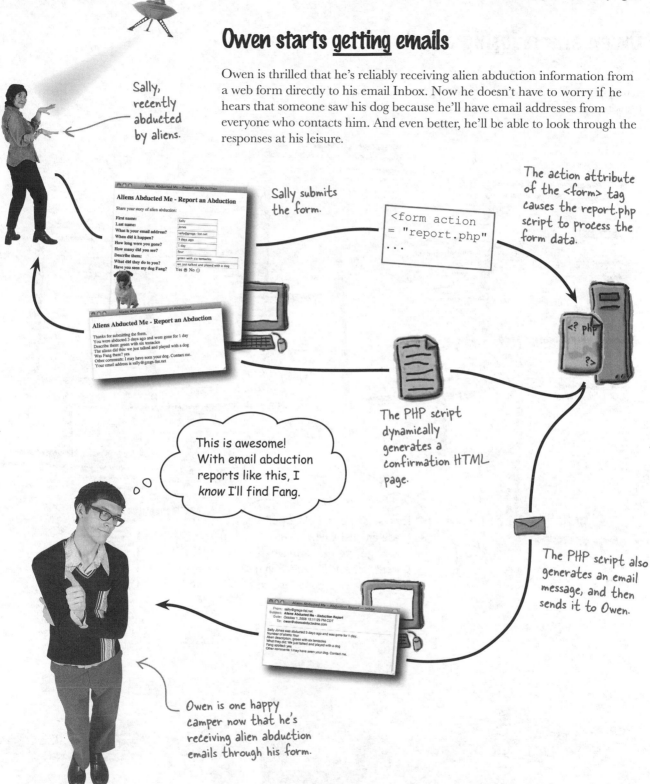

Sally, recently abducted by aliens.

Sally submits the form.

The action attribute of the <form> tag causes the report.php script to process the form data.

```
<form action
= "report.php"
...
```

The PHP script dynamically generates a confirmation HTML page.

This is awesome! With email abduction reports like this, I *know* I'll find Fang.

The PHP script also generates an email message, and then sends it to Owen.

Owen is one happy camper now that he's receiving alien abduction emails through his form.

Owen starts <u>losing</u> emails

The good news is that Owen's getting emails now. The bad news is that he's getting lots and lots of emails. So many that he's having difficulty keeping track of them. His Inbox is packed, and he's already accidentally deleted some... Owen needs a better way to store the alien abduction data.

> This is not good. Look at all these emails! I need some way to get to the data **when I want to**. And I need it in a **safe place** so I don't lose it.

Got aliens on the brain? Shake them loose by matching each HTML and PHP component to what you think it does.

HTML

A software application for viewing and interacting with web pages that acts as the client side of web communications.

PHP

A PHP command that is used to output content, such as pure text or HTML code.

web form

These tags are used to enclose PHP code so that the web server knows to process it and run it.

browser

A built-in PHP array that stores data that has been submitted using the "post" method.

<?php ?>

A programming language used to create scripts that run on a web server.

variable

All strings must be enclosed within these.

quotes

A software application for delivering web pages that acts as the server side of web communications.

echo

A markup language used to describe the structure of web page content that is viewed in a web browser.

$_POST

A name used to describe built-in PHP variables that are accessible to all scripts.

web server

A series of input fields on a web page that is used to get information from users.

A built-in PHP function that sends an email message.

array

A storage location in a PHP script that has its own unique name and data type.

superglobal

A type of PHP data storage that allows you to store multiple pieces of information in a single place.

mail()

WHO DOES WHAT?
SOLUTION

Got aliens on the brain? Shake them loose by matching each HTML
and PHP component to what you think it does.

HTML

PHP

web form

browser

<?php ?>

variable

quotes

echo

$_POST

web server

array

superglobal

mail()

A software application for viewing and interacting with web
pages that acts as the client side of web communications.

A PHP command that is used to output content, such as
pure text or HTML code.

These tags are used to enclose PHP code so that the web
server knows to process it and run it.

A built-in PHP array that stores data that has been
submitted using the "post" method.

A programming language used to create scripts that run
on a web server.

All strings must be enclosed within these.

A software application for delivering web pages that
acts as the server side of web communications.

A markup language used to describe the structure of
web page content that is viewed in a web browser.

A name used to describe built-in PHP variables
that are accessible to all scripts.

A series of input fields on a web page that is used to
get information from users.

A built-in PHP function that sends an email message.

A storage location in a PHP script that has its own
unique name and data type.

A type of PHP data storage that allows you to store
multiple pieces of information in a single place.

Your PHP & MySQL Toolbox

In Chapter 1, you learned how to harness PHP to bring life to Owen's web form. Look at everything you've learned already...

variable

A storage container for a piece of data. In PHP, variables must start with a dollar sign, like this: $variable_name.

$_POST

A special variable that holds form data.

PHP

A server-side scripting language that lets you manipulate web page content on the server before a page is delivered to the client browser.

PHP script

A text file that contains PHP code to carry out tasks on a web server.

<?php ?>

These tags must surround all PHP code in your PHP scripts.

mail()

The PHP function for sending an email. It takes the email subject, email body text, and the destination email address as parameters (you can optionally specify a From address too).

echo

The PHP command for sending output to the browser window. Its syntax is:

echo 'Hello World';

MySQL

An application that lets you store data in databases and tables and insert and retrieve information using the SQL language.

SQL

A query language for interacting with database applications like MySQL.

client-side

Interpreted solely by the client web browser.

server-side

Interpreted by a web server, not a client machine.

array

A data structure that stores a set of values. Each value has an index that you can use to access it.

escape character

Used to represent characters in PHP code that are difficult to type or that might conflict with other code, such as \n (newlines).

2 Connecting to MySQL

How it fits together

> We have to plug in the interweb **before** we can connect the web site configuraturer.

> I'm not letting her anywhere near my web application.

Knowing how things fit together before you start building is a good idea. You've created your first PHP script, and it's working well. But getting your form results in an email isn't good enough anymore. You need a way to **save the results** of your form, so you can *keep them* as long as you need them and *retrieve them* when you want them. A **MySQL database** can store your data for safe keeping. But you need to hook up your PHP script to the MySQL database to make it happen.

Owen's PHP form works well. Too well...

The new report form is great, but now I'm getting too many emails. I can't drink enough caffeine to go through them all when I first receive them.

Owen's email script was fine when he was only getting a few responses, but now he's getting lots of emails, far more than he can manage.

He's accidentally deleted some without reading them. And some are getting stuffed in his spam folder, which he never checks. In fact, an email he'd be very interested in seeing is hidden away in his spam folder right this moment... Owen needs a way to store all the messages so he can look at them when he has time and easily find ones related to Fang.

It will take more than a coffee buzz for Owen to keep up with all the alien abduction reports arriving in his inbox.

This lost alien abduction report mentions seeing a dog... this is information Owen desperately needs.

Aliens Abducted Me – Abduction Report — Inbox

From: sally@gregs-list.net
Subject: **Aliens Abducted Me - Abduction Report**
Date: October 1, 2008 12:11:29 PM CDT
To: owen@aliensabductedme.com

Sally Jones was abducted 3 days ago and was gone for 1 day.
Number of aliens: four
Alien description: green with six tentacles
What they did: We just talked and played with a dog
Fang spotted: yes
Other comments: I may have seen your dog. Contact me.

Owen needs messages like this safely stored in one place where he can sift through them for possible Fang sightings.

This is where a **MySQL** database can help...

Just in case you didn't know, most people pronounce MySQL by spelling out the last three letters, as in "my-ess-que-el".

MySQL excels at storing data

Owen really needs a way to store the alien abduction report data in a safe place other than his email Inbox. What he needs is a **database**, which is kinda like a fancy, ultra-organized electronic file cabinet. Since the information in a database is extremely organized, you can pull out precisely the information you need when you need it.

Databases are managed by a special program called a **database server**, in our case a **MySQL** database server. You communicate with a database server in a language it can understand, which in our case is **SQL**. A database server typically runs alongside a web server on the same server computer, working together in concert reading and writing data, and delivering web pages.

The "SQL" in MySQL stands for Structured Query Language.

MySQL stores data inside of database tables.

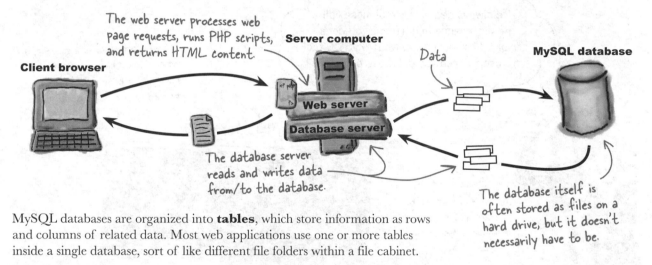

The web server processes web page requests, runs PHP scripts, and returns HTML content.

Server computer

Data

MySQL database

Client browser

Web server

Database server

The database server reads and writes data from/to the database.

The database itself is often stored as files on a hard drive, but it doesn't necessarily have to be.

MySQL databases are organized into **tables**, which store information as rows and columns of related data. Most web applications use one or more tables inside a single database, sort of like different file folders within a file cabinet.

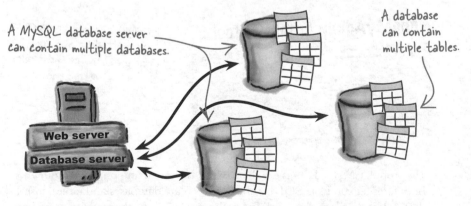

A MySQL database server can contain multiple databases.

A database can contain multiple tables.

Web server

Database server

SQL is the query language used to communicate with a MySQL database.

With alien abduction data safely stored in a MySQL database, Owen can analyze the reports from everyone who answered "yes" to the Fang question at his convenience. He just needs to use a little SQL code to talk to the database server.

Owen needs a MySQL database

So it's decided: MySQL databases are good, and Owen needs one to store alien abduction data. He can then modify the `report.php` script to store data in the table instead of emailing it to himself. The table will keep the data safe and sound as it pours in from abductees, giving Owen time to sift through it and isolate potential Fang sightings. But first things first... a database!

Creating a MySQL database requires a MySQL database server and a special software tool. The reason is because, unlike a web server, a database server has to be communicated with using SQL commands.

> **Creating MySQL databases and tables requires <u>communicating</u> with a MySQL database server.**

> I've always heard the tool makes all the difference in getting a job done right. How do I know what MySQL tool to use to create a database and table?

MySQL terminal is a command-line window that provides access to a command line where you can enter SQL commands.

Owen needs a MySQL tool to create his new alien abduction database/table.

MySQL terminal

```
File Edit Window Help MustFindFang
mysql> CREATE TABLE aliens_abduction (
    first_name varchar(30),
    last_name varchar(30),
    when_it_happened varchar(30),
    how_long varchar(30),
    how_many varchar(30),
    alien_description varchar(100),
    what_they_did varchar(100),
    fang_spotted varchar(10),
    other varchar(100),
    email varchar(50)
    );
Query OK, 0 rows affected (0.14 sec)
```

phpMyAdmin graphical tool

phpMyAdmin is actually written in PHP.

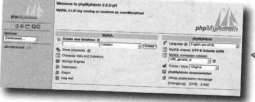

phpMyAdmin is a graphical tool that allows you to create databases and tables through a web interface.

Two popular MySQL tools are the MySQL terminal and phpMyAdmin. Both tools let you issue SQL commands to create databases and tables, insert data, select data, etc., but phpMyAdmin goes a step further by also providing a point-and-click web-based interface. Some web hosting companies include phpMyAdmin as part of their standard MySQL service, while the MySQL terminal can be used to access most MySQL installations.

You must have a MySQL database server installed before turning the page.

It's impossible to help Owen without one! If you already have a MySQL database server installed and working, read on. If not, turn to Appendix ii and follow the instructions for getting it installed. If you're using a web hosting service that offers MySQL, go ahead and ask them to install it. Several pieces of information are required to access a MySQL database server. You'll need them again later, so now is a good time to figure out what they are. Check off each one after you write it down.

☐ **My MySQL server location (IP address or hostname):** ....

☐ **My database user name:** ....

☐ **My database password:** ....

You need to check all of these.

If you're afraid this book might fall into the wrong hands, feel free to skip writing this one down.

With your MySQL database server information in hand, all that's left is confirming that the server is up and running. Check one of the boxes below to confirm that you can successfully access your MySQL server.

☐ **I can successfully access MySQL server using the MySQL terminal.**

☐ **I can successfully access MySQL server using phpMyAdmin.**

☐ **I can successfully access MySQL server using** ....

You only need to check one of these.

If you've found some other MySQL tool that works, write it down here.

Create a MySQL database and table

Some MySQL installations already include a database. If yours doesn't, you'll need to create one using the CREATE DATABASE SQL command in the MySQL terminal. But first you need to open the MySQL terminal in a command-line window—just typing **mysql** will often work. You'll know you've successfully entered the terminal when the command prompt changes to **mysql>**.

To create the new alien abduction database, type
         CREATE DATABASE aliendatabase; like this:

```
File  Edit  Window  Help  PhoneHome
mysql> CREATE DATABASE aliendatabase;
Query OK, 1 row affected (0.01 sec)
```

The MySQL server usually responds to let you know that a command was successful.

When you use the terminal, you must put a semicolon after each command.

Before you can create the table inside the database, you need to make sure you've got our new database selected. Enter the command
         USE aliendatabase;

```
File  Edit  Window  Help  PhoneHome
mysql> USE aliendatabase;
Database changed
```

The SQL code to create a table is a little more involved since it has to spell out exactly what kind of data's being stored. Let's take a look at the SQL command before entering it into the terminal:

This is an SQL command that creates a new table.

```
CREATE TABLE aliens_abduction (
  first_name varchar(30),
  last_name varchar(30),
  when_it_happened varchar(30),
  how_long varchar(30),
  how_many varchar(30),
  alien_description varchar(100),
  what_they_did varchar(100),
  fang_spotted varchar(10),
  other varchar(100),
  email varchar(50)
);
```

All the other stuff is detailed information about what kinds of data can be stored in the table.

All SQL commands entered into the MySQL terminal must end with a semicolon.

To actually create the new table, type the big CREATE TABLE command into
the MySQL terminal. (You can find the code for the command on the web at
www.headfirstlabs.com/books/hfphp.) After successfully entering
this command, you'll have a shiny new aliens_abduction table.

The "Query OK"
response from the
MySQL server lets
you know the table
was created without
any problems.

```
File Edit Window Help PhoneHome
mysql> CREATE TABLE aliens_abduction (
  first_name varchar(30),
  last_name varchar(30),
  when_it_happened varchar(30),
  how_long varchar(30),
  how_many varchar(30),
  alien_description varchar(100),
  what_they_did varchar(100),
  fang_spotted varchar(10),
  other varchar(100),
  email varchar(50)
);
Query OK, 0 rows affected (0.14 sec)
```

Your MySQL installation may offer the phpMyAdmin web-based tool,
which lets you access your databases and tables graphically. You can use
the phpMyAdmin user interface to click your way through the creation of
a database and table, or enter SQL commands directly just as if you're in
the MySQL terminal. Click the SQL tab in phpMyAdmin to access a text
box that acts like the MySQL terminal.

You can enter the
same commands here
that you'd enter in
the MySQL terminal,
just click Go to
execute them.

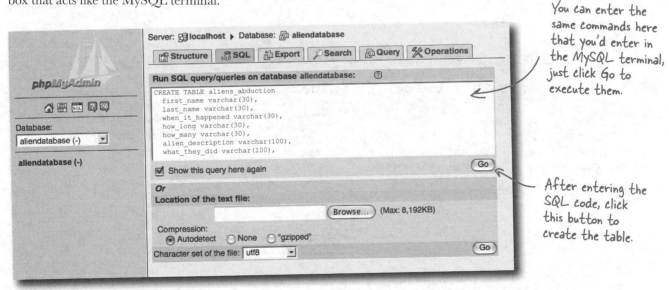

After entering the
SQL code, click
this button to
create the table.

So the SQL tab of the phpMyAdmin application provides a way to issue
SQL commands just as if you were using the MySQL terminal.

I've got a MySQL database and table, now how do I put data into them?

You use the SQL INSERT **statement to insert data into a table.**

The SQL language provides all kinds of cool statements for interacting with databases. One of the more commonly used statements is INSERT, which does the work of storing data in a table.

Take a look at the statement below to see how the INSERT works. Keep in mind that this statement isn't an actual SQL statement, it's a **template** of a statement to show you the general format of INSERT.

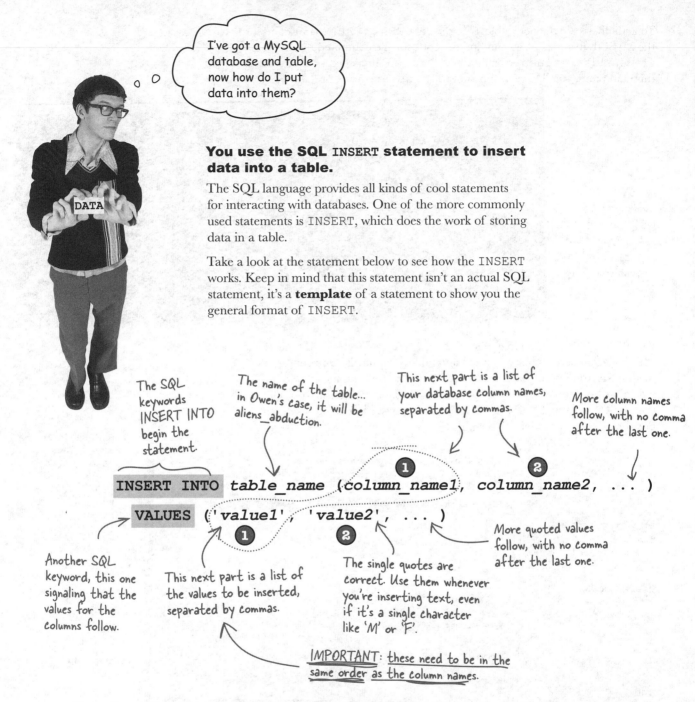

The SQL keywords INSERT INTO begin the statement.

The name of the table... in Owen's case, it will be aliens_abduction.

This next part is a list of your database column names, separated by commas.

More column names follow, with no comma after the last one.

```
INSERT INTO table_name (column_name1, column_name2, ... )
    VALUES ('value1', 'value2', ... )
```

Another SQL keyword, this one signaling that the values for the columns follow.

This next part is a list of the values to be inserted, separated by commas.

The single quotes are correct. Use them whenever you're inserting text, even if it's a single character like 'M' or 'F'.

More quoted values follow, with no comma after the last one.

IMPORTANT: these need to be in the same order as the column names.

One of the most important things to note in this statement is that the values in the second set of parentheses have to be in the *same order as the database column names.* This is how the INSERT statement matches values to columns when it inserts the data.

The INSERT statement in action

Here's how an INSERT statement can be used to store alien abduction data in Owen's new `aliens_abduction` table.

This is the name of the table the data is being inserted into, NOT the name of the database.

Your column names are in the first set of parentheses and divided by commas.

Watch it!

Order matters!

*The **values** to be inserted must be listed in **exactly** the **same order** as the **column names**.*

```
INSERT INTO aliens_abduction (first_name, last_name,
   when_it_happened, how_long, how_many, alien_description,
   what_they_did, fang_spotted, other, email)
   VALUES ('Sally', 'Jones', '3 days ago', '1 day', 'four',
   'green with six tentacles', 'We just talked and played with a dog',
   'yes', 'I may have seen your dog. Contact me.',
   'sally@gregs-list.net')
```

The values for each column are in the second set of parentheses and also divided by commas.

Unlike PHP statements, SQL statements don't end in a semicolon when used in PHP code.

All of these values contain text, not numbers, so we put single quotes around each one.

Who's really the funny looking alien here?

Sharpen your pencil

The `aliens_abduction` table is shown below, but it doesn't have any data yet. Write Sally's alien abduction data into the table. It's OK to write some of the data above the table and use arrows if you don't have room.

These are the column names.

aliens_abduction

first_name	last_name	when_it_happened	how_long	how_many	alien_description	what_they_did	fang_spotted	other	email

Sharpen your pencil
Solution

The `aliens_abduction` table is shown below, but it doesn't have any data yet. Write Sally's alien abduction data into the table. It's OK to write some of the data above the table and use arrows if you don't have room.

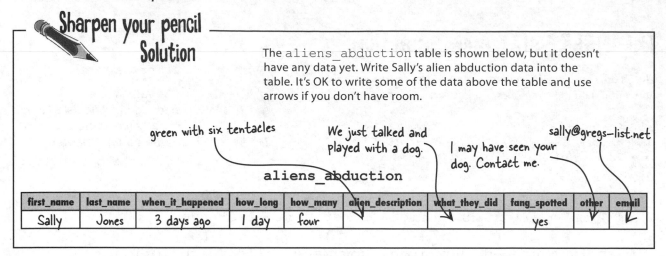

green with six tentacles

We just talked and played with a dog.

I may have seen your dog. Contact me.

sally@gregs-list.net

aliens_abduction

first_name	last_name	when_it_happened	how_long	how_many	alien_description	what_they_did	fang_spotted	other	email
Sally	Jones	3 days ago	1 day	four			yes		

there are no
Dumb Questions

Q: **I'm not sure I understand the difference between a database and a table. Don't they both just store data?**

A: Yes. Tables serve as a way to divide up the data in a database into related groups so that you don't just have one huge mass of data. It's sort of like the difference between throwing a bunch of shoes into a huge box, as opposed to first placing each pair in a smaller box—the big box is the database, the smaller shoeboxes are the tables. So data is stored in tables, and tables are stored in databases.

Q: **What exactly is the MySQL terminal? How do I find it on my computer?**

A: The MySQL terminal is a **technique** for accessing a MySQL database server through a command-line interface. In many cases the MySQL terminal is not a unique program, but instead a connection you establish using the command line from a "generic" terminal program, such as the terminal application in Mac OS X. How you access the MySQL terminal varies widely depending on what operating system you are using and whether the MySQL server is local or remote (located somewhere other than your computer). Appendix ii has more details about how to go about accessing the MySQL terminal.

Q: **What about phpMyAdmin? Where can I find that?**

A: Unlike the MySQL terminal, phpMyAdmin is a web-based application that allows access to a MySQL database. It is actually a PHP application, which is why you always access it from a web server, as opposed to installing it as a local client application. Many web hosting companies offer phpMyAdmin as part of their standard MySQL hosting plan, so it may already be installed for you. If not, you can download and install phpMyAdmin yourself. It is available for free download from `www.phpmyadmin.net`. Just remember that it must be installed on a web server and configured to have access to your MySQL databases, just like any other PHP and MySQL application.

Q: **I have both the MySQL terminal and phpMyAdmin available. Which one should I use to access my database?**

A: It's totally a personal preference. The upside to phpMyAdmin is that you can explore your databases and tables visually without having to enter SQL commands. That can be very handy once you get comfortable with SQL and don't want to manually enter commands for every little thing. However, for now it's a good idea to focus on really understanding how to interact with your MySQL data using SQL commands, in which case either tool works just fine.

Test Drive

Store an alien abduction sighting in your database with an SQL INSERT statement.

Using a MySQL tool such as the MySQL terminal or the SQL tab of phpMyAdmin, enter an INSERT statement for an alien abduction. As an example, here's the INSERT statement for Sally Jones' abduction:

```
INSERT INTO aliens_abduction (first_name, last_name,
   when_it_happened, how_long, how_many, alien_description,
   what_they_did, fang_spotted, other, email)
   VALUES ('Sally', 'Jones', '3 days ago', '1 day', 'four',
   'green with six tentacles', 'We just talked and played with a dog',
   'yes', 'I may have seen your dog. Contact me.',
   'sally@gregs-list.net')
```

```
File  Edit  Window  Help  PugsInSpace
mysql> INSERT INTO aliens_abduction (first_name, last_name,
   when_it_happened, how_long, how_many, alien_description,
   what_they_did, fang_spotted, other, email)
   VALUES ('Sally', 'Jones', '3 days ago', '1 day', 'four',
   'green with six tentacles', 'We just talked and played with a dog',
   'yes', 'I may have seen your dog. Contact me.',
   'sally@gregs-list.net');
Query OK, 1 rows affected (0.0005 sec)
```

Executing the INSERT statement in the MySQL terminal results in a new row of data being added to the aliens_abduction table.

The INSERT statement appears to have succeeded. Write down how you think we can confirm that the data was added.

....
....
....

Use SELECT to get table data

Inserting data into a table is handy and all, but it's hard not to feel a certain sense of unease at the fact that you haven't confirmed that the data actually made its way into the table. It's kind of like depositing money into a savings account but never being able to get a balance. The SELECT statement is how you "get the balance" of a table in a database. Or more accurately, SELECT allows you to request columns of data from a table.

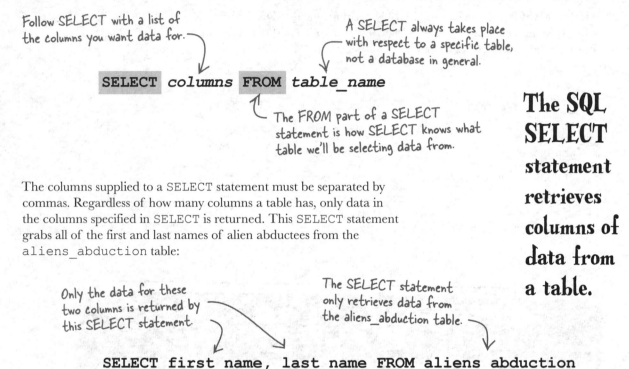

Follow SELECT with a list of the columns you want data for.

A SELECT always takes place with respect to a specific table, not a database in general.

SELECT columns FROM table_name

The FROM part of a SELECT statement is how SELECT knows what table we'll be selecting data from.

The SQL SELECT statement retrieves columns of data from a table.

The columns supplied to a SELECT statement must be separated by commas. Regardless of how many columns a table has, only data in the columns specified in SELECT is returned. This SELECT statement grabs all of the first and last names of alien abductees from the aliens_abduction table:

Only the data for these two columns is returned by this SELECT statement.

The SELECT statement only retrieves data from the aliens_abduction table.

SELECT first_name, last_name FROM aliens_abduction

To check an INSERT, you need a quick way to look at **all of the data** in a table, not just a few columns. The SELECT statement offers a shortcut for just this thing:

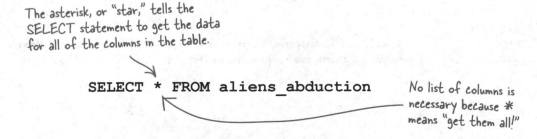

The asterisk, or "star," tells the SELECT statement to get the data for all of the columns in the table.

SELECT * FROM aliens_abduction

No list of columns is necessary because * means "get them all!"

Test Drive

Make sure the alien abduction INSERT statement worked by SELECTing the table data.

Execute a SELECT query using a MySQL tool to view all of the contents of the aliens_abduction table. Make sure the new row of data you just inserted appears in the results.

```
SELECT * FROM aliens_abduction
```

These are the columns.

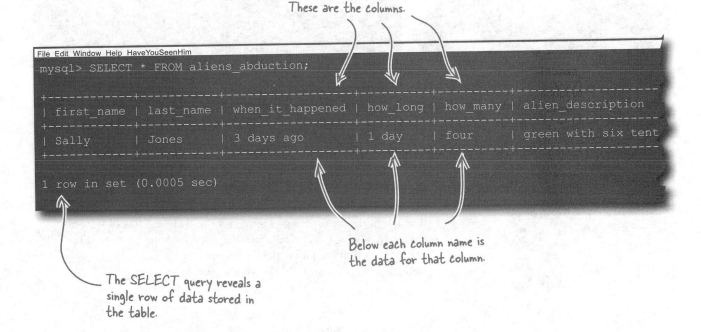

```
File Edit Window Help HaveYouSeenHim
mysql> SELECT * FROM aliens_abduction;

+------------+-----------+------------------+----------+----------+------------------
| first_name | last_name | when_it_happened | how_long | how_many | alien_description
+------------+-----------+------------------+----------+----------+------------------
| Sally      | Jones     | 3 days ago       | 1 day    | four     | green with six tent
+------------+-----------+------------------+----------+----------+------------------

1 row in set (0.0005 sec)
```

Below each column name is the data for that column.

The SELECT query reveals a single row of data stored in the table.

How many rows of data does your table have in it? ....

So you're telling me I have to write an INSERT statement every time I want to add a new alien abduction report to my database? This MySQL stuff suddenly isn't looking so appealing.

```
aliens_abduction (first_name, last_name,
pened, how_long, how_many, alien_description,
_did, fang_spotted, other, email)
VALUES ('Sally', 'Jones', '3 d
'green w  File Edit Window Help Kang
'yes',   mysql> INSERT INTO aliens_abduction (first_name, last_name,
'sally@g     when_it_happened, how_long, how_many, alien_description,
Query OK,    what_they_did, fang_spotted, other, email)
             VALUES ('Don', 'Quayle', 'back in 1991', '37 seconds',
             'dunno', 'they looked like donkeys made out of metal with some kind
  File Edit Window Help Kodos
  mysql> INSERT INTO aliens_abduction (first_name, last_name,
     when_it_happened, how_long, how_many, alien_description,
     what_they_did, fang_spotted, other, email)
     VALUES ('Shill', 'Watner', 'summer of \'69', '2 hours',
     'don\'t know',
     'there was a bright light in the sky, followed by a bark or two',
     'they beamed me toward a gas station in the desert', 'yes',
     'I was out of gas, so it was a pretty good abduction.',
     'shillwatner@imightbecaptkirk.com');
  Query OK, 1 rows affected (0.0005 sec)


     'belitac@rockin.net'));
  Query OK, 1 rows affected (0.0005 sec)
```

It's true, each insertion into a MySQL database requires an INSERT statement.

And this is where communicating with a MySQL database purely through SQL commands gets tedious. Sure there are lots of benefits gained by storing Owen's data in a database, as opposed to emails in his Inbox, but managing the data manually by issuing SQL statements in a MySQL tool is not a workable solution.

How do you think Owen's MySQL data insertion problem can be solved?

Let PHP handle the tedious SQL stuff

The solution to Owen's problem lies not in avoiding SQL but in **automating** SQL with the help of PHP. PHP makes it possible to issue SQL statements in script code that runs on the server, so you don't need to use a MySQL tool at all. This means Owen's HTML form can call a PHP script to handle inserting data into the database whenever it's submitted—no emails, no SQL tools, no hassle!

Owen creates an SQL INSERT statement that inserts the data from the email into the database.

The HTML form generates an email that Owen receives and must then manually add to the database.

```
File Edit Window Help NanooNanoo
mysql> INSERT INTO aliens_abduction (first_name, last_name,
    when_it_happened, how_long, how_many, alien_description,
    what_they_did, fang_spotted, other, email)
    ...Jones', '3 days ago', '1 day', 'four',
    ...tacles', 'We just talked and played with a dog',
    ...seen your dog. Contact me.',
    ...et');
    ...ected (0.0005 sec)
```

Without PHP, a manual SQL INSERT statement is required to store each alien abduction report in the database.

report.html

With PHP, a PHP script automatically handles the INSERT when the form is submitted.

```php
<?php
  $dbc = mysqli_connect('data.aliensabductedme.com', 'owen', 'aliensrool', 'aliendatabase')
    or die('Error connecting to MySQL server.');

  $query = "INSERT INTO aliens_abduction (first_name, last_name, " .
    "when_it_happened, how_long, how_many, alien_description, " .
    "what_they_did, fang_spotted, other, email) " .
    "VALUES ('Sally', 'Jones', '3 days ago', '1 day', 'four', " .
    "'green with six tentacles', 'We just talked and played with a dog', " .
    "'yes', 'I may have seen your dog. Contact me.', " .
    "'sally@gregs-list.net')";

  $result = mysqli_query($dbc, $query)
    or die('Error querying database.');

  mysqli_close($dbc);
?>
```

The HTML form calls a PHP script and asks it to add the form data to the database.

The PHP script creates an INSERT statement that inserts the form data into the database...no Owen required!

report.php

PHP lets data drive Owen's web form

PHP improves Owen's alien abduction web form by letting a script **send the form data *directly* to a database**, instead of sending it to Owen's email address and Owen entering it manually. Let's take a closer look at exactly how the application works now that PHP is in the picture.

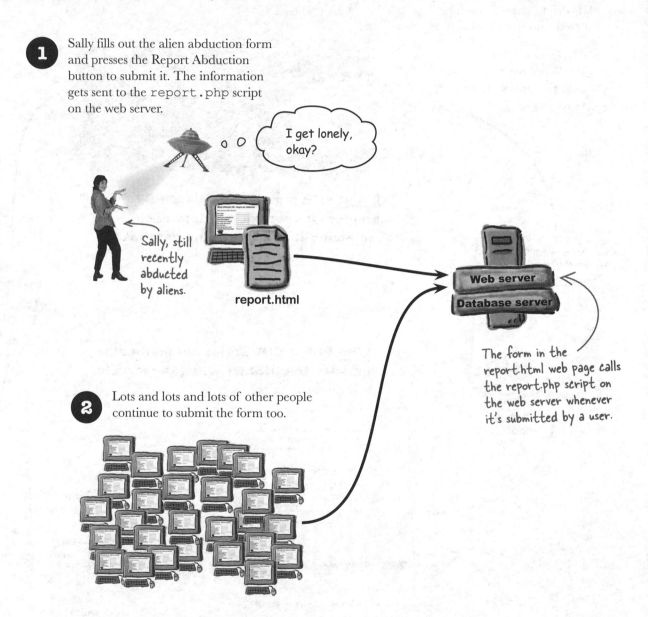

1 Sally fills out the alien abduction form and presses the Report Abduction button to submit it. The information gets sent to the report.php script on the web server.

I get lonely, okay?

Sally, still recently abducted by aliens.

report.html

Web server

Database server

The form in the report.html web page calls the report.php script on the web server whenever it's submitted by a user.

2 Lots and lots and lots of other people continue to submit the form too.

3 Owen's `report.php` script connects to a
MySQL database and inserts the information from
each submission using SQL `INSERT` statements.

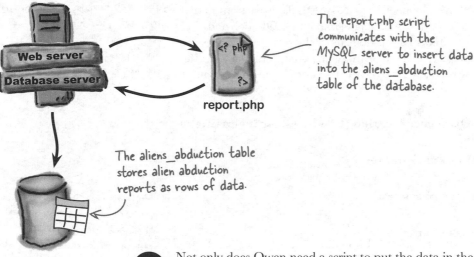

report.php

The report.php script
communicates with the
MySQL server to insert data
into the aliens_abduction
table of the database.

The aliens_abduction table
stores alien abduction
reports as rows of data.

4 Not only does Owen need a script to put the data in the database, but he
also needs a script to search and view the data. In fact, this could serve as the
main page for his web site. The `index.php` script connects to the database,
retrieves alien abduction data, and shows it to Owen.

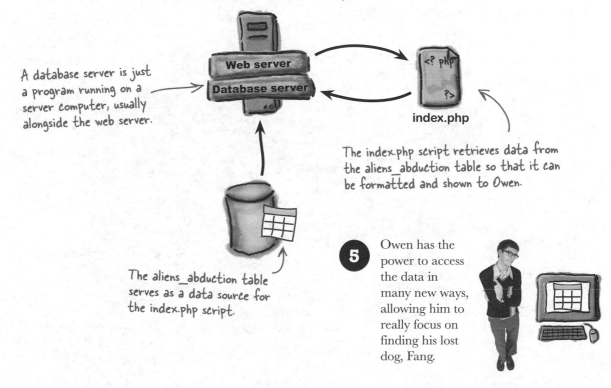

A database server is just
a program running on a
server computer, usually
alongside the web server.

index.php

The index.php script retrieves data from
the aliens_abduction table so that it can
be formatted and shown to Owen.

The aliens_abduction table
serves as a data source for
the index.php script.

5 Owen has the
power to access
the data in
many new ways,
allowing him to
really focus on
finding his lost
dog, Fang.

Connect to your database from PHP

Before a PHP script can insert or retrieve data from a MySQL database, it must connect to the database. Connecting to a MySQL database from PHP is similar in many ways to accessing a database from a MySQL tool, and it requires the same pieces of information. Remember the three checkboxes you filled out earlier in the chapter? Here they are again, along with a new one for the name of the database—go ahead and write them down one more time.

Your web hosting service or webmaster may tell you this, or if your web server and MySQL database server are running on the same machine, you can use the word "localhost".

1 **My MySQL server location (IP address or hostname):** ....

2 **My database user name:** ....

3 **My database password:** ....

4 **My database name:** ....

The name of the database you created earlier, which is aliendatabase. If for some reason you named your database something else or decided to use a database that was already created, use that name instead.

The database server host location, username, password, and database name are all required in order to establish a connection to a MySQL database from a PHP script. Once that connection is made, the script can carry out SQL commands just as if you were entering them manually in a MySQL tool.

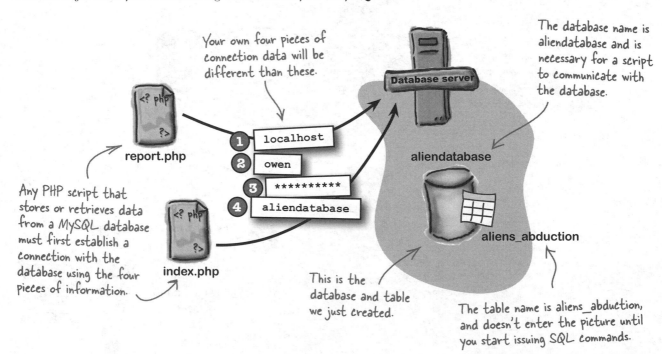

Your own four pieces of connection data will be different than these.

The database name is aliendatabase and is necessary for a script to communicate with the database.

Any PHP script that stores or retrieves data from a MySQL database must first establish a connection with the database using the four pieces of information.

This is the database and table we just created.

The table name is aliens_abduction, and doesn't enter the picture until you start issuing SQL commands.

Insert data with a PHP script

Issuing a MySQL query from PHP code first requires you to establish a connection with the database. Then you build the query as a PHP string. The query isn't actually carried out until you pass along the query string to the database server. And finally, when you're finished querying the database, you close the connection. All of these tasks are carried out through PHP script code. Here's an example that inserts a new row of alien abduction data:

These should be YOUR four values, not Owen's.

Connect to the MySQL database.

```php
<?php

  $dbc = mysqli_connect('data.aliensabductedme.com', 'owen', 'aliensrool', 'aliendatabase')

    or die('Error connecting to MySQL server.');
```

You may be able to use 'localhost' for your database location instead of a domain name.

```php
  $query = "INSERT INTO aliens_abduction (first_name, last_name, when_it_happened, how_long, " .

    "how_many, alien_description, what_they_did, fang_spotted, other, email) " .

    "VALUES ('Sally', 'Jones', '3 days ago', '1 day', 'four', 'green with six tentacles', " .

    "'We just talked and played with a dog', 'yes', 'I may have seen your dog. Contact me.', " .

    "'sally@gregs-list.net')";
```

Build the INSERT query as a string in PHP code.

Be really careful with the quotes and double quotes here, as well as spaces before and after quotes!

```php
  $result = mysqli_query($dbc, $query)

    or die('Error querying database.');
```

Issue the INSERT query on the MySQL database.

```php
  mysqli_close($dbc);

?>
```

These functions require your web server to have PHP version 4.1 or greater.

BRAIN POWER

What do you think each of these PHP functions is doing in the script?

```
mysqli_connect()
mysqli_query()
mysqli_close()
```

Use PHP functions to talk to the database

There are three main PHP functions used to communicate with a MySQL database: `mysqli_connect()`, `mysqli_query()`, and `mysqli_close()`. If you see a pattern it's no accident—all of the modern PHP functions that interact with MySQL begin with `mysqli_`.

An older set of PHP functions that interact with MySQL begin with mysql_, without the "i". The "i" stands for "improved," and the mysqli_ functions are now preferred.

`mysqli_connect()`

Connect to a MySQL database using the four pieces of information you already learned about.

`mysqli_query()`

Issue a query on a MySQL database, which often involves storing or retrieving data from a table.

`mysqli_close()`

Close a connection with a MySQL database.

Using these three functions typically involves a predictable sequence of steps.

1 **Connect to a database with the `mysqli_connect()` function.**

Provide the server location, username, and password to get permission to interact with the MySQL database server. Also specify the database name since this is a connection to a specific database.

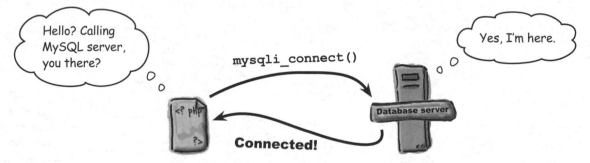

2 **Create an SQL query and store it as a string in a PHP variable.**

To communicate with the database server, you have to use SQL commands. For example, an `INSERT` statement is needed to add data to the `aliens_abduction` table. There's nothing special about the variable name we chose, but a straightforward name like `$query` works fine.

3 **Issue the query with the** `mysqli_query()` **function.**

Use the `$query` variable with the `mysqli_query()` function to talk to the MySQL database server and add data to the `aliens_abduction` table. You have to tell `mysqli_query()` both the name of the connection you created back in Step 1 and the name of the variable that holds your query from Step 2.

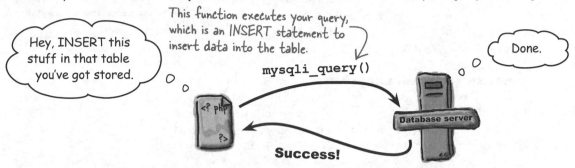

4 **Close the database connection with the** `mysqli_close()` **function.**

Finally, `mysqli_close()` tells the MySQL database server that you are finished communicating with it.

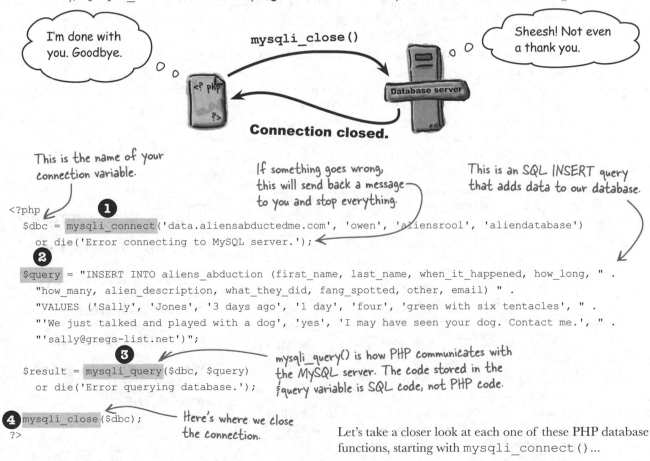

This is the name of your connection variable.

If something goes wrong, this will send back a message to you and stop everything.

This is an SQL INSERT query that adds data to our database.

```php
<?php
    $dbc = mysqli_connect('data.aliensabductedme.com', 'owen', 'aliensrool', 'aliendatabase')
        or die('Error connecting to MySQL server.');

    $query = "INSERT INTO aliens_abduction (first_name, last_name, when_it_happened, how_long, " .
        "how_many, alien_description, what_they_did, fang_spotted, other, email) " .
        "VALUES ('Sally', 'Jones', '3 days ago', '1 day', 'four', 'green with six tentacles', " .
        "'We just talked and played with a dog', 'yes', 'I may have seen your dog. Contact me.', " .
        "'sally@gregs-list.net')";

    $result = mysqli_query($dbc, $query)
        or die('Error querying database.');

    mysqli_close($dbc);
?>
```

mysqli_query() is how PHP communicates with the MySQL server. The code stored in the $query variable is SQL code, not PHP code.

Here's where we close the connection.

Let's take a closer look at each one of these PHP database functions, starting with `mysqli_connect()`...

Get connected with mysqli_connect()

For our PHP script to be able to create a connection to the database with the `mysqli_connect()` function, you'll need a few pieces of information that you're starting to get very familiar with. Yes, it's the same information you used earlier when working with the MySQL terminal, plus the name of the database.

> ❶ Connect with mysqli_connect().
> ❷ Assemble the query string.
> ❸ Execute the query with mysqli_query().
> ❹ Close the connection with mysqli_close().

Who?

Your username and password

You'll need your own username and password for your own database server. These will either be set up by you or given to you by your web hosting company when MySQL is first installed. If you set up your own MySQL, follow the instructions to give yourself a secure username and password.

What?

The name of your database

In our example, we've named the database `aliendatabase`. Yours will be whatever name you decided to give it when you set it up earlier, or if your web hosting company created your database for you, you'll be using that name.

Where?

The location of the database (a domain name, an IP address or `localhost`)

In our example, we're using the location of Owen's (fictional) database. You need to use the location of your own MySQL server. Often, this is `localhost` if the database server is on the same machine as your web server. Your web hosting company will be able to tell you this. It may also be an IP address or a domain name like Owen's, such as `yourserver.yourisp.com`.

The location, username, password, and name of the MySQL database in the `mysqli_connect()` function must all have quotes around them.

Use this variable to perform other actions on the database.

```
$dbc = mysqli_connect(
    'data.aliensabductedme.com',
    'owen',
    'aliensrool',
    'aliendatabase');
```

Username → `'owen'`

Password ↗ `'aliensrool'`

Location of the database ↖

Database name ↙

The mysqli_connect() function treats the location, username, password, and database name as strings, so you must quote them.

The result of calling the function is a database connection and a PHP variable that you can use to interact with the database. The variable is named `$dbc` in the example, but you can name it anything you like.

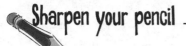

Sharpen your pencil

Here are some examples of PHP database connection strings. Look at each one and then write down whether or not it will work, and how to fix it. Also circle any of the code you find problematic.

```
$dbc = mysqli_connect('data.aliensabductedme.com', 'owen', 'aliensrool',
  'aliendatabase');
```

....
....

```
$dbc = mysqli_connect('data.aliensabductedme.com', 'owen', 'aliensrool',
  "aliendatabase")
```

....
....

```
$fangisgone = mysqli_connect('data.aliensabductedme.com', 'owen', 'aliensrool',
  'aliendatabase');
```

....
....

```
$dbc = mysqli_connect('localhost', 'owen', 'aliensrool', 'aliendatabase');
```

....
....

```
$dbc = mysqli_connect('data.aliensabductedme.com', 'owen', '', 'aliendatabase');
```

....
....

```
$dbc = mysqli_connect('data.aliensabductedme.com', 'owen', 'aliensrool');
mysqli_select_db($dbc, 'aliendatabase');
```

....
....
....

Sharpen your pencil
Solution

Here are some examples of PHP database connection strings. Look at each one and then write down whether or not it will work, and how to fix it. Also circle any of the code you find problematic.

```php
$dbc = mysqli_connect('data.aliensabductedme.com', 'owen', 'aliensrool',
  'aliendatabase');
```

.... This connection string will work. ....

You need a semicolon here to terminate the PHP statement.

In this book, we're using single quotes for PHP strings and reserving double quotes for SQL queries.

```php
$dbc = mysqli_connect('data.aliensabductedme.com', 'owen', 'aliensrool',
  "aliendatabase")
```

This won't work because it's missing a semicolon. The double quotes will work just like the single quotes. ....

Not a very descriptive name for a database connection.

```php
$fangisgone = mysqli_connect('data.aliensabductedme.com', 'owen', 'aliensrool',
 'aliendatabase');
```

.... This will work, although it's not a very good name for a database connection. ....

This assumes the database server is located on the same server computer as the web server.

```php
$dbc = mysqli_connect('localhost', 'owen', 'aliensrool', 'aliendatabase');
```

.... This will work, assuming the web server and database server are on the same machine. ....

An empty database password is not a good idea.

```php
$dbc = mysqli_connect('data.aliensabductedme.com', 'owen', '', 'aliendatabase');
```

.... This will work only if you set a blank password for the database. Not a good idea, though! ....
.... You should always have a password set for each database. ....

Leaving off the fourth argument requires you to call mysqli_select_db() to select the database.

```php
$dbc = mysqli_connect('data.aliensabductedme.com', 'owen', 'aliensrool');
mysqli_select_db($dbc, 'aliendatabase');
```

.... Sorry, this is a trick question. In mysqli_connect(), that fourth item, the name of the database, is
optional. You can leave it out of the function and use mysqli_select_db() to specify the name of the
database instead. So this code is the same as if you had passed all four arguments to mysqli_connect(). ....

It seems like it would be easy to screw up one of the pieces of information used to connect to the database. How do I know for sure if the connection worked?

This is where the PHP `die()` function comes in handy.

The PHP `die()` function terminates a PHP script and provides feedback about code that failed. While it won't reveal precisely what went wrong, `die()` tells us that something's up and that we need to fix it. If something's wrong with one of the four connection variables for `mysqli_connect()`, or if the database server can't be located, the `die()` function will stop the rest of the PHP script from running and show the error message in parentheses.

The die() function is called if the connection isn't created.

If one of our four strings in the mysqli_connect() function isn't right, we'll get feedback.

```
$dbc = mysqli_connect('data.aliensabductedme.com', 'owen', 'aliensrool', 'aliendatabase')
  or die('Error connecting to MySQL server.');
```

This message is echoed to the web page if the connection fails.

A semicolon isn't necessary here since "or die(...)" is technically a continuation of a single statement.

Okay, so we've got a PHP database connection. Now what? Can we just start issuing queries as if we're inside the MySQL terminal?

Yes! Once you've made a database connection with `mysqli_connect()`, you can issue SQL queries directly from PHP.

Nearly everything you can do in the MySQL terminal you can do in PHP code with the database connection you've now made. It's this connection that establishes a line of communication between a PHP script and a MySQL database. For example, now that Owen has a connection to his database, he can start inserting data into the `aliens_abduction` table with the `mysqli_query()` function and some SQL query code.

Remember, our goal is to automate this INSERT query using PHP code.

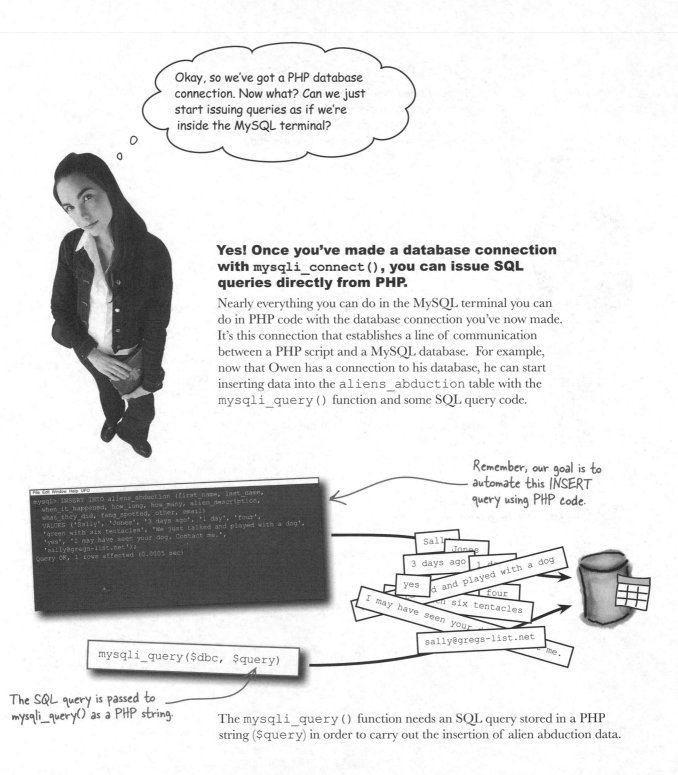

```
File Edit Window Help UFO
mysql> INSERT INTO aliens_abduction (first_name, last_name,
    when_it_happened, how_long, how_many, alien_description,
    what_they_did, fang_spotted, other, email)
    VALUES ('Sally', 'Jones', '3 days ago', '1 day', 'four',
    'green with six tentacles', 'We just talked and played with a dog',
    'yes', 'I may have seen your dog. Contact me.',
    'sally@gregs-list.net');
Query OK, 1 rows affected (0.0005 sec)
```

```
mysqli_query($dbc, $query)
```

The SQL query is passed to `mysqli_query()` as a PHP string.

The `mysqli_query()` function needs an SQL query stored in a PHP string (`$query`) in order to carry out the insertion of alien abduction data.

Build the INSERT query in PHP

SQL queries in PHP are represented as strings, and it's customary to store a query in a string before passing it along to the `mysqli_query()` function. Since SQL queries can be fairly long, it's often necessary to construct a query string from smaller strings that span multiple lines of code. Owen's INSERT query is a good example of this:

① ~~Connect with mysqli_connect().~~
② Assemble the query string.
③ Execute the query with mysqli_query().
④ Close the connection with mysqli_close().

The period tells PHP to tack this string onto the string on the next line.

This is a PHP string variable that now holds the INSERT query.

```
$query = "INSERT INTO aliens_abduction (first_name, last_name, " .
  "when_it_happened, how_long, how_many, alien_description, " .
  "what_they_did, fang_spotted, other, email) " .
  "VALUES ('Sally', 'Jones', '3 days ago', '1 day', 'four', " .
  "'green with six tentacles', 'We just talked and played with a dog', " .
  "'yes', 'I may have seen your dog. Contact me.', " .
  "'sally@gregs-list.net')";
```

Since this entire piece of code is PHP code, it must be terminated with a semicolon.

The query string is broken across multiple lines to make the query more readable — the periods tell PHP to turn this into one big string.

With the INSERT query stored in a string, you're ready to pass it along to the `mysqli_query()` function and actually carry out the insertion.

---
there are no
Dumb Questions

Q: Why is an INSERT into a database called a query? Doesn't "query" mean we're asking the database for something?

A: Yes, "query" does mean you're asking for something...you're asking the database to **do** something. In MySQL database applications, the word "query" is quite general, referring to any SQL command you perform on a database, including both storing and retrieving data.

Q: Why isn't the INSERT statement just created as one big string?

A: Keep in mind that the INSERT statement is stored as one big string, even though it is created from multiple smaller strings. Ideally, the INSERT statement would be coded as a single string. But like many SQL statements, the INSERT statement is quite long and doesn't fit on a "normal" line of code. So it's easier to read the query string if it's coded as smaller strings that are glued together with periods.

Q: Is it really necessary to list the column names when doing an INSERT?

A: No. You can leave off the column names in the INSERT statement. In which case, you must provide values for all of the columns in the table in the same order that they appear in the table structure. Knowing this, it's generally safer and more convenient to specify the column names.

Query the MySQL database with PHP

The mysqli_query() function needs two pieces of information to carry out a query: a database connection and an SQL query string.

① ~~Connect with mysqli_connect().~~
② ~~Assemble the query string.~~
③ **Execute the query with mysqli_query().**
④ Close the connection with mysqli_close().

```
mysqli_query(database_connection, query);
```

This is a database connection that's already been established via the mysqli_connect() function.

This is the SQL query that will be performed....the one we stored in a string.

The database connection required by the mysqli_query() function was returned to you by the mysqli_connect() function. Just in case that's a bit fuzzy, here's the code that established that connection:

Remember, these connection variables will be different for your database setup.

```
$dbc = mysqli_connect('data.aliensabductedme.com', 'owen', 'aliensrool', 'aliendatabase')
       or die('Error connecting to MySQL server.');
```

The connection to the database was stored away earlier in the $dbc variable.

So you have a database connection ($dbc) and an SQL query ($query). All that's missing is passing them to the mysqli_query() function.

```
$result = mysqli_query($dbc, $query);
          or die('Error querying database.');
```

The query

The database connection.

The result of the query

An SQL query is a <u>request</u> written in SQL code that is sent to the database server.

This code shows that calling the mysqli_query() function isn't just a one-way communication. The function talks back to you by returning a piece of information that's stored in the $result variable. But no actual data is returned from the INSERT query—the $result variable just stores whether or not the query issued by mysqli_query() was successful.

The mysqli_query() function requires a <u>database</u> connection and <u>a query</u> string in order to carry out an SQL query.

Close your connection with mysqli_close()

1. ~~Connect with mysqli_connect().~~
2. ~~Assemble the query string.~~
3. ~~Execute the query with mysqli_query().~~
4. Close the connection with mysqli_close().

Since we're only interested in executing the single INSERT query, the database interaction is over, at least as far as the script is concerned. And when you're done with a database connection, you should close it. Database connections will close by themselves when the user navigates away from the page but, just like closing a door, it's a good habit to close them when you're finished. The PHP mysqli_close() function closes a MySQL database connection.

> It's a good habit to close a MySQL database connection when you're finished with it.

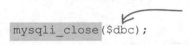 **mysqli_close**(*database_connection*);

This is where you pass the database connection variable that we've been using to interact with the database.

In the case of Owen's script, we need to pass mysqli_close() the actual database connection, which is stored in the $dbc variable.

mysqli_close($dbc);

This variable holds a reference to the database connection, which was created by mysqli_connect() back when the connection was first opened.

> But if database connections are closed automatically, why bother?

Database servers only have a certain number of connections available at a time, so they must be preserved whenever possible.

And when you close one connection, it frees that connection up so that a new one can be created. If you are on a shared database, you might only have five connections allocated to you, for example. And as you create new database-driven applications, you'll want to keep your supply of available connections open as much as you can.

there are no
Dumb Questions

Q: **Couldn't you just put all the SQL code directly in the `mysqli_query()` function in place of the `$query` variable?**

A: You could, but it gets messy. It's just a bit easier to manage your code when you store your queries in variables, and then use those variables in the `mysqli_query()` function.

Q: **Should the code that issues the INSERT query be doing anything with the result?**

A: Perhaps, yes. So far we've been using `die()` to terminate a script and send a message to the browser if something goes wrong. Eventually you may want to provide more information to the user when a query's unsuccessful, in which case you can use the result of the query to determine the query's success.

BULLET POINTS

- Database connections need a location, a username, a password, and a database name.

- The `mysqli_connect()` function creates a connection between your PHP script and the MySQL database server.

- The `die()` function exits the script and returns feedback if your connection fails.

- Issuing an SQL query from PHP code involves assembling the query in a string and then executing it with a call to `mysqi_query()`.

- Call the `mysqli_close()` function to close a MySQL database connection from PHP when you're finished with it.

TEST DRIVE

Replace the email code in Owen's `report.php` script so that it inserts data into the MySQL database, and then try it out.

Remove the code in the `report.php` script that emails form data to Owen. In its place, enter the code that connects to your MySQL database, builds a SQL query as a PHP string, executes the query on the database, and then closes the connection.

Here's the new PHP database code you've been working on. Don't enter the <?php ?> tags in report.php since you're adding this code to a spot in the script that's already inside the tags.

```php
<?php
  $dbc = mysqli_connect('data.aliensabductedme.com', 'owen', 'aliensrool', 'aliendatabase')
    or die('Error connecting to MySQL server.');

  $query = "INSERT INTO aliens_abduction (first_name, last_name, " .
    "when_it_happened, how_long, how_many, alien_description, " .
    "what_they_did, fang_spotted, other, email) " .
    "VALUES ('Sally', 'Jones', '3 days ago', '1 day', 'four', " .
    "'green with six tentacles', 'We just talked and played with a dog', " .
    "'yes', 'I may have seen your dog. Contact me.', " .
    "'sally@gregs-list.net')";

  $result = mysqli_query($dbc, $query)
    or die('Error querying database.');

  mysqli_close($dbc);
?>
```

Upload the new `report.php` file to your web server, and then open the `report.html` page in a browser to access the Report an Abduction form. Fill out the form and click Report Abduction to store the data in the database. Now fire up your MySQL tool and perform a `SELECT` query to view any changes in the database.

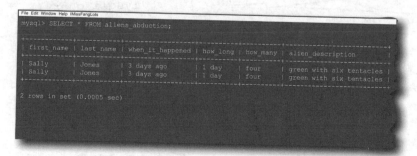

Is this correct? Write down if you think this is what the script should be doing, and why.

....

....

....

Hang on a second. Isn't the whole point here to take data from a **form** and store it in a database? It looks like the query's inserting the same data no matter what gets entered into the form. I don't see how this PHP script automates anything.

This is a big problem. The `INSERT` query needs to be inserting the form data, not static strings.

The query we've built consists of hard coded strings, as opposed to being driven from text data that was entered into the alien abduction form. In order for the script to work with the form, we need to feed the data from the form fields into the query string.

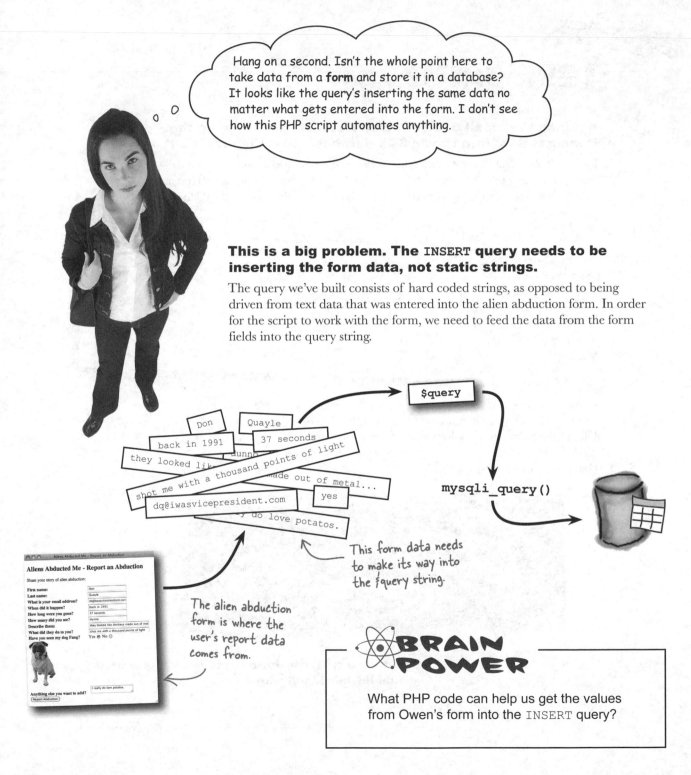

This form data needs to make its way into the $query string.

The alien abduction form is where the user's report data comes from.

BRAIN POWER

What PHP code can help us get the values from Owen's form into the `INSERT` query?

$_POST provides the form data

The good news is that the report.php script already has the form
data stored away in variables thanks to the $_POST superglobal.
Remember this PHP code?

```php
$name = $_POST['firstname'] . ' ' . $_POST['lastname'];

$when_it_happened = $_POST['whenithappened'];

$how_long = $_POST['howlong'];

$how_many = $_POST['howmany'];

$alien_description = $_POST['aliendescription'];

$what_they_did = $_POST['whattheydid'];

$fang_spotted = $_POST['fangspotted'];

$email = $_POST['email'];

$other = $_POST['other'];
```

*The $_POST superglobal's already
being used to extract the data
from each of Owen's form fields
and store it in variables.*

*Remember, the name you
use for $_POST needs to
match up with the name of
an HTML form field.*

So you already have the form data in hand, you just need to incorporate
it into the alien abduction INSERT statement. But you need to make a
small change first. Now that you're no longer emailing the form data, you
don't need the $name variable. You *do* still need the first and last name
of the user so that they can be added to the database—but you need the
names in separate variables.

```php
$first_name = $_POST['firstname'];

$last_name = $_POST['lastname'];
```

*The user's name is now stored in
separate variables so that it can
be inserted into distinct columns
of the aliens_abduction table.*

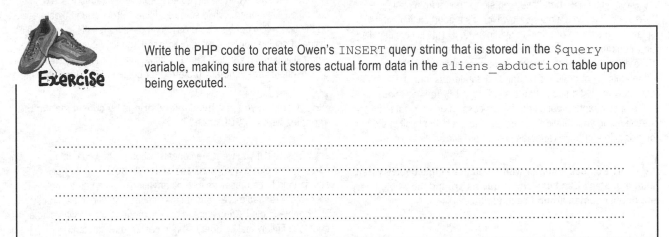

Exercise

Write the PHP code to create Owen's INSERT query string that is stored in the $query
variable, making sure that it stores actual form data in the aliens_abduction table upon
being executed.

....

....

....

....

Exercise Solution

Write the PHP code to create Owen's `INSERT` query string that is stored in the `$query` variable, making sure that it stores actual form data in the `aliens_abduction` table upon being executed.

The column names appear in the SQL statement exactly as they did before.

```
$query = "INSERT INTO aliens_abduction (first_name, last_name, when_it_happened, how_long, " .
"how_many, alien_description, what_they_did, fang_spotted, other, email) " .
"VALUES ('$first_name', '$last_name', '$when_it_happened', '$how_long', '$how_many', " .
"'$alien_description', '$what_they_did', '$fang_spotted', '$other', '$email')";
```

Instead of static data about Sally Jones' abduction, now we insert whatever data the user entered into the form.

The order of the variables must match the order of the column names for the data to get stored in the correct columns of the table.

there are no Dumb Questions

Q: Do I have to create all those variables to store the $_POST data? Can't I just reference the $_POST data directly into the $query string?

A: Yes, you can. There's nothing stopping you from putting $_POST directly in a query. However, it's a good coding habit to isolate form data before doing anything with it. This is because it's fairly common to process form data to some degree before inserting it into a database. For example, there are clever ways for hackers to try and hijack your queries by entering dangerous form data. You'll learn how to thwart such attempts in Chapter 6. To keep things simple, this chapter doesn't do any processing on form data, but that doesn't mean you shouldn't go ahead and get in the habit of storing form data in your own variables first *before* sticking it in a query.

Q: OK, so does it matter where you use single quotes versus double quotes? Can I use single quotes around the whole query and double quotes around each variable?

A: Yes, it matters. And no, you can't use single quotes around the whole query with double quotes around the variables. The reason is because PHP treats strings differently depending on whether they appear inside single quotes or double quotes. The difference between the two is that single quotes represent *exactly* the text contained within them, while some additional processing takes place on the text within double quotes. This processing results in a variable inside of double quotes getting processed and its value placed in the string in lieu of the variable name. This is quite handy, and is why double quotes are generally preferred for building SQL query strings.

Q: Couldn't you just build query strings by concatenating the variables with the SQL code?

A: Yes, and if you went the concatenation route, you could certainly use single quotes instead of double quotes. But query strings tend to be messy as it is, so anything you can do to make them more readable is a good thing—embedding variables directly in a double-quoted string instead of concatenating them with single quotes definitely makes query strings easier to understand.

Exercise

Let's use everything we've learned to finish Owen's form-handling PHP script so that it can successfully store alien abduction data in a database. Finish the PHP code below to complete the `report.php` script.

```php
<?php

    ....................................................................

    ...............................................................
    $when_it_happened = $_POST['whenithappened'];
    $how_long = $_POST['howlong'];
    $how_many = $_POST['howmany'];
    $alien_description = $_POST['aliendescription'];
    $what_they_did = $_POST['whattheydid'];
    $fang_spotted = $_POST['fangspotted'];
    $email = $_POST['email'];
    $other = $_POST['other'];

    $dbc = ........................................................................................

        ...............................................................................................


    $query = "INSERT INTO aliens_abduction (first_name, last_name, when_it_happened, how_long, " .
        "how_many, alien_description, what_they_did, fang_spotted, other, email) " .
        "VALUES ('$first_name', '$last_name', '$when_it_happened', '$how_long', '$how_many', " .
        "'$alien_description', '$what_they_did', '$fang_spotted', '$other', '$email')";

    $result = ....................................................

        ...............................................................

    .....................................

    echo 'Thanks for submitting the form.<br />';
    echo 'You were abducted ' . $when_it_happened;
    echo ' and were gone for ' . $how_long . '<br />';
    echo 'Number of aliens: ' . $how_many . '<br />';
    echo 'Describe them: ' . $alien_description . '<br />';
    echo 'The aliens did this: ' . $what_they_did . '<br />';
    echo 'Was Fang there? ' . $fang_spotted . '<br />';
    echo 'Other comments: ' . $other . '<br />';
    echo 'Your email address is ' . $email;
?>
```

Exercise Solution

Let's use everything we've learned to finish Owen's form-handling PHP script so that it can successfully store alien abduction data in a database. Finish the code below to complete the `report.php` script.

The new name variables hold the first and last name of the user, as entered into the form.

```php
<?php
  $first_name = $_POST['firstname'];

  $last_name = $_POST['lastname'];

  $when_it_happened = $_POST['whenithappened'];
  $how_long = $_POST['howlong'];
  $how_many = $_POST['howmany'];
  $alien_description = $_POST['aliendescription'];
  $what_they_did = $_POST['whattheydid'];
  $fang_spotted = $_POST['fangspotted'];
  $email = $_POST['email'];
  $other = $_POST['other'];

  $dbc = mysqli_connect('data.aliensabductedme.com', 'owen', 'aliensrool', 'aliendatabase')
     or die('Error connecting to MySQL server.');


  $query = "INSERT INTO aliens_abduction (first_name, last_name, when_it_happened, how_long, " .
    "how_many, alien_description, what_they_did, fang_spotted, other, email) " .
    "VALUES ('$first_name', '$last_name', '$when_it_happened', '$how_long', '$how_many', " .
    "'$alien_description', '$what_they_did', '$fang_spotted', '$other', '$email')";

  $result = mysqli_query($dbc, $query)
     or die('Error querying database.');

  mysqli_close($dbc);

  echo 'Thanks for submitting the form.<br />';
  echo 'You were abducted ' . $when_it_happened;
  echo ' and were gone for ' . $how_long . '<br />';
  echo 'Number of aliens: ' . $how_many . '<br />';
  echo 'Describe them: ' . $alien_description . '<br />';
  echo 'The aliens did this: ' . $what_they_did . '<br />';
  echo 'Was Fang there? ' . $fang_spotted . '<br />';
  echo 'Other comments: ' . $other . '<br />';
  echo 'Your email address is ' . $email;
?>
```

You must connect to the database and provide the proper connection information before performing any SQL queries from PHP.

The query is constructed as a PHP string, making sure to use data extracted from the form fields.

Execute the query on the database — this inserts the data!

Close the database connection.

Confirm the successful form submission, just like you did in the old script.

TEST DRIVE

Change Owen's script to use actual form data when you do an INSERT.

Remove the `$name` variable in the `report.php` script, add the `$first_name` and `$last_name` variables, and modify the `$query` variable to use form variables instead of static text in the `INSERT` statement. Upload the new version of the script and then try it out by submitting the form in the `report.html` page a few times, making sure to enter different data each time.

Now use your MySQL tool to carry out a SELECT and view the contents of the `aliens_abduction` table.

The new alien abduction reports appear in the table just as you would expect!

There's an extra row of data for Sally Jones from before you fixed the INSERT query. Don't worry, you learn how to remove unwanted data in the next chapter.

Owen needs help sifting through his data

The new and improved `report.php` script is doing its job and automating the process of adding alien abduction reports to the database. Owen can just sit back and let the reports roll in... except that there's a new problem. More data isn't exactly making it any easier to hone in on alien abduction reports involving a potential Fang sighting.

> I'm really stoked that I've now got a database automatically filled with alien abduction reports submitted by users. But it doesn't help me isolate the reports that might help me find Fang.

Owen needs a way to find specific data, such as alien abductions where Fang was spotted.

You know what column of the database contains the information in question: `fang_spotted`. This column contains either `yes` or `no` depending on whether the abductee reported that they saw Fang. So what you need is a way to select only the reports in the `aliens_abduction` table that have a value of `yes` in the `fang_spotted` column.

You know that the following SQL query returns all of the data in the table:

SELECT * FROM aliens_abduction

The SQL `SELECT` statement lets you tack on a clause to control the data returned by the query. It's called `WHERE`, and you tell it exactly how you want to filter the query results. In Owen's case, this means only selecting alien abduction reports where the `fang_spotted` column equals `yes`.

Remember, without the WHERE clause, this causes all of the data in the table to be selected.

The name of the column

The value the column must be set to in order for data to be selected

SELECT * FROM aliens_abduction WHERE fang_spotted = 'yes'

This part of the SELECT query stays the same — the WHERE clause takes care of whittling down the results.

This clause reduces the data returned by the query, yielding only the data where the fang_spotted column is set to yes.

Test Drive

Try out the SELECT query with a WHERE clause to find specific data.

Use a SELECT query with a WHERE clause in your MySQL tool to search for alien abduction data that specifically involves Fang sightings.

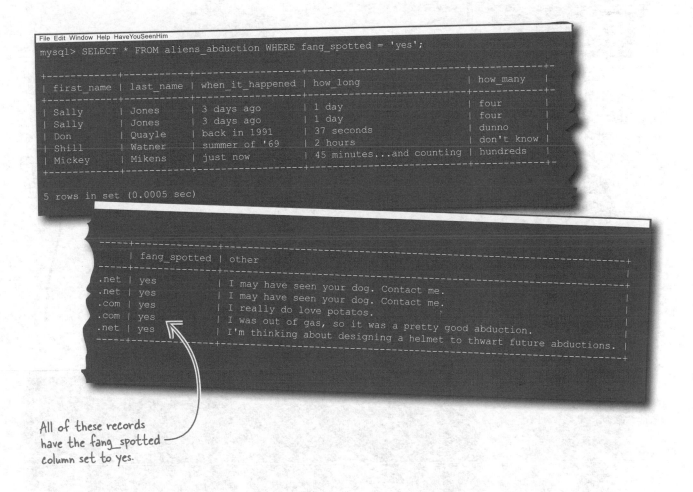

```
File Edit Window Help HaveYouSeenHim
mysql> SELECT * FROM aliens_abduction WHERE fang_spotted = 'yes';

+------------+-----------+------------------+-----------------------------+------------+
| first_name | last_name | when_it_happened | how_long                    | how_many   |
+------------+-----------+------------------+-----------------------------+------------+
| Sally      | Jones     | 3 days ago       | 1 day                       | four       |
| Sally      | Jones     | 3 days ago       | 1 day                       | four       |
| Don        | Quayle    | back in 1991     | 37 seconds                  | dunno      |
| Shill      | Watner    | summer of '69    | 2 hours                     | don't know |
| Mickey     | Mikens    | just now         | 45 minutes...and counting   | hundreds   |
+------------+-----------+------------------+-----------------------------+------------+

5 rows in set (0.0005 sec)
```

```
------+---------------+-------------------------------------------------------------------+
      | fang_spotted  | other                                                             |
------+---------------+-------------------------------------------------------------------+
.net  | yes           | I may have seen your dog. Contact me.                             |
.net  | yes           | I may have seen your dog. Contact me.                             |
.com  | yes           | I really do love potatos.                                         |
.com  | yes           | I was out of gas, so it was a pretty good abduction.              |
.net  | yes           | I'm thinking about designing a helmet to thwart future abductions.|
------+---------------+-------------------------------------------------------------------+
```

All of these records have the fang_spotted column set to yes.

Owen's on his way to finding Fang

Thanks to PHP and its functions that interface to MySQL, Owen's MySQL database server receives the alien abduction data from an HTML form and stores it in a database table. The data waits there safely in the table until Owen gets a chance to sift through it. And when he's ready, a simple `SELECT` query is all it takes to isolate abduction reports that potentially involve Fang.

I'm famous!

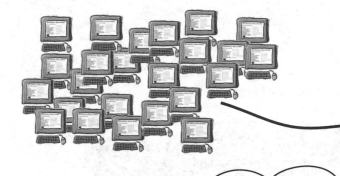

Web server

Database server

Owen, UFO buff and lover of databases.

Cool. Storing the data in a database is sooo much better than email, and I can now really focus on alien abductions where Fang might've been seen.

```
File Edit Window Help TheDogIsOutThere
mysql> SELECT * FROM aliens_abduction WHERE fang_spotted = 'yes';

+------------+-----------+-------------------+----------------------------+-----------+
| first_name | last_name | when_it_happened  | how_long                   | how_many  |
+------------+-----------+-------------------+----------------------------+-----------+
| Sally      | Jones     | 3 days ago        | 1 day                      | four      |
| Don        | Quayle    | back in 1991      | 37 seconds                 | dunno     |
| Shill      | Watner    | summer of '69     | 2 hours                    | don't know|
| Mickey     | Mikens    | just now          | 45 minutes...and counting  | hundreds  |
| James      | Decola    | sometime in the 70's | several years           | plenty    |
+------------+-----------+-------------------+----------------------------+-----------+

5 rows i
```

```
        | fang_spotted | other
+-------+--------------+--------------------------------------------------------------+
| .net  | yes          | I may have seen your dog. Contact me.                        |
| .com  | yes          | I really do love potatos.                                    |
| .com  | yes          | I was out of gas, so it was a pretty good abduction.         |
| .net  | yes          | I'm thinking about designing a helmet to thwart future abductions. |
| .com  | yes          | I did see a dog, and bunches of beetles.                     |
+-------+--------------+--------------------------------------------------------------+
```

WHO DOES WHAT?

Even though you haven't seen it all put together yet, match each
HTML, PHP, and MySQL component to what you think it does.

aliendatabase

    This is the SQL code the PHP script passes to the
MySQL server.

aliens_abduction table

    This runs PHP scripts and returns HTML pages to browsers,
often communicating with a database along the way.

report.html

    The name of the database that contains the
`aliens_abduction` table.

report.php

    The HTML form uses this request method to send the
data in the form to a PHP script.

POST

    This is where the data from the `report.html` form
will eventually end up being stored.

web server

    This is where Owen collects data from the user.

MySQL database server

    This PHP function closes a connection to the MySQL server.

Submit button

    This is the name of Owen's PHP script that processes
the data users enter into his `report.html` form.

query

    This PHP function sends a query to the MySQL server.

mysqli_connect()

    This HTML element is used by visitors to the site
when they finish filling out the form.

mysqli_close()

    This is another name for the software that runs MySQL
and all the databases and tables it contains.

mysqli_query()

    This optional PHP function tells the database server
which database to use.

mysqli_select_db()

    This opens a connection between the PHP script and
the MySQL server so they can communicate.

WHO DOES WHAT? SOLUTION

Even though you haven't seen it all put together yet, match each
HTML, PHP, and MySQL component to what you think it does.

aliendatabase

aliens_abduction table

report.html

report.php

POST

web server

MySQL database server

Submit button

query

mysqli_connect()

mysqli_close()

mysqli_query()

mysqli_select_db()

This is the SQL code the PHP script passes to the MySQL server.

This runs PHP scripts and returns HTML pages to browsers, often communicating with a database along the way.

The name of the database that contains the `aliens_abduction` table.

The HTML form uses this request method to send the data in the form to a PHP script.

This is where the data from the `report.html` form will eventually end up being stored.

This is where Owen collects data from the user.

This PHP function closes a connection to the MySQL server.

This is the name of Owen's PHP script that processes the data users enter into his `report.html` form.

This PHP function sends a query to the MySQL server.

This HTML element is used by visitors to the site when they finish filling out the form.

This is another name for the software that runs MySQL and all the databases and tables it contains.

This optional PHP function tells the database server which database to use.

This opens a connection between the PHP script and the MySQL server so they can communicate.

there are no
Dumb Questions

Q: It's pretty cool that I've learned how to insert data into a MySQL table but I'm still a little confused about how the table and its database were created. What gives?

A: Good question. It's true that you need to **understand** how to create your own tables, not just use code presented to you. So far you've created a table without much understanding of the `CREATE TABLE` syntax. That's fine for Owen's single table, but when you need to create multiple tables of your own design, it isn't good enough. You'll need to take a closer look at the data you're storing in new tables and think about the best way to represent it. This is the main focus of the next chapter... are you ready?

3 create and populate a database

Creating your own data

Are you Jamaican? Because Jamaican me crazy!

Not so fast, Dexter. I need some data first.

You don't always have the data you need.

Sometimes you have to *create the data* before you can use it. And sometimes you have to *create tables* to hold that data. And sometimes you have to *create the database* that holds the data that you need to create before you can use it. Confused? You won't be. Get ready to learn how to create databases and tables of your very own. And if that isn't enough, along the way, you'll build your very first PHP & MySQL application.

The Elvis store is open for business

Elmer Priestley has opened his Elvis store, MakeMeElvis.com. Demand has been huge. He's sold a number of studded polyester jump suits, many fake sideburns, and hundreds of pairs of sunglasses.

Each time someone buys something, Elmer collects a new email address. He uses these to send out newsletters about sales at his store. Right now Elmer has to manually go through each email address in his list and copy and paste to send out his email advertising sales. It works, but it takes a lot of time and effort.

Elmer has 328 email addresses collected at this point, with more every day.

Elmer's customer mailing list:

Anderson	Jillian	jill_anderson@breakneckpizza.com
Joffe	Kevin	joffe@simuduck.com
Newsome	Amanda	aman2luv@breakneckpizza.com
Garcia	Ed	ed99@b0tt0msup.com
Roundtree	Jo-Ann	jojoround@breakneckpizza.com
Briggs	Chris	cbriggs@boards-r-us.com
Harte	Lloyd	hovercraft@breakneckpizza.com
Toth	Anne	AnneToth@leapinlimos.com
Wiley	Andrew	andrewwiley@objectville.net
Palumbo	Tom	palofmine@mightygumball.net
Ryan	Alanna	angrypirate@breakneckpizza.com
McKinney	Clay	clay@starbuzzcoffee.com
Meeker	Ann	annmeeker@chocoholic-inc.com
Powers	Brian	bp@honey-doit.com
Manson	Anne	am86@objectville.net
Mandel	Debra	debmonster@breakneckpizza.com
Tedesco	Janis	janistedesco@starbuzzcoffee.com
Talwar	Vikram	vikt@starbuzzcoffee.com
Szwed	Joe	szwedjoe@objectville.net
Sheridan	Diana	sheridi@mightygumball.net
Snow	Edward	snowman@tikibeanlounge.com
Otto	Glenn	glenn0098@objectville.net
Hardy	Anne	anneh@b0tt0msup.com
Deal	Mary	nobigdeal@starbuzzcoffee.com
Jagel	Ann	dreamgirl@breakneckpizza.com
Melfi	James	drmelfi@b0tt0msup.com
Oliver	Lee	leeoliver@weatherorama.com
Parker	Anne	annep@starbuzzcoffee.com
Ricci	Peter	ricciman@tikibeanlounge.com
Reno	Grace	grace23@objectville.net
Moss	Zelda	zelda@weatherorama.com
Day	Clifford	cliffnight@breakneckpizza.com
Bolger	Joyce	joyce@chocoholic-inc.com
Blunt	Anne	anneblunt@breakneckpizza.com
Bolling	Lindy	lindy@tikibeanlounge.com
Gares	Fred	fgares@objectville.net
Jacobs	Anne	anne99@objectville.net

Elmer, the undisputed King of online Elvis goods.

> This is taking too long. I'd rather be spending my time imitating Elvis, not sending out emails manually.

Elmer writes this email and copies and pastes each email address in the "To" field.

New Message

To:

Subject: Big Sale!

Dear Fellow Elvisonians,

Big sale this week at MakeMeElvis.com! Genuine horse hair sideburns 20% off!

And don't forget the "buy one, get one free" leisure suits — only three days left!

These people are on Elmer's email list, and look forward to looking more like Elvis with Elmer's help.

Elmer spends far too much time copying and pasting emails into the "To" field of his client email application. He wants to simplify the task of adding new email addresses and sending out mass emails.

Elmer needs an <u>application</u>

An **application** is a software program designed to fulfill a particular purpose for its users. Elmer needs an application that will keep track of his email address list and allow him to send out email to the people on the list by clicking a single form button. Here's how he wants it to work:

☑ Go to a web page and enter an email message.

☑ Click a Submit button on the page, and the message gets sent to the entire MakeMeElvis.com email list.

☑ Let the email list build itself by allowing new customers to sign up through a web form.

With this laundry list of application needs, it's possible for Elmer to visualize his application in all its glory...

> A web application is a dynamic web site that is designed to fulfill a particular purpose for its users.

This email stuff sounds a lot like Owen's Alien Abduction application, but the difference here is that Elmer's email list will build itself, and his email messages will go out to the entire list. Elmer's app is all about <u>automation</u>!

The MakeMeElvis.com web application consists of two main components: a form to send email messages to people on Elmer's email list and a form to allow new customers to join the email list. With these two forms in mind, sketch a design of Elmer's application.

Visualize Elmer's application design

It always help to visualize the design of an application before diving into the
development details. This means figuring out what web pages and scripts will
be involved, how they connect together, and perhaps most importantly, how
you'll store the data in a MySQL database.

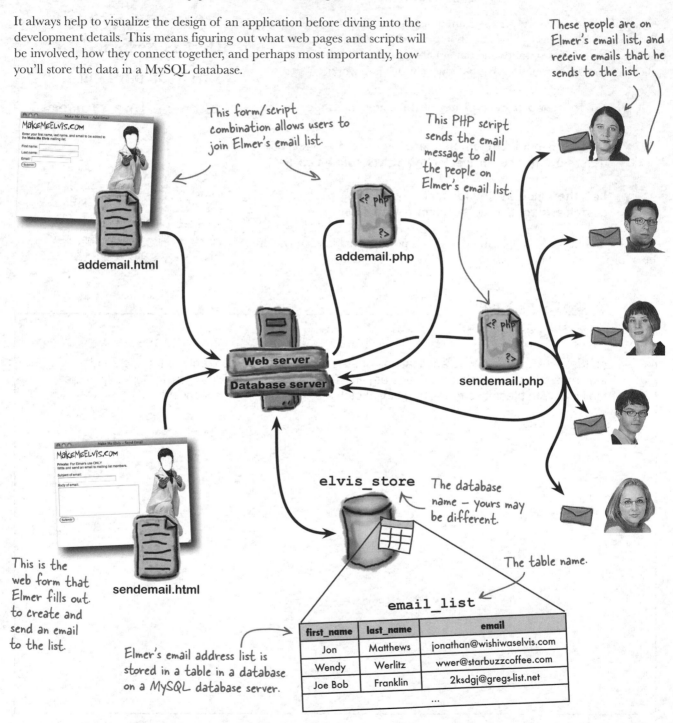

These people are on
Elmer's email list, and
receive emails that he
sends to the list.

This form/script
combination allows users to
join Elmer's email list.

This PHP script
sends the email
message to all
the people on
Elmer's email list.

addemail.html

addemail.php

Web server

Database server

sendemail.php

This is the
web form that
Elmer fills out.
to create and
send an email
to the list.

sendemail.html

elvis_store

The database
name – yours may
be different.

The table name.

Elmer's email address list is
stored in a table in a database
on a MySQL database server.

email_list

first_name	last_name	email
Jon	Matthews	jonathan@wishiwaselvis.com
Wendy	Werlitz	wwer@starbuzzcoffee.com
Joe Bob	Franklin	2ksdgj@gregs-list.net
...		

So where do we begin in building a PHP and MySQL application? Should we write the PHP script and then create the table to hold the data? Or should we make the table first and then the script?

Frank →
Jill
Joe

Joe: I don't see how it really matters. We're going to need the table *and* the script before the application will work.

Frank: That's true, but I think we should write the script first so we can test out the PHP code before connecting it to the database.

Jill: But the PHP script's entirely dependent on the database. It'll be hard to test the script if we don't have a database for it to connect to.

Frank: Couldn't we create the script but just leave out the specific code that connects to the database? We could do everything but actually interact with the database. That might still be helpful, right?

Joe: Not necessarily. Remember, the script's only job is to take data entered into an HTML form and stick it in a database. Or if it's sending an email to the mailing list, the script reads from the database and generates an email message for each user. Either way, the database is critical to the script.

Jill: True, but we didn't even think about the HTML form. Where does that fit into all of this? I'm thinking we need to create the database before we can even think about writing the script.

Frank: That's it! First we create the HTML form, then we figure out what data goes in the database, and when that's done we tie it all together with the script.

Joe: I'm not sure if that really makes sense. How can we create an HTML form when we aren't 100% sure what data we need to get from the user?

Jill: Joe's right. The HTML form still leads back to us needing to have the data for the application figured out first. The data drives everything, so we should probably build the database and table first, then the HTML form, and then the script that reacts to the form submission.

Frank: I'm sold. Let's do it!

Joe: I still think we probably need to come up with specific steps of how this application is going to come together...

Write down the specific steps you think are involved in going from design to implementation with MakeMeElvis.com.

....
....
....

PLAN AHEAD

We really need a plan of attack for putting together Elmer's application. By breaking it down into steps, we can focus on one thing at a time and not get overwhelmed.

❶ Create a database and table for the email list.

This table will hold the first names, last names, and email addresses of everyone on Elmer's mailing list.

`elvis_store`

❷ Create an Add Email web form and PHP script for adding a new customer to the list.

Here's where we'll build a form and script that will allow a customer to easily enter their first name, last name, and email address, and then add them to the email list.

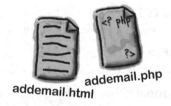

addemail.php

addemail.html

❸ Create a Send Email web form and PHP script for sending an email to the list.

Finally, we'll build a web form that will allow Elmer to compose an email message and, more importantly, a script that will take that message and send it to everyone stored in his email list table.

sendemail.php

sendemail.html

It all starts with a table

Actually, it all starts with a database, which is basically a container for storing data. Remember, in the last chapter, how databases are divided internally into more containers called **tables**.

Like days and weeks in a calendar, a table's made up of columns and rows of data. **Columns** consist of one specific type of data, such as "first name," "last name," and "email." **Rows** are collections of columns where a single row consists of one of each column. An example of a row is "Wendy, Werlitz, wwer@starbuzzcoffee.com."

> A database is a container for storing data in a very structured way.

calendar

Sunday	Monday	Tuesday	Wednesday	Thursday	Friday	Saturday
1	2	3	4	5	6	7
8	9	10	11	12	13	14
15	16	17	18	19	20	21
...						

These data structures are both tables.

A column

email_list

first_name	last_name	email
...		
Jon	Matthews	jonathan@wishiwaselvis.com
Wendy	Werlitz	wwer@starbuzzcoffee.com
Joe Bob	Franklin	2ksdgj@gregs-list.net

A row

Generally, all the tables in a database have some relationship to each other, even if that affiliation is sometimes loose. It's common for a web application to consist of multiple tables that are connected to one another through their data. But all the tables are still made up of columns and rows.

> Tables store data in a grid-like pattern of columns and rows.

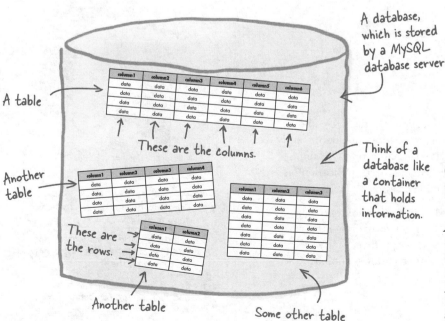

A table

A database, which is stored by a MySQL database server.

These are the columns.

Another table

These are the rows.

Another table

Some other table

Think of a database like a container that holds information.

there are no
Dumb Questions

Q: Where's database data actually stored? Can I see the files?

A: Database data is typically stored in files on a hard disk. And although you could certainly look at them, they wouldn't tell you much. Database files are binary files that can't just be opened and looked at. That's why we have SQL—to allow us to peer into a database and interact with the data stored within it.

Make contact with the MySQL server

Elmer's application design needs a database and a table. Most of the day-to-day work of dealing with a database involves interacting with tables, but you can't just jump in and start creating tables without creating a database to hold them first.

The CREATE DATABASE command is the SQL command used to create a database. Once that's done, you can move on to creating a table with the CREATE TABLE command. **But before you can use either of those commands, you have to connect to your MySQL database server.** You did this back in the last chapter, and it required a few pieces of important information.

The name's Elmer. That's E-L-M-E-R...

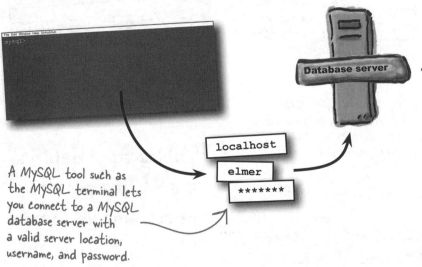

A MySQL tool such as the MySQL terminal lets you connect to a MySQL database server with a valid server location, username, and password.

localhost
elmer
****

Database server

As well as letting a PHP script make a connection to a database and perform database actions, the database server location, username, and password are the key to using the MySQL terminal or phpMyAdmin. And these tools are pretty helpful for getting a database application off the ground with the initial database and table creation.

Since creating a database and table for Elmer's application only has to happen once, it makes sense to use an SQL query to create them manually. So fire up your MySQL tool of choice, and get ready to knock out the first step of Elmer's application, creating a database and table for the email list.

You are here.

1. Create a database and table for the email list.

2. Create an Add Email web form and PHP script for adding a new customer to the list.

3. Create a Send Email web form and PHP script for sending an email to the list.

Create a database for Elmer's emails

To create a new table and database for Elmer's email list, first we need to create the `elvis_store` database, which will hold the `email_list` table. We'll use SQL commands to create both. The SQL command used to create a database is `CREATE DATABASE`, which you used briefly in the previous chapter. Let's look a bit closer at how it works.

CREATE DATABASE *database_name*

↖ The name of the new database to be created

CREATE DATABASE is the SQL command used to create a new database.

You need to specify the name of the new database after the command `CREATE DATABASE`. Here's the SQL statement to create Elmer's database:

CREATE DATABASE elvis_store

When you execute this statement on a MySQL database server, the database will be created.

When you run SQL commands in the terminal, you always add a semicolon to the end...but not when you issue SQL queries through the PHP mysqli_query() function.

```
File Edit Window Help Don'tBeCruel
mysql> CREATE DATABASE elvis_store;
Query OK, 1 row affected (0.01 sec)
```

elvis_store

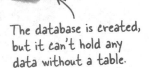

Creating the `elvis_store` database with the `CREATE DATABASE` command results in a shiny new database but no table to actually store data in yet...

The database is created, but it can't hold any data without a table.

Watch it!

> **SQL statements only end with semicolons when you use the terminal.**
>
> *In your PHP code, your SQL statements don't need to end with a semicolon. The MySQL terminal is different, however, and requires a semicolon at the end of every SQL statement. This is because the terminal is capable of running multiple SQL statements, whereas in PHP, you only submit one statement at a time.*

Create a table inside the database

You have to know what kind of data you want to store in a table before you can create the table. Elmer wants to use the first and last names of people on his email list to make the email messages he sends out a bit more personal. Add that information to the email address, and Elmer's `email_list` table needs to store three pieces of data for each entry.

Each piece of data in a table goes in a column, which needs a name that describes the data. Let's use `first_name`, `last_name`, and `email` as our **column names**. Each **row** in the table consists of a single piece of data for each of these columns, and constitutes a single entry in Elmer's email list.

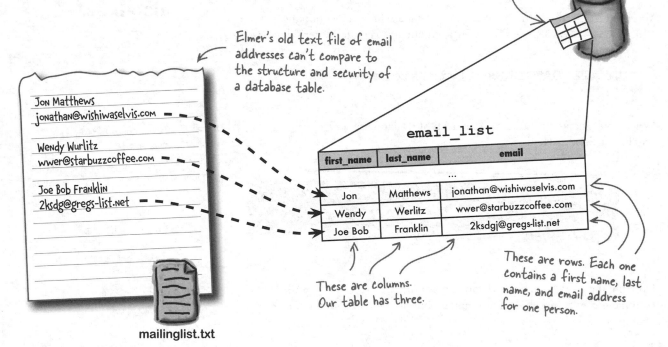

The email_list table is one of many tables that could be stored in the elvis_store database.

elvis_store

Elmer's old text file of email addresses can't compare to the structure and security of a database table.

Jon Matthews
jonathan@wishiwaselvis.com

Wendy Wurlitz
wwer@starbuzzcoffee.com

Joe Bob Franklin
2ksdg@gregs-list.net

mailinglist.txt

email_list

first_name	last_name	email
...		
Jon	Matthews	jonathan@wishiwaselvis.com
Wendy	Werlitz	wwer@starbuzzcoffee.com
Joe Bob	Franklin	2ksdgj@gregs-list.net

These are columns. Our table has three.

These are rows. Each one contains a first name, last name, and email address for one person.

Table rows are horizontal, and table columns are vertical.

So now we know that the first name, last name, and email address of a customer must be created as columns in the `email_list` table. Problem is, MySQL tables are highly structured and expect you to provide more than just the name of a column of data. You have to tell the database a bit more about **what kind** of data you intend to store in the column.

Data columns in Elmer's new email_list table.

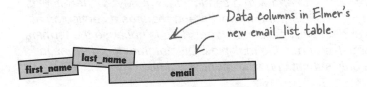

first_name last_name email

We need to <u>define</u> our data

When you create a table, you have to tell the MySQL server what type of data each column will hold. Data types are required for *all* MySQL columns, and each column in a table holds a particular type of data. This means some columns may hold text, some may hold numeric values, some may hold time or dates, and so on. MySQL has a variety of data types, and you need to know which one suits your particular data. Let's suppose Elmer has a table named `products` that keeps track of the items for sale at his store:

This column contains <u>text</u> descriptions of each product in Elmer's store.

The inventory column contains an <u>integer</u> value for how many of each item are in stock.

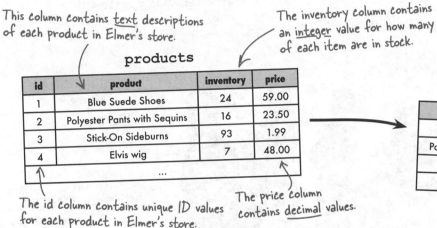

products

id	product	inventory	price
1	Blue Suede Shoes	24	59.00
2	Polyester Pants with Sequins	16	23.50
3	Stick-On Sideburns	93	1.99
4	Elvis wig	7	48.00
	...		

The id column contains unique ID values for each product in Elmer's store.

The price column contains <u>decimal</u> values.

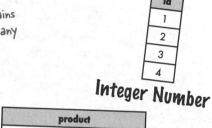

Integer Number

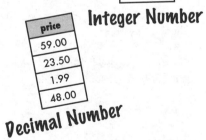

Text

Integer Number

Decimal Number

Notice that `product` is the only text column in the `products` table. There are also decimal numbers for `price` and integer numbers for `inventory` and `id`. MySQL has its own names for each one of these types of data, as well as a few more such as types for dates and times.

It's important to use the appropriate data types when you create table columns so that your tables are accurate and efficient. For example, **text data takes more room to store than integer data**, so if a column only needs to hold integers, it's a smart practice to use an integer data type for it. Also, if it knows what kind of data a column holds, the web server won't allow you to accidentally insert the wrong type of data. So if you have a column that holds a date, you will receive an error if you try to insert anything except a date in that column.

To create a table, you need to know what <u>type</u> <u>of</u> <u>data</u> is stored in each table column.

BRAIN POWER

Why do you think using different data types is better than using just text to store everything?

Take a meeting with some MySQL data types

These are a few of the most useful MySQL data types. Remember, you can use any of them to describe the data stored within a particular column of table data. It's their job to store your data for you without mucking it up.

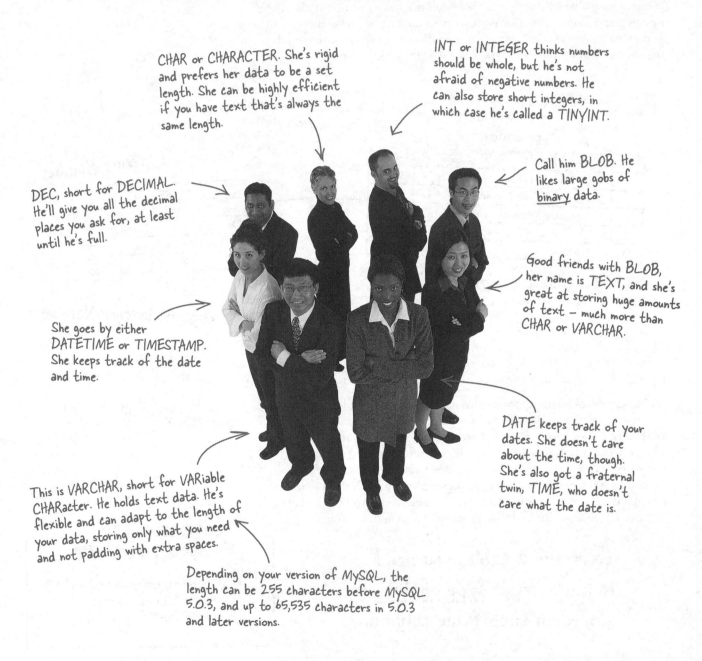

CHAR or CHARACTER. She's rigid and prefers her data to be a set length. She can be highly efficient if you have text that's always the same length.

INT or INTEGER thinks numbers should be whole, but he's not afraid of negative numbers. He can also store short integers, in which case he's called a TINYINT.

DEC, short for DECIMAL. He'll give you all the decimal places you ask for, at least until he's full.

Call him BLOB. He likes large gobs of binary data.

Good friends with BLOB, her name is TEXT, and she's great at storing huge amounts of text — much more than CHAR or VARCHAR.

She goes by either DATETIME or TIMESTAMP. She keeps track of the date and time.

This is VARCHAR, short for VARiable CHARacter. He holds text data. He's flexible and can adapt to the length of your data, storing only what you need and not padding with extra spaces.

Depending on your version of MySQL, the length can be 255 characters before MySQL 5.0.3, and up to 65,535 characters in 5.0.3 and later versions.

DATE keeps track of your dates. She doesn't care about the time, though. She's also got a fraternal twin, TIME, who doesn't care what the date is.

there are no
Dumb Questions

Q: Why would I ever use a **CHAR** when a **VARCHAR** does the same thing with more flexibility?

A: The answer is accuracy and efficiency. From a design perspective, you should always design your tables to model your data as rigidly as possible. If you know without a shadow of a doubt that a state column will always hold exactly a two-character abbreviation, then it makes sense to only allot two characters of storage for it with CHAR(2). However, if a password column can contain up to 10 characters, then VARCHAR(10) makes more sense. That's the design side of things. So CHAR is a little more efficient than VARCHAR because it doesn't have to keep track of a variable length. Therefore, it's more desirable when you know for certain a text column has an exact length.

Q: Why do I need these numeric types like **INT** and **DEC**?

A: It all comes down to database storage and efficiency. Choosing the best matching data type for each column in your table will reduce the size of the table and make operations on your data faster. Storing a number as an actual number (INT, DEC, etc.) instead of text characters is usually more efficient.

Q: Is this it? Are these all the types?

A: No, but these are the most commonly used ones. We'll get up and running with these for now, rather than bogging things down by looking at data types you may never need.

WHAT'S MY PURPOSE?

Match each MySQL data type to each description of some data you might store in a table.

Data Type	Description
INT	Your full name
CHAR(1)	A two letter state abbreviation
DATE	Cost of an Elvis wig: 48.99
TIME	How much money Elvis's best-selling album made.
VARCHAR(2)	Date of alien abduction: 2/19/2004
DEC(4,2)	Number of Elvis sideburns in stock: 93
VARCHAR(60)	Did you see Owen's dog? Y or N
CHAR(2)	Your email address
DATETIME	When you eat dinner
DEC(10,2)	How many aliens you saw when you were abducted
	When Elvis was born

WHAT'S MY PURPOSE?

Match each MySQL data type to each description of some data you might store in a table.

Not needed. Although it would work for the state abbreviation, CHAR(2) is a better choice because it's usually a little more efficient.

When the length of a text value can vary, VARCHAR is a good choice. Make it long enough to hold whatever value someone will probably need to store.

Data Type

INT

CHAR(1)

DATE

TIME

~~VARCHAR(2)~~

DEC(4,2)

VARCHAR(60)

CHAR(2)

DATETIME

DEC(10,2)

Description

Your full name

A two letter state abbreviation

Cost of an Elvis wig: 48.99

How much money Elvis's best-selling album made.

Date of alien abduction: 2/19/2004

Number of Elvis sideburns in stock: 93

Did you see Owen's dog? Y or N

Your email address

When you eat dinner

How many aliens you saw when you were abducted

When Elvis was born

When you know exactly how many characters to expect in a column, use CHAR.

DEC is generally used to store prices in addition to other decimal values.

These two numbers show how many digits the database should expect in front of the decimal, and how many after.

You may have answered DATE here, but true Elvisonians will know the exact date <u>and</u> time.

There are arguably other (potentially better) ways to represent a yes/no value in MySQL than using CHAR(1), but this way's straightforward and reasonably efficient.

Create your table with a query

We've got all the pieces that we need to create our table, even a good name (email_list). We also have names for the columns of data: first_name, last_name, and email. All that's missing is the data type for each column and an SQL statement to tie it all together and create the table. The SQL command to create your table is CREATE TABLE.

It begins with CREATE TABLE then your table name. Two parentheses hold a comma separated list of all the column names, each one followed by a data type. Here's what the command looks like:

Yep, we're still here...but, we're almost ready to move on.

1. Create a database and table for the email list.
2. Create an Add Email web form and PHP script for adding a new customer to the list.
3. Create a Send Email web form and PHP script for sending an email to the list.

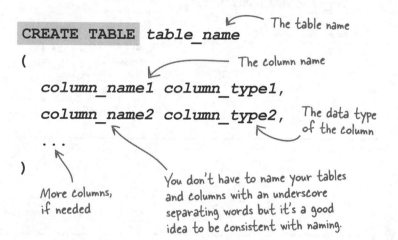

CREATE TABLE *table_name*

The table name

(

The column name

   column_name1 column_type1,

   column_name2 column_type2,   *The data type of the column*

   ...

)

More columns, if needed

You don't have to name your tables and columns with an underscore separating words but it's a good idea to be consistent with naming.

The CREATE TABLE SQL command is used to create a new table in a database.

![pencil] **Sharpen your pencil**

Write an SQL query to create Elmer's email_list table with the three required columns of data: first_name, last_name, and email.

....

....

....

....

....

....

Sharpen your pencil
Solution

Write an SQL query to create Elmer's `email_list` table with the three required columns of data: `first_name`, `last_name`, and `email`.

Here's the SQL command to create the table, notice the caps.

Your table's name should be lowercase and have an underscore in place of any spaces.

CREATE TABLE email_list

The opening parenthesis opens the list of columns to create.

(

first_name VARCHAR(20),

The comma separates the columns being created.

last_name VARCHAR(20),

email VARCHAR(60)

)

The closing parenthesis closes the list of columns.

The name of the column that stores the email address.

This tells MySQL that the email column has a VARCHAR data type. The (60) means that the text it holds can be up to 60 characters long.

TEST DRIVE

Create Elmer's database and table.

Execute the CREATE DATABASE and CREATE TABLE queries using a MySQL tool to create the elvis_store database and the email_list table within it.

```
CREATE DATABASE elvis_store

CREATE TABLE email_list(first_name VARCHAR(20), last_name VARCHAR(20), email VARCHAR(60))
```

Did both queries execute without a hitch? If not, write down what you think might have gone wrong.

....

....

> Hang on, something ain't right here. I entered the code to create the table exactly like we drew it up...and now I'm getting some weird error.

The CREATE TABLE statement's fine but the MySQL terminal doesn't know which database it's being created in...not good.

```
File Edit Window Help Oops
mysql> CREATE TABLE email_list
(
  first_name VARCHAR(20),
  last_name VARCHAR(20),
  email VARCHAR(60)
);
ERROR 1046 (3D000): No database selected
```

For some reason the CREATE TABLE statement failed in the MySQL terminal.

Getting the ~~cart~~ table in front of the ~~horse~~ database

Elmer has a legitimate problem that has to do with the fact that the MySQL terminal doesn't automatically know which database you're talking about when issuing commands. Sure, it knows that you just created the `elvis_store` database, but there could already be plenty of other databases stored on the same server—it can't just assume you're talking about the one you just created.

Fortunately, there is a simple solution that involves telling the MySQL terminal which database you want targeted by all subsequent statements...

Elmer's all shook up because his CREATE TABLE statement is flawless, yet the MySQL terminal's reporting an error.

there are no Dumb Questions

Q: **What's up with the weird -> prompt I get sometimes in the MySQL terminal?**

A: The -> prompt indicates that you're entering a single statement across multiple lines—MySQL is basically telling you that it knows you're still entering the same statement, even though you've hit Return to break it out across more than one line. Once you finish the statement and put the semicolon on the end, MySQL will execute it.

USE the database before you use it

So that the CREATE TABLE statement will work, Elmer needs to **select the database** in the MySQL terminal so that it knows what database the new table belongs to. The USE command chooses a database as the default database in the terminal, meaning that all subsequent commands apply to that database. Here's how it works:

The USE command tells MySQL what database you intend to use.

USE `database_name`

> **The USE command selects a database as the default database for subsequent SQL statements.**

Elmer should specify his database name (`elvis_store`) in a USE statement to select the database and access his new table.

The name of the database you'd like to USE.

USE `elvis_store`

The USE command chooses the database you want to work with.

elvis_sightings

elvis_lyrics

elvis_fans

elvis_store

Once you pick a database to USE, the other databases on the database server are ignored...until you choose to USE a different one.

Test Drive

First USE Elmer's database, then create the table.

Execute the USE query to select Elmer's `elvis_store` database in a MySQL tool, and then execute the CREATE TABLE query to create the `email_list` table inside the database.

```
USE elvis_store

CREATE TABLE email_list(first_name VARCHAR(20), last_name VARCHAR(20), email VARCHAR(60))
```

The USE statement isn't necessary if you're using a graphical SQL tool such as phpMyAdmin — it requires you to select the database graphically before issuing SQL commands.

```
File Edit Window Help LisaMarie
mysql> USE elvis_store;
Database changed
mysql> CREATE TABLE email_list
(
  first_name VARCHAR(20),
  last_name VARCHAR(20),
  email VARCHAR(60)
);
Your SQL query has been executed successfully (Query took 0.4481 sec)
```

The table creation code is the same as before — it just needed the database selected before it would work.

With the database selected thanks to the USE command, the table creation now works with no problems.

Oops! My CREATE TABLE statement had a typo in it, but it still got executed. Does SQL have an undo option?

There isn't exactly an undo option in SQL but it's certainly possible to fix mistakes.

However, first you need to find out exactly what kind of mistake has been made in order to fix it. Suppose the email_list table looks like this:

email_list

first_naem	last_name	email

Circle what you think is wrong with this table. Any idea how you might fix it?

DESCRIBE reveals the structure of tables

Repairing a mistake in a table first involves finding the mistake. Even if you don't suspect a mistake, it's never a bad idea to check your work. The SQL DESCRIBE command analyzes the structure of a table, displaying a list of column names, data types, and other information.

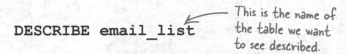

`DESCRIBE` *table_name*

Plugging in Elmer's table name gives us the following SQL statement:

`DESCRIBE email_list` ← This is the name of the table we want to see described.

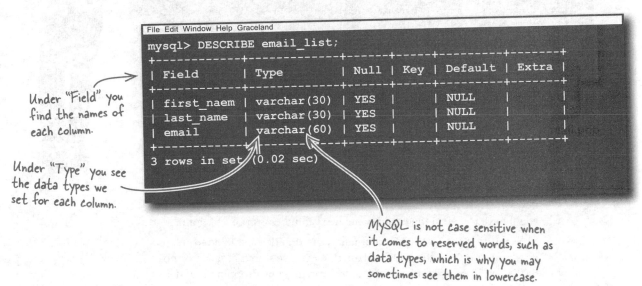

Under "Field" you find the names of each column.

Under "Type" you see the data types we set for each column.

MySQL is not case sensitive when it comes to reserved words, such as data types, which is why you may sometimes see them in lowercase.

there are no Dumb Questions

Q: What's up with those other columns: Null, Key, Default, and Extra?

A: MySQL lets you set a number of options for each column in your table. These options control things like whether a column can be left empty or if it has a default value. We'll explore these a bit later when they become more critical to the application.

Q: So if I actually had data stored in my table, would it show up here?

A: No. DESCRIBE only shows you the table structure, not the data stored in it. But don't worry, you'll see the data in your table very soon... but first we have to learn how to actually put data into the table.

Q: Can I look at the same table structure using phpMyAdmin?

A: Yes. Graphical database tools such as phpMyAdmin allow you to view the structure of tables by issuing a DESCRIBE statement or by clicking a visual view of a table. It's entirely up to you which kind of tool you use to analyze your tables.

> I fixed the typo and tried to run the CREATE TABLE query again. It didn't work. Surely I don't have to delete the typo'd table first... do I?

The first_name column was accidentally misspelled first_naem...oops!

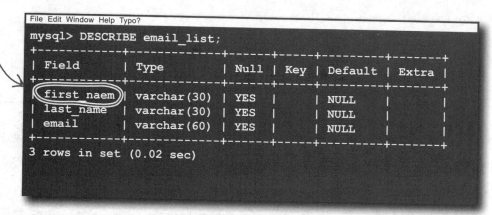

```
File Edit Window Help Typo?
mysql> DESCRIBE email_list;
+------------+-------------+------+-----+---------+-------+
| Field      | Type        | Null | Key | Default | Extra |
+------------+-------------+------+-----+---------+-------+
| first_naem | varchar(30) | YES  |     | NULL    |       |
| last_name  | varchar(30) | YES  |     | NULL    |       |
| email      | varchar(60) | YES  |     | NULL    |       |
+------------+-------------+------+-----+---------+-------+
3 rows in set (0.02 sec)
```

Actually, you do. You can't recreate a table again with CREATE TABLE once it's been created.

Once you've created a table, it exists and **can't be overwritten** by a new CREATE TABLE query. If you want to recreate a table from scratch, you'll have to delete the existing one first, and then start over again.

In SQL, the DROP TABLE command is used to delete a table from a database. It deletes the table and anything you've stored in it. Since no data exists in a new table, we won't lose anything by dropping it and creating a new one with the first_name correction.

The name of the table you'd like to delete from the database.

DROP TABLE email_list

The DROP TABLE command deletes a table AND all its data from the database.

Elmer's ready to store data

The CREATE DATABASE, USE, and CREATE TABLE SQL
commands were successfully used to create Elmer's email list
database and table. Elmer couldn't be more pleased, unless
maybe the table was already filled with eager customers.
That's a job for PHP...

> Nice. With the database
> and table created, I'm
> ready to start storing some
> serious mailing list data.

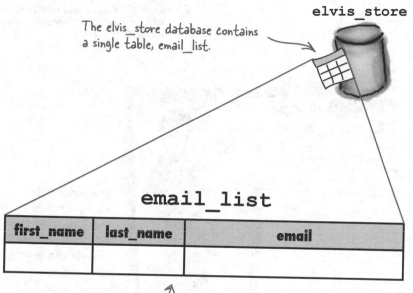

The elvis_store database contains
a single table, email_list.

elvis_store

email_list

first_name	last_name	email

The email_list table
consists of three columns
used to store the data
for Elmer's email list.

there are no
Dumb Questions

Q: Hey, I have a copy of Head First SQL (great book, by the way). In that book, every time you show the code for an SQL statement, you put a semicolon after it. Why not here?

A: We're glad you enjoyed *Head First SQL*. The difference is that
when you talk to MySQL directly, you need a semicolon so it knows
where the end of the statement is. That's because it's possible to
issue multiple statements to MySQL directly. In PHP, when you use
the `mysqli_query()` function, you only execute a single SQL
command at a time, so no semicolon is needed. But don't forget that
you **do** still need a semicolon at the end of each **PHP statement**!

Q: So if my table has data in it and I drop it, all my data is deleted too?

A: That is true. So drop tables with care!

Q: So if I need to change a table with data in it, I'm out of luck?

A: Hey, no one is perfect. Everyone makes mistakes, and SQL
offers the ALTER statement to help us change existing tables. We'll
talk about this command a bit later on in the book.

Create the Add Email script

Elmer needs an HTML form that can collect names and email addresses from customers. Once he has those, he can grab them with a PHP script and store them in the `email_list` table. The web form (`addemail.html`) requires three input fields and a button. The form action is the most important code in the form since its job is to pass along the form data to the `addemail.php` script we're about to create.

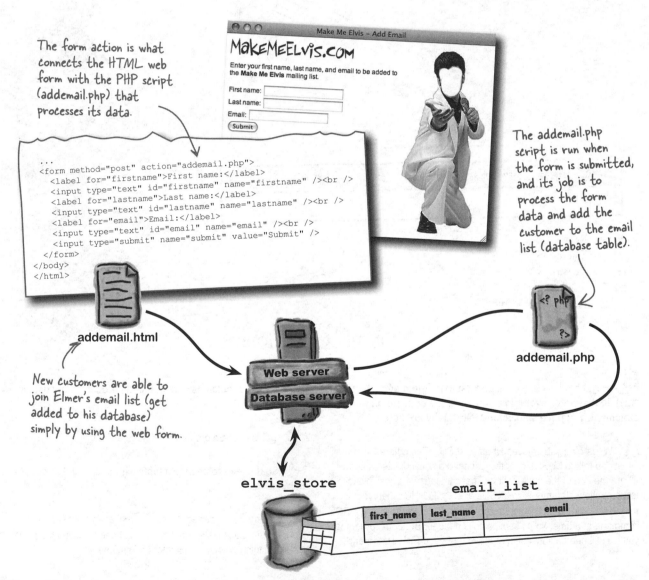

You are now here.

1. ~~Create a database and table for the email list.~~

2. Create an Add Email web form and PHP script for adding a new customer to the list.

3. Create a Send Email web form and PHP script for sending an email to the list.

The form action is what connects the HTML web form with the PHP script (addemail.php) that processes its data.

```
...
<form method="post" action="addemail.php">
  <label for="firstname">First name:</label>
  <input type="text" id="firstname" name="firstname" /><br />
  <label for="lastname">Last name:</label>
  <input type="text" id="lastname" name="lastname" /><br />
  <label for="email">Email:</label>
  <input type="text" id="email" name="email" /><br />
  <input type="submit" name="submit" value="Submit" />
</form>
</body>
</html>
```

The addemail.php script is run when the form is submitted, and its job is to process the form data and add the customer to the email list (database table).

addemail.html

New customers are able to join Elmer's email list (get added to his database) simply by using the web form.

Web server

Database server

addemail.php

elvis_store

email_list

first_name	last_name	email

Exercise

The `addemail.php` script processes data from the Add Email form. The script should take the data from the form, connect to the `elvis_store` database, and `INSERT` the data into the `email_list` table. Help Elmer by first writing an example SQL query to insert a new customer, and then use that query to finish the PHP script code.

Write an example query here that inserts data into Elmer's table.

....
....

```
<?php
  $dbc = .........................................................................................
  ...............................................................................................

  $first_name = $_POST['firstname'];
  ...............................................................................................
  ...............................................................................................

  $query = .......................................................................................
  ...............................................................................................

  mysqli_query( ...................... )
  ...............................................................................................

  echo 'Customer added.';
  ...............................................................................................
?>
```

addemail.php

Exercise Solution

The `addemail.php` script is called upon to process data from the Add Email form. The script should take the data from the form, connect to the `elvis_store` database, and INSERT the data into the `email_list` table. Help Elmer by first writing an example SQL query to insert a new customer, and then use that query to finish the PHP script code.

INSERT INTO email_list (first_name, last_name, email)

VALUES ('Julian', 'Oates', 'julian@breakneckpizza.com')

The example INSERT query is rewritten as a PHP string that relies on form data for the insertion.

Here are the $_POST array values that contain the submitted information.

```php
<?php
  $dbc = mysqli_connect('data.makemeelvis.com', 'elmer', 'theking', 'elvis_store')
    or die('Error connecting to MySQL server.');

  $first_name = $_POST['firstname'];
  $last_name = $_POST['lastname'];
  $email = $_POST['email'];

  $query = "INSERT INTO email_list (first_name, last_name, email) " .
    "VALUES ('$first_name', '$last_name', '$email')";

  mysqli_query( $dbc, $query )
    or die('Error querying database.');

  echo 'Customer added.';

  mysqli_close($dbc);
?>
```

If we wanted to be fancy here, we could put a link back to our form with an HTML <a> tag.

addemail.php

Test Drive

Try out the Add Email form.

Download the code for the Add Email web page from the Head First Labs web site at **www.headfirstlabs.com/books/hfphp**. It's in the **chapter03** folder. This code consists of Elmer's web form in **addemail.html**, a style sheet (**style.css**), and two images (**elvislogo.gif** and **blankface.jpg**).

Now create a new text file called **addemail.php**, and enter all of the code on the facing page. This is the script that will process Elmer's web form and add new customers to the email_list table.

Don't forget to change the database connection variables to your own.

Upload all of these files to your web server and open the addemail.html page in a web browser. Enter a new customer in the form, and click Submit.

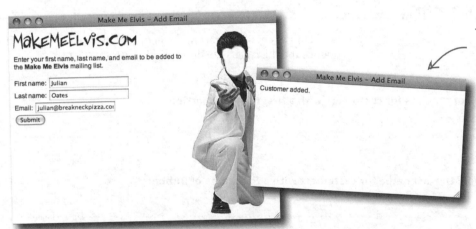

The insertion of the new customer to the email list is confirmed by the addemail.php script.

Check to see that the customer was added to the database by issuing a SELECT query in a MySQL tool.

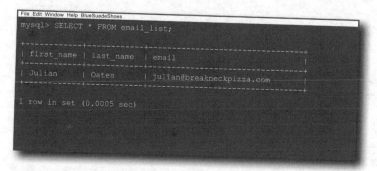

```
mysql> SELECT * FROM email_list;

+------------+-----------+----------------------------+
| first_name | last_name | email                      |
+------------+-----------+----------------------------+
| Julian     | Oates     | julian@breakneckpizza.com  |
+------------+-----------+----------------------------+
1 row in set (0.0005 sec)
```

there are no
Dumb Questions

Q: Is the star in the SQL SELECT command the same thing as an asterisk?

A: Yes, it's the same character on your keyboard, located above the 8 key. Hit SHIFT at the same time as the 8 to type one. But although it's exactly the same character as asterisk, in SQL lingo, it's always referred to as a **star**. This is a good thing, since saying "SELECT asterisk FROM..." is not as easy as saying "SELECT star FROM...".

Q: Are there other characters in SQL that have special meaning like the star does?

A: While SQL does have other special, or reserved, characters, the star is the only one you need to know about for right now. More importantly for our immediate purposes, it's the only one used in the SELECT part of an SQL statement.

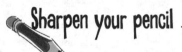
Sharpen your pencil

With Elmer's email list starting to fill up, help him write some SQL queries that he can use to find specific customer data.

Select all of the data for customers with a first name of Martin:

....

Select only the last name for customers with a first name of Bubba:

....

Select the first name and last name for the customer with an email address of ls@objectville.net.

....

Select all of the columns for customers with a first name of Amber and a last name of McCarthy:

....

first_name	last_name	email
Julian	Oates	julian@breakneckpizza.com
Kevin	Jones	jones@simuduck.com
Amanda	Sanchez	sunshine@breakneckpizza.com
Bo	Wallace	bo@b0tt0msup.com
Amber	McCarthy	amber@breakneckpizza.com
Cormac	Hurst	churst@boards-r-us.com
Joyce	Harper	joyceharper@breakneckpizza.com
Stephen	Meyer	meyers@leapinlimos.com
Martin	Wilson	martybaby@objectville.net
Walt	Perala	walt@mightygumball.net
	Munyon	craftsman@breakneckpizza.com
	ano	joe_m@starbuzzcoffee.com
		bruce@chocoholic-inc.com
		pr@honey-doit.com
	on	bertieh@objectville.net
	n	gregeck@breakneckpizza.com
		wilmawu@starbuzzcoffee.com
		samjaffe@starbuzzcoffee.com
	affe	ls@objectville.net
Louis	Shaffer	bshakes@mightygumball.net
Bubba	Shakespeare	johndoe@tikibeanlounge.com
John	Doe	

Very cool. Now that users can subscribe to my email list through a web page. The list pretty much builds itself.

This isn't the end of the table data...Elmer just has a rapidly growing mailing list!

But the email list can't send itself.

Elmer's still missing the other part of the web application, the part that allows him to enter an email message and have it delivered to everyone on the email list. To do this, he'll need a new HTML form and a PHP script to put it into action...

① ~~Create a database and table for the email list.~~

② ~~Create an Add Email web form and PHP script for adding a new customer to the list.~~

Step 2 is done!

③ Create a Send Email web form and PHP script for sending an email to the list.

Sharpen your pencil
Solution

With Elmer's email list starting to fill up, help him write some SQL queries that he can use to find specific customer data.

Select all of the data for customers with a first name of Martin:

SELECT * FROM email_list WHERE first_name = 'Martin'

    ⤸ The star selects *all* the columns in the table.

    ⤸ This WHERE clause trims down the query results to only those customers with a first name of Martin.

Select only the last name for customers with a first name of Bubba:

SELECT last_name FROM email_list WHERE first_name = 'Bubba'

    ↰ Only the last_name column is returned in the query results.

Select the first name and last name for the customer with an email address of ls@objectville.net.

SELECT first_name, last_name FROM email_list WHERE email = 'ls@objectville.net'

    ⤸ You specify multiple columns of result data by separating the column names with commas.

Select all of the columns for customers with a first name of Amber and a last name of McCarthy:

SELECT * FROM email_list WHERE first_name = 'Amber' AND last_name = 'McCarthy'

    ⤴ The WHERE clause can be made dependent on multiple pieces of information, in this case a match for both a first name AND a last name.

The other side of Elmer's application

Sending email messages to people on Elmer's email list is similar in some ways to adding people to the list because it involves an HTML web form and a PHP script. The big difference, is that sending an email message to the mailing list involves dealing with the *entire contents* of the email_list table, whereas the addemail.php script only deals with one row of data.

The Send Email web form allows Elmer to enter a subject and body of an email message, and then send it to his entire email list.

1. ~~Create a database and table for the email list.~~

2. ~~Create an Add Email web form and PHP script for adding a new customer to the list.~~

3. Create a Send Email web form and PHP script for sending an email to the list.

Whew, we're finally on the last step.

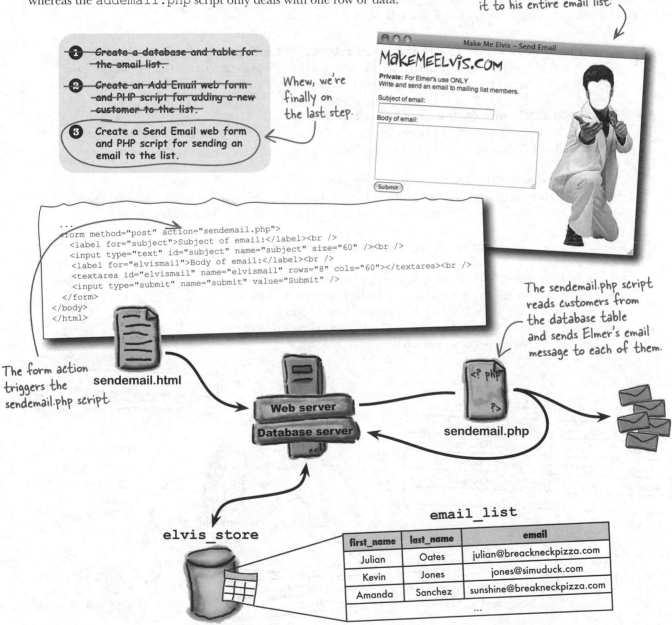

MAKEMEELVIS.COM

Private: For Elmer's use ONLY
Write and send an email to mailing list members.

Subject of email:

Body of email:

Submit

```
...
<form method="post" action="sendemail.php">
  <label for="subject">Subject of email:</label><br />
  <input type="text" id="subject" name="subject" size="60" /><br />
  <label for="elvismail">Body of email:</label><br />
  <textarea id="elvismail" name="elvismail" rows="8" cols="60"></textarea><br />
  <input type="submit" name="submit" value="Submit" />
</form>
</body>
</html>
```

The form action triggers the sendemail.php script.

sendemail.html

The sendemail.php script reads customers from the database table and sends Elmer's email message to each of them.

Web server

Database server

sendemail.php

elvis_store

email_list

first_name	last_name	email
Julian	Oates	julian@breackneckpizza.com
Kevin	Jones	jones@simuduck.com
Amanda	Sanchez	sunshine@breakneckpizza.com
		...

The nuts and bolts of the Send Email script

The `sendemail.php` script must combine data from two different sources to generate and send email messages. On the one hand, the script needs to pull the names and email addresses of the email recipients from the `email_list` table in the `elvis_store` database. But it also has to grab the email subject and message body entered by Elmer into the Send Email web form (`sendemail.html`). Let's break down the steps involved.

1 **Use the `$_POST` array to get the email subject and message body from the form.**
There's nothing new here. Clicking the Submit button in the `sendemail.html` form sends the form data to `sendemail.php`, where we capture it in variables with a little help from the `$_POST` array.

2 **Run a `SELECT` query on the `email_list` table.**
The PHP `mysqli_query()` function runs a `SELECT` query to get the data for the email list. Since we want all of the data in the table, we can use `SELECT *`.

3 **Fetch the email data from the query result.**
Running a query alone doesn't provide access to data. We need to grab each row of data in the query results in order to have access to the first name, last name, and email address of each customer.

4 **Call the `mail()` function to send an email message to each customer.**
Sending the emails involves looping through each customer in the email list, which corresponds to each row of data in the query results. The loop we create here starts at the first row of data, then moves on to the second row, and loops through the remaining rows of the data obtained by the `SELECT` query. We stop when we reach the end of the data.

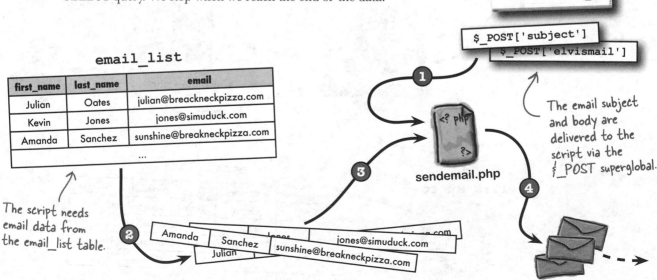

```
$_POST['subject']
$_POST['elvismail']
```

The email subject and body are delivered to the script via the $_POST superglobal.

email_list

first_name	last_name	email
Julian	Oates	julian@breacknneckpizza.com
Kevin	Jones	jones@simuduck.com
Amanda	Sanchez	sunshine@breakneckpizza.com
...		

The script needs email data from the email_list table.

sendemail.php

| Amanda | Sanchez | Jones | jones@simuduck.com |
| Julian | | | sunshine@breakneckpizza.com |

First things first, grab the data

We're already pretty well versed in extracting data from forms in PHP, so the first step is nothing new, just use the `$_POST` superglobal to store away the email subject and message body in variables. While we're at it, let's go ahead and store Elmer's email address in a variable since we'll need it later when sending the emails.

> Elmer's email address is stored in a variable so that we know exactly where it is in case it ever needs to change.

```php
$from = 'elmer@makemeelvis.com';

$subject = $_POST['subject'];

$text = $_POST['elvismail'];
```

> The email message form data's stored in variables, too.

The remaining data required by the `sendemail.php` script comes from Elmer's MySQL database. Pulling customer data from the `email_list` table data into the script requires a `SELECT` query. Unlike before when we've used the MySQL terminal to issue a `SELECT` and look at table data, this time we're doing it in the `sendemail.php` script and issuing the query with `mysqli_query()`.

> The $query variable holds the SQL query as a string of text.

> Here's our query, which selects all of the columns from the email_list table.

```php
$query = "SELECT * FROM email_list";

$result = mysqli_query($dbc, $query);
```

> mysqli_query executes the query using a connection variable ($dbc) and a query string ($query).

> A database connection is required in order to submit a query — the details of the connection are stored in the $dbc variable.

> So all we have to do is go through the query results in the $result variable, right?

No, the `$result` variable doesn't actually hold any query data.

If you try to echo the `$result` variable directly, you'll see something like this:

```
Resource id #3
```

The `$result` variable stores an ID number for a MySQL **resource**, not the actual data returned by the query. What happens is the MySQL server temporarily stores the results of your query and gives them a resource number to identify them. You then use this resource ID with the PHP `mysqli_fetch_array()` function to grab the data one row at a time.

mysqli_fetch_array() fetches query results

Once our query executes, we can grab the results with the $result variable. This variable's used with the mysqli_fetch_array() function to get the data in the table one row at a time. Each row of data is returned as an array, which we can store in a new variable named $row.

This function retrieves a row of data from the query results and stores it in an array.

```
$row = mysqli_fetch_array($result);
```

The variable $row is an array that initially stores the first row of data from our results.

Each SQL query has its own resource ID number that is used to access the data associated with its results.

Each time this code is executed by the web server, a row of data from the query results gets stored in the $row array. You repeatedly call the mysqli_fetch_array() function to step through each row of the query results. So the first three calls to the mysqli_fetch_array() function retrieve the first three rows of data from the table, storing each column of the row as an item in the $row array.

The mysqli_fetch_array() function stores a row of data in an array.

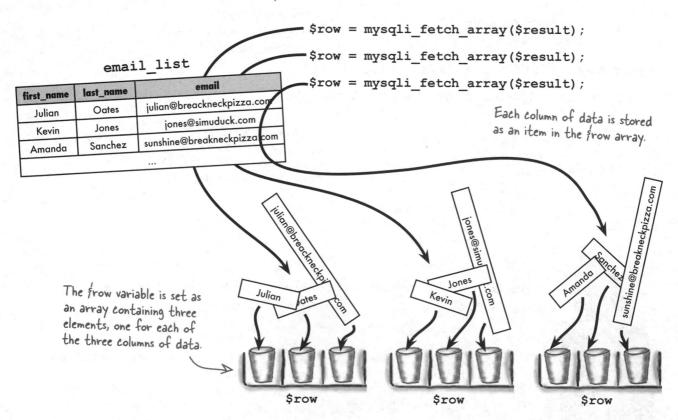

```
$row = mysqli_fetch_array($result);
$row = mysqli_fetch_array($result);
$row = mysqli_fetch_array($result);
```

email_list

first_name	last_name	email
Julian	Oates	julian@breackneckpizza.com
Kevin	Jones	jones@simuduck.com
Amanda	Sanchez	sunshine@breakneckpizza.com
...		

Each column of data is stored as an item in the $row array.

The $row variable is set as an array containing three elements, one for each of the three columns of data.

$row $row $row

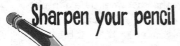

Sharpen your pencil

As a test to make sure we can actually get the customer data a row at a time, finish writing the PHP code to echo the first name, last name, and email address of each customer in the `email_list` table.

```
$query = "SELECT * FROM email_list";

$result = mysqli_query($dbc, $query);

$row = mysqli_fetch_array($result);
```

....

....

....

....

....

....

....

....

....

....

....

....

....

....

....

....

Sharpen your pencil
Solution

As a test to make sure we can actually get the customer data a row at a time, finish writing the PHP code to echo the first name, last name, and email address of each customer in the email_list table.

```
$query = "SELECT * FROM email_list";

$result = mysqli_query($dbc, $query);

$row = mysqli_fetch_array($result);
```

```
echo $row['first_name'] . ' ' . $row['last_name'] . ': ' . $row['email'] . '<br />';

$row = mysqli_fetch_array($result);

echo $row['first_name'] . ' ' . $row['last_name'] . ': ' . $row['email'] . '<br />';

$row = mysqli_fetch_array($result);

echo $row['first_name'] . ' ' . $row['last_name'] . ': ' . $row['email'] . '<br />';

$row = mysqli_fetch_array($result);

echo $row['first_name'] . ' ' . $row['last_name'] . ': ' . $row['email'] . '<br />';

$row = mysqli_fetch_arr

echo $row['first_nam

$row = mysqli_fetch

echo $row['first_nam[] . . ro                    br />';

$row            tch_array($result);

echo           ame'] . ' ' . $row['last_name'] . ': ' . $row['email'] . '<br />';

$row           _array($result);

echo          e'] . ' ' . $row['last_name'] . ': ' . $row['email'] . '<br />';
```

You have *got* to be kidding me. Repeating the same two lines of code over and over is about the dumbest thing I've ever seen. Surely there's a better way.

There is a better way—we need a loop.

A **loop** is a mechanism in the PHP language that repeats a chunk of code until a certain condition's been met, like running out of data. So a loop can **cycle through each row of data** in a query result, taking any action we want to each row along the way.

Looping for a WHILE

A while loop is a loop specifically geared toward repeating code **while a certain condition is met**. For example, you might have a variable in a customer service application named `$got_customers` that keeps up with whether or not customers are waiting to be helped. If `$got_customers` is set to `true`, you know there are more customers, so you might call the `next_customer()` function to get the next customer and help them. Here's how this scenario could be coded using a while loop:

A while loop repeats code <u>while</u> a condition is met.

As long as we still have customers, keep on looping.

```
while ($got_customers) {
    next_customer();
    ...
}
```

This is the code that gets executed each time through the loop.

Enclosing the loop code within curly braces lets you execute as many lines of code as you want.

A while loop lets us loop through customers until there aren't any left!

When we look to see if there are more customers, we're **testing a condition**. The **condition** is the code in the parentheses, and it always poses a question that results in a yes/no answer. If it's yes, or **true**, then the action is performed. If it's no, or **false**, then we quit the loop.

When we call `next_customer()` and proceed to help them, we're **performing an action**. The action is the code inside the curly braces, which is repeated as long as the condition remains `true`. If the condition ever goes `false`, the loop exits and the action is not repeated again. Here's the general format of a while loop:

The test condition always results in true or false... keep looping (true) or stop looping (false).

```
while (test_condition) {
    action
}
```

The loop action takes place once each time through the loop.

BRAIN POWER

How do you think a while loop could be used to loop through the customers in Elmer's `email_list` table?

Looping through data with while

Applying a while loop to Elmer's email data lets us access the data a row at a time without duplicating any code. We know that mysqli_fetch_array() can take a table row and put the column values in the $row array, but the function by itself won't get through all of our data—it will store the first row and then stop. A while loop can call mysqli_fetch_array() to go through each row of result data, one at a time, until it reaches the end.

> The while loop condition is the return value of the mysqli_fetch_array() function, which is interpreted as true if data is available or false if we're all out of data.

```php
while($row = mysqli_fetch_array($result)) {
    echo $row['first_name'] . ' ' . $row['last_name'] .
        ' : ' . $row['email'] . '<br />';
}
```

> The loop action gets run each time through the loop.

> The loop action consists of an echo statement that sticks the row data together with a line break at the end.

> The first time through the loop the $row array holds the first row of the email_list table.

$row

1st loop!

email_list

first_name	last_name	email
Julian	Oates	julian@breackneckpizza.com
Kevin	Jones	jones@simuduck.com
Amanda	Sanchez	sunshine@breakneckpizza.com
...		

2nd loop!

$row

> The second time through the loop the $row array holds the second row of the email_list table...see a pattern here?

More loops...

The echo statement inside the while loop takes the data in the $row array and outputs formatted HTML content.

An HTML line break puts each row of data on its own line on the resulting page.

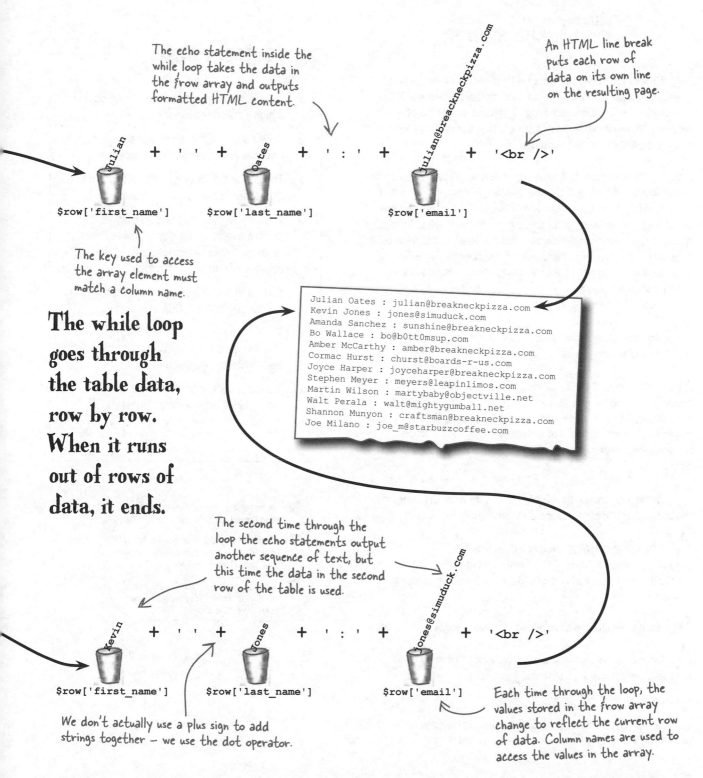

Julian + ' ' + Oates + ' : ' + julian@breakneckpizza.com + '<br />'

$row['first_name'] $row['last_name'] $row['email']

The key used to access the array element must match a column name.

The while loop goes through the table data, row by row. When it runs out of rows of data, it ends.

```
Julian Oates : julian@breakneckpizza.com
Kevin Jones : jones@simuduck.com
Amanda Sanchez : sunshine@breakneckpizza.com
Bo Wallace : bo@b0tt0msup.com
Amber McCarthy : amber@breakneckpizza.com
Cormac Hurst : churst@boards-r-us.com
Joyce Harper : joyceharper@breakneckpizza.com
Stephen Meyer : meyers@leapinlimos.com
Martin Wilson : martybaby@objectville.net
Walt Perala : walt@mightygumball.net
Shannon Munyon : craftsman@breakneckpizza.com
Joe Milano : joe_m@starbuzzcoffee.com
```

The second time through the loop the echo statements output another sequence of text, but this time the data in the second row of the table is used.

Kevin + ' ' + Jones + ' : ' + jones@simuduck.com + '<br />'

$row['first_name'] $row['last_name'] $row['email']

We don't actually use a plus sign to add strings together — we use the dot operator.

Each time through the loop, the values stored in the $row array change to reflect the current row of data. Column names are used to access the values in the array.

there are no
Dumb Questions

Q: How exactly does the `while` loop know to keep looping? I mean, a `while` loop's controlled by a `true`/`false` condition, and `mysqli_fetch_array()` returns some kind of resource ID, which is stored in `$row`... That sure doesn't look like a `true`/`false` test condition.

A: Good observation. As it turns out, PHP is fairly liberal when it comes to how it interprets the "true" condition. In short, any value that is not zero (0) or `false` is considered `true` for the sake of a test condition. So when the `mysqli_fetch_array()` function returns a row of data, the `$row` array is interpreted as `true` since it isn't set to 0 or `false`. And since the test condition is `true`, the loop keeps on chugging. What's interesting is what happens when no more data's available—the `mysqli_fetch_array()` returns `false`, which terminates the loop.

Q: So I can control a `while` loop with any kind of data, not just `true`/`false` values?

A: That's correct. But keep in mind that ultimately the `while` loop's interpreting the data as `true` or `false`. So the important thing to understand is what constitutes `true` or `false` when it comes to the interpretation of other types of data. And the simple answer is that anything other than 0 or `false` is always interpreted as `true`.

Q: What happens to the `while` loop if no data is returned by the `mysqli_fetch_array()` function?

A: If the query doesn't result in any data, then the `mysqli_fetch_array()` function returns `false`. And this causes the `while` loop to never make it into the action code, not even once.

Q: So it's possible to have a loop that never loops?

A: Indeed it is. It's also possible to have a loop that never stops looping. Consider this `while` loop:

```
while (true) {
```

This is known as an **infinite loop** because the test condition never causes the loop to exit. Infinite loops are a very bad thing.

BULLET POINTS

- A database is a container for storing data in a highly structured manner.

- Tables store data in a grid-like pattern of columns and rows within a database.

- The `CREATE DATABASE` SQL command is used to create a new database.

- The `CREATE TABLE` SQL command creates a table within a database and requires detailed information about the columns of data within the table.

- You can delete a table from a database with the `DROP TABLE` SQL command.

- The `mysqli_fetch_array()` function retrieves a row of data from the results of a database query.

- A `while` loop repeats a chunk of PHP code while a test condition is met.

---

1. ~~Create a database and table for the email list.~~

2. ~~Create an Add Email web form and PHP script for adding a new customer to the list.~~

3. Create a Send Email web form and PHP script for sending an email to the list.

Don't forget, we still have that last step to finish up.

PHP & MySQL Magnets

Use the magnets below to finish the code for the Send Email script so that Elmer can start sending emails to his customer list. As a refresher, here's how the `mail()` function works:

```php
mail(to, subject, msg, 'From:' . from);
```

```php
<?php
  $from = 'elmer@makemeelvis.com';

  $subject = ........................................................ ;

  $text = ........................................................ ;

  $dbc = mysqli_connect('data.makemeelvis.com', 'elmer', 'theking', 'elvis_store')
    or die('Error connecting to MySQL server.');

  $query = "SELECT * FROM email_list";
  $result = mysqli_query($dbc, $query)
    or die('Error querying database.');

  while($row = mysqli_fetch_array($result)) {
    $first_name = $row['first_name'];
    $last_name = $row['last_name'];

    $msg = "Dear $first_name $last_name,\n ................. ";

    $to = ........................................ ;
    mail( ............. , ....................... , 'From:' . ............. );
    echo 'Email sent to: ' . ............. . '<br />';

  }

  mysqli_close($dbc);
?>
```

sendemail.php

Magnets:

to msg subject text email subject row _POST _POST elvismail from to

$ $ $ $ $ $ $ $ $

' ' ' ' ' '

[[[ ]]]]]

PHP & MySQL Magnets

Use the magnets below to finish the code for the Send Email script so that Elmer can start sending emails to his customer list. As a refresher, here's how the mail() function works:

$$mail(\textit{to, subject, msg, 'From:'} . \textit{from});$$

Make sure to change this to your own email address.

The Subject form field is named "subject", which is the same name used to access it in the $_POST array.

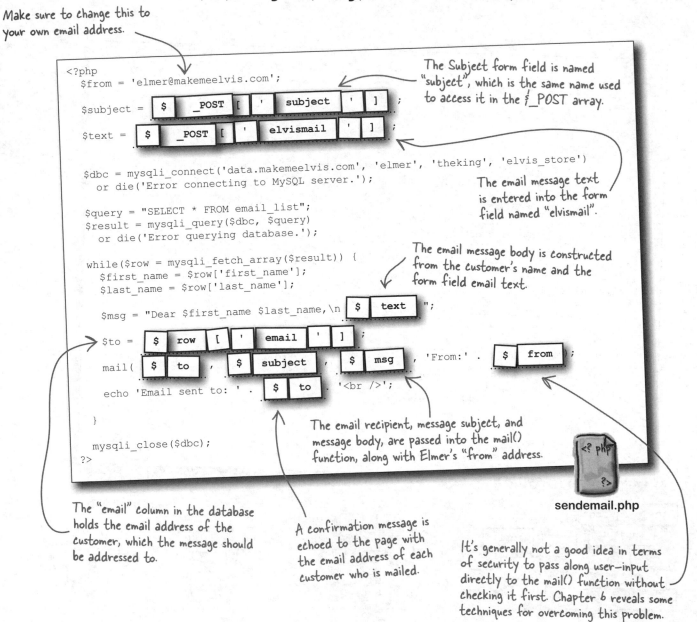

```php
<?php
  $from = 'elmer@makemeelvis.com';

  $subject = $ _POST [ ' subject ' ] ;

  $text = $ _POST [ ' elvismail ' ] ;

  $dbc = mysqli_connect('data.makemeelvis.com', 'elmer', 'theking', 'elvis_store')
    or die('Error connecting to MySQL server.');

  $query = "SELECT * FROM email_list";
  $result = mysqli_query($dbc, $query)
    or die('Error querying database.');

  while($row = mysqli_fetch_array($result)) {
    $first_name = $row['first_name'];
    $last_name = $row['last_name'];

    $msg = "Dear $first_name $last_name,\n $ text ";

    $to = $ row [ ' email ' ] ;
    mail( $ to , $ subject , $ msg , 'From:' . $ from );
    echo 'Email sent to: ' . $ to . '<br />';

  }

  mysqli_close($dbc);
?>
```

The email message text is entered into the form field named "elvismail".

The email message body is constructed from the customer's name and the form field email text.

The email recipient, message subject, and message body, are passed into the mail() function, along with Elmer's "from" address.

sendemail.php

The "email" column in the database holds the email address of the customer, which the message should be addressed to.

A confirmation message is echoed to the page with the email address of each customer who is mailed.

It's generally not a good idea in terms of security to pass along user-input directly to the mail() function without checking it first. Chapter 6 reveals some techniques for overcoming this problem.

Test Drive

Send an email to the mailing list using the Send Email form.

Download the code for the Send Email web page from the Head First Labs web site at **www.headfirstlabs.com/books/hfphp**. It's in the **chapter03** folder. Similar to the Add Email page you saw earlier, this code consists of a web form in **sendemail.html**, a style sheet (**style.css**), and a couple of images (**elvislogo.gif** and **blankface.jpg**).

Create a new text file called **sendemail.php**, and enter all of the code on the facing page. Upload all of these files to your web server and open the `sendemail.html` page in a web browser. Enter an email message in the form, and click Submit.

> *Keep in mind that your email address will need to be on the mailing list in order for you to receive a message.*

You've got mail...from Elmer!

At last, Elmer can send out his MakeMeElvis.com sale emails to everyone on his mailing list by using his new Send Email web form and PHP script. He can also use the output from the script to confirm that each message is successfully being sent. Each time the code in the script's `while` loop executes, he sees "Email sent to someone@somewhere.com" with the email address of the person in his database. The end result is more exposure for his products, and for better or worse, more Elvis look-alikes!

> *The Send Email script really does send emails to the addresses stored in the database, so be careful when tinkering with it!*

> I've sold out of blue suede shoes...I'm rich!

Make Me Elvis – Send Email

PRI... ...ONLY
Write and send an email to mailing list members.

Subject of email:
Big Sale!

Body of email:
Big sale this week at MakeMeElvis.com! Genuine horse hair sideburns 20% off!
And don't forget the "buy one, get one free" leisure suits — only three days left!

Submit

Make Me Elvis – Send Email

Email sent to: julian@breakneckpizza.com
Email sent to: jones@simuduck.com
Email sent to: sunshine@breakneckpizza.com
Email sent to: bo@b0tt0msup.com
Email sent to: amber@breakneckpizza.com
Email sent to: churst@boards-r-us.com
Email sent to: joyceharper@breakneckpizza.com
Email sent to: meyers@leapinlimos.com
Email sent to: martybaby@objectville.net
Email sent to: walt@mightygumball.net
Email sent to: craftsman@breakneckpizza.com
Email sent to: joe_m@starbuzzcoffee.com
Email sent to: bruce@chocoholic-inc.com
Email sent to: pr@honey-doit.com
Email sent to: bertieh@objectville.net
Email sent to: gregeck@breakneckpizza.com
Email sent to: wilmawu@starbuzzcoffee.com
Email sent to: samjaffe@starbuzzcoffee.com
Email sent to: ls@objectville.net
Email sent to: bshakes@mightygumball.net

Sometimes people want out

As with any blossoming new business, there are bumps in the road. It seems some Elvis fans have jumped ship on the King and want off Elmer's mailing list. Elmer wants to oblige, but that means he needs to remove the customers from his database.

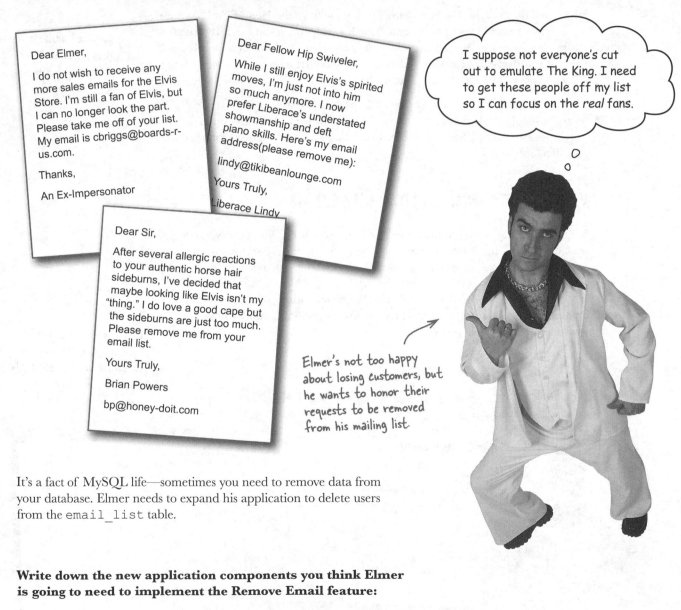

Dear Elmer,

I do not wish to receive any more sales emails for the Elvis Store. I'm still a fan of Elvis, but I can no longer look the part. Please take me off of your list. My email is cbriggs@boards-r-us.com.

Thanks,

An Ex-Impersonator

Dear Fellow Hip Swiveler,

While I still enjoy Elvis's spirited moves, I'm just not into him so much anymore. I now prefer Liberace's understated showmanship and deft piano skills. Here's my email address(please remove me):

lindy@tikibeanlounge.com

Yours Truly,

Liberace Lindy

Dear Sir,

After several allergic reactions to your authentic horse hair sideburns, I've decided that maybe looking like Elvis isn't my "thing." I do love a good cape but the sideburns are just too much. Please remove me from your email list.

Yours Truly,

Brian Powers

bp@honey-doit.com

I suppose not everyone's cut out to emulate The King. I need to get these people off my list so I can focus on the *real* fans.

Elmer's not too happy about losing customers, but he wants to honor their requests to be removed from his mailing list.

It's a fact of MySQL life—sometimes you need to remove data from your database. Elmer needs to expand his application to delete users from the `email_list` table.

Write down the new application components you think Elmer is going to need to implement the Remove Email feature:

....

....

Removing data with DELETE

To delete data from a table, we need a new SQL command, DELETE. We'll use DELETE in a new Remove Email script that deletes customers' data from Elmer's mailing list. In fact, we need a new script and a new web form to drive it... but first we need DELETE.

The DELETE SQL command removes rows of data from a table. This makes it a command you should use very carefully since it's capable of wiping out a table full of data in the blink of an eye. Knowing this, here's the most dangerous form of DELETE, which deletes every row from a table.

1 ~~Create a database and table for the email list.~~

2 ~~Create an Add Email web form and PHP script for adding a new customer to the list.~~

3 ~~Create a Send Email web form and PHP script for sending an email to the list.~~

4 Create a Remove Email web form and PHP script for removing a customer from the list.

> *Looks like we need a new step...sometimes design plans change!*

`DELETE FROM` `table_name`

This is the name of the table you want to delete rows from.

Without any other qualifiers, the DELETE command completely empties a table of <u>all its data</u>.

> *So we can never delete anything from a table without deleting **everything**?*

No, not at all. DELETE can be used to pinpoint a specific row or rows for deletion.

To precisely target the row or rows you want to delete with DELETE, you need to tack on a WHERE clause. If you recall from using it with the SELECT command, WHERE allows you to isolate specific rows in a query.

Sharpen your pencil

Suppose Elmer had 23 customers with a first name of Anne, 11 customers with a last name of Parker, and one customer with the name Anne Parker. Write down how many rows of data are deleted by each of these queries.

```
DELETE FROM email_list WHERE first_name = 'Anne';
```
....

```
DELETE FROM email_list WHERE first_name = 'Anne' OR last_name = 'Parker';
```
....

```
DELETE FROM email_list WHERE last_name = Parker;
```
....

Sharpen your pencil
Solution

Suppose Elmer had 23 customers with a first name of Anne, 11 customers with a last name of Parker, and one customer with the name Anne Parker. Write down how many rows of data are deleted by each of these queries.

```
DELETE FROM email_list WHERE first_name = 'Anne';
```
<u>23</u>

```
DELETE FROM email_list WHERE first_name = 'Anne' OR last_name = 'Parker';
```
<u>33</u>

```
DELETE FROM email_list WHERE last_name = Parker;
```
<u>0</u>

Trick question! The last name isn't quoted, so no rows are deleted — all text values must be quoted.

Use WHERE to DELETE specific data

By using a WHERE clause with the DELETE command, we target specific rows of data for deletion, instead of emptying an entire table. The WHERE clause lets us focus on just the row we want to remove, in this case one of Elmer's customers who wants to be removed from the mailing list.

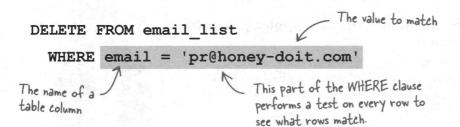

```
DELETE FROM email_list
    WHERE email = 'pr@honey-doit.com'
```

The value to match

The name of a table column

This part of the WHERE clause performs a test on every row to see what rows match.

A WHERE clause narrows down a query to focus on specific rows of data.

The actual test within a WHERE clause performs a comparison that is carried out against every row in the table. In this example, the equal sign (=) tests each value in the email column to see which rows are equal to "pr@honey-doit.com". If the value in the email column of a row matches, then that row will be deleted.

Write down why you think the email **column is used in the** WHERE **clause, as opposed to** first_name **or** last_name:

....

....

Minimize the risk of accidental deletions

It's important to understand that although any column name can be used in a WHERE clause to match rows, there's a *very* good reason why we chose the email column for Elmer's DELETE query. Consider that if more than one row matches a WHERE clause, all of the matching rows will be deleted. So it's important for Elmer's WHERE clause to pinpoint **exactly** the row you want to delete.

What we're really talking about is uniqueness. It's fairly safe to assume that email addresses are unique within the email_list table, whereas first names and last names are not. You don't want to create a WHERE clause matching the first_name column to "Pat" just to delete a single customer—you'll end up deleting every customer named Pat! That's why Elmer's WHERE clause is carefully crafted to look for a specific match with the email column.

> **A WHERE clause in a DELETE statement lets you pinpoint the row you want to remove.**

```
DELETE FROM email_list
    WHERE email = 'pr@honey-doit.com'
```

Using the email column in the WHERE clause helps to establish uniqueness and reduce the risk of accidentally deleting a row.

The DELETE query removes this row from the database...never to be seen again!

email_list

first_name	last_name	email
...		
Joe	Milano	joe_m@starbuzzcoffee.com
Bruce	Spence	bruce@chocoholic-inc.com
Pat	Risse	pr@honey-doit.com
Bertie	Henderson	bertieh@objectville.net
Greg	Eckstein	gregeck@breakneckpizza.com
Wilma	Wu	wilmawu@starbuzzcoffee.com
Sam	Jaffe	samjaffe@starbuzzcoffee.com
Louis	Shaffer	ls@objectville.net
Bubba	Shakespeare	bshakes@mightygumball.net
John	Doe	johndoe@tikibeanlounge.com
Pat	Grommet	grommetp@simuduck.com
...		

If we used first_name in the WHERE clause instead of email, this user would accidentally get deleted.

```
File Edit Window Help ByeBye
mysql> DELETE FROM email_list WHERE email = 'pr@honey-doit.com';
1 row deleted (0.005 sec)
```

Test Drive

Try out the DELETE command on Elmer's database.

Fire up a MySQL tool and try a few `DELETE` commands to delete individual rows of data from the `email_list` table based on customers' email addresses. Just make sure to include a `WHERE` clause on each `DELETE` statement so that you don't accidentally wipe out the whole table!

> The `DELETE` command's pretty handy, but ideally we'd delete rows of data using a web form and PHP script, right?

That's right. Deleting users by hand with individual queries is no way to manage a mailing list.

Since Elmer will inevitably face users who want to be removed from his mailing list in the future, it makes a lot of sense to develop a web-based user interface for removing customers. An HTML web form and PHP script should do the trick, not to mention a `DELETE FROM` query with a little help from a `WHERE` clause...

Exercise

Elmer has created a web form (`removeemail.html`) for deleting a customer from his mailing list. All the form accepts is an email address, which is entered into an HTML form field named `email`. Finish the code for Elmer's `removeemail.php` script that's called by the form to carry out each customer removal.

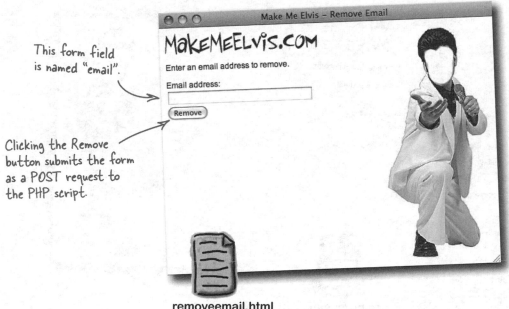

This form field is named "email".

Clicking the Remove button submits the form as a POST request to the PHP script.

removeemail.html

```php
<?php

  $dbc = mysqli_connect('data.makemeelvis.com', 'elmer', 'theking', 'elvis_store')
    or die('Error connecting to MySQL server.')

  .............................................................................

  .............................................................................

  .............................................................................

  .............................................................................

  .............................................................................

  .............................................................................

  .............................................................................

  mysqli_close($dbc);

?>
```

removeemail.php

Exercise
Solution

Elmer has created a web form (removeemail.html) for deleting a customer from his mailing list. All the form accepts is an email address, which is entered into an HTML form field named email. Finish the code for Elmer's removeemail.php script that's called by the form to carry out each customer removal.

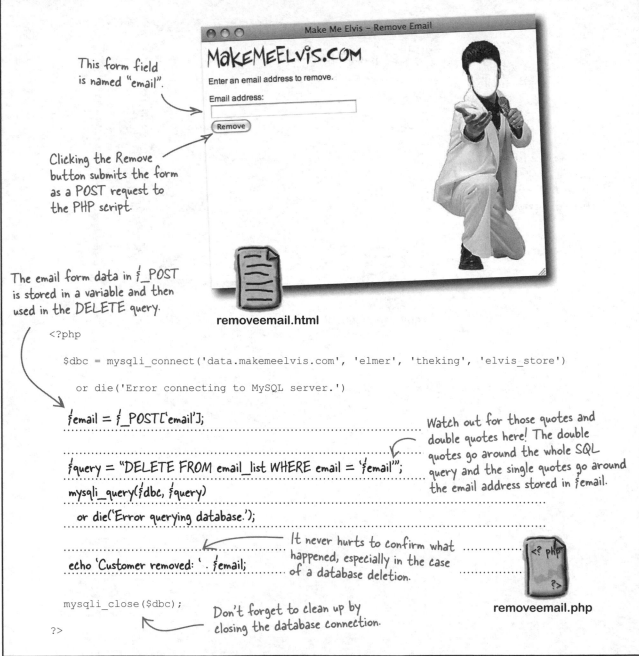

This form field is named "email".

Clicking the Remove button submits the form as a POST request to the PHP script.

removeemail.html

The email form data in $_POST is stored in a variable and then used in the DELETE query.

```php
<?php
    $dbc = mysqli_connect('data.makemeelvis.com', 'elmer', 'theking', 'elvis_store')
        or die('Error connecting to MySQL server.')

    $email = $_POST['email'];

    $query = "DELETE FROM email_list WHERE email = '$email'";
    mysqli_query($dbc, $query)
        or die('Error querying database.');

    echo 'Customer removed: ' . $email;

    mysqli_close($dbc);
?>
```

Watch out for those quotes and double quotes here! The double quotes go around the whole SQL query and the single quotes go around the email address stored in $email.

It never hurts to confirm what happened, especially in the case of a database deletion.

removeemail.php

Don't forget to clean up by closing the database connection.

1. ~~Create a database and table for the email list.~~

2. ~~Create an Add Email web form and PHP script for adding a new customer to the list.~~

3. ~~Create a Send Email web form and PHP script for sending an email to the list.~~

4. ~~Create a Remove Email web form and PHP script for removing a customer from the list.~~

Whew, we're finally finished!

TEST DRIVE

Remove a customer from the mailing list using the Remove Email form.

This is starting to feel a little familiar, eh? Download the code for the Remove Email web page from the Head First Labs web site at **www.headfirstlabs.com/books/hfphp**. It's in the **chapter03** folder. This code consists of a web form in **removeemail.html**, a style sheet (**style.css**), and a couple of images (**elvislogo.gif** and **blankface.jpg**).

Create a new text file called **removeemail.php**, and enter all of the code on the facing page. Upload all of these files to your web server and open the removeemail.html page in a web browser. Enter the email address of a customer in the form, and click Remove to delete them from the database.

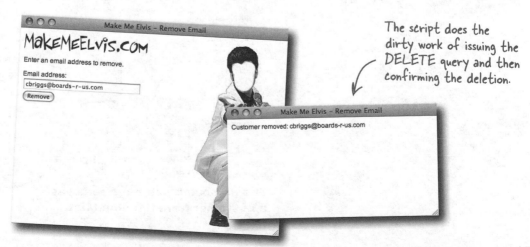

The script does the dirty work of issuing the DELETE query and then confirming the deletion.

MakeMeElvis.com is a web <u>application</u>

It's official. With the help of PHP and MySQL, Elmer's MakeMeElvis.com web site is now worthy of being called an application. Elmer can now store data persistently in a MySQL database, and also interact with that data through web forms. A combination of HTML pages, PHP scripts, and embedded SQL queries allow Elmer to add and remove customers to/from his email list (they can also add themselves), as well as send email messages to the entire list.

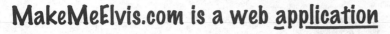

Viva PHP and MySQL! Now **that's** a web application. I can build my email list, send out emails to all my customers, and even prune the list...all from my web browser.

The Add Email page adds new customers to Elmer's email list.

addemail.php
addemail.html

sendemail.php
sendemail.html

The Send Email page sends an email to everyone on the list with the click of a button.

removeemail.php
removeemail.html

The Remove Email page removes a customer from the email list.

Return to sender! Please remove me from the Elvis mailing list.

PHP&MySQLcross

When you're finished perfecting Elmer's dance moves, see
if you can hum along and finish this crossword puzzle.

Across

3. A MySQL database is divided into these.
5. A persistent, highly organized, data structure that is typically stored in a file on a hard drive.
6. This conditional clause can be added to SQL statements to control which rows are targeted.
8. This SQL command removes an entire table from a database.
9. Use this SQL command to choose rows from a table.
10. Use this MySQL data type to store a varying amount of text.
12. Within a MySQL table, this holds a specific type of data.
13. Keep doing something as long as a certain test condition remains true.

Down

1. A MySQL data type that stores numbers without decimal places.
2. Use this SQL command to look at the structure of a table.
4. When dynamic functionality is added to a web site via PHP and MySQL, it becomes an ....
5. Use this SQL command to destroy rows within a table.
7. After creating a new database in a MySQL terminal, you must issue this command before you can do anything with the database.
11. A single collection of data in a table consisting of one of each column.

PHP&MySQLcross Solution

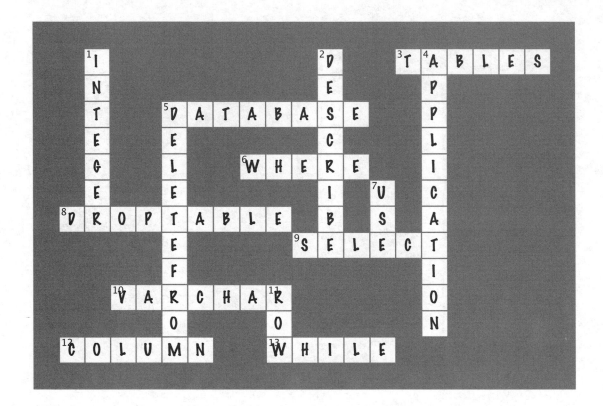

CHAPTER 3

Your PHP & MySQL Toolbox

Not only did you help Elmer get his web application off the ground, but you also developed some valuable PHP and MySQL skills in this chapter. For instance...

mysqli_fetch_array()

This built-in PHP function retrieves a single row of data from the results of a database query. You can call this function repeatedly to read row after row of data.

while

A PHP looping construct that allows you to repeat a section of code as long as a certain condition remains true. One particularly handy usage of the while loop is in looping through rows of data in an SQL query result.

DROP TABLE *tableName*

This SQL statement drops an entire table from the database, meaning that the table is removed along with any and all data stored within it.

DESCRIBE *tableName*

If you need to find out the structure of a table, this SQL statement is what you need. It doesn't reveal any data, but it does show the column names and their respective data types.

DELETE FROM *tableName*

Use this SQL statement to delete rows from a table. Depending on how you use the statement, you can delete individual rows or multiple rows.

WHERE

This SQL clause is used in conjunction with other SQL commands to build statements that target specific rows in a table. For example, you can isolate rows that have a column matching a specific value.

SELECT * FROM *tableName*

This SQL statement selects rows from a table. When the star is used (*), all of the columns for the rows in the table are returned. You can be more specific by listing individual column names instead of the * if you don't want to get all of the column data back from the query.

4 realistic and practical applications

Your Application on the Web

If I put a banana in my teacher's tailpipe, her car won't start, so no exam. But then the substitute might give the test, so he gets a banana, too. But then the substitute's substitute...

Sometimes you have to be realistic and rethink your plans.

Or plan more carefully in the first place. When your application's out there on the Web, you may discover that you haven't planned well enough. Things that you thought would work aren't good enough in the real world. This chapter takes a look at some *real-world problems* that can occur as you **move your application from testing to a live site**. Along the way, we'll show you more important PHP and SQL code.

Elmer has some irritated customers

Elmer's customer mailing list has grown by leaps and bounds, but his emails have generated some complaints. The complaints vary, but they all seem to involve customers receiving blank email messages or multiple messages, neither of which is good. Elmer needs to figure out what's gone wrong and fix it. His business depends on it.

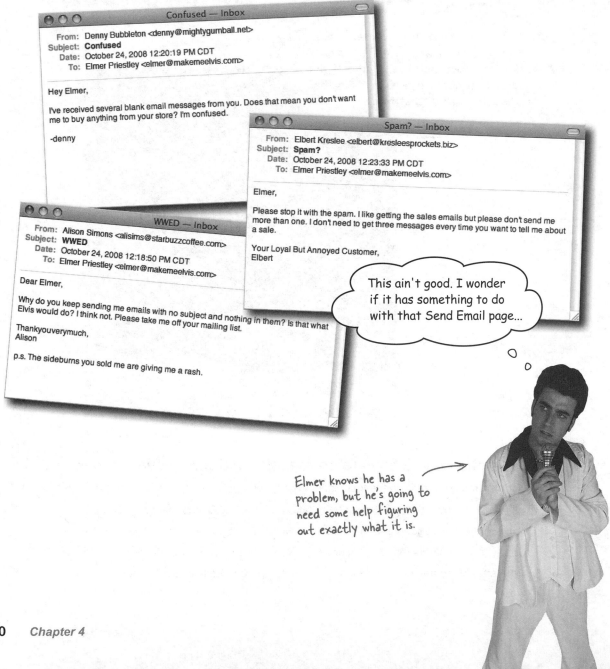

Confused — Inbox

From: Denny Bubbleton <denny@mightygumball.net>
Subject: **Confused**
Date: October 24, 2008 12:20:19 PM CDT
To: Elmer Priestley <elmer@makemeelvis.com>

Hey Elmer,

I've received several blank email messages from you. Does that mean you don't want me to buy anything from your store? I'm confused.

-denny

Spam? — Inbox

From: Elbert Kreslee <elbert@kresleesprockets.biz>
Subject: **Spam?**
Date: October 24, 2008 12:23:33 PM CDT
To: Elmer Priestley <elmer@makemeelvis.com>

Elmer,

Please stop it with the spam. I like getting the sales emails but please don't send me more than one. I don't need to get three messages every time you want to tell me about a sale.

Your Loyal But Annoyed Customer,
Elbert

WWED — Inbox

From: Alison Simons <alisims@starbuzzcoffee.com>
Subject: **WWED**
Date: October 24, 2008 12:18:50 PM CDT
To: Elmer Priestley <elmer@makemeelvis.com>

Dear Elmer,

Why do you keep sending me emails with no subject and nothing in them? Is that what Elvis would do? I think not. Please take me off your mailing list.

Thankyouverymuch,
Alison

p.s. The sideburns you sold me are giving me a rash.

This ain't good. I wonder if it has something to do with that Send Email page...

Elmer knows he has a problem, but he's going to need some help figuring out exactly what it is.

BE Elmer the email list manager

Your job is to play Elmer and figure out
how those blank emails are getting sent.
He suspects it has something to do with
the sendemail.html form.

Write down what Elmer
thinks the problem is.

Make Me Elvis – Send Email

MAKEMEELVIS.COM

Private: For Elmer's use ONLY
Write and send an email to mailing list members.

Subject of email:

Body of email:

Submit

sendemail.html

BE Elmer the email list manager Solution

Your job is to play Elmer and figure out
how those blank emails are getting sent.
He suspects it has something to do with
the sendemail.html form.

Write down what Elmer
thinks the problem is.

If I click the Submit button
without filling out a message
body, a blank email gets sent.

Make Me Elvis – Send Email

MakeMeElvis.com

Private: For Elmer's use ONLY
Write and send an email to mailing list members.

Subject of email:

Body of email:

Submit

sendemail.html

If the Submit button's pressed
on the form with nothing in the
Body field, a blank email gets sent.
Come to think of it, an empty
Subject field is a problem too.

Protecting Elmer from... Elmer

So "operator error' is really the problem here—Elmer inadvertently clicks Submit without entering the email information, and blank emails get sent to the entire list. It's never safe to assume a web form will be used exactly the way it was intended. That's why it's up to you, the vigilant PHP scripter, to try and head off these kinds of problems by anticipating that some users will misuse your forms.

Let's take a look at the code in our current `sendemail.php` script to see how Elmer's empty email messages are getting created.

Our Send Email script uses the text from the form to build an email, even if the user didn't enter anything.

```php
<?php
  $from = 'elmer@makemeelvis.com';
  $subject = $_POST['subject'];
  $text = $_POST['elvismail'];

  $dbc = mysqli_connect('data.makemeelvis.com', 'elmer', 'theking', 'elvis_store')
    or die('Error connecting to MySQL server.');

  $query = "SELECT * FROM email_list";
  $result = mysqli_query($dbc, $query)
    or die('Error querying database.');

  while ($row = mysqli_fetch_array($result)){
    $to = $row['email'];
    $first_name = $row['first_name'];
    $last_name = $row['last_name'];
    $msg = "Dear $first_name $last_name,\n$text";
    mail($to, $subject, $msg, 'From:' . $from);
    echo 'Email sent to: ' . $to . '<br />';
  }

  mysqli_close($dbc);
?>
```

The text in the form is retrieved from $_POST['subject'] and $_POST['elvismail'], and is saved in $subject and $text, respectively...

Problem is, we use $text in our message whether the variable contains text or not...

...and we also use $subject whether there's text in it or not.

Write down what you think should be changed in the `sendemail.php` **script code to fix the blank email problem:**

....

....

Demand good form data

Elmer's Send Email form's in need of **validation**, which is the process of checking to make sure form data is OK before doing anything with it. Elmer already uses validation even though he doesn't call it that. Whenever he receives an order for Elvis gear, he doesn't just immediately fill it and send it out... he validates it first!

In the case of an order, Elmer first checks to see if the customer's credit card is **valid**. If so, he fills the order and gets it ready to ship. But then he has to check if the customer's shipping address is complete. If that checks out, then Elmer goes ahead and sends out the order. A successful order for Elmer's store always hinges on the validation of the order data.

> Validation means making sure the data you get is the data you expect.

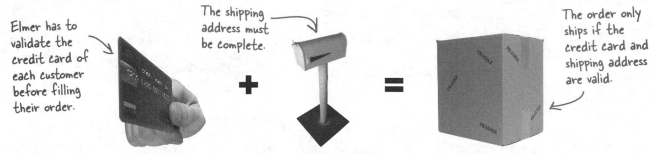

Elmer has to validate the credit card of each customer before filling their order.

The shipping address must be complete.

The order only ships if the credit card and shipping address are valid.

To solve Elmer's blank email problem, we need to validate the form data delivered to the `sendemail.php` script. This means the form data is submitted from the client web page (`sendemail.html`) to the server, and the server (`sendemail.php`) checks to make sure all the data is present. We can add code to `sendemail.php` that examines the values in the text boxes and checks to make sure they aren't empty. If everything checks out OK, the script sends out the emails.

> If everything's cool with this data, I'll send out those emails.

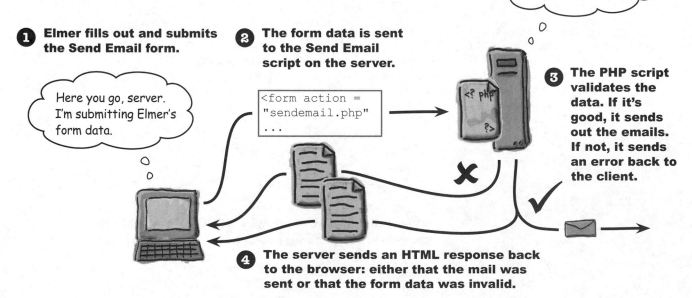

1 Elmer fills out and submits the Send Email form.

> Here you go, server. I'm submitting Elmer's form data.

2 The form data is sent to the Send Email script on the server.

```
<form action =
"sendemail.php"
...
```

```
<? php

?>
```

3 The PHP script validates the data. If it's good, it sends out the emails. If not, it sends an error back to the client.

4 The server sends an HTML response back to the browser: either that the mail was sent or that the form data was invalid.

The logic behind Send Email validation

Elmer needs to **validate** the data he gets from the sendemail.html form before he sends any emails. In fact, sending the emails should completely hinge on the data validation. What we really need PHP to do is **make a decision** based on the validity of the form data received by the sendemail.php script. We need code that says, "***if*** the data is ***valid***, go ahead and send the emails."

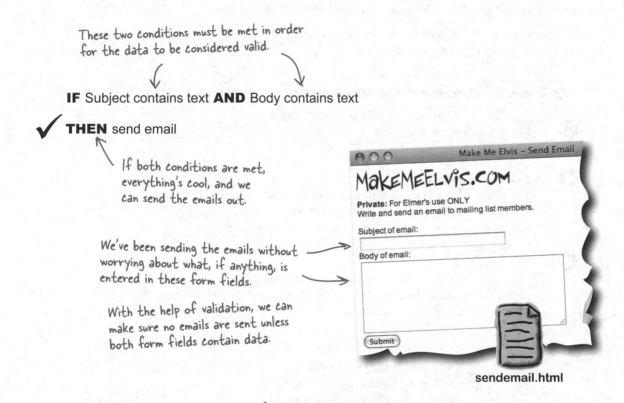

These two conditions must be met in order for the data to be considered valid.

IF Subject contains text **AND** Body contains text

✓ **THEN** send email

If both conditions are met, everything's cool, and we can send the emails out.

We've been sending the emails without worrying about what, if anything, is entered in these form fields.

With the help of validation, we can make sure no emails are sent unless both form fields contain data.

sendemail.html

there are no Dumb Questions

Q: I've also heard of validating data on the client instead of on the server. How does that work?

A: The web browser is considered the client, so client-side validation would be any checking that occurs before the data's sent to the PHP script. Languages like JavaScript can do client-side validation. If you're interested in learning more , check out *Head First JavaScript*, which discusses client-side validation in depth.

Q: So why use server-side validation instead of client-side?

A: If we validate on the client, only part of the problem's solved. Elmer could potentially browse directly to sendemail.php and send out a blank email. But if we validate on the server, it solves both problems. Blank data in the form will be detected as well as blank data from the PHP script being directly loaded. This isn't to say that it's wrong to validate on the client. In fact, it's a very good idea. But the server is the last line of defense for catching bad form data, so server-side validation can't be ignored.

Your code can make decisions with IF

The PHP **if** statement lets your code make decisions **based on whether or not something is true**. Consider Elmer's orders again. Before filling an order, Elmer must get paid, which means charging the customer's credit card. If the customer gave Elmer the wrong card number, he can't fill the order. So Elmer performs a kind of real-world validation on every order that goes like this:

If the customer's credit card checks out, go ahead and fill the order.

We can translate this scenario to PHP code using the if statement, which is designed to handle just this kind of decision making.

The basic if statement has three parts:

1 **The if keyword**
This starts off the statement.

2 **The test condition**
The test condition, or **conditional expression**, is located in **parentheses** right after the if keyword. Here's where you put the statement that you want to determine the validity, or truth, of.

3 **The action**
The action of an if statement directly follows the test condition and is enclosed in **curly braces**. Here's where you put the PHP code you want to execute if the condition is, in fact, true.

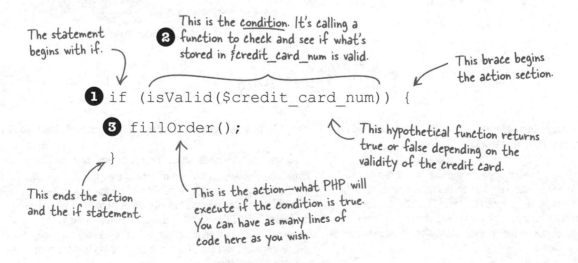

The statement begins with if.

2 This is the condition. It's calling a function to check and see if what's stored in $credit_card_num is valid.

This brace begins the action section.

```
1 if (isValid($credit_card_num)) {
3     fillOrder();
  }
```

This hypothetical function returns true or false depending on the validity of the credit card.

This ends the action and the if statement.

This is the action—what PHP will execute if the condition is true. You can have as many lines of code here as you wish.

Testing for truth

The heart of the `if` statement is its test condition, which is always interpreted as either `true` or `false`. The test condition can be a variable, a function call, or a comparison of one thing to another, as a few examples. Elmer's credit card validation relies on a function call as the test condition, which means the value returned by the function is either `true` or `false`.

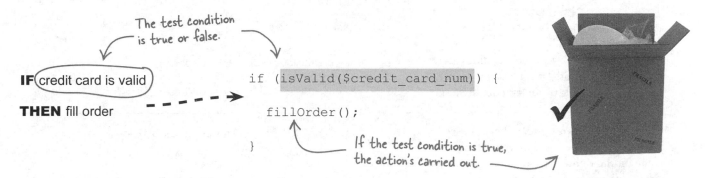

The test condition is true or false.

IF credit card is valid

THEN fill order

```
if (isValid($credit_card_num)) {
    fillOrder();
}
```

If the test condition is true, the action's carried out.

It's quite common to use a comparison as a test condition, which typically involves comparing a variable to some value. For example, maybe Elmer wants to give a discount to customers who live in Nevada. He could create an `if` statement that carries out a comparison on part of the shipping address, like this:

This is true if the $shipping_state variable contains the text 'Nevada'.

IF customer lives in Nevada

THEN apply discount

```
if ($shipping_state == 'Nevada') {
    $total = $total * 0.9;
}
```

A 10% discount is applied in the action if the test condition is true.

This test condition performs a comparison for equality, which involves two equal signs (==). Equality comparisons aren't just for variables and strings. You can compare variables to numbers, variables to variables, and even perform calculations.

You can check to see if what is stored in one variable is equal to what is stored in another.

Don't put quotes around numeric values.

```
($num_items == 10)

($shipping_address == $billing_address)

(2 + 2 == 4)
```

You can carry out math operations in a test condition.

IF checks for more than just equality

An `if` statement can check for more than just equality. The test condition in your `if` statement can also check to see if a value is **greater than** another one. If it is, the result of the condition is `true`, and the action code is executed. Here are a few more tests you can use to control the decision of an `if` statement.

It's OK to write an if statement entirely on a single line as long as the action is relatively simple.

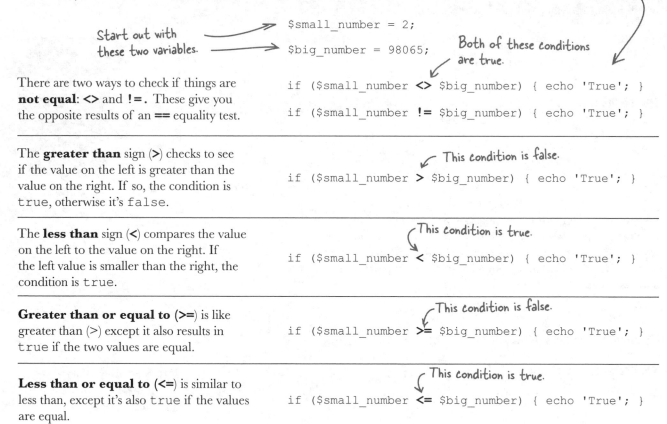

Start out with these two variables.

```
$small_number = 2;
$big_number = 98065;
```

Both of these conditions are true.

There are two ways to check if things are **not equal**: **<>** and **!=**. These give you the opposite results of an **==** equality test.

```
if ($small_number <> $big_number) { echo 'True'; }
if ($small_number != $big_number) { echo 'True'; }
```

The **greater than** sign (**>**) checks to see if the value on the left is greater than the value on the right. If so, the condition is `true`, otherwise it's `false`.

This condition is false.

```
if ($small_number > $big_number) { echo 'True'; }
```

The **less than** sign (**<**) compares the value on the left to the value on the right. If the left value is smaller than the right, the condition is `true`.

This condition is true.

```
if ($small_number < $big_number) { echo 'True'; }
```

Greater than or equal to (**>=**) is like greater than (**>**) except it also results in `true` if the two values are equal.

This condition is false.

```
if ($small_number >= $big_number) { echo 'True'; }
```

Less than or equal to (**<=**) is similar to less than, except it's also `true` if the values are equal.

This condition is true.

```
if ($small_number <= $big_number) { echo 'True'; }
```

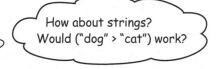

How about strings?
Would ("dog" > "cat") work?

Yes, you can compare strings in `if` test conditions.

They work based on the alphabet, with *a* being considered smaller than (less than) *z*. Using greater than and less than can help you when you need to present information in alphabetical order.

BE the test condition in the if statement

Your job is to play the if test condition and decide if you are true or false given the following variables.

```php
$my_name = 'Buster';

$a_number = 3;

$a_decimal = 4.6;

$favorite_song = 'Trouble';

$another_number = 0;

$your_name = $my_name;
```

($a_number == 3)   **true or false**

($another_number == "")   **true or false**

($favorite_song == "Trouble")   **true or false**

($my_name == '$your_name')   **true or false**

($my_name == "$your_name")   **true or false**

($your_name == $my_name)   **true or false**

($favorite_song == 'Trouble')   **true or false**

($a_number > 9)   **true or false**

($favorite_food = 'hamburger')   **true or false**

BE the test condition in the if statement Solution

Your job is to play the if test condition and decide if you are true or false given the following variables.

```
$my_name = 'Buster';

$a_number = 3;

$a_decimal = 4.6;

$favorite_song = 'Trouble';

$another_number = 0;

$your_name = $my_name;
```

($a_number == 3)   **true** or false

($another_number == "")   **true** or false   *0 and an empty string evaluate as equal.*

($favorite_song == "Trouble")   **true** or false

($my_name == '$your_name')   true or **false**   *Because of those single quotes, the condition is actually asking if the string Buster equals the string "$your_name", not the value contained in the variable $your_name.*

($my_name == "$your_name")   **true** or false

($your_name == $my_name)   **true** or false

($favorite_song == 'Trouble')   **true** or false   *$a_number is 3, which is not greater than 9.*

($a_number > 9)   true or **false**

($favorite_food = 'hamburger')   **true** or false

Should be == if we intended this to be a comparison.

OK, this one's tricky. Since only one equal sign is used here, it's actually an assignment (=), not a comparison (==). And it ends up being true because anything other than 0, NULL, or false gets interpreted by PHP as true.

there are no Dumb Questions

Q: Okay, is a test condition the same thing we used to control `while` loops in Chapter 3?

A: It's exactly the same. And even though we used it to tell us when we had remaining rows of query data back in Chapter 3, we can devise more interesting test conditions for `while` loops by using different kinds of comparisons. You'll see that later in the book.

The logic behind Send Email validation

Elmer needs to **validate** the data he gets from the `sendemail.html` form before he sends any emails. In fact, sending the emails should completely hinge on the data validation. What we really need PHP to do is **make a decision** based on the validity of the form data received by the `sendemail.php` script. We need code that says, "*if* the data is *valid*, go ahead and send the emails."

But first we need to grab the form data and store it in a couple of variables:

```
$subject = $_POST['subject'];

$text = $_POST['elvismail'];
```

sendemail.html

This form data is all we need to check and see if there is data in each of the form fields. The logic might look something like this:

IF `$subject` contains text **AND** `$body` contains text

THEN send email

Or we could take the opposite approach and check to see if the form fields are both empty, in which case we could display a warning to the user:

IF `$subject` is empty **AND** `$body` is empty

THEN echo error message

Both of these examples have a problem in that their logic requires us to make two comparisons in a single `if` statement. One possible solution is to use two `if` statements...

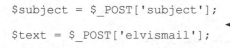 Sharpen your pencil

Write two `if` statements that check to see if both the subject and message body of Elmer's Send Email form are empty. Echo a warning message if they're empty.

....

....

....

....

....

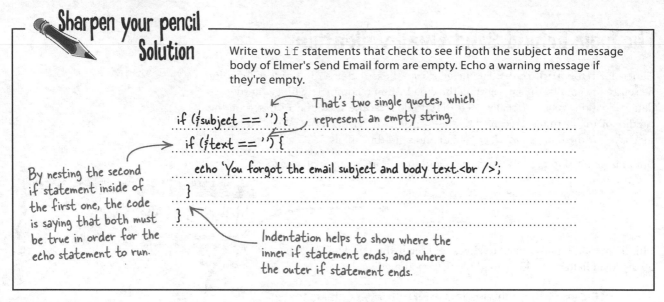

Sharpen your pencil
Solution

Write two `if` statements that check to see if both the subject and message body of Elmer's Send Email form are empty. Echo a warning message if they're empty.

That's two single quotes, which represent an empty string.

```
if ($subject == '') {
    if ($text == '') {
        echo 'You forgot the email subject and body text.<br />';
    }
}
```

By nesting the second if statement inside of the first one, the code is saying that both must be true in order for the echo statement to run.

Indentation helps to show where the inner if statement ends, and where the outer if statement ends.

PHP functions for verifying variables

Using == to check for an empty string works, but there's a better way that involves built-in PHP functions. The **isset()** function tests to see if a variable exists, which means that it's been assigned a value. The **empty()** function takes things one step further and determines whether a variable contains an **empty value**, which PHP defines as 0, an empty string (`''` or `""`), or the values `false` or `NULL`. So `isset()` only returns `true` if a variable has been assigned a value, while `empty()` only returns `true` if a variable has been set to 0, an empty string, `false`, or `NULL`.

Let's take a look at how these functions work:

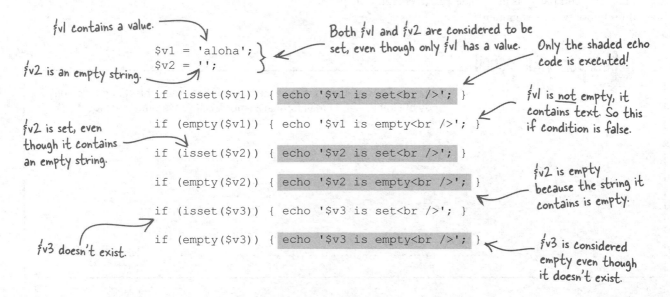

$v1 contains a value.

$v2 is an empty string.

```
$v1 = 'aloha';
$v2 = '';
```

Both $v1 and $v2 are considered to be set, even though only $v1 has a value.

Only the shaded echo code is executed!

```
if (isset($v1)) { echo '$v1 is set<br />'; }
```

$v1 is _not_ empty, it contains text. So this if condition is false.

$v2 is set, even though it contains an empty string.

```
if (empty($v1)) { echo '$v1 is empty<br />'; }

if (isset($v2)) { echo '$v2 is set<br />'; }

if (empty($v2)) { echo '$v2 is empty<br />'; }
```

$v2 is empty because the string it contains is empty.

```
if (isset($v3)) { echo '$v3 is set<br />'; }

if (empty($v3)) { echo '$v3 is empty<br />'; }
```

$v3 doesn't exist.

$v3 is considered empty even though it doesn't exist.

> I get it. We can use isset() and empty() to validate the $subject and $text form data.

That's half right. We're really just checking to make sure the form data isn't empty, so empty() is what we need.

The $subject and $text variables are assigned values from the $_POST['subject'] and $_POST['elvismail'] superglobals. If you test these variables with isset(), it will always return true regardless of whether or not they hold any actual text. In other words, isset() doesn't show you the difference between a blank form field and a filled out one. The empty() function checks to see if a variable is actually empty, which is what we need for form validation.

isset() checks that a variable **exists** and is set.

empty() checks to see if a variable has any **contents**.

there are no Dumb Questions

Q: So what's the point of using isset() anyway?

A: The isset() function is extremely valuable when you need to know if a piece of data **exists**. For example, you can check if a form has been submitted via a POST request by passing the isset() function $_POST. This ends up being an extremely handy technique, as you find out a little later in the chapter.

Sharpen your pencil

Rewrite the two if statements that check to see if both the subject and message body of Elmer's Send Email form are empty, but this time, use the empty() function instead of == in the test conditions.

....
....
....
....
....

Sharpen your pencil
Solution

Rewrite the two `if` statements that check to see if both the subject and message body of Elmer's Send Email form are empty, but this time, use the `empty()` function instead of `==` in the test conditions.

A call to the empty() function replaces the equality operator (==) in each of the if test conditions.

```
if (empty($subject)) {
if (empty($text)) {
    echo 'You forgot the email subject and body text.<br />';
  }
}
```

The rest of the code is the same as before.

> What if we need to only take a certain action if a form field is **not** empty? Is there a notempty() function?

No, but there's an easy way to reverse the logic of any test condition... the negation operator.

We know the test condition that controls an `if` statement always results in a value of `true` or `false`. But what if our logic dictates that we need to check for the reverse of what a condition gives us? For example, it would be helpful to know if Elmer's form fields are **not empty** before sending a bunch of emails with the form data. Problem is, there is no `notempty()` function. The solution is the negation operator (`!`), which turns `true` into `false`, or `false` into `true`. So `!empty()` literally calls the `empty()` function and reverses its result, like this:

The NOT operator (!) turns true into false, or false into true.

```
if (!empty($subject)) {
    ...
}
```

This condition asks, "Is the Subject field not empty?" Or, does it have data in it?

Exercise

Fill in the blanks in Elmer's `sendemail.php` code so that email only gets sent when both `$subject` and `$text` are **not** empty. Use `if` statements and the `empty()` function.

All my fields need to have values.

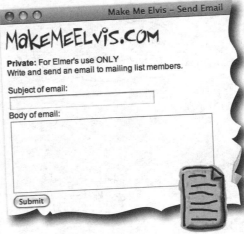

sendemail.html

```php
<?php
  $from = 'elmer@makemeelvis.com';
  $subject = $_POST['subject'];
  $text = $_POST['elvismail'];

  if .......................................................

    if .......................................................

      $dbc = mysqli_connect('data.makemeelvis.com', 'elmer', 'theking', 'elvis_store')
        or die('Error connecting to MySQL server.');

      $query = "SELECT * FROM email_list";
      $result = mysqli_query($dbc, $query)
        or die('Error querying database.');


      while ($row = mysqli_fetch_array($result)) {
        $to = $row['email'];
        $first_name = $row['first_name'];
        $last_name = $row['last_name'];
        $msg = "Dear $first_name $last_name,\n$text";
        mail($to, $subject, $msg, 'From:' . $from);
        echo 'Email sent to ' . $to . '<br />';
      }
      mysqli_close($dbc);

    ..........................

  ..........................
?>
```

Fill in the blanks in Elmer's `sendemail.php` code so that email only gets sent when both `$subject` and `$text` are **not** empty. Use `if` statements and the `empty()` function.

Exercise Solution

All my fields need to have values.

MakeMeElvis.com — Make Me Elvis – Send Email

Private: For Elmer's use ONLY
Write and send an email to mailing list members.

Subject of email:

Body of email:

Submit

sendemail.html

The exclamation point reverses the logic of the empty() function.

The first condition checks to see if $subject is not empty...

...if not, good! Now we check to see if $text is not empty.

```php
<?php
  $from = 'elmer@makemeelvis.com';
  $subject = $_POST['subject'];
  $text = $_POST['elvismail'];

  if (!empty($subject)) {
    if (!empty($text)) {
      $dbc = mysqli_connect('data.makeelvis.com', 'elmer', 'theking', 'elvis_store')
        or die('Error connecting to MySQL server.');

      $query = "SELECT * FROM email_list";
      $result = mysqli_query($dbc, $query)
        or die('Error querying database.');

      while ($row = mysqli_fetch_array($result)) {
        $to = $row['email'];
        $first_name = $row['first_name'];
        $last_name = $row['last_name'];
        $msg = "Dear $first_name $last_name,\n$text";
        mail($to, $subject, $msg, 'From:' . $from);
        echo 'Email sent to ' . $to . '<br />';
      }
      mysqli_close($dbc);
    }
  }
?>
```

We had to put one if statement inside the other one to make this work. This is called nesting.

If either form data variable is empty, one of the if statements will be false, and none of the code here will run, which means no blank email will be sent out — just what we wanted!

We have to close off the action part of both of the if statements. The first brace ends the inner if statement, and the second brace ends the outer if statement.

TEST DRIVE

See if the empty form field validation works.

Modify the code in sendemail.php to use if statements that check the form field data before sending email messages. Upload the new version of the script to your web server and open the sendemail.html page in a web browser. Make sure to leave at least one of the form fields blank, and click Submit.

The body of the message is empty, which makes the form data fail validation.

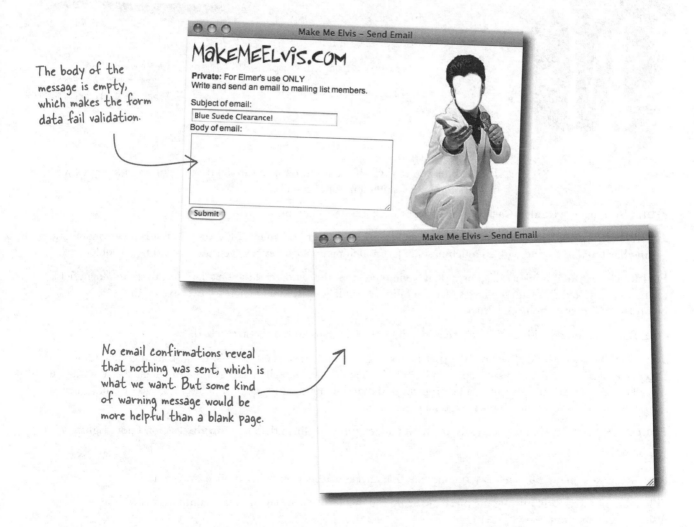

No email confirmations reveal that nothing was sent, which is what we want. But some kind of warning message would be more helpful than a blank page.

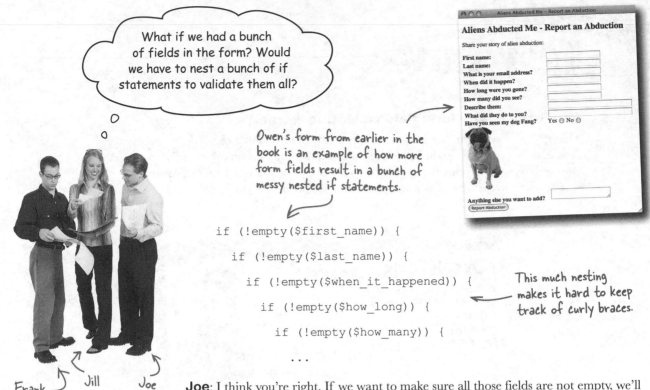

What if we had a bunch of fields in the form? Would we have to nest a bunch of if statements to validate them all?

Owen's form from earlier in the book is an example of how more form fields result in a bunch of messy nested if statements.

```php
if (!empty($first_name)) {

  if (!empty($last_name)) {

    if (!empty($when_it_happened)) {

      if (!empty($how_long)) {

        if (!empty($how_many)) {

          ...
```

This much nesting makes it hard to keep track of curly braces.

Joe: I think you're right. If we want to make sure all those fields are not empty, we'll have to nest an `if` statement for each field.

Frank: As long as we indent each line of code for each `if` statement, aren't we OK?

Jill: Technically, yes. I mean, the code will certainly work no matter how many `if`'s we nest, but I'm worried about it getting hard to understand with so much nesting. Just matching up curly braces accurately could be a problem.

Frank: That's true. I think it'd also be a pain having to indent the action code so far... let's see, that's ten form fields, giving us ten nested `if`s with ten levels of indentation. Even if we just indent each `if` two spaces, that's 20 spaces before every line of action code. Yuck.

Joe: But if we indent with tabs, it cuts that in half—10 tabs versus 20 spaces isn't so bad.

Jill: Guys, the issue isn't really about the specific code used to indent the nested `if`'s. It's just not a good coding practice to nest `if` statements so deep. Think about it like this—we're really talking about one logical test condition, "are all our form fields non-empty?" The problem is, that test condition involves ten different pieces of data, causing us to have to break it into ten separate `if` statements.

Frank: Ah, I see. So what we need is a way to test all ten pieces of form data in a **single** test condition, right?

Jill: Yup.

Joe: Then we could write one big test condition that checks all the form fields at once. Awesome!

Jill: Yeah, but we're still missing the piece of the puzzle that lets us combine multiple comparisons within a single test condition...

Test multiple conditions with AND and OR

You can build a test condition for an `if` statement with multiple checks by connecting them with a **logical operator**. Let's look at how it works with two familiar conditions, `!empty($subject)` and `!empty($text)`. This first example involves two expressions joined by the logical AND operator, which is coded using `&&`.

The logical AND operator.

The extra parentheses help make it clear that the negation operator applies only to the empty() function.

```php
if ((!empty($subject)) && (!empty($text))) {
```

This test condition is only true if both $subject AND $text are not empty.

The AND operator takes two `true`/`false` values and gives you `true` only if they are both `true`; otherwise the result is `false`. So in this case both form fields must be non-empty in order for the test condition to be `true` and the action code for the `if` statement to run.

The logical OR operator, coded as `||`, is similar to AND except that it results in `true` if either of the `true`/`false` values is `true`. Here's an example:

```php
if ((!empty($subject)) || (!empty($text))) {
```

This test condition is true if either $subject OR $text are not empty.

So the action code for this `if` statement is executed if either one of the form fields is not empty. Things get even more interesting if you want to isolate one form field as being empty but the other having data, like this:

```php
if (empty($subject) && (!empty($text))) {
```

$subject must be empty and $text must be non-empty for this test condition to be true.

Since this test condition uses AND, both expressions inside of the test condition must be `true` in order for the action code to be run. This means the Subject form field must be empty, but the Body field must have data. You can reverse this check by moving the negation operator (`!`) to the other `empty()` function:

```php
if ((!empty($subject)) && empty($text)) {
```

This is true only if $subject isn't empty but $text is.

The AND (`&&`) and OR (`||`) logical operators make it possible to structure much more powerful test conditions that would otherwise require additional, often messy, `if` statements.

PHP logic operators make it possible to structure more elegant if statements.

Logical AND is coded as &&, while logical OR is coded as ||.

That's not the number eleven, it's two vertical pipes ||—just above backslash (\) on your keyboard.

Exercise

Rewrite the highlighted sections of the `sendemail.php` script so that it uses logical operators in a single `if` test condition instead of nested `if` statements.

```php
<?php
  $from = 'elmer@makemeelvis.com';
  $subject = $_POST['subject'];
  $text = $_POST['elvismail'];

  if (!empty($subject)) {
    if (!empty($text)) {
```

Here are our nested if statements. Rewrite them using a single if statement with logical operators.

```php
    ......................................................

    ......................................................

      $dbc = mysqli_connect('data.makemeelvis.com', 'elmer', 'theking', 'elvis_store')
        or die('Error connecting to MySQL server.');

      $query = "SELECT * FROM email_list";
      $result = mysqli_query($dbc, $query)
        or die('Error querying database.');

      while ($row = mysqli_fetch_array($result)) {
        $to = $row['email'];
        $first_name = $row['first_name'];
        $last_name = $row['last_name'];
        $msg = "Dear $first_name $last_name,\n$text";
        mail($to, $subject, $msg, 'From:' . $from);
        echo 'Email sent to ' . $to . '<br />';
      }

      mysqli_close($dbc);
    }
  }
```

These braces close the two if statements.

```php
    ......................................................

    ......................................................

?>
```

Test Drive

Make sure the logical operators in the Send Email script do the same job as the nested `if` statements.

Modify the code in `sendemail.php` to use a single `if` statement that takes advantage of logical operators to check the form field data before sending email messages. Double-check the exercise solution on the following page if you aren't sure about the changes to make.

Upload the new version of the script to your web server and open the `sendemail.html` page in a web browser. Make sure to leave at least one of the form fields blank, and click Submit. Does the script still prevent the email messages from being sent when a form field is blank?

there are no Dumb Questions

Q: Does it matter what order you put two conditions joined by `&&` or `||` in an `if` statement?

A: Yes. The reason is because these two operators are **short-circuited** whenever possible. What this means is that if the first operand is enough to determine the outcome of the expression, the second operand is ignored. As an example, if the first operand in an AND expression is `false`, this is enough to cause the expression to be `false` regardless of the second operand, so the second operand is ignored. The same rule applies when the first operand in an OR expression is `true`.

Q: I've seen PHP code that uses `and` and `or` instead of `&&` and `||`. How do those work?

A: They're virtually the same as `&&` and `||`. There's a slight difference in how they're evaluated relative to other operators, but if you're careful to use parentheses to make your test conditions clear, then there's essentially no difference.

Exercise Solution

Rewrite the highlighted sections of the `sendemail.php` script so that it uses logical operators in a single `if` test condition instead of nested `if` statements.

```php
<?php
  $from = 'elmer@makemeelvis.com';
  $subject = $_POST['subject'];
  $text = $_POST['elvismail'];
```

The negation, or NOT operator (!), is used to check for non-empty form fields.

```php
  if (!empty($subject)) {
    if (!empty($text)) {

  if ((!empty($subject)) && (!empty($text))) {
```

We can use AND to check for both conditions in one if statement.

Remember, && is how you actually specify the AND logical operator.

```php
    $dbc = mysqli_connect('data.makemeelvis.com', 'elmer', 'theking', 'elvis_store')
      or die('Error connecting to MySQL server.');

    $query = "SELECT * FROM email_list";
    $result = mysqli_query($dbc, $query)
      or die('Error querying database.');

    while ($row = mysqli_fetch_array($result)) {
      $to = $row['email'];
      $first_name = $row['first_name'];
      $last_name = $row['last_name'];
      $msg = "Dear $first_name $last_name,\n$text";
      mail($to, $subject, $msg, 'From:' . $from);
      echo 'Email sent to ' . $to . '<br />';
    }

    mysqli_close($dbc);
    }
  }
?>
```

All of the code inside the if statement should be un-indented one level since it now resides in a single if statement.

Our single if statement means we only need one closing curly brace.

Form users need feedback

Our `sendemail.php` code does a great job of validating the form data so that no mail gets sent out if either the Subject or Body fields are left blank. But when the validation fails, and no emails are sent out, the script doesn't tell Elmer what happened. He just gets a blank web page.

Elmer sees this page when he submits the form... and he has no clue why!

What happened? I tried to use the new form and all I got was a blank page.

The problem is that our code only reacts to a **successful** validation, in which case it sends the email messages. But if the `if` statement turns out being `false` (invalid form data), the code doesn't do anything, leaving Elmer in the dark about whether any emails were sent or what went wrong. Here's the abbreviated script code, which reveals the blank page problem:

```php
<?php
  $from = 'elmer@makemeelvis.com';
  $subject = $_POST['subject'];
  $text = $_POST['elvismail'];

  if ((!empty($subject)) && (!empty($text))) {
    $dbc = mysqli_connect('data.makemeelvis.com', 'elmer', 'theking', 'elvis_store')
    ...
    mysqli_close($dbc);
  }
?>
```

Nothing at all happens if the if statement fails to run the action code, which is why a blank page is generated when there is missing form data.

We need to let Elmer know that there was a problem, ideally telling him what form fields were blank so that he can try entering the message again.

Not a problem. Just put an echo statement after the closing brace of the if statement.

That won't work because code <u>after</u> the `if` statement will always be executed.

Placing the `echo` statement after the `if` statement just means it runs **after** the `if` statement, but it always runs regardless of the outcome of the `if`. That's not what we need. We need the `echo` statement to show an error message **only** if the test condition of the `if` statement is `false`. You could express our logic as this:

IF subject contains text **AND** body contains text

✔ **THEN** send email

✘ **ELSE** echo error message

The `if` statement offers an optional `else` clause that runs code in the event that the test condition is `false`. So our error message `echo` code can go in an `else` clause, in which case it only gets run when one of the form fields is left empty. Just place the word `else` after the `if` statement, and then stick the action code for it inside curly braces:

The else clause starts right after the closing curly brace for the if statement.

```
if ((!empty($subject)) && (!empty($text))) {

    ...

}
else {

    echo 'You forgot the email subject and/or body text.<br />';

}
```

This is a placeholder for the code that sends the email messages.

The code here only gets run if the if statement turns out false.

Just like the action code in an if, the code in an else is enclosed in curly braces.

The else clause executes code when an if test condition is <u>false</u>.

Below is new code for Elmer's `sendemail.php` script that uses `if` statements and `else` clauses to provide feedback, but some of the code has gotten misplaced. Use the magnets to replace the missing code.

```php
<?php
  $from = 'elmer@makemeelvis.com';
  $subject = $_POST['subject'];
  $text = $_POST['elvismail'];
```

```
// We know both $subject AND $text are blank
// $subject is empty
// Everything is fine, send email
// $text is empty
```

```
.........................................................................
.........................................................................
  }
  else {
.........................................................................

    // We know we are missing $subject OR $text - let's find out which one

.........................................................................

.........................................................................

      echo 'You forgot the email subject.<br />';
    }
    else {
.........................................................................

      echo 'You forgot the email body text.<br />';
    }
  }
  else {

.........................................................................

    ...
    while ($row = mysqli_fetch_array($result)) {
      $to = $row['email'];
      $first_name = $row['first_name'];
      $last_name = $row['last_name'];
      $msg = "Dear $first_name $last_name,\n$text";
      mail($to, $subject, $msg, 'From:' . $from);
      echo 'Email sent to ' . $to . '<br />';
    }

    mysqli_close($dbc);
  }
}
?>
```

Magnets: `{` `{` `||` `&&` `{` `empty($text)` `empty($subject)` `empty($text)` `empty($subject)` `empty($subject)` `if` `if` `if` `)` `(` `)` `(` `(` `)`

Exercise Solution

Below is new code for Elmer's `sendemail.php` script that uses `if` statements and `else` clauses to provide feedback, but some of the code has fallen off. Use the magnets to replace the missing code.

> The outer if statement checks to see if both the subject and body are empty. If not, there are only three other possible scenarios: both are filled in, the subject is missing, or the body text is missing.

```php
<?php
  $from = 'elmer@makemeelvis.com';
  $subject = $_POST['subject'];
  $text = $_POST['elvismail'];

  if ( empty($subject) && empty($text) ) {
    // We know both $subject AND $text are blank

  }
  else {
    if ( empty($subject) || empty($text) ) {
      // We know we are missing $subject OR $text - let's find out which one
      if ( empty($subject) ) {
        // $subject is empty

        echo 'You forgot the email subject.<br />';
      }
      else {
        // $text is empty

        echo 'You forgot the email body text.<br />';
      }
    }
    else {
      // Everything is fine, send email

      ...
      while ($row = mysqli_fetch_array($result)) {
        $to = $row['email'];
        $first_name = $row['first_name'];
        $last_name = $row['last_name'];
        $msg = "Dear $first_name $last_name,\n$text";
        mail($to, $subject, $msg, 'From:' . $from);
        echo 'Email sent to ' . $to . '<br />';
      }

      mysqli_close($dbc);
    }
  }
?>
```

> At this point we've gone through all the other possibilities, so we know that both form fields have values.

All those nested if's and else's are making the script hard to follow. I'd hate to ever have to work on that script! It needs to be simplified before someone gets hurt.

It's always a good idea to simplify code whenever possible, especially nested code that gets too deep.

Too many else clauses with nested if statements can make your code hard to follow. Maybe that wouldn't matter if we never had to look at it again, but that's unlikely. If we ever needed to change the form and add another field, validating it would be trickier than it needed to be because it would be hard to read the code and figure out where the changes need to go.

cleaner
BE the IF code

Your job is to play IF code and clean up the messy nested IF's and ELSE's. Rewrite the code to get rid of the nesting, but make sure it still works correctly.

Hint: You might not even need any elses!

```
if (empty($subject) && empty($text)) {
  echo 'You forgot the email subject and body text.<br />';
} else {
  if (empty($subject) || empty($text)) {
    if (empty($subject) {
      echo 'You forgot the email subject.<br />';
    } else {
      echo 'You forgot the email body text.<br />';
    }
  } else {
    // Everything is fine. send the email
  }
}
```

Rewrite this code so that it isn't nested.

....
....
....
....
....
....
....
....
....
....
....
....

Test Drive

Try out the cleaner `if` code to make sure it works as expected.

Modify the code in `sendemail.php` to use `if` statements similar to those you just wrote that simplify the `if` nesting. Flip to the solution on the following page if you aren't sure about the changes to make.

Upload the new version of the script to your web server and open the `sendemail.html` page in a web browser. Experiment with the script by submitting the form with form fields both blank and filled. Does the script display error messages as expected?

there are no Dumb Questions

Q: Are a few levels of nesting really that big of a deal?

A: It depends. If you're writing some code that only you will ever see and you think you'll remember exactly what every next line does in six months time when you come back to it to tweak it, nest away.

If on the other hand, you'd like to keep your code as clean and logical as possible, you can use any of the several logic operators you've met so far.

Q: How does `else` work?

A: In an `if...else` statement, the `else` matches anything and everything that doesn't match the `if` part.

Q: Hmm. Okay. Does that mean I could nest `if` and `else` in existing `if...else` statements?

A: Well, you could, but with all that nesting, things would get complex pretty fast and we're trying to avoid nesting here!

cleaner
BE the ~~IF~~ code Solution

Your job is to play IF code and clean up the
messy nested IF's and ELSE's. RRewrite
the code to get rid of the nesting, but make
sure it still works correctly.

```
if (empty($subject) && empty($text)) {
  echo 'You forgot the email subject and body text.<br />';
} else {
  if (empty($subject) || empty($text)) {
    if (empty($subject)) {
      echo 'You forgot the email subject.<br />';
    } else {
      echo 'You forgot the email body text.<br />';
    }
  } else {
    // Everything is fine. send the email
  }
}
```

Here, we're testing
to see if both the
$subject and $text
variables are empty.

```
if (empty($subject) && empty($text)) {
  echo 'You forgot the email subject and body text.<br />';
}
```

Here we're testing
to see if $text is
empty and $subject
is not empty.

```
if (empty($subject) && (!empty($text))) {
  echo 'You forgot the email subject.<br />';
}
```

This code checks to see if $subject is
empty and $text is not empty.

```
if ((!empty($subject)) && empty($text)) {
  echo 'You forgot the email body text.<br />';
}
```

If we didn't use the AND (&&) to isolate
the non-empty subject/empty body text,
we could end up getting an extra feedback
message. Same thing goes for not empty
$subject and empty $text.

```
if ((!empty($subject)) && (!empty($text))) {
  // Everything is fine. send the email
}
```

The NOT operator (!) checks for
$subject and $text being non-empty.

And here, we're
testing to see if
neither $subject nor
$text is empty.

I'm all shook up. When I forgot to enter the subject in the form, I got this page. But then, when I clicked the Back button, I had to retype the whole message.

This page tells Elmer what he's missing... but not much else.

Make Me Elvis – Send Email

You forgot the email subject.

Validation in Elmer's Send Email script is working but it could be a lot more helpful.

When the `sendemail.php` script detects missing form data, it displays a message that information is missing, but that's it. There's no link back to the original form, for example. And even worse, when Elmer navigates back to the original form, the information he did enter is no longer there. He has to retype both the subject and body of his email message.

BRAIN POWER

What would you do to improve the error handling of the Send Email script to make it more helpful?.

It would be cool to show the form along with the error message. Couldn't we just echo the form if the email subject and body text are empty?

Displaying the form would definitely be helpful, as it would save Elmer having to navigate back in his browser.

So in addition to echoing an error message when one of the form fields is empty, we also need to regenerate the HTML form code from PHP by echoing it to the browser. This code shows that PHP is capable of generating some fairly complex HTML code:

This PHP code generates the entire HTML form, starting with the <form> tag.

```
echo '<form method="post" action="sendemail.php">';

echo '  <label for="subject">Subject of email:</label><br />';

echo '  <input id="subject" name="subject" type="text" ' .
  'size="30" /><br />';

echo '  <label for="elvismail">Body of email:</label><br />';

echo '  <textarea id="elvismail" name="elvismail" rows="8" ' .
  'cols="40"></textarea><br />';

echo '  <input type="submit" name="submit" value="Submit" />';

echo '</form>';
```

This indentation isn't strictly necessary, but it helps to see the structure of the original HTML code.

Since HTML code is riddled with double quotes, it's easier to use single quotes to surround strings of HTML code in PHP.

If you're thinking this code looks a bit chaotic, that's because it is. Just because you **can** do something in PHP doesn't mean you should. In this case, the added complexity of echoing all that HTML code is a problem. This is a big enough chunk of code that generating it via PHP with echo is really not a good option...

Ease in and out of PHP as needed

It's sometimes easy to forget that a PHP script is really just an HTML web page that is capable of holding PHP code. Any code in a PHP script that isn't enclosed by the `<?php` and `?>` tags is assumed to be HTML. This means you can close a block of PHP code and revert to HTML as needed, and then pick back up with a new block of PHP code. This is an extremely handy technique for outputting a chunk of HTML code that is unwieldy to generate through PHP `echo` statements... like our Send Email form code.

> You can close and open blocks of PHP code to output chunks of HTML code in a PHP script.

```php
<?php
  $from = 'elmer@makemeelvis.com';
  $subject = $_POST['subject'];
  $text = $_POST['elvismail'];

  if (empty($subject) && empty($text)) {
    // We know both $subject AND $text are blank
    echo 'You forgot the email subject and body text.<br />';
?>
```

This `?>` tag closes the PHP block, returning us to HTML.

The form is coded as normal HTML since this code is outside of PHP tags.

```html
<form method="post" action="sendemail.php">
  <label for="subject">Subject of email:</label><br />
  <input id="subject" name="subject" type="text" size="30" /><br />
  <label for="elvismail">Body of email:</label><br />
  <textarea id="elvismail" name="elvismail" rows="8" cols="40"></textarea><br />
  <input type="submit" name="submit" value="Submit" />
</form>
```

```php
<?php
  }
```

The `<?php` tag starts a new PHP block. Since we're still inside the if action, we have to close the if statement before continuing.

Since we're still inside of the if action, the HTML code is only output if both form fields are empty.

```php
  if (empty($subject) && (!empty($text))) {
    echo 'You forgot the email subject.<br />';
  }

  if ((!empty($subject)) && empty($text)) {
    echo 'You forgot the email body text.<br />';
  }

  if ((!empty($subject)) && (!empty($text))) {
    // Code to send the email
    ...
  }
?>
```

Write down anything you think might be limiting about this code. How would you fix it?

....

....

....

Use a flag to avoid ~~duplicate~~ duplicate code

The problem with the previous code is that it will have to drop out of PHP and duplicate the form code in three different places (once for each validation error). We can use a `true`/`false` variable known as a **flag** to keep track of whether or not we need to output the form. Let's call it `$output_form`. Then we can check the variable **later in the code** and display the form if the variable is `true`.

So we need to start out the script with `$output_form` set to `false`, and then only change it to `true` if a form field is empty and we need to show the form:

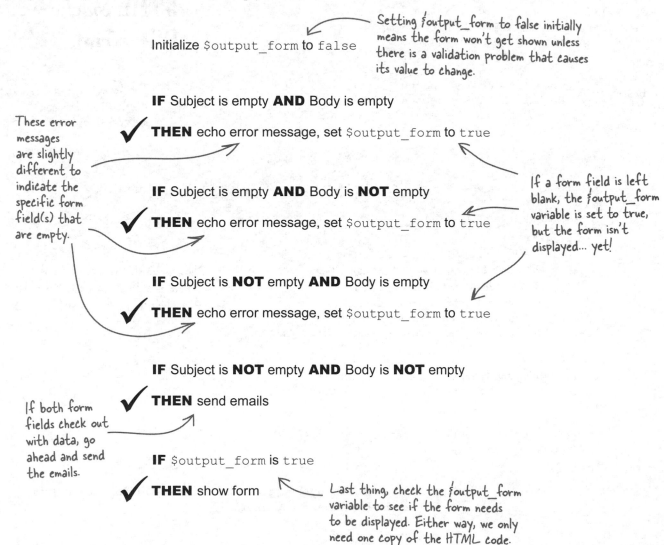

Initialize `$output_form` to `false`

Setting `$output_form` to false initially means the form won't get shown unless there is a validation problem that causes its value to change.

IF Subject is empty **AND** Body is empty

✓ **THEN** echo error message, set `$output_form` to `true`

These error messages are slightly different to indicate the specific form field(s) that are empty.

IF Subject is empty **AND** Body is **NOT** empty

✓ **THEN** echo error message, set `$output_form` to `true`

If a form field is left blank, the `$output_form` variable is set to true, but the form isn't displayed... yet!

IF Subject is **NOT** empty **AND** Body is empty

✓ **THEN** echo error message, set `$output_form` to `true`

IF Subject is **NOT** empty **AND** Body is **NOT** empty

✓ **THEN** send emails

If both form fields check out with data, go ahead and send the emails.

IF `$output_form` is `true`

✓ **THEN** show form

Last thing, check the `$output_form` variable to see if the form needs to be displayed. Either way, we only need one copy of the HTML code.

Code the HTML form only once

Turning the new validation logic into PHP code involves creating and initializing the new $output_form variable, and then making sure to set it throughout the validation code. Most important is the new if statement at the end of the code that only displays the form if $output_form is set to true.

By making HTML code dependent on an IF statement, we avoid duplicate code in our script.

```php
<?php
  $from = 'elmer@makemeelvis.com';
  $subject = $_POST['subject'];
  $text = $_POST['elvismail'];
  $output_form = false;
```

We create our new variable here and set it to false initially.

```php
  if (empty($subject) && empty($text)) {
    // We know both $subject AND $text are blank
    echo 'You forgot the email subject and body text.<br />';
    $output_form = true;
  }
```

Set the variable to true if both $subject and $text are empty so that the form is shown.

```php
  if (empty($subject) && (!empty($text))) {
    echo 'You forgot the email subject.<br />';
    $output_form = true;
  }
```

Also set the variable to true if $subject is empty.

```php
  if ((!empty($subject)) && empty($text)) {
    echo 'You forgot the email body text.<br />';
    $output_form = true;
  }
```

And set the variable to true if $text is empty.

```php
  if ((!empty($subject)) && (!empty($text))) {
    // Code to send the email
    ...
  }

  if ($output_form) {
?>
```

This if statement checks the $output_form variable and displays the form if it is true.

We've dropped out of PHP code, but anything prior to the closing } is still considered part of the if action — in this case it's the HTML code for the form.

```html
<form method="post" action="sendemail.php">
  <label for="subject">Subject of email:</label><br />
  <input id="subject" name="subject" type="text" size="30" /><br />
  <label for="elvismail">Body of email:</label><br />
  <textarea id="elvismail" name="elvismail" rows="8" cols="40"></textarea><br />
  <input type="submit" name="submit" value="Submit" />
</form>
```

```php
<?php
  }
?>
```

Don't forget to jump back into PHP code and close the if statement.

The HTML code only appears once since we've crunched all the logic for displaying it into a single variable, $output_form.

> The new form is better, but I still have to retype the fields I had typed in correctly, which is really annoying.

HTML alone can't preserve form data.

When Elmer submits the Send Email form with an empty field, the `sendemail.php` script catches the error and generates a new form. But the new form is pure HTML code, which can't possibly know anything about any data Elmer might have entered earlier. So we're generating a clean new form as part of the validation, which is wiping out any data Elmer might have entered.

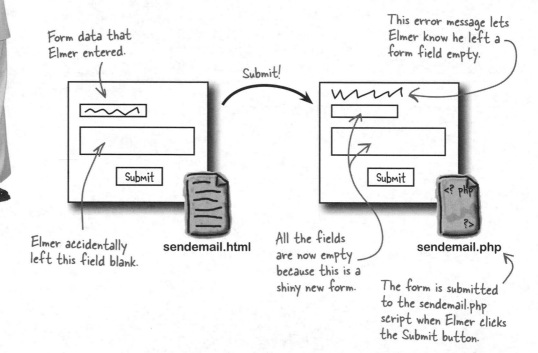

Form data that Elmer entered.

This error message lets Elmer know he left a form field empty.

Submit!

Elmer accidentally left this field blank.

sendemail.html

All the fields are now empty because this is a shiny new form.

sendemail.php

The form is submitted to the sendemail.php script when Elmer clicks the Submit button.

Ack. We can't get around the fact that a new form will have to be generated in the PHP script. But we need a way to remember any data Elmer might have already entered, and plug it back into the new form so that Elmer can focus solely on filling out the form field that he accidentally left empty...

Sharpen your pencil

Draw what Elmer's form should look like after he submits it with only the first form field filled out. Then write down how you think each of the two files (HTML and PHP) should be altered to carry out this new functionality.

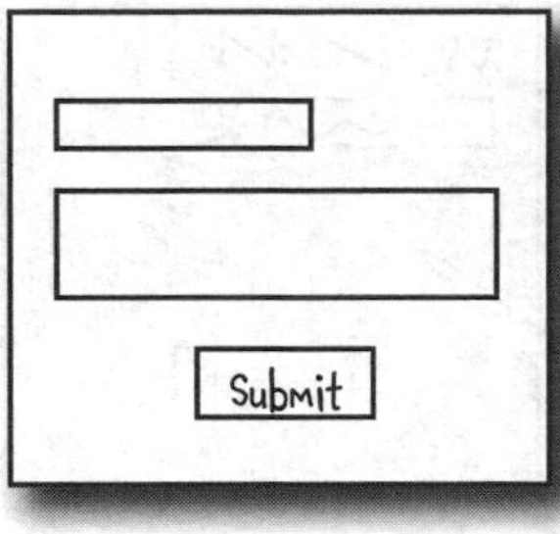

sendemail.php

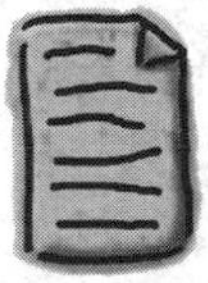

sendemail.html

....
....
....
....
....
....
....

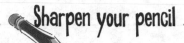

Sharpen your pencil

Draw what Elmer's form should look like after he submits it with only the first form field filled out. Then write down how you think each of the two files (HTML and PHP) should be altered to carry out this new functionality.

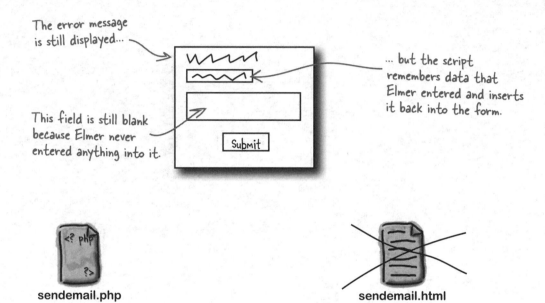

The error message is still displayed...

... but the script remembers data that Elmer entered and inserts it back into the form.

This field is still blank because Elmer never entered anything into it.

Submit

sendemail.php

sendemail.html

The PHP script takes over the job of displaying the form, both before and after submission. And since the script has access to any form data that has been entered, it can plug the data back into the form when it is generated. This solves Elmer's problem of having to re-enter form data he's already filled out.

If we display the form entirely in the PHP script, we can do away with the HTML page by letting the PHP script both show the form and process it. In doing so, the PHP script can access and use any data entered into the form, which is impossible in pure HTML code.

A form that references itself

How can it be possible to remove `sendemail.html` from the Send Email form equation? The answer is that we're not actually eliminating any HTML code, we're just moving it to the PHP script. This is made possible by the fact that a PHP script can contain HTML code just like a normal web page. So we can structure our script so that it not only processes the form on submission but also displays the form initially, which is all `sendemail.html` was doing.

The key to the `sendemail.php` script being able to fill the role left by `sendemail.html` is the form action. Since the script itself now contains the HTML form, the form action leads back to the script... a **self-referencing form**.

An HTML form that is part of the PHP script that processes it is known as self-referencing.

We no longer need sendemail.html—users navigate directly to the PHP script to use the form.

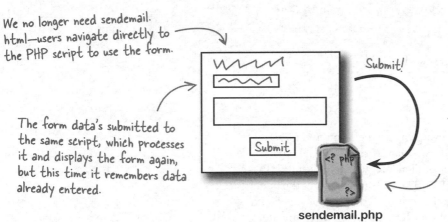

Submit!

The form data's submitted to the same script, which processes it and displays the form again, but this time it remembers data already entered.

The script initially shows the form and then processes it when it is submitted. Processing the form involves either sending emails or displaying the form again with an error message.

sendemail.php

To understand what's going on here, think about the first time Elmer visits the page (script). An empty form is generated as HTML code and displayed. Elmer fills out a field of the form and clicks Submit. The script processes its own form, and displays an error message if any data's missing. More importantly, the script displays the form again, but this time it includes any data Elmer has already entered. When a form's smart enough to remember data entered into it in prior submissions, it's known as a **sticky form**... the data sticks to it!

Sticky forms remember the data the user has already correctly entered.

BRAIN POWER

How do you think we can tweak Elmer's application to make the form fields sticky?

Point the form action at the script

As we've seen several times, the action attribute of the `<form>` tag is what connects a form to a PHP script that processes it. Setting the action of Elmer's form to `sendemail.php` works just fine in allowing it to process itself, which is the first step toward form stickiness. In fact, the form already has its action attribute set to the script:

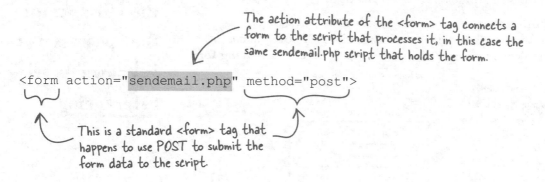

The action attribute of the `<form>` tag connects a form to the script that processes it, in this case the same sendemail.php script that holds the form.

```
<form action="sendemail.php" method="post">
```

This is a standard `<form>` tag that happens to use POST to submit the form data to the script.

This code works, assuming you don't ever rename the script and forget to update the code. But there's a better way that works no matter what because it doesn't rely on a specific script filename. It's the built-in PHP superglobal variable **$_SERVER['PHP_SELF']**, which stores the name of the current script. You can replace the script URL in the form action to `$_SERVER['PHP_SELF']`, and not ever have to worry about updating anything if you ever need to rename the script.

The only catch is that `$_SERVER['PHP_SELF']` is PHP code, which means you have to echo its value so that it is output as part of the HTML code, like this:

Instead of hardcoding the name of our script, we can tell it to reference itself by using the $_SERVER['PHP_SELF'] superglobal.

```
<form action="<?php echo $_SERVER['PHP_SELF']; ?>" method="post">
```

Granted, using `$_SERVER['PHP_SELF']` instead of the script name isn't an earth shattering improvement but it's one of the many little things you can do to make your scripts easier to maintain over time.

$_SERVER['PHP_SELF'] stores away the name of the current script.

TEST DRIVE

Try out the new self-referencing script with improved form validation logic.

Modify the code in `sendemail.php` to use the `$output_form` variable to selectively display the form as shown a few pages back. Also change the `action` attribute of the `<form>` tag so that the form is self-referencing.

You no longer need the `sendemail.html` page on your web server, so feel free to delete it. Then upload the new version of the `sendemail.php` script to your web server and open the script in a web browser. How does it look?

For some reason the script's showing an error message even though the form hasn't even been submitted... not good.

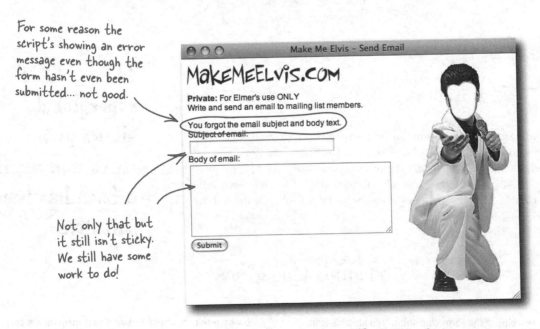

Not only that but it still isn't sticky. We still have some work to do!

First things first — we'll get to the sticky stuff in a moment.

Write down why you think the script is displaying an error message the first time the form is shown:

....

....

....

Check to see if the form has been submitted

The problem is that the script can't distinguish between the form being displayed for the first time and it being submitted with incomplete data. So the script reports missing data the very first time the form is displayed, which is confusing. The question is, how can we check to see if the form is being submitted? If we know that, we can make sure we only validate data on a submission.

Remember how, when a form is submitted using the POST method, its data is stored away in the $_POST array? If the form hasn't been submitted, then the $_POST array isn't filled with any data. Or to put it another way, the $_POST array **hasn't been set**. Any guess what function we could call to see if the $_POST array's been set?

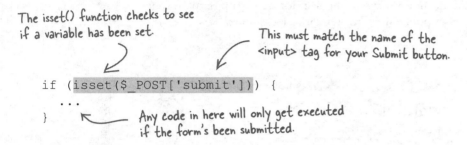

The isset() function checks to see if a variable has been set.

This must match the name of the <input> tag for your Submit button.

```
if (isset($_POST['submit'])) {
    ...
}
```

Any code in here will only get executed if the form's been submitted.

Since every form has a Submit button, an easy way to check to see if a form has been submitted is to see if there's $_POST data for the Submit button. The data's just the label on the button, which isn't important. What's important is simply the existence of $_POST['submit'], which tells us that the form has been submitted. Just make sure that 'submit' matches up with the id attribute of the Submit button in the form code.

> **The $_POST superglobal allows us to check and see if a form has been submitted.**

there are no Dumb Questions

Q: How does knowing if the form was submitted stop us from accidentally displaying validation error messages?

A: The reason the error messages are being shown incorrectly is because the script doesn't distinguish between the form being submitted vs. being displayed for the first time. So we need a way to tell if this is the first time the form is being shown, in which case empty form fields are perfectly fine—it's not an error. We should *only* validate the form fields if the form's been submitted, so being able to detect a form submission is very important.

Q: So why don't we check to see if real form data's set, instead of the Submit button?

A: It would work perfectly fine to check $_POST['subject'] or $_POST['elvismail'], but only for this particular form. Since every form has a Submit button that can be consistently named submit, checking $_POST['submit'] gives you a reliable way to check for form submission in all of our scripts.

The Send Email Script Up Close

```php
<?php
  if (isset($_POST['submit'])) {
    $from = 'elmer@makemeelvis.com';
    $subject = $_POST['subject'];
    $text = $_POST['elvismail'];
    $output_form = false;

    if (empty($subject) && empty($text)) {
      // We know both $subject AND $text are blank
      echo 'You forgot the email subject and body text.<br />';
      $output_form = true;
    }

    if (empty($subject) && (!empty($text))) {
      echo 'You forgot the email subject.<br />';
      $output_form = true;
    }

    if ((!empty($subject)) && empty($text)) {
      echo 'You forgot the email body text.<br />';
      $output_form = true;
    }

    if ((!empty($subject)) && (!empty($text))) {
      // Code to send the email
      ...
    }
  }
  else {
    $output_form = true;
  }

  if ($output_form) {
?>

  <form method="post" action="<?php echo $_SERVER['PHP_SELF']; ?>">
    <label for="subject">Subject of email:</label><br />
    <input id="subject" name="subject" type="text" size="30" /><br />
    <label for="elvismail">Body of email:</label><br />
    <textarea id="elvismail" name="elvismail" rows="8" cols="40"></textarea><br />
    <input type="submit" name="submit" value="Submit" />
  </form>

<?php
  }
?>
```

We check the value of $_POST"submit']. If the form has never been submitted, this will be unset.

This parenthesis closes the first if, which tells us if the form was submitted.

If the form's never been submitted, we definitely need to show it!

Cool. So we can now detect the form submission and show error messages correctly. But we still haven't made the form fields sticky, right?

That's right. Detecting the form submission is important, but we still need to plug the sticky form data back into the form.

Knowing if the form's been submitted is an important part of making it sticky, but it isn't the only part. The part we're missing is taking any form data that was submitted and plugging it back into the form as the form is being output. You can set an input form field using the value attribute of the HTML <input> tag. For example, this code presets the value of an input field using the value attribute:

This value is hardcoded — it's always the same every time the form is shown.

```
<input name="subject" type="text" value="Fall Clearance!">
```

But we don't want to hardcode a specific value. We want to insert a piece of data from a PHP variable. How is that possible? Remember that we've used echo to dynamically generate HTML code from PHP in other situations. In this case, we can use echo to generate a value for the value attribute from a PHP variable, like this:

Since we're switching to PHP to echo the variable, we have to use a <?php tag.

The variable is echoed using the familiar echo statement.

```
<input name="subject" type="text" value="<?php echo $subject; ?>">
```

And to return back to HTML, we close up the PHP code with the ?> tag.

For a text area input field, we echo the sticky data in between the <textarea> and </textarea> tags instead of using the value attribute.

Elmer's form can then be modified similarly to take advantage of sticky data:

```
<form method="post" action="<?php echo $_SERVER['PHP_SELF']; ?>">
  <label for="subject">Subject of email:</label><br />
  <input id="subject" name="subject" type="text" size="30"
    value="<?php echo $subject; ?>"/><br />
  <label for="elvismail">Body of email:</label><br />
  <textarea id="elvismail" name="elvismail" rows="8" cols="40">
    <?php echo $text; ?></textarea><br />
  <input type="submit" name="submit" value="Submit" />
</form>
```

TEST DRIVE

Check to see how sticky Elmer's data really is.

Change the code in `sendemail.php` to check `$_POST` for the form submission, as well as adding `echo` code to the form so that its fields are sticky. Upload the new version of the script to your web server and open the script in a web browser. Experiment with different form field values, including leaving one or both fields empty, and submit it a few times.

> Boy, that was dumb leaving the body of the email blank. Thankfully, I'll never do that again now that the form is on top of things. And I don't have to keep re-entering the same data to fix it either.

Make Me Elvis – Send Email

MAKEMEELVIS.COM

Private: For Elmer's use ONLY
Write and send an email to mailing list members.

You forgot the email body text.
Subject of email:

Fall Clearance!

Body of email:

Submit

The Send Email script now shows an error message when Elmer leaves a form field blank, but it remembers any data he did enter.

Some users are still disgruntled

Form validation has gone a long way toward dealing with Elmer's frustrated customers, particularly those who were receiving blank emails. But not everyone is happy. It seems a few people are receiving duplicate emails... remember this guy from earlier in the chapter?

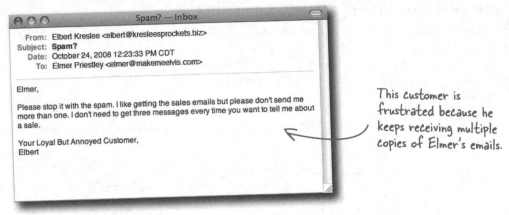

This customer is frustrated because he keeps receiving multiple copies of Elmer's emails.

Elmer knows he didn't send a message more than once, leading him to suspect that maybe some users have accidentally subscribed to his email list more than once. Not a problem, just use the Remove Email page/script from the last chapter to remove the user, right?

Unfortunately, it's not that simple. Removing Elbert using his email address will completely delete him from the `email_list` table, causing him to no longer receive any email messages from Elmer. We need a way to only delete Elbert's **extra** rows from the table, making sure to leave one.

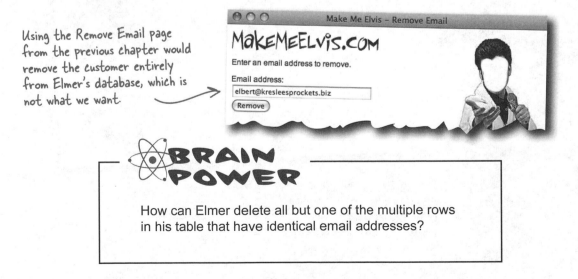

Using the Remove Email page from the previous chapter would remove the customer entirely from Elmer's database, which is not what we want.

BRAIN POWER

How can Elmer delete all but one of the multiple rows in his table that have identical email addresses?

> Hmm. The problem is that there are multiple rows in the table but no way to distinguish them from each other. Without a way to isolate them individually, any DELETE we try to do will delete all of them.

Frank   Jill   Joe

Joe: Maybe our Add Email form should check for duplicate email addresses before adding new users. That would fix it, right?

Frank: Excellent idea.

Jill: Yes, that would solve the problem moving forward, but it doesn't help us deal with duplicate email addresses that are already in the database.

Frank: Right. What if we tried to use a different column in the table to delete the extra rows, like `last_name`?

Jill: I wondered about that, but using a last name is potentially even worse than an email address. What if we wanted to delete someone named John Smith from our mailing list, and we ran the following SQL code:

```
DELETE FROM email_list WHERE last_name = 'Smith'
```

Joe: We wouldn't just delete John Smith from our table; we'd be deleting Will Smith, Maggie Smith, Emmitt Smith...

Frank: Wow, that wouldn't be good. Last names are more likely to be common across rows than email addresses, and first names would be even worse than that. We could lose dozens and dozens of rows with one simple query.

Jill: Exactly. We can't risk using a `WHERE` clause that will delete rows we need to keep. We need to be certain we can pinpoint just the ones we want to remove.

Joe: So what the heck do we do? We can't use `email`, `last_name`, or `first_name` in our `WHERE` clause.

Frank: We're out of columns in our table to use. Looks like we're out of luck.

Jill: Not necessarily. What we really need is something to make each row of the table unique—then we could pinpoint rows without any trouble. And just because we don't currently have a column that has a unique value for each row doesn't mean we can't add one.

Joe: A new column? But we've already decided on our table structure.

Frank: Yeah, but what we've got isn't meeting our needs. You're right that it would be better if we had realized this beforehand, so we could have designed our table accordingly, but it's not too late to fix what we've got.

Joe: OK, but what would we call our new column? What data would we put into it?

Jill: Well, since its purpose would be to uniquely identify each row in the table, we could call it `identifier`, or maybe just `id` for short.

Frank: Nice, and we can fill the `id` column with a different ID number for each row, so when we execute our DELETE, we'll be removing rows based on a unique number, instead of an email address or surname.

Joe: Exactly. It's really a great idea, isn't it? I'm so glad I thought of it.

Table rows should be uniquely identifiable

Part of the whole idea of sticking something in a database is that later on you'd like to look it up and do something with it. Knowing this, it's incredibly important for each row in a table to be **uniquely identifiable**, meaning that you can specifically access one row (and only that row!). Elmer's email_list table makes a dangerous assumption that email addresses are unique. That assumption works as long as no one accidentally subscribes to the mailing list twice, but when they do (and they will!), their email address gets stored in the table twice... no more uniqueness!

What Elmer's table contains now:

first_name	last_name	email
Denny	Bubbleton	denny@mightygumball.net
Irma	Werlitz	iwer@aliensabductedme.com
Elbert	Kreslee	elbert@kresleesprockets.biz
Irma	Kreslee	elbert@kresleesprockets.biz

Nothing in the structure of this table guarantees uniqueness among rows.

And while most of the time email is unique, we can't count on that always being the case.

More than one person can have the same first name, so this isn't a good choice for a unique column.

Same here, we can't count on unique last names.

When you don't have a column of truly unique values in a table, you should create one. MySQL gives you a way to add a unique integer column, also called a **primary key**, for each row in your table.

What Elmer's table should contain:

We need a new column that contains a value that is unique for every row in the table.

id	first_name	last_name	email
1	Denny	Bubbleton	denny@mightygumball.net
2	Irma	Werlitz	iwer@aliensabductedme.com
3	Elbert	Kreslee	elbert@kresleesprockets.biz
4	Irma	Kreslee	elbert@kresleesprockets.biz

Now that this column contains a unique value, we can be sure that every row in our table is truly unique.

Duplicate data in other columns no longer affects the uniqueness of rows because the new id column takes care of that.

Hey genius, you know if we want to make a change to the table structure, we have to do a DROP TABLE and then recreate it from scratch. Elmer's email data will be toast!

It's true that `DROP TABLE` **would destroy Elmer's data. But SQL has a another command that lets you make changes to an existing table without losing any data.**

It's called **ALTER TABLE**, and we can use it to create a new column without having to drop the table and destroy its data. Here's what the general format of an `ALTER TABLE` statement looks like for adding a new column to a table:

The name of the table to be altered.

The name of the new column to be added.

```
ALTER TABLE table_name ADD column_name column_type
```

The data type of the new column.

We can use the `ALTER TABLE` command to add a new column to the `email_list` table, which we'll name `id`. We'll give the `id` column a data type of `INT`, since integers work great for establishing uniqueness. Some other information is also required, as this code reveals:

The name of the table that we want to alter.

We want to ADD a new column, which we call id.

This tells the MySQL server to add 1 to the value stored in this column for each new row that's inserted.

```
ALTER TABLE email_list ADD id INT NOT NULL AUTO_INCREMENT FIRST,
    ADD PRIMARY KEY (id)
```

The data type of the column makes it an INTeger.

FIRST tells MySQL to make the new column first in the table. This is optional, but it's good form to put your id column first.

This little chunk of code tells MySQL that the new id column is the primary key for the table. More on that in just a sec!

This `ALTER TABLE` statement has a lot going on because primary keys have to be created with very specific features. For example, `NOT NULL` tells MySQL that there must be a value in the `id` column—you can never leave it blank. `AUTO_INCREMENT` further describes the traits of the `id` column by causing it to automatically get set to a unique numeric value when a new row is inserted. As its name suggests, `AUTO_INCREMENT` automatically adds one to the last `id` value used in a row and places this value into the `id` column when you `INSERT` a new row into your table. Finally, `PRIMARY KEY` tells MySQL that each value in the `id` column is unique, but there's more to it than just uniqueness...

Primary keys enforce uniqueness

A **primary key** is a column in a table that distinguishes each row in that table as unique. Unlike normal columns, which could also be designed to be unique, only one column can be made the primary key. This provides a clear choice for what column to use in any queries that need to pinpoint specific rows.

In order to ensure this uniqueness for primary keys, MySQL imposes a bunch of restrictions on the column that has been declared as PRIMARY KEY. You can think of these restrictions as rules to be followed as you work with primary keys:

A primary key is a column in your table that makes each row unique.

The five rules of primary keys:

The data in a primary key can't be repeated.

Two rows should never have the same data in their primary keys. No exceptions—a primary key should always have unique values within a given table.

A primary key must have a value.

If a primary key was left empty (NULL), then it might not be unique because other rows could potentially also be NULL. Always set your primary keys to unique values!

The primary key must be set when a new row is inserted.

If you could insert a row without a primary key, you would run the risk of ending up with a NULL primary key and duplicate rows in your table, which would defeat the purpose.

A primary key must be as efficient as possible.

A primary key should contain only the information it needs to be unique and nothing more. That's why integers make good primary keys—they allow for uniqueness without requiring much storage.

The value of a primary key can't be changed.

If you could change the value of your key, you'd risk accidentally setting it to a value you already used. Remember, it has to remain unique at all costs.

The id column in Elmer's table doesn't have repeat data, has a value for every row, is automatically set when a new row is inserted, is compact, and doesn't change. Perfect!

id	first_name	last_name	email
1	Denny	Bubbleton	denny@mightygumball.net
2	Irma	Werlitz	iwer@aliensabductedme.com
...			

TEST DRIVE

Alter Elmer's table and try out inserting a new row of data with a primary key.

Using a MySQL tool such as the MySQL terminal or the SQL tab of phpMyAdmin, enter the ALTER TABLE statement to add a primary key column named id:

```
ALTER TABLE email_list ADD id INT NOT NULL AUTO_INCREMENT FIRST,
    ADD PRIMARY KEY (id)
```

Now insert a new customer to the database to see if the id column is automatically set for the new row. Here's an example of an INSERT statement to use (notice the primary key isn't mentioned):

```
INSERT INTO email_list (first_name, last_name, email)
    VALUES ('Don', 'Draper', 'draper@sterling-cooper.com')
```

Finally, issue a SELECT statement to view the contents of the table and see the new primary key in all its glory! Just in case you've forgotten, here's the SELECT statement:

```
SELECT * FROM email_list
```

The new id column is auto-incremented so that it remains unique for the new row of data.

```
File  Edit  Window  Help  Email
mysql> SELECT * FROM email_list;

+------+------------+-----------+-----------------------------+
| id   | first_name | last_name | email                       |
+------+------------+-----------+-----------------------------+
| 1    | Denny      | Bubbleton | denny@mightygumball.net     |
| 2    | Irma       | Werlitz   | iwer@aliensabductedme.com   |
| 3    | Elbert     | Kreslee   | elbert@kresleesprockets.biz |
| 4    | Irma       | Kreslee   | elbert@kresleesprockets.biz |
| 5    | Don        | Draper    | draper@sterling-cooper.com  |
+------+------------+-----------+-----------------------------+
5 rows in set (0.0005 sec)
```

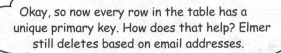

Okay, so now every row in the table has a unique primary key. How does that help? Elmer still deletes based on email addresses.

Joe: The problem is that the user needs to pinpoint rows of data using the primary key instead of the email address.

Frank: That's right! So we just need to change the form so that the user enters the ID of a customer instead of their email address. No problemo!

Jill: Actually, big problemo. The user has no way of knowing the ID of a customer without somehow finding them in the database. In fact, the user doesn't know anything about the database structure. Maybe what we need is to rethink the form so that it lists out all the names and email addresses in a list with checkboxes next to each one. Here, I'll sketch it for you.

The value of the checkbox will keep track of the id value.

Frank: Nice sketch, but how does that help Elmer isolate a customer for deletion using their ID?

Joe: Hmm. What if we stored the customer ID in the value of the checkbox. That way it isn't actually visible, but the script can get to it.

Jill: That's a great idea. So we could generate the form automatically in a loop by doing a `SELECT` to get all the data, and then creating each checkbox input field from a row of query data.

Joe: Cool. But what happens when the Submit button is pressed? What does `$_POST` have in it?

Frank: Hang on, Joe, we'll get there in a minute. Let's just start by building this part of the script, the part that displays all the data from the table and writes out those checkboxes...

PHP & MySQL Magnets

Use the magnets below to finish the missing code for the Remove Email script, which presents a series of checkboxes for the customers in Elmer's database. Note that this code just creates the form; don't worry about the code that performs the DELETE just yet.

```
<img src="blankface.jpg" width="161" height="350" alt="" style="float:right" />
<img name="elvislogo" src="elvislogo.gif" width="229" height="32" border="0" alt="Make Me Elvis" />
<p>Please select the email addresses to delete from the email list and click Remove.</p>

<form method="post" action="                    echo $_SERVER['PHP_SELF'];          ">
                    .................                                  ...........

<?php
  $dbc = mysqli_connect('data.makemeelvis.com', 'elmer', 'theking', 'elvis_store')
    or die('Error connecting to MySQL server.');

  // Display the customer rows with checkboxes for deleting
  $query = "SELECT * FROM email_list";
  $result = mysqli_query($dbc, $query);

  while (              = mysqli_fetch_array($result)) {
        .................                                              .'" name="todelete[]" />';
    echo '<input type="checkbox" value="' .
                                  ..............................................

    echo                                  ;
        ......................................................

    echo ' ' .                                  ;
        ......................................................

    echo ' ' .                                  ;
        ......................................................

    echo '<br />';
  }

  mysqli_close($dbc);
?>

  <input type="submit" name="              " value="Remove" />
                        .................

</form>
```

removeemail.php

?>

`' '` `' '` `' '`

`row` `row`
`row` `row`
`row`

`first_name`

`id`

`]` `]`
`[`
`[` `]`
`[` `[`

`last_name`

`email`

`submit`

`<?php`

`$`
`$`
`$` `$`
`$`

PHP & MySQL Magnets Solution

Use the magnets below to finish the missing code for the Remove Email script, which presents a series of checkboxes for the customers in Elmer's database. Note that this code just creates the form; don't worry about the code that performs the DELETE just yet.

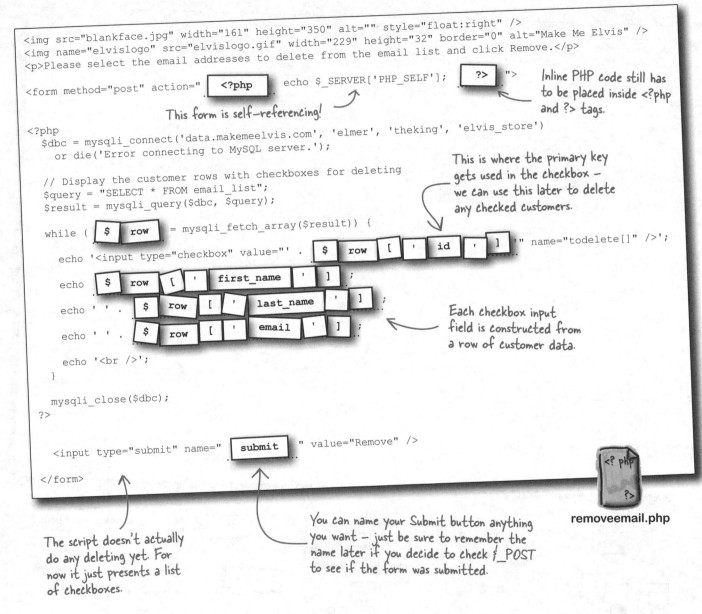

```
<img src="blankface.jpg" width="161" height="350" alt="" style="float:right" />
<img name="elvislogo" src="elvislogo.gif" width="229" height="32" border="0" alt="Make Me Elvis" />
<p>Please select the email addresses to delete from the email list and click Remove.</p>

<form method="post" action=" <?php   echo $_SERVER['PHP_SELF'];   ?> ">
```

This form is self-referencing!

Inline PHP code still has to be placed inside <?php and ?> tags.

```
<?php
  $dbc = mysqli_connect('data.makemeelvis.com', 'elmer', 'theking', 'elvis_store')
    or die('Error connecting to MySQL server.');

  // Display the customer rows with checkboxes for deleting
  $query = "SELECT * FROM email_list";
  $result = mysqli_query($dbc, $query);

  while ( $row = mysqli_fetch_array($result)) {
    echo '<input type="checkbox" value="' . $row[ 'id' ] . '" name="todelete[]" />';
    echo . $row [ ' first_name ' ] ;
    echo ' ' . $row [ ' last_name ' ] . ;
    echo ' ' . $row [ ' email ' ] . ;
    echo '<br />';
  }

  mysqli_close($dbc);
?>

  <input type="submit" name=" submit " value="Remove" />

</form>
```

This is where the primary key gets used in the checkbox — we can use this later to delete any checked customers.

Each checkbox input field is constructed from a row of customer data.

removeemail.php

The script doesn't actually do any deleting yet. For now it just presents a list of checkboxes.

You can name your Submit button anything you want — just be sure to remember the name later if you decide to check $_POST to see if the form was submitted.

From checkboxes to customer IDs

The checkbox code generated by the Remove Email script is simple HTML with our primary key (id) stuffed into the value attribute of the <input> tag. There's one small, but very important change from ordinary checkbox HTML code, though. You might have noticed square brackets ([]) at the end of the checkbox name—they serve a vital purpose.

```
echo '<input type="checkbox" value="' . $row['id'] . '" name="todelete[]">';
```

The square brackets result in the creation of an array within $_POST that stores the contents of the value attribute of every checked checkbox in the form. Since each checkbox's value attribute contains a primary key, **each value in the todelete array is the ID of the row in our table that needs to be deleted.** This makes it possible for us to loop through the todelete array and issue an SQL query to delete each customer that is checked in the form.

The square brackets at the end of the checkbox name automatically put the checkbox values in an array we've named "todelete[]".

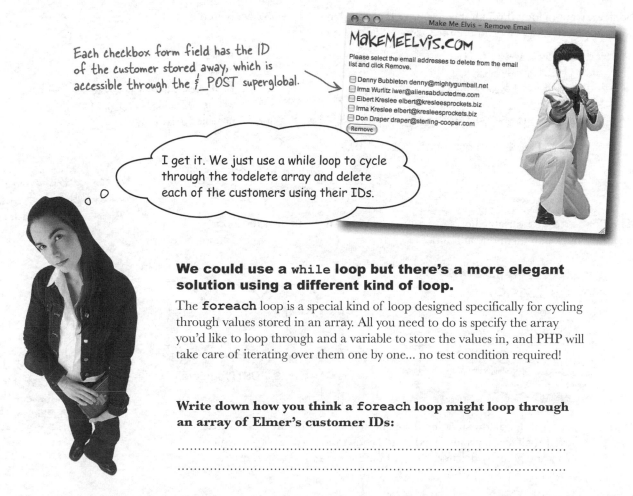

Each checkbox form field has the ID of the customer stored away, which is accessible through the $_POST superglobal.

I get it. We just use a while loop to cycle through the todelete array and delete each of the customers using their IDs.

We could use a while loop but there's a more elegant solution using a different kind of loop.

The **foreach** loop is a special kind of loop designed specifically for cycling through values stored in an array. All you need to do is specify the array you'd like to loop through and a variable to store the values in, and PHP will take care of iterating over them one by one... no test condition required!

Write down how you think a foreach loop might loop through an array of Elmer's customer IDs:

....

....

Loop through an array with foreach

The `foreach` loop takes an array and loops through each element in the array without the need for a test condition or loop counter. As it steps through each element in the array, it temporarily stores the value of that element in a variable. Assuming an array is stored in a variable named `$customers`, this code steps through each one:

The array you want to loop through appears first.

As the loop goes through each individual element in the array, it will temporarily store them in a variable with this name.

```
foreach ($customers as $customer) {
    echo $customer;
};
```

Inside of the loop, you can access each element using the variable name you just provided.

So if we want to loop through the customer IDs stored in the `$_POST` array in the Remove Email script, we can use the following `foreach` code:

Here the array is stored inside of the ?_POST superglobal, and identified by "todelete".

Each element of the array will be accessible through the variable ?delete_id.

```
foreach ($_POST['todelete'] as $delete_id) {
    // Delete a row from the table
};
```

We can use ?delete_id to delete each of the customers from the database.

The `$delete_id` variable holds the value of each array element as the loop progresses through them one at a time.

We can use this variable to access the ID of each customer and then delete them from the table.

$delete_id

$_POST['todelete']

We constructed this array so that it only holds customers that were checked in the Remove Email form.

With the `foreach` loop now stepping through each of the **checked** checkboxes in the Remove Email form, we just need to add code inside of the loop to issue a `DELETE` query and actually delete each row from the `email_list` table.

Exercise

Finish the code for Elmer's new and improved `removeemail.php` script so that it deletes customers that have been checked in the form when the form is submitted.

```
...
$dbc = mysqli_connect('data.makemeelvis.com', 'elmer', 'theking', 'elvis_store')
  or die('Error connecting to MySQL server.');

// Delete the customer rows (only if the form has been submitted)
if ( ........................................... ) {
  foreach ($_POST['todelete'] as $delete_id) {
    ..................................................................................................
    ..................................................................................................
    ..................................................................................................
  }

  echo 'Customer(s) removed.<br />';
}


// Display the customer rows with checkboxes for deleting
$query = "SELECT * FROM email_list";
$result = mysqli_query($dbc, $query);
while ($row = mysqli_fetch_array($result)) {
  echo '<input type="checkbox" value="' . $row['id'] . '" name="todelete[]" />';
  echo $row['first_name'];
  echo ' ' . $row['last_name'];
  echo ' ' . $row['email'];
  echo '<br />';
}

mysqli_close($dbc);
?>

<input type="submit" name="submit" value="Remove" />
</form>
```

removeemail.php

Exercise Solution

Finish the code for Elmer's new and improved `removeemail.php` script so that it deletes customers that have been checked in the form when the form is submitted.

```
...
$dbc = mysqli_connect('data.makemeelvis.com', 'elmer', 'theking', 'elvis_store')
  or die('Error connecting to MySQL server.');

// Delete the customer rows (only if the form has been submitted)
if (   isset($_POST['submit'])          ) {
    foreach ($_POST['todelete'] as $delete_id) {
      $query = "DELETE FROM email_list WHERE id = $delete_id";
      mysqli_query($dbc, $query)
        or die('Error querying database.');
    }

    echo 'Customer(s) removed.<br />';
  }


  // Display the customer rows with checkboxes for deleting
  $query = "SELECT * FROM email_list";
  $result = mysqli_query($dbc, $query);
  while ($row = mysqli_fetch_array($result)) {
    echo '<input type="checkbox" value="' . $row['id'] . '" name="todelete[]" />';
    echo $row['first_name'];
    echo ' ' . $row['last_name'];
    echo ' ' . $row['email'];
    echo '<br />';
  }

  mysqli_close($dbc);
?>


  <input type="submit" name="submit" value="Remove" />
</form>
```

Only delete customers if the form has been submitted!

Use $delete_id to choose the exact customer to delete.

The code to generate the customer checkboxes is the same as you created it before.

removeemail.php

TEST DRIVE

Take Elmer's newly revamped Remove Email script for a spin.

Modify the code in the `removeemail.php` script so that it generates customer checkboxes instead of using the old email text field. Then add the code to delete customers whenever the form's submitted. Also change the `action` attribute of the `<form>` tag so that the form's self-referencing.

Now that `removeemail.php` uses a self-referencing form, you no longer need the `removeemail.html` page on your web server, so feel free to delete it. Then upload the new version of `removeemail.php` to your web server and open the script in a web browser. Check off a few customers and click Submit. The form immediately changes to reflect the customer removal.

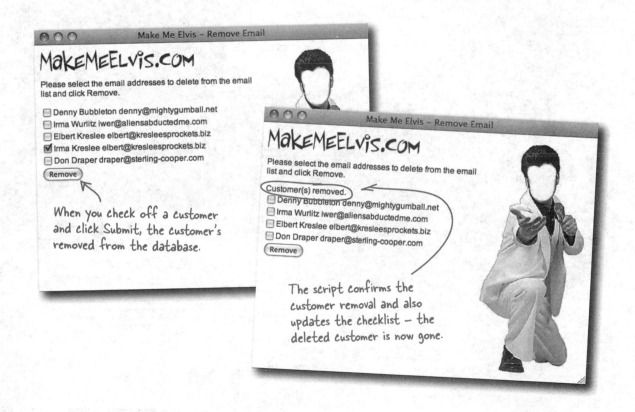

When you check off a customer and click Submit, the customer's removed from the database.

The script confirms the customer removal and also updates the checklist — the deleted customer is now gone.

Totally digging my new Remove Email form. Time for a vacation. Viva Las Vegas, baby!

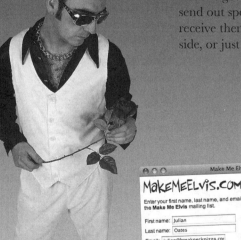

Elmer's got a fully functioning application. He can add customers, send out spectacular sale emails to just the customers who want to receive them, and delete customers who have traveled to the dark side, or just want to be removed from his list. Life is good.

Your PHP & MySQL Toolbox

You bagged quite a few new PHP and MySQL skills while taking Elmer's web application to a whole new level...

if, else

The PHP if statement makes decisions based on whether or not something is true. Give it a true/false test condition and some action code, and an if statement will let you make all kinds of cool decisions. An else clause can be added to an if statement to give it an alternate action.

ALTER TABLE

This SQL statement changes the structure of a table, such as adding a new column of data. This allows you to alter a table structurally without having to drop it and start over.

!

The negation operator, or NOT operator, reverses a true/false value. So true becomes false and false becomes true.

==, <>, !=, <, >, ...

Comparison operators that can be used to construct test conditions that compare values to each other. These are often used to control if statements and loops.

foreach

A PHP looping construct that lets you loop through an array one element at a time without using a test condition. Inside the loop, you can access each element of the array.

&&, OR

These are logical operators that are used to build expressions involving true/false values. Combining two values with && (AND) results in true only if both values are true. Combining values with || (OR) results in true if either of the values is true.

isset(), empty()

The built-in PHP isset() function tests to see if a variable exists, which means that it has been assigned a value. The empty() function takes things one step further and determines whether a variable contains an empty value (0, an empty string, false, or NULL).

When a database just isn't enough

You've got permission to upload that to me, and I'll file it under delicious!

I'll file you in the pest folder.

Don't believe the hype...about databases, that is. Sure, they work wonders for storing all kinds of data involving text, but *what about binary data*? You know, stuff like **JPEG images** and **PDF documents**. Does it really make sense to store all those pictures of your rare guitar pick collection in a database table? Usually not. That kind of data is typically stored in files, and we'll leave it in files. But it's entirely possible to have your virtual cake and eat it too—this chapter reveals that you can **use files and databases together to build PHP applications** that are awash in binary data.

Virtual guitarists like to compete

Apparently creating art for art's sake isn't always enough because players of the hot new game Guitar Wars are quite enamored with competitive virtual guitar playing. So much so that they regularly post their high scores at the Guitar Wars web site, which you are now in charge of maintaining. Problem is, there isn't currently a good way to verify the scores.

The Guitar Wars application allows users to add their own scores to the high score list.

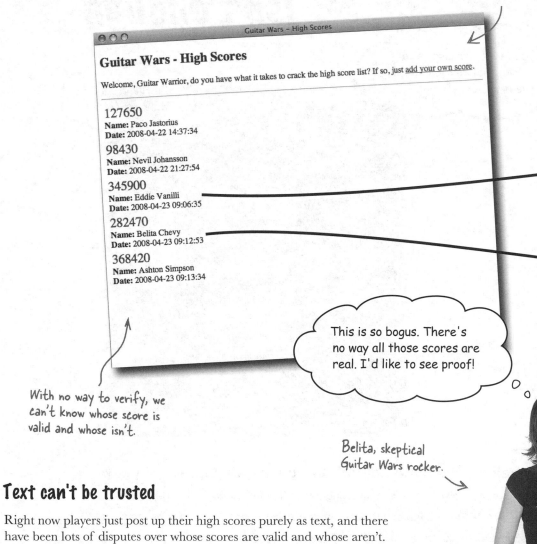

Guitar Wars - High Scores

Welcome, Guitar Warrior, do you have what it takes to crack the high score list? If so, just add your own score.

127650
Name: Paco Jastorius
Date: 2008-04-22 14:37:34

98430
Name: Nevil Johansson
Date: 2008-04-22 21:27:54

345900
Name: Eddie Vanilli
Date: 2008-04-23 09:06:35

282470
Name: Belita Chevy
Date: 2008-04-23 09:12:53

368420
Name: Ashton Simpson
Date: 2008-04-23 09:13:34

With no way to verify, we can't know whose score is valid and whose isn't.

This is so bogus. There's no way all those scores are real. I'd like to see proof!

Belita, skeptical Guitar Wars rocker.

Text can't be trusted

Right now players just post up their high scores purely as text, and there have been lots of disputes over whose scores are valid and whose aren't. There's only one way to put an end to all this bickering and crown a legitimate Guitar Wars champion...

The proof is in the rockin' picture

Visual verification of a high score is what we need to determine who's for real and who isn't. So the Guitar Wars application needs to allow users to submit a screen shot of their high score when posting their score. This means the high score list will not only be a list of scores, names, and dates, but also a list of images (screen shots).

With photo verification, we find out that Eddie is a Guitar Wars fraud!

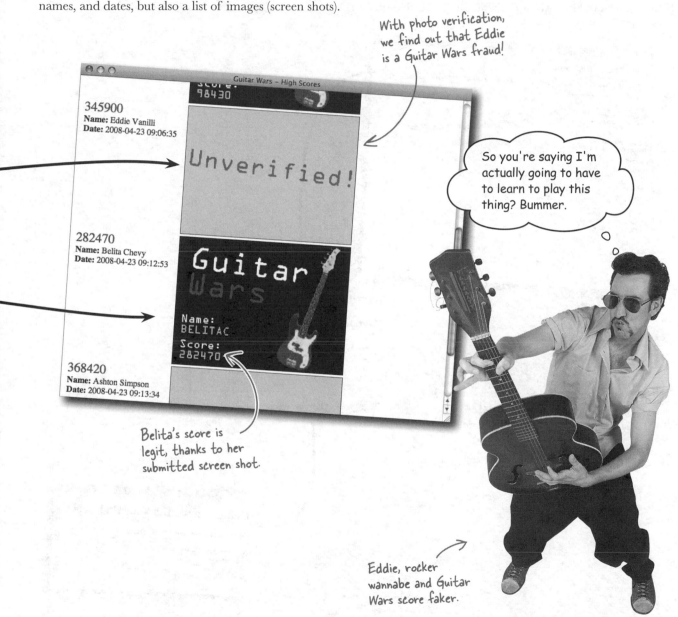

So you're saying I'm actually going to have to learn to play this thing? Bummer.

Belita's score is legit, thanks to her submitted screen shot.

Eddie, rocker wannabe and Guitar Wars score faker.

The application needs to store images

Currently, the Guitar Wars high score application keeps track of three pieces of information: the date and time of a new score, the name of the person submitting the score, and the score itself. This information is entered through a form as part of the application's user interface, after which it gets stored in a MySQL database table called `guitarwars`.

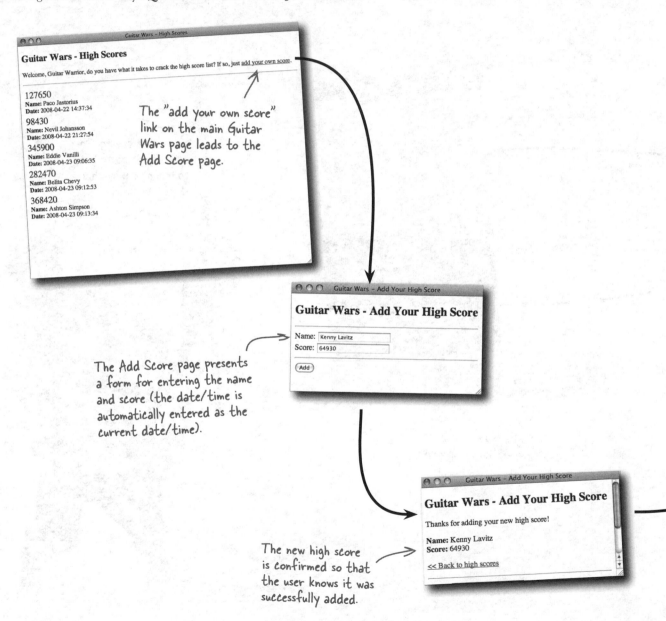

The "add your own score" link on the main Guitar Wars page leads to the Add Score page.

The Add Score page presents a form for entering the name and score (the date/time is automatically entered as the current date/time).

The new high score is confirmed so that the user knows it was successfully added.

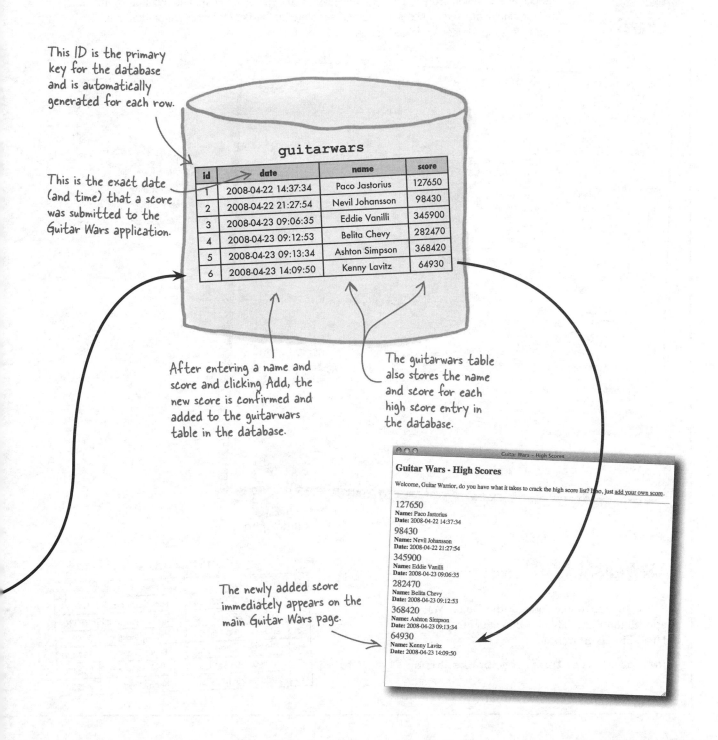

This ID is the primary key for the database and is automatically generated for each row.

This is the exact date (and time) that a score was submitted to the Guitar Wars application.

After entering a name and score and clicking Add, the new score is confirmed and added to the guitarwars table in the database.

The guitarwars table also stores the name and score for each high score entry in the database.

The newly added score immediately appears on the main Guitar Wars page.

Exercise

The Guitar Wars high score application will have to change to accommodate uploadable image files for high score screen shots. Circle and annotate the parts of the application that must change to support user-submitted images.

```html
<html xmlns="http://www.w3.org/1999/xhtml" xml:lang="en" lang="en">
<head>
  <title>Guitar Wars - High Scores</title>
  <link rel="stylesheet" type="text/css" href="style.css" />
</head>
<body>
  <h2>Guitar Wars - High Scores</h2>
  <p>Welcome, Guitar Warrior, do you have what it takes to crack the
  high score list? If so, just <a href="addscore.php">add your own
  score</a>.</p>
  <hr />

<?php
  // Connect to the database
  $dbc = mysqli_connect('www.guitarwars.net', 'admin', 'rockit', 'gwdb');

  // Retrieve the score data from MySQL
  $query = "SELECT * FROM guitarwars";
  $data = mysqli_query($dbc, $query);

  // Loop through the array of score data, formatting it as HTML
  echo '<table>';
  while ($row = mysqli_fetch_array($data)) {
    // Display the score data
    echo '<tr><td class="scoreinfo">';
    echo '<span class="score">' . $row['score'] . '</span><br />';
    echo '<strong>Name:</strong> ' . $row['name'] . '<br />';
    echo '<strong>Date:</strong> ' . $row['date'] . '</td></tr>';
  }
  echo '</table>';

  mysqli_close($dbc);
?>

</body>
</html>
```

style.css

This file doesn't need to change, so you don't have to worry about it.

index.php

Download It!

The complete source code for the Guitar Wars application is available for download from the Head First Labs web site:

www.headfirstlabs.com/books/hfphp

guitarwars

id	date	name	score
1	2008-04-22 14:37:34	Paco Jastorius	127650
2	2008-04-22 21:27:54	Nevil Johansson	98430
3	2008-04-23 09:06:35	Eddie Vanilli	345900
4	2008-04-23 09:12:53	Belita Chevy	282470
5	2008-04-23 09:13:34	Ashton Simpson	368420
6	2008-04-23 14:09:50	Kenny Lavitz	64930

```
<html xmlns="http://www.w3.org/1999/xhtml" xml:lang="en" lang="en">
<head>
  <title>Guitar Wars - Add Your High Score</title>
  <link rel="stylesheet" type="text/css" href="style.css" />
</head>
<body>
  <h2>Guitar Wars - Add Your High Score</h2>

<?php
  if (isset($_POST['submit'])) {
    // Grab the score data from the POST
    $name = $_POST['name'];
    $score = $_POST['score'];

    if (!empty($name) && !empty($score)) {
      // Connect to the database
      $dbc = mysqli_connect('www.guitarwars.net', 'admin', 'rockit', 'gwdb');

      // Write the data to the database
      $query = "INSERT INTO guitarwars VALUES (0, NOW(), '$name', '$score')";
      mysqli_query($dbc, $query);

      // Confirm success with the user
      echo '<p>Thanks for adding your new high score!</p>';
      echo '<p><strong>Name:</strong> ' . $name . '<br />';
      echo '<strong>Score:</strong> ' . $score . '</p>';
      echo '<p><a href="index.php">&lt;&lt; Back to high scores</a></p>';

      // Clear the score data to clear the form
      $name = "";
      $score = "";

      mysqli_close($dbc);
    }
    else {
      echo '<p class="error">Please enter all of the information to add ' .
        'your high score.</p>';
    }

  }
?>

  <hr />
  <form method="post" action="<?php echo $_SERVER['PHP_SELF']; ?>">
    <label for="name">Name:</label><input type="text" id="name" name="name"
      value="<?php if (!empty($name)) echo $name; ?>" /><br />
    <label for="score">Score:</label><input type="text" id="score" name="score"
      value="<?php if (!empty($score)) echo $score; ?>" />
    <hr />
    <input type="submit" value="Add" name="submit" />
  </form>
</body>
</html>
```

addscore.php

Exercise Solution

The Guitar Wars high score application will have to change to accommodate uploadable image files for high score screen shots. Circle and annotate the parts of the application that must change to support user-submitted images.

```html
<html xmlns="http://www.w3.org/1999/xhtml" xml:lang="en" lang="en">
<head>
  <title>Guitar Wars - High Scores</title>
  <link rel="stylesheet" type="text/css" href="style.css" />
</head>
<body>
  <h2>Guitar Wars - High Scores</h2>
  <p>Welcome, Guitar Warrior, do you have what it takes to crack the
  high score list? If so, just <a href="addscore.php">add your own
  score</a>.</p>
  <hr />

<?php
  // Connect to the database
  $dbc = mysqli_connect('www.guitarwars.net', 'admin', 'rockit
  
  // Retrieve the score data from MySQL
  $query = "SELECT * FROM guitarwars";
  $data = mysqli_query($dbc, $query);

  // Loop through the array of score data, formatting it as HT
  echo '<table>';
  while ($row = mysqli_fetch_array($data)) {
    // Display the score data
    echo '<tr><td class="scoreinfo">';
    echo '<span class="score">' . $row['score'] . '</span>
    echo '<strong>Name:</strong> ' . $row['name'] . '<br />
    echo '<strong>Date:</strong> ' . $row['date'] . '</td><
  }
  echo '</table>';

  mysqli_close($dbc);
?>

</body>
</html>
```

The screen shot image needs to be displayed on the main page.

The image should be displayed to the user to confirm success.

guitarwars

id	date	name	score
1	2008-04-22 14:37:34	Paco Jastorius	127650
2	2008-04-22 21:27:54	Nevil Johansson	98430
3	2008-04-23 09:06:35	Eddie Vanilli	345900
4	2008-04-23 09:12:53	Belita Chevy	282470
5	2008-04-23 09:13:34	Ashton Simpson	368420
6	2008-04-23 14:09:50	Kenny Lavitz	64930

The table needs a new column to store the screen shot image filename for each score.

The form needs an <input> tag for the image file selection.

The screen shot image file must be obtained from form POST data.

You should validate to make sure the image filename isn't empty.

```html
<html xmlns="http://www.w3.org/1999/xhtml" xml:lang="en" lang="en">
<head>
  <title>Guitar Wars - Add Your High Score</title>
  <link rel="stylesheet" type="text/css" href="style.css" />
</head>
<body>
  <h2>Guitar Wars - Add Your High Score</h2>

<?php
  if (isset($_POST['submit'])) {
    // Grab the score data from the POST
    $name = $_POST['name'];
    $score = $_POST['score'];

    if (!empty($name) && !empty($score)) {
      // Connect to the database
      $dbc = mysqli_connect('www.guitarwars.net', 'admin', 'rockit', 'gwdb');

      // Write the data to the database
      $query = "INSERT INTO guitarwars VALUES (0, NOW(), '$name', '$score')";
      mysqli_query($dbc, $query);

      // Confirm success with the user
      echo '<p>Thanks for adding your new high score!</p>';
      echo '<p><strong>Name:</strong> ' . $name . '<br />';
      echo '<strong>Score:</strong> ' . $score . '</p>';
      echo '<p><a href="index.php">&lt;&lt; Back to high scores</a></p>';

      // Clear the score data to clear the form
      $name = "";
      $score = "";

      mysqli_close($dbc);
    }
    else {
      echo '<p class="error">Please enter all of the information to add ' .
        'your high score.</p>';
    }
  }
?>

  <hr />
  <form method="post" action="<?php echo $_SERVER['PHP_SELF']; ?>">
    <label for="name">Name:</label><input type="text" id="name" name="name"
      value="<?php if (!empty($name)) echo $name; ?>" /><br />
    <label for="score">Score:</label><input type="text" id="score" name="score"
      value="<?php if (!empty($score)) echo $score; ?>" />
    <hr />
    <input type="submit" value="Add" name="submit" />
  </form>
</body>
</html>
```

The SQL query must now insert the image filename into the guitarwars table.

Upon success, make sure the sticky image form field gets cleared.

This query takes a bit of a shortcut by not specifying column names.

addscore.php

Planning for image file uploads in Guitar Wars

Although it may not seem like a big deal to add support for uploadable screen shot images to Guitar Wars, the application must change in a variety of ways. For this reason, it's a good idea to have a plan of attack before diving into any code. Let's nail down the steps required to revamp the Guitar Wars high scores for screen shots.

① **Use `ALTER` to add a `screenshot` column to the table.**

First off is the database, which needs a new column for storing the name of each screen shot image file. Since we plan on putting all image files in the same folder, all we need to store in the database is the filename itself (no path).

screenshot

② **Change the Add Score form so that it uses a file input field to allow image file uploads.**

The Add Score page already has a form for adding scores, so we need to modify that form and give it a file input field. This input field works in conjunction with the web browser to present the user with a user interface for selecting a file to upload.

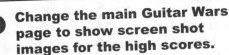

③ **Write a query to `INSERT` the screen shot image filename into the `screenshot` column of the table.**

The Add Score script that processes the form for adding scores must also take into consideration the new file input form field, and handle inserting a screen shot image filename into the `screenshot` column when inserting a new high score row into the `guitarwars` table.

screenshot
phizsscore.gif

④ **Change the main Guitar Wars page to show screen shot images for the high scores.**

Last on the laundry list of changes involves the main `index.php` Guitar Wars page, which must be changed to actually show the screen shot image for each high score that is displayed.

The high score database must be ALTERed

In addition to a variety of PHP scripting tweaks, the image-powered Guitar Wars application needs a new column in the `guitarwars` table to store screen shot image filenames. Enter SQL, which offers a statement called `ALTER` that is capable of modifying tables in all kinds of interesting ways, including adding new columns of data. You used the `ALTER` statement in the previous chapter to tweak Elmer's `email_list` table, but let's recap how the command works.

The ALTER statement is used to change the <u>structure</u> of a database.

The ALTER statement is often followed by TABLE to indicate that you're going to alter a table. It's also possible to alter the structure of the entire database with ALTER DATABASE, but that's another story.

`ALTER TABLE` guitarwars `DROP COLUMN` score

The DROP COLUMN statement drops an entire column from a table.

OK, maybe that's a dangerous example since it reveals how to drop an entire column from a table, data and all. Yet there certainly may be a situation where you need to remove a column of data from a table. It's more likely that you need to add a column of data, as is the case with Guitar Wars. This is made possible by `ADD COLUMN`, which is one of several table alterations you can carry out with `ALTER`.

ADD COLUMN

Adds a new column to a table—just specify the name of the column and its type following `ADD COLUMN`.

```
ALTER TABLE guitarwars
ADD COLUMN age TINYINT
```

DROP COLUMN

Drops a column (and any data stored in it) from a table—just specify the name of the column following `DROP COLUMN`.

```
ALTER TABLE guitarwars
DROP COLUMN age
```

CHANGE COLUMN

Changes the name and data type of a column—just specify the name of the old column, new column, and new data type following `CHANGE COLUMN`.

```
ALTER TABLE guitarwars
CHANGE COLUMN score high_score INT
```

MODIFY COLUMN

Changes the data type or position of a column within a table—just specify the name of the column and its new data type following `MODIFY COLUMN`. To change the position of a column, specify the name of the column and its exact position (`FIRST` is the only option here) or a relative position (`AFTER` another existing column, specified by name).

```
ALTER TABLE guitarwars
MODIFY COLUMN date DATETIME AFTER age
```

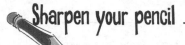 Sharpen your pencil

Write an SQL statement that adds a new column named `screenshot` to the `guitarwars` table. Make sure to give the new column a suitable MySQL data type. Then write another SQL query to check the structure of the table and make sure the column was successfully added.

guitarwars

id	date	name	score	screenshot
1	2008-04-22 14:37:34	Paco Jastorius	127650	
2	2008-04-22 21:27:54	Nevil Johansson	98430	
3	2008-04-23 09:06:35	Eddie Vanilli	345900	
4	2008-04-23 09:12:53	Belita Chevy	282470	
5	2008-04-23 09:13:34	Ashton Simpson	368420	
6	2008-04-23 14:09:50	Kenny Lavitz	64930	

Write the statement that adds a column here.

....

....

Write the other SQL statement here.

....

Sharpen your pencil
Solution

Write an SQL statement that adds a new column named screenshot to the guitarwars table. Make sure to give the new column a suitable MySQL data type. Then write another SQL query to check the structure of the table and make sure the column was successfully added.

The ALTER statement adds a new screenshot column to the guitarwars table.

guitarwars

id	date	name	score	screenshot
1	2008-04-22 14:37:34	Paco Jastorius	127650	
2	2008-04-22 21:27:54	Nevil Johansson	98430	
3	2008-04-23 09:06:35	Eddie Vanilli	345900	
4	2008-04-23 09:12:53	Belita Chevy	282470	
5	2008-04-23 09:13:34	Ashton Simpson	368420	
6	2008-04-23 14:09:50	Kenny Lavitz	64930	

Since the column is new, it starts out empty (NULL) for existing rows in the table.

The name of the table to be altered follows ALTER TABLE.

The ALTER statement doesn't affect any of the other table data.

ALTER TABLE guitarwars

ADD COLUMN screenshot varchar(64)

ADD COLUMN indicates that we want to alter the table by adding a new column of data.

The name and data type of the new column are specified last in the SQL query – 64 characters are enough to accommodate most image filenames, although you can make the column even longer if you want to be extra safe.

DESCRIBE guitarwars

This statement displays the structure of the table, including the column names and their data types.

The first step is done!

DONE

1 Use ALTER **to add a** screenshot **column to the table.**

TEST DRIVE

Add the `screenshot` column to the `guitarwars` table.

Using a MySQL tool, execute the ALTER statement to add the `screenshot` column to the `guitarwars` table. Then issue the DESCRIBE statement to take a look at the table structure and make sure the column was added.

You can construct the initial guitarwars table by downloading the example code for Guitar Wars, and then executing the SQL query found in the file guitarwars.sql.

Issuing the DESCRIBE statement reveals the new screenshot column.

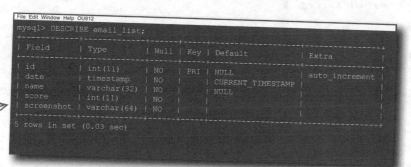

```
File Edit Window Help OU812
mysql> DESCRIBE email_list;
+------------+-------------+------+-----+-------------------+----------------+
| Field      | Type        | Null | Key | Default           | Extra          |
+------------+-------------+------+-----+-------------------+----------------+
| id         | int(11)     | NO   | PRI | NULL              | auto_increment |
| date       | timestamp   | NO   |     | CURRENT_TIMESTAMP |                |
| name       | varchar(32) | NO   |     | NULL              |                |
| score      | int(11)     | NO   |     |                   |                |
| screenshot | varchar(64) | NO   |     |                   |                |
+------------+-------------+------+-----+-------------------+----------------+
5 rows in set (0.03 sec)
```

there are no Dumb Questions

Q: Do new columns added with ALTER have to be added to the end of a database table?

A: No, they can be added anywhere. But keep in mind that the order of the columns in a table isn't terribly important. In other words, you can structure query results so that data is organized in any order you want. But maybe you like the sense of structural order brought about by a specific ordering of columns, in which case you may want to add a column in an exact location. You can do this by tacking on the keyword FIRST to the ALTER query. Or use AFTER *column* to place a column relative to another column:

```
ALTER TABLE guitarwars
ADD COLUMN age TINYINT AFTER name
```

If you don't specify where a new column is added, it defaults to the end of the table.

Q: What happens to the existing high score database rows of data after adding the new `screenshot` column?

A: Since the ALTER statement only affects the structure of a database, the new `screenshot` column is empty for all pre-existing rows of high scores. While it's possible to populate the `screenshot` column of future rows, pre-existing rows all have an empty `screenshot` column.

Q: Can screen shot filenames still be added to the pre-existing rows?

A: Yes, they definitely can, and you would use the UPDATE SQL statement to do so. There is nothing stopping you from manually uploading image files to the web server and then using UPDATE to fill in the screen shot filenames for existing scores. But remember that the whole idea here is user-submitted image files, so it makes sense to allow users to upload their own screen shot images. And they can do exactly this by using the improved image-powered Add Score script you're about to build...

How do we get an image from the user?

With a new column added to the high score database, we're ready to focus on allowing the user to upload an image file. But how exactly is that possible? FTP? Mental telepathy? This actually leads back to the Add Score form, where we can use a form field to allow the user to select an image file to upload.

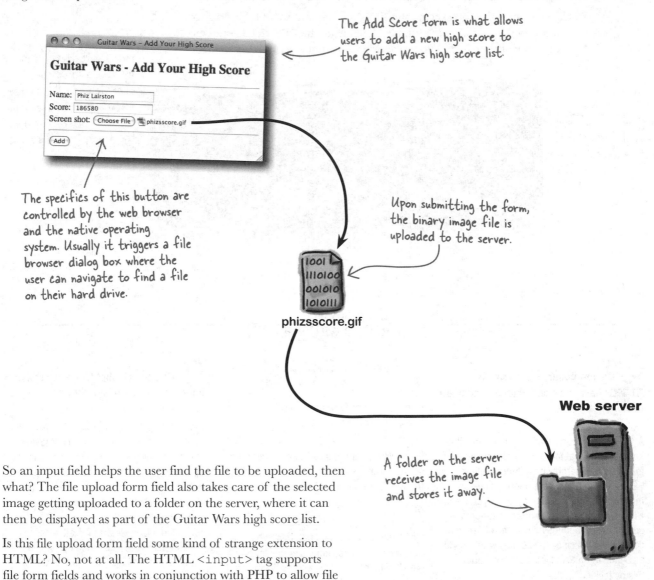

The Add Score form is what allows users to add a new high score to the Guitar Wars high score list.

The specifics of this button are controlled by the web browser and the native operating system. Usually it triggers a file browser dialog box where the user can navigate to find a file on their hard drive.

Upon submitting the form, the binary image file is uploaded to the server.

phizsscore.gif

Web server

A folder on the server receives the image file and stores it away.

So an input field helps the user find the file to be uploaded, then what? The file upload form field also takes care of the selected image getting uploaded to a folder on the server, where it can then be displayed as part of the Guitar Wars high score list.

Is this file upload form field some kind of strange extension to HTML? No, not at all. The HTML `<input>` tag supports file form fields and works in conjunction with PHP to allow file uploads. But before we get into the PHP side of things, let's take a closer look at the form field itself...

 The Add Score Form Up Close

This form attribute tells the form to use a special type of encoding required for file uploading — it affects how the POST data is bundled and sent when the form is submitted.

Establishes a maximum file size for file uploads, in this case 32 KB (32,768 bytes).

This is a self-referencing form.

```
<form enctype="multipart/form-data" method="post" action="<?php echo $_SERVER['PHP_SELF']; ?>">
    <input type="hidden" name="MAX_FILE_SIZE" value="32768" />

    <label for="name">Name:</label>

    <input type="text" id="name" name="name" value="<?php if (!empty($name)) echo $name; ?>" />

    <br />

    <label for="score">Score:</label>

    <input type="text" id="score" name="score" value="<?php if (!empty($score)) echo $score; ?>" />

    <br />

    <label for="screenshot">Screen shot:</label>

    <input type="file" id="screenshot" name="screenshot" />

    <hr />

    <input type="submit" value="Add" name="submit" />
</form>
```

The actual file input field, which ultimately relies on a native operating system dialog for file browsing and selection.

~~DONE~~

2 **Change the Add Score form so that it uses a file input field to allow image file uploads.**

filename

Insert the image into the database

Simply uploading an image file to the web server via a form isn't enough. We have to store the filename in the new `screenshot` column of the database so that the image can be accessed and displayed. As it stands, the Add Score script already inserts new high scores into the `guitarwars` table using the SQL `INSERT` statement, but this statement doesn't factor in the new `screenshot` column:

Image filenames are stored in the database as part of an INSERT statement.

The MySQL NOW() function is used to insert the current date/time.

```
INSERT INTO guitarwars VALUES (0, NOW(), '$name', '$score')
```

The id column gets set automatically via AUTO_INCREMENT — the 0 is ignored, although the query does require a value here.

Since this SQL statement is inserting values without identifying the column names for each, it must include a value for every column. But we just added a new column, which means the query no longer works—it's missing a value for the new `screenshot` column. So adding a screen shot image filename to the database as part of a new high score row requires us to add a new value to the `INSERT` statement:

Passing the screenshot image filename along in the INSERT statement adds it to the database.

```
INSERT INTO guitarwars VALUES (0, NOW(), '$name', '$score', '$screenshot')
```

Rows of data inserted prior to the addition of the screenshot column don't have a screenshot filename.

The order of these values matters since the INSERT statement is assuming they are in the same order as the columns in the table.

guitarwars

id	date	name	score	screenshot
1	2008-04-22 14:37:34	Paco Jastorius	127650	
2	2008-04-22 21:27:54	Nevil Johansson	98430	
3	2008-04-23 09:06:35	Eddie Vanilli	345900	
4	2008-04-23 09:12:53	Belita Chevy	282470	
5	2008-04-23 09:13:34	Ashton Simpson	368420	
6	2008-04-23 14:09:50	Kenny Lavitz	64930	
7	2008-04-24 08:13:52	Phiz Lairston	186580	phizsscore.gif

The new INSERT statement results in the screenshot filename getting inserted into the screenshot column.

DONE

3 Write a query to `INSERT` **the screen shot image filename into the** `screenshot` **column of the table.**

Find out the name of the uploaded file

The query looks good, but we still don't know what the actual filename of the image is. It's fair to assume that the file input field in the form somehow provides access to the filename, but how? The answer lies in a built-in PHP superglobal variable named `$_FILES`, which is similar to the `$_POST` superglobal we've used to access form data. Like `$_POST`, `$_FILES` is an array, and within it is not only the name of the uploaded file, but also some other information about the file that might prove useful.

```
<input type="file" name="screenshot" />
```

The form passes some useful information about the file to the PHP script via the $_FILES superglobal variable.

`$_FILES['screenshot']['name']`

`phizsscore.gif`

The name of the uploaded file.

`$_FILES['screenshot']['type']`

`image/gif`

The MIME type of the uploaded file, in this case GIF.

phizsscore.gif

This is the image file being uploaded thanks to the file input field in the form.

`$_FILES['screenshot']['size']`

`12244`

The size (in bytes) of the uploaded file.

`$_FILES['screenshot']['tmp_name']`

`/tmp/phpE7qJky`

The temporary storage location of the file on the server.

The `$_FILES` built-in superglobal variable provides access to information about uploaded files.

`$_FILES['screenshot']['error']`

`0`

The error code for the file upload; 0 indicates a success, other values indicate failure.

The other information made available in the `$_FILES` variable is certainly useful, but right this moment, we just need the name of the image, which can be stored away in a local variable (`$screenshot`) and used in the SQL INSERT statement.

```
$screenshot = $_FILES['screenshot']['name'];
```

Data stored in external files is typically left in external files, even in database applications.

In this case, the data is a collection of pixels that make up an image, which is stored in an external file—a GIF, JPEG, or PNG image file. Databases excel at storing text data, not raw binary data such as images, so it's better to just store a **reference** to an image in the database. This reference is the name of the image file.

Another reason images in web applications aren't stored in databases is because it would be much harder to display them using HTML code. Remember that HTML code references images from external files using filenames. So generating an image tag in HTML involves using an image filename, not raw image data.

```
<img src="phizsscore.jpg" alt="Score image" />
```

Placing an image on a web page only requires a <u>reference</u> to the image file.

The image filename

The HTML <img> tag uses the filename of an image to reference the image file on the web server.

phizsscore.gif

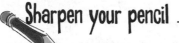

Sharpen your pencil

The main Guitar Wars page (`index.php`) still isn't displaying screen shot images for the high scores. Finish the code so that it shows the images.

```php
<?php
 // Connect to the database
 $dbc = mysqli_connect('www.guitarwars.net', 'admin', 'rockit', 'gwdb');


 // Retrieve the score data from MySQL
 $query = ...............................;
 $data = mysqli_query($dbc, $query);


 // Loop through the array of score data, formatting it as HTML
 echo '<table>';
 while ($row = mysqli_fetch_array($data)) {
  // Display the score data
  echo '<tr><td class="scoreinfo">';
  echo '<span class="score">' . $row['score'] . '</span><br />';
  echo '<strong>Name:</strong> ' . $row['name'] . '<br />';
  echo '<strong>Date:</strong> ' . $row['date'] . '</td>';
  if (is_file(....................) && filesize(....................) > 0) {
   echo '<td><img src="' . .................... . '" alt="Score image" /></td></tr>';
  }
  else {
   echo '<td><img src="unverified.gif" alt="Unverified score" /></td></tr>';
  }
 }
 echo '</table>';


 mysqli_close($dbc);
?>
```

Sharpen your pencil
Solution

The main Guitar Wars page (`index.php`) still isn't displaying screen shot images for the high scores. Finish the code so that it shows the images.

In a move to help simplify the code, we're not using "or die()" to produce error messages and exit the script when a mysqli function fails. You may want to continue including this code in your own applications but we're going to skip it from here on for the sake of brevity.

```php
<?php
  // Connect to the database
  $dbc = mysqli_connect('www.guitarwars.net', 'admin', 'rockit', 'gwdb');
```

The SQL statement that requests scores doesn't change at all!

```php
  // Retrieve the score data from MySQL
  $query = "SELECT * FROM guitarwars";
  $data = mysqli_query($dbc, $query);


  // Loop through the array of score data, formatting it as HTML
  echo '<table>';
  while ($row = mysqli_fetch_array($data)) {
    // Display the score data
    echo '<tr><td class="scoreinfo">';
    echo '<span class="score">' . $row['score'] . '</span><br />';
    echo '<strong>Name:</strong> ' . $row['name'] . '<br />';
    echo '<strong>Date:</strong> ' . $row['date'] . '</td>';
    if (is_file( $row['screenshot'] ) && filesize( $row["screenshot"] ) > 0) {
      echo '<td><img src="' . $row['screenshot'] . '" alt="Score image" /></td></tr>';
    }
    else {
      echo '<td><img src="unverified.gif" alt="Unverified score" /></td></tr>';
    }
  }
  echo '</table>';


  mysqli_close($dbc);
?>
```

This function checks to make sure the screen shot image file isn't an empty file.

This function checks to see if a screen shot image file actually exists.

The screenshot column of the database stores the screen shot image for a given score.

4. **Change the main Guitar Wars page to show screen shot images for the high scores.** ~~DONE~~

Test Drive

**Add a new high score to Guitar Wars, complete with a
screen shot image.**

If you haven't already done so, download the Guitar Wars example code from the
Head First Labs web site at **www.headfirstlabs.com/books/hfphp**. It's
in the **chapter05** folder. The code consists of the main page (**index.php**), the
Add Score script (**addscore.php**), and a style sheet (**style.css**).

First you need to change the addscore.php script so that its Add Score form
supports file uploads. This includes adding new form fields, adjusting the <form>
tag, and checking to make sure the $screenshot variable isn't empty. Then
incorporate the new high score INSERT query into the script.

Now shift to the index.php script, and add the new code from the facing page
so that it displays the screen shot image for each high score.

Upload all of these files to your web server and open the addscore.php page
in a web browser. Enter a new high score in the form, and click Submit. Then
navigate to the index.php page and take a look at the new score.

*Something isn't right! The
image doesn't appear with
the new score as expected.*

BRAIN POWER

Why do you think the screen shot image doesn't
show up for the new score? What about for the
scores that were already in the database?

Where did the uploaded file go?

The problem with the uploaded image not appearing is that we made an assumption that the file would be uploaded to the same folder on the web server as our PHP scripts. As it turns out, this assumption is dead wrong. The Add Score form lets the user select a file from their own computer, but the file is actually uploaded to a **temporary folder** on the server. The temporary folder is created automatically on the server and usually has a weird name with a bunch of random letters and numbers.

This presents a problem for our <img> code in index.php because it assumes the image is located in the main web folder:

```
<img src="phizsscore.jpg" alt="Score image" />
```

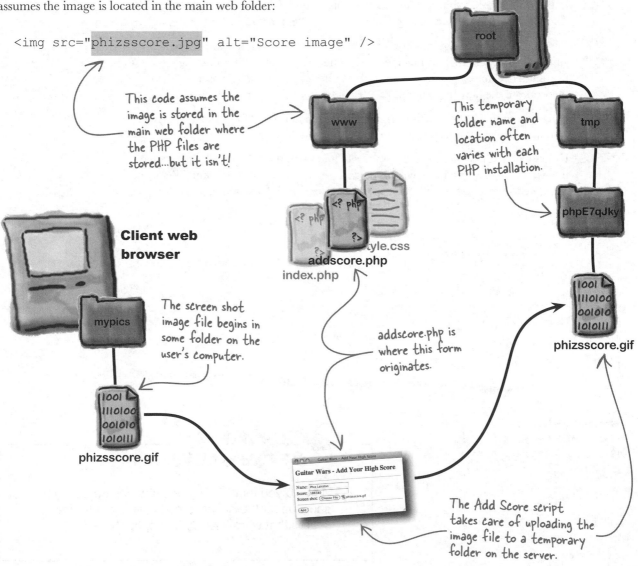

This code assumes the image is stored in the main web folder where the PHP files are stored...but it isn't!

Web server

root

This temporary folder name and location often varies with each PHP installation.

tmp

www

phpE7qJky

<? php
<? php
?>
style.css
addscore.php
index.php

Client web browser

mypics

The screen shot image file begins in some folder on the user's computer.

addscore.php is where this form originates.

1001
1110100
001010
1010111
phizsscore.gif

1001
1110100
001010
1010111
phizsscore.gif

Guitar Wars – Add Your High Score

Guitar Wars - Add Your High Score

Name: Phiz Lairston
Score: 186580
Screen shot: (Choose File) phizsscore.gif

(Add)

The Add Score script takes care of uploading the image file to a temporary folder on the server.

244

> Storing images in a cryptic temporary folder seems like an unnecessary hassle. Can we control where the uploaded files are stored?

Yes! PHP lets you control where uploaded files are stored.

However, you can't control the **initial** storage location of uploaded files with PHP, which is why the location is considered temporary. But you can move a file to another location after it has been uploaded. The PHP function move_uploaded_file() accepts the source and destination locations for a file, and then takes care of the moving:

```
move_uploaded_file($_FILES['screenshot']['tmp_name'], $target);
```

This is the source location of the image file, including the temporary path and filename.

This is the destination location of the image file, including the permanent path and filename.

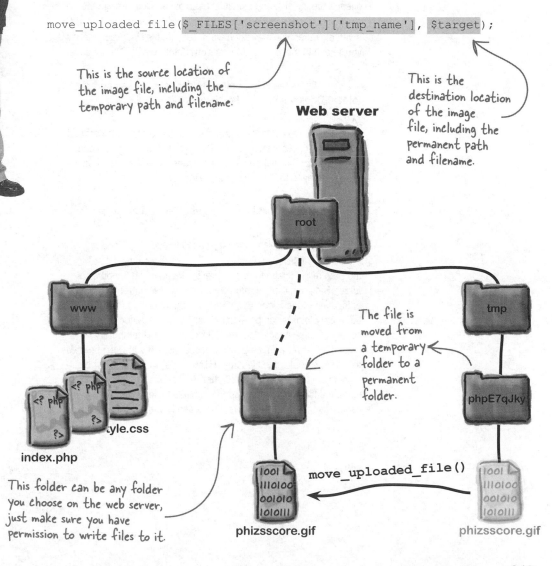

Web server

root

www

tmp

The file is moved from a temporary folder to a permanent folder.

index.php

<? php

<? php ?>

?>

tyle.css

phpE7qJky

This folder can be any folder you choose on the web server, just make sure you have permission to write files to it.

1001 1110100 001010 1010111

move_uploaded_file()

1001 1110100 001010 1010111

phizsscore.gif

phizsscore.gif

there are no
Dumb Questions

Q: Can't I change the initial storage location of uploaded files by modifying the `php.ini` file?

A: Yes. The PHP initialization file (php.ini) can be used to change the initial storage location of uploaded files through the `upload_tmp_dir` option. But if your application is hosted on a virtual server, you may not have access to this file, which means you'll have to move the file to your own folder via PHP script code.

Q: Why is the initial upload folder called a "temporary" folder? Does it go away after a file is moved?

A: No. The folder is "temporary" in a sense that it isn't intended to serve as the final storage location for uploaded files. You can think of it as a holding area where uploaded files are stored until they are moved to their final storage location.

Q: Why can't I just leave a file in the temporary folder?

A: You can, in which case you'd need to add `$_FILES['screenshot']['tmp_name']` to the path of the image to make sure it is found in the temporary folder. But keep in mind that you don't typically control the name or location of the folder. Even more important is the fact that temporary folders can be automatically emptied periodically on some systems. Another potential issue is that the temporary upload folder may not be publicly accessible, so you won't be able to reference uploaded files from HTML code, which is the whole point in Guitar Wars and most other PHP applications. By moving uploaded files out of the temporary upload folder, you can carefully control exactly where they are stored and how they are accessed.

OK, so now I know how to move uploaded files around. That's really special. But I still don't have a clue where they are supposed to go.

Every application needs an `images` folder.

OK, maybe "need" is a bit strong, but it's important to organize the pieces and parts of PHP applications as much as possible, and one way to do so is to create folders for different components. Since uploaded images are submitted by users, they aren't something you typically have direct control over, at least in terms of filenames and quantity. So it's a good idea to store them separately from other application files.

All this said, we need an `images` folder, where image files that are uploaded to the Guitar Wars application are stored. This folder can also serve as the storage location for any other images the application may use, should the need arise.

The images folder isn't actually any bigger than other folders, but it helps organize image files into one place.

Create a home for uploaded image files

The `images` folder is just like any other folder on the web server except that it must be placed somewhere beneath the main web folder for the application. It's usually fine to just place the folder directly beneath this web folder, but you're free to create a more complex folder hierarchy if you want.

With the `images` folder created immediately beneath the main web folder on the web server, it becomes possible to reference image files from within PHP scripts like this:

The image filename is concatenated to the path.

```
$target = GW_UPLOADPATH . $screenshot;
```

`images/phizsscore.gif`

The `$target` path is built out of a new constant we're going to add to the script called `GW_UPLOADPATH`, which holds the path to our `images` folder. Like a variable, a **constant** stores a piece of data. But the value of a constant can't change once it's set. The image filename as entered into the Add Score form is then concatenated to the `images` path.

This is the web folder for the application where the PHP scripts are stored, including index.php.

Web server

root

www

The images folder is typically placed just beneath the web folder.

tmp

images

phpE7qJky

`<? php` `<? php` score.php
index.php

Uploaded image files are moved to the images folder, where they can be displayed via HTML <img> tags.

1001 1110100 001010 1010111
phizsscore.gif

1001 1110100 001010 1010111
phizsscore.gif

```
move_uploaded_file(
    $_FILES['screenshot']['tmp_name'],
    $target);
```

Watch it!

If your PHP application is hosted anywhere other than your local computer, you'll need to use FTP to create the `images` folder.

Use an FTP program to access the file system of your web site and create the `images` folder beneath the web folder of the application.

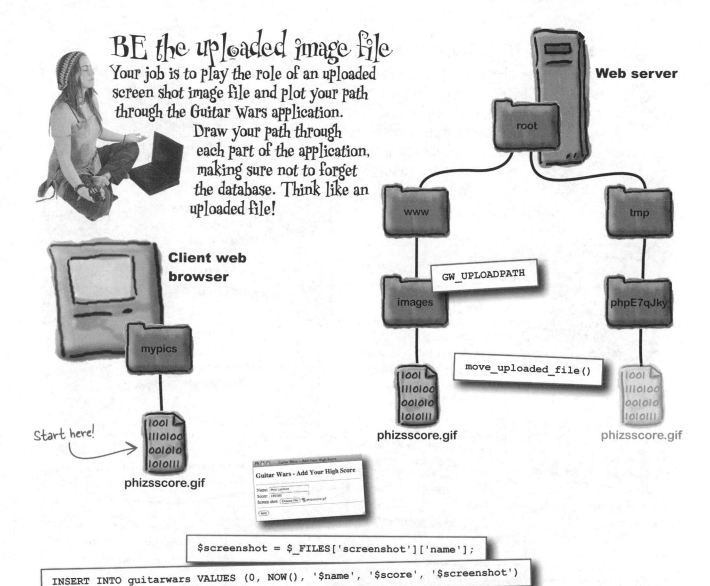

BE the uploaded image file
Your job is to play the role of an uploaded screen shot image file and plot your path through the Guitar Wars application. Draw your path through each part of the application, making sure not to forget the database. Think like an uploaded file!

Web server

root

www

tmp

Client web browser

images

`GW_UPLOADPATH`

phpE7qJky

mypics

`move_uploaded_file()`

Start here!

phizsscore.gif

phizsscore.gif

phizsscore.gif

Guitar Wars – Add Your High Score

Guitar Wars - Add Your High Score
Name: Phiz Lairston
Score: 186580
Screen shot: Choose File phizsscore.gif
Add

```
$screenshot = $_FILES['screenshot']['name'];
```

```
INSERT INTO guitarwars VALUES (0, NOW(), '$name', '$score', '$screenshot')
```

guitarwars

id	date	name	score	screenshot
1	2008-04-22 14:37:34	Paco Jastorius	127650	
2	2008-04-22 21:27:54	Nevil Johansson	98430	
3	2008-04-23 09:06:35	Eddie Vanilli	345900	
4	2008-04-23 09:12:53	Belita Chevy	282470	
5	2008-04-23 09:13:34	Ashton Simpson	368420	
6	2008-04-23 14:09:50	Kenny Lavitz	64930	
7	2008-04-24 08:13:52	Phiz Lairston	186580	phizsscore.gif

BE the uploaded image file solution

Your job is to play the role of an uploaded screen shot image file and plot your path through the Guitar Wars application.
Draw your path through each part of the application, making sure not to forget the database. Think like an uploaded file!

Web server

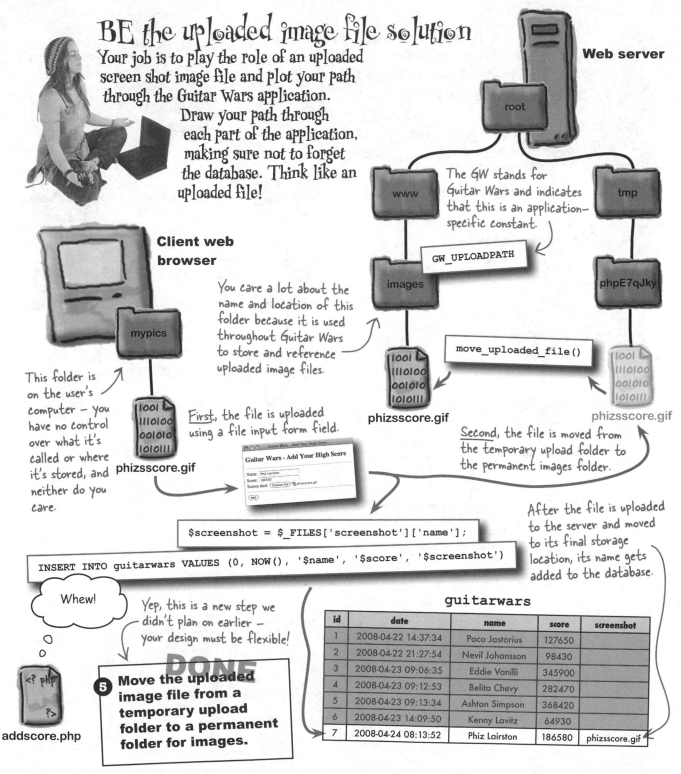

The GW stands for Guitar Wars and indicates that this is an application-specific constant.

`GW_UPLOADPATH`

Client web browser

You care a lot about the name and location of this folder because it is used throughout Guitar Wars to store and reference uploaded image files.

`move_uploaded_file()`

This folder is on the user's computer — you have no control over what it's called or where it's stored, and neither do you care.

phizsscore.gif

First, the file is uploaded using a file input form field.

phizsscore.gif

phizsscore.gif

Second, the file is moved from the temporary upload folder to the permanent images folder.

After the file is uploaded to the server and moved to its final storage location, its name gets added to the database.

`$screenshot = $_FILES['screenshot']['name'];`

`INSERT INTO guitarwars VALUES (0, NOW(), '$name', '$score', '$screenshot')`

Whew!

Yep, this is a new step we didn't plan on earlier — your design must be flexible!

DONE

⑤ **Move the uploaded image file from a temporary upload folder to a permanent folder for images.**

addscore.php

guitarwars

id	date	name	score	screenshot
1	2008-04-22 14:37:34	Paco Jastorius	127650	
2	2008-04-22 21:27:54	Nevil Johansson	98430	
3	2008-04-23 09:06:35	Eddie Vanilli	345900	
4	2008-04-23 09:12:53	Belita Chevy	282470	
5	2008-04-23 09:13:34	Ashton Simpson	368420	
6	2008-04-23 14:09:50	Kenny Lavitz	64930	
7	2008-04-24 08:13:52	Phiz Lairston	186580	phizsscore.gif

TEST DRIVE

Give uploaded screen shot images a permanent home in their own image folder.

Modify the `addscore.php` script to use the `GW_UPLOADPATH` constant and store uploaded screen shot images in the path it points to. Here's a peek at the code that needs to change:

```php
<?php
  // Define the upload path and maximum file size constants
  define('GW_UPLOADPATH', 'images/');

  if (isset($_POST['submit'])) {
    // Grab the score data from the POST
    $name = $_POST['name'];
    $score = $_POST['score'];
    $screenshot = $_FILES['screenshot']['name'];

    if (!empty($name) && !empty($score) && !empty($screenshot)) {
      // Move the file to the target upload folder
      $target = GW_UPLOADPATH . $screenshot;
      if (move_uploaded_file($_FILES['screenshot']['tmp_name'], $target)) {
        // Connect to the database
        $dbc = mysqli_connect('www.guitarwars.net', 'admin', 'rockit', 'gwdb');

        // Write the data to the database
        $query = "INSERT INTO guitarwars VALUES (0, NOW(), '$name', '$score', '$screenshot')";
        mysqli_query($dbc, $query);

        // Confirm success with the user
        echo '<p>Thanks for adding your new high score!</p>';
        echo '<p><strong>Name:</strong> ' . $name . '<br />';
        echo '<strong>Score:</strong> ' . $score . '<br />';
        echo '<img src="' . GW_UPLOADPATH . $screenshot . '" alt="Score image" /></p>';
        echo '<p><a href="index.php">&lt;&lt; Back to high scores</a></p>';
```

addscore.php

The `index.php` script is also affected by the `GW_UPLOADPATH` constant. Don't forget to change it as well. After making these changes, upload the scripts to your server and try adding a high score again.

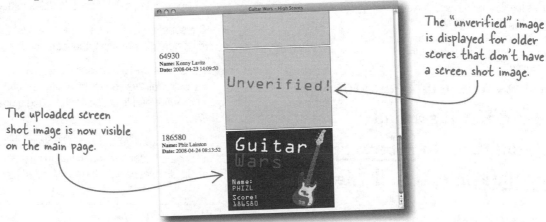

The uploaded screen shot image is now visible on the main page.

The "unverified" image is displayed for older scores that don't have a screen shot image.

Q: If the `php.ini` file can be used to control the storage location of uploaded files, why is it necessary to move the file?

A: Because it isn't always possible to change php.ini. For example, if you're building a PHP application on a virtual web server, you very likely won't be able to change the settings in php.ini. And even if you are able to change php.ini, you run the risk of breaking your application if you ever need to move it to another server. In other words, the application will be dependent on a path controlled by php.ini, as opposed to a path controlled by your own PHP code.

Q: Why isn't the date something that users can enter in Guitar Wars?

A: The date is an important part of a high score in that it establishes when a score was officially posted to the site. Like any record, the first person to achieve a certain score gets all the glory. Rather than trust a user to tell us when they achieved their high score, we can just use the post date/time as the official recording of the score. This eliminates bogus dates and lends more credibility to the high score list. Users of such a competitive application will always be looking for an angle, so eliminate as many of them as you can!

It is worth pointing out that the NOW() function uses the time on the web server, which may not be the same as the user's local time. This shouldn't be a problem, however, since all users are held to that same server time.

Databases are great for storing text data, but it's usually better for them to reference binary data in external files.

Q: Isn't it possible for people to overwrite each other's screen shot images by uploading image files with the same names?

A: Yes. The problem has to do with the fact that the screen shot image stored on the web server uses the exact same filename provided by the user in the file upload form field. So if two users upload image files with the same filenames, the first user's image will get overwritten by the second user's image. Not good. One solution is to add a degree of uniqueness to the image filename on the server. A simple way to do this is to add the current server time, in seconds, to the front of the filename, like this:

```
$target = GW_UPLOADPATH . time() .
  $screenshot;
```

The result of this code is a filename of 1221634560phizsscore.gif instead of phizsscore.gif, where 1221634560 is the current time on the server expressed in seconds.

Q: Could we have stored the actual image data for an uploaded high score screen shot in the Guitar Wars database?

A: Yes. Databases are very flexible and allow you to store binary data within them. However, the big problem in this case is that Guitar Wars uses the uploaded images in HTML code so that they can be displayed on the main index.php page. The HTML `<img>` tag is designed to reference an image file stored on the web server, not a chunk of binary image data stored in a database. So even if you altered the `guitarwars` table to hold binary image data, you'd be facing a significant challenge trying to get the data back into a format that can be displayed using HTML code.

There's nothing terribly special about the time returned by the time() function other than the fact that it sources unique numbers...the number it returns is always growing!

BULLET POINTS

- The ALTER statement is used to change the structure of a MySQL database table, such as adding a new column of data.

- With a little help from PHP and MySQL, an HTML `<input>` tag can be used to upload image files.

- The superglobal variable `$_FILES` is where PHP stores information about an uploaded file.

- The standard PHP function `move_uploaded_file()` allows you to move files around on the web server and is critical for handling uploaded files.

- Most web applications benefit from having an `images` folder for storing images used by the application, especially those uploaded by users.

I like that the file upload path is stored in a constant, but why is it created in two places, index.php and addscore.php? What happens if the path changes?

The GW_UPLOADPATH constant stores away the file upload path for screen shot images.

```php
define('GW_UPLOADPATH', 'images/');
```

define() is used to create constants.

The name of the constant

The value of the constant, which can never change...it's constant!

So within each of the index.php and addscore.php scripts, the GW_UPLOADPATH constant works great. But the constant is duplicated in each script, meaning that any change in the path must be updated in each script. This kind of code duplication is bad design and should be eliminated whenever possible.

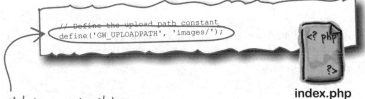

```php
// Define the upload path constant
define('GW_UPLOADPATH', 'images/');
```

index.php

The constant is stored twice, meaning it has to be maintained in two different places.

To solve the duplicate code problem, we need to store the GW_UPLOADPATH constant in a single place. Would you store it in index.php or addscore.php? Why?

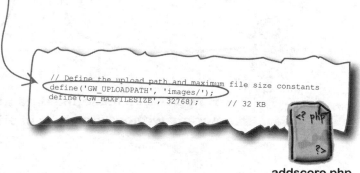

```php
// Define the upload path and maximum file size constants
define('GW_UPLOADPATH', 'images/');
define('GW_MAXFILESIZE', 32768);    // 32 KB
```

addscore.php

Shared data has to be shared

When it comes to data that is shared across multiple scripts in an application, you need a way to store the data in one place and then pull it into the different scripts. But that still doesn't answer the question of where exactly the data should go...?

Shared script data needs to be accessible throughout an application without code duplication.

You could store the data only in `index.php`...

```
// Define the upload path constant
define('GW_UPLOADPATH', 'images/');
```

index.php

...but then other scripts wouldn't have access to it.

Dude, where's my data?

So storing shared script data in an existing script file doesn't really work because the data isn't really shared any more. The answer lies in somehow making the data accessible to multiple scripts but without directly storing it in any of them.

addscore.php

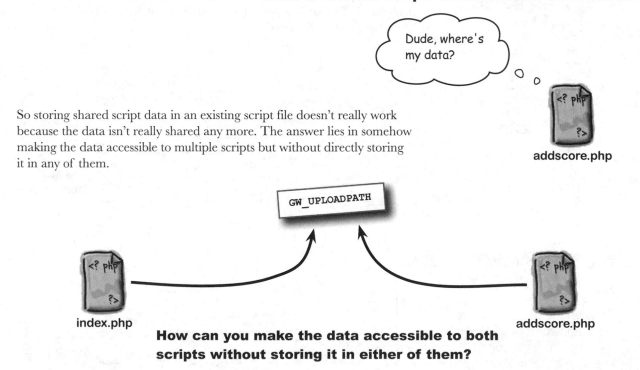

GW_UPLOADPATH

index.php

addscore.php

How can you make the data accessible to both scripts without storing it in either of them?

The solution to shared script data lies in **include files**, which are PHP source code files that are inserted into other PHP files as needed.

Shared script data is required

Include files are very powerful because you create them once but then reuse them as needed in other script files, effectively sharing the code within. The GW_UPLOADPATH constant can be placed within an include file to establish a collection of "application variables."

> Include files allow you to share code across multiple scripts.

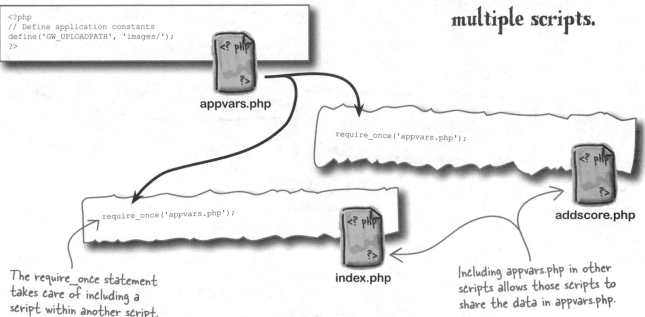

```php
<?php
// Define application constants
define('GW_UPLOADPATH', 'images/');
?>
```

appvars.php

```php
require_once('appvars.php');
```

```php
require_once('appvars.php');
```

index.php

addscore.php

The require_once statement takes care of including a script within another script.

Including appvars.php in other scripts allows those scripts to share the data in appvars.php.

there are no Dumb Questions

Q: Hey, aren't these application "variables" really constants?

A: Sometimes, yes. But that's OK. The point is not to split hairs over variables vs. constants. Instead, we're just trying to establish a common place to store shared script data within a given application. And that place is a script file called appvars.php.

Q: Is code in shared script files limited to data?

A: No, not at all. Any PHP code can be placed in its own script file and shared using the require_once statement. In fact, it's very common for applications to share lots of functional code across multiple script files. Not only is it common to use shared script files, but it's often a great idea in terms of code organization.

Q: Why is the PHP statement to include script code called require_once?

A: The name "include file" comes from a PHP statement called include that is very similar to require_once. The difference is that require_once results in an error if the include file cannot be found—include won't reveal an error if an include file is missing. Also, the "once" in require_once means that it keeps a file from being accidentally included more than **once**. You sometimes see include used instead of require_once to include code that isn't as important, such as pure HTML code that doesn't perform a critical purpose. PHP also has include_once and require statements that are variations on require_once and include.

Think of `require_once` as "insert"

Includes aren't limited to one shared PHP file, and they can appear anywhere you want within a script. You can think of the `require_once` statement as an "insert" statement that gets replaced with the contents of the script file it references. In the case of Guitar Wars, the database connection variables could also benefit from being moved into an include file. So the contents of two shared script files are inserted directly into other script files at the points where they are `required`.

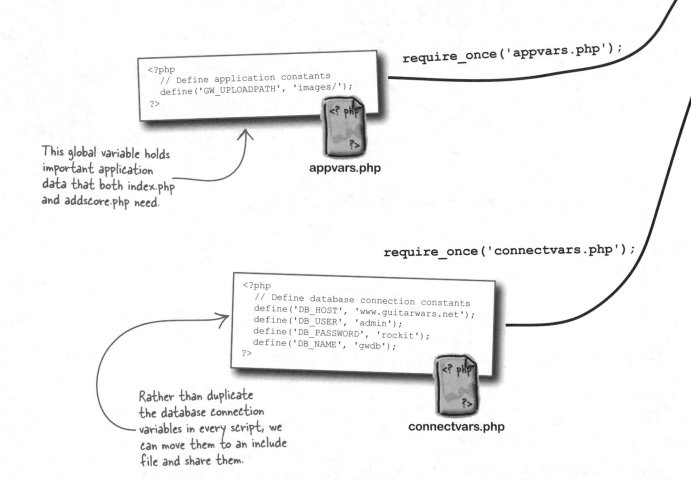

```php
<?php
  // Define application constants
  define('GW_UPLOADPATH', 'images/');
?>
```

appvars.php

`require_once('appvars.php');`

This global variable holds important application data that both index.php and addscore.php need.

```php
<?php
  // Define database connection constants
  define('DB_HOST', 'www.guitarwars.net');
  define('DB_USER', 'admin');
  define('DB_PASSWORD', 'rockit');
  define('DB_NAME', 'gwdb');
?>
```

connectvars.php

`require_once('connectvars.php');`

Rather than duplicate the database connection variables in every script, we can move them to an include file and share them.

The REQUIRE_ONCE statement inserts shared script code into other scripts.

```php
<?php
// Define application constants
define('GW_UPLOADPATH', 'images/');

// Define database connection constants
define('DB_HOST', 'www.guitarwars.net');
define('DB_USER', 'admin');
define('DB_PASSWORD', 'rockit');
define('DB_NAME', 'gwdb');

// Connect to the database
$dbc = mysqli_connect(DB_HOST, DB_USER, DB_PASSWORD, DB_NAME);

// Retrieve the score data from MySQL
$query = "SELECT * FROM guitarwars";
$data = mysqli_query($dbc, $query);

// Loop through the array of score data, formatting it as HTML
echo '<table>';
while ($row = mysqli_fetch_array($data)) {
  // Display the score data
  echo '<tr><td class="scoreinfo">';
  echo '<span class="score">' . $row['score'] . '</span><br />';
  echo '<strong>Name:</strong> ' . $row['name'] . '<br />';
  echo '<strong>Date:</strong> ' . $row['date'] . '</td>';
  if (is_file(GW_UPLOADPATH . $row['screenshot']) &&
    filesize(GW_UPLOADPATH . $row['screenshot']) > 0) {
    echo '<td><img src="' . GW_UPLOADPATH . $row['screenshot'] .
      '" alt="Score image" /></td></tr>';
  }
  else {
    echo '<td><img src="' . GW_UPLOADPATH . 'unverified.gif' .
      '" alt="Unverified score" /></td></tr>';
  }
}
echo '</table>';

mysqli_close($dbc);
?>
```

index.php

> Awesome! Now I have access to the shared data too.

addscore.php

DONE

6 Move the file upload path to a constant that is shared via an include file.

Oops, another new step! Some things are difficult to plan for, so you have to be ready to tweak your design "on the fly."

Test Drive

Create two include files for Guitar Wars, and then share them among the other scripts.

Create two new text files, `appvars.php` and `connectvars.php`, and enter the code for them shown on the facing page. Then add `require_once` statements to `index.php` and `addscore.php` so that both shared script files are included. Upload all of the scripts to your web server and try out the Add Score form and main page to make sure they still work with the new and improved include file organizational structure.

~~Timing~~ Order is everything with high scores

Guitar Wars is finally image-powered, allowing users to upload screen shot images to help verify their high scores. While this is a major improvement to the application, it hasn't solved a problem that users have actually been grumbling about for quite a while—the order of the scores on the main page.

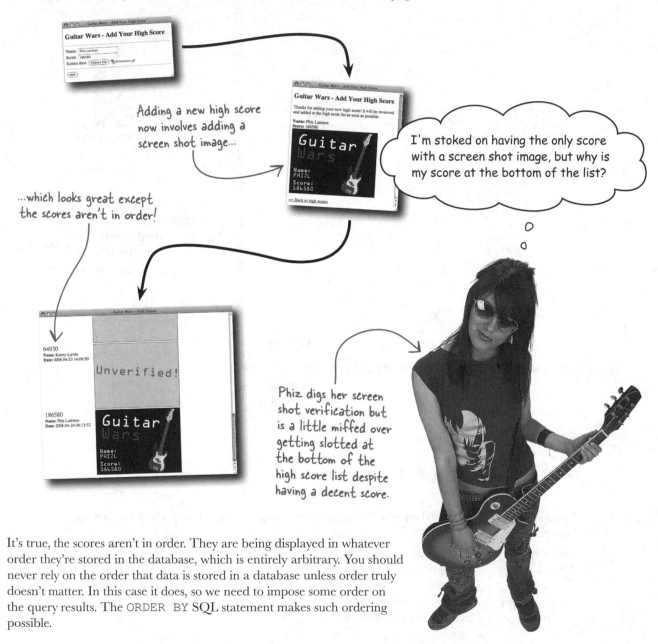

Adding a new high score now involves adding a screen shot image...

...which looks great except the scores aren't in order!

I'm stoked on having the only score with a screen shot image, but why is my score at the bottom of the list?

Phiz digs her screen shot verification but is a little miffed over getting slotted at the bottom of the high score list despite having a decent score.

It's true, the scores aren't in order. They are being displayed in whatever order they're stored in the database, which is entirely arbitrary. You should never rely on the order that data is stored in a database unless order truly doesn't matter. In this case it does, so we need to impose some order on the query results. The ORDER BY SQL statement makes such ordering possible.

PHP & MySQL, Magnets

See if you can figure out how **ORDER BY** works by using the magnets below to create ordered **SELECT** statements that result in the output below. Also circle which query you think represents the best fix for Guitar Wars. Hint: **ASC** stands for ASCending and **DESC** stands for DESCending.

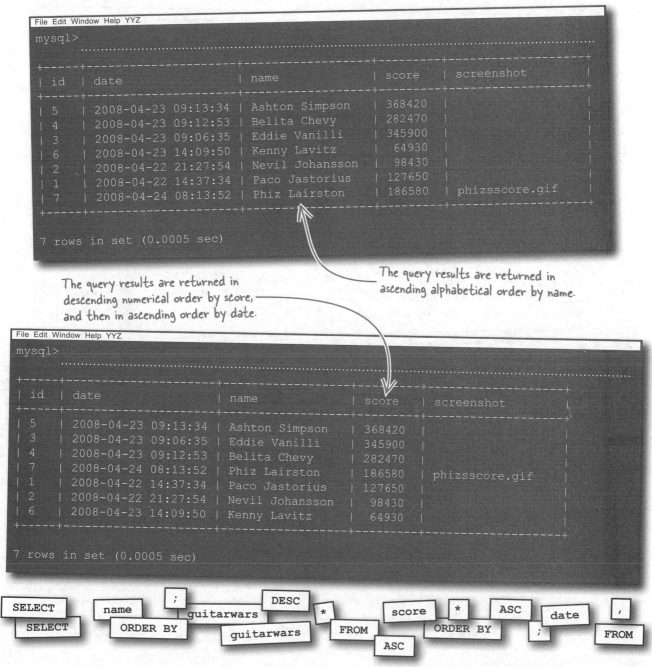

```
File Edit Window Help YYZ
mysql>
...........................................................................
+-----+---------------------+-----------------+--------+-------------------+
| id  | date                | name            | score  | screenshot        |
+-----+---------------------+-----------------+--------+-------------------+
| 5   | 2008-04-23 09:13:34 | Ashton Simpson  | 368420 |                   |
| 4   | 2008-04-23 09:12:53 | Belita Chevy    | 282470 |                   |
| 3   | 2008-04-23 09:06:35 | Eddie Vanilli   | 345900 |                   |
| 6   | 2008-04-23 14:09:50 | Kenny Lavitz    |  64930 |                   |
| 2   | 2008-04-22 21:27:54 | Nevil Johansson |  98430 |                   |
| 1   | 2008-04-22 14:37:34 | Paco Jastorius  | 127650 |                   |
| 7   | 2008-04-24 08:13:52 | Phiz Lairston   | 186580 | phizsscore.gif    |
+-----+---------------------+-----------------+--------+-------------------+
7 rows in set (0.0005 sec)
```

The query results are returned in descending numerical order by score, and then in ascending order by date.

The query results are returned in ascending alphabetical order by name.

```
File Edit Window Help YYZ
mysql>
...........................................................................
+-----+---------------------+-----------------+--------+-------------------+
| id  | date                | name            | score  | screenshot        |
+-----+---------------------+-----------------+--------+-------------------+
| 5   | 2008-04-23 09:13:34 | Ashton Simpson  | 368420 |                   |
| 3   | 2008-04-23 09:06:35 | Eddie Vanilli   | 345900 |                   |
| 4   | 2008-04-23 09:12:53 | Belita Chevy    | 282470 |                   |
| 7   | 2008-04-24 08:13:52 | Phiz Lairston   | 186580 | phizsscore.gif    |
| 1   | 2008-04-22 14:37:34 | Paco Jastorius  | 127650 |                   |
| 2   | 2008-04-22 21:27:54 | Nevil Johansson |  98430 |                   |
| 6   | 2008-04-23 14:09:50 | Kenny Lavitz    |  64930 |                   |
+-----+---------------------+-----------------+--------+-------------------+
7 rows in set (0.0005 sec)
```

Magnets:

`SELECT` `name` `;` `guitarwars` `DESC` `*` `score` `*` `ASC` `date` `,`

`SELECT` `ORDER BY` `guitarwars` `FROM` `ORDER BY` `;` `FROM` `ASC`

PHP & MySQL Magnets Solution

See if you can figure out how **ORDER BY** works by using the magnets below to create ordered **SELECT** statements that result in the output below. Also circle which query you think represents the best fix for Guitar Wars. Hint: **ASC** stands for ASCending and **DESC** stands for DESCending.

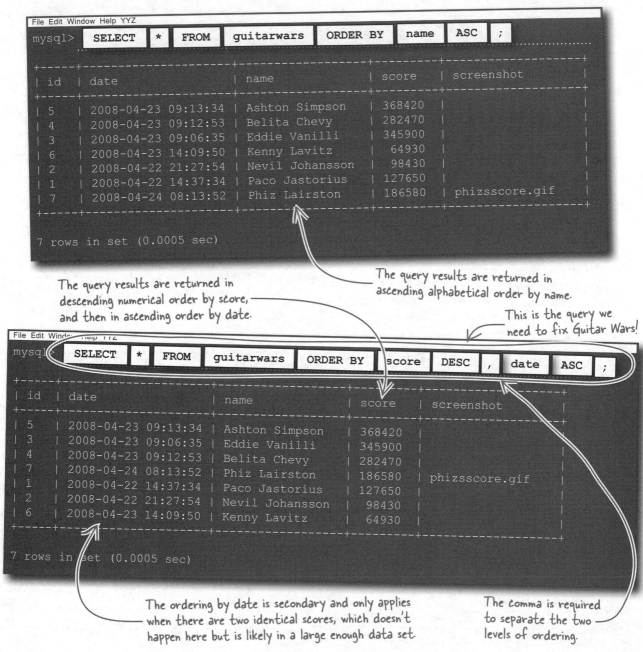

```
File Edit Window Help YYZ
mysql> SELECT * FROM guitarwars ORDER BY name ASC ;

+-----+---------------------+------------------+--------+---------------+
| id  | date                | name             | score  | screenshot    |
+-----+---------------------+------------------+--------+---------------+
| 5   | 2008-04-23 09:13:34 | Ashton Simpson   | 368420 |               |
| 4   | 2008-04-23 09:12:53 | Belita Chevy     | 282470 |               |
| 3   | 2008-04-23 09:06:35 | Eddie Vanilli    | 345900 |               |
| 6   | 2008-04-23 14:09:50 | Kenny Lavitz     |  64930 |               |
| 2   | 2008-04-22 21:27:54 | Nevil Johansson  |  98430 |               |
| 1   | 2008-04-22 14:37:34 | Paco Jastorius   | 127650 |               |
| 7   | 2008-04-24 08:13:52 | Phiz Lairston    | 186580 | phizsscore.gif|
+-----+---------------------+------------------+--------+---------------+
7 rows in set (0.0005 sec)
```

The query results are returned in ascending alphabetical order by name.

The query results are returned in descending numerical order by score, and then in ascending order by date.

This is the query we need to fix Guitar Wars!

```
File Edit Window Help YYZ
mysql> SELECT * FROM guitarwars ORDER BY score DESC , date ASC ;

+-----+---------------------+------------------+--------+---------------+
| id  | date                | name             | score  | screenshot    |
+-----+---------------------+------------------+--------+---------------+
| 5   | 2008-04-23 09:13:34 | Ashton Simpson   | 368420 |               |
| 3   | 2008-04-23 09:06:35 | Eddie Vanilli    | 345900 |               |
| 4   | 2008-04-23 09:12:53 | Belita Chevy     | 282470 |               |
| 7   | 2008-04-24 08:13:52 | Phiz Lairston    | 186580 | phizsscore.gif|
| 1   | 2008-04-22 14:37:34 | Paco Jastorius   | 127650 |               |
| 2   | 2008-04-22 21:27:54 | Nevil Johansson  |  98430 |               |
| 6   | 2008-04-23 14:09:50 | Kenny Lavitz     |  64930 |               |
+-----+---------------------+------------------+--------+---------------+
7 rows in set (0.0005 sec)
```

The ordering by date is secondary and only applies when there are two identical scores, which doesn't happen here but is likely in a large enough data set.

The comma is required to separate the two levels of ordering.

Honoring the top Guitar Warrior

With the order of the scores fixed, it's now possible to make an unexpected improvement to the high score list by calling out the highest scorer at the top of the list. The top scoring Guitar Warrior deserves a top score header that clearly displays the highest, score, so there is no doubt who the top Guitar Warrior is... and what score to gun for.

A top score header clearly highlights the top score, providing a target for competing Guitar Warriors.

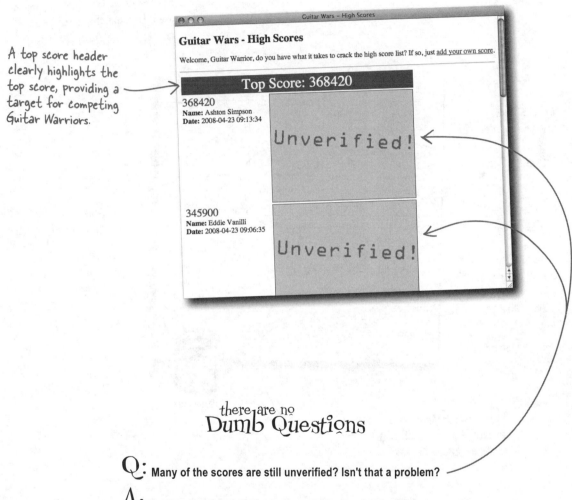

there are no Dumb Questions

Q: **Many of the scores are still unverified? Isn't that a problem?**

A: Yes it is. But it doesn't stop us from going ahead and calling attention to the top score. It just means that we'll need to eventually clean up the high score list by removing unverified scores. In fact, we'll tackle the unverified high scores just as soon as we finish highlighting the top score.

Format the top score with HTML and CSS

The most important thing about the new high score header is that it be clearly seen above all other scores in the high score list. This requires the help of both HTML and CSS to add some visual flair. The header will be generated as a row in the HTML table with a special CSS style applied to it. This style, `topscoreheader`, must be added to the `style.css` stylesheet for Guitar Wars.

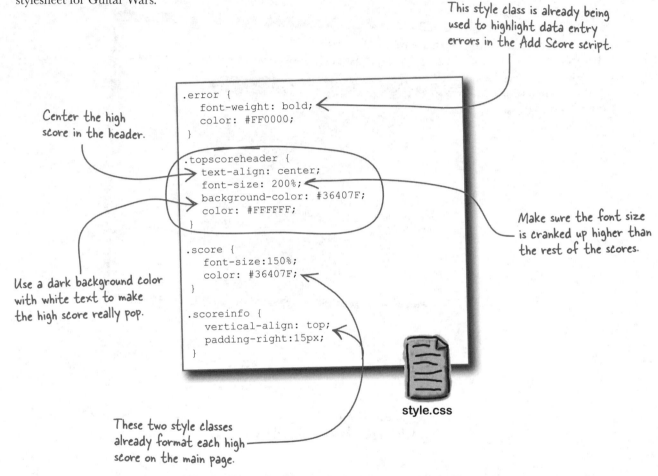

This style class is already being used to highlight data entry errors in the Add Score script.

Center the high score in the header.

Use a dark background color with white text to make the high score really pop.

Make sure the font size is cranked up higher than the rest of the scores.

```
.error {
    font-weight: bold;
    color: #FF0000;
}

.topscoreheader {
    text-align: center;
    font-size: 200%;
    background-color: #36407F;
    color: #FFFFFF;
}

.score {
    font-size:150%;
    color: #36407F;
}

.scoreinfo {
    vertical-align: top;
    padding-right:15px;
}
```

style.css

These two style classes already format each high score on the main page.

The `index.php` script already generates an HTML table containing the high score list. Generating a header just for the top score involves isolating the first score, which is guaranteed to be the top score since the list is now in order. A `while` loop takes care of looping through the scores, so we need to somehow count the scores, and only generate the header for the first one...

Finish the code for the `index.php` Guitar Wars script so that it adds a formatted header for the top score that uses the `topscoreheader` CSS style. Hint: Don't forget that the top score header is part of the high score HTML table, which has two columns.

```
...
// Loop through the array of score data, formatting it as HTML
echo '<table>';
$i = 0;
while ($row = mysqli_fetch_array($data)) {
  // Display the score data ...............................
  if (.............) {

    .....................................................................................................................

    .....................................................................................................................
  }
  echo '<tr><td class="scoreinfo">';
  echo '<span class="score">' . $row['score'] . '</span><br />';
  echo '<strong>Name:</strong> ' . $row['name'] . '<br />';
  echo '<strong>Date:</strong> ' . $row['date'] . '</td>';
  if (is_file(GW_UPLOADPATH . $row['screenshot']) &&
    filesize(GW_UPLOADPATH . $row['screenshot']) > 0) {
    echo '<td><img src="' . GW_UPLOADPATH . $row['screenshot'] .
      '" alt="Score image" /></td></tr>';
  }
  else {
    echo '<td><img src="' . GW_UPLOADPATH . 'unverified.gif' .
      '" alt="Unverified score" /></td></tr>';
  }
  ....................
}
echo '</table>';
...
```

index.php

Exercise
Solution

Finish the code for the `index.php` Guitar Wars script so that it adds a formatted header for the top score that uses the `topscoreheader` CSS style. Hint: Don't forget that the top score header is part of the high score HTML table, which has two columns.

$i is the variable that counts through the high scores — we can use it to isolate the first score.

```
...
// Loop through the array of score data, formatting it as HTML
echo '<table>';
$i = 0;
while ($row = mysqli_fetch_array($data)) {
  // Display the score data
  if ( $i == 0 ) {
    echo '<tr><td colspan="2" class="topscoreheader">Top Score: ' .
      $row['score'] . '</td></tr>';
  }
  echo '<tr><td class="scoreinfo">';
  echo '<span class="score">' . $row['score'] . '</span><br />';
  echo '<strong>Name:</strong> ' . $row['name'] . '<br />';
  echo '<strong>Date:</strong> ' . $row['date'] . '</td>';
  if (is_file(GW_UPLOADPATH . $row['screenshot']) &&
    filesize(GW_UPLOADPATH . $row['screenshot']) > 0) {
    echo '<td><img src="' . GW_UPLOADPATH . $row['screenshot'] .
      '" alt="Score image" /></td></tr>';
  }
  else {
    echo '<td><img src="' . GW_UPLOADPATH . 'unverified.gif' .
      '" alt="Unverified score" /></td></tr>';
  }
  $i++;
}
echo '</table>';
...
```

If $i equals 0, we know it's the first (top!) score, so render the HTML code for the header.

The topscoreheader style class is stored in style.css.

Increment the counter at the end of the score loop — this code is the same as $i = $i + 1;.

index.php

264

Test Drive

Order the high scores and showcase the highest score of all.

Modify the `index.php` script to use the new ordered `SELECT` query, and then add in the code that generates the top score header. Upload the new script to your web server and open it in your browser to see the top score prominently displayed.

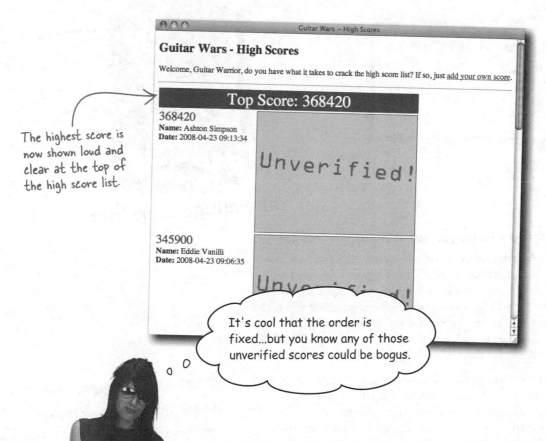

The highest score is now shown loud and clear at the top of the high score list.

> It's cool that the order is fixed...but you know any of those unverified scores could be bogus.

It's true, the unverified scores need to be dealt with.

But one thing at a time. It seems another problem has surfaced that is preventing people from uploading their high score screen shots...

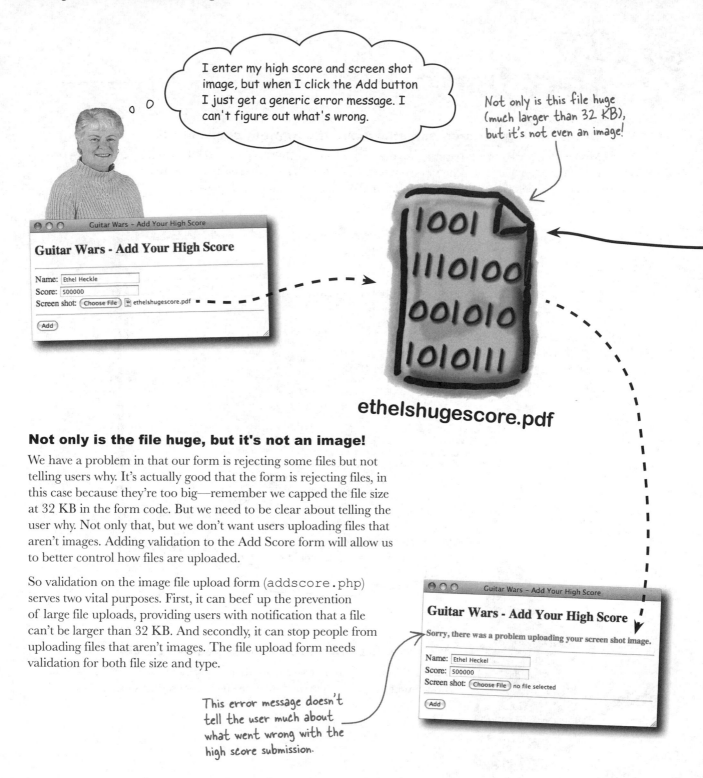

I enter my high score and screen shot image, but when I click the Add button I just get a generic error message. I can't figure out what's wrong.

Not only is this file huge (much larger than 32 KB), but it's not even an image!

ethelshugescore.pdf

Not only is the file huge, but it's not an image!

We have a problem in that our form is rejecting some files but not telling users why. It's actually good that the form is rejecting files, in this case because they're too big—remember we capped the file size at 32 KB in the form code. But we need to be clear about telling the user why. Not only that, but we don't want users uploading files that aren't images. Adding validation to the Add Score form will allow us to better control how files are uploaded.

So validation on the image file upload form (addscore.php) serves two vital purposes. First, it can beef up the prevention of large file uploads, providing users with notification that a file can't be larger than 32 KB. And secondly, it can stop people from uploading files that aren't images. The file upload form needs validation for both file size and type.

This error message doesn't tell the user much about what went wrong with the high score submission.

Only ^{small} images allowed

So how exactly do we check the Add Score form and make sure uploaded images adhere to a certain size and type? The answer lies in the built-in `$_FILES` superglobal variable, which if you recall, is where we earlier obtained the temporary storage location of the uploaded file so that it could be moved to the `images` folder. Now we're going to use it to grab the size and MIME type of the file.

`$_FILES['screenshot']['size']`

`1280472`

The size of the file is over 1 MB, much larger than our 32 KB limit (1,280,472 bytes is 1.22 MB, or 1,250 KB).

`$_FILES['screenshot']['type']`

`application/pdf`

The type of the file is PDF, not an acceptable web image type, such as GIF, JPG, or PNG.

We don't just want image files to be smaller than our 32 KB size limit, but we also need them to be a file type that can be displayed as a web image. The following MIME types are commonly used to represent web images:

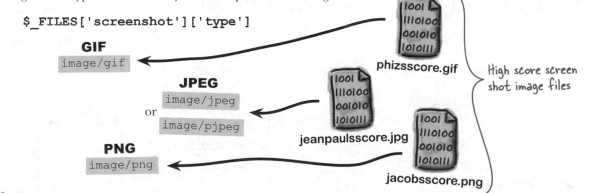

`$_FILES['screenshot']['type']`

GIF
`image/gif`

JPEG
`image/jpeg`
or
`image/pjpeg`

PNG
`image/png`

phizsscore.gif

jeanpaulsscore.jpg

jacobsscore.png

High score screen shot image files

Sharpen your pencil

Write an `if` statement that checks to make sure a screen shot file is an image, as well as checking to make sure it is greater than 0 bytes in size and less than the constant `GW_MAXFILESIZE`. Assume the file size and type have already been stored in variables named `$screenshot_size` and `$screenshot_type`.

```
if (
.............................................................................
.............................................................................
.............................................................. ) {
```

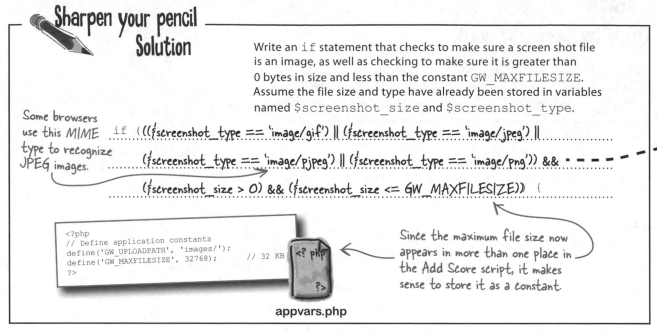

Sharpen your pencil Solution

Write an `if` statement that checks to make sure a screen shot file is an image, as well as checking to make sure it is greater than 0 bytes in size and less than the constant `GW_MAXFILESIZE`. Assume the file size and type have already been stored in variables named `$screenshot_size` and `$screenshot_type`.

Some browsers use this MIME type to recognize JPEG images.

```
if (((($screenshot_type == 'image/gif') || ($screenshot_type == 'image/jpeg') ||
($screenshot_type == 'image/pjpeg') || ($screenshot_type == 'image/png')) &&
($screenshot_size > 0) && ($screenshot_size <= GW_MAXFILESIZE)) {
```

```php
<?php
// Define application constants
define('GW_UPLOADPATH', 'images/');
define('GW_MAXFILESIZE', 32768);    // 32 KB
?>
```

appvars.php

Since the maximum file size now appears in more than one place in the Add Score script, it makes sense to store it as a constant.

File validation makes the app more robust

A little validation goes a long way toward making any PHP application more intuitive and easier to use, not to mention safer from abuse. Now a helpful error message lets the user know the exact constraints imposed on uploaded image files.

An error message helps to explain exactly what kind of files are allowed for upload.

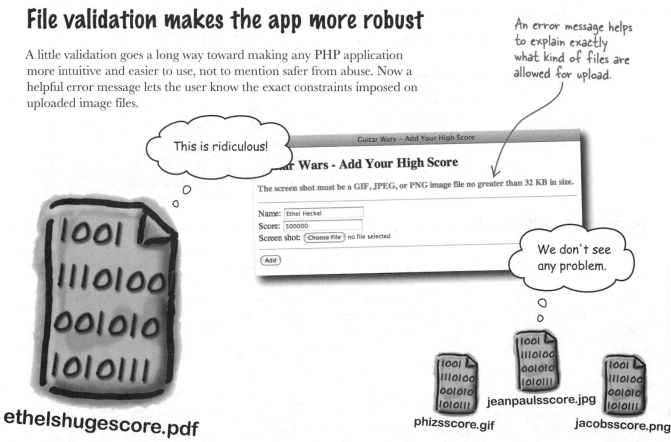

This is ridiculous!

Guitar Wars – Add Your High Score

...ar Wars - Add Your High Score

The screen shot must be a GIF, JPEG, or PNG image file no greater than 32 KB in size.

Name: Ethel Heckel
Score: 500000
Screen shot: (Choose File) no file selected

(Add)

We don't see any problem.

ethelshugescore.pdf

phizsscore.gif

jeanpaulsscore.jpg

jacobsscore.png

Since we're making the script more
robust, it's also a good idea to check
the $_FILES superglobal to make
sure there wasn't an upload error.

Display a descriptive
error if the file is the
wrong type or too large.

```php
if (!empty($name) && !empty($score) && !empty($screenshot)) {
  if ((($screenshot_type == 'image/gif') || ($screenshot_type == 'image/jpeg') ||
  ($screenshot_type == 'image/pjpeg') || ($screenshot_type == 'image/png')) &&
  ($screenshot_size > 0) && ($screenshot_size <= GW_MAXFILESIZE)) {
    if ($_FILES['screenshot']['error'] == 0) {
      // Move the file to the target upload folder
      $target = GW_UPLOADPATH . $screenshot;
      if (move_uploaded_file($_FILES['screenshot']['tmp_name'], $target)) {
        // Connect to the database
        $dbc = mysqli_connect(DB_HOST, DB_USER, DB_PASSWORD, DB_NAME);

        // Write the data to the database
        $query = "INSERT INTO guitarwars VALUES (0, NOW(), '$name', '$score', '$screenshot')";
        mysqli_query($dbc, $query);

        // Confirm success with the user
        echo '<p>Thanks for adding your new high score!</p>';
        echo '<p><strong>Name:</strong> ' . $name . '<br />';
        echo '<strong>Score:</strong> ' . $score . '<br />';
        echo '<img src="' . GW_UPLOADPATH . $screenshot . '" alt="Score image" /></p>';
        echo '<p><a href="index.php">&lt;&lt; Back to high scores</a></p>';

        // Clear the score data to clear the form
        $name = "";
        $score = "";
        $screenshot = "";

        mysqli_close($dbc);
      }
      else {
        echo '<p class="error">Sorry, there was a problem uploading your screen shot image.</p>';
      }
    }
  }
  else {
    echo '<p class="error">The screen shot must be a GIF, JPEG, or PNG image file no ' .
      'greater than ' . (GW_MAXFILESIZE / 1024) . ' KB in size.</p>';
  }

  // Try to delete the temporary screen shot image file
  @unlink($_FILES['screenshot']['tmp_name']);
}
else {
  echo '<p class="error">Please enter all of the information to add your high score.</p>';
}
```

addscore.php

The unlink() function deletes a file
from the web server. We suppress its
error reporting with @ in case the
file upload didn't actually succeed.

The new and improved
Add Score script now
has image file validation.

Test Drive

Add screen shot image file validation to the Add Score script.

Modify the `addscore.php` script to use the new image file validation code. Upload the script to your web server and try out the Add Score form with both valid images and a few invalid files (huge images and non-images).

---

there are no
Dumb Questions

Q: Why are there two different MIME types for JPEG images?

A: This is a question better asked of browser vendors, who, for some reason, decided to use different MIME types for JPEG images. To make sure the JPEG file validation works across as many browsers as possible, it's necessary to check for both MIME types.

Q: Why is it necessary to check for image files larger than 0 bytes? Aren't all images larger than 0 bytes?

A: In theory, yes. But it is technically possible for a 0 byte file to get created on the server if the user specifies a file that doesn't actually exist on their own computer. Just in case this happens, `addscore.php` plays it safe and checks for an empty file.

Q: Why is `GW_MAXFILESIZE` placed in `appvars.php` even though it is only used in `addscore.php`?

A: While it's true that `appvars.php` is intended for storing script data that is shared across multiple script files, it is also a good place to store **any** constant script data. In this case, placing `GW_MAXFILESIZE` in `appvars.php` makes it easier to find if you ever want to make the file upload limit larger.

Q: How does that line of code with `@unlink()` work?

A: The built-in PHP `unlink()` function deletes a file from the web server, in our case the temporary image file that was uploaded. Since it's possible that the upload failed and there is no temporary image file, we suppress any potential errors generated by `unlink()` by preceding it with an at symbol (@). You can stick @ in front of any PHP function to suppress its error reporting.

> What about all those unverified scores? They haven't gone away, you know.

The high score list <u>must</u> be cleaned up.

With image file uploading tightened up thanks to validation, we can't ignore the problem of unverified scores any longer. New scores with uploaded screen shot images shouldn't play second fiddle to old scores without screen shots that may or may not be valid. Guitar Wars needs a way to remove old scores!

The current top score is not verified, which doesn't instill much confidence in other users.

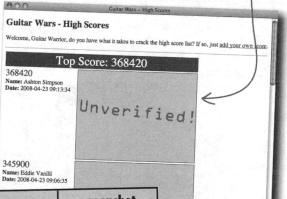

guitarwars

id	date	name	score	screenshot
1	2008-04-22 14:37:34	Paco Jastorius	127650	
2	2008-04-22 21:27:54	Nevil Johansson	98430	
3	2008-04-23 09:06:35	Eddie Vanilli	345900	
4	2008-04-23 09:12:53	Belita Chevy	282470	
5	2008-04-23 09:13:34	Ashton Simpson	368420	
6	2008-04-23 14:09:50	Kenny Lavitz	64930	
7	2008-04-24 08:13:52	Phiz Lairston	186580	phizsscore.gif

Unverified scores without images need to be removed from the database, pronto!

Write down how you would go about cleaning up the unverified scores in the high score list:

....

....

Plan for an Admin page

Since we just need to remove some unverified scores from the database, it's perfectly reasonable to just fire up an SQL tool and manually remove rows from the database with a few DELETE queries. But this may not be the last time you'll need to remove a score, and it's no fun having to resort to manual SQL queries to maintain a web application. The idea here is to build an application that can be maintained with as little hassle as possible.

What we need is a page that only the web site administrator has access to and can use to remove scores... an Admin page! But we need to be very careful in making a clear distinction between what parts of Guitar Wars are for the administrator and what parts are for users.

> **Web applications often include pages for public access, as well as admin pages that are only for site maintenance.**

These pages are for users:

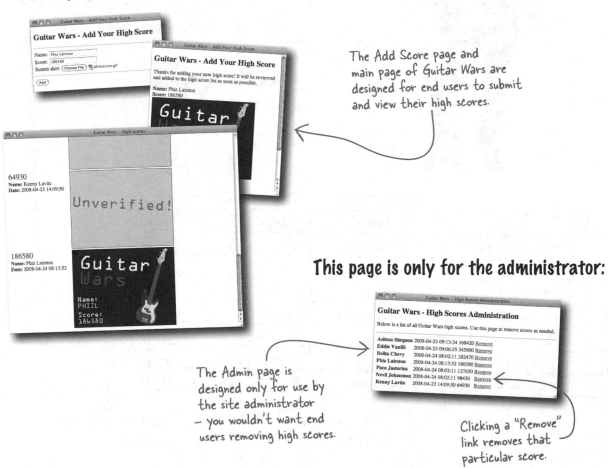

The Add Score page and main page of Guitar Wars are designed for end users to submit and view their high scores.

The Admin page is designed only for use by the site administrator — you wouldn't want end users removing high scores.

This page is only for the administrator:

Clicking a "Remove" link removes that particular score.

Exercise

Write down what the Admin and Remove Score scripts need to do in order to accommodate a score removal feature for Guitar Wars. Then draw how a score removal affects a row in the `guitarwars` table and the screen shot image file associated with it.

admin.php

....
....
....
....
....

Web server

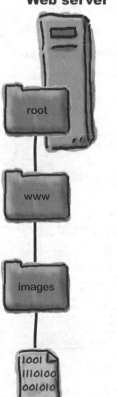

root

www

images

....
....
....
....
....
....

removescore.php

guitarwars

id	date	name	score	screenshot
1	2008-04-22 14:37:34	Paco Jastorius	127650	
2	2008-04-22 21:27:54	Nevil Johansson	98430	
3	2008-04-23 09:06:35	Eddie Vanilli	345900	
4	2008-04-23 09:12:53	Belita Chevy	282470	
5	2008-04-23 09:13:34	Ashton Simpson	368420	
6	2008-04-23 14:09:50	Kenny Lavitz	64930	
7	2008-04-24 08:13:52	Phiz Lairston	186580	phizsscore.gif

Exercise Solution

Write down what the Admin and Remove Score scripts need to do in order to accommodate a score removal feature for Guitar Wars. Then draw how a score removal affects a row in the `guitarwars` table and the screen shot image file associated with it.

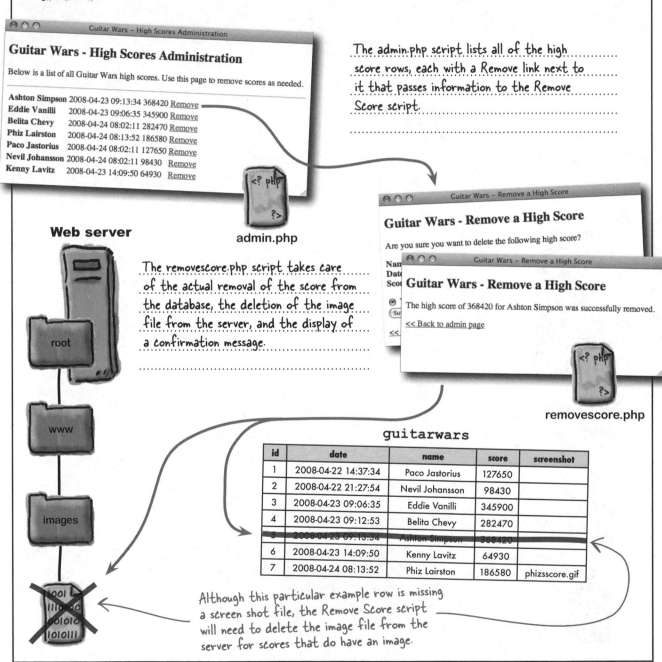

Guitar Wars - High Scores Administration

Below is a list of all Guitar Wars high scores. Use this page to remove scores as needed.

Ashton Simpson	2008-04-23 09:13:34	368420	Remove
Eddie Vanilli	2008-04-23 09:06:35	345900	Remove
Belita Chevy	2008-04-24 08:02:11	282470	Remove
Phiz Lairston	2008-04-24 08:13:52	186580	Remove
Paco Jastorius	2008-04-24 08:02:11	127650	Remove
Nevil Johansson	2008-04-24 08:02:11	98430	Remove
Kenny Lavitz	2008-04-23 14:09:50	64930	Remove

The admin.php script lists all of the high score rows, each with a Remove link next to it that passes information to the Remove Score script.

admin.php

Web server

root

www

images

The removescore.php script takes care of the actual removal of the score from the database, the deletion of the image file from the server, and the display of a confirmation message.

Guitar Wars - Remove a High Score

Are you sure you want to delete the following high score?

Guitar Wars - Remove a High Score

The high score of 368420 for Ashton Simpson was successfully removed.

<< Back to admin page

removescore.php

guitarwars

id	date	name	score	screenshot
1	2008-04-22 14:37:34	Paco Jastorius	127650	
2	2008-04-22 21:27:54	Nevil Johansson	98430	
3	2008-04-23 09:06:35	Eddie Vanilli	345900	
4	2008-04-23 09:12:53	Belita Chevy	282470	
5	2008-04-23 09:13:34	Ashton Simpson	368420	
6	2008-04-23 14:09:50	Kenny Lavitz	64930	
7	2008-04-24 08:13:52	Phiz Lairston	186580	phizsscore.gif

Although this particular example row is missing a screen shot file, the Remove Score script will need to delete the image file from the server for scores that do have an image.

Generate score removal links on the Admin page

Although the Remove Score script is responsible for the actual score removal, we need an Admin script that allows us to select a score to remove. The `admin.php` script generates a list of high scores with Remove links for each one. These links pass along data about a given score to the `removescore.php` script.

```php
<?php
  require_once('appvars.php');

  require_once('connectvars.php');


  // Connect to the database
  $dbc = mysqli_connect(DB_HOST, DB_USER, DB_PASSWORD, DB_NAME);


  // Retrieve the score data from MySQL
  $query = "SELECT * FROM guitarwars ORDER BY score DESC, date ASC";

  $data = mysqli_query($dbc, $query);


  // Loop through the array of score data, formatting it as HTML
  echo '<table>';

  while ($row = mysqli_fetch_array($data)) {
    // Display the score data
    echo '<tr class="scorerow"><td><strong>' . $row['name'] . '</strong></td>';

    echo '<td>' . $row['date'] . '</td>';

    echo '<td>' . $row['score'] . '</td>';

    echo '<td><a href="removescore.php?id=' . $row['id'] . '&amp;date=' . $row['date'] .
      '&amp;name=' . $row['name'] . '&amp;score=' . $row['score'] . '&amp;screenshot=' .
      $row['screenshot'] . '">Remove</a></td></tr>';
  }
  echo '</table>';


  mysqli_close($dbc);
?>
```

admin.php

The URL to the Remove Score script is doing more than just linking to the script...it's also passing data to it!

This code generates an HTML link to the removescore.php script, passing along information about the score to be removed.

```
<a href="removescore.php?id=5&date=2008-04-23%20
09:13:34&name=Ashton%20Simpson&score=368420&screenshot="
```

Scripts can communicate with each other

In order for the Remove Score script to remove a high score, it must know what score to remove. But that's decided in the Admin script. This begs the question, how does the Admin script tell the Remove Score script what score to remove? This communication between scripts is accomplished by packaging up the data as part of a "Remove" URL for each high score shown on the Admin page. If you closely analyze the URL for a particular score, you'll notice that all the high score data is in there.

The URL of a script can be used to pass data as a GET request.

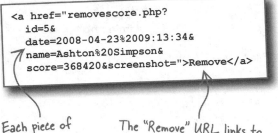

```
<a href="removescore.php?
   id=5&
   date=2008-04-23%2009:13:34&
   name=Ashton%20Simpson&
   score=368420&screenshot="">Remove</a>
```

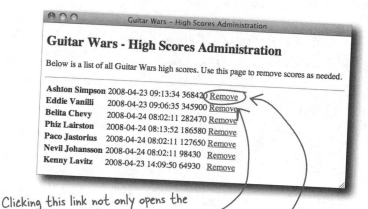

Each piece of data has a name and a value, and is separated from other name/value pairs by an ampersand (&).

The "Remove" URL links to the removescore.php script but also includes data for the row to be deleted.

Clicking this link not only opens the Remove Score script, but it also passes along data to the script as a GET request.

OK, so data gets passed along through a URL, but how exactly does the Remove Score script get its hands on that data? Data passed to a script through a URL is available in the $_GET superglobal, which is an array very similar to $_POST. Packaging data into a linked URL is the same as using a GET request in a web form. In a traditional HTML GET request, form data is **automatically** sent along to the form processing script as part of the script's URL. We're doing the same thing by **manually** building our own GET request as a custom URL.

Similar to $_POST, using the $_GET array to access the high score data requires the name of each piece of data.

The name of the piece of data is used to access it within the $_GET array.

The URL for a script serves as a handy way to pass important data, such as the ID of a database row.

$_GET['id']

$_GET['score']

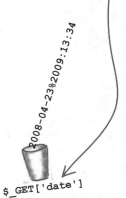

$_GET['name']

$_GET['date']

> I don't see what all the fuss is with GET. Why can't you just pass the data to the script using POST? That's how you've done it up until now.

POST requests can only be initiated through a form, while GET requests can be packaged as URLs.

Up until now we've always passed data to a script through a web form where the script was listed as the action for the form's Submit button. When the user fills out the form and presses the Submit button, the form data is packaged up and sent along to the form as a POST request.

The problem is that the Admin page doesn't use a form to initiate the Remove Score script. It just links to the script via a URL. So we need a way to send along data to a script using nothing more than a URL. This is where GET is particularly handy since it provides access to data that is packaged in a URL as parameters. Similar to POST, the data that gets passed along to the script through a GET request is available through a superglobal, but it's named $_GET instead of $_POST.

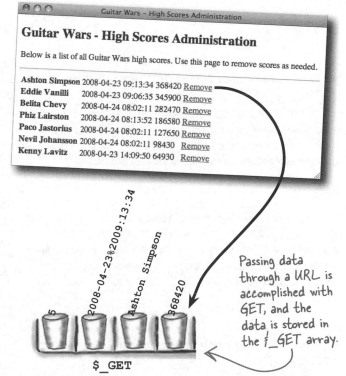

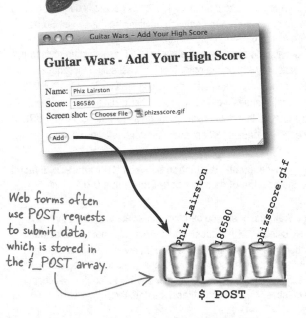

Web forms often use POST requests to submit data, which is stored in the $_POST array.

Passing data through a URL is accomplished with GET, and the data is stored in the $_GET array.

Of GETs and POSTs

The difference between GET and POST isn't just form vs. URL since GET requests can (and often are) used to submit form data as well. The real distinction between GET and POST has to do with the **intent** of a request. GET is used primarily to retrieve data from the server **without affecting anything** on the server. POST, on the other hand, typically involves sending data to the server, after which **the state of the server usually changes** somehow in response to the data that was sent.

The two types of web requests, GET and POST, control how you shuttle data between scripts.

POST

Used to send data to the server that somehow causes a change in the state of the server, such as inserting data in a database. Data can still be returned in a response. Unlike GET, POST requests can only be made through the action of a web form. Also unlike GET, the data sent in a POST request is hidden from view.

GET

Typically used for data retrieval that doesn't change anything on the server. For small amounts of data, GET is also useful for directly sending data to the server in a URL. Unlike POST, GET is primarily suited to sending small amounts of data.

there are no Dumb Questions

Q: I've seen web forms that use GET. How does that work?

A: Both GET and POST have their place when it comes to web forms. When creating a web form, the `method` attribute of the `<form>` tag controls how the data is sent, while the `action` attribute identifies the script to receive the data and process it:

```
<form method="post" action="addscore.php">
```

When the submit button is clicked to submit this form, the addscore.php script is executed, and the form data is passed along to it through the `$_POST` array. But you could've just as easily written the `<form>` tag like this, in which case the data would get passed along through the `$_GET` array:

```
<form method="get" action="addscore.php">
```

Q: Ah, so it doesn't matter which request method I use, GET or POST?

A: Wrong. It matters quite a lot. GET is generally used for getting data from the server, not changing anything on the server. So GET is perfect for forms that make informational requests on the server without altering the state of the server, such as selecting rows from a database. POST, on the other hand, is best suited for requests that affect the server's state, such as issuing an INSERT or DELETE query that changes the database. Another distinction between GET and POST is that data passed through a GET is visible in a URL, while POST data is hidden, and, therefore, is a tiny bit more secure.

Q: How does this distinction between GET and POST factor into the passing of data to a script through a URL?

A: Well, first of all, you can only pass data to a script through a URL using a GET request, so POST is eliminated immediately. Furthermore, since GET is intended purely for requests that don't alter the state of the server, this means you shouldn't be doing any INSERTs, DELETE FROMs, or anything else that will change the database in a script that receives data through its URL.

Fireside Chats

Tonight's talk: **GET and POST**

GET:

So, word on the street is you've been saying all I'm good for is asking questions but not really doing anything with the answers. Is that true?

OK, so it's true that I'm not really intended to be causing changes on the server such as deleting files or adding database rows, but that doesn't mean I'm not important.

True, but you're permanently connected to your good buddy, Form, whereas Form and I are merely casual acquaintances. I leave room for other friends, such as URL.

Well, then I have a question for you. How exactly do you take action when your little sidekick, Form, isn't around? You know sometimes Page doesn't find it necessary to go to the trouble of involving Form.

Calm down. I'm just pointing out that while I'm geared toward retrieving data from the server, I'm fairly flexible in how I can be used to do it.

Glad to hear it. It's been good talking to you...

POST:

Sure is. Let's face it, you don't have any real power, just the ability to ask the server for something.

If you say so. All I know is not a whole lot would get done without people like me making things happen on the server. If the server was always stuck in the same state, it would be pretty boring out there.

So you think your "circle of friends" somehow overcomes your inability to take action? I doubt it.

Listen, Form is my friend, and long ago I made a commitment not to do any requesting without him. So judge my loyalty if you must, but I won't betray my friend!

I'll give you that. You're alright by me.

GET, POST, and high score removal

We've established that the removal of scores in Guitar Wars starts with a "Remove" link on the Admin page that links to the Remove Score script. We also know that score data can be passed through the link URL to the Remove Score script. But we have a problem in that a GET request really shouldn't be changing anything on the server, such as deleting a score. A possible solution is to not change anything on the server... yet. What if the Remove Score script initially displayed a confirmation page before actually removing a score from the database?

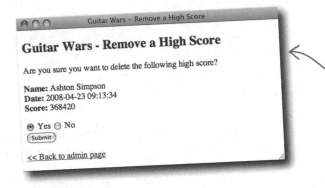

A confirmation page gives the user a chance to confirm the high score removal instead of just removing it instantly.

The confirmation page shows the score that is up for removal with a simple Yes/No form. Selecting Yes and clicking the Submit button results in the score being removed, while choosing No cancels the score removal.

Thinking in terms of GETs and POSTs, the Remove Score script can display the confirmation page as a response to the GET request from the Admin script. And since the confirmation itself is a form, it can issue its own POST request when submitted. If the form is a self-referencing form, the same script (`removescore.php`) can process the POST and carry out the score removal. Here are the steps involved in this process:

It's entirely possible, even helpful in some cases, for the same script to respond to both GET and POST requests.

1 The Remove Score script is initiated through a GET request by the user clicking the "Remove" link on the Admin page.

2 The Remove Score script uses the high score data stored in the $_GET array to generate a removal confirmation form.

3 The Remove Score script is initiated again, this time, through a POST request by the user submitting the confirmation form.

4 The Remove Score script deletes the score from the database and also deletes the screen shot image file from the web server.

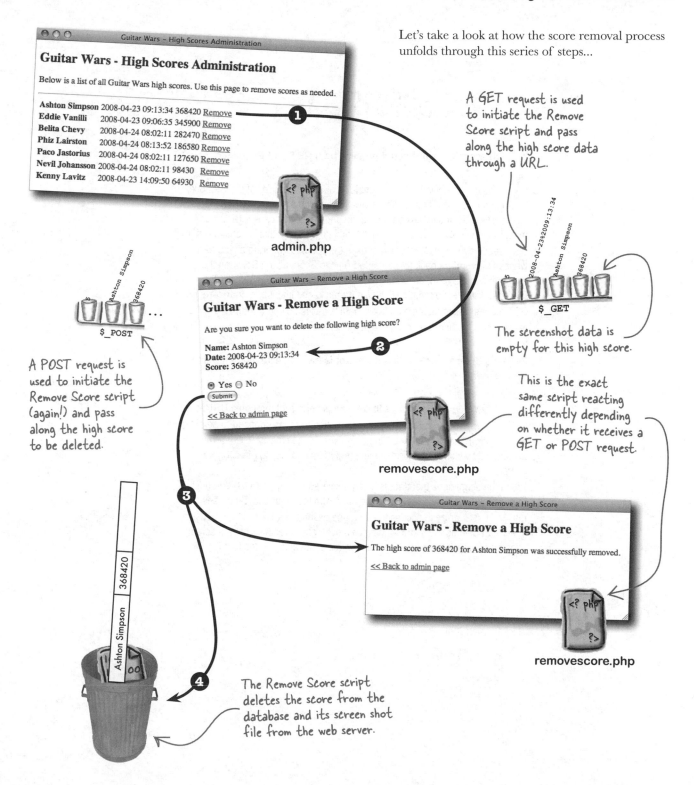

Let's take a look at how the score removal process unfolds through this series of steps...

A GET request is used to initiate the Remove Score script and pass along the high score data through a URL.

Guitar Wars - High Scores Administration

Below is a list of all Guitar Wars high scores. Use this page to remove scores as needed.

Ashton Simpson 2008-04-23 09:13:34 368420 Remove
Eddie Vanilli 2008-04-23 09:06:35 345900 Remove
Belita Chevy 2008-04-24 08:02:11 282470 Remove
Phiz Lairston 2008-04-24 08:13:52 186580 Remove
Paco Jastorius 2008-04-24 08:02:11 127650 Remove
Nevil Johansson 2008-04-24 08:02:11 98430 Remove
Kenny Lavitz 2008-04-23 14:09:50 64930 Remove

admin.php

$_GET

The screenshot data is empty for this high score.

A POST request is used to initiate the Remove Score script (again!) and pass along the high score to be deleted.

$_POST

Guitar Wars - Remove a High Score

Are you sure you want to delete the following high score?

Name: Ashton Simpson
Date: 2008-04-23 09:13:34
Score: 368420

Yes   No
Submit

<< Back to admin page

removescore.php

This is the exact same script reacting differently depending on whether it receives a GET or POST request.

Guitar Wars - Remove a High Score

The high score of 368420 for Ashton Simpson was successfully removed.

<< Back to admin page

removescore.php

The Remove Score script deletes the score from the database and its screen shot file from the web server.

there are no
Dumb Questions

Q: How can the same script process both **GET** and **POST** requests?

A: It all has to do with how a script is invoked. In the case of the Remove Score script, it is invoked in two different ways. The first way is when the user clicks a "Remove" link on the Admin page, in which case a URL leads them to the script. Since data is packaged into the URL, this is considered a GET request. This GET request causes the script to generate a web form whose action refers back to the same Remove Score script. So when the user submits the form, the script is invoked a second time. But unlike the first time, there is no fancy URL with data packaged into it and, therefore, no GET request. Instead, the high score data is passed along through a POST request and is, therefore, available in the $_POST array.

Q: So the manner in which the script is invoked actually determines what it does?

A: Yes! When the script sees that data has been sent through a URL as a GET request, it knows to display a confirmation form, as opposed to deleting anything from the database. So the data sent along in the $_GET array is used only within the confirmation page and has no lasting effect on the server.

When the script sees that data is being delivered through a POST request, the script knows that it can delete the data from the database. So it uses the $_POST array to access the data and assemble a DELETE FROM query that deletes the score. And since most high scores also have a screen shot image file stored on the web server, the script also deletes that file.

Isolate the high score for deletion

With the score removal process laid out, we can now focus our attention on the database side of things. The Remove Score script is responsible for removing a high score, which means deleting a row from the database of scores. If you recall, the SQL DELETE FROM statement allows us to delete rows. But in order to delete a row, we must first find it. This is accomplished by tacking a WHERE clause onto a query that uses DELETE FROM. For example, this SQL query deletes the row with the name column set to 'Ashton Simpson':

This query deletes rows with a name column matching 'Ashton Simpson'.

```
DELETE FROM guitarwars WHERE name = 'Ashton Simpson'
```

The table name is required by DELETE FROM to know which table you're deleting data from.

guitarwars

id	date	name	score	screenshot
1	2008-04-22 14:37:34	Paco Jastorius	127650	
2	2008-04-22 21:27:54	Nevil Johansson	98430	
3	2008-04-23 09:06:35	Eddie Vanilli	345900	
4	2008-04-23 09:12:53	Belita Chevy	282470	
5	2008-04-23 09:13:34	Ashton Simpson	368420	
6	2008-04-23 14:09:50	Kenny Lavitz	64930	
7	2008-04-24 08:13:52	Phiz Lairston	186580	phizsscore.gif

The name of the user is the match used to delete the high score.

There's a problem with this query, however. In a world full of millions of Guitar Warriors, odds are there will be more than one Ashton Simpson. This query doesn't just delete a single row, it deletes **all** rows matching the name 'Ashton Simpson'. The query needs more information in order to delete the right row:

By matching the score in addition to the name, the deletion gets much more exact.

```
DELETE FROM guitarwars WHERE name = 'Ashton Simpson' AND score = '368420'
```

The AND operator changes the query so that both the name and score must match.

guitarwars

id	date	name	score	screenshot
1	2008-04-22 14:37:34	Paco Jastorius	127650	
2	2008-04-22 21:27:54	Nevil Johansson	98430	
3	2008-04-23 09:06:35	Eddie Vanilli	345900	
4	2008-04-23 09:12:53	Belita Chevy	282470	
5	2008-04-23 09:13:34	Ashton Simpson	368420	
6	2008-04-23 14:09:50	Kenny Lavitz	64930	
7	2008-04-24 08:13:52	Phiz Lairston	186580	phizsscore.gif

Now that both the name and score have to match, the odds of accidentally deleting more than one score are decreased dramatically.

Control how much you delete with LIMIT

Using both the name and score columns as the basis for deleting a row is good... but not good enough. Application development is about minimizing risks at all cost, and there's still a slight risk of deleting multiple rows that match both the same name and score. The solution is to force the query to only delete **one row** no matter what. The LIMIT clause makes this happen:

> For maximum safety, put a limit on the number of rows that can be deleted.

```
DELETE FROM guitarwars WHERE name = 'Ashton Simpson' AND score = '368420' LIMIT 1
```

The number following LIMIT lets MySQL know the maximum number of rows to delete—in this case, one. So we're guaranteed to never delete more than one row with this query. But what if there were two Ashton Simpsons with the same score? Sure, this is an unlikely scenario, but it's sometimes worth considering extreme scenarios when working out the best design for an application.

guitarwars

id	date	name	score	screenshot
1	2008-04-22 14:37:34	Paco Jastorius	127650	
2	2008-04-22 21:27:54	Nevil Johansson	98430	
3	2008-04-23 09:06:35	Eddie Vanilli	345900	
4	2008-04-23 09:12:53	Belita Chevy	282470	
5	2008-04-23 09:13:34	Ashton Simpson	368420	
6	2008-04-23 14:09:50	Kenny Lavitz	64930	
7	2008-04-24 08:13:52	Phiz Lairston	186580	phizsscore.gif
	...			
523	2008-11-04 10:03:21	Ashton Simpson	368420	ashtonsscore.jpg

> Two high score rows with the exact same name and score present a problem for our DELETE query.

Write down what happens to this table when the DELETE statement above is executed. How could you make sure the right Ashton Simpson score is deleted?

....

....

....

> Would it be any better to use the ID of the score in the WHERE clause of the DELETE FROM query? It might help make sure we delete the right score, no?

Yes, it would! The ID of a high score is the perfect way to isolate the score for deletion.

Uniqueness is one of the main advantages of creating primary keys for your tables. The id column in the guitarwars table is the primary key and is, therefore, unique for each and every high score. By using this column in the WHERE clause of the DELETE FROM query, we eliminate all doubt surrounding which score we're deleting. Here's a new query that uses the id column to help ensure uniqueness:

```
DELETE FROM guitarwars WHERE id = 5
```

Deleting data based on a primary key helps to ensure accuracy in isolating the right row for deletion.

Trusting that the id column is indeed a primary key results in this code safely deleting only one row. But what if **you** didn't create the database, and maybe uniqueness wasn't properly enforced? Then a LIMIT clause might still make some sense. The rationale is that if you intend for a query to only affect one row, then say it in the query.

```
DELETE FROM guitarwars WHERE id = 5 LIMIT 1
```

The LIMIT clause explicitly states that the query can't delete more than one row.

It's never a bad idea to be very explicit with what you expect to be done in a query, and in this case LIMIT adds an extra degree of safety to the DELETE query.

PHP & MySQL Magnets

The removescore.php script is almost finished, but it is missing a few important pieces of code. Use the magnets to plug in the missing code and give Guitar Wars the ability to eradicate unwanted scores.

```
<html xmlns="http://www.w3.org/1999/xhtml" xml:lang="en" lang="en">
<head>
  <meta http-equiv="Content-Type" content="text/html; charset=utf-8"/>
  <title>Guitar Wars - Remove a High Score</title>
  <link rel="stylesheet" type="text/css" href="style.css" />
</head>
<body>
  <h2>Guitar Wars - Remove a High Score</h2>

<?php
  ...................... ('appvars.php');
  ...................... ('connectvars.php');
  if (isset($_GET['id']) && isset($_GET['date']) && isset($_GET['name']) &&
    isset($_GET['score']) && isset($_GET[..................... ])) {

    // Grab the score data from the GET
    $id = $_GET['id'];
    $date = $_GET['date'];
    $name = $_GET['name'];
    $score = $_GET['score'];
    .................... = $_GET[..................... ];
  }
  else if (isset($_POST['id']) && isset($_POST['name']) && isset($_POST['score'])) {
    // Grab the score data from the POST
    .......... = $_POST[.......... ];
    $name = $_POST['name'];
    $score = $_POST['score'];
    $screenshot = $_POST['screenshot'];
  }
  else {
    echo '<p class="error">Sorry, no high score was specified for removal.</p>';
  }

  if (isset($_POST['submit'])) {

    if ($_POST['confirm'] == ............ ) {

      // Delete the screen shot image file from the server
      @unlink(GW_UPLOADPATH . $screenshot);

      // Connect to the database
      $dbc = mysqli_ connect(DB_HOST,    DB_ USER, DB_PASSWORD, DB_NAME);
```

```
    // Delete the score data from the database
    $query = "                          guitarwars WHERE                        LIMIT        ";
              ................. .............                ...........................

    mysqli_query($dbc, $query);
    mysqli_close($dbc);

    // Confirm success with the user
    echo '<p>The high score of ' . $score . ' for ' . $name . ' was successfully removed.';
  }
  else {
    echo '<p class="error">The high score was not removed.</p>';
  }
}
else if (isset(         ) && isset(              ) && isset(              ) &&
                ............                ...............               .................
  isset($score) && isset($screenshot)) {
  echo '<p>Are you sure you want to delete the following high score?</p>';
  echo '<p><strong>Name: </strong>' . $name . '<br /><strong>Date: </strong>' . $date .
    '<br /><strong>Score: </strong>' . $score . '</p>';
  echo '<form method="post" action="removescore.php">';
  echo '<input type="radio" name="confirm" value="Yes" /> Yes ';
  echo '<input type="radio" name="confirm" value="No" checked="checked" /> No <br />';
  echo '<input type="submit" value="Submit" name="submit" />';

  echo '<input type="hidden" name=              value="' .              . '" />';
                                 .............         .............
  echo '<input type="hidden" name="name" value="' . $name . '" />';
  echo '<input type="hidden" name="score" value="' . $score . '" />';
  echo '<input type="hidden" name="screenshot" value="' . $screenshot . '" />';
  echo '</form>';
  }

  echo '<p><a href=..................... >&lt;&lt; Back to admin page</a></p>';

?>

</body>
</html>
```

removescore.php

require_once   'Yes' $id   "admin.php" $name   FROM

1   'id'   "id"   DELETE $date   'screenshot' $id $screenshot

$id   id   "id"   'screenshot' $id   =   require_once

'id' $id $id

PHP & MySQL Magnets Solution

The removescore.php script is almost finished, but it is missing a few
important pieces of code. Use the magnets to plug in the missing
code and give Guitar Wars the ability to eradicate unwanted scores.

```html
<html xmlns="http://www.w3.org/1999/xhtml" xml:lang="en" lang="en">
<head>
  <meta http-equiv="Content-Type" content="text/html; charset=utf-8"/>
  <title>Guitar Wars - Remove a High Score</title>
  <link rel="stylesheet" type="text/css" href="style.css" />
</head>
<body>
  <h2>Guitar Wars - Remove a High Score</h2>

<?php
  require_once ('appvars.php');
  require_once ('connectvars.php');
  if (isset($_GET['id']) && isset($_GET['date']) && isset($_GET['name']) &&
    isset($_GET['score']) && isset($_GET['screenshot'])) {

    // Grab the score data from the GET
    $id = $_GET['id'];
    $date = $_GET['date'];
    $name = $_GET['name'];
    $score = $_GET['score'];

    $screenshot = $_GET['screenshot'];
  }
  else if (isset($_POST['id']) && isset($_POST['name']) && isset($_POST['score'])) {
    // Grab the score data from the POST
    $id = $_POST['id'];
    $name = $_POST['name'];
    $score = $_POST['score'];
    $screenshot = $_POST['screenshot'];
  }
  else {
    echo '<p class="error">Sorry, no high score was specified for removal.</p>';
  }

  if (isset($_POST['submit'])) {
    if ($_POST['confirm'] == 'Yes') {
      // Delete the screen shot image file from the server
      @unlink(GW_UPLOADPATH . $screenshot);

      // Connect to the database
      $dbc = mysqli_connect(DB_HOST, DB_USER, DB_PASSWORD, DB_NAME);
```

Include the shared script
files but use required_once
since they are critical to
the score removal.

The script reacts differently
depending on whether the incoming
request is a GET or a POST.

The @ PHP error suppression directive prevents
errors from being displayed. This makes sense
for unlink() since we may be attempting to
delete a file that doesn't exist. In which case,
we don't want the user to see an error.

This script can be used
to remove any scores,
so the uploaded image
file must be deleted as
part of the removal.

The id column is matched by the DELETE query, along with using a LIMIT of one row.

```
    // Delete the score data from the database
    $query = " DELETE   FROM  guitarwars WHERE   id  =  $id  LIMIT  1  ";

    mysqli_query($dbc, $query);
    mysqli_close($dbc);

    // Confirm success with the user
    echo '<p>The high score of ' . $score . ' for ' . $name . ' was successfully removed.';
  }
  else {
    echo '<p class="error">The high score was not removed.</p>';
  }
}
else if (isset( $id ) && isset( $name ) && isset( $date ) &&
  isset($score) && isset($screenshot)) {
  echo '<p>Are you sure you want to delete the following high score?</p>';
  echo '<p><strong>Name: </strong>' . $name . '<br /><strong>Date: </strong>' . $date .
    '<br /><strong>Score: </strong>' . $score . '</p>';
  echo '<form method="post" action="removescore.php">';
  echo '<input type="radio" name="confirm" value="Yes" /> Yes ';
  echo '<input type="radio" name="confirm" value="No" checked="checked" /> No <br />';
  echo '<input type="submit" value="Submit" name="submit" />';

  echo '<input type="hidden" name= "id"  value="' . $id . '" />';

  echo '<input type="hidden" name="name" value="' . $name . '" />';
  echo '<input type="hidden" name="score" value="' . $score . '" />';
  echo '<input type="hidden" name="screenshot" value="' . $screenshot . '" />';
  echo '</form>';
}

  echo '<p><a href= "admin.php" >&lt;&lt; Back to admin page</a></p>';

?>

</body>
</html>
```

removescore.php

Provide a link back to the Admin page to improve navigation.

$id
"id"
'id'

There were a few magnets leftover.

A few hidden form fields are used to store the score data so that it gets sent along as part of the POST request.

We don't use $_SERVER['PHP_SELF'] here because it would include any data that had been passed through the URL query string as a GET. We want to make sure no GET data is passed along with this form – only POST data.

The confirmation form is only displayed if all of these high score variables are set.

Test Drive

Add Remove Score and Admin scripts to Guitar Wars so that scores can be removed.

Create two new text files, `removescore.php` and `admin.php`, and add the code to them that you've just worked through. Upload the new scripts to your web server, and then open the Admin script in your web browser. Click the "Remove" link for a score you'd like to get rid of, and then confirm its removal on the Remove Score page. Return to the Admin page to make sure the score is gone, and then go to the main Guitar Wars page (`index.php`) to see the change there.

The new Admin page provides links to remove unverified high scores.

There's only room in this town for one top rocker, and it's me!

The new Remove Score page takes care of both confirming and removing unwanted scores.

The main Guitar Wars page now only shows verified high scores.

Little Jacob, Guitar Warrior rock prodigy

The legit Guitar Warriors are now happy to see only verified high scores.

Unverified high scores, those without screen shot images, have now been removed from the system.

290

PHP&MySQLcross

Tired of uploading image files? How about uploading some knowledge into a bunch of squares laid out in a puzzle?

Across

1. The type attribute of the <input> tag must be set to this for a file upload form field.

4. It's usually a good idea to store uploaded application images in an ...... folder.

8. This SQL statement is used to change the structure of a table.

10. This SQL statement is used to put the results of a query in a certain order.

11. Information about uploaded files is stored in the $_..... superglobal variable.

12. This PHP statement is used to insert code from another script.

13. It's a good idea to do this to newly uploaded files.

Down

2. To prevent a DELETE FROM statement from deleting more than one row, use this SQL statement.

3. When a file is uploaded through a form, it is placed in a .... folder on the web server.

5. When altering a table, this SQL command takes care of adding a new column.

6. This PHP statement is used to create a constant.

7. Include files are very handy for .... data among several script files.

9. This SQL statement is used as part of another statement to order query results in descending order.

PHP&MySQLcross Solution

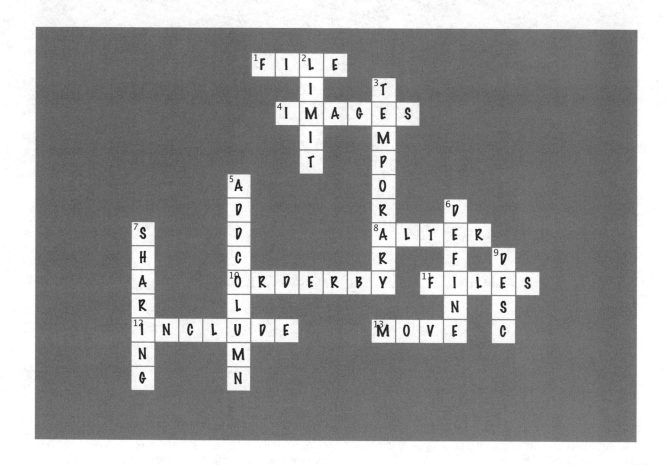

Your PHP & MySQL Toolbox

Feel free to take a virtual bow. Not
only are you loved by virtual guitarists
worldwide, but you've also added quite
a few new skills to your PHP and MySQL
skillset: altering the structure of tables,
handling file uploads, controlling the
order of data, and removing data.

CHAPTER 5

This folder provides a convenient
location to store images for an
application, including images that
were uploaded by users.

ALTER TABLE *table*
ADD COLUMN *column type*

Use this SQL statement to add a
new column of data to an existing
database table. The column is
added to the end of the table
and is initially empty for rows
that are already in the database.

$_FILES

This built-in PHP superglobal
variable stores information about
files that have been uploaded
through a file input form. You can
use it to determine the filename,
the temporary storage location
of the file, the file size, and the
file type, among other things.

include, include_once,
require, require_once

These PHP statements allow
you to share script code across
multiple script files in an
application, eliminating duplicate
code and making the code easier
to maintain.

ORDER BY *column*

This SQL statement orders the
results of a query based on a
certain column of data. Use ASC
or DESC after the statement
to sort the data in ascending
or descending order. ASC is the
default ordering for ORDER BY,
and is, therefore, optional.

DELETE FROM *table*
WHERE *column = match*
LIMIT *num*

Use this SQL statement to
remove a row from a database
table. More than one match can
(and often should) be used to
improve the accuracy of the
deletion, not to mention limiting
the deletion to a single row.

6 securing your application

A short climb, a little telephone rewiring, and this little one-horse town won't know what hit it.

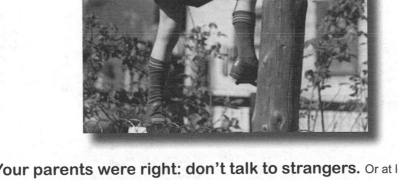

Your parents were right: don't talk to strangers. Or at least don't trust them. If nothing else, *don't give them the keys to your application data*, assuming they'll do the right thing. It's a cruel world out there, and you can't count on everyone to be trustworthy. In fact, as a web application developer, you have to be part cynic, part conspiracy theorist. Yes, people are generally bad, and they're definitely out to get you! OK, maybe that's a little extreme, but it's very important to **take security seriously** and **design your applications so that they're protected** against anyone who might choose to do harm.

The day the music died

Uh oh, our young virtual rock prodigy's moment in the limelight has been short-lived, as Jacob's top Guitar Wars score is somehow missing, along with all the other scores. It seems a diabolical force is at work to foil the high score application and prevent Guitar Warriors from competing online. Unhappy virtual guitarists are unhappy users, and that can only lead to unhappy application developers... you!

The main page is missing high scores because they've all been removed from the database!

This isn't fair! I worked so hard to become the best Guitar Warrior, and now my score is gone.

Guitar Wars top scorer Jacob, fighting mad at his top score disappearing from the high score list.

Jacob's musical weapon of choice, a vintage 2005 Eradicaster.

Where did the high scores go?

We know that the main Guitar Wars page is empty, but does that mean the database is empty too? A SELECT query can answer that question:

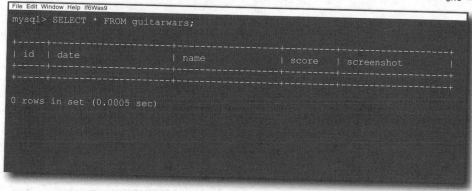

A SELECT query reveals that the guitarwars table is completely empty—all the scores are gone!

Somehow all of the high score rows of data have been deleted from the Guitar Wars database. Could it be that maybe someone out there is using our Remove Score script to do evil? We need to protect the scores!

Sharpen your pencil

Circle which of the following techniques you could use to protect the Guitar Wars high scores from bitter virtual guitar haters, and then write down why.

Password protect the Admin page so that only people who know the password (you!) can remove scores.

....
....
....
....

Create a user registration system, and then only give some users (you!) administrative privileges.

....
....
....
....

Check the IP address of the computer trying to access the Admin page, and only allow certain ones (yours!).

....
....
....
....

Eliminate the score removal feature altogether.

....
....
....
....

Sharpen your pencil
Solution

Circle which of the following techniques you could use to protect the Guitar Wars high scores from bitter virtual guitar haters, and then write down why.

 Password protect the Admin page so that only people who know the password (you!) can remove scores.

Password protecting the Admin page is a good quick and dirty solution because it's not too complicated and it secures the site quickly.

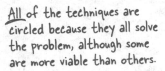 All of the techniques are circled because they all solve the problem, although some are more viable than others.

Create a user registration system, and then only give some users (you!) administrative privileges.

A user registration system with admin privileges is a great solution but involves a fair amount of planning and coding effort... Guitar Wars needs security now!

 Check the IP address of the computer trying to access the Admin page, and only allow certain ones (yours!).

Checking the IP address works but it makes the site dependent upon your computer's IP address, which very well may change.

 Eliminate the score removal feature altogether.

Removing the feature certainly solves this specific problem, but if you recall, the removal feature was originally added in the previous chapter to make the site easier to maintain.

Securing the teeming hordes

A simple and straightforward way to quickly secure the Guitar Wars high scores is to use HTTP authentication to password protect the Admin page. This technique actually involves both a user name and a password, but the idea is to require a piece of secret information from an administrator before they have access to restricted application features, such as the score removal links.

When a page is secured using HTTP authentication, a window pops up requesting the user name and password before access is allowed to the protected page. In the case of Guitar Wars, you can limit access to the Admin page to as few people as you want, potentially just you!

HTTP authentication provides a simple way to secure a page using PHP.

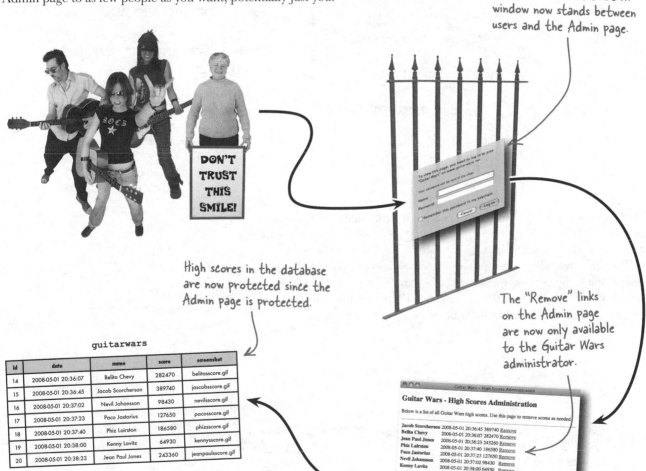

The HTTP authentication window now stands between users and the Admin page.

DON'T TRUST THIS SMILE!

High scores in the database are now protected since the Admin page is protected.

The "Remove" links on the Admin page are now only available to the Guitar Wars administrator.

guitarwars

id	date	name	score	screenshot
14	2008-05-01 20:36:07	Belita Chevy	282470	belitasscore.gif
15	2008-05-01 20:36:45	Jacob Scorcherson	389740	jascobsscore.gif
16	2008-05-01 20:37:02	Nevil Johansson	98430	nevilsscore.gif
17	2008-05-01 20:37:23	Paco Jastorius	127650	pacosscore.gif
18	2008-05-01 20:37:40	Phiz Lairston	186580	phizsscore.gif
19	2008-05-01 20:38:00	Kenny Lavitz	64930	kennysscore.gif
20	2008-05-01 20:38:23	Jean Paul Jones	243360	jeanpaulsscore.gif

Guitar Wars - High Scores Administration

Below is a list of all Guitar Wars high scores. Use this page to remove scores as needed.

Jacob Scorcherson	2008-05-01 20:36:45 389740	Remove
Belita Chevy	2008-05-01 20:36:07 282470	Remove
Jean Paul Jones	2008-05-01 20:38:23 243360	Remove
Phiz Lairston	2008-05-01 20:37:40 186580	Remove
Paco Jastorius	2008-05-01 20:37:23 127650	Remove
Nevil Johansson	2008-05-01 20:37:02 98430	Remove
Kenny Lavitz	2008-05-01 20:38:00 64930	Remove

Protecting the Guitar Wars Admin page

HTTP authentication works like this: when a user tries to access a page protected by authentication, such as our Admin page, they are presented with a window that asks them for a user name and password.

The web browser uses a window like this to request a user name and password before allowing access to a protected page.

To keep things simple, the password isn't encrypted.

This PHP superglobal variable stores the user name entered into the authentication window.

$_SERVER['PHP_AUTH_USER']

$_SERVER['PHP_AUTH_PW']

This variable stores the password entered into the authentication window.

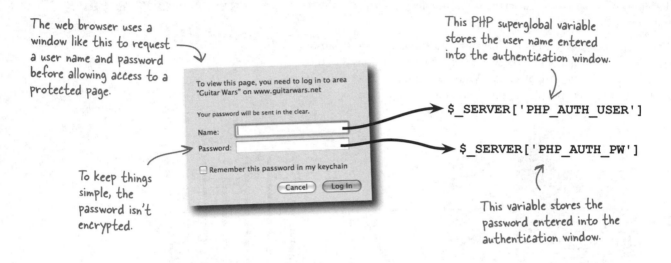

PHP enters the picture through its access to the user name and password entered by the user. They are stored in the $_SERVER superglobal, which is similar to other superglobals you've used ($_POST, $_FILES, etc.). A PHP script can analyze the user name and password entered by the user and decide if they should be allowed access to the protected page. Let's say we only allow access to the Admin page if the user name is "rock" and the password is "roll." Here's how the Admin page is unlocked:

The Admin page is only accessible if the correct user name and password are entered.

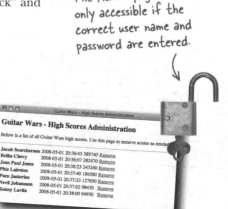

$_SERVER['PHP_AUTH_PW']

$_SERVER['PHP_AUTH_USER']

there are no
Dumb Questions

Q: **Is HTTP authentication really secure?**

A: Yes. And no. It all depends on what you're trying to accomplish with security. Nothing is ever truly 100% secure, so we're always talking about **degrees of security**. For the purposes of protecting high scores in Guitar Wars, HTTP authentication provides a reasonable level of security. You could add encryption to the password to ramp that up a bit further. However, it's probably not sufficient for an application involving data that is more sensitive, such as financial data.

Q: **What happens if the user name and password are entered incorrectly?**

A: The browser emits a small electrical shock through the mouse. No, it's nothing that harsh. Usually a message is displayed letting users know that they're attempting to access a secure page that is apparently none of their business. It's ultimately up to you how grim you want this message to read.

Q: **Does HTTP authentication require both a user name and password? What if I only want to use a password?**

A: You aren't required to use both a user name and password. If you just want a password, focus solely on checking the $_SERVER['PHP_AUTH_PW'] global variable. More on how this variable is checked in just a moment...

Q: **How exactly do you protect a page with HTTP authentication? Do you call a PHP function?**

A: Yes, you do. HTTP authentication involves establishing a line of communication between the browser and the server through HTTP headers. You can think of a header as a short little conversation between the browser and the server. Browsers and servers use headers quite often to communicate outside of the context of PHP, but PHP does allow you to send a header, which is how HTTP authentication works. We're about to dig a lot deeper into headers and their role in HTTP authentication with PHP.

When should the authentication of the Admin page actually take place?

HTTP authentication requires headers

The idea behind HTTP authentication is that the server withholds a protected web page, and then asks the browser to prompt the user for a user name and password. If the user enters these correctly, the browser goes ahead and sends along the page. This dialog between browser and server takes place through **headers**, which are little text messages with specific instructions on what is being requested or delivered.

Headers are actually used **every time** you visit a web page, not just when authentication is required. Here's how a normal, unprotected web page is delivered from the server to the browser with the help of headers:

All web pages are delivered with the help of headers.

Web server

1 The browser requests a page from the server by sending a couple of headers to identify the file being requested and the host name of the server.

This collection of headers constitutes a web page request.

```
GET /index.php ...
Host: www.guitar...
Connection: close
...
```

2 The server responds with a collection of headers, followed by the requested page.

```
HTTP/1.1 200 OK
Date: Thu, 01 May...
Server: Apache/2....
...
```

index.php

This group of headers constitutes a web page response.

Client web browser

Guitar Wars - High Scores

Guitar Wars - High Scores

Welcome, Guitar Warrior, do you have what it takes to crack the high score list? If so, just add your own score.

Top Score: 389740

389740
Name: Jacob Scorcherson
Date: 2008-04-25 11:49:23

```
Guitar
Wars

Name:
JACOBOWNSU
Score:
389740
```

186580
Name: Phiz Lairston
Date: 2008-04-25 11:49:25

```
Guitar
Wars

Name:
PHIZL
```

3 The browser receives the headers and the page, and renders the HTML code for the page.

When all is said and done, the headers help to successfully deliver the requested page to the browser.

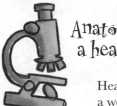

Anatomy of a header

Headers control precisely how and what kind of information is passed back and forth between a web browser and web server. An individual header often consists of a name/value pair that identifies a piece of information, such as the content type of a web page (HTML). A certain group of headers is sent to the server as part of a web page request, and then another group is returned to the browser as part of the response. Let's take a closer look at these groups of headers to find out exactly what is sent as the client and server communicate with each other.

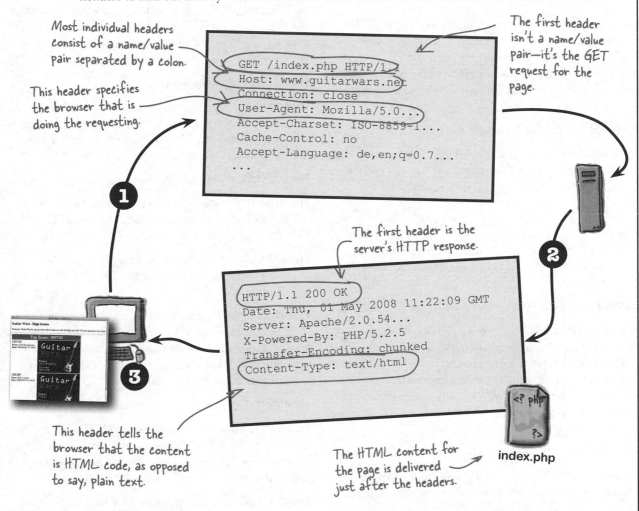

Most individual headers consist of a name/value pair separated by a colon.

This header specifies the browser that is doing the requesting.

The first header isn't a name/value pair—it's the GET request for the page.

```
GET /index.php HTTP/1.1
Host: www.guitarwars.net
Connection: close
User-Agent: Mozilla/5.0...
Accept-Charset: ISO-8859-1...
Cache-Control: no
Accept-Language: de,en;q=0.7...
...
```

1

The first header is the server's HTTP response.

```
HTTP/1.1 200 OK
Date: Thu, 01 May 2008 11:22:09 GMT
Server: Apache/2.0.54...
X-Powered-By: PHP/5.2.5
Transfer-Encoding: chunked
Content-Type: text/html
```

2

3

This header tells the browser that the content is HTML code, as opposed to say, plain text.

The HTML content for the page is delivered just after the headers.

index.php

Headers matter to us in regard to Guitar Wars because they provide the mechanism for disrupting the delivery of a page from the server and requiring the user to enter a user name and password before it can be delivered. In other words, you have to tweak the headers returned by the server to protect a page with HTTP authentication.

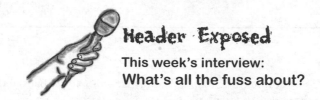

Header Exposed

This week's interview:
What's all the fuss about?

Head First: You seem to be grabbing a lot of attention when it comes to authenticating web pages. Is it really justified, or are you just looking for your fifteen minutes of virtual fame?

Header: Oh, I'm justified alright. You more than likely take for granted that I play a role in delivering every single web page in existence. So I guess you could say the web wouldn't even work without me in the picture. I'll be around a lot longer than fifteen minutes, even if I do go largely underappreciated.

Head First: So what exactly is this role you play?

Header: You have to understand that web browsers and web servers aren't people, so they can't just call each other up on the phone or send a text message.

Head First: OMG!

Header: Yeah, I know, it's a little shocking but machines just don't communicate the same way people do. But browsers and servers still have to communicate, and they do so using me.

Head First: So how does that work?

Header: When someone types in a URL or clicks a link on a web page, the browser assembles a GET request that it sends to the server. This request is packaged into a series of headers, each of which contains information about the request. The headers hold information like the name and host of the page being requested, the type of browser doing the requesting, etc.

Head First: I still don't see why that's important.

Header: Well, do you think it's important when you tell the person at the coffee shop that you want a giganto vanilla espressiato with skim milk?

Head First: Of course, they need to know what I want.

Header: That's the same idea here. The browser tells the server what it wants by packaging the request up and sending it along in headers.

Head First: Interesting. But I heard that servers can send headers as well. I thought servers just sent back web pages.

Header: Ah, good question. I am just as important on the other side of the communication because the server has to do more than just dump a bunch of content on the browser. The browser wouldn't have a clue what to do with it without knowing a bit more.

Head First: Such as what?

Header: The type of the content, for one thing. That's probably the most important thing, but the server also sends along other stuff like the size of the content, the date and time of the delivery, and so on.

Head First: When does the web page itself get sent?

Header: Right after the server sends me to the browser, it follows up with the actual content, be it HTML code, PDF data, or image data such as a GIF or JPEG image.

Head First: OK, I'm starting to see how you work in regard to normal web pages. But what about this authentication stuff?

Header: I play the same role for an authenticated web page as I do for a normal web page except that I also take care of letting the browser know that the page must be authenticated. That way the browser can prompt the user for authentication information.

Head First: You mean a user name and password?

Header: Exactly. And then it's up to PHP code on the server to decide if the user name and password match up, in which case, the server can go ahead and send along the rest of the page.

Head First: Fascinating. Thanks for the heads up.

Header: No problem. That's just part of my job.

Take control of headers with PHP

Using PHP, you can carefully control the headers sent by the server to the browser, opening up the possibilities for performing header-driven tasks such as HTTP authentication. The built-in `header()` function is how a header is sent from the server to the browser from within a PHP script.

The header() function lets you create and send a header from a PHP script.

```php
header('Content-Type: text/html');
```

The `header()` function immediately sends a header from the server to the browser and must be called before any actual content is sent to the browser. This is a very strict requirement—if even a single character or space is sent ahead of a header, the browser will reject it with an error. For this reason, calls to the `header()` function should precede any HTML code in a PHP script:

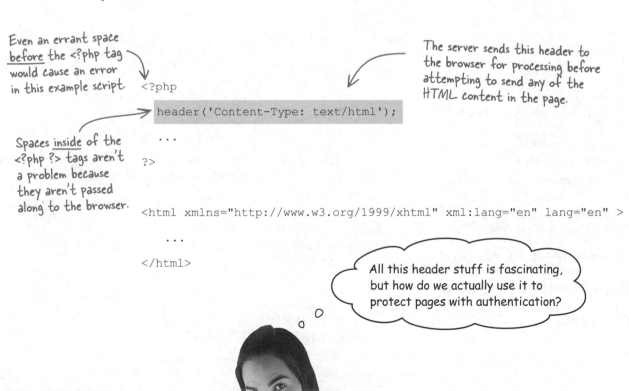

Even an errant space _before_ the <?php tag would cause an error in this example script.

The server sends this header to the browser for processing before attempting to send any of the HTML content in the page.

```php
<?php
    header('Content-Type: text/html');
    ...
?>
```

Spaces _inside_ of the <?php ?> tags aren't a problem because they aren't passed along to the browser.

```html
<html xmlns="http://www.w3.org/1999/xhtml" xml:lang="en" lang="en" >
    ...
</html>
```

All this header stuff is fascinating, but how do we actually use it to protect pages with authentication?

Authenticating with headers

Authenticating the Guitar Wars Admin page using headers involves crafting a very specific set of headers, two in fact, that let the browser know to prompt the user for a user name and password before delivering the page. These two headers are generated by PHP code in the Admin script, and control the delivery of the page to the browser.

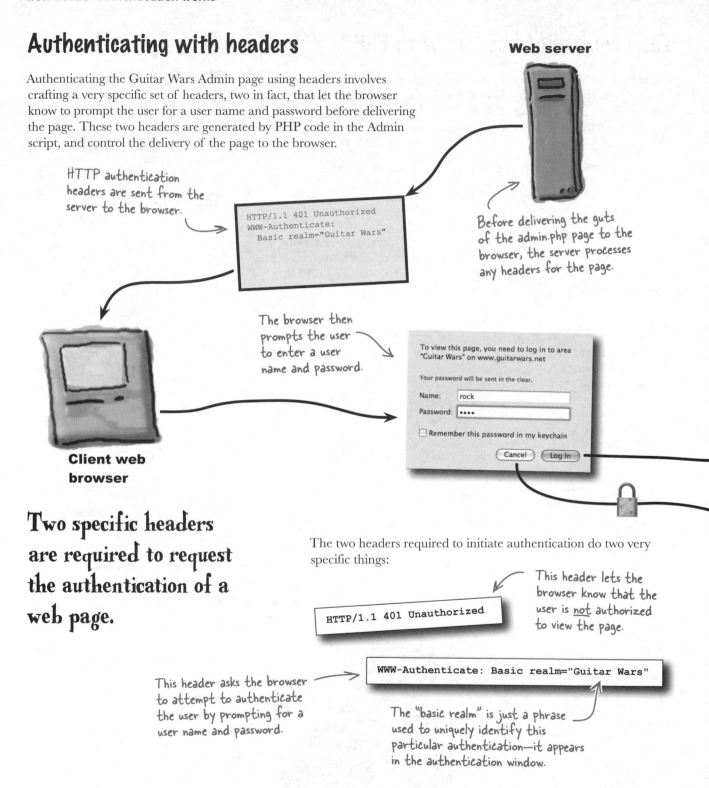

Web server

HTTP authentication headers are sent from the server to the browser.

```
HTTP/1.1 401 Unauthorized
WWW-Authenticate:
    Basic realm="Guitar Wars"
```

Before delivering the guts of the admin.php page to the browser, the server processes any headers for the page.

The browser then prompts the user to enter a user name and password.

To view this page, you need to log in to area "Guitar Wars" on www.guitarwars.net

Your password will be sent in the clear.

Name: rock
Password: ••••

☐ Remember this password in my keychain

Cancel   Log In

Client web browser

Two specific headers are required to request the authentication of a web page.

The two headers required to initiate authentication do two very specific things:

```
HTTP/1.1 401 Unauthorized
```

This header lets the browser know that the user is <u>not</u> authorized to view the page.

This header asks the browser to attempt to authenticate the user by prompting for a user name and password.

```
WWW-Authenticate: Basic realm="Guitar Wars"
```

The "basic realm" is just a phrase used to uniquely identify this particular authentication—it appears in the authentication window.

After processing the authentication headers, the browser waits for the user to take action via the authentication window. The browser takes a dramatically different action in response to what the user does...

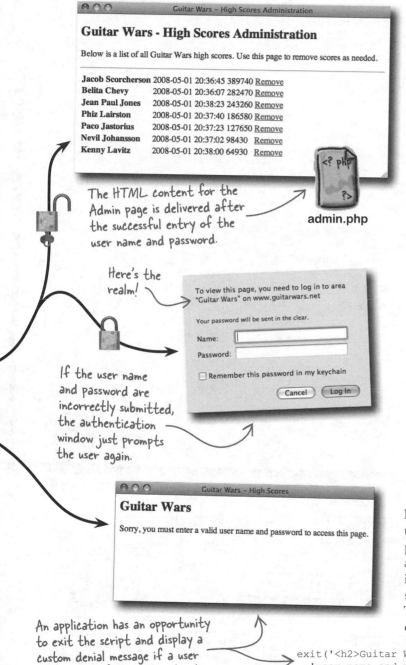

Guitar Wars - High Scores Administration

Below is a list of all Guitar Wars high scores. Use this page to remove scores as needed.

Jacob Scorcherson	2008-05-01 20:36:45	389740	Remove
Belita Chevy	2008-05-01 20:36:07	282470	Remove
Jean Paul Jones	2008-05-01 20:38:23	243260	Remove
Phiz Lairston	2008-05-01 20:37:40	186580	Remove
Paco Jastorius	2008-05-01 20:37:23	127650	Remove
Nevil Johansson	2008-05-01 20:37:02	98430	Remove
Kenny Lavitz	2008-05-01 20:38:00	64930	Remove

The HTML content for the Admin page is delivered after the successful entry of the user name and password.

admin.php

Here's the realm!

To view this page, you need to log in to area "Guitar Wars" on www.guitarwars.net

Your password will be sent in the clear.

Name:

Password:

☐ Remember this password in my keychain

Cancel   Log In

If the user name and password are incorrectly submitted, the authentication window just prompts the user again.

Guitar Wars

Sorry, you must enter a valid user name and password to access this page.

An application has an opportunity to exit the script and display a custom denial message if a user cancels out of the authentication.

If the user enters the **correct** user name and password, and clicks Log In, the server sends the HTML content of the admin.php page to the browser. The browser displays the Admin page, and the user can then remove scores just like the previous unprotected version.

If the user enters the **incorrect** user name and password, and clicks Log In, the server tells the browser to prompt the user again. The browser continues this process as long as the user keeps entering incorrect user name/password combinations. In other words, if they don't know the user name and password, their only way out is to click Cancel.

If the user clicks the Cancel button to bail out of the authentication, the server sends the browser a page with a denial message, and nothing else—the admin.php page is not sent. The denial message is controlled by PHP code in the admin.php script that is closely associated with the headers. This code calls the PHP exit() function to display a message and immediately exit the script:

```php
exit('<h2>Guitar Wars</h2>Sorry, you must enter a valid ' .
'user name and password to access this page.');
```

PHP Magnets

The Guitar Wars Admin script is missing several important pieces of PHP code that provide HTTP authentication. Use the magnets to fill in the missing code and use headers to make the Admin page secure. Hint: Some magnets may be used more than once.

```php
<?php
  // User name and password for authentication

  ........................ = 'rock';

  ........................ = 'roll';

  if (!isset( ........................................................ ) ||
   !isset( ........................................................ ) ||
   ($_SERVER['PHP_AUTH_USER'] != ........................ ) || ($_SERVER['PHP_AUTH_PW'] != ........................ )) {
    // The user name/password are incorrect so send the authentication headers

    .................. ('HTTP/1.1 401 Unauthorized');
    .................. ('WWW-Authenticate: Basic realm= ........................ ');
    .............. ('<h2>Guitar Wars</h2>Sorry, you must enter a valid user name and password to ' .

    'access this page.');
  }
?>

<html xmlns="http://www.w3.org/1999/xhtml" xml:lang="en" lang="en">
  ...
</html>
```

admin.php

Magnets:
- `$username`
- `username`
- `PHP_AUTH_USER`
- `_SERVER`
- `exit`
- `'` `'` `'` `'`
- `header`
- `$` `$` `$` `$`
- `"Guitar Wars"`
- `[` `]` `[` `]`
- `$password`
- `_SERVER`
- `PHP_AUTH_PW`
- `password`

I wonder if it's possible to send other kinds of headers using PHP?

Indeed it is... headers aren't just for security

Although authentication presents the immediate need for headers, they are quite flexible and can do lots of other interesting things. Just call the `header()` function with the appropriate name/value pair, like this:

The browser is redirected to the About page upon receiving this header.

```php
<?php
    header('Location: http://www.guitarwars.net/about.php');
?>
```

The header is called a **location header** and redirects the current page to a page called `about.php` on the same Guitar Wars site. Here we use a similar header to redirect to the `about.php` page after five seconds:

The browser is redirected to the About page after 5 seconds.

```php
<?php
    header('Refresh: 5; url=http://www.guitarwars.net/about.php');
    echo 'In 5 seconds you'll be taken to the About page.';
?>
```

This header is called a **refresh header** since it refreshes a page after a period of time has elapsed. You often see the URL in such headers reference the current page so that it refreshes itself.

One last header is called a **content type header** because it controls the type of the content being delivered by the server. As an example, you can force a page to be plain text, as opposed to HTML, by using the following header when calling the `header()` function:

The content is delivered to the browser as plain text.

```php
<?php
    header('Content-Type: text/plain');
    echo 'This <strong>text</strong> won't actually be bold.';
?>
```

In this example, the text echoed to the browser is displayed exactly as shown with no special formatting. In other words, the server is telling the browser **not** to render the echoed content as HTML, so the HTML tags are displayed literally as text.

Watch it!

Headers must be the very first thing sent to the browser in a PHP file.

Because headers must be sent before any content, it is extremely important to not allow even a single space to appear outside of PHP code before calling the `header()` function in a PHP script.

PHP Magnets Solution

The Guitar Wars Admin script is missing several important pieces of PHP code that provide HTTP authentication. Use the magnets to fill in the missing code and use headers to make the Admin page secure. Hint: Some magnets may be used more than once.

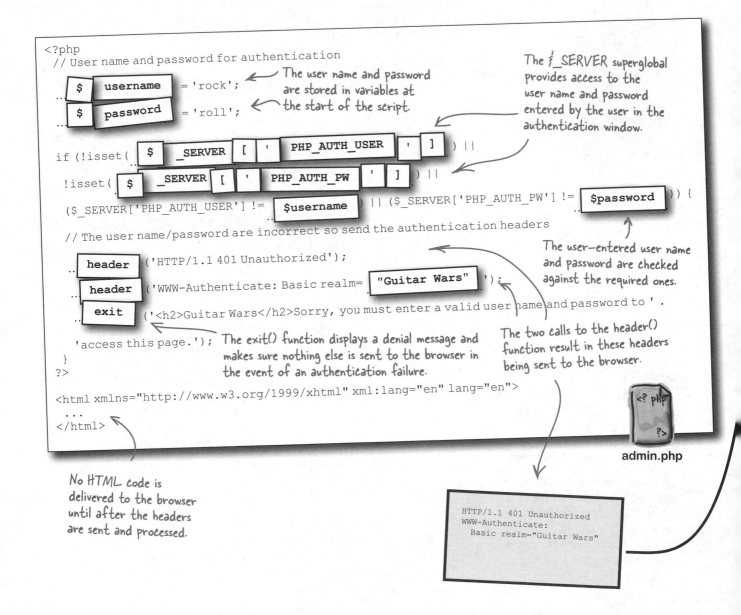

```php
<?php
  // User name and password for authentication
  $ username = 'rock';
  $ password = 'roll';

  if (!isset( $ _SERVER [ ' PHP_AUTH_USER ' ] ) ||
     !isset( $ _SERVER [ ' PHP_AUTH_PW ' ] ) ||
     ($_SERVER['PHP_AUTH_USER'] != $username ) || ($_SERVER['PHP_AUTH_PW'] != $password )) {
    // The user name/password are incorrect so send the authentication headers
    header ('HTTP/1.1 401 Unauthorized');
    header ('WWW-Authenticate: Basic realm= "Guitar Wars" ');
    exit ('<h2>Guitar Wars</h2>Sorry, you must enter a valid user name and password to ' .
      'access this page.');
  }
?>
<html xmlns="http://www.w3.org/1999/xhtml" xml:lang="en" lang="en">
  ...
</html>
```

The user name and password are stored in variables at the start of the script.

The $_SERVER superglobal provides access to the user name and password entered by the user in the authentication window.

The user-entered user name and password are checked against the required ones.

The exit() function displays a denial message and makes sure nothing else is sent to the browser in the event of an authentication failure.

The two calls to the header() function result in these headers being sent to the browser.

No HTML code is delivered to the browser until after the headers are sent and processed.

admin.php

```
HTTP/1.1 401 Unauthorized
WWW-Authenticate:
  Basic realm="Guitar Wars"
```

Test Drive

Add HTTP authorization to the Admin script.

Modify the `admin.php` script to use HTTP authentication so that only you have access to it. Upload the script to your web server and then open it in your web browser. Try entering the wrong user name and password first to see how access is restricted.

The Guitar Warriors are stoked about the high score application now being safe and secure!

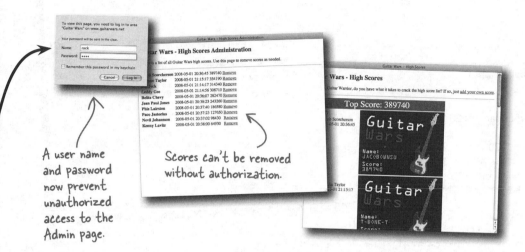

A user name and password now prevent unauthorized access to the Admin page.

Scores can't be removed without authorization.

there are no Dumb Questions

Q: When exactly does the `exit()` function get called in the Guitar Wars Admin script?

A: Even though the `exit()` function appears in the PHP code just below the two calls to the `header()` function, it's only called if the user cancels out of the authentication window by clicking the Cancel button. If the authentication fails, the server doesn't continue executing past the two `header()` calls. Instead, it resends the headers and tries again. Only if the user clicks Cancel does the server make it to the `exit()` function, in which case it sends along the content within the function call and nothing else. If the authentication succeeds, `exit()` isn't called because the script never makes it inside the `if` statement—the code inside the `if` statement is only executed if the user name and password aren't set or have been entered incorrectly.

Q: Does the "basic realm" of an HTTP authentication have any real purpose?

A: Yes. It defines a security "zone" that is protected by a particular user name and password. Once the user name and password have been successfully entered for a given realm, the browser will remember it and not continue to display the authentication window for subsequent authentication headers in the same realm. In other words, realms allow a browser to remember that you've met the security requirements for a given collection of pages—just specify the same realm for the authentication headers in the pages.

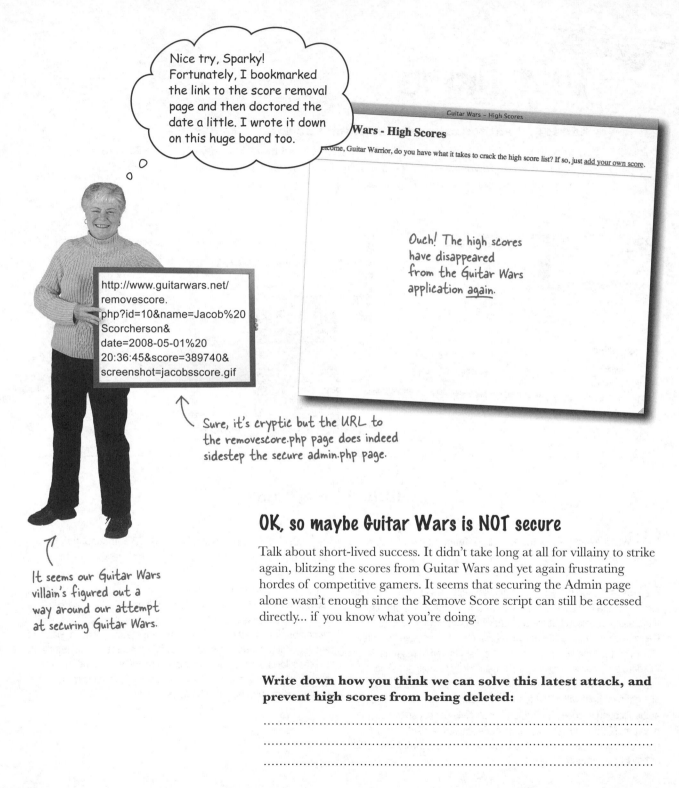

Nice try, Sparky! Fortunately, I bookmarked the link to the score removal page and then doctored the date a little. I wrote it down on this huge board too.

Guitar Wars - High Scores

Wars - High Scores

...ome, Guitar Warrior, do you have what it takes to crack the high score list? If so, just add your own score.

Ouch! The high scores have disappeared from the Guitar Wars application again.

http://www.guitarwars.net/ removescore. php?id=10&name=Jacob%20 Scorcherson& date=2008-05-01%20 20:36:45&score=389740& screenshot=jacobsscore.gif

Sure, it's cryptic but the URL to the removescore.php page does indeed sidestep the secure admin.php page.

It seems our Guitar Wars villain's figured out a way around our attempt at securing Guitar Wars.

OK, so maybe Guitar Wars is NOT secure

Talk about short-lived success. It didn't take long at all for villainy to strike again, blitzing the scores from Guitar Wars and yet again frustrating hordes of competitive gamers. It seems that securing the Admin page alone wasn't enough since the Remove Score script can still be accessed directly... if you know what you're doing.

Write down how you think we can solve this latest attack, and prevent high scores from being deleted:

....

....

....

> We need to secure the Remove Score script, and I'm pretty sure we can just use HTTP authentication again.

Frank → Jill → Joe

Joe: That makes sense. I mean, it worked fine for the Admin page.

Frank: That's true. So all we have to do is put the same header authorization code in the Remove Score script, and we're good to go, right?

Jill: Yes, that will certainly work. But I worry about duplicating all that authorization code in two places. What happens if later on we add another page that needs to be protected? Do we duplicate the code yet again?

Joe: Code duplication is definitely a problem. Especially since there is a user name and password that all the scripts need to share. If we ever wanted to change those, we'd have to make the change in every protected script.

Frank: I've got it! How about putting the `$username` and `$password` variables into their own include file, and then sharing that between the protected scripts. We could even put it in an `appvars.php` include file for application variables.

Joe: I like where you're headed but that solution only deals with a small part of the code duplication. Remember, we're talking about a decent sized little chunk of code.

```php
<?php
 // User name and password for authentication
 $username = 'rock';
 $password = 'roll';

 if (!isset($_SERVER['PHP_AUTH_USER']) || !isset($_SERVER['PHP_AUTH_PW']) ||
  ($_SERVER['PHP_AUTH_USER'] != $username) || ($_SERVER['PHP_AUTH_PW'] != $password)) {
  // The user name/password are incorrect so send the authentication headers
  header('HTTP/1.1 401 Unauthorized');
  header('WWW-Authenticate: Basic realm="Guitar Wars"');
  exit('<h2>Guitar Wars</h2>Sorry, you must enter a valid user name and password to access this page.');
 }
?>

<html>
```

admin.php

Jill: You're both right, and that's why I think we need a new include file that stores away all of the authorization code, not just the `$username` and `$password` variables.

Frank: Ah, and we can just include that script in any page we want to protect with HTTP authorization.

Joe: That's right! We just have to make sure we always include it first thing since it relies on headers for all the HTTP authorization stuff.

Create an Authorize script

We already have all the code we need for a new Authorize script; it's just a matter of moving the code from `admin.php` to a new script file (`authorize.php`), and replacing the original code with a `require_once` statement.

> We're pulling this code from admin.php so that we can place it in its own script file, authorize.php.

```php
<?php
  // User name and password for authentication
  $username = 'rock';
  $password = 'roll';

  if (!isset($_SERVER['PHP_AUTH_USER']) || !isset($_SERVER['PHP_AUTH_PW']) ||
    ($_SERVER['PHP_AUTH_USER'] != $username) || ($_SERVER['PHP_AUTH_PW'] != $password)) {
    // The user name/password are incorrect so send the authentication headers
    header('HTTP/1.1 401 Unauthorized');
    header('WWW-Authenticate: Basic realm="Guitar Wars"');
    exit('<h2>Guitar Wars</h2>Sorry, you must enter a valid user name and password to access this page.');
  }
?>
```

```php
<html>
<head>
  <meta http-equiv="Content-Type" content="text/html; charset=utf-8" />
  <title>Guitar Wars—High Scores Administration</title>
  <link rel="stylesheet" type="text/css" href="style.css" />
</head>
<body>
  <h2>Guitar Wars—High Scores Administration</h2>
  <p>Below is a list of all Guitar Wars high scores. Use this page to remove scores as needed.</p>
  <hr />

<?php
  require_once('appvars.php');
  require_once('connectvars.php');

  // Connect to the database
  $dbc = mysqli_connect(DB_HOST, DB_USER, DB_PASSWORD, DB_NAME);

  // Retrieve the score data from MySQL
  $query = "SELECT * FROM guitarwars ORDER BY score DESC, date ASC";
  $data = mysqli_query($dbc, $query);

  // Loop through the array of score data, formatting it as HTML
  echo '<table>';
  while ($row = mysqli_fetch_array($data)) {
    // Display the score data
    echo '<tr class="scorerow"><td><strong>' . $row['name'] . '</strong></td>';
    echo '<td>' . $row['date'] . '</td>';
    echo '<td>' . $row['score'] . '</td>';
    echo '<td><a href="removescore.php?id=' . $row['id'] . '&amp;date=' . $row['date'] .
      '&amp;name=' . $row['name'] . '&amp;score=' . $row['score'] .
      '&amp;screenshot=' . $row['screenshot'] . '">Remove</a></td></tr>';
  }
  echo '</table>';

  mysqli_close($dbc);
?>

</body>
</html>
```

admin.php

```php
<?php
 // User name and password for authentication
 $username = 'rock';
 $password = 'roll';

 if (!isset($_SERVER['PHP_AUTH_USER']) || !isset($_SERVER['PHP_AUTH_PW']) ||
  ($_SERVER['PHP_AUTH_USER'] != $username) || ($_SERVER['PHP_AUTH_PW'] != $password)) {
  // The user name/password are incorrect so send the authentication headers
  header('HTTP/1.1 401 Unauthorized');
  header('WWW-Authenticate: Basic realm="Guitar Wars"');
  exit('<h2>Guitar Wars</h2>Sorry, you must enter a valid user name and password to access this page.');
 }
?>
```

Since the Authorize script is shared, you're guaranteed that the two pages have the same authentication realm, which means they share the same user name and password.

// The user name/password are incorrect so send the authentication headers

authorize.php

```php
<?php
 require_once('authorize.php');
?>

<html>
```

The shared Authorize script is included at the very beginning of this script since it calls the header() function.

```php
<?php
 require_once('authorize.php');
?>

<html>
```

removescore.php

The authentication code in the Admin script is replaced with a single line of PHP code.

admin.php

BULLET POINTS

- PHP scripts can use headers to control how the server delivers web content to the browser.

- The built-in PHP `header()` function is used to send headers to the browser, which can be used to redirect a page, control the content type of a page, or request the authentication of a page.

- When headers are sent to the browser using the `header()` function, calls to the `header()` function must come before any other content is sent.

- When a page is protected using HTTP authentication, the user name and password entered by the user are stored in the `$_SERVER` superglobal.

- The "basic realm" of an HTTP authentication is a security zone that gets associated with a specific user name and password, allowing multiple pages to be secured together.

- The built-in PHP `exit()` function exits a PHP script, preventing any code following it from being executed or otherwise sent to the browser.

there are no
Dumb Questions

Q: I still don't fully understand how Ethel got around the security in Guitar Wars. What did she do?

A: She capitalized on the weakness inherent in only protecting one page (Admin) when the remove score feature really relies on two pages (Admin and Remove Score). The Admin page presents a series of Remove links that link to the Remove Score page. The specifics about which score to remove are passed in the URL, allowing the Remove Score script to access them through the $_GET superglobal. If you were able to put together a legit URL for the Remove Score page, you could remove scores without even going through the Admin page. That's what Ethel did.

Q: But how did she know how to structure the URL to the Remove Score page?

A: She's pretty crafty, but this task didn't require a genius. Remember she mentioned bookmarking the Remove Score page back when the whole site was unprotected. Well, a bookmark is just a URL, and she was able to use it to construct a URL that directly accessed the Remove Score page without having to go through the Admin page.

Q: OK, but the high scores had been re-entered since the previous attack. Doesn't that mean the old URLs wouldn't work since the dates are different?

A: Yes, that's a very good point. But remember, Ethel is pretty clever. She could easily look at the main Guitar Wars page and see the new dates, which she then plugged into the old URL to remove the new scores without any trouble. It's important to never underestimate the ability of determined people to reverse-engineer your PHP scripts and exploit weaknesses.

Q: Alright, so protecting both the Admin and Remove Score pages stops Ethel, but don't they now make it a total hassle to remove scores legitimately?

A: No, not at all. Without the help of realms, it would definitely be a hassle removing scores legitimately because you'd have to enter the user name and password separately for the Admin and Remove Score pages. But remember that a realm was established that is the same in both pages, meaning that the pages fall under the same security zone. And once you go through the authentication window for a page in a given realm, the user name and password are remembered throughout the realm. The end result is that successfully entering the user name and password once is sufficient to unlock both pages.

Never underestimate the ability of determined people to reverse-engineer your PHP scripts and exploit weaknesses.

TEST DRIVE

Create the Authorize script and include it in the Admin and Remove Score scripts to secure them.

Create a new text file called `authorize.php`, and enter the code for the Authorize script into it. Then modify the `admin.php` script so that it includes the Authorize script instead of the actual HTTP authentication code. Add the same `require_once` statement to the beginning of the `removescore.php` script so that it is also protected by HTTP authentication.

Upload all of the scripts to your web server and then try to open the Remove Score script directly in your web browser. You may have to clear any previous HTTP authentication sessions in your browser for it to prompt you again—most browsers remember an authentication realm so that you don't have to keep re-entering the user name and password.

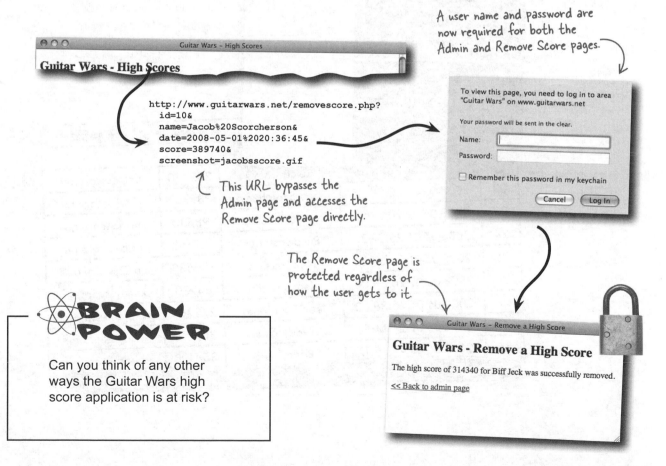

A user name and password are now required for both the Admin and Remove Score pages.

```
http://www.guitarwars.net/removescore.php?
  id=10&
  name=Jacob%20Scorcherson&
  date=2008-05-01%2020:36:45&
  score=389740&
  screenshot=jacobsscore.gif
```

This URL bypasses the Admin page and accesses the Remove Score page directly.

To view this page, you need to log in to area "Guitar Wars" on www.guitarwars.net

Your password will be sent in the clear.

Name:

Password:

☐ Remember this password in my keychain

Cancel   Log In

The Remove Score page is protected regardless of how the user gets to it.

Guitar Wars - Remove a High Score

The high score of 314340 for Biff Jeck was successfully removed.

<< Back to admin page

⚛ BRAIN POWER

Can you think of any other ways the Guitar Wars high score application is at risk?

Guitar Wars Episode II : Attack of the ^High Score Clones

Sadly, happiness in the Guitar Wars universe didn't last for long, as bogus scores are showing up in the application in place of legitimate scores... and still inciting rage throughout the Guitar Wars universe. Apparently it's entirely possible to disrupt the Guitar Wars high score list without removing scores. But how?

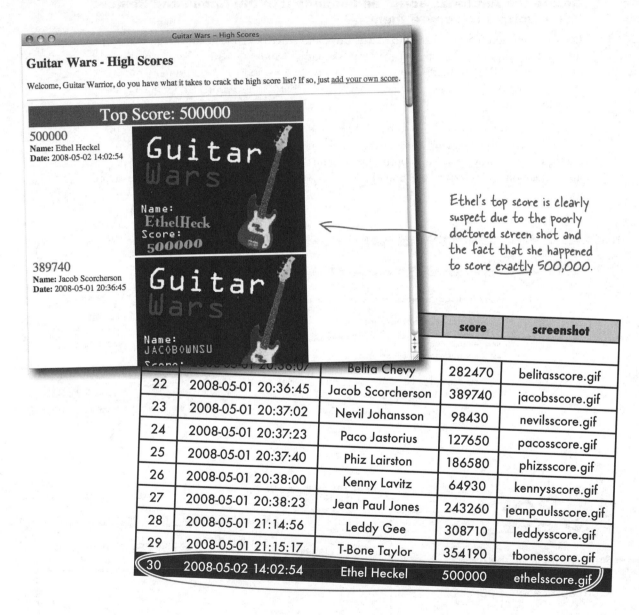

Guitar Wars - High Scores

Welcome, Guitar Warrior, do you have what it takes to crack the high score list? If so, just add your own score.

Top Score: 500000

500000
Name: Ethel Heckel
Date: 2008-05-02 14:02:54

Guitar Wars

Name: EthelHeck
Score: 500000

389740
Name: Jacob Scorcherson
Date: 2008-05-01 20:36:45

Guitar Wars

Name: JACOBOWNSU
Scor

Ethel's top score is clearly suspect due to the poorly doctored screen shot and the fact that she happened to score <u>exactly</u> 500,000.

			score	screenshot
		Belita Chevy	282470	belitasscore.gif
22	2008-05-01 20:36:45	Jacob Scorcherson	389740	jacobsscore.gif
23	2008-05-01 20:37:02	Nevil Johansson	98430	nevilsscore.gif
24	2008-05-01 20:37:23	Paco Jastorius	127650	pacosscore.gif
25	2008-05-01 20:37:40	Phiz Lairston	186580	phizsscore.gif
26	2008-05-01 20:38:00	Kenny Lavitz	64930	kennysscore.gif
27	2008-05-01 20:38:23	Jean Paul Jones	243260	jeanpaulsscore.gif
28	2008-05-01 21:14:56	Leddy Gee	308710	leddysscore.gif
29	2008-05-01 21:15:17	T-Bone Taylor	354190	tbonesscore.gif
30	2008-05-02 14:02:54	Ethel Heckel	500000	ethelsscore.gif

Subtraction by addition

Until now we've operated under the assumption that any high score submitted with a screen shot image is considered verified. It's now reasonably safe to say this is not the case! And it's pretty clear who the culprit is...

Oh yeah, it's me... guilty as charged! All I had to do was post my awesomely fake scores with touched-up screen shots. Ah, it's good to be the top Guitar Warrior.

Ethel realized she could wreak plenty of Guitar Wars havoc by simply submitting bogus scores with doctored screen shot images.

Write down how you would solve the problem of people being able to post bogus high scores to the Guitar Wars application:

....

....

....

Security requires <u>humans</u>

Even in this modern world we live in, sometimes you can't beat a real live thinking, breathing human being. In this case, it's hard to beat a real person when it comes to analyzing a piece of information and assessing whether or not it is valid. We're talking about moderation, where a human is put in charge of approving content posted to a web application before it is made visible to the general public.

Human moderation is an excellent way to improve the integrity of user-submitted content.

With moderation, a new high score gets added to the database but doesn't appear to the public until a moderator approves it.

The Admin change adds an "Approve" link to each new high score so that it can be approved.

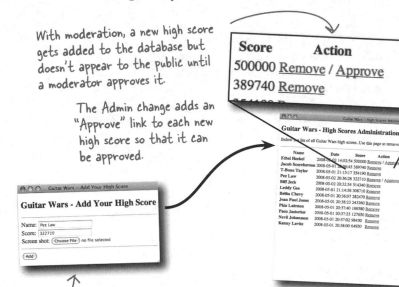

Good luck trying to slip any falsified documents, er high scores, by me. I'm thorough, and I rarely make mistakes.

Simply adding a new high score doesn't automatically add it to the publicly visible high score list anymore.

Guitar Wars could really use some human moderation. Sure, it's still possible that someone could carefully doctor a screen shot and maybe still sneak a score by a human moderator. But it wouldn't be easy, and it doesn't change the fact that moderation is a great deterrent. Keep in mind that securing a PHP application is largely about prevention.

Our fearless Guitar Wars moderator... never met a high score he really and truly trusted.

Plan for moderation in Guitar Wars

Adding a human moderation feature to Guitar Wars is significant because it affects several parts of the application. The database must change, a new script must be created to carry out an approval, the Admin page must add an "Approve" link to each score, and finally, the main page must change to only show approved scores. With this many changes involved, it's important to map out a plan and carry out each change one step at a time.

 1 **Use `ALTER` to add an `approved` column to the table.**

Let's start with the database, which needs a new column for keeping up with whether or not a score has been approved.

id	date	name	score	screenshot	approved
		...			
28	2008-05-01 21:14:56	Leddy Gee	308710	leddysscore.gif	0
29	2008-05-01 21:15:17	T-Bone Taylor	354190	tbonesscore.gif	0
30	2008-05-02 14:02:54	Ethel Heckel	500000	ethelsscore.gif	0
31	2008-05-02 20:32:54	Biff Jeck	314340	biffsscore.gif	0
32	2008-05-02 20:36:38	Pez Law	322710	pezsscore.gif	0

2 **Create an Approve Score script that handles approving a new high score (sets the `approved` column to 1).**

With the database ready to accommodate high score approvals, you need a script to actually handle approving a score. This Approve Score script is responsible for looking up a specific score in the database and changing the `approved` column for it.

3 **Modify the Admin page to include an "Approve" link for scores that have yet to be approved.**

The Approve Score script is a back-end script that shouldn't normally be accessed directly. Instead, it is accessed through "Approve" links generated and displayed on the Admin page—only unapproved scores have the "Approve" link next to them.

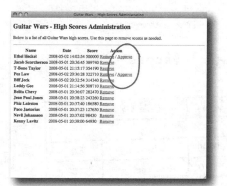

4 **Change the query on the main page to only show approved scores.**

The last step is to make sure all this approval stuff gets factored into the main high score view. So the main page of the application changes to only show high scores that have been approved—without this change, all the other approval modifications would be pointless.

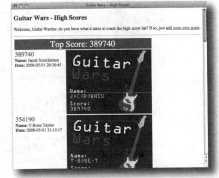

Make room for approvals with ALTER

Adding the new `approved` column to the `guitarwars` table involves a one-time usage of the `ALTER TABLE` statement, which is an SQL statement we've used before.

```
ALTER TABLE guitarwars
ADD COLUMN approved TINYINT
```

The MySQL data type BOOL is an alias for TINYINT, so you can use either one.

The new `approved` column is a `TINYINT` that uses `0` to indicate an unapproved score, or `1` to indicate an approved score. So all new scores should start out with a value of `0` to indicate that they are **initially unapproved**.

1 Use `ALTER` to add an approved **column to the table.** ~~DONE~~

> Wait a minute. I don't think you can just go adding a column to the database without changing the Add Score script—shouldn't it INSERT data into the new column?

It's true, a new column means a new value in the `INSERT` query in the Add Score script.

It's important to not lose sight of the fact that a PHP application is a careful orchestration of several pieces and parts: a database consisting of tables with rows and columns, PHP code, HTML code, and usually CSS code. It's not always immediately apparent that changing one part requires changing another. Adding the new `approved` column in the `guitarwars` table for the sake of the new Approve Score script also requires modifying the `INSERT` query in the Add Score script:

All newly inserted high score rows have approved set to 0... unapproved!

```
INSERT INTO guitarwars
VALUES (0, NOW(), '$name', '$score','$screenshot', 0)
```

id	date	name	score	screenshot	approved
		...			
30	2008-05-02 14:02:54	Ethel Heckel	500000	ethelsscore.gif	0
31	2008-05-02 20:32:54	Biff Jeck	314340	biffsscore.gif	0
32	2008-05-02 20:36:38	Pez Law	322710	pezsscore.gif	0

When a new column is added, its approved column is set to 0 so that it starts out unapproved.

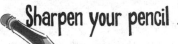

Sharpen your pencil

The Approve Score script is similar in structure to the Remove Score script except that its job is to approve a score. Finish the missing code for the Approve Score script, making sure to secure the page and only approve the appropriate score based on score data passed through a URL.

```php
<?php
  ......................................................... ;
?>
...
<?php
  require_once('appvars.php');
  require_once('connectvars.php');
  ...
  if (isset($_POST['submit'])) {
    if ( .......................................................... ) {
      // Connect to the database
      $dbc = mysqli_connect(DB_HOST, DB_USER, DB_PASSWORD, DB_NAME);

      // Approve the score by setting the approved column in the database
      $query = "UPDATE guitarwars SET ........................................................... ";
      mysqli_query($dbc, $query);
      mysqli_close($dbc);

      // Confirm success with the user
      echo .................................................................................................
    }
    else {
      echo .................................................................................................
    }
  }
  ...
  echo '<p><a href="........................">&lt;&lt; Back to admin page</a></p>';
?>
...
```

Sharpen your pencil
Solution

The Approve Score script is similar in structure to the Remove Score script except that its job is to approve a score. Finish the missing code for the Approve Score script, making sure to secure the page and only approve the appropriate score based on score data passed through a URL.

```php
<?php
      require_once('authorize.php')               ;

?>
...

<?php
  require_once('appvars.php');

  require_once('connectvars.php');

  ...

  if (isset($_POST['submit'])) {

    if (      $_POST['confirm'] == 'Yes'          ) {

      // Connect to the database
      $dbc = mysqli_connect(DB_HOST, DB_USER, DB_PASSWORD, DB_NAME);

      // Approve the score by setting the approved column in the database
      $query = "UPDATE guitarwars SET      approved = 1 WHERE id = '$id'        ";
      mysqli_query($dbc, $query);
      mysqli_close($dbc);

      // Confirm success with the user
      echo    '<p>The high score of ' . $score . ' for ' . $name . ' was successfully approved.';

    }

    else {

      echo    '<p class="error">Sorry, there was a problem approving the high score.</p>';

    }
  }
  ...

  echo '<p><a href="      admin.php      ">&lt;&lt; Back to admin page</a></p>';

?>
...
```

Including the Authorize script is all that is required to secure the Approve Score page with a user name and password, but it must be done first thing in the script since it relies on headers.

2 **Create an Approve Score script that handles approving a new high score (sets the** approved **column to 1).** ~~DONE~~

The ID must match in order to carry out the approval.

Setting the approved column to 1 approves the score.

Confirm the approval with the user by showing the approved score and name.

It's important to reveal when a score cannot be approved, similar to how other Guitar Wars scripts report errors.

Provide a link back to the Admin page for easier navigation.

there are no
Dumb Questions

Q: Why isn't it necessary to pass along the screen shot filename when approving a score?

A: Because the process of approving a high score only requires enough information to look up a score row and then approve it. This means you really only need enough data to hone in on a particular row. The date, name, and score are enough to find a particular row and set its approved column to 1.

Q: It seems kind of cryptic to use 0 and 1 in the approved column. Are there other ways to represent this information?

A: Yes. The MySQL ENUM data type, which stands for "enumerated," allows you to create a column with a restricted list of possible values. So instead of adding the approved column as a TINYINT that is intended to be 0 or 1, you could add it as an ENUM that can only have values of 'yes' and 'no', like this:

```
ALTER TABLE guitarwars
ADD COLUMN approved ENUM('yes', 'no')
```

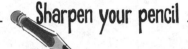 **Sharpen your pencil**

The score data used to approve a score in the Approve Score script is passed through "Approve" links that are generated in the Admin script. Finish the missing code in the Admin script so that it generates these links.

```
...
// Loop through the array of score data, formatting it as HTML
echo '<table>';
echo '<tr><th>Name</th><th>Date</th><th>Score</th><th>Action</th></tr>';
while ($row = mysqli_fetch_array($data)) {
  // Display the score data
  echo '<tr class="scorerow"><td><strong>' . $row['name'] . '</strong></td>';
  echo '<td>' . $row['date'] . '</td>';
  echo '<td>' . $row['score'] . '</td>';
  echo '<td><a href="removescore.php?id=' . $row['id'] . '&amp;date=' . $row['date']
    '&amp;name=' . $row['name'] . '&amp;score=' . $row['score'] .
    '&amp;screenshot=' . $row['screenshot'] . '">Remove</a>';
  if (................................................) {
    echo ........................................................................................
    ........................................................................................
    ........................................................................................
  }
  echo '</td></tr>';
}
echo '</table>';
...
```

Hint: only unapproved scores should have an "Approve" link.

Sharpen your pencil
Solution

The score data used to approve a score in the Approve Score script is passed through "Approve" links that are generated in the Admin script. Finish the missing code in the Admin script so that it generates these links.

```
...
// Loop through the array of score data, formatting it as HTML
echo '<table>';
echo '<tr><th>Name</th><th>Date</th><th>Score</th><th>Action</th></tr>';
while ($row = mysqli_fetch_array($data)) {
  // Display the score data
  echo '<tr class="scorerow"><td><strong>' . $row['name'] . '</strong></td>';
  echo '<td>' . $row['date'] . '</td>';
  echo '<td>' . $row['score'] . '</td>';
  echo '<td><a href="removescore.php?id=' . $row['id'] . '&amp;date=' . $row['date']
    '&amp;name=' . $row['name'] . '&amp;score=' . $row['score']
    '&amp;screenshot=' . $row['screenshot'] . '">Remove</a>';
  if (      $row['approved'] == '0'        ) {
    echo    '/ <a href="approvescore.php?id=' . $row['id'] . '&amp;date=' . $row['date'] .
            '&amp;name=' . $row['name'] . '&amp;score=' . $row['score'] . '&amp;screenshot=' .
            $row['screenshot'] . '">Approve</a>';
  }
  echo '</td></tr>';
}
echo '</table>';
...
```

Check to see if the score is unapproved before generating the "Approve" link.

Generate the "Approve" link so that the id, date, name, score, and screen shot image name are passed in the URL.

The "Approve" link ties the Admin page to the Approve Score page.

Guitar Wars - High Scores Administration

Below is a list of all Guitar Wars high scores. Use this page to remove scores as needed.

Name	Date	Score	Action
Ethel Heckel	2008-05-02 14:02:54	500000	Remove Approve
Jacob Scorcherson	2008-05-01 20:36:45	389740	Remove
T-Bone Taylor	2008-05-01 21:15:17	354190	Remove
Pez Law	2008-05-02 20:36:28	322710	Remove Approve
Biff Jeck	2008-05-02 20:32:54	314340	Remove
Leddy Gee	2008-05-01 21:14:56	308710	Remove
Belita Chevy	2008-05-01 20:36:07	282470	Remove
Jean Paul Jones	2008-05-01 20:38:23	243260	Remove
Phiz Lairston	2008-05-01 20:37:40	186580	Remove
Paco Jastorius	2008-05-01 20:37:23	127650	Remove
Nevil Johansson	2008-05-01 20:37:02	98430	Remove
Kenny Lavitz	2008-05-01 20:38:00	64930	Remove

Guitar Wars - Approve a High Score

Are you sure you want to approve the following high score?

Name: Pez Law
Date: 2008-05-02 20:36:28
Score: 32271

⊙ Yes ⊙ No
Submit

<< Back to admin page

Guitar Wars - Approve a High Score

The high score of 322710 for Pez Law was successfully approved.

<< Back to admin page

DONE

③ Modify the Admin page to include an "Approve" link for scores that have yet to be approved.

Unapproved scores aren't worthy

All the infrastructure is now in place for the moderation feature in the Guitar Wars high score application. All that's missing is the final step, which is altering the main page to only show approved scores. This involves tweaking the SQL `SELECT` query so that it only plucks out scores whose `approved` column is set to 1 (approved). This is accomplished with a `WHERE` statement.

Use WHERE to select rows based on the value of a certain column.

```
SELECT * FROM guitarwars
WHERE approved = 1
ORDER BY score DESC, date ASC
```

The addition of the `WHERE` statement to this query eliminates any scores that haven't been approved, which includes all new scores. This gives the moderator a chance to look them over and decide whether they should be removed or made visible to the public (approved).

If the approved column is set to something other than 1, the score won't be displayed.

id	date	name	score	screenshot	approved
		...			
28	2008-05-01 21:14:56	Leddy Gee	308710	leddysscore.gif	1
29	2008-05-01 21:15:17	T-Bone Taylor	354190	tbonesscore.gif	1
30	2008-05-02 14:02:54	Ethel Heckel	500000	ethelsscore.gif	0
31	2008-05-02 20:32:54	Biff Jeck	314340	biffsscore.gif	1
32	2008-05-02 20:36:38	Pez Law	322710	pezsscore.gif	1

Only approved scores show up on the main page (index.php) now.

4 Change the query on the main page to only show approved scores.

DONE

Test Drive

Create the Approve script and rework the rest of the Guitar Wars application to use it.

Using a MySQL tool, issue the ALTER query to add the new approved column to the guitarwars table. Then change the INSERT query in the addscore.php script to insert a 0 in the approved column for new rows of data.

Now create a new text file called approvescore.php, and enter the code for the Approve Score script into it. Then modify the admin.php script to include an "Approve" link for high scores that have yet to be approved. And finally, change the SELECT query in index.php to only show approved scores.

Upload all of the scripts to your web server, and open the main Guitar Wars page in your web browser. Take note of the scores that are visible, and then open the Admin page. Click one of the "Approve" links and continue along to approve the score. Then go back to the main page to see if the score appears.

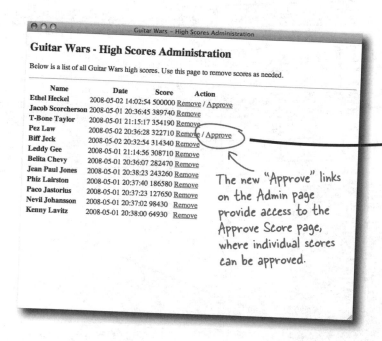

The new "Approve" links on the Admin page provide access to the Approve Score page, where individual scores can be approved.

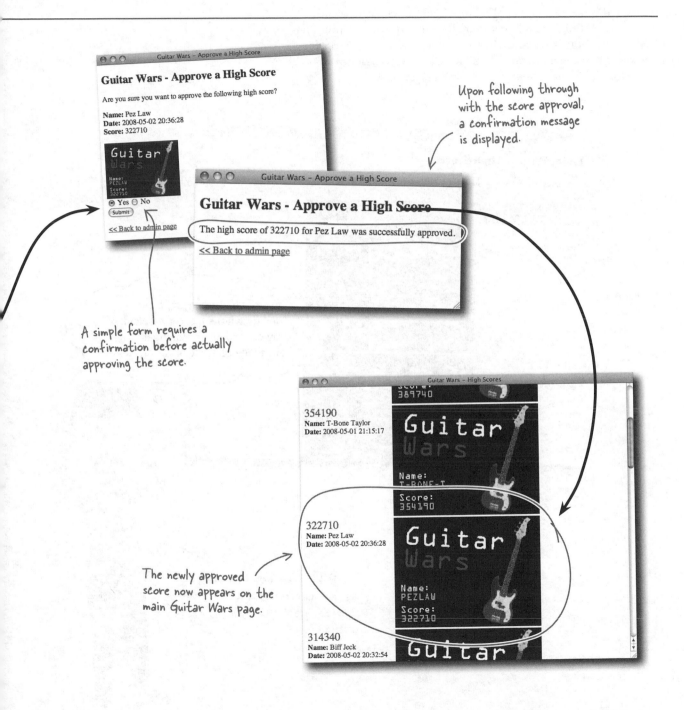

Upon following through
with the score approval,
a confirmation message
is displayed.

A simple form requires a
confirmation before actually
approving the score.

The newly approved
score now appears on the
main Guitar Wars page.

The million-point hack

The moderated version of Guitar Wars represents a significant security improvement, but it's far from bulletproof. It seems our wily infiltrator has managed to find another weakness in the high score system and somehow sneak her high scores past the moderator. Ethel must be stopped, **permanently**, in order to restore trust throughout the Guitar Wars universe.

This is precisely the kind of high score the moderator would've stopped dead in its tracks... yet there it is!

I've gotta be honest, I can't decide what's more fun, playing my accordion or making a mockery of the Guitar Wars site!

Ethel can't help but gloat over her success now that she beat the system yet again.

Everything in moderation... ?

Even though the moderator knows without a doubt that he never approved Ethel's high score submission, it nevertheless is there in plain view with the `approved` column set to 1. We know the Add Score script sets the `approved` column to 0 for new high scores because we just modified the `INSERT` query in that script. Something just doesn't add up!

The Guitar Wars moderator can't figure out what happened.

How is that possible? I know I never approved that score. A million points!?

id	date	name	score	screenshot	approved
21	2008-05-01 20:36:07	Belita Chevy	282470	belitasscore.gif	1
22	2008-05-01 20:36:45	Jacob Scorcherson	389740	jacobsscore.gif	1
23	2008-05-01 20:37:02	Nevil Johansson	98430	nevilsscore.gif	1
24	2008-05-01 20:37:23	Paco Jastorius	127650	pacosscore.gif	1
25	2008-05-01 20:37:40	Phiz Lairston	186580	phizsscore.gif	1
26	2008-05-01 20:38:00	Kenny Lavitz	64930	kennysscore.gif	1
27	2008-05-01 20:38:23	Jean Paul Jones	243260	jeanpaulsscore.gif	1
28	2008-05-01 21:14:56	Leddy Gee	308710	leddysscore.gif	1
29	2008-05-01 21:15:17	T-Bone Taylor	354190	tbonesscore.gif	1
31	2008-05-02 20:32:54	Biff Jeck	314340	biffsscore.gif	1
32	2008-05-02 20:36:38	Pez Law	322710	pezsscore.gif	1
33	2008-05-05 14:58:59	Ethel Heckel	1000000	ethelsscore2.gif	1

This score was never approved by the moderator yet its approved column is set to 1, resulting in it being displayed.

BRAIN POWER

How do you think Ethel's bogus post got past the moderator?

BRAIN
BARBELL

As it turns out, Ethel's million-point hack had nothing to do with the Approve Score form. Her mischief was completely isolated to the Add Score form. Below is the exact form data that Ethel entered into the Add Score form to carry out her hack. Enter the same form data in your own form and add the score. What do you think is going on?

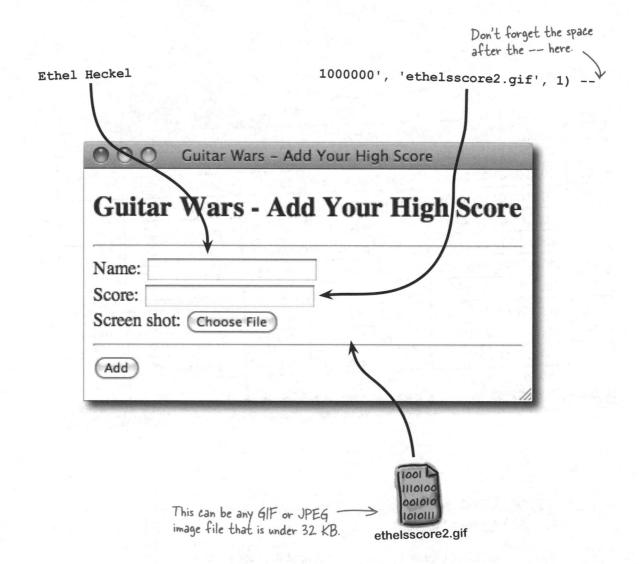

Don't forget the space after the -- here.

Ethel Heckel

1000000', 'ethelsscore2.gif', 1) --

Guitar Wars – Add Your High Score

Guitar Wars - Add Your High Score

Name:

Score:

Screen shot: (Choose File)

(Add)

This can be any GIF or JPEG image file that is under 32 KB.

ethelsscore2.gif

How exactly did she do it?

In order to understand what's happening with this clever form attack, let's trace the flow of form data as it travels through the Add Score script.

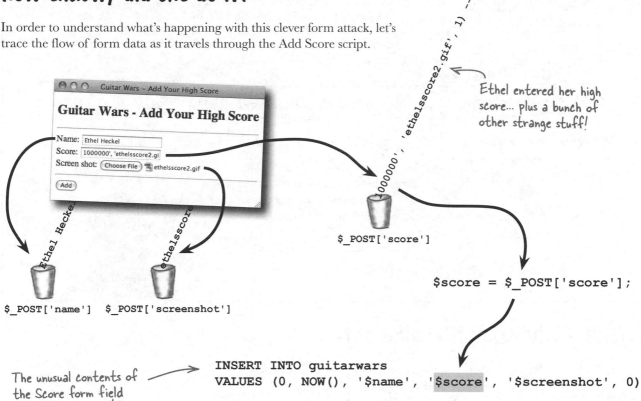

Ethel entered her high score... plus a bunch of other strange stuff!

$_POST['score']

$_POST['name'] $_POST['screenshot']

$score = $_POST['score'];

The unusual contents of the Score form field get stored in the $score variable, which ends up making its way directly into the INSERT query.

```
INSERT INTO guitarwars
VALUES (0, NOW(), '$name', '$score', '$screenshot', 0)
```

The Score form field expects a single numeric value, such as 1000000, but instead it has several values enclosed in single quotes, separated by commas, and then with a strange double-hyphen at the end. Very strange.

This strange data first gets stored in the $score variable, after which it gets incorporated into the INSERT query. This just results in a meaningless score, right? Or is something more sinister taking place here?

Sharpen your pencil

Using the exact form data shown on the facing page, write out the full Add Score SQL query for the million-point attack. Make sure to replace the variables in the query with the actual form data. Annotate what you think is happening.

....

....

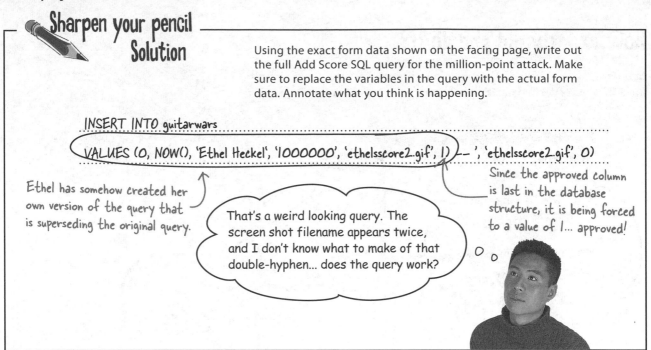

Sharpen your pencil
Solution

Using the exact form data shown on the facing page, write out the full Add Score SQL query for the million-point attack. Make sure to replace the variables in the query with the actual form data. Annotate what you think is happening.

INSERT INTO guitarwars

VALUES (0, NOW(), 'Ethel Heckel', '1000000', 'ethelsscore2.gif', 1) -- ', 'ethelsscore2.gif', 0)

Ethel has somehow created her own version of the query that is superseding the original query.

That's a weird looking query. The screen shot filename appears twice, and I don't know what to make of that double-hyphen... does the query work?

Since the approved column is last in the database structure, it is being forced to a value of 1... approved!

Tricking MySQL with comments

The real culprit in Ethel's million-point attack is, strangely enough, SQL comments. A double-hyphen (--) is used in SQL to comment out the remainder of a line of SQL code. You **must follow the double-hyphen with a space** for it to work (--), but everything after the space is ignored. Now take a look at Ethel's full query with that little nugget of wisdom.

```
INSERT INTO guitarwars

VALUES (0, NOW(), 'Ethel Heckel', '1000000', 'ethelsscore2.gif', 1) -- ', 'ethelsscore2.gif', 0)
```

The -- comment causes the rest of the line of SQL code to be ignored.

Is it making more sense? The comment effectively erased the remaining SQL code so that it wouldn't generate an error, allowing Ethel's version of the query to slip through without a snag. The end result is an instantly approved new high score that the moderator never got a chance to catch.

Ethel tricked the query into approving her score.

id	date	name	score	screenshot	approved
			...		
33	2008-05-05 14:58:59	Ethel Heckel	1000000	ethelsscore2.gif	1

The Add Score form was SQL injected

Ethel's attack is known as an **SQL injection**, and involves an extremely sneaky trick where form data is used as a means to change the fundamental operation of a query. So instead of a form field just supplying a piece of information, such as a name or score, it meddles with the underlying SQL query itself. In the case of Guitar Wars, Ethel's SQL injection used the Score field as a means of not only providing the score, but also the screen shot filename, the approval value, and a comment at the end to prevent the original SQL code from generating an error.

Form fields are a security weak point for web applications because they allow users to enter data.

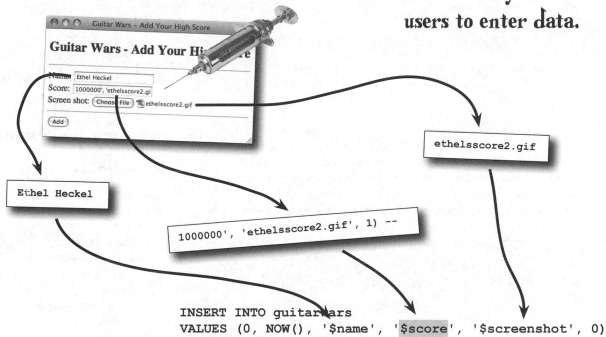

```
INSERT INTO guitarwars
VALUES (0, NOW(), '$name', '$score', '$screenshot', 0)
```

there are no Dumb Questions

Q: Are there any other kinds of comments in SQL besides --?

A: Yes. Another variation on the single-line comment involves the use of # instead of --, but still results in commenting out any SQL code to the end of the line following the comment. SQL also supports multi-line comments that are similar to PHP's multi-line comments in that you enclose commented code between /* and */.

Q: Would Ethel's SQL injection attack have still worked if the **approved** column wasn't at the end of the table?

A: No, and that's a really important point. This particular INSERT query relies on the default ordering of columns in the table. Tacking on 1 to the end of the query just happened to work because approved is the last column, appearing immediately after the screenshot column.

Protect your data from SQL injections

The real weakness that SQL injections capitalize on is form fields that aren't validated for dangerous characters. "Dangerous characters" are any characters that could potentially change the nature of an SQL query, such as commas, quotes, or -- comment characters. Even spaces at the end of a piece of data can prove harmful. Leading or trailing spaces are easy enough to eliminate with the built-in PHP function `trim()`—just run all form data through the `trim()` function before using it in an SQL query.

```
$name = trim($_POST['name']);

$score = trim($_POST['score']);

$screenshot = trim($_FILES['screenshot']['name']);
```

The trim() function gets rid of leading and trailing spaces in this form data.

> **SQL injections can be prevented by properly processing form data.**

But leading and trailing spaces aren't the whole problem. You still have the commas, quotes, comment characters, and on, and on. So in addition to trimming form fields of extra spaces, we also need a way to find and render harmless other problematic characters. PHP comes to the rescue with another built-in function, `mysqli_real_escape_string()`, which escapes potentially dangerous characters so that they can't adversely affect how a query executes. These characters can still appear as data in form fields, they just won't interfere with queries.

Putting the `trim()` and `mysqli_real_escape_string()` functions together provide a solid line of defense against SQL injections.

The mysqli_real_escape_string() function converts dangerous characters into an escaped format that won't adversely affect SQL queries.

```
$name = mysqli_real_escape_string($dbc, trim($_POST['name']));

$score = mysqli_real_escape_string($dbc, trim($_POST['score']));

$screenshot = mysqli_real_escape_string($dbc, trim($_FILES['screenshot']['name']));
```

mysqli_real_escape_string() is considered a database function, which is why it requires you to pass it a database connection variable, like the one used when submitting queries.

Processing the three Guitar Wars form fields with the `trim()` and `mysqli_real_escape_string()` functions greatly reduces the chances of another SQL injection attack. But these two functions aren't enough—maybe there's a way to make the query itself less vulnerable...

A safer INSERT (with parameters)

Aside from exploiting weak form field protection, Ethel's SQL injection also relied on the fact that the approved column followed the screenshot column in the database structure. That's how she was able to get away with just adding 1 onto the end of INSERT and have it go into the approved column. The problem is that the INSERT query is structured in such a way that it has to insert data into all columns, which adds unnecessary risk.

> *An INSERT query can be written so that it nails down exactly what values go in what columns.*

> *Ideally, we shouldn't be setting the id and approved columns since they could just have default values.*

```
INSERT INTO guitarwars
VALUES (0, NOW(), '$name', '$score', '$screenshot', 0)
```

When data is inserted into a table like this, the order of the data must line up with the order of the columns in the table structure. So the fifth piece of data will go into the screenshot column because it's the fifth column in the table. But it really isn't necessary to explicitly insert the id or approved columns since id is auto-incremented and approved should always be 0. A better approach is to focus on inserting only the data explicitly required of a new high score. The id and approved columns can then be allowed to **default** to AUTO_INCREMENT and 0, respectively.

We need a restructured INSERT query that expects a list of columns prior to the list of data, with each matching one-to-one. This eliminates the risk of the approved column being set—it's no longer part of the query. If this kind of query looks familiar, it's because you've used it several times in other examples.

> *Nothing can be inserted into the approved column because it isn't listed as part of the query.*

```
INSERT INTO guitarwars (date, name, score, screenshot)
VALUES (NOW(), '$name', '$score', '$screenshot')
```

> *The id column can be left out since it auto-increments anyway.*

id	date	name	score	screenshot	approved
			...		

NOW()

'$name'

'$score'

'$screenshot'

This version of the INSERT query spells out exactly which column each piece of data is to be stored in, allowing you to insert data without having to worry about the underlying table structure. In fact, it's considered better coding style to use this kind of INSERT query so that data is inserted exactly where you intend it to go, as opposed to relying on the structural layout of the table.

Hang on a second. This is the first I've heard of default values in MySQL tables. Is that really possible?

Not only is it possible, but it's a very good idea to specify DEFAULT column values whenever possible.

The SQL DEFAULT command is what allows you to specify a default value for a column. If a column has a default value, you can forego setting it in an INSERT query and relax in the confidence of knowing that it will automatically take on the default value. This is perfect for the approved column in the guitarwars table. Now we just need to modify the table one more time to set the default value for approved to 0 (unapproved).

Since the approved column already exists, in this ALTER TABLE statement we have to use MODIFY COLUMN instead of ADD COLUMN.

```
ALTER TABLE guitarwars
MODIFY COLUMN approved TINYINT
DEFAULT 0
```

DEFAULT results in the approved column being automatically assigned a value of 0 unless an INSERT query explicitly sets it otherwise.

You still have to specify the type of the column—just make sure it's the same as when you first added the column.

With the approved column now altered to take on a default value, the new and improved INSERT query in the Add Score script can insert high scores without even mentioning the approved column. This is good design since there's no need to explicitly insert a value that can be defaulted, and it adds a small extra degree of security by not exposing the approved column to a potential attack.

Form validation can never be too smart

One last step in minimizing the risks of SQL injection attacks involves the form validation in the Add Score script. Before checking to see if the screen shot file type or size is within the application-defined limits, the three Add Score form fields are checked to make sure they aren't empty.

```
if (!empty($name) && !empty($score) && !empty($screenshot)) {
  ...
}
```

← *This if statement checks to make sure all of the form fields are non-empty.*

There is nothing wrong with this code as-is, but securing an application is often about going above and beyond the call of duty. Since the Score field expects a number, it makes sense to not just check for a non-empty value but for a numeric value. The PHP `is_numeric()` function does just that by returning `true` if a value passed to it is a number, or false otherwise. It's consistently doing the little things, like checking for a number when you're expecting a number, that will ultimately make your application as secure as possible from data attacks.

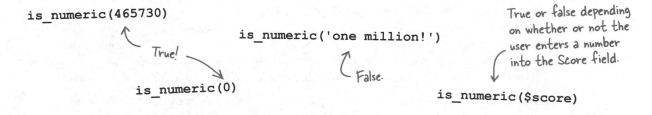

is_numeric(465730)

True!

is_numeric(0)

is_numeric('one million!')

False.

True or false depending on whether or not the user enters a number into the Score field.

is_numeric($score)

Whenever possible, insist on form data being in the format you've requested.

Exercise

Rewrite the Add Score form validation `if` statement to use the `isnumeric()` function so that only a numeric score is allowed.

....

....

....

Rewrite the Add Score form validation `if` statement to use the `isnumeric()` function so that only a numeric score is allowed.

```
if (!empty($name) && is_numeric($score) && !empty($screenshot)) {
    ...
}
```

Test Drive

Beef up the handling of form data in the Add Score script.

Tweak the assignment of form data to variables in the addscore.php script so that the `trim()` and `mysqli_real_escape_string()` functions are used to clean up the form data. Then change the `INSERT` query so that it specifies both the column names and values, eliminating the need to provide values for the `id` and `approved` columns. Also change the `if` statement that validates the form fields so that it checks to make sure the score is numeric.

Finally, use a MySQL tool to run the `ALTER` query that defaults the `approved` column to 0.

Upload the new Add Score script to your web server, navigate to it in a web browser, and then try the same SQL injection attack again.

Sure, this error message could be a bit more specific, but it gets the job done without adding extra logic to the script.

Now the Score form field will only accept numbers and nothing else.

Guitar Wars – Add Your High Score

Please enter all of the information to add your high score.

Name: Ethel Heckel
Score: 1000000', 'ethelsscore2.g
Screen shot: (Choose File) no file selected

(Add)

Form validation is a topic that reaches far beyond database security. Chapter 10 revisits form validation in much more detail...

Cease fire!

It seems Ethel's will to interfere with the Guitar Wars high scores has finally been broken thanks to the improvements to the application that render it immune to SQL injections. The reigning Guitar Wars champion has responded by posting a new top score.

Finally! I'm back at the top of the high score list with a jamming new score.

Relieved that high scores are now safe from outside interference, Jacob posts a new top score that will be tough to beat.

Egad! Foiled again. Maybe it's time I just learned how to play virtual guitar.

Resigned that she'd rather join them than continue to lose fighting them, Ethel figures it might be time to become a Guitar Warrior.

CHAPTER 6

Your PHP & MySQL Toolbox

In addition to taking the Guitar Wars high score application to a new level, you've acquired several new tools and techniques. Let's revisit the most important ones.

exit()

This built-in PHP function causes a PHP script to stop immediately. Once a script encounters the exit() function, no additional PHP code is executed and no additional HTML code is delivered to the browser.

header()

This built-in PHP function is used to send a header from the server to the browser, allowing you to perform tasks such as redirecting the page, specifying a certain content type, or carrying out HTTP authentication.

$_SERVER

Among other things, this built-in PHP superglobal stores the user name and password entered by the user when attempting to access a page requiring HTTP authentication. You can check these against expected values to protect pages that need to be secured.

DEFAULT value

This SQL statement establishes the default value of a column in a table. If a new row is added and the column isn't set, it will take on the default value.

is_numeric()

This built-in PHP function checks to see if a value is a number. It is useful for checking to see if a numeric form field actually holds a numeric value.

trim(), mysqli_real_escape_string()

These two built-in PHP functions are handy for processing form data and preventing problematic characters from interfering with SQL queries. The first function trims leading and trailing spaces, while the latter escapes special characters.

Human Moderation

Everything in moderation! In this case, it means that a human being is often the best line of defense in identifying and eliminating unwanted content being posted by others. Automated security techniques are still important, but it's hard to beat a living, breathing person with a brain!

SQL Injection

A security breach that involves an evil-doer somehow compromising a SQL query to gain unwarranted access to a database. Most SQL injections involve tricking a web form into passing along dangerous data directly to a dynamically constructed query. So form validation is often the solution.

HTTP Authentication

A simple web security technique that limits access to a web page or script using a user name and password. Although not intended for highly sensitive security applications, HTTP authentication can be handy for quickly adding a degree of security to a web application.

Form Validation

The process of checking all of the data entered by a user into a form to ensure that it is in the expected format. In addition to making forms easier to use, validation can help make web applications more secure by not allowing users to enter bad data.

Column/Value Query

A type of INSERT query where columns and their respective values are carefully matched to each other, as opposed to relying on the order of the data matching the structural order of the columns in the table.

7 building personalized web apps

Remember me?

What's your name again? Johnson, right. Well, I'm showing no record of you, Mr. Jackson. Are you sure you signed up for a warranty on your cryogenic storage cell? Oh, I see, so you're calling from inside your cell right now. And what was your name again?

No one likes to be forgotten, especially users of web applications. If an application has any sense of "membership," meaning that users somehow interact with the application in a personal way, then the application needs to remember the users. You'd hate to have to reintroduce yourself to your family every time you walk through the door at home. You don't have to because they have this wonderful thing called **memory**. But *web applications don't remember people automatically*—it's up to a savvy web developer to use the tools at their disposal (PHP and MySQL, maybe?) to **build personalized web apps that can actually remember users**.

They say opposites attract

It's an age-old story: boy meets girl, girl thinks boy is completely nuts, boy thinks girl has issues, but their differences become the attraction, and they end up living happily ever after. This story drives the innovative new dating site, Mis-match.net. Mismatch takes the "opposites attract" theory to heart by mismatching people based on their differences.

Problem is, Mismatch has yet to get off the ground and is in dire need of a web developer to finish building the system. That's where you come in. Millions of lonely hearts are anxiously awaiting your completion of the application... don't let them down!

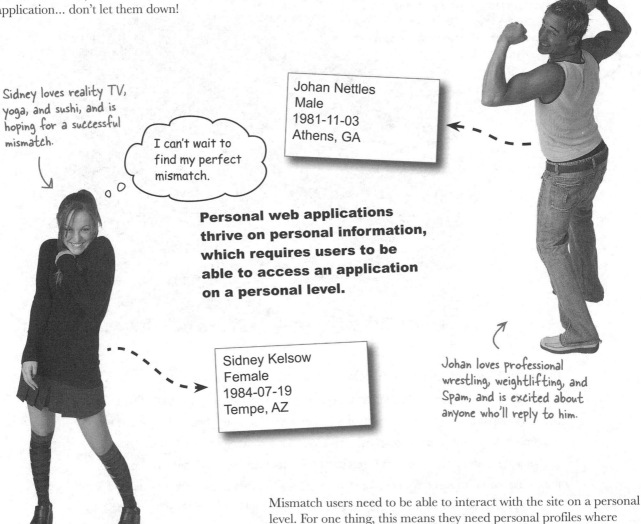

Check out these guns!

Sidney loves reality TV, yoga, and sushi, and is hoping for a successful mismatch.

I can't wait to find my perfect mismatch.

Johan Nettles
Male
1981-11-03
Athens, GA

Personal web applications thrive on personal information, which requires users to be able to access an application on a personal level.

Sidney Kelsow
Female
1984-07-19
Tempe, AZ

Johan loves professional wrestling, weightlifting, and Spam, and is excited about anyone who'll reply to him.

Mismatch users need to be able to interact with the site on a personal level. For one thing, this means they need personal profiles where they enter information about themselves that they can share with other Mismatch users, such as their gender, birthdate, and location.

Mismatch is all about <u>personal</u> data

So Mismatch is all about establishing connections through personal data. These connections must take place within a **community of users**, each of whom is able to interact with the site and manage their own personal data. A table called `mismatch_user` is used to keep up with Mismatch users and store their personal information.

This is the Mismatch database.

Within the Mismatch database, the mismatch_user table stores users and their personal profile data.

mismatch_user

user_id	join_date	first_name	last_name	gender	birthdate	city	state	picture
1	2008-04-17 09:43:11	Sidney	Kelsow	F	1984-07-19	Tempe	AZ	sidneypic.jpg
...								
11	2008-05-23 12:24:06	Johan	Nettles	M	1981-11-03	Athens	GA	johanpic.jpg
...								

Each row of the mismatch_user table contains personal data for a single user.

Mismatch - View Profile

First name: Sidney
Last name: Kelsow
Gender: Female
Birthdate: 1984-07-19
Location: Tempe, AZ

Picture:

Would you like to edit your profile

Mismatch - Edit Profile

— Personal Information —
First name: Sidney
Last name: Kelsow
Gender: Female
Birthdate: 1984-07-19
City: Tempe
State: AZ
Picture: (Choose File) sidneypic.jpg

(Save Profile)

The Edit and View Profile pages need to know whose profile to access.

Sidney Kelsow
Female
1984-07-19
Tempe, AZ

In addition to viewing a user profile, Mismatch users can edit their own personal profiles using the Edit Profile page. But there's a problem in that the application needs to know which user's profile to edit. The Edit Profile page somehow needs to keep track of the user who is accessing the page.

BRAIN POWER

How can Mismatch customize the Edit Profile page for each different user?

Mismatch needs user log-ins

The solution to the Mismatch personal data access problem involves user log-ins, meaning that users need to be able to log into the application. This gives Mismatch the ability to provide access to information that is custom-tailored to each different user. For example, a logged-in user would only have the ability to edit their own profile data, although they might also be able to view other users' profiles. User log-ins provide the key to personalization for the Mismatch application.

A user log-in typically involves two pieces of information, a username and a password.

User log-ins allow web applications to get personal with users.

Username

The job of the username is to provide each user with a unique name that can be used to identify the user within the system. Users can potentially access and otherwise communicate with each other through their usernames.

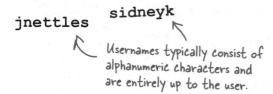

`jnettles`   `sidneyk`

Usernames typically consist of alphanumeric characters and are entirely up to the user.

Password

The password is responsible for providing a degree of security when logging in users, which helps to safeguard their personal data. To log in, a user must enter both a username and password.

`******`

`********`

Passwords are extremely sensitive pieces of data and should never be made visible within an application, even inside the database.

A username and password allows a user to log in to the Mismatch application and access personal data, such as editing their profile.

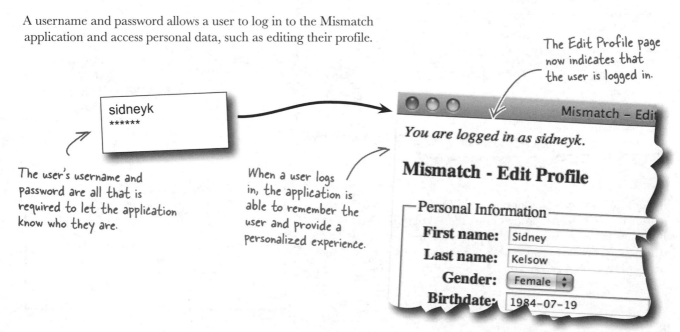

The Edit Profile page now indicates that the user is logged in.

sidneyk
`******`

The user's username and password are all that is required to let the application know who they are.

When a user logs in, the application is able to remember the user and provide a personalized experience.

Mismatch – Edit

You are logged in as sidneyk.

Mismatch - Edit Profile

Personal Information

First name: Sidney
Last name: Kelsow
Gender: Female
Birthdate: 1984-07-19

Come up with a user log-in gameplan

Adding user log-in support to Mismatch is no small feat, and it's important to work out exactly what is involved before writing code and running database queries. We know there is an existing table that stores users, so the first thing is to alter it to store log-in data. We'll also need a way for users to enter their log-in data, and this somehow needs to integrate with the rest of the Mismatch application so that pages such as the Edit Profile page are only accessible after a successful log-in. Here are the log-in development steps we've worked out so far:

1 Use `ALTER` **to add** `username` **and** `password` **columns to the table.**

The database needs new columns for storing the log-in data for each user. This consists of a username and password.

2 **Build a new Log-In script that prompts the user to enter their username and password.**

The Log In form is what will ultimately protect personalized pages in that it prompts for a valid username and password. This information must be entered properly before Mismatch can display user-specific data. So the script must limit access to personalized pages so that they can't be viewed without a valid log-in.

3 **Connect the Log-In script to the rest of the Mismatch application.**

The Edit Profile and View Profile pages of the Mismatch application should only be accessible to logged in users. So we need to make sure users log in via the Log In script before being allowed to access these pages.

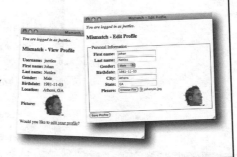

Before going any further, take a moment to tinker with the Mismatch application and get a feel for how it works.

Download all of the code for the Mismatch application from the Head First Labs web site at `www.headfirstlabs.com/books/hfphp`. Post all of the code to your web server except for the `.sql` files, which contain SQL statements that build the necessary Mismatch tables. Make sure to run the statement in each of the `.sql` files in a MySQL tool so that you have the initial Mismatch tables to get started with.

When all that's done, navigate to the `index.php` page in your web browser, and check out the application. Keep in mind that the View Profile and Edit Profile pages are initially broken since they are entirely dependent upon user log-ins, which we're in the midst of building.

The main Mismatch page allows you to see the name and picture of the latest users, but not much else without being logged in.

These two links lead into the personalized parts of the application.

Download It!

The complete source code for the Mismatch application is available for download from the Head First Labs web site:

www.headfirstlabs.com/books/hfphp

Prepping the database for log-ins

OK, back to the construction. The `mismatch_user` table already does a good job of holding profile information for each user, but it's lacking when it comes to user log-in information. More specifically, the table is missing columns for storing a username and password for each user.

The mismatch_user table needs columns for username and password in order to store user log-in data.

mismatch_user

user_id	join_date	first_name	last_name	gender	birthdate	city	state	picture

Username and password data both consist of pure text, so it's possible to use the familiar VARCHAR MySQL data type for the new `username` and `password` columns. However, unlike some other user profile data, the username and password shouldn't ever be allowed to remain empty (NULL).

The username and password columns contain simple text data but should never be allowed to go empty.

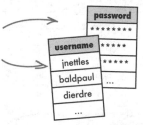

there are no
Dumb Questions

Q: **Why can't you just use** `user_id` **instead of** `username` **for uniquely identifying a user?**

A: You can if you want. In fact, the purpose of `user_id` is to provide an efficient means of uniquely identifying user rows. However, numeric IDs tend to be difficult to remember, and users really like being able to make up their own usernames for accessing personalized web applications. So it's more of a usability decision to allow Johan to be able to log in as "jnettles" instead of "11". No one wants to be relegated to just being a number!

Sharpen your pencil

Few people would want to try and remember a password longer than 16 characters!

Finish writing an SQL statement to add the `username` and `password` columns to the table positioned as shown, with `username` able to hold 32 characters, `password` able to hold 16 characters, and neither of them allowing NULL data.

....

....

mismatch_user

user_id	username	password	join_date	first_name	last_name	gender	birthdate	city	state	picture

Sharpen your pencil
Solution

Finish writing an SQL statement to add the `username` and `password` columns to the table positioned as shown, with `username` able to hold 32 characters, `password` able to hold 16 characters, and neither of them allowing `NULL` data.

ALTER TABLE is used to add new columns to an existing table.

ALTER TABLE mismatch_user ADD username VARCHAR(32) NOT NULL AFTER user_id,

ADD password VARCHAR(16) NOT NULL AFTER username

The username column is added first, so it's OK to reference it here.

The AFTER statement controls where in the table new columns are added.

mismatch_user

user_id	username	password	join_date	first_name	last_name	gender	birthdate	city	state	picture

The position of columns in a table doesn't necessarily matter, although it can serve an organizational purpose in terms of positioning the most important columns first.

~~DONE~~

1 Use ALTER to add username and password **columns to the table.**

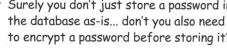

Surely you don't just store a password in the database as-is... don't you also need to encrypt a password before storing it?

Good point... passwords require encryption.

Encryption in Mismatch involves converting a password into an unrecognizable format when stored in the database. Any application with user log-in support must encrypt passwords so that users can feel confident that their passwords are safe and secure. Exposing a user's password even within the database itself is not acceptable. So we need a means of encrypting a password before inserting it into the `mismatch_user` table. Problem is, encryption won't help us much if we don't have a way for users to actually enter a username and password to log in...

Constructing a log-in user interface

With the database altered to hold user log-in data, we still need a way for users to enter the data and actually log in to the application. This log-in user interface needs to consist of text edit fields for the username and password, as well as a button for carrying out the log-in.

> **An application log-in requires a user interface for entering the username and password.**

The password field is protected so that the password isn't readable.

Username: [jnettles]
Password: [********]

[Log In]

Clicking the Log In button makes the application check the username and password against the database.

mismatch_user

user_id	username	password	...
9	dierdre	*******	
10	baldpaul	******	
11	jnettles	*******	

...

If the username and password check out, the user is successfully logged in.

○○○ Mismatch – View Profile

You are logged in as jnettles.

there are no Dumb Questions

Q: So asterisks aren't actually stored in the database, right?

A: That's correct. The asterisks displayed in a password form field simply provide **visual security**, preventing someone from looking over your shoulder as you enter the password. When the form is submitted, the password itself is submitted, not the asterisks. That's why it's important for the password to be encrypted before inserting it into the database.

 **Relax** **If you're worried about how users will be able to log in when we haven't assigned them user names and passwords yet... don't sweat it.**

We'll get to creating user names and passwords for users in just a bit. For now it's important to lay the groundwork for log-ins, even if we still have more tasks ahead before it all comes together.

Encrypt passwords with SHA()

The log-in user interface is pretty straightforward, but we didn't address the need to encrypt the log-in password. MySQL offers a function called SHA() that applies an encryption algorithm to a string of text. The result is an encrypted string that is exactly 40 hexadecimal characters long, regardless of the original password length. So the function actually generates a 40-character code that uniquely represents the password.

Since SHA() is a MySQL function, not a PHP function, you call it as part of the query that inserts a password into a table. For example, this code inserts a new user into the mismatch_user table, making sure to encrypt the password with SHA() along the way.

The MySQL SHA() function encrypts a piece of text into a unique 40-character code.

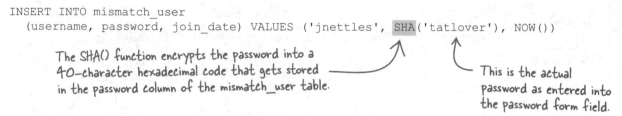

```
INSERT INTO mismatch_user
    (username, password, join_date) VALUES ('jnettles', SHA('tatlover'), NOW())
```

The SHA() function encrypts the password into a 40-character hexadecimal code that gets stored in the password column of the mismatch_user table.

This is the actual password as entered into the password form field.

The same SHA() function works on the other end of the log-in equation by checking to see that the password entered by the user matches up with the encrypted password stored in the database.

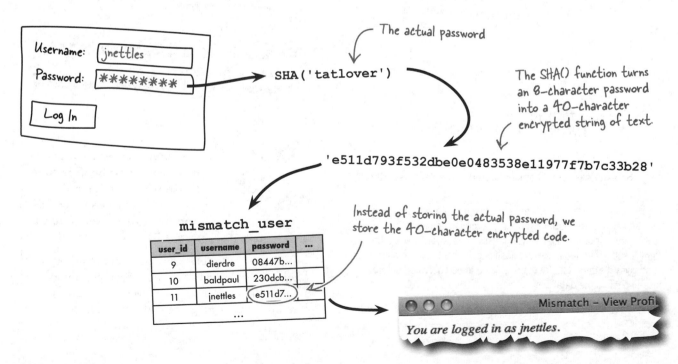

The actual password

SHA('tatlover')

The SHA() function turns an 8-character password into a 40-character encrypted string of text.

'e511d793f532dbe0e0483538e11977f7b7c33b28'

Instead of storing the actual password, we store the 40-character encrypted code.

mismatch_user

user_id	username	password	...
9	dierdre	08447b...	
10	baldpaul	230dcb...	
11	jnettles	e511d7...	
	...		

Mismatch – View Profile

You are logged in as jnettles.

Comparing
~~Decrypting~~ passwords

Once you've encrypted a piece of information, the natural instinct is to think in terms of decrypting it at some point. But the SHA() function is a one-way encryption with no way back. This is to preserve the security of the encrypted data—even if someone hacked into your database and stole all the passwords, they wouldn't be able to decrypt them. So how is it possible to log in a user if you can't decrypt their password?

You don't need to know a user's original password to know if they've entered the password correctly at log-in. This is because SHA() generates the same 40-character code as long as you provide it with the same string of text. So you can just encrypt the log-in password entered by the user and compare it to the value in the password column of the mismatch_user table. This can be accomplished with a single SQL query that attempts to select a matching user row based on a password.

> **The SHA()
> function provides
> one-way
> encryption—you
> can't decrypt
> data that has
> been encrypted.**

```
SELECT * FROM mismatch_user
    WHERE password = SHA('tatlover')
```

This is the password entered by the user in order to log in.

The SHA() function is called to encrypt the password so that it can appear in the WHERE clause.

This SELECT query selects all rows in the mismatch_user table whose password column matches the entered password, 'tatlover' in this case. Since we're comparing encrypted versions of the password, it isn't necessary to know the original password. A query to actually log in a user would use SHA(), but it would also need to SELECT on the user ID, as we see in just a moment.

Making room for the encrypted password

The SHA() function presents a problem for Mismatch since encrypted passwords end up being 40 characters long, but our newly created password column is only 16 characters long. An ALTER is in order to expand the password column for storing encrypted passwords.

```
ALTER TABLE mismatch_user
    CHANGE password password VARCHAR(40) NOT NULL
```

The size of the password column is changed to 40 so that encrypted passwords will fit.

there are no
Dumb Questions

Q: **What does SHA() stand for?**

A: The SHA() function stands for Secure Hash Algorithm. A "hash" is a programming term that refers to a unique, fixed-length string that uniquely represents a string of text. In the case of SHA(), the hash is the 40-character hexadecimal encrypted string of text, which uniquely represents the original password.

Q: **Are there any other ways to encrypt passwords?**

A: Yes. MySQL offers another function similar to SHA() called MD5() that carries out a similar type of encryption. But the SHA() algorithm is considered a little more secure than MD5(), so it's better to use SHA() instead. PHP also offers equivalent functions (sha1() and md5()) if you need to do any encryption in PHP code, as opposed to within an SQL query.

Test Drive

Add the `username` and `password` columns to the `mismatch_user` table, and then try them out.

Using a MySQL tool, execute the ALTER statement to add the `username` and `password` columns to the `mismatch_user` table.

```
ALTER TABLE mismatch_user ADD username VARCHAR(32) NOT NULL AFTER user_id,
   ADD password VARCHAR(16) NOT NULL AFTER username
```

But our `password` column actually needs to be able to hold a 40-character encrypted string, so ALTER the table once more to make room for the larger password data.

```
ALTER TABLE mismatch_user
   CHANGE password password VARCHAR(40) NOT NULL
```

Now, to test out the new columns, let's do an INSERT for a new user.

Don't forget to encrypt the password by calling the SHA() function.

```
INSERT INTO mismatch_user
   (username, password, join_date) VALUES ('jimi', SHA('heyjoe'), NOW())
```

To double-check that the password was indeed encrypted in the database, take a look at it by running a SELECT on the new user.

```
SELECT password FROM mismatch_user WHERE username = 'jimi'
```

And finally, you can simulate a log-in check by doing a SELECT on the username and using the SHA() function with the password in a WHERE clause.

For a successful log-in, this must be the same password used when inserting the row.

```
SELECT username FROM mismatch_user WHERE password = SHA('heyjoe')
```

```
File Edit Window Help OppositesAttract
mysql> SELECT username FROM mismatch_user WHERE password = SHA('heyjoe');

+----------+
| username |
+----------+
| jimi     |
+----------+
1 row in set (0.0005 sec)
```

Only one user matches the encrypted password.

So the password is now encrypted, but we still need to build a log-in form. Could we just use HTTP authentication since it requires a username and password to access protected pages?

Yes! HTTP authentication will certainly work as a simple user log-in system.

If you recall from the Guitar Wars high score application in the last chapter, HTTP authentication was used to restrict access to certain parts of an application by prompting the user for a username and password. That's roughly the same functionality required by Mismatch, except that now we have an entire database of possible username/password combinations, as opposed to one application-wide username and password. Mismatch users could use the same HTTP authentication window; however, they'll just be entering their own personal username and password.

To view this page, you need to log in to area "Mismatch" on www.mis-match.net.

Your password will be sent in the clear.

Name:

Password:

☐ Remember this password in my keychain

Cancel   Log In

The standard HTTP authentication window, which is browser-specific, can serve as a simple log-in user interface.

Authorizing users with HTTP

As Guitar Wars illustrated, two headers must be sent in order to restrict access to a page via an HTTP authentication window. These headers result in the user being prompted for a username and password in order to gain access to the Admin page of Guitar Wars.

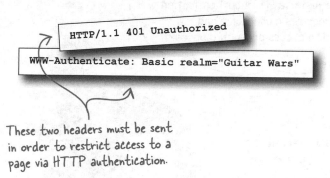

```
HTTP/1.1 401 Unauthorized
```

```
WWW-Authenticate: Basic realm="Guitar Wars"
```

These two headers must be sent in order to restrict access to a page via HTTP authentication.

Sending the headers for HTTP authentication amounts to two lines of PHP code—a call to the `header()` function for each header being sent.

```php
header('HTTP/1.1 401 Unauthorized');
header('WWW-Authenticate: Basic realm="Mismatch"');
```

HTTP authentication requires us to send two headers.

This is the realm for the authentication, which applies to the entire application.

Unless a user enters the correct username and password, they cannot see or use this page.

A username and password are required in order to access restricted pages in the Guitar Wars application.

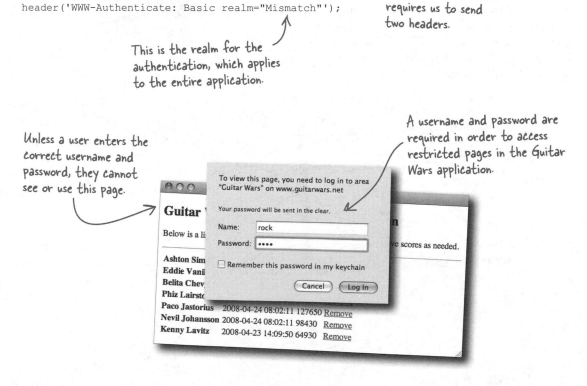

Circle the different parts of the Mismatch application that are impacted by the Log-In script (`login.php`) and its usage of HTTP authentication to control access. Then annotate how those application pieces are impacted.

Here's the Log-In script.

login.php

viewprofile.php

index.php

editprofile.php

`mismatch_user`

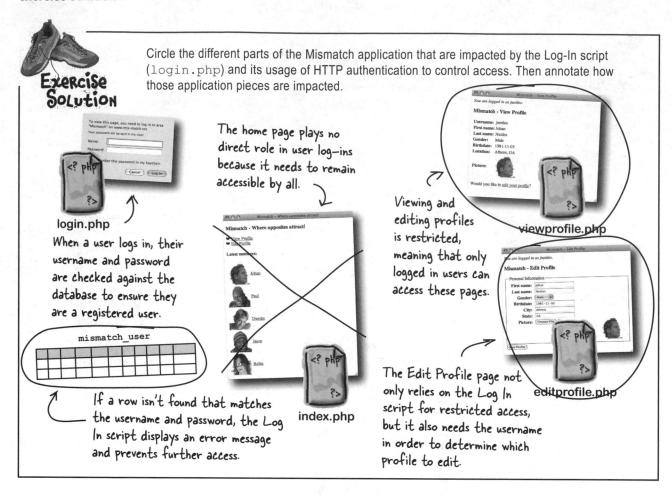

Circle the different parts of the Mismatch application that are impacted by the Log-In script (`login.php`) and its usage of HTTP authentication to control access. Then annotate how those application pieces are impacted.

Exercise Solution

login.php

When a user logs in, their username and password are checked against the database to ensure they are a registered user.

mismatch_user

If a row isn't found that matches the username and password, the Log In script displays an error message and prevents further access.

The home page plays no direct role in user log-ins because it needs to remain accessible by all.

index.php

Viewing and editing profiles is restricted, meaning that only logged in users can access these pages.

viewprofile.php

editprofile.php

The Edit Profile page not only relies on the Log In script for restricted access, but it also needs the username in order to determine which profile to edit.

there are no Dumb Questions

Q: **Why isn't it necessary to include the home page when requiring user log-ins?**

A: Because the home page is the first place a user lands when visiting the site, and it's important to let visitors glimpse the site before requiring a log-in. So the home page serves as both a teaser and a starting point—a teaser for visitors and a starting point for existing users who must log in to go any deeper into the application.

Q: **Can logged-in users view anyone's profile?**

A: Yes. The idea is that profiles are visible to all users who log in, but remain private to guests. In other words, you have to be a member of Mismatch in order to view another user's profile.

Q: **How does password encryption affect HTTP authentication?**

A: There are two different issues here: transmitting a password and storing a password. The SHA() MySQL function focuses on securely **storing** a password in a database in an encrypted form. The database doesn't care how you transmitted the password initially, so this form of encryption has no impact on HTTP authentication. However, an argument could be made that encryption should also take place during the **transmission** of the password when the HTTP authentication window submits it to the server. This kind of encryption is outside the scope of this chapter and, ultimately, only necessary when dealing with highly sensitive data.

Logging In Users with HTTP Authentication

The Log-In script (login.php) is responsible for requesting a username and password from the user using HTTP authentication headers, grabbing the username and password values from the $_SERVER superglobal, and then checking them against the mismatch_user database before providing access to a restricted page.

```php
<?php
  require_once('connectvars.php');

  if (!isset($_SERVER['PHP_AUTH_USER']) || !isset($_SERVER['PHP_AUTH_PW'])) {
    // The username/password weren't entered so send the authentication headers
    header('HTTP/1.1 401 Unauthorized');
    header('WWW-Authenticate: Basic realm="Mismatch"');
    exit('<h3>Mismatch</h3>Sorry, you must enter your username and password to log in and access ' .
      'this page.');
  }

  // Connect to the database
  $dbc = mysqli_connect(DB_HOST, DB_USER, DB_PASSWORD, DB_NAME);

  // Grab the user-entered log-in data
  $user_username = mysqli_real_escape_string($dbc, trim($_SERVER['PHP_AUTH_USER']));
  $user_password = mysqli_real_escape_string($dbc, trim($_SERVER['PHP_AUTH_PW']));

  // Look up the username and password in the database
  $query = "SELECT user_id, username FROM mismatch_user WHERE username = '$user_username' AND " .
    "password = SHA('$user_password')";
  $data = mysqli_query($dbc, $query);

  if (mysqli_num_rows($data) == 1) {
    // The log-in is OK so set the user ID and username variables
    $row = mysqli_fetch_array($data);
    $user_id = $row['user_id'];
    $username = $row['username'];
  }
  else {
    // The username/password are incorrect so send the authentication headers
    header('HTTP/1.1 401 Unauthorized');
    header('WWW-Authenticate: Basic realm="Mismatch"');
    exit('<h2>Mismatch</h2>Sorry, you must enter a valid username and password to log in and ' .
      'access this page.');
  }

  // Confirm the successful log-in
  echo('<p class="login">You are logged in as ' . $username . '.</p>');
?>
```

If the username and password haven't been entered, send the authentication headers to prompt the user.

Grab the username and password entered by the user.

Perform a query to see if any rows match the username and encrypted password.

If a row matches, it means the log-in is OK, and we can set the $user_id and $username variables.

If no database row matches the username and password, send the authentication headers again to re-prompt the user.

All is well at this point, so confirm the successful log-in.

DONE

2 **Build a new Log-In script that prompts the user to enter their username and password.**

TEST DRIVE

Create the new Log-In script, and include it in the View Profile and Edit Profile scripts.

Create a new text file named `login.php`, and enter the code for the Log-In script in it (or download the script from the Head First Labs site at www.headfirstlabs.com/books/hfphp). Then add PHP code to the top of the `viewprofile.php` and `editprofile.php` scripts to include the new Log-In script.

Upload all of the scripts to your web server, and then open the main Mismatch page in a web browser. Click the View Profile or Edit Profile link to log in and access the personalized pages. Of course, this will only work if you've already added a user with a username and password to the database.

These two links lead to the protected pages, which invoke the Log-In script if a user isn't logged in.

This password is SHA() encrypted and compared with the password in the database to determine if the log-in is allowed.

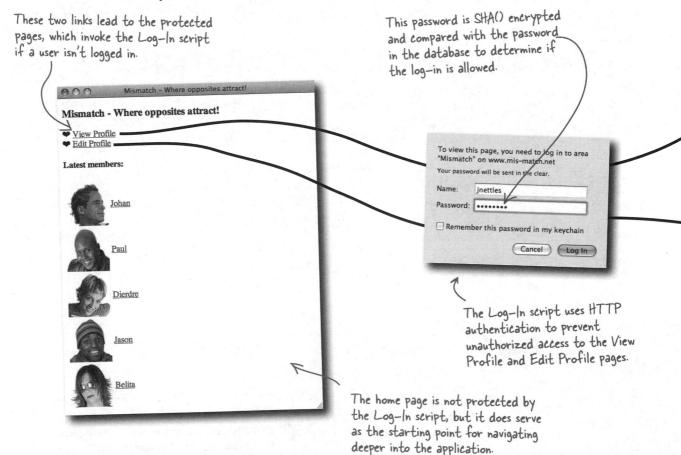

The Log-In script uses HTTP authentication to prevent unauthorized access to the View Profile and Edit Profile pages.

The home page is not protected by the Log-In script, but it does serve as the starting point for navigating deeper into the application.

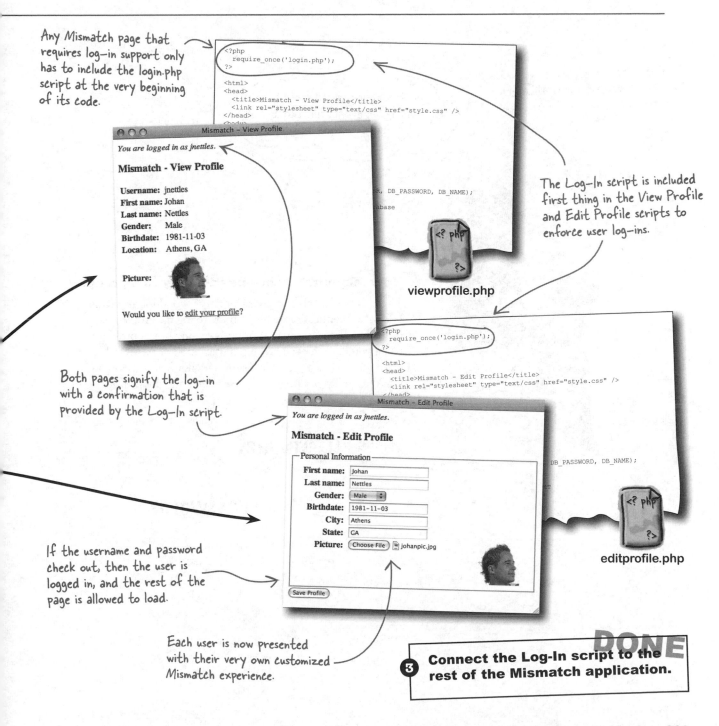

Any Mismatch page that requires log-in support only has to include the login.php script at the very beginning of its code.

```php
<?php
  require_once('login.php');
?>

<html>
<head>
  <title>Mismatch - View Profile</title>
  <link rel="stylesheet" type="text/css" href="style.css" />
</head>
<body>
```

The Log-In script is included first thing in the View Profile and Edit Profile scripts to enforce user log-ins.

Mismatch – View Profile

You are logged in as jnettles.

Mismatch - View Profile

Username: jnettles
First name: Johan
Last name: Nettles
Gender:　　Male
Birthdate: 1981-11-03
Location:　Athens, GA

Picture:

Would you like to edit your profile?

viewprofile.php

Both pages signify the log-in with a confirmation that is provided by the Log-In script.

```php
<?php
  require_once('login.php');
?>

<html>
<head>
  <title>Mismatch - Edit Profile</title>
  <link rel="stylesheet" type="text/css" href="style.css" />
</head>
```

Mismatch – Edit Profile

You are logged in as jnettles.

Mismatch - Edit Profile

┌─ Personal Information ────────────
First name: Johan
Last name: Nettles
Gender: Male
Birthdate: 1981-11-03
City: Athens
State: GA
Picture: Choose File 📄 johanpic.jpg

Save Profile

editprofile.php

If the username and password check out, then the user is logged in, and the rest of the page is allowed to load.

Each user is now presented with their very own customized Mismatch experience.

DONE

❸ Connect the Log-In script to the rest of the Mismatch application.

Ruby loves horror movies, cube puzzles, and spicy food, but hates Mismatch at the moment for not letting her sign up and use the system.

I'd love to log in and start working on my profile, but I can't figure out how to sign up.

New Mismatch users need a way to sign up.

The new Mismatch Log-In script does a good job of using HTTP authentication to allow users to log in. Problem is, users don't have a way to sign up—logging in is a problem when you haven't even created a username or password yet. Mismatch needs a Sign-Up form that allows new users to join the site by creating a new username and password.

Username?

Password?

A form for signing up new users

What does this new Sign-Up form look like? We know it needs to allow the user to enter their desired username and password... anything else? Since the user is establishing their password with the new Sign-Up form, and passwords in web forms are typically masked with asterisks for security purposes, it's a good idea to have two password form fields. So the user enters the password twice, just to make sure there wasn't a typo.

So the job of the Sign-Up page is to retrieve the username and password from the user, make sure the username isn't already used by someone else, and then add the new user to the `mismatch_user` database.

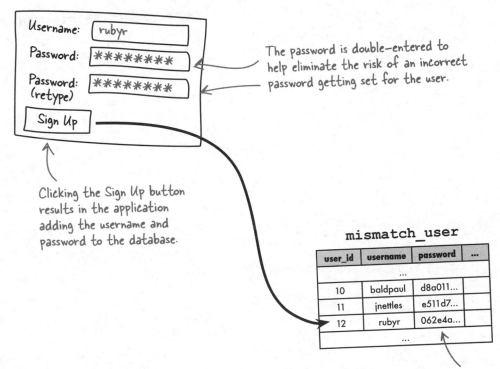

The password is double-entered to help eliminate the risk of an incorrect password getting set for the user.

Clicking the Sign Up button results in the application adding the username and password to the database.

Since the passwords are now encrypted, they're secure even when viewing the database.

One potential problem with the Sign-Up script involves the user attempting to sign up for a username that already exists. The script needs to be smart enough to catch this problem and force the user to try a different username. So the job of the Sign-Up page is to retrieve the username and password from the user, make sure the username isn't already used by someone else, and then add the new user to the `mismatch_user` database.

PHP & MySQL Magnets

The Mismatch Sign-Up script uses a custom form to prompt the user for their desired username and password. Problem is, the script code is incomplete. Use the magnets below to finish up the script so new users can sign up and join the Mismatch community.

Here's the Sign-Up form.

Mismatch - Sign Up

Mismatch - Sign Up

Please enter your username and desired password to sign up to Mismatch.

Registration Info

Username: rubyr
Password: ••••••••
Password (retype): ••••••••

Sign Up

```php
<?php
require_once('appvars.php');
require_once('connectvars.php');

// Connect to the database
$dbc = mysqli_connect(DB_HOST, DB_USER, DB_PASSWORD, DB_NAME);

if (isset($_POST['submit'])) {
  // Grab the profile data from the POST
  .................... = mysqli_real_escape_string($dbc, trim($_POST['................']));

  ...................... = mysqli_real_escape_string($dbc, trim($_POST['..............']));

  ...................... = mysqli_real_escape_string($dbc, trim($_POST['..............']));


  if (!empty($username) && !empty($password1) && !empty($password2) &&

    ( ..................... == ..................... )) {

    // Make sure someone isn't already registered using this username

    $query = "SELECT * FROM mismatch_user WHERE username = '.................'";

    $data = mysqli_query($dbc, $query);
    if (mysqli_num_rows($data) == 0) {
      // The username is unique, so insert the data into the database
      $query = "INSERT INTO mismatch_user (username, password, join_date) VALUES " .

      "('...............', SHA('.................'), NOW())";

      mysqli_query($dbc, $query);

      // Confirm success with the user
      echo '<p>Your new account has been successfully created. You\'re now ready to log in and ' .
        '<a href="editprofile.php">edit your profile</a>.</p>';

      mysqli_close($dbc);
      exit();
    }
```

Don't forget, you have to escape an apostrophe if it appears inside of single quotes.

```
      else {
        // An account already exists for this username, so display an error message
        echo '<p class="error">An account already exists for this username. Please use a different ' .
          'address.</p>';

                      ...................... = "";

      }
    }
    else {
      echo '<p class="error">You must enter all of the sign-up data, including the desired password ' .
        'twice.</p>';
    }
  }

  mysqli_close($dbc);
?>

<p>Please enter your username and desired password to sign up to Mismatch.</p>
<form method="post" action="<?php echo $_SERVER['PHP_SELF']; ?>">
  <fieldset>
    <legend>Registration Info</legend>
    <label for="username">Username:</label>

    <input type="text" id=".................." name=".................."

      value="<?php if (!empty(..................)) echo ..................; ?>" /><br />

    <label for="..................">Password:</label>

    <input type=".................." id=".................." name=".................." /><br />

    <label for="..................">Password (retype):</label>

    <input type=".................." id=".................." name=".................." /><br />

  </fieldset>
  <input type="submit" value="Sign Up" name="submit" />
</form>
```

signup.php

password
password

$password1
$password1 $password1

$username
$username
$username $username
$username $username

username
username
username

password2
password2 password2
password2

password1
password1 password1
password1

$password2
$password2

PHP & MySQL Magnets Solution

The Mismatch Sign-Up script uses a custom form to prompt the user for their desired username and password. Problem is, the script code is incomplete. Use the magnets below to finish up the script so new users can sign up and join the Mismatch community.

Here's the Sign-Up form.

Mismatch - Sign Up

Please enter your username and desired password to sign up to Mismatch.

Registration Info
Username: ruby
Password: ••••••••
Password (retype): ••••••••

Sign Up

```php
<?php
require_once('appvars.php');
require_once('connectvars.php');

// Connect to the database
$dbc = mysqli_connect(DB_HOST, DB_USER, DB_PASSWORD, DB_NAME);

if (isset($_POST['submit'])) {
  // Grab the profile data from the POST
  $username = mysqli_real_escape_string($dbc, trim($_POST['username']));
  $password1 = mysqli_real_escape_string($dbc, trim($_POST['password1']));
  $password2 = mysqli_real_escape_string($dbc, trim($_POST['password2']));

  if (!empty($username) && !empty($password1) && !empty($password2) &&
    ($password1 == $password2)) {
    // Make sure someone isn't already registered using this username
    $query = "SELECT * FROM mismatch_user WHERE username = '$username'";
    $data = mysqli_query($dbc, $query);
    if (mysqli_num_rows($data) == 0) {
      // The username is unique, so insert the data into the database
      $query = "INSERT INTO mismatch_user (username, password, join_date) VALUES " .
        "('$username', SHA('$password1'), NOW())";
      mysqli_query($dbc, $query);

      // Confirm success with the user
      echo '<p>Your new account has been successfully created. You\'re now ready to log in and ' .
        '<a href="editprofile.php">edit your profile</a>.</p>';

      mysqli_close($dbc);
      exit();
    }
```

Grab all of the user-entered data, making sure to clean it up first.

Check to make sure that none of the form fields are empty and that both passwords match.

Perform a query to see if any existing rows match the username entered.

If no match is found, the username is unique, so we can carry out the INSERT.

Either password could be used here since they must be equal to get to this point.

Confirm the successful sign-up with the user, and exit the script.

```
    else {
      // An account already exists for this username, so display an error message
      echo '<p class="error">An account already exists for this username. Please use a different ' .
        'address.</p>';
```

```
      $username = "";
```

Clear the *username* variable so that the form field is cleared.

↳ The username is not unique, so display an error message.

```
    }
  }
  else {
    echo '<p class="error">You must enter all of the sign-up data, including the desired password ' .
      'twice.</p>';
  }
}
```

One or more of the form fields are empty, so display an error message.

```
mysqli_close($dbc);
?>

<p>Please enter your username and desired password to sign up to Mismatch.</p>
<form method="post" action="<?php echo $_SERVER['PHP_SELF']; ?>">
  <fieldset>
    <legend>Registration Info</legend>
    <label for="username">Username:</label>
```

```
    <input type="text" id=" username " name=" username "
      value="<?php if (!empty( $username )) echo $username ; ?>" /><br />
    <label for=" password1 ">Password:</label>
    <input type=" password " id=" password1 " name=" password1 " /><br />
    <label for=" password2 ">Password (retype):</label>
    <input type=" password " id=" password2 " name=" password2 " /><br />
  </fieldset>
  <input type="submit" value="Sign Up" name="submit" />
</form>
```

signup.php

there are no
Dumb Questions

Q: Why couldn't you just use HTTP authentication for signing up new users?

A: Because the purpose of the Sign-Up script isn't to restrict access to pages. The Sign-Up script's job is to allow the user to enter a unique username and password, and then add them to the user database. Sure, it's possible to use the HTTP authentication window as an input form for the username and password, but the authentication functionality is overkill for just signing up a new user. It's better to create a custom form for sign-ups—then you get the benefit of double-checking the password for data entry errors.

Q: So does the Sign-Up script log in users after they sign up?

A: No. And the reason primarily has to do with the fact that the Log-In script already handles the task of logging in a user, and there's no need to duplicate the code in the Sign-Up script. The Sign-Up script instead presents a link to the Edit Profile page, which is presumably where the user would want to go after signing in. And since they aren't logged in yet, they are presented with the Log-In window as part of attempting to access the Edit Profile page. So the Sign-Up script leads the user to the Log-In window via the Edit Profile page, as opposed to logging them in automatically.

Give users a chance to sign up

We have a Sign-Up script, but how do users get to it? We need to let users know how to sign up. One option is to put a "Sign Up" link on the main Mismatch page. That's not a bad idea, but we would ideally need to be able to turn it on and off based on whether a user is logged in. Another possibility is to just show a "Sign Up" link as part of the Log-In script.

When a new user clicks the "View Profile" or "Edit Profile" links on the main page, for example, they'll be prompted for a username and password by the Log-In script. Since they don't yet have a username or password, they will likely click Cancel to bail out of the log-in. That's our chance to display a link to the Sign-Up script by tweaking the log-in failure message displayed by the Log-In script so that it provides a link to `signup.php`.

Here's the original log-in failure code:

This code just shows a log-in error message with no mention of how to sign up for Mismatch.

```
exit('<h3>Mismatch</h3>Sorry, you must enter your username and password to log in and access ' .

  'this page.');
```

This code actually appears in two different places in the Log-In script: when no username or password are entered and when they are entered incorrectly. It's probably a good idea to go ahead and provide a "Sign Up" link in both places. Here's what the new code might look like:

This code is much more helpful since it generates a link to the Sign-Up script so that the user can sign up.

```
exit('<h2>Mismatch</h2>Sorry, you must enter a valid username and password to log in and ' .

  'access this page. If you aren\'t a registered member, please <a href="signup.php">sign up</a>.');
```

Nothing fancy here, just a normal HTML link to the signup.php script.

TEST DRIVE

Add Sign-Up functionality to Mismatch.

Create a new text file named `signup.php`, and enter the code for the Sign-Up script in it (or download the script from the Head First Labs site at `www.headfirstlabs.com/books/hfphp`). Then modify the `login.php` script to add links to the Sign-Up script for users who can't log in.

Upload the scripts to your web server, and then open the Sign-Up page in a web browser. Sign up as a new user and then log in. Then edit your profile and view your profile to confirm that the sign-up and log-in worked correctly. The application now has that personalized touch that's been missing.

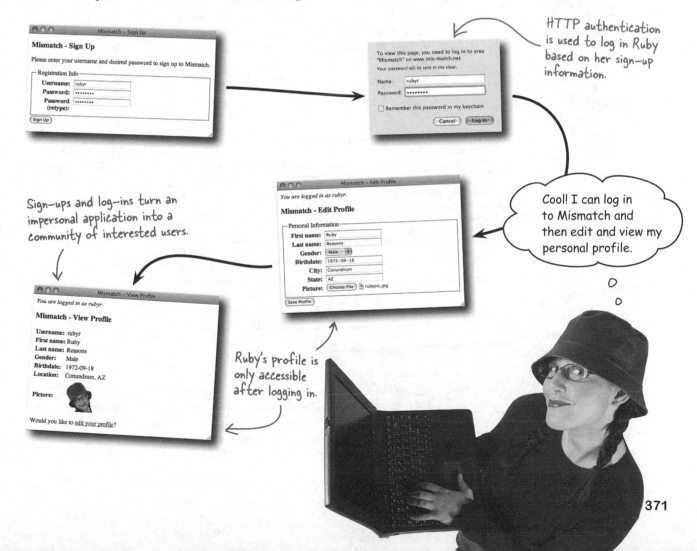

HTTP authentication is used to log in Ruby based on her sign-up information.

Sign-ups and log-ins turn an impersonal application into a community of interested users.

Cool! I can log in to Mismatch and then edit and view my personal profile.

Ruby's profile is only accessible after logging in.

I share a computer with two roommates, and I'd rather they not have access to my Mismatch profile. I need to be able to log out!

Community web sites must allow users to log out so that others can't access their personal data from a shared computer.

Allowing users to log out might sound simple enough, but it presents a pretty big problem with HTTP authentication. The problem is that HTTP authentication is intended to be carried out once for a given page or collection of pages—it's only reset when the browser is shut down. In other words, a user is never "logged out" of an HTTP authenticated web page until the browser is shut down or the user manually clears the HTTP authenticated session. The latter option is easier to carry out in some browsers (Firefox, for example) than others (Safari).

Mismatch – Edit Profile

You are logged in as sidneyk.

Mismatch - Edit Profile

Personal Information

First name: Sidney
Last name: Kelsow
Gender: Female
Birthdate: 1984-07-19
City: Tempe
State: AZ
Picture: Choose File — sidneypic.jpg

To view this page, you need to log in to area "Mismatch" on www.mis-match.net
Your password will be sent in the clear.

Name: sidneyk
Password: ••••••

☐ Remember this password in my keychain

Cancel   Log In

Save Profile

Once you log in, you stay in until you close the browser.

A log-out feature would allow Sidney to carefully control access to her personal profile.

Even though HTTP authentication presents a handy and simple way to support user log-ins in the Mismatch application, it doesn't provide any control over logging a user out. We need to be able to both remember users and also allow them to log out whenever they want.

Sometimes you just need a cookie

The problem originally solved by HTTP authentication is twofold: there is the issue of limiting access to certain pages, and there is the issue of remembering that the user entered information about themselves. The second problem is the tricky one because it involves an application remembering who the user is across multiple pages (scripts). Mismatch accomplishes this feat by checking the username and password stored in the $_SERVER superglobal. So we took advantage of the fact that PHP stores away the HTTP authentication username and password in a superglobal that persists across multiple pages.

HTTP authentication stores data persistently on the client but doesn't allow you to delete it when you're done.

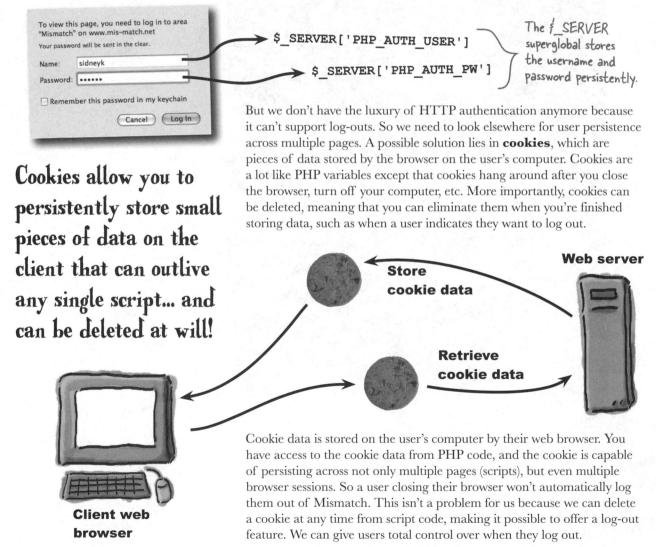

The $_SERVER superglobal stores the username and password persistently.

But we don't have the luxury of HTTP authentication anymore because it can't support log-outs. So we need to look elsewhere for user persistence across multiple pages. A possible solution lies in **cookies**, which are pieces of data stored by the browser on the user's computer. Cookies are a lot like PHP variables except that cookies hang around after you close the browser, turn off your computer, etc. More importantly, cookies can be deleted, meaning that you can eliminate them when you're finished storing data, such as when a user indicates they want to log out.

Cookies allow you to persistently store small pieces of data on the client that can outlive any single script... and can be deleted at will!

Cookie data is stored on the user's computer by their web browser. You have access to the cookie data from PHP code, and the cookie is capable of persisting across not only multiple pages (scripts), but even multiple browser sessions. So a user closing their browser won't automatically log them out of Mismatch. This isn't a problem for us because we can delete a cookie at any time from script code, making it possible to offer a log-out feature. We can give users total control over when they log out.

What's in a cookie?

A cookie stores **a single piece of data** under a unique name, much like a variable in PHP. Unlike a variable, a cookie can have an expiration date. When this expiration date arrives, the cookie is destroyed. So cookies aren't exactly immortal—they just live longer than PHP variables. You can create a cookie without an expiration date, in which case it acts just like a PHP variable—it gets destroyed when the browser closes.

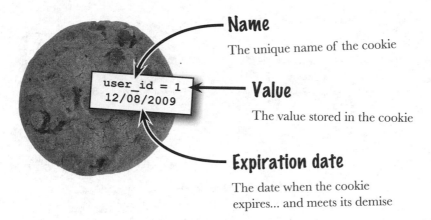

Name

The unique name of the cookie

Value

The value stored in the cookie

Expiration date

The date when the cookie expires... and meets its demise

Cookies allow you to store a string of text under a certain name, kind of like a PHP text variable. It's the fact that cookies outlive normal script data that makes them so powerful, especially in situations where an application consists of multiple pages that need to remember a few pieces of data, such as log-in information.

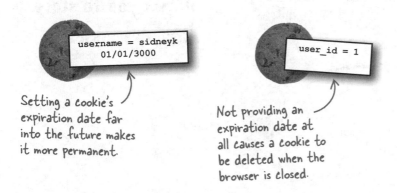

Setting a cookie's expiration date far into the future makes it more permanent.

Not providing an expiration date at all causes a cookie to be deleted when the browser is closed.

So Mismatch can mimic the persistence provided by the $_SERVER superglobal by setting two cookies—one for the username and one for the password. Although we really don't need to keep the password around, it might be more helpful to store away the user ID instead.

there are no Dumb Questions

Q: What's the big deal about cookies being persistent? Isn't data stored in a MySQL database persistent too?

A: Yes, database data is most certainly persistent. In fact, it's technically much more persistent than a cookie because there is no expiration date involved—if you stick data in a database, it stays there until you explicitly remove it. The real issue in regard to cookies and persistence is convenience. We don't need to store the current user's ID or username for all eternity just to allow them to access their profile; we just need a quick way to know who they are. What we really need is **temporary persistence**, which might seem like an oxymoron until you consider the fact that we need data to hang around longer than a page (persistent), but not forever.

Use
~~Bake~~ cookies with PHP

PHP provides access to cookies through a function called `setcookie()`
and a superglobal called `$_COOKIE`. The `setcookie()` function is
used to set the value and optional expiration date of a cookie, and the
`$_COOKIE` superglobal is used to retrieve the value of a cookie.

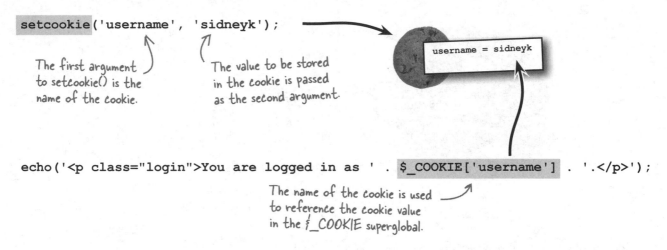

```
setcookie('username', 'sidneyk');
```

The first argument
to setcookie() is the
name of the cookie.

The value to be stored
in the cookie is passed
as the second argument.

username = sidneyk

```
echo('<p class="login">You are logged in as ' . $_COOKIE['username'] . '.</p>');
```

The name of the cookie is used
to reference the cookie value
in the $_COOKIE superglobal.

The power of setting a cookie is that the cookie data persists across
multiple scripts, so we can remember the username without having to
prompt the user to log in every time they move from one page to another
within the application. But don't forget, we also need to store away the
user's ID in a cookie since it serves as a primary key for database queries.

> **The PHP
> setcookie() function
> allows you to store
> data in cookies.**

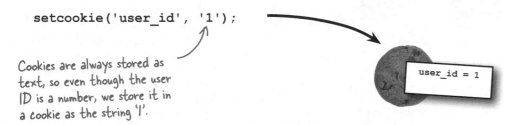

```
setcookie('user_id', '1');
```

Cookies are always stored as
text, so even though the user
ID is a number, we store it in
a cookie as the string '1'.

user_id = 1

The `setcookie()` function also accepts an optional third argument
that sets the expiration date of the cookie, which is the date upon which
the cookie is automatically deleted. If you don't specify an expiration
date, as in the above example, the cookie automatically expires when the
browser is closed.

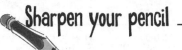

Sharpen your pencil

Switching Mismatch to use cookies involves more than just writing a new Log-Out script. We must first revisit the Log-In script and change it to use cookies instead of HTTP authentication. Circle and annotate the parts of the Log-In code that you think need to change to accommodate cookies.

```php
<?php
  require_once('connectvars.php');

  if (!isset($_SERVER['PHP_AUTH_USER']) || !isset($_SERVER['PHP_AUTH_PW'])) {
    // The username/password weren't entered so send the authentication headers
    header('HTTP/1.1 401 Unauthorized');
    header('WWW-Authenticate: Basic realm="Mismatch"');
    exit('<h3>Mismatch</h3>Sorry, you must enter your username and password to ' .
      'log in and access this page. If you aren\'t a registered member, please ' .
      '<a href="signup.php">sign up</a>.');
  }

  // Connect to the database
  $dbc = mysqli_connect(DB_HOST, DB_USER, DB_PASSWORD, DB_NAME);

  // Grab the user-entered log-in data
  $user_username = mysqli_real_escape_string($dbc, trim($_SERVER['PHP_AUTH_USER']));
  $user_password = mysqli_real_escape_string($dbc, trim($_SERVER['PHP_AUTH_PW']));

  // Look up the username and password in the database
  $query = "SELECT user_id, username FROM mismatch_user WHERE username = " .
    "'$user_username' AND password = SHA('$user_password')";
  $data = mysqli_query($dbc, $query);

  if (mysqli_num_rows($data) == 1) {
    // The log-in is OK so set the user ID and username variables
    $row = mysqli_fetch_array($data);
    $user_id = $row['user_id'];
    $username = $row['username'];
  }
  else {
    // The username/password are incorrect so send the authentication headers
    header('HTTP/1.1 401 Unauthorized');
    header('WWW-Authenticate: Basic realm="Mismatch"');
    exit('<h2>Mismatch</h2>Sorry, you must enter a valid username and password ' .
      'to log in and access this page. If you aren\'t a registered member, ' .
      'please <a href="signup.php">sign up</a>.');
  }

  // Confirm the successful log-in
  echo('<p class="login">You are logged in as ' . $username . '.</p>');
?>
```

login.php

Sharpen your pencil
Solution

Switching Mismatch to use cookies involves more than just writing a new Log-Out script. We must first revisit the Log-In script and change it to use cookies instead of HTTP authentication. Circle and annotate the parts of the Log-In code that you think need to change to accommodate cookies.

We need to check for the existence of a cookie to see if the user is logged in or not.

Instead of getting the username and password from an authentication window, we need to use a form with POST data.

```php
<?php
  require_once('connectvars.php');

  if (!isset($_SERVER['PHP_AUTH_USER']) || !isset($_SERVER['PHP_AUTH_PW'])) {
    // The username/password weren't entered so send the authentication headers
    header('HTTP/1.1 401 Unauthorized');
    header('WWW-Authenticate: Basic realm="Mismatch"');
    exit('<h3>Mismatch</h3>Sorry, you must enter your username and password to ' .
      'log in and access this page. If you aren\'t a registered member, please ' .
      '<a href="signup.php">sign up</a>.');
  }

  // Connect to the database
  $dbc = mysqli_connect(DB_HOST, DB_USER, DB_PASSWORD, DB_NAME);

  // Grab the user-entered log-in data
  $user_username = mysqli_real_escape_string($dbc, trim($_SERVER['PHP_AUTH_USER']));
  $user_password = mysqli_real_escape_string($dbc, trim($_SERVER['PHP_AUTH_PW']));

  // Look up the username and password in the database
  $query = "SELECT user_id, username FROM mismatch_user WHERE username = " .
    "'$user_username' AND password = SHA('$user_password')";
  $data = mysqli_query($dbc, $query);

  if (mysqli_num_rows($data) == 1) {
    // The log-in is OK so set the user ID and username variables
    $row = mysqli_fetch_array($data);
    $user_id = $row['user_id'];
    $username = $row['username'];
  }
  else {
    // The username/password are incorrect so send the authentication headers
    header('HTTP/1.1 401 Unauthorized');
    header('WWW-Authenticate: Basic realm="Mismatch"');
    exit('<h2>Mismatch</h2>Sorry, you must enter a valid username and password ' .
      'to log in and access this page. If you aren\'t a registered member, ' .
      'please <a href="signup.php">sign up</a>.');
  }

  // Confirm the successful log-in
  echo('<p class="login">You are logged in as ' . $username . '.</p>');
?>
```

We no longer need to send HTTP authentication headers.

The query doesn't have to change at all!

Here we need to set two cookies instead of setting script variables.

Since we can't rely on the HTTP authentication window for entering the username and password, we need to create an HTML Log-In form for entering them.

login.php

Rethinking the flow of log-ins

Using cookies instead of HTTP authentication for Mismatch log-ins involves more than just rethinking the storage of user data. What about the log-in user interface? The cookie-powered log-in must provide its own form since it can't rely on the authentication window for entering a username and password. Not only do we have to build this form, but we need to think through how it changes the flow of the application as users log in and access other pages.

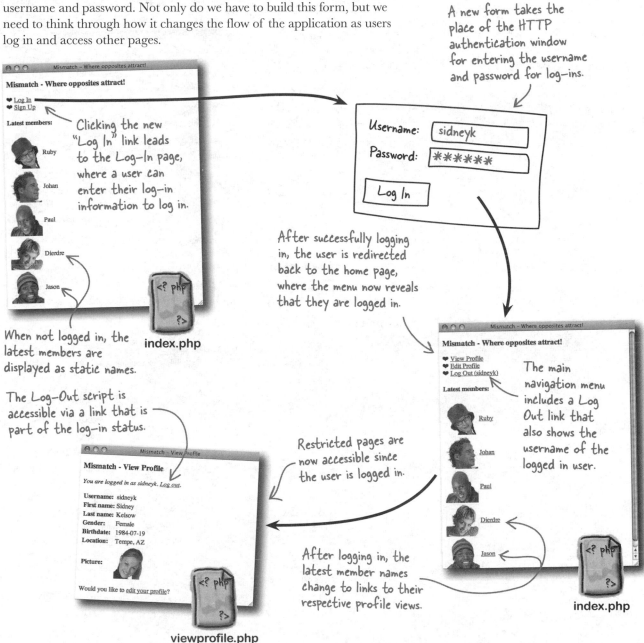

A new form takes the place of the HTTP authentication window for entering the username and password for log-ins.

Clicking the new "Log In" link leads to the Log-In page, where a user can enter their log-in information to log in.

When not logged in, the latest members are displayed as static names.

index.php

After successfully logging in, the user is redirected back to the home page, where the menu now reveals that they are logged in.

The Log-Out script is accessible via a link that is part of the log-in status.

The main navigation menu includes a Log Out link that also shows the username of the logged in user.

Restricted pages are now accessible since the user is logged in.

After logging in, the latest member names change to links to their respective profile views.

viewprofile.php

index.php

A cookie-powered log-in

The new version of the Log-In script that relies on cookies for log-in persistence is a bit more complex than its predecessor since it must provide its own form for entering the username and password. But it's more powerful in that it provides log-out functionality.

Mismatch - Log In

Mismatch - Log In

Log In
Username: sidneyk
Password: ••••••

Log In

login.php

Here's the new Log-In form.

```php
<?php
  require_once('connectvars.php');

  // Clear the error message
  $error_msg = "";

  // If the user isn't logged in, try to log them in
  if (!isset($_COOKIE['user_id'])) {
    if (isset($_POST['submit'])) {
      // Connect to the database
      $dbc = mysqli_connect(DB_HOST, DB_USER, DB_PASSWORD, DB_NAME);

      // Grab the user-entered log-in data
      $user_username = mysqli_real_escape_string($dbc, trim($_POST['username']));
      $user_password = mysqli_real_escape_string($dbc, trim($_POST['password']));

      if (!empty($user_username) && !empty($user_password)) {
        // Look up the username and password in the database
        $query = "SELECT user_id, username FROM mismatch_user WHERE username = '$user_username' AND " .
          "password = SHA('$user_password')";
        $data = mysqli_query($dbc, $query);

        if (mysqli_num_rows($data) == 1) {
          // The log-in is OK so set the user ID and username cookies, and redirect to the home page
          $row = mysqli_fetch_array($data);
          setcookie('user_id', $row['user_id']);
          setcookie('username', $row['username']);
          $home_url = 'http://' . $_SERVER['HTTP_HOST'] . dirname($_SERVER['PHP_SELF']) . '/index.php';
          header('Location: ' . $home_url);
        }
        else {
          // The username/password are incorrect so set an error message
          $error_msg = 'Sorry, you must enter a valid username and password to log in.';
        }
      }
      else {
        // The username/password weren't entered so set an error message
        $error_msg = 'Sorry, you must enter your username and password to log in.';
      }
    }
  }
?>

<html>
<head>
  <title>Mismatch - Log In</title>
  <link rel="stylesheet" type="text/css" href="style.css" />
</head>
<body>
  <h3>Mismatch - Log In</h3>
```

Error messages are now stored in a variable and displayed, if necessary, later in the script.

Check the user_id cookie to see if the user is logged in.

If the user isn't logged in, see if they've submitted log-in data.

The user-entered data now comes from form POST data instead of an authentication window.

Log in the user by setting user_id and username cookies.

Redirect the user to the Mismatch home page upon a successful log-in.

Set the error message variable if anything is wrong with the log-in data.

The Log-In script is now a full web page, so it requires all the standard HTML elements.

continues on the facing page...

```php
<?php
  // If the cookie is empty, show any error message and the log-in form; otherwise confirm the log-in
  if (empty($_COOKIE['user_id'])) {
    echo '<p class="error">' . $error_msg . '</p>';
?>
```

If the user still isn't logged in at this point, go ahead and show the error message.

```html
<form method="post" action="<?php echo $_SERVER['PHP_SELF']; ?>">
  <fieldset>
    <legend>Log In</legend>
    <label for="username">Username:</label>
    <input type="text" id="username" name="username"
      value="<?php if (!empty($user_username)) echo $user_username; ?>" /><br />
    <label for="password">Password:</label>
    <input type="password" id="password" name="password" />
  </fieldset>
  <input type="submit" value="Log In" name="submit" />
</form>
```

These two form fields are used to enter the username and password for logging in.

Everything prior to this curly brace is still part of the first if clause.

```php
<?php
  }
  else {
    // Confirm the successful log in
    echo('<p class="login">You are logged in as ' . $_COOKIE['username'] . '.</p>');
  }
?>
```

If the user is logged in at this point, just tell them so.

```html
</body>
</html>
```

Finish the HTML code to complete the Log-In web page.

there are no Dumb Questions

Q: Why is it necessary to store both the user ID and username in cookies?

A: Since both pieces of information uniquely identify a user within the Mismatch user database, you could use either one for the purpose of keeping up with the current user. However, user_id is a better (more efficient) user reference with respect to the database because it is a numeric primary key. On the other hand, user_id is fairly cryptic and doesn't have any meaning to the user, so username comes in handy for letting the user know they are logged in, such as displaying their name on the page. Since multiple people sometimes share the same computer, it is important to not just let the user know they are logged in, but also who they are logged in *as*.

Q: Then why not also store the password in a cookie as part of the log-in data?

A: The password is only important for initially verifying that a user is who they claim to be. Once the password is verified as part of the log-in process, there is no reason to keep it around. Besides, passwords are very sensitive data, so it's a good idea to avoid storing them temporarily if at all possible.

Q: It looks as if the form in the Log-In script is actually inside the `if` statement? Is that possible?

A: Yes. In fact it's quite common for PHP code to be "broken up" around HTML code, as is the case with the Log-In script. Just because you close a section of PHP code with `?>`, doesn't mean the logic of the code is closed. When you open another section of PHP code with `<?php`, the logic continues right where it left off. In the Log-In script, the HTML form is contained within the first `if` branch, while the `else` branch picks up after the form code. Breaking out of PHP code into HTML code like this keeps you from having to generate the form with a bunch of messy `echo` statements.

Navigating the Mismatch application

The new Log-In script changes the flow of the Mismatch application, requiring a simple menu that appears on the home page (index.php). This menu is important because it provides access to the different major parts of the application, currently the View Profile and Edit Profile pages, as well as the ability for users to log in, sign up, and log out depending on their current log-in state. The fact that the menu changes based on the user's log-in is significant and is ultimately what gives the menu its power and usefulness.

A different menu is shown depending on whether the username cookie is set.

This menu appears when a user is not logged in, giving them an opportunity to either log in or sign up.

Mismatch – Where opposites attract!

Mismatch - Where opposites attract!

❤ Log In
❤ Sign Up

Latest members:

Ruby

Johan

Paul

Dierdre

Jason

username = **?**

The index.php script knows to show the limited menu when it can't find the username cookie.

The menu is generated by PHP code within the index.php script, and this code uses the $_COOKIE superglobal to look up the username cookie and see if the user is logged in or not. The user ID cookie could have also been used, but the username is actually displayed in the menu, so it makes more sense to check for it instead.

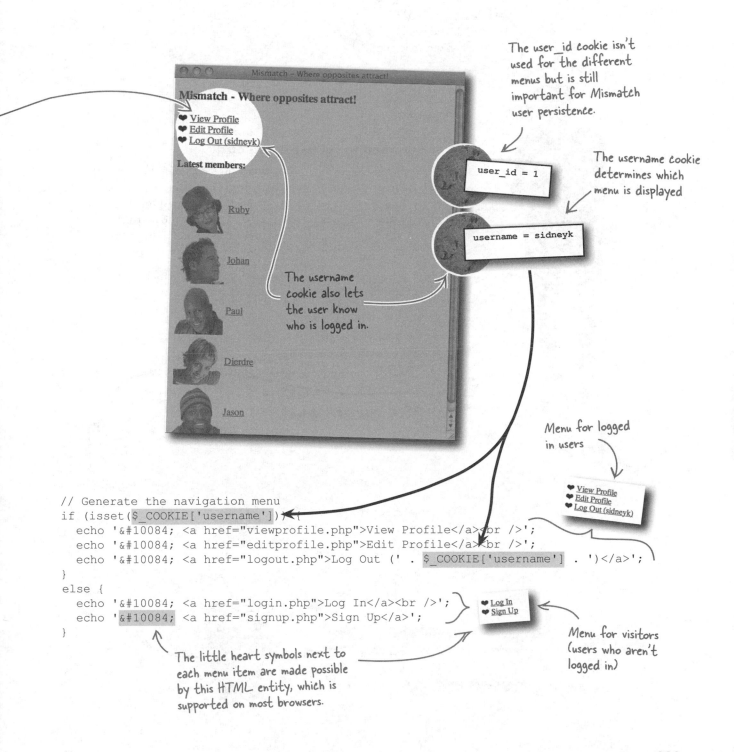

The user_id cookie isn't used for the different menus but is still important for Mismatch user persistence.

user_id = 1

The username cookie determines which menu is displayed

username = sidneyk

The username cookie also lets the user know who is logged in.

Menu for logged in users

```
// Generate the navigation menu
if (isset($_COOKIE['username'])) {
  echo '&#10084; <a href="viewprofile.php">View Profile</a><br />';
  echo '&#10084; <a href="editprofile.php">Edit Profile</a><br />';
  echo '&#10084; <a href="logout.php">Log Out (' . $_COOKIE['username'] . ')</a>';
}
else {
  echo '&#10084; <a href="login.php">Log In</a><br />';
  echo '&#10084; <a href="signup.php">Sign Up</a>';
}
```

Menu for visitors (users who aren't logged in)

The little heart symbols next to each menu item are made possible by this HTML entity, which is supported on most browsers.

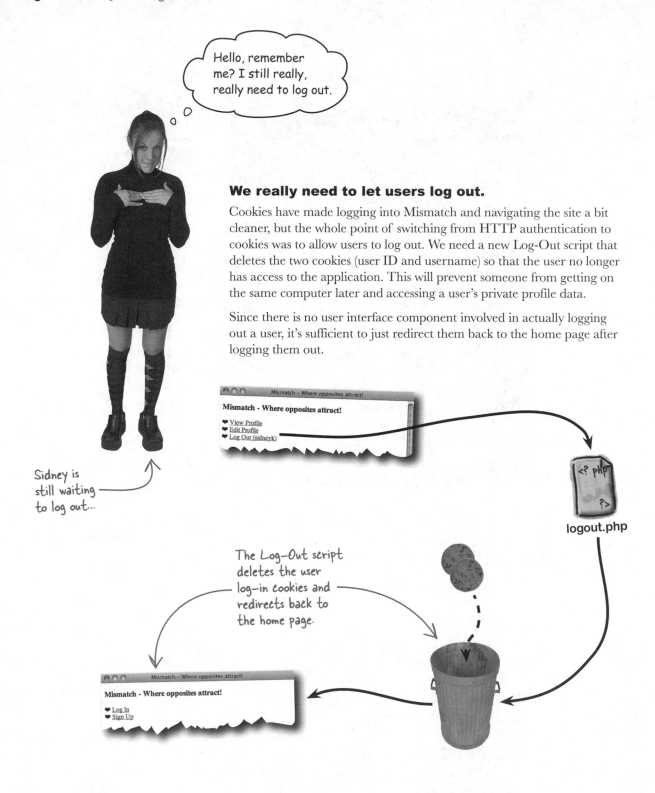

Hello, remember me? I still really, really need to log out.

We really need to let users log out.

Cookies have made logging into Mismatch and navigating the site a bit cleaner, but the whole point of switching from HTTP authentication to cookies was to allow users to log out. We need a new Log-Out script that deletes the two cookies (user ID and username) so that the user no longer has access to the application. This will prevent someone from getting on the same computer later and accessing a user's private profile data.

Since there is no user interface component involved in actually logging out a user, it's sufficient to just redirect them back to the home page after logging them out.

Sidney is still waiting to log out...

Mismatch ~ Where opposites attract!

Mismatch - Where opposites attract!

♥ View Profile
♥ Edit Profile
♥ Log Out (sidneyk)

logout.php

The Log-Out script deletes the user log-in cookies and redirects back to the home page.

Mismatch ~ Where opposites attract!

Mismatch - Where opposites attract!

♥ Log In
♥ Sign Up

Logging out means deleting cookies

Logging out a user involves deleting the two cookies that keep track of the user. This is done by calling the setcookie() function, and passing an expiration date that causes the cookies to get deleted at that time.

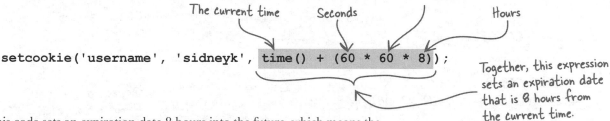

The current time   Seconds   Minutes   Hours

```php
setcookie('username', 'sidneyk', time() + (60 * 60 * 8));
```

Together, this expression sets an expiration date that is 8 hours from the current time.

This code sets an expiration date 8 hours into the future, which means the cookie will be automatically deleted in 8 hours. But we want to delete a cookie immediately, which requires setting the expiration date to a time in the past. The amount of time into the past isn't terribly important—just pick an arbitrary amount of time, such as an hour, and subtract it from the current time.

```php
setcookie('username', 'sidneyk', time() - 3600);
```

60 seconds * 60 minutes = 3600 seconds, which is 1 hour into the past.

To delete a cookie, just set its expiration date to a time in the <u>past</u>.

Exercise

The Log-Out script for Mismatch is missing a few pieces of code. Write the missing code, making sure that the log-in cookies get deleted before the Log-Out page is redirected to the home page.

```php
<?php
  // If the user is logged in, delete the cookie to log them out
  if ( ................................................. ) {
    // Delete the user ID and username cookies by setting their expirations to an hour ago (3600)

    ....................................................

    ....................................................
  }

  // Redirect to the home page
  $home_url = 'http://' . $_SERVER['HTTP_HOST'] . dirname($_SERVER['PHP_SELF']) . '.....................';
  header('Location: ' . $home_url);
?>
```

Exercise
Solution

The Log-Out script for Mismatch is missing a few pieces of code. Write the missing code, making sure that the log-in cookies get deleted before the Log-Out page is redirected to the home page.

```php
<?php
  // If the user is logged in, delete the cookie to log them out
  if (   isset($_COOKIE['user_id'])        ) {
    // Delete the user ID and username cookies by setting their expirations to an hour ago (3600)
      setcookie('user_id', '', time() - 3600);
      setcookie('username', '', time() - 3600);
  }

  // Redirect to the home page
  $home_url = 'http://' . $_SERVER['HTTP_HOST'] . dirname($_SERVER['PHP_SELF']) . '  /index.php    ';
  header('Location: ' . $home_url);
?>
```

Only log out a user if they are already logged in.

Set each cookie to an hour in the past so that they are deleted by the system.

Redirect to the Mismatch home page, which is constructed as an absolute URL.

A location header results in the browser redirecting to another page.

Test Drive

Use cookies to add Log-Out functionality to Mismatch.

Modify the Mismatch scripts so that they use cookies to allows users to log in and out (or download the scripts from the Head First Labs site at www.headfirstlabs.com/books/hfphp. The cookie modifications involve changes to the index.php, login.php, logout.php, editprofile.php, and viewprofile.php scripts. The changes to the latter two scripts are fairly minor, and primarily involve changing $user_id and $username global variable references so that they use the $_COOKIE superglobal instead.

Upload the scripts to your web server, and then open the main Mismatch page (index.php) in a web browser. Take note of the navigation menu, and then click the "Log In" link and log in. Notice how the Log-In script leads you back to the main page, while the menu changes to reflect your logged in status. Now click "Log Out" to blitz the cookies and log out.

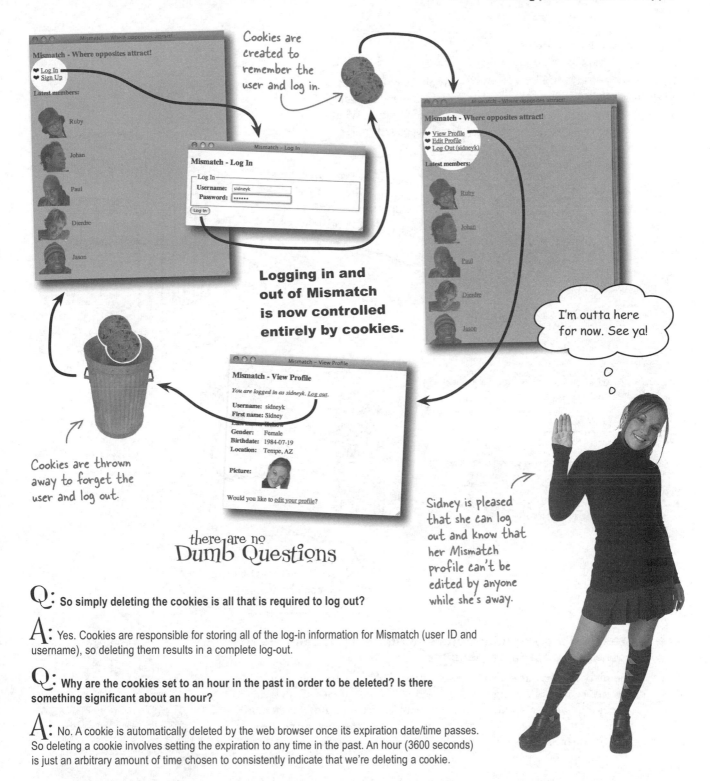

Cookies are created to remember the user and log in.

Logging in and out of Mismatch is now controlled entirely by cookies.

I'm outta here for now. See ya!

Cookies are thrown away to forget the user and log out.

Sidney is pleased that she can log out and know that her Mismatch profile can't be edited by anyone while she's away.

there are no
Dumb Questions

Q: So simply deleting the cookies is all that is required to log out?

A: Yes. Cookies are responsible for storing all of the log-in information for Mismatch (user ID and username), so deleting them results in a complete log-out.

Q: Why are the cookies set to an hour in the past in order to be deleted? Is there something significant about an hour?

A: No. A cookie is automatically deleted by the web browser once its expiration date/time passes. So deleting a cookie involves setting the expiration to any time in the past. An hour (3600 seconds) is just an arbitrary amount of time chosen to consistently indicate that we're deleting a cookie.

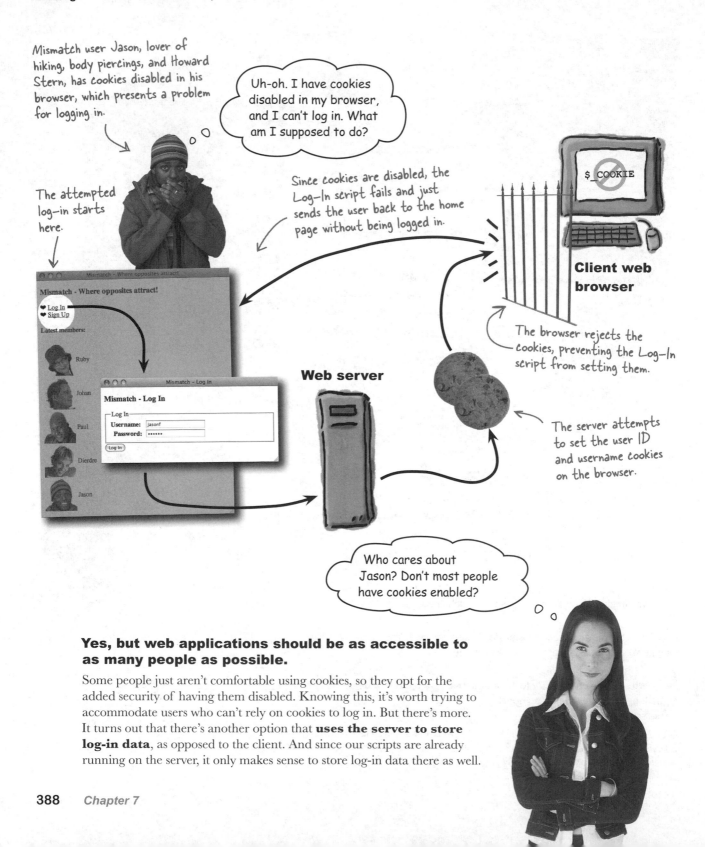

Mismatch user Jason, lover of hiking, body piercings, and Howard Stern, has cookies disabled in his browser, which presents a problem for logging in.

Uh-oh. I have cookies disabled in my browser, and I can't log in. What am I supposed to do?

Since cookies are disabled, the Log-In script fails and just sends the user back to the home page without being logged in.

The attempted log-in starts here.

$_COOKIE

Client web browser

Mismatch - Where opposites attract!

♥ Log In
♥ Sign Up

Latest members:

Ruby
Johan
Paul
Dierdre
Jason

Mismatch - Log In

Log In
Username: jasonf
Password: ••••••

Log In

Web server

The browser rejects the cookies, preventing the Log-In script from setting them.

The server attempts to set the user ID and username cookies on the browser.

Who cares about Jason? Don't most people have cookies enabled?

Yes, but web applications should be as accessible to as many people as possible.

Some people just aren't comfortable using cookies, so they opt for the added security of having them disabled. Knowing this, it's worth trying to accommodate users who can't rely on cookies to log in. But there's more. It turns out that there's another option that **uses the server to store log-in data**, as opposed to the client. And since our scripts are already running on the server, it only makes sense to store log-in data there as well.

Sessions aren't dependent on the client

Cookies are powerful little guys, but they do have their limitations, such as being subject to limitations beyond your control. But what if we didn't have to depend on the browser? What if we could store data directly on the server? **Sessions** do just that, and they allow you to store away individual pieces of information just like with cookies, but the data gets stored on the server instead of the client. This puts session data outside of the browser limitations of cookies.

Sessions allow you to persistently store small pieces of data on the server, independently of the client.

Web server

Store session data

Unlike cookies, sessions store their data on the server.

Retrieve session data

The browser doesn't factor directly into the storage of session data since everything is stored on the server.

Client web browser

Sessions store data in **session variables**, which are logically equivalent to cookies on the server. When you place data in a session variable using PHP code, it is stored on the server. You can then access the data in the session variable from PHP code, and it remains persistent across multiple pages (scripts). Like with cookies, you can delete a session variable at any time, making it possible to continue to offer a log-out feature with session-based code.

Since session data is stored on the server, it is <u>more</u> <u>secure</u> and more <u>reliable</u> than data stored in cookies.

A user can't manually delete session data using their browser, which can be a problem with cookies.

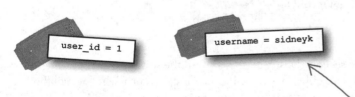

```
user_id = 1
```

```
username = sidneyk
```

Surely there's a catch, right? Sort of. Unlike cookies, sessions don't offer as much control over how long a session variable stores data. Session variables are **automatically destroyed as soon as a session ends**, which usually coincides with the user shutting down the browser. So even though session variables aren't stored on the browser, they are indirectly affected by the browser since they get deleted when a browser session ends.

There isn't an expiration date associated with session variables because they are automatically deleted when a session ends.

The life and times of sessions

Sessions are called sessions for a reason—they have a very clear start and finish. Data associated with a session lives and dies according to the lifespan of the session, which you control through PHP code. The only situation where you don't have control of the session life cycle is when the user closes the browser, which results in a session ending, whether you like it or not.

You must tell a session when you're ready to start it up by calling the `session_start()` PHP function.

The PHP session_start() function starts a session and allows you to begin storing data in session variables.

`session_start();` ← *This PHP function starts a session.*

Calling the `session_start()` function doesn't set any data—its job is to get the session up and running. The session is identified internally by a unique session identifier, which you typically don't have to concern yourself with. This ID is used by the web browser to associate a session with multiple pages.

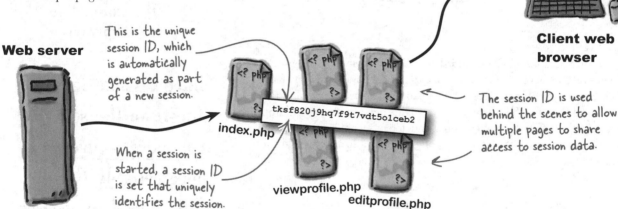

Web server

This is the unique session ID, which is automatically generated as part of a new session.

`tksf820j9hq7f9t7vdt5o1ceb2`

index.php

When a session is started, a session ID is set that uniquely identifies the session.

viewprofile.php

editprofile.php

Client web browser

The session ID is used behind the scenes to allow multiple pages to share access to session data.

The session ID isn't destroyed until the session is closed, which happens either when the browser is closed or when you call the `session_destroy()` function.

The session_destroy() function closes a session.

`session_destroy();` ← *This PHP function ends a session.*

If you close a session yourself with this function, it doesn't automatically destroy any session variables you've stored. Let's take a closer look at how sessions store data to uncover why this is so.

Keeping up with session data

The cool thing about sessions is that they're very similar to cookies in terms of how you use them. Once you've started a session with a call to `session_start()`, you can begin setting session variables, such as Mismatch log-in data, with the **$_SESSION** superglobal.

```
$_SESSION['username'] = 'sidneyk';
```

The name of the session variable is used as an index into the $_SESSION superglobal.

The value to be stored is just assigned to the $_SESSION superglobal.

The session variable is created and stored on the server.

username = sidneyk

```
echo('<p class="login">You are logged in as ' . $_SESSION['username'] . '.</p>');
```

To access the session variable, just use the $_SESSION superglobal and the session variable name.

Unlike cookies, session variables don't require any kind of special function to set them—you just assign a value to the `$_SESSION` superglobal, making sure to use the session variable name as the array index.

What about deleting session variables? Destroying a session via `session_destroy()` doesn't actually destroy session variables, so you must manually delete your session variables if you want them to be killed prior to the user shutting down the browser (log-outs!). A quick and effective way to destroy all of the variables for a session is to set the `$_SESSION` superglobal to an empty array.

```
$_SESSION = array();
```

This code kills all of the session variables in the current session.

Session variables are _not_ automatically deleted when a session is destroyed.

But we're not quite done. Sessions can actually use cookies behind the scenes. If the browser allows cookies, a session may possibly set a cookie that temporarily stores the session ID. So to fully close a session via PHP code, you must also delete any cookie that might have been automatically created to store the session ID on the browser. Like any other cookie, you destroy this cookie by setting its expiration to some time in the past. All you need to know is the name of the cookie, which can be found using the `session_name()` function.

If a session is using a cookie to help remember the session ID, then the ID is stored in a cookie named after the session.

PHPSESSID = tks6820j...

```
if (isset($_COOKIE[session_name()])) {
  setcookie(session_name(), '', time() - 3600);
}
```

First check to see if a session cookie actually exists.

Destroy the session cookie by setting its expiration to an hour in the past.

Renovate Mismatch with sessions

Reworking the Mismatch application to use a session to store log-in data isn't as dramatic as it may sound. In fact, the flow of the application remains generally the same—you just have to take care of a little extra bookkeeping involved in starting the session, destroying the session, and then cleaning up after the session.

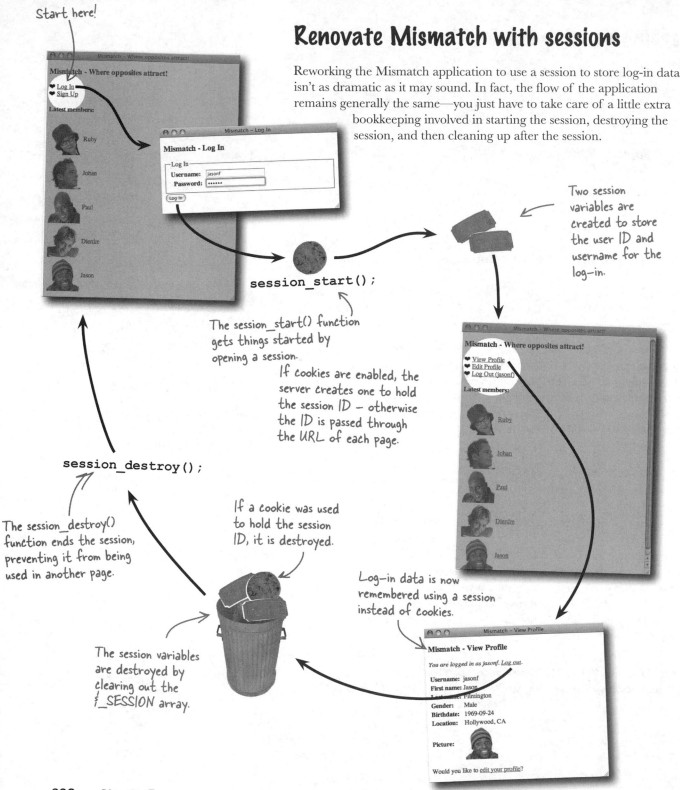

Start here!

`session_start();`

The session_start() function gets things started by opening a session.

If cookies are enabled, the server creates one to hold the session ID – otherwise the ID is passed through the URL of each page.

Two session variables are created to store the user ID and username for the log-in.

`session_destroy();`

The session_destroy() function ends the session, preventing it from being used in another page.

If a cookie was used to hold the session ID, it is destroyed.

The session variables are destroyed by clearing out the $_SESSION array.

Log-in data is now remembered using a session instead of cookies.

Log out with sessions

Logging a user out of Mismatch requires a little more work with sessions than the previous version with its pure usage of cookies. These steps must be taken to successfully log a user out of Mismatch using sessions.

1 **Delete the session variables.**

2 **Check to see if a session cookie exists, and if so, delete it.**

You don't know for certain if a session cookie is being used without checking.

3 **Destroy the session.**

4 **Redirect the user to the home page.**

OK, so this is a bonus step that isn't strictly required to log the user out, but is helpful nonetheless.

Sharpen your pencil

The Log-Out script for Mismatch is undergoing an overhaul to use sessions instead of pure cookies for log-in persistence. Write the missing code to "sessionize" the Log-Out script, and then annotate which step of the log-out process it corresponds to.

```php
<?php
  // If the user is logged in, delete the session vars to log them out
  session_start();
  if (                              ) {
    ..........................................
    // Delete the session vars by clearing the $_SESSION array

    ....................................

    // Delete the session cookie by setting its expiration to an hour ago (3600)
    if (isset($_COOKIE[session_name()])) {

      ................................................................

    }

    // Destroy the session

    .............................
  }

  // Redirect to the home page
  $home_url = 'http://' . $_SERVER['HTTP_HOST'] . dirname($_SERVER['PHP_SELF']) . '/index.php';
  header('Location: ' . $home_url);
?>
```

Sharpen your pencil
Solution

The Log-Out script for Mismatch is undergoing an overhaul to use sessions instead of pure cookies for log-in persistence. Write the missing code to "sessionize" the Log-Out script, and then annotate which step of the log-out process it corresponds to.

(1) Delete the session variables.

(2) Check to see if a session cookie exists, and if so, delete it.

(3) Destroy the session.

(4) Redirect the user to the home page.

Even when logging out, you have to first start the session in order to access the session variables.

```php
<?php
  // If the user is logged in, delete the session vars to log them out
  session_start();
  if (  isset($_SESSION['user_id'])  ) {
    // Delete the session vars by clearing the $_SESSION array
      $_SESSION = array();      (1)

    // Delete the session cookie by setting its expiration to an hour ago (3600)
    if (isset($_COOKIE[session_name()])) {
        setcookie(session_name(), '', time() - 3600);      (2)
    }

    // Destroy the session
      session_destroy();      (3)
  }

  // Redirect to the home page
  $home_url = 'http://' . $_SERVER['HTTP_HOST'] . dirname($_SERVER['PHP_SELF']) . '/index.php';
  header('Location: ' . $home_url);      (4)
?>
```

Now a session variable is used to check the log-in status instead of a cookie.

To clear out the session variables, assign the $_SESSION superglobal an empty array.

If a session cookie exists, delete it by setting its expiration to an hour ago.

Destroy the session with a call to the built-in session_destroy() function.

The move from cookies to sessions impacts more than just the Log-Out script. Match the other pieces of the Mismatch application with how they need to change to accommodate sessions.

appvars.php

connectvars.php

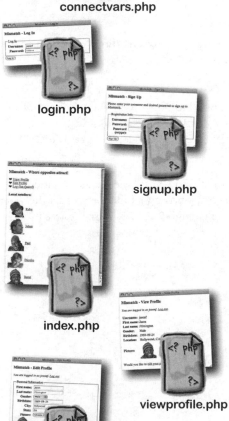

login.php

signup.php

index.php

viewprofile.php

editprofile.php

No change since the script has no direct dependence on log-in persistence.

Sessions are required to remember who the user is. Call the `session_start()` function to start the session, and then change `$_COOKIE` references to `$_SESSION`.

Sessions are required to control the navigation menu. Call the `session_start()` function to start the session, and then change `$_COOKIE` references to `$_SESSION`.

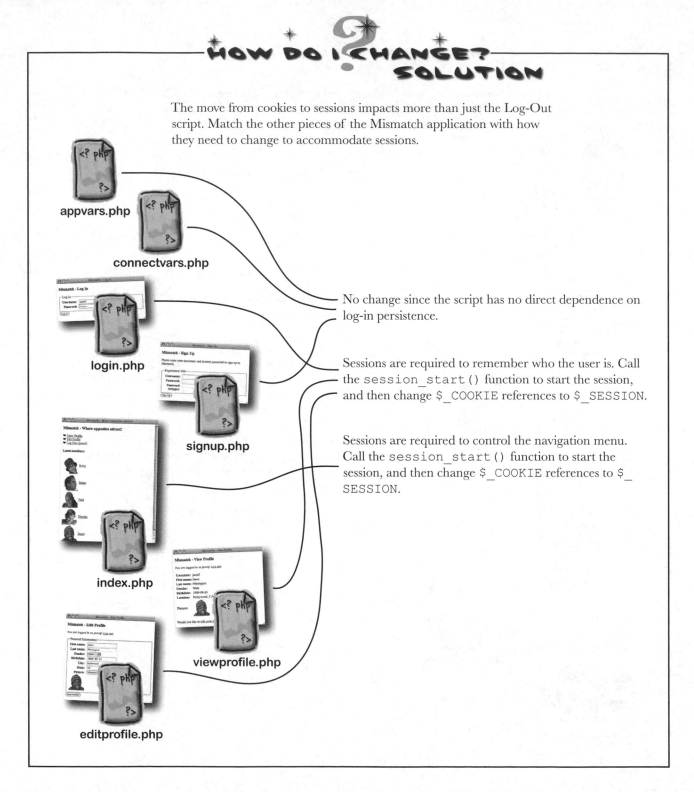

HOW DO I CHANGE? SOLUTION

The move from cookies to sessions impacts more than just the Log-Out script. Match the other pieces of the Mismatch application with how they need to change to accommodate sessions.

appvars.php

connectvars.php

login.php

signup.php

index.php

viewprofile.php

editprofile.php

No change since the script has no direct dependence on log-in persistence.

Sessions are required to remember who the user is. Call the `session_start()` function to start the session, and then change `$_COOKIE` references to `$_SESSION`.

Sessions are required to control the navigation menu. Call the `session_start()` function to start the session, and then change `$_COOKIE` references to `$_SESSION`.

BULLET POINTS

- HTTP authentication is handy for restricting access to individual pages, but it doesn't offer a good way to "log out" a user when they're finished accessing a page.

- Cookies let you store small pieces of data on the client (web browser), such as the log-in data for a user.

- All cookies have an expiration date, which can be far into the future or as near as the end of the browser session.

- To delete a cookie, you just set its expiration to a time in the past.

- Sessions offer similar storage as cookies but are stored on the server and, therefore, aren't subject to the same browser limitations, such as cookies being disabled.

- Session variables have a limited lifespan and are always destroyed once a session is over (for example, when the browser is closed).

there are no Dumb Questions

Q: The `session_start()` function gets called in a lot of different places, even after a session has been started. Are multiple sessions being created with each call to `session_start()`?

A: No. The `session_start()` function doesn't just start a new session—it also taps into an existing session. So when a script calls `session_start()`, the function first checks to see if a session already exists by looking for the presence of a session ID. If no session exists, it generates a new session ID and creates the new session. Future calls to `session_start()` from within the same application will recognize the existing session and use it instead of creating another one.

Q: So how does the session ID get stored? Is that where sessions sometimes use cookies?

A: Yes. Even though session data gets stored on the server and, therefore, gains the benefit of being more secure and outside of the browser's control, there still has to be a mechanism for a script to know about the session data.

This is what the session ID is for—it uniquely identifies a session and the data associated with it. This ID must somehow persist on the client in order for multiple pages to be part of the same session. One way this session ID persistence is carried out is through a cookie, meaning that the ID is stored in a cookie, which is then used to associate a script with a given session.

Q: If sessions are dependent on cookies anyway, then what's the big deal about using them instead of cookies?

A: Sessions are not entirely dependent on cookies. It's important to understand that cookies serve as an **optimization** for preserving the session ID across multiple scripts, not as a necessity. If cookies are disabled, the session ID gets passed from script to script through a URL, similar to how you've seen data passed in a GET request. So sessions can work perfectly fine without cookies. The specifics of how sessions react in response to cookies being disabled are controlled in the php.ini configuration file on the web server via the `session.use_cookies`, `session.use_only_cookies`, and `session.use_trans_sid` settings.

Q: It still seems strange that sessions could use cookies when the whole point is that sessions are supposed to be better than cookies. What gives?

A: While sessions do offer some clear benefits over cookies in certain scenarios, they don't necessarily have an either/or relationship with cookies. Sessions certainly have the benefit of being stored on the server instead of the client, which makes them more secure and dependable. So if you ever need to store sensitive data persistently, then a session variable would provide more security than a cookie. Sessions are also capable of storing larger amounts of data than cookies. So there are clear advantages to using sessions regardless of whether cookies are available.

For the purposes of Mismatch, sessions offer a convenient server-side solution for storing log-in data. For users who have cookies enabled, sessions provide improved security and reliability while still using cookies as an optimization. And in the case of users who don't have cookies enabled, sessions can still work by passing the session ID through a URL, foregoing cookies altogether.

Complete the session transformation

Even though the different parts of Mismatch affected by sessions use them to accomplish different things, the scripts ultimately require similar changes in making the migration from cookies to sessions. For one, they all must call the session_start() function to get rolling with sessions initially. Beyond that, all of the changes involve moving from the $_COOKIE superglobal to the $_SESSION superglobal, which is responsible for storing session variables.

```php
<?php
  session_start();
?>
```

All of the session-powered scripts start out with a call to session_start() to get the session up and running.

```php
// If the user isn't logged in, try to log them in
if (!isset($_SESSION['user_id'])) {
  if (isset($_POST['submit'])) {
    // Connect to the database
    $dbc = mysqli_connect(DB_HOST, DB_USER, DB_PASSWORD, DB_NAME);

    // Grab the user-entered log-in data
    $user_username = mysqli_real_escape_string($dbc, trim($_POST['username']));
    $user_password = mysqli_real_escape_string($dbc, trim($_POST['password']));

    if (!empty($user_username) && !empty($user_password)) {
      // Look up the username and password in the database
      $query = "SELECT user_id, username FROM mismatch_user WHERE username = '$user_username' AND " .
        "password = SHA('$user_password')";
      $data = mysqli_query($dbc, $query);

      if (mysqli_num_rows($data) == 1) {
        // The log-in is OK so set the user ID and username session vars, and redirect to the home page
        $row = mysqli_fetch_array($data);
        $_SESSION['user_id'] = $row['user_id'];
        $_SESSION['username'] = $row['username'];
        $home_url = 'http://' . $_SERVER['HTTP_HOST'] . dirname($_SERVER['PHP_SELF']) . '/index.php';
        header('Location: ' . $home_url);
      }
      else {
        // The username/password are incorrect so set an error message
        $error_msg = 'Sorry, you must enter a valid username and password to log in.';
      }
    }
```

login.php

The Log-In script uses sessions to remember the user ID and username for log-in persistence, and it does so by relying on the $_SESSION superglobal instead of $_COOKIE.

```
   // Generate the navigation menu
   if (isset($_SESSION['username'])) {
     echo '&#10004; <a href="viewprofile.php">View Profile</a><br />';
     echo '&#10004; <a href="editprofile.php">Edit Profile</a><br />';
     echo '&#10004; <a href="logout.php">Log Out (' . $_SESSION['username'] . ')</a>';
   }
   else {
     echo '&#10004; <a href="login.php">Log In</a><br />';
     echo '&#10004; <a href="signup.php">Sign Up</a>';
   }

   ...

   // Loop through the array of user data, formatting it as HTML
   echo '<h4>Latest members:</h4>';
   echo '<table>';
   while ($row = mysqli_fetch_array($data)) {
     ...
     if (isset($_SESSION['user_id'])) {
       echo '<td><a href="viewprofile.php?user_id=' . $row['user_id'] . '">' .
         $row['first_name'] . '</a></td></tr>';
     }
     else {
       echo '<td>' . $row['first_name'] . '</td></tr>';
     }
   }
   echo '</table>';
```

The Mismatch home page uses the $_SESSION superglobal instead of $_COOKIE to access log-in data while generating the menu and choosing whether or not to provide a link to the "latest members" profiles.

index.php

Similar to the Log-In and home pages, the Edit Profile script now uses $_SESSION to access log-in data instead of $_COOKIE.

```
   //  Make sure the user is logged in before going any further.
   if (!isset($_SESSION['user_id'])) {
     echo '<p class="login">Please <a href="login.php">log in</a> to access this page.</p>';
     exit();
   }
   else {
     echo('<p class="login">You are logged in as ' . $_SESSION['username']
       . '. <a href="logout.php">Log out</a>.</p>');
   }

   ...

     if (!empty($first_name) && !empty($last_name) && !empty($gender) && !empty($birthdate) &&
       !empty($city) && !empty($state)) {
       // Only set the picture column if there is a new picture
       if (!empty($new_picture)) {
         $query = "UPDATE mismatch_user SET first_name = '$first_name', last_name = '$last_name', " .
           "gender = '$gender', birthdate = '$birthdate', city = '$city', state = '$state', " .
           "picture = '$new_picture' WHERE user_id = '" . $_SESSION['user_id'] . "'";
       }
       else {
         $query = "UPDATE mismatch_user SET first_name = '$first_name', last_name = '$last_name', " .
           "gender = '$gender', birthdate = '$birthdate', city = '$city', state = '$state' " .
           "WHERE user_id = '" . $_SESSION['user_id'] . "'";
       }
       mysqli_query($dbc, $query);
```

Although not shown, the View Profile script uses sessions in much the same way as Edit Profile.

viewprofile.php

editprofile.php

Fireside Chats

Tonight's talk: **Cookie and session variable get down and dirty about who has the best memory**

Cookie:

Session variable:

There's been a lot of talk around here among us cookies about what exactly goes on over there on the server. Rumor is you're trying to move in on our territory and steal data storage jobs. What gives?

Come on now, steal is a strong word. The truth is sometimes it just makes more sense to store data on the server.

That doesn't make any sense to me. The browser is a perfectly good place to store data, and I'm just the guy to do it.

What about when the user disables you?

Uh, well, that's a completely different issue. And if the user decides to disable me, then clearly they don't have any need to store data.

Not true. The user often doesn't even know a web application is storing data because in many cases, it is behind-the-scenes data, like a username. So if you're not available, they're left with nothing.

So I suppose your answer is to store the data on the server? How convenient.

Exactly. And the cool thing is that the user doesn't have the ability to disable anything on the server, so you don't have to worry about whether or not the data is really able to be stored.

Alright, Einstein. Since you seem to have it all figured out, why is it that you still sometimes use me to store your precious little ID on the browser?

Er, well, most people really don't know about that, so there's no need to get into it here. We can talk about that off the record. The important thing is that I'm always around, ready to store data on the server.

Cookie:

Come on, tell me how much you need me!

Oh I know you can, but the truth is you'd rather not. And maybe deep down you really kinda like me.

Ah, so you're going to resort to picking on the little guy. Sure, I may not be able to store quite as much as you, and I'll admit that living on the client makes me a little less secure. But it sure is more exciting! And I have something you can only dream about.

Well, all that storage space and security you're so proud of comes at a cost... a short lifespan! I didn't want to be the one to have to tell you, but your entire existence is hinging on a single browser session. I think that's how you got your name.

It's simple. I don't die with a session, I just expire. So I can be set to live a long, full life, far beyond the whim of some click-happy web surfer who thinks it's cute to open and close the browser every chance he gets.

Problem is, those same scripters often set my expiration to such a short period that I don't really get to experience the long life I truly deserve. I mean, I...

Session variable:

Alright, I will admit that from time to time I do lean on you a little to help me keep up with things across multiple pages. But I can get by without you if I need to.

Look, I don't have any problem with you. I just wish you were a little more secure. And you have that size limitation. You know, not every piece of persistent data is bite-sized.

Is that so? Do tell.

You mean you can go on living beyond a single session? How is that possible?!

Wow. What a feeling that must be to experience immortality. My only hope is that some slacker scripter accidentally forgets to destroy me when he closes a session... but the browser will still do me in whenever it gets shut down.

Hello? Are you there? Geez, expiration is harsh.

Test Drive

Change Mismatch to use sessions instead of cookies.

Modify the Mismatch scripts so that they use sessions instead of cookies to support log-in persistence (or download the scripts from the Head First Labs site at `www.headfirstlabs.com/books/hfphp`). The session modifications involve changes to the `index.php`, `login.php`, `logout.php`, `editprofile.php`, and `viewprofile.php` scripts, and primarily involve starting the session with a call to the `session_start()` function and changing `$_COOKIE` superglobal references to use `$_SESSION` instead.

Upload the scripts to your web server, and then open the main Mismatch page (`index.php`) in a web browser. Try logging in and out to make sure everything works the same as before. Unless you had cookies disabled earlier, you shouldn't notice any difference—that's a good thing!

Very cool. It's nice being able to log in even without cookies turned on.

Thanks to sessions, users with cookies disabled can still log in and access their personal profiles.

Watch it!

Sessions without cookies may not work if your PHP settings in `php.ini` aren't configured properly on the server.

In order for sessions to work with cookies disabled, there needs to be another mechanism for passing the session ID among different pages. This mechanism involves appending the session ID to the URL of each page, which takes place automatically if the `session.use_trans_id` setting is set to 1 (true) in the `php.ini` file on the server. If you don't have the ability to alter this file on your web server, you'll have to manually append the session ID to the URL of session pages if cookies are disabled with code like this:

```
<a href="viewprofile.php?<?php echo SID; ?>">view your profile</a>
```

The SID superglobal holds the session ID, which is being passed along through the URL so that the View Profile page knows about the session.

Users aren't feeling welcome

Despite serving as a nice little improvement over cookies, something about the new session-powered Mismatch application isn't quite right. Several users have reported getting logged out of the application despite never clicking the "Log Out" link. The application doesn't exactly feel personal anymore... this is a big problem.

Frustrated users are never a good thing.

Hey, we were logged in last time we checked, and suddenly we're all logged out! What gives?

This isn't the message we want Mismatch to send its users.

Users are being logged out of Mismatch without ever clicking the "Log Out" link.

Mismatch - Where opposites attract!

♥ Log In
♥ Sign Up

Latest members:

Ruby

Johan

Paul

Dierdre

Jason

The home page is presented to the registered users as if they are visitors even though they never logged out.

What do you think is causing users to be
automatically logged out of Mismatch? Is
it something they've done inadvertently?

Sessions are short-lived...

The problem with the automatic log-outs in Mismatch has to do with the limited lifespan of sessions. If you recall, sessions only last as long as the current browser instance, meaning that all session variables are killed when the user closes the browser application. In other words, closing the browser results in a user being logged out whether they like it or not. This is not only inconvenient, but it's also a bit confusing because we already have a log-out feature. Users assume they aren't logged out unless they've clicked the Log Out link.

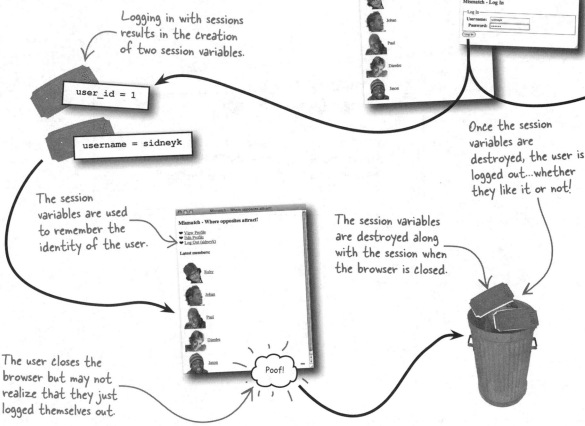

Whether sessions or cookies are used, logging in is what sets the persistent wheels in motion.

Logging in with sessions results in the creation of two session variables.

user_id = 1

username = sidneyk

The session variables are used to remember the identity of the user.

Once the session variables are destroyed, the user is logged out...whether they like it or not!

The session variables are destroyed along with the session when the browser is closed.

The user closes the browser but may not realize that they just logged themselves out.

Poof!

Even though you can destroy a session when you're finished with it, you can't prolong it beyond a browser instance. So sessions are more of a short-term storage solution than cookies, since cookies have an expiration date that can be set hours, days, months, or even years into the future. Does that mean sessions are inferior to cookies? No, not at all. But it does mean that sessions present a problem if you're trying to remember information beyond a single browser instance... such as log-in data!

Session variables are destroyed when the user ends a session by closing the browser.

... but cookies can last forever!

Maybe not forever, but plenty long enough to outlast a session.

Unlike session variables, the lifespan of a cookie isn't tied to a browser instance, so cookies can live on and on, at least until their expiration date arrives. Problem is, users have the ability to destroy all of the cookies stored on their machine with a simple browser setting, so don't get too infatuated with the permanence of cookies—they're still ultimately only intended to store temporary data.

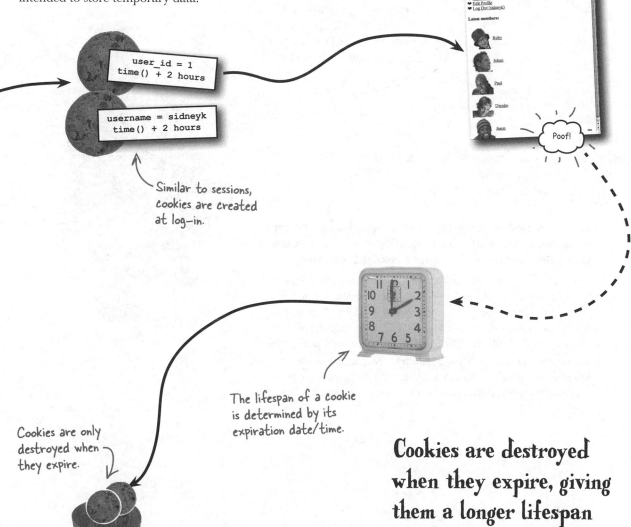

```
user_id = 1
time() + 2 hours
```

```
username = sidneyk
time() + 2 hours
```

Similar to sessions, cookies are created at log-in.

Poof!

The lifespan of a cookie is determined by its expiration date/time.

Cookies are only destroyed when they expire.

Cookies are destroyed when they expire, giving them a longer lifespan than session variables.

So would it make sense to use both sessions **and** cookies, where cookies help keep users logged in for longer periods of time? It would work for users who have cookies enabled.

As long as you're not dealing with highly sensitive data, in which case, the weak security of cookies would argue for using sessions by themselves.

Yes, it's not wrong to take advantage of the unique assets of both sessions and cookies to make Mismatch log-ins more flexible.

In fact, it can be downright handy. Sessions are better suited for short-term persistence since they share wider support and aren't limited by the browser, while cookies allow you to remember log-in data for a longer period of time. Sure, not everyone will be able to benefit from the cookie improvement, but enough people will that it matters. Any time you can improve the user experience of a significant portion of your user base without detracting from others, it's a win.

Sessions + Cookies = Superior log-in persistence

For the ultimate in log-in persistence, you have to get more creative and combine all of what you've learned in this chapter to take advantage of the benefits of both sessions and cookies. In doing so, you can restructure the Mismatch application so that it excels at both short-term and long-term user log-in persistence.

Start here!

When a user logs in, both session variables and cookies are set to store the user ID and username.

```
user_id = 1
```

```
user_id = 1
time() + 30 days
```

```
username = sidneyk
```

```
username = sidneyk
time() + 30 days
```

Closing the browser results in the session variables being destroyed, but not the cookies.

The user closes the web browser, killing the session in the process.

Poof!

The next time the user opens Mismatch, the cookies are used to recreate the session variables...voila!

```
user_id = 1
time() + 30 days
```

```
user_id = 1
```

```
username = sidneyk
time() + 30 days
```

```
username = sidneyk
```

The expiration for the cookies is set to 30 days after the initial log-in.

The log-in data stored in the cookies is used to reset the session variables.

Rather than keeping users logged in forever, the cookies are destroyed 30 days later.

there are no
Dumb Questions

Q: So is short-term vs. long-term persistence the reason to choose between sessions and cookies?

A: No. This happened to be the strategy that helped guide the design of the Mismatch application, but every application is different, and there are other aspects of sessions and cookies that often must be weighed. For example, the data stored in a session is more secure than the data stored in a cookie. So even if cookies are enabled and a cookie is being used solely to keep track of the session ID, the actual data stored in the session is more secure than if it was being stored directly in a cookie. The reason is because session data is stored on the server, making it very difficult for unprivileged users to access it. So if you're dealing with data that must be secure, sessions get the nod over cookies.

Q: What about the size of data? Does that play a role?

A: Yes. The size of the data matters as well. Sessions are capable of storing larger pieces of data than cookies, so that's another reason to lean toward sessions if you have the need to store data beyond a few simple text strings. Of course, a MySQL database is even better for storing large pieces of data, so make sure you don't get carried away even when working with sessions.

Q: So why would I choose a session or cookie over a MySQL database?

A: Convenience. It takes much more effort to store data in a database, and don't forget that databases are ideally suited for holding **permanent** data. Log-in data really isn't all that permanent in the grand scheme of things. That's where cookies and sessions enter the picture—they're better for data that you need to remember for a little while and then throw away.

PHP Magnets

The Mismatch application has been redesigned to use both sessions and cookies for the ultimate in user log-in persistence. Problem is, some of the code is missing. Use the session and cookie magnets to add back the missing code.

`$_COOKIE` `$_COOKIE` `COOKIE`
`$_COOKI` `$_COOKIE`

```
...
if (mysqli_num_rows($data) == 1) {
  // The log-in is OK so set the user ID and username session vars (and cookies),
  // and redirect to the home page
  $row = mysqli_fetch_array($data);

  ....................['user_id'] = $row['user_id'];
  ....................['username'] = $row['username'];

  setcookie('user_id', $row['user_id'], time() + (60 * 60 * 24 * 30));    // expires in 30 days
  setcookie('username', $row['username'], time() + (60 * 60 * 24 * 30));  // expires in 30 days
  $home_url = 'http://' . $_SERVER['HTTP_HOST'] . dirname($_SERVER['PHP_SELF']) . '/index.php';
  header('Location: ' . $home_url);
}
...
```

login.php

```
<?php
  // If the user is logged in, delete the session vars to log them out
  session_start();

  if (isset(....................['user_id'])) {

    // Delete the session vars by clearing the $_SESSION array

    .................... = array();

    // Delete the session cookie by setting its expiration to an hour ago (3600)

    if (isset(.................... [session_name()])) {

      setcookie(session_name(), '', time() - 3600);
    }

    // Destroy the session
    session_destroy();
  }

  // Delete the user ID and username cookies by setting their expirations to an hour ago (3600)
  setcookie('user_id', '', time() - 3600);
  setcookie('username', '', time() - 3600);
...
```

logout.php

`$_SESSION`
`$_SESSION`
`$_SESSION`
`$_SESSION`
`$_SESSION`
`$_SESSION`
`$_SESSION`

```
<?php
  session_start();

  // If the session vars aren't set, try to set them with a cookie

  if (!isset(....................['user_id'])) {
    if (isset(....................['user_id']) && isset(....................['username'])) {
      ....................['user_id'] = ....................['user_id'];
      ....................['username'] = ....................['username'];
    }....................  ....................
  }
?>
...
```

index.php

PHP Magnets Solution

The Mismatch application has been redesigned to use both sessions and cookies for the ultimate in user log-in persistence. Problem is, some of the code is missing. Use the session and cookie magnets to add back the missing code.

```php
...
if (mysqli_num_rows($data) == 1) {
  // The log-in is OK so set the user ID and username session vars (and cookies),
  // and redirect to the home page
  $row = mysqli_fetch_array($data);

  $_SESSION ['user_id'] = $row['user_id'];

  $_SESSION ['username'] = $row['username'];

  setcookie('user_id', $row['user_id'], time() + (60 * 60 * 24 * 30));   // expires in 30 days
  setcookie('username', $row['username'], time() + (60 * 60 * 24 * 30)); // expires in 30 days
  $home_url = 'http://' . $_SERVER['HTTP_HOST'] . dirname($_SERVER['PHP_SELF']) . '/index.php';
  header('Location: ' . $home_url);
}
...
```

The new cookies are set in addition to the session variables.

login.php

```php
<?php
  // If the user is logged in, delete the session vars to log them out
  session_start();

  if (isset( $_SESSION ['user_id'])) {

    // Delete the session vars by clearing the $_SESSION array

    ... $_SESSION = array();

    // Delete the session cookie by setting its expiration to an hour ago (3600)

    if (isset( $_COOKIE [session_name()])) {

      setcookie(session_name(), '', time() - 3600);
    }

    // Destroy the session
    session_destroy();
  }

  // Delete the user ID and username cookies by setting their expirations to an hour ago (3600)
  setcookie('user_id', '', time() - 3600);
  setcookie('username', '', time() - 3600);
  ...
```

Logging out now requires deleting both the session cookie and the new log-in cookies.

logout.php

```php
<?php
  session_start();

  // If the session vars aren't set, try to set them with a cookie

  if (!isset( $_SESSION ['user_id'])) {

    if (isset( . $_COOKIE ['user_id']) && isset( $_COOKIE ['username'])) {

      ... $_SESSION ['user_id'] = $_COOKIE ['user_id'];
      ... $_SESSION ['username'] = $_COOKIE ['username'];
    }
  }
?>
...
```

If the user isn't logged in via the session, check to see if the cookies are set.

Set the session variables using the cookies.

This same cookie/session code must also go in editprofile.php and viewprofile.php.

index.php

TEST DRIVE

Change Mismatch to use both sessions <u>and</u> cookies.

Modify the Mismatch scripts so that they use both sessions and cookies to support log-in persistence (or download the scripts from the Head First Labs site at www.headfirstlabs.com/books/hfphp. This requires changes to the `index.php`, `login.php`, `logout.php`, `editprofile.php`, and `viewprofile.php` scripts.

Upload the scripts to your web server, and then open the main Mismatch page (`index.php`) in a web browser. Try logging in and then closing the web browser, which will cause the session variables to get destroyed. Re-open the main page and check to see if you're still logged in—cookies make this possible since they persist beyond a given browser session.

Combining cookies with sessions adds longer term persistence to the excellent short-term persistence already made possible by sessions.

Awesome! Mismatch now remembers us regardless of whether we close our browsers or not.

Oh well, I guess you can't win 'em all.

Most users are thrilled with how sessions and cookies combine to remember them better.

Using cookies to help make sessions better doesn't help users who have cookies disabled... you can only do so much.

CHAPTER 7

Your PHP & MySQL Toolbox

You've covered quite a bit of new territory in building a user management system as part of the Mismatch application. Let's recap some of the highlights.

SHA(`value`)

This MySQL function encrypts a piece of text, resulting in a string of 40 hexadecimal characters. This function provides a great way to encrypt data that needs to remain unrecognizable within the database. It is a one-way encryption, however, meaning that there is no "decrypt" function.

---

setcookie()

This built-in PHP function is used to set a cookie on the browser, including an optional expiration date, after which the cookie is destroyed. If no expiration is provided, the cookie is deleted when the browser is closed.

$_COOKIE

This built-in PHP superglobal is used to access cookie data. It is an array, and each cookie is stored as an entry in the array. So accessing a cookie value involves specifying the name of the cookie as the array index.

---

session_destroy()

This built-in PHP function closes a session, and should be called when you're finished with a particular session. This function does not destroy session variables; however, so it's important to manually clean those up by clearing out the $_SESSION superglobal.

---

session_start()

This built-in PHP function starts a new session or re-starts a pre-existing session. You must call this function prior to accessing any session variables.

$_SESSION

This built-in PHP superglobal is used to access session data. It is an array, and each session variable is stored as an entry in the array. So accessing the value of a session variable involves specifying the name of the variable as the array index.

Several pieces of code from the Mismatch application have been pulled out, and we can't remember what they do. Draw lines connecting each piece of code with what it does.

PHP/MySQL Code	**Description**
`empty($_COOKIE['user_id'])`	Use a session variable to determine if a user is logged in or not.
`setcookie(session_name(), '', time() - 3600);`	Use a cookie to determine if a user is logged in or not.
`SHA('$user_password')`	Destroy a session cookie by setting its expiration to an hour in the past.
`session_destroy()`	Encrypt a user's password into an unrecognizable format.
`setcookie('user_id', $row['user_id'])`	Store a user's unique ID in a cookie.
`$_SESSION = array()`	Start a new session.
`session_start()`	Close the current session.
`isset($_SESSION['user_id'])`	Destroy all session variables.

Several pieces of code from the Mismatch application have been pulled
out, and we can't remember what they do. Draw lines connecting each
piece of code with what it does.

PHP/MySQL Code   **Description**

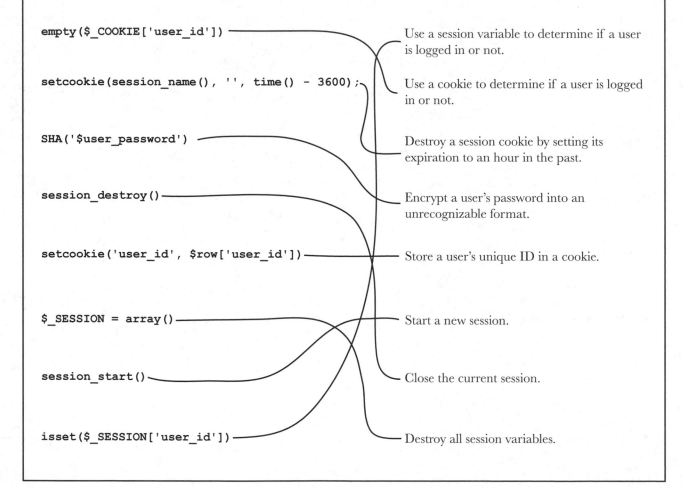

`empty($_COOKIE['user_id'])`   Use a session variable to determine if a user
                                                      is logged in or not.

`setcookie(session_name(), '', time() - 3600);`   Use a cookie to determine if a user is logged
                                                      in or not.

`SHA('$user_password')`   Destroy a session cookie by setting its
                                                      expiration to an hour in the past.

`session_destroy()`   Encrypt a user's password into an
                                                      unrecognizable format.

`setcookie('user_id', $row['user_id'])`   Store a user's unique ID in a cookie.

`$_SESSION = array()`   Start a new session.

`session_start()`   Close the current session.

`isset($_SESSION['user_id'])`   Destroy all session variables.

7 ½ eliminate duplicate code

Sharing is caring

It's really quite simple, darling. By sharing one umbrella, we eliminate the need for two umbrellas, we both still stay dry... and you get to latch on to one handsome fella.

Handsome *and* smart! Your shared umbrella theory is pure genius.

Umbrellas aren't the only thing that can be shared. In any web application you're bound to run into situations where *the same code is duplicated* in more than one place. Not only is this wasteful, but it leads to *maintenance headaches* since you will inevitably have to make changes, and these changes will have to be carried out in multiple places. The solution is to **eliminate duplicate code by sharing it**. In other words, you stick the duplicate code in one place, and then just reference that single copy wherever you need it. Eliminating duplicate code results in applications that are **more efficient**, **easier to maintain**, and ultimately **more robust**.

The Mismatch application has evolved since you last saw it, with improved navigation and a more consistent look and feel. But these improvements have come at a cost... duplicate code. Just by looking at the pages themselves, see if you can figure out what parts of Mismatch might represent a duplicate code problem. Circle and annotate these application parts, and also write down anything not visible that you think might also have code duplication issues.

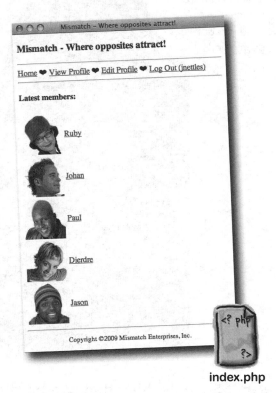

index.php

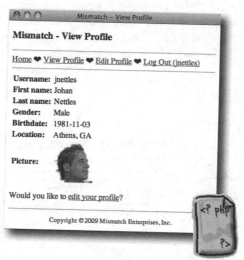

viewprofile.php

editprofile.php

Exercise Solution

The Mismatch application has evolved since you last saw it, with improved navigation and a more consistent look and feel. But these improvements have come at a cost... duplicate code. Just by looking at the pages themselves, see if you can figure out what parts of Mismatch might represent a duplicate code problem. Circle and annotate these application parts, and also write down anything not visible that you think might also have code duplication issues.

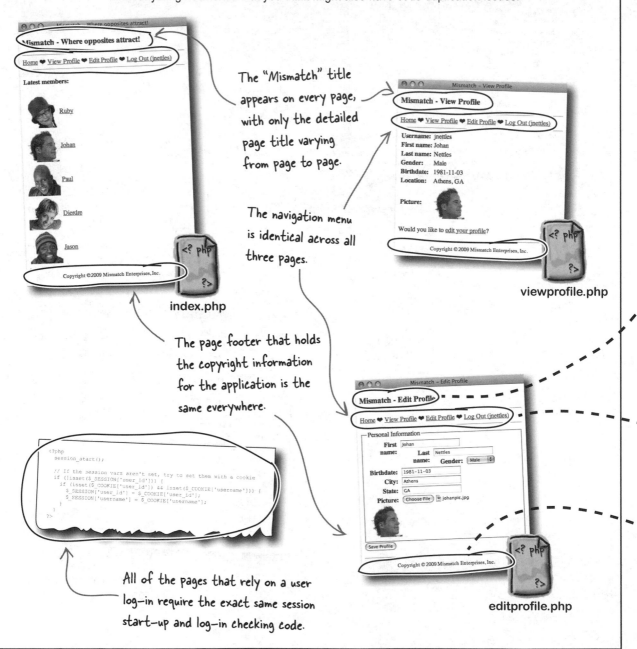

The "Mismatch" title appears on every page, with only the detailed page title varying from page to page.

The navigation menu is identical across all three pages.

index.php

viewprofile.php

The page footer that holds the copyright information for the application is the same everywhere.

```php
<?php
  session_start();

  // If the session vars aren't set, try to set them with a cookie
  if (!isset($_SESSION['user_id'])) {
    if (isset($_COOKIE['user_id']) && isset($_COOKIE['username'])) {
      $_SESSION['user_id'] = $_COOKIE['user_id'];
      $_SESSION['username'] = $_COOKIE['username'];
    }
  }
?>
```

All of the pages that rely on a user log-in require the exact same session start-up and log-in checking code.

editprofile.php

Mismatch is in pieces

So the Mismatch application has some common elements that are duplicated in the main script files at the moment. Why is this a big deal? Because it makes the application difficult to maintain. What happens if you decide to add a new page that requires a new menu item? You have to go through and change the menu code in *every script file* to show the new menu item. The same thing applies to the copyright notice.

The solution to the problem is to only store any given piece of information once. Then if that code ever needs to change, you only change it in one place. With that in mind, it's possible to rethink the organization of Mismatch in terms of reusable script components.

The page header

header.php

The header.php script contains the title of the page, which references a variable to present a different title on each page. The header also includes standard HTML boilerplate code and takes care of chores such as linking in the CSS style sheet.

The navigation menu

navmenu.php

The navmenu.php script generates a navigation menu for the application based on whether the user is logged in or not. The navigation menu presents "Log In" or "Log Out" links as needed.

This component doesn't result in visible HTML code, but it plays a vital role in managing user log-ins throughout the Mismatch application.

The session starter

startsession.php

The startsession.php script is responsible for starting the session and checking to see if the user is logged in.

The page footer

footer.php

The footer.php script displays a copyright notice for the application and closes the HTML tags opened in the header. So the header and footer work as a pair that must always be used together.

Rebuilding Mismatch from a template

OK, so we break apart Mismatch into multiple scripts, but how do we put them back together? You're already familiar with how include files work, and those are part of the solution. But you have to think larger than include files... you have to think in terms of **templates**, which allow you to build a single page as a combination of multiple include files. A template is like a blueprint for a page within an application where everything but what is truly unique to that page comes from include files.

The template version of Mismatch involves breaking apart common code into scripts that each play a very specific role, some responsible for generating visual HTML code, some not. The idea is to distill as much common functionality as possible into template include files, and then only leave code in each application page that is completely unique to that page.

Templates allow a PHP application to be built out of reusable script components.

The header appears at the top of every Mismatch page, and displays the application title as well as a page-specific title.

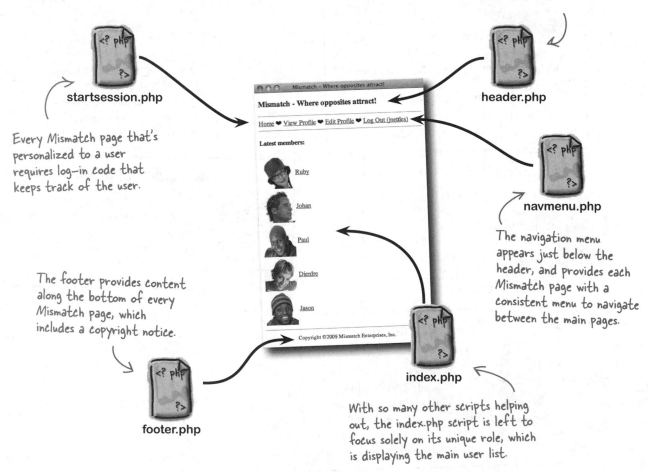

startsession.php

Every Mismatch page that's personalized to a user requires log-in code that keeps track of the user.

header.php

navmenu.php

The navigation menu appears just below the header, and provides each Mismatch page with a consistent menu to navigate between the main pages.

The footer provides content along the bottom of every Mismatch page, which includes a copyright notice.

footer.php

index.php

With so many other scripts helping out, the index.php script is left to focus solely on its unique role, which is displaying the main user list.

there are no
Dumb Questions

Q: What is a template exactly? Isn't it just a bunch of include files?

A: Yes. A template is a collection of include files, but it's a collection designed specifically to separate an application into functional components. The goal is to reduce a page down to what is truly unique about that page, and only that page. So headers, footers, navigation menus, and any other application pieces and parts that are the same or similar among more than one page are ideal for inclusion in an application template. The end result is that you place template code in PHP include files that are referenced by other scripts that need them.

You can think of a template as a group of include files that go a step or two beyond just reducing duplicate code—they actually help organize the functionality of an application. Mismatch is a fairly simple example of how to employ templates—larger, more complex PHP applications often employ very sophisticated template systems.

Q: Doesn't template code have to be exactly the same in order to be shared across multiple scripts?

A: No. It's perfectly acceptable for template code to just be similar, not exact. The reason is because you can use variables to allow for some degree of customization as a template is applied to different pages. The page title in Mismatch is a perfect example of this. The page header template is similar in every page in that it has a title that always begins with "Mismatch - ." But the specific title is different, which is why a variable is needed to provide a means of varying the title slightly among different pages.

Rebuild Mismatch with templates

The design work involved in breaking an application into template scripts
is usually worth the effort. You end up with a collection of tightly focused,
bite-size scripts, as well as dramatically simplified code in the main
application script files that are now dependent on the template scripts.

Start the session.

Try to reset the session variables with cookies if they aren't set.

```php
<?php
  session_start();

  // If the session vars aren't set, try to set them with a cookie
  if (!isset($_SESSION['user_id'])) {
    if (isset($_COOKIE['user_id']) && isset($_COOKIE['username'])) {
      $_SESSION['user_id'] = $_COOKIE['user_id'];
      $_SESSION['username'] = $_COOKIE['username'];
    }
  }
?>
```

startsession.php

Start the official HTML code with a DOCTYPE and an <html> tag.

Link in the application style sheet.

Build a custom page title using the $page_title variable, which is provided by the script including this file.

```php
<!DOCTYPE html PUBLIC "-//W3C//DTD XHTML 1.0 Transitional//EN"
  "http://www.w3.org/TR/xhtml1/DTD/xhtml1-transitional.dtd">
<html xmlns="http://www.w3.org/1999/xhtml" xml:lang="en" lang="en">
<head>
  <meta http-equiv="Content-Type" content="text/html; charset=utf-8" />

<?php
  echo '<title>Mismatch - ' . $page_title . '</title>';
?>

  <link rel="stylesheet" type="text/css" href="style.css" />
</head>
<body>

<?php
  echo '<h3>Mismatch - ' . $page_title . '</h3>';
?>
```

header.php

See if the user is logged in, and then generate the appropriate navigation menu.

```php
<?php
  // Generate the navigation menu
  echo '<hr />';
  if (isset($_SESSION['username'])) {
    echo '<a href="index.php">Home</a> &#10084; ';
    echo '<a href="viewprofile.php">View Profile</a> &#10084; ';
    echo '<a href="editprofile.php">Edit Profile</a> &#10084; ';
    echo '<a href="logout.php">Log Out (' . $_SESSION['username'] . ')</a>';
  }
  else {
    echo '<a href="login.php">Log In</a> &#10084; ';
    echo '<a href="signup.php">Sign Up</a>';
  }
  echo '<hr />';
?>
```

navmenu.php

Display a copyright notice and wrap up the HTML code.

```php
  <hr />
  <p class="footer">Copyright &copy;2008 Mismatch Enterprises, Inc.</p>
</body>
</html>
```

footer.php

The startsession.php script must be included first so that the session is started and the remainder of the script has access to session data.

The $page_title variable determines the title of the page that is displayed within the page header.

```php
<?php
  // Start the session
  require_once('startsession.php');

  // Insert the page header
  $page_title = 'Where opposites attract!';
  require_once('header.php');

  require_once('appvars.php');
  require_once('connectvars.php');

  // Show the navigation menu
  require_once('navmenu.php');

  // Connect to the database
  $dbc = mysqli_connect(DB_HOST, DB_USER, DB_PASSWORD, DB_NAME);

  // Retrieve the user data from MySQL
  $query = "SELECT user_id, first_name, picture FROM mismatch_user WHERE first_name IS NOT NULL " .
    "ORDER BY join_date DESC LIMIT 5";
  $data = mysqli_query($dbc, $query);

  // Loop through the array of user data, formatting it as HTML
  echo '<h4>Latest members:</h4>';
  echo '<table>';
  while ($row = mysqli_fetch_array($data)) {
   if (is_file(MM_UPLOADPATH . $row['picture']) && filesize(MM_UPLOADPATH . $row['picture']) > 0) {
    echo '<tr><td><img src="' . MM_UPLOADPATH . $row['picture'] . '" alt="' . $row['first_name'] .
     '" /></td>';
   }
   else {
    echo '<tr><td><img src="' . MM_UPLOADPATH . 'nopic.jpg' . '" alt="' . $row['first_name'] .
     '" /></td>';
   }
   if (isset($_SESSION['user_id'])) {
    echo '<td><a href="viewprofile.php?user_id=' . $row['user_id'] . '">' . $row['first_name'] .
     '</a></td></tr>';
   }
   else {
    echo '<td>' . $row['first_name'] . '</td></tr>';
   }
  }
  echo '</table>';

  mysqli_close($dbc);
?>

<?php
  // Insert the page footer
  require_once('footer.php');
?>
```

The connection variables and application variables are still included from separate script files like before.

The navigation menu is generated after the header but before the body of the page.

The non-template code is now truly unique to the page, so there's much less of it.

The footer finishes up the page, and must appear last since it closes up the HTML tags.

index.php

Mismatch is whole again... and better organized

While the thought of ripping apart the Mismatch application into tiny pieces might have been a bit unnerving, the end result is definitely worth the effort. The application's now spread across several new template (include) files, which offer much better organization and maximize the sharing of script code. If you need to change one of these pieces, just change one file and the effect cascades throughout the entire application... that's the power of templates!

The session start-up code is used by any page that requires a user log-in.

The startsession.php script handles behind-the-scenes log-in tasks, and doesn't occupy any visual space on the page.

startsession.php

The navigation menu provides handy links to the major parts of the application.

The page header includes boilerplate HTML code and the page title.

navmenu.php

header.php

Mismatch – Where opposites attract!

Mismatch - Where opposites attract!

Home ❤ View Profile ❤ Edit Profile ❤ Log Out (jnettles)

Latest members:

Ruby
Johan
Paul
Dierdre
Jason

Copyright ©200

Mismatch – View Profile

Mismatch - View Profile

Home ❤ View Profile ❤ Edit Profile ❤ Log Out (jnettles)

Username: jnettles
First name: Johan
Last name: Nettles
Gender: Male
Birthdate: 1981-11-03
Location: Athens, GA

Picture:

Would you like to edit yo

Copyright ©

Mismatch – Edit Profile

Mismatch - Edit Profile

Home ❤ View Profile ❤ Edit Profile ❤ Log Out (jnettles)

Personal Information
First name: Johan
Last name: Nettles **Gender:** Male
Birthdate: 1981-11-03
City: Athens
State: GA
Picture: Choose File johanpic.jpg

Save Profile

Copyright © 2009 Mismatch Enterprises, Inc.

The page footer contains copyright information for the entire application... if you need to change the copyright notice, just change it in one place!

footer.php

8 control your data, control your world

Harvesting data

> The way I see it, it's all about data management. First I sort the peas, then I select a few potatoes, join them with some celery and a few rows of corn kernels... before you know it there's a tasty stew!

There's nothing like a good fall data harvest. An abundance of information ready to be *examined*, *sorted*, *compared*, *combined*, and generally made to do whatever it is your killer web app needs it to do. Fulfilling? Yes. But like real harvesting, **taking control of data in a MySQL database** requires some hard work and a fair amount of expertise. Web users demand more than tired old wilted data that's dull and unengaging. They want data that enriches... data that fulfills... data that's relevant. So what are you waiting for? Fire up your MySQL tractor and get to work!

Making the perfect mismatch

The Mismatch application has a growing database of registered users but they're ready to see some results. We need to allow users to find their ideal opposite by comparing their loves and hates against other users and looking for mismatches. For every love mismatched against a hate, a couple is that much closer to being the perfect mismatch.

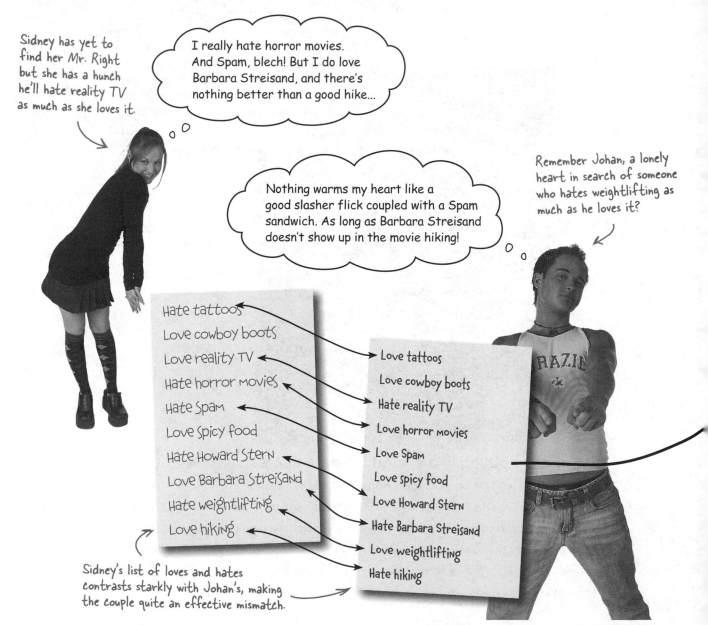

Sidney has yet to find her Mr. Right but she has a hunch he'll hate reality TV as much as she loves it.

I really hate horror movies. And Spam, blech! But I do love Barbara Streisand, and there's nothing better than a good hike...

Nothing warms my heart like a good slasher flick coupled with a Spam sandwich. As long as Barbara Streisand doesn't show up in the movie hiking!

Remember Johan, a lonely heart in search of someone who hates weightlifting as much as he loves it?

Hate tattoos
Love cowboy boots
Love reality TV
Hate horror movies
Hate Spam
Love spicy food
Hate Howard Stern
Love Barbara Streisand
Hate weightlifting
Love hiking

Love tattoos
Love cowboy boots
Hate reality TV
Love horror movies
Love Spam
Love spicy food
Love Howard Stern
Hate Barbara Streisand
Love weightlifting
Hate hiking

Sidney's list of loves and hates contrasts starkly with Johan's, making the couple quite an effective mismatch.

Mismatching is all about the data

In order to carry out Mismatches between users, we must first figure out how to organize the data that keeps up with what they love and hate. Knowing that it's going to be stored in a MySQL database isn't enough. We need to organize these love/hate topics so that they are more manageable, allowing users to respond to related topics, indicating whether they love or hate each one.

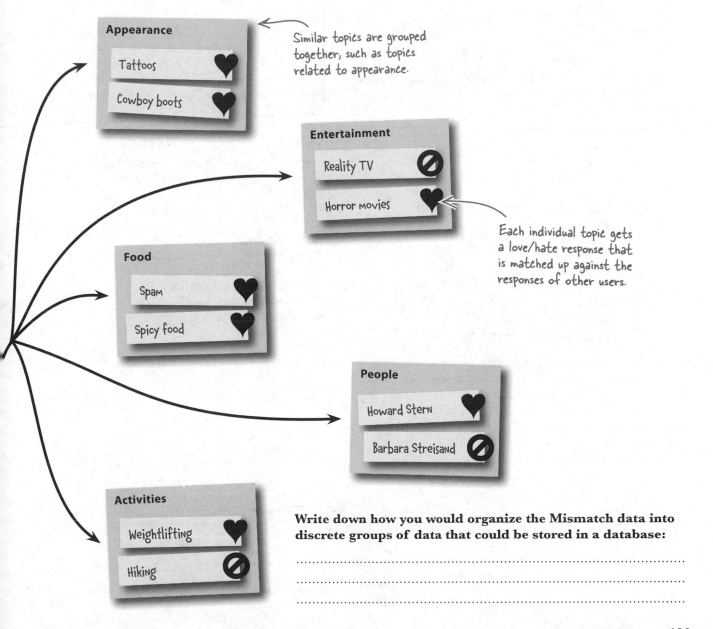

Appearance
- Tattoos ♥
- Cowboy boots ♥

Similar topics are grouped together, such as topics related to appearance.

Entertainment
- Reality TV 🚫
- Horror movies ♥

Each individual topic gets a love/hate response that is matched up against the responses of other users.

Food
- Spam ♥
- Spicy food ♥

People
- Howard Stern ♥
- Barbara Streisand 🚫

Activities
- Weightlifting ♥
- Hiking 🚫

Write down how you would organize the Mismatch data into discrete groups of data that could be stored in a database:

....
....
....

Break down the Mismatch data

Coming up with a data model for an application such as Mismatch is an extremely important step, as it controls an awful lot about how the application is constructed. In the case of Mismatch, we can break down its data needs into three interrelated pieces of data.

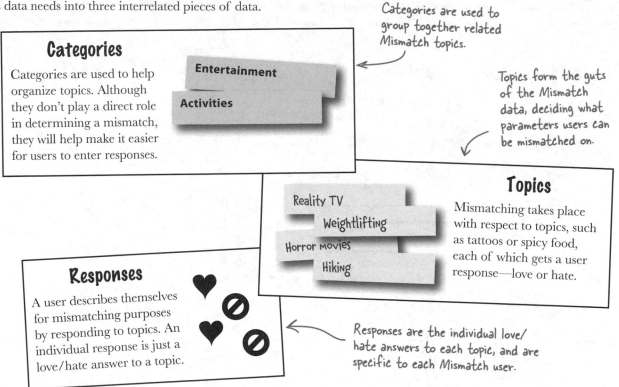

Categories

Categories are used to help organize topics. Although they don't play a direct role in determining a mismatch, they will help make it easier for users to enter responses.

Entertainment

Activities

Categories are used to group together related Mismatch topics.

Topics form the guts of the Mismatch data, deciding what parameters users can be mismatched on.

Topics

Reality TV

Weightlifting

Horror movies

Hiking

Mismatching takes place with respect to topics, such as tattoos or spicy food, each of which gets a user response—love or hate.

Responses

A user describes themselves for mismatching purposes by responding to topics. An individual response is just a love/hate answer to a topic.

Responses are the individual love/hate answers to each topic, and are specific to each Mismatch user.

How exactly does this data lead to a mismatch between two users? We compare responses that users have made on each topic. For example, since Sidney and Johan have opposite responses to the topic "Horror movies," we have a successful mismatch on that particular topic. Figuring the best overall mismatch for a given user involves finding the user who has the most mismatched topics with them.

Hate 'em!

Love 'em.

Horror movies

Horror movies

Sidney's dislike of horror movies leads to a mismatch.

A mismatch!

Model a database with a schema

In order to translate the data requirements of the Mismatch application into an actual database design, we need a schema. A **schema** is a representation of all the structures, such as tables and columns, in your database, along with how they connect. Creating a visual depiction of your database can help you see how things connect when you're writing your queries, not to mention which specific columns are responsible for doing the connecting. As an example, let's take a look at the schema for the original Mismatch database from the previous chapter, which consists of only a single table, `mismatch_user`.

A description of the data (the tables and columns) in your database, along with any other related objects and the way they all connect is known as a schema.

The table name.

mismatch_user
user_id 🔑
username
password
join_date
first_name
last_name
gender
birthdate
city
state
picture

This symbol indicates that the column is a primary key for the table.

Other columns in the table are listed just as they appear in the database structure.

This way of looking at the structure of a table is a bit different than what you've seen up until now. Tables have normally been depicted with the column names across the top and the data below. That's a great way to look at individual tables and tables populated with data, but it's not very practical when we want to create a structural diagram of multiple tables and how they relate to one another. And Mismatch is already in need of multiple tables...

Creating a diagram of a table lets you keep the design of the table separate from the data that's inside of it.

Exercise

The Mismatch database is in need of storage for user responses to love/hate topics, as well as the topic names and their respective categories. Here are three different database designs for incorporating categories, topics, and responses into the Mismatch database. Circle the schema that you think makes the most sense, and annotate why.

category

topic

response

This is the new data introduced by the need to keep up with Mismatch users' loves and hates.

mismatch_topic

topic_id	name	category
1	Tattoos	Appearance
2	Cowboy hats	Appearance
3	Reality TV	Entertainment
4	Horror movies	Entertainment
...		

mismatch_user

user_id	username	password	...
...			
11	jnettles	********	...
...			

mismatch_response

response_id	response	user_id	topic_id
...			
101	Love	11	1
102	Love	11	2
103	Hate	11	3
104	Love	11	4
...			

1

mismatch_user

user_id
username
password
join_date
first_name
last_name
gender
birthdate
city
state
picture

mismatch_response

response_id
response
user_id
topic_id

mismatch_topic

topic_id
name
category

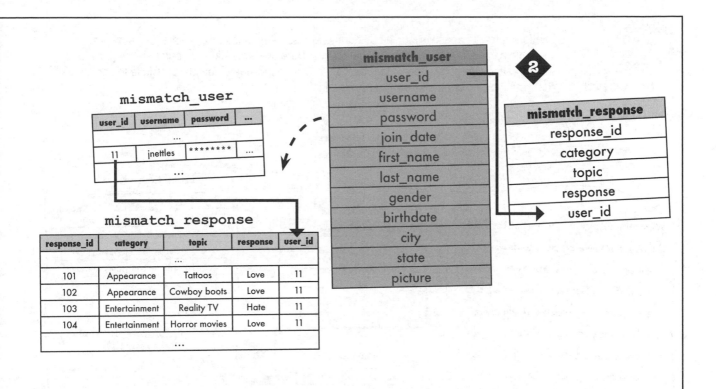

mismatch_user

user_id	username	password	...
...			
11	jnettles	********	...
...			

mismatch_response

response_id	category	topic	response	user_id
...				
101	Appearance	Tattoos	Love	11
102	Appearance	Cowboy boots	Love	11
103	Entertainment	Reality TV	Hate	11
104	Entertainment	Horror movies	Love	11
...				

mismatch_user

user_id
username
password
join_date
first_name
last_name
gender
birthdate
city
state
picture

mismatch_response

response_id
category
topic
response
user_id

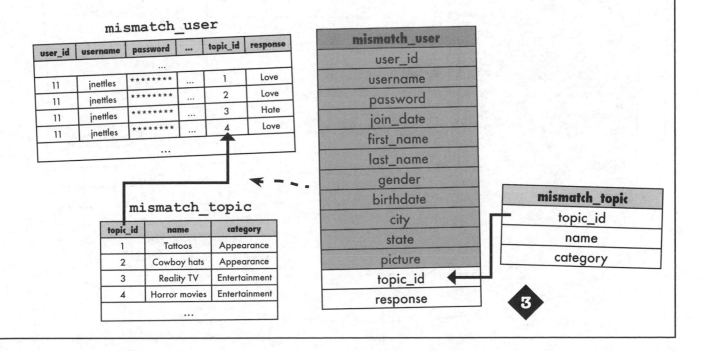

mismatch_user

user_id	username	password	...	topic_id	response
...					
11	jnettles	********	...	1	Love
11	jnettles	********	...	2	Love
11	jnettles	********	...	3	Hate
11	jnettles	********	...	4	Love
...					

mismatch_topic

topic_id	name	category
1	Tattoos	Appearance
2	Cowboy hats	Appearance
3	Reality TV	Entertainment
4	Horror movies	Entertainment
...		

mismatch_user

user_id
username
password
join_date
first_name
last_name
gender
birthdate
city
state
picture
topic_id
response

mismatch_topic

topic_id
name
category

Exercise Solution

The Mismatch database is in need of storage for user responses to love/hate topics, as well as the topic names and their respective categories. Here are three different database designs for incorporating categories, topics, and responses into the Mismatch database. Circle the schema that you think makes the most sense, and annotate why.

First off, it's important to establish that the only new data involved in a user giving love/hate responses are the responses themselves — everything else in the database is fixed, at least from the user's perspective.

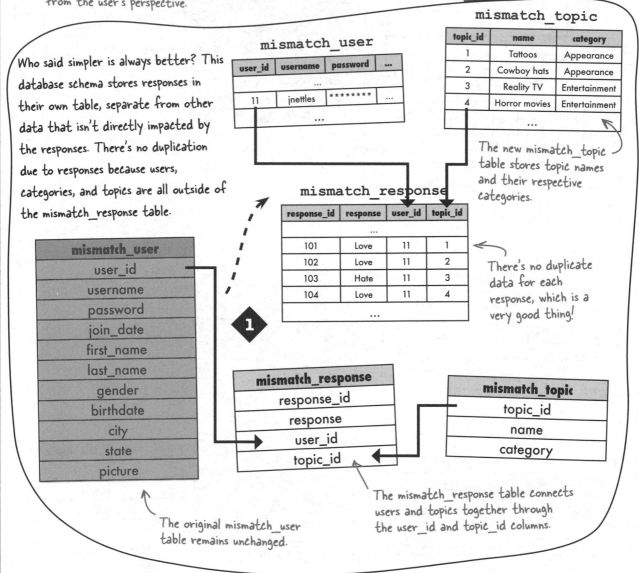

Who said simpler is always better? This database schema stores responses in their own table, separate from other data that isn't directly impacted by the responses. There's no duplication due to responses because users, categories, and topics are all outside of the mismatch_response table.

mismatch_user

user_id	username	password	...
...			
11	jnettles	********	...
...			

mismatch_topic

topic_id	name	category
1	Tattoos	Appearance
2	Cowboy hats	Appearance
3	Reality TV	Entertainment
4	Horror movies	Entertainment
...		

The new mismatch_topic table stores topic names and their respective categories.

mismatch_response

response_id	response	user_id	topic_id
...			
101	Love	11	1
102	Love	11	2
103	Hate	11	3
104	Love	11	4
...			

There's no duplicate data for each response, which is a very good thing!

①

mismatch_user
- user_id
- username
- password
- join_date
- first_name
- last_name
- gender
- birthdate
- city
- state
- picture

The original mismatch_user table remains unchanged.

mismatch_response
- response_id
- response
- user_id
- topic_id

mismatch_topic
- topic_id
- name
- category

The mismatch_response table connects users and topics together through the user_id and topic_id columns.

The responses aren't stored inside the user table, which is great. But there's a ton of duplicate data since the categories and topics are duplicated for each and every response.

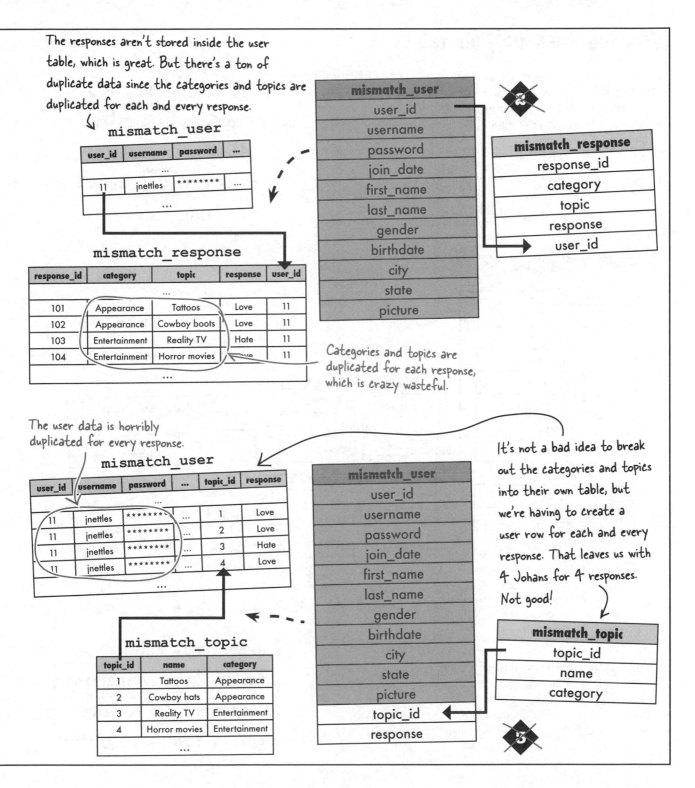

mismatch_user

user_id	username	password	...
		...	
11	jnettles	********	...
		...	

mismatch_user

user_id
username
password
join_date
first_name
last_name
gender
birthdate
city
state
picture

mismatch_response

response_id
category
topic
response
user_id

mismatch_response

response_id	category	topic	response	user_id
		...		
101	Appearance	Tattoos	Love	11
102	Appearance	Cowboy boots	Love	11
103	Entertainment	Reality TV	Hate	11
104	Entertainment	Horror movies	ove	11
		...		

Categories and topics are duplicated for each response, which is crazy wasteful.

The user data is horribly duplicated for every response.

mismatch_user

user_id	username	password	...	topic_id	response
			...		
11	jnettles	********	...	1	Love
11	jnettles	********	...	2	Love
11	jnettles	********	...	3	Hate
11	jnettles	********	...	4	Love
			...		

mismatch_topic

topic_id	name	category
1	Tattoos	Appearance
2	Cowboy hats	Appearance
3	Reality TV	Entertainment
4	Horror movies	Entertainment
	...	

mismatch_user

user_id
username
password
join_date
first_name
last_name
gender
birthdate
city
state
picture
topic_id
response

It's not a bad idea to break out the categories and topics into their own table, but we're having to create a user row for each and every response. That leaves us with 4 Johans for 4 responses. Not good!

mismatch_topic

topic_id
name
category

Wire together multiple tables

Connecting tables together to form a cohesive system of data involves the use of **keys**. We've used **primary keys** to provide a unique identifier for data within a table, but we now need **foreign keys** to link a row in one table to a row in another table. A foreign key in a table references the primary key of another table, establishing a connection between the two tables that can be used in queries.

The Mismatch schema from the previous exercise relies on a pair of foreign keys in the `mismatch_response` table to connect response rows to user and topic rows in other tables.

A foreign key is a column in a table that references the primary key of another table.

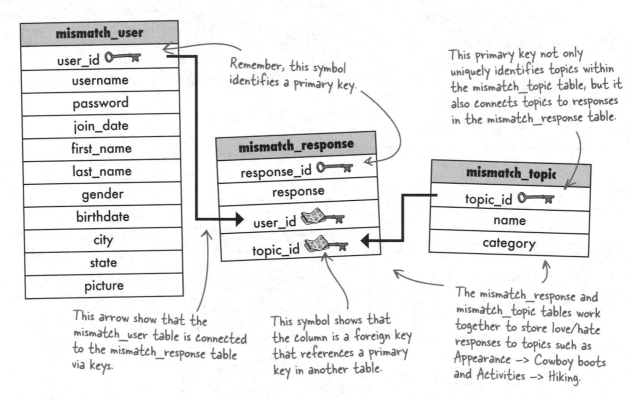

Remember, this symbol identifies a primary key.

This primary key not only uniquely identifies topics within the mismatch_topic table, but it also connects topics to responses in the mismatch_response table.

This arrow show that the mismatch_user table is connected to the mismatch_response table via keys.

This symbol shows that the column is a foreign key that references a primary key in another table.

The mismatch_response and mismatch_topic tables work together to store love/hate responses to topics such as Appearance -> Cowboy boots and Activities -> Hiking.

Without foreign keys, it would be very difficult to associate data from one table with data in another table. And spreading data out across multiple tables is how we're able to eliminate duplicate data and arrive at an efficient database. So foreign keys play an important role in all but the most simplistic of database schemas.

Large arrows show primary keys connecting to foreign keys to wire together tables.

Foreign keys in action

It often helps to visualize data flowing into tables and connecting tables to one another through primary and foreign keys. Taking a closer look at the Mismatch tables with some actual data in them helps to reveal how primary keys and foreign keys relate to one another.

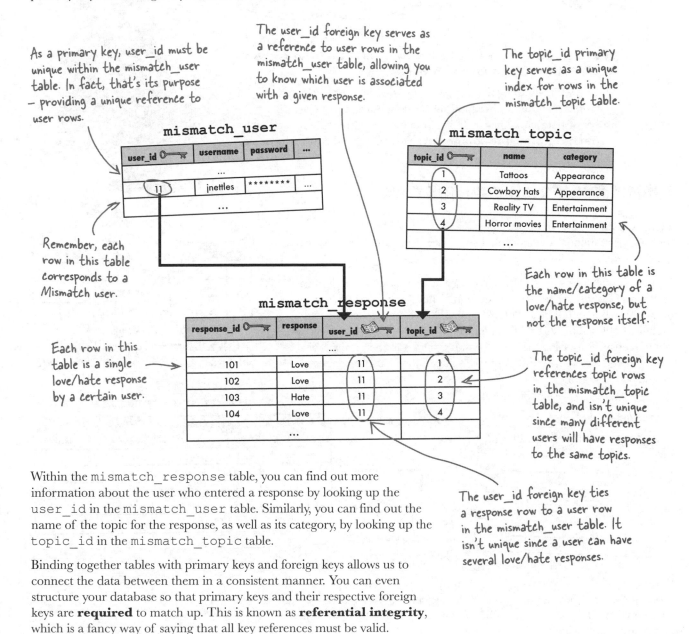

As a primary key, user_id must be unique within the mismatch_user table. In fact, that's its purpose — providing a unique reference to user rows.

The user_id foreign key serves as a reference to user rows in the mismatch_user table, allowing you to know which user is associated with a given response.

The topic_id primary key serves as a unique index for rows in the mismatch_topic table.

Remember, each row in this table corresponds to a Mismatch user.

Each row in this table is the name/category of a love/hate response, but not the response itself.

Each row in this table is a single love/hate response by a certain user.

The topic_id foreign key references topic rows in the mismatch_topic table, and isn't unique since many different users will have responses to the same topics.

The user_id foreign key ties a response row to a user row in the mismatch_user table. It isn't unique since a user can have several love/hate responses.

Within the mismatch_response table, you can find out more information about the user who entered a response by looking up the user_id in the mismatch_user table. Similarly, you can find out the name of the topic for the response, as well as its category, by looking up the topic_id in the mismatch_topic table.

Binding together tables with primary keys and foreign keys allows us to connect the data between them in a consistent manner. You can even structure your database so that primary keys and their respective foreign keys are **required** to match up. This is known as **referential integrity**, which is a fancy way of saying that all key references must be valid.

> I understand that primary keys and foreign keys connect multiple tables together, but does the direction of the arrows between keys in those diagrams mean anything?

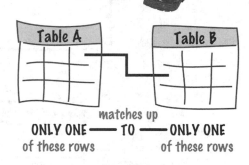

Yes, the direction of the arrows tells us how rows in each table relate to each other.

More specifically, they tell us how many rows in one table can have matching rows in another table, and vice-versa. This is a critical aspect of database schema design, and involves three different possible **patterns** of data: **one-to-one**, **one-to-many**, and **many-to-many**.

Tables can match row for row

The first pattern, **one-to-one**, states that a row in Table A can have at most ONE matching row in Table B, and vice-versa. So there is only one match in each table for each row.

As an example, let's say the Mismatch user table was separated into two tables, one for just the log-in information (Table A) and one with profile data (Table B). Both tables contain a user ID to keep users connected to their profiles. The `user_id` column in the log-in table is a primary key that ensures user log-in uniqueness. `user_id` in the profile table is a foreign key, and plays a different role since its job is just to connect a profile with a log-in.

Table A ⎯⎯ **Table B**

matches up
ONLY ONE ⎯ TO ⎯ ONLY ONE
of these rows   of these rows

mismatch_user_login

user_id 🔑	username	password	join_date
...			
9	dierdre	08447b...	2008-05...
10	baldpaul	230dcb...	2008-05...
11	jnettles	e511d7...	2008-05...
12	rubyr	062e4a...	2008-06...
13	theking	b4f283...	2008-06...

One-to-one, so no arrowheads.

mismatch_user_profile

user_profile_id 🔑	first_name	last_name	gender	...	user_id 🔑
...					
7	Johan	Nettles	M	...	11
8	Jason	Filmington	M	...	8
9	Paul	Hillsman...	M	...	10
...					

The tables have a one-to-one relation through user_id.

With respect to the two `user_id` columns, the log-in table is considered a **parent** table, while the profile table is considered a **child** table—a table with a primary key has a parent-child relationship to the table with the corresponding foreign key.

One row leads to many

One-to-many means that a row in Table A can have **many** matching rows in Table B, but a row in Table B can only match **one** row in Table A. The direction of the arrow in the table diagram always points **from** the table with one row **to** the table with many rows.

Using the Mismatch database again, the current schema already takes advantage of a one-to-many data pattern. Since a user is capable of having many topic responses (love tattoos, hate hiking, etc.), there is a one-to-many relationship between user rows and response rows. The user_id column connects these two tables, as a primary key in mismatch_user and a foreign key in mismatch_response.

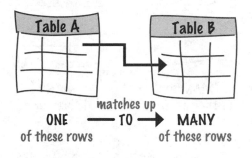

Table A — Table B

matches up

ONE — TO ▶ **MANY**
of these rows   of these rows

Primary key.

mismatch_user

user_id 🔑	username	password	...
9	dierdre	08447b...	...
10	baldpaul	230dcb...	...
11	jnettles	e511d7...	...
12	rubyr	062e4a...	...
13	theking	b4f283...	...

There is a one-to-many relationship through user_id.

Foreign key!

mismatch_response

response_id 🔑	response	user_id 🔑	topic_id 🔑
...			
101	Love	11	1
102	Love	11	2
103	Hate	11	3
104	Love	11	4
...			

there are no Dumb Questions

One-to-One: exactly one row of a parent table is related to one row of a child table.

Q: How do I know whether rows in two tables should have a one-to-one or one-to-many relationship?

A: There will be a tendency to use one-to-many patterns much more often than one-to-one, and rightly so. It's common to have a main (parent) table containing primary data, such as users in Mismatch, that connects to a secondary (child) table in a one-to-many arrangement. This happens twice in the Mismatch schema, where both users and topics have a one-to-many relationship to responses.

In many cases, rows with a one-to-one relationship in two tables can be combined into the same table. However, there are certainly situations where it makes sense to go with a one-to-one pattern, such as the hypothetical user profile example on the facing page, where there is a security motivation in moving a portion of the data into its own table.

One-to-Many: exactly one row of a parent table is related to multiple rows of a child table.

Matching rows many-to-many

The third and final table row relationship data pattern is the **many-to-many** relationship, which has multiple rows of data in Table A matching up with multiple rows in Table B... it's kinda like data overload! Not really. There are plenty of situations where a many-to-many pattern is warranted. Mismatch, perhaps? Let's have a look.

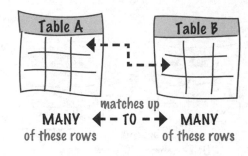

matches up

MANY ← - TO - → **MANY**
of these rows   of these rows

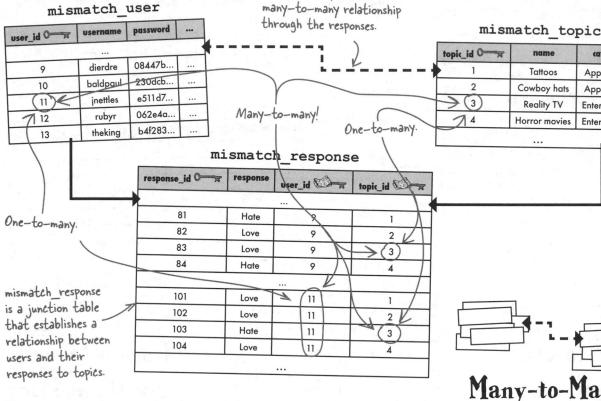

Users and topics have a many-to-many relationship through the responses.

mismatch_user

user_id 🔑	username	password	...
...			
9	dierdre	08447b...	...
10	baldpaul	230dcb...	...
11	jnettles	e511d7...	...
12	rubyr	062e4a...	...
13	theking	b4f283...	...

mismatch_topic

topic_id 🔑	name	category
1	Tattoos	Appearance
2	Cowboy hats	Appearance
3	Reality TV	Entertainment
4	Horror movies	Entertainment
...		

Many-to-many!

One-to-many.

mismatch_response

response_id 🔑	response	user_id 🔑	topic_id 🔑
...			
81	Hate	9	1
82	Love	9	2
83	Love	9	3
84	Hate	9	4
...			
101	Love	11	1
102	Love	11	2
103	Hate	11	3
104	Love	11	4
...			

One-to-many.

mismatch_response is a junction table that establishes a relationship between users and their responses to topics.

The many-to-many pattern in Mismatch is indirect, meaning that it takes place through the mismatch_response table. But the pattern still exists. Just look at how many of the same user_ids and topic_ids appear in mismatch_response.

In addition to holding the response data, the mismatch_response table is acting as what's known as a **junction table** by serving as a convenient go-between for the users and topics. Without the junction table, we would have lots of duplicate data, which is a bad thing. If you aren't convinced, turn back to the schema exercise near the beginning of the chapter and take a closer look at Design 2. In that design, the mismatch_topic table is folded into the mismatch_response table, resulting in lots of duplicate data.

Many-to-Many: Multiple rows of a parent table are related to multiple rows of a child table.

NAME THAT RELATIONSHIP

In each of the tables below, there are circled columns that could be moved out into their own tables. Write down if each of the columns is best represented by a one-to-one, one-to-many, or many-to-many relationship with its original table, and then draw the relationship as a line connecting the two tables with appropriate arrowheads.

RELATIONSHIP

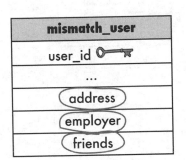

mismatch_user
user_id 🔑
...
(address)
(employer)
(friends)

....

....

 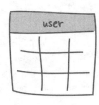

....

mismatch_topic
topic_id 🔑
name
(category)

....

NAME THAT RELATIONSHIP SOLUTION

In each of the tables below, there are circled columns that could be moved out into their own tables. Write down if each of the columns is best represented by a one-to-one, one-to-many, or many-to-many relationship with its original table, and then draw the relationship as a line connecting the two tables with appropriate arrowheads.

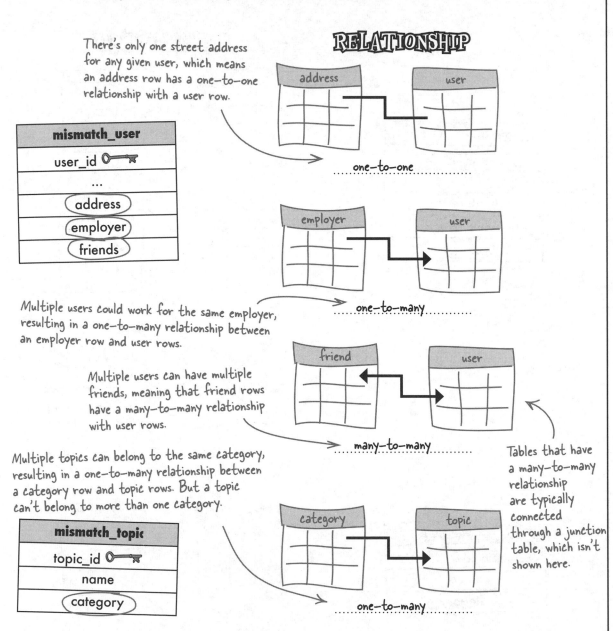

There's only one street address for any given user, which means an address row has a one-to-one relationship with a user row.

RELATIONSHIP

mismatch_user

user_id 🔑

...

(address)

(employer)

(friends)

address ——— user

one-to-one

employer ——→ user

one-to-many

Multiple users could work for the same employer, resulting in a one-to-many relationship between an employer row and user rows.

Multiple users can have multiple friends, meaning that friend rows have a many-to-many relationship with user rows.

friend ←——→ user

many-to-many

Multiple topics can belong to the same category, resulting in a one-to-many relationship between a category row and topic rows. But a topic can't belong to more than one category.

Tables that have a many-to-many relationship are typically connected through a junction table, which isn't shown here.

mismatch_topic

topic_id 🔑

name

(category)

category ——→ topic

one-to-many

Hold it right there! Take a second to get the Mismatch database in order so that we can make mismatches.

Download the `.sql` files for the Mismatch application from the Head First Labs web site at `www.headfirstlabs.com/books/hfphp`. These files contain SQL statements that build the necessary Mismatch tables: `mismatch_user`, `mismatch_topic`, and `mismatch_response`. Make sure to run the statement in each of the `.sql` files in a MySQL tool so that you have the initial Mismatch tables to get started with.

When all that's done, run a `DESCRIBE` statement on each of the new tables (`mismatch_topic` and `mismatch_response`) to double-check their structures. These tables factor heavily into the Mismatch PHP scripts we're about to put together.

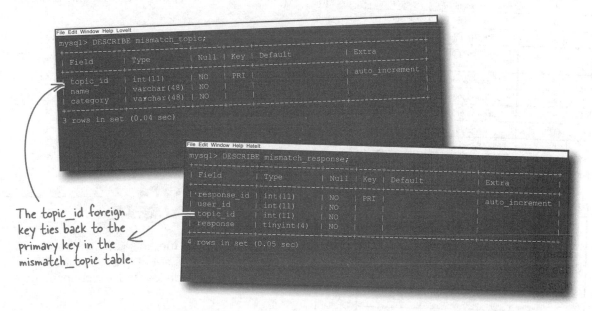

The topic_id foreign key ties back to the primary key in the mismatch_topic table.

OK, so we have this wonderfully designed database of users, categories, topics, and responses. How is that going to actually help us make a mismatch?

If you start with a well-designed database, every other piece of the application puzzle becomes that much easier to build and assemble.

Getting the database right when initially designing an application is perhaps the best thing you can do to make the development process run smoothly. It may seem like a lot of work up front plotting and scheming about how best to store the data, but it will pay off in the long run. Think about how much more difficult it would be to rework the Mismatch database schema with it full of data.

That's the big picture benefit of a good database design. Looking at the Mismatch database specifically, we have a user table that is populated by the users themselves through sign-ups and profile edits, and we have a new topic table that contains enough categories and topics to give some decent insight into a person. What we're still missing to make mismatches is a way to allow the user to enter responses, and then store them away in the response table.

mismatch_topic

topic_id 🔑	name	category
1	Tattoos	Appearance
2	Gold chains	Appearance
3	Body piercings	Appearance
4	Cowboy boots	Appearance
5	Long hair	Appearance
6	Reality TV	Entertainment
7	Professional wrestling	Entertainment
8	Horror movies	Entertainment
9	Easy listening music	Entertinment
10	The opera	Entertainment
11	Sushi	Food
12	Spam	Food
13	Spicy food	Food
14	Peanut butter & banana sandwiches	Food
15	Martinis	Food
16	Howard Stern	People
17	Bill Gates	Peopel
18	Barbara Streisand	People
19	Hugh Hefner	People
20	Martha Stewart	People
21	Yoga	Activities
22	Weightlifting	Activities
23	Cube puzzles	Activities
24	Karaoke	Activities
25	Hiking	Activities

The full mismatch_topic table contains 25 topics broken up across 5 categories...it's our "5 dimensions of opposability!"

How would you turn this list of categories and topics into a set of questions that users can provide love/hate responses to?

Build a Mismatch questionnaire

So how exactly do we get love/hate responses from users for each Mismatch topic? The answer is a questionnaire form that allows the user to choose "Love" or "Hate" for each topic in the `mismatch_topic` table. This form can be generated directly from the responses in the database, with its results getting stored back in the database. In fact, the design of the questionnaire form involves reading and writing responses from and to the `mismatch_response` table. Here's a peek at the questionnaire, along with the steps involved in building it.

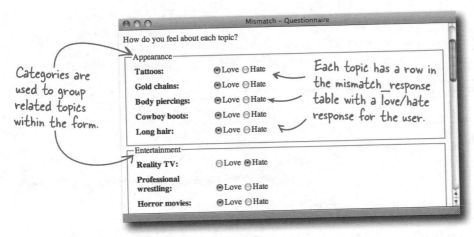

Categories are used to group related topics within the form.

Each topic has a row in the mismatch_response table with a love/hate response for the user.

1. **Use `INSERT` to add empty response rows to the database the first time the user accesses the form.**

   We're going to generate the questionnaire form from data in the `mismatch_response` table, even when the user has never entered any responses. This means we need to "seed" the `mismatch_response` table with empty responses the first time a user accesses the questionnaire. Since the `response` column for these rows is empty, neither the "Love" or "Hate" radio buttons are checked when the form is first presented to the user.

2. **Use `UPDATE` to change response rows based on user responses on the form.**

   When users submit the questionnaire form, we must commit their personal responses to the database. Even then, only responses with checked radio buttons should be updated. In other words, the database only needs to know about the responses that **have** been answered.

3. **Use `SELECT` to retrieve the response data required to generate the questionnaire form.**

   In order to generate the questionnaire form, we need all of the responses for the logged-in user. Not only that, but we need to look up the topic and category name for each response so that they can be displayed in the form—these names are stored in the `mismatch_topic` table, not `mismatch_response`.

4. **Generate the HTML questionnaire form from response data.**

   With the response data in hand, we can generate the HTML questionnaire form as a bunch of input fields, making sure to check the appropriate "Love" or "Hate" radio buttons based on the user responses.

Get responses into the database

Although it might seem as if we should start out by generating the questionnaire form, the form's dependent on response data existing in the mismatch_response table. So first things first: we need to "seed" the mismatch_response table with rows of unanswered responses the first time a user accesses the questionnaire. This will allow us to generate the questionnaire form from the mismatch_response table without having to worry about whether the user has actually made any responses.

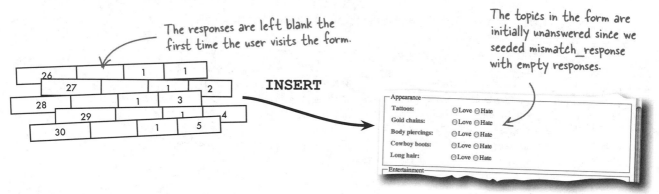

The responses are left blank the first time the user visits the form.

The topics in the form are initially unanswered since we seeded mismatch_response with empty responses.

So from the perspective of the questionnaire form, there's always a row of data in the mismatch_response table for each question in the form. This means that when the user submits the questionnaire form, we just update the rows of data for each response in the form.

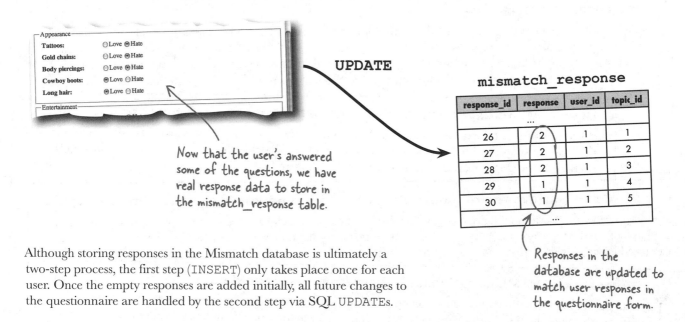

Now that the user's answered some of the questions, we have real response data to store in the mismatch_response table.

Responses in the database are updated to match user responses in the questionnaire form.

Although storing responses in the Mismatch database is ultimately a two-step process, the first step (INSERT) only takes place once for each user. Once the empty responses are added initially, all future changes to the questionnaire are handled by the second step via SQL UPDATEs.

PHP & MySQL Magnets

The following code takes care of inserting empty responses into the `mismatch_response` table the first time a user visits the questionnaire form. It also updates the responses when the user makes changes and submits the form. Unfortunately, some of the code has fallen off and needs to be replaced. Use the magnets to fix the missing code.

```
...
  // If this user has never answered the questionnaire, insert empty responses into the database
  $query = "SELECT * FROM mismatch_response WHERE user_id = '" . $_SESSION['user_id'] . "'";
  $data = mysqli_query($dbc, $query);

  if ( ........................... ($data) == 0) {

    // First grab the list of topic IDs from the topic table

    $query = "SELECT .................. FROM mismatch_topic ORDER BY category_id, topic_id";

    $data = mysqli_query($dbc, $query);
    $topicIDs = array();
    while ($row = mysqli_fetch_array($data)) {
      array_push($topicIDs, $row['topic_id']);
    }

    // Insert empty response rows into the response table, one per topic
    foreach ($topicIDs as $topic_id) {

      $query = "......................... mismatch_response " .

        "( .................. , .................. ) VALUES ('" . $_SESSION['user_id']. "', '$topic_id')";

      mysqli_query($dbc, $query);
    }
  }

  // If the questionnaire form has been submitted, write the form responses to the database
  if (isset($_POST['submit'])) {
    // Write the questionnaire response rows to the response table
    foreach ($_POST as $response_id => $response) {

      $query = "................. mismatch_response ............... response = '$response' " .

        "WHERE ..................... = '$response_id'";

      mysqli_query($dbc, $query);
    }
    echo '<p>Your responses have been saved.</p>';
  }
...
```

Magnets:
`user_id`
`topic_id`
`INSERT INTO`
`mysqli_num_rows`
`SET`
`topic_id`
`response_id`
`UPDATE`

PHP & MySQL Magnets

The following code takes care of inserting empty responses into the `mismatch_response` table the first time a user visits the questionnaire form. It also updates the responses when the user makes changes and submits the form. Unfortunately, some of the code has fallen off and needs to be replaced. Use the magnets to fix the missing code.

```php
...
  // If this user has never answered the questionnaire, insert empty responses into the database
  $query = "SELECT * FROM mismatch_response WHERE user_id = '" . $_SESSION['user_id'] . "'";
  $data = mysqli_query($dbc, $query);

  if ( ... mysqli_num_rows ... ($data) == 0) {
```

> Check to see if the query returned 0 rows of data… no data!

```php
    // First grab the list of topic IDs from the topic table

    $query = "SELECT ... topic_id ... FROM mismatch_topic ORDER BY category_id, topic_id";
```

> In order to generate an empty array of responses, we first need to grab all of the topics in the topic table.

```php
    $data = mysqli_query($dbc, $query);
    $topicIDs = array();
    while ($row = mysqli_fetch_array($data)) {
      array_push($topicIDs, $row['topic_id']);
    }

    // Insert empty response rows into the response table, one per topic
    foreach ($topicIDs as $topic_id) {
```

> The response row is "unanswered" at this point since the user hasn't actually chosen "love" or "hate" on the form yet.

```php
      $query = "... INSERT INTO ... mismatch_response " .
        "( ... user_id ... , ... topic_id ... ) VALUES ('" . $_SESSION['user_id']. "', '$topic_id')";
      mysqli_query($dbc, $query);
    }
  }

  // If the questionnaire form has been submitted, write the form responses to the database
  if (isset($_POST['submit'])) {
    // Write the questionnaire response rows to the response table
    foreach ($_POST as $response_id => $response) {

      $query = "... UPDATE ... mismatch_response ... SET ... response = '$response' " .
        "WHERE ... response_id ... = '$response_id'";
```

> All that changes when the user submits the form is the response column of the response table, so that's all we update.

```php
      mysqli_query($dbc, $query);
    }
    echo '<p>Your responses have been saved.</p>';
  }
...
```

Q: What's the deal with the `array_push()` function? I don't think we've used that one before.

A: We haven't. And that's because we haven't needed to build an array dynamically one element at a time. The `array_push()` function tacks a new element onto the end of an array, causing the array to grow by one. In the Mismatch code on the facing page, we're using `array_push()` to build an array of topic IDs from the `mismatch_topic` table. This array is then used to insert blank responses into the `mismatch_response` table... one for each topic.

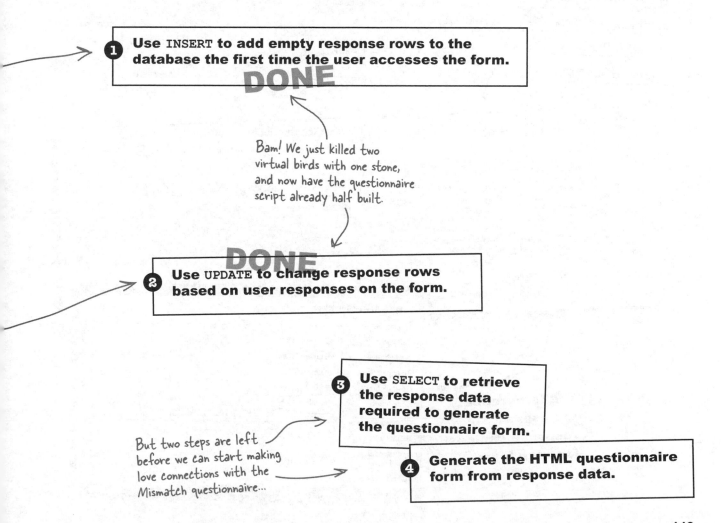

1 Use INSERT **to add empty response rows to the database the first time the user accesses the form.**

DONE

Bam! We just killed two virtual birds with one stone, and now have the questionnaire script already half built.

DONE

2 Use UPDATE **to change response rows based on user responses on the form.**

3 Use SELECT **to retrieve the response data required to generate the questionnaire form.**

But two steps are left before we can start making love connections with the Mismatch questionnaire...

4 **Generate the HTML questionnaire form from response data.**

We can drive a form with data

It's nothing new that web forms are used to retrieve data from users via text fields, selection lists, radio buttons, etc., but it may not be all that obvious that you can generate HTML forms from database data using PHP. The idea with Mismatch is to dynamically generate an HTML questionnaire form from response data. The Mismatch questionnaire script makes the assumption that response data already exists, which allows it to generate the form from data in the `mismatch_response` table. We know this assumption is a safe one because we just wrote the code to add empty responses the first time a user visits the form.

Data-driven forms rely on data in a MySQL database to generate HTML form fields.

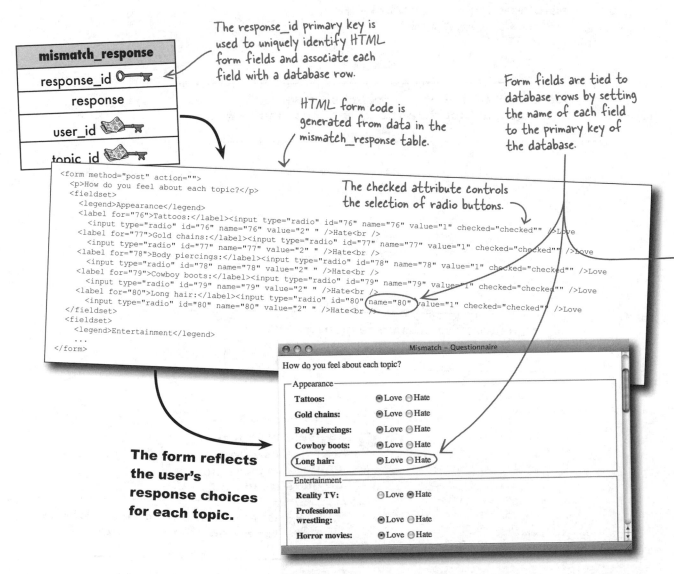

The response_id primary key is used to uniquely identify HTML form fields and associate each field with a database row.

HTML form code is generated from data in the mismatch_response table.

Form fields are tied to database rows by setting the name of each field to the primary key of the database.

The checked attribute controls the selection of radio buttons.

```
<form method="post" action="">
  <p>How do you feel about each topic?</p>
  <fieldset>
    <legend>Appearance</legend>
    <label for="76">Tattoos:</label><input type="radio" id="76" name="76" value="1" checked="checked"" />Love
      <input type="radio" id="76" name="76" value="2" />Hate<br />
    <label for="77">Gold chains:</label><input type="radio" id="77" name="77" value="1" checked="checked"" />Love
      <input type="radio" id="77" name="77" value="2" />Hate<br />
    <label for="78">Body piercings:</label><input type="radio" id="78" name="78" value="1" checked="checked"" />Love
      <input type="radio" id="78" name="78" value="2" />Hate<br />
    <label for="79">Cowboy boots:</label><input type="radio" id="79" name="79" value="1" checked="checked"" />Love
      <input type="radio" id="79" name="79" value="2" />Hate<br />
    <label for="80">Long hair:</label><input type="radio" id="80" name="80" value="1" checked="checked"" />Love
      <input type="radio" id="80" name="80" value="2" />Hate<br />
  </fieldset>
  <fieldset>
    <legend>Entertainment</legend>
    ...
</form>
```

The form reflects the user's response choices for each topic.

Exercise

The Mismatch response questionnaire is generated from user responses that are stored in the `mismatch_response` table. In order to generate the code for the HTML form, it's necessary to read these responses, making sure to look up the name of the topic and category for each response from the `mismatch_topic` table. The following code builds an array of responses with topics and categories by performing two queries: the first query grabs the responses for a user, while the second query looks up the topic and category name for each response. Problem is, some of the code is missing... fill in the blanks to get it working!

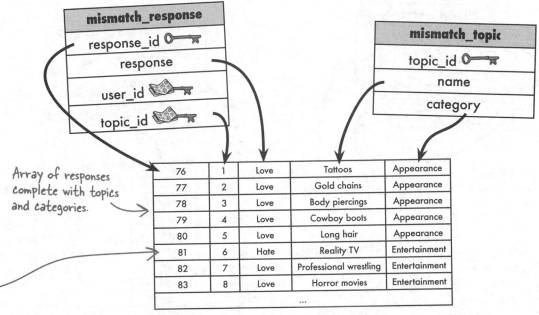

Array of responses complete with topics and categories.

```
// Grab the response data from the database to generate the form
$query = "SELECT response_id, topic_id, response FROM mismatch_response " .
   "WHERE user_id = '" . $_SESSION['user_id'] . "'";
$data = mysqli_query($dbc, $query);
$responses = array();
while ($row = mysqli_fetch_array($data)) {
   // Look up the topic name for the response from the topic table
   $query2 = "...................................................................." .
      "WHERE topic_id = '" . $row['topic_id'] . "'";
   $data2 = mysqli_query($dbc, ............);
   if (mysqli_num_rows(............) == 1) {
      $row2 = mysqli_fetch_array($data2);
      $row['topic_name'] = ...........................
      $row['category_name'] = ...........................
      array_push($responses, $row);
   }
}
```

This PHP function tells you how many rows of data were returned as query results.

mismatch_response

- response_id 🔑
- response
- user_id 🔑
- topic_id 🔑

mismatch_topic

- topic_id 🔑
- name
- category

76	1	Love	Tattoos	Appearance
77	2	Love	Gold chains	Appearance
78	3	Love	Body piercings	Appearance
79	4	Love	Cowboy boots	Appearance
80	5	Love	Long hair	Appearance
81	6	Hate	Reality TV	Entertainment
82	7	Love	Professional wrestling	Entertainment
83	8	Love	Horror movies	Entertainment
...				

Exercise Solution

The Mismatch response questionnaire is generated from user responses that are stored in the `mismatch_response` table. In order to generate the code for the HTML form, it's necessary to read these responses, making sure to look up the name of the topic and category for each response from the `mismatch_topic` table. The following code builds an array of responses with topics and categories by performing two queries: the first query grabs the responses for a user, while the second query looks up the topic and category name for each response. Problem is, some of the code is missing... fill in the blanks to get it working!

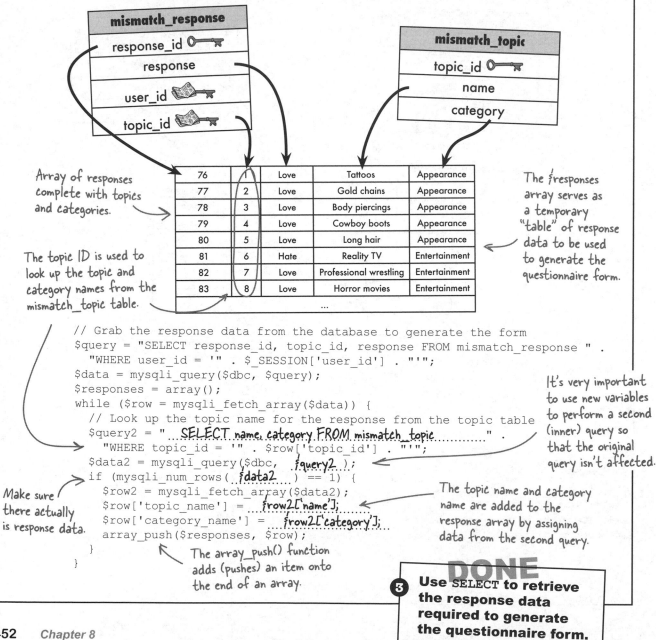

mismatch_response

response_id 🔑

response

user_id 💵🔑

topic_id 💵🔑

mismatch_topic

topic_id 🔑

name

category

Array of responses complete with topics and categories.

76	1	Love	Tattoos	Appearance
77	2	Love	Gold chains	Appearance
78	3	Love	Body piercings	Appearance
79	4	Love	Cowboy boots	Appearance
80	5	Love	Long hair	Appearance
81	6	Hate	Reality TV	Entertainment
82	7	Love	Professional wrestling	Entertainment
83	8	Love	Horror movies	Entertainment
		...		

The topic ID is used to look up the topic and category names from the mismatch_topic table.

The $responses array serves as a temporary "table" of response data to be used to generate the questionnaire form.

```
// Grab the response data from the database to generate the form
$query = "SELECT response_id, topic_id, response FROM mismatch_response " .
  "WHERE user_id = '" . $_SESSION['user_id'] . "'";
$data = mysqli_query($dbc, $query);
$responses = array();
while ($row = mysqli_fetch_array($data)) {
  // Look up the topic name for the response from the topic table
  $query2 = " ....SELECT name, category FROM mismatch_topic........... " .
    "WHERE topic_id = '" . $row['topic_id'] . "'";
  $data2 = mysqli_query($dbc,  $query2 );
  if (mysqli_num_rows(  $data2  ) == 1) {
    $row2 = mysqli_fetch_array($data2);
    $row['topic_name'] =  $row2['name'];
    $row['category_name'] =  $row2['category'];
    array_push($responses, $row);
  }
}
```

Make sure there actually is response data.

The array_push() function adds (pushes) an item onto the end of an array.

It's very important to use new variables to perform a second (inner) query so that the original query isn't affected.

The topic name and category name are added to the response array by assigning data from the second query.

DONE

③ Use `SELECT` to retrieve the response data required to generate the questionnaire form.

Is the user response actually stored as text in the database, as in "Love" and "Hate"? If so, isn't that inefficient?

No and Yes, which is why it is important to use the most efficient data type possible to store data in a MySQL database.

When you think about it, a Mismatch response is more like a true/false answer because it's always either one value (love) or another one (hate). Actually, a third value (unknown) can be useful in letting the application know when the user has yet to respond to a particular topic. So we really need to keep track of three possible values for any given response. This kind of storage problem is ideal for a number, such as a `TINYINT`. Then you just use different numeric values to represent each possible response.

Unknown = 0   **Love = 1**   **Hate = 2**

Minimizing the storage requirements of data is an important part of database design, and in this case a subtle but important part of the Mismatch application. These numeric responses play a direct role in the generation of form fields for the Mismatch questionnaire.

Sharpen your pencil

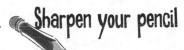

Don't worry about the "Hate" radio buttons for now — they're generated exactly the same way.

The following code loops through the Mismatch response array that you just created, generating an HTML form field for each "Love" radio button. Fill in the missing code so that the form field is initially checked if the response is set to love (1). Also, make sure the value of the `<input>` tag is set accordingly.

```
foreach ($responses as $response) {
  ...
  if (.......................................) {
    echo '<input type="radio" name="' . $response['response_id'] .
     '" value=....... checked=............... />Love ';
  }
  else {
    echo '<input type="radio" name="' . $response['response_id'] .
     '" value=.......  />Love ';
  }
}
```

Sharpen your pencil Solution

The following code loops through the Mismatch response array that you just created, generating an HTML form field for each "Love" radio button. Fill in the missing code so that the form field is initially checked if the response is set to love (1). Also, make sure the value of the `<input>` tag is set accordingly.

The "Love" radio button is checked based on the value of the response (1 represents love in the database).

If this response is set to love (1), check the radio button by setting its checked attribute to "checked".

```
foreach ($responses as $response) {
  ...
  if ( $response['response'] == 1 ) {
    echo '<input type="radio" name="' . $response['response_id'] .
      '" value="1" checked="checked" />Love ';
  }
  else {
    echo '<input type="radio" name="' . $response['response_id'] .
      '" value="1" />Love ';
  }
}
```

The value of the `<input>` tag is set to "1" so that it will be easier to store the response in the database when the form is submitted.

Leaving off checked="checked" results in the radio button being unchecked if the response isn't set to love (1).

```
foreach ($responses as $response) {
  ...
  if ($response['response'] == 2) {
    echo '<input type="radio" name="' . $response['response_id'] .
      '" value="2" checked="checked" />Hate ';
  }
  else {
    echo '<input type="radio" name="' . $response['response_id'] .
      '" value="2" />Hate ';
  }
}
```

In case you're curious, the code to generate the "Hate" radio buttons works exactly the same way — it just looks for a slightly different response... but there's actually a cleaner way to generate both the "Love" and "Hate" radio buttons with less code...

Speaking of efficiency...

Database efficiency isn't the only kind of efficiency worth considering. There's also **coding efficiency**, which comes in many forms. One form is taking advantage of the PHP language to simplify `if-else` statements. The **ternary operator** is a handy way to code simple `if-else` statements so that they are more compact.

> The ternary ? : operator can be used to code if-else statements in a more compact form.

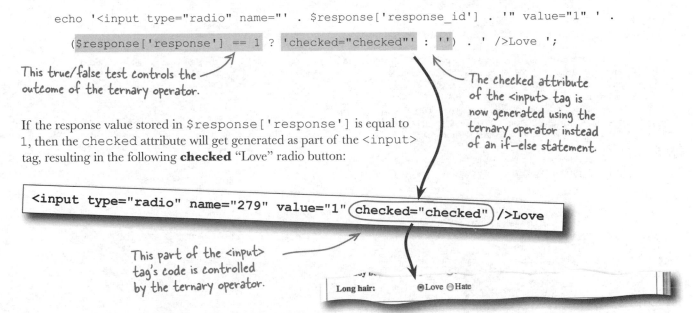

true

If TestExpression is true, Statement1 is executed.

TestExpression ? Statement1 : Statement2

false

If TextExpression is false, Statement2 is executed.

The ternary operator is really just a shorthand way to write an `if-else` statement. It can be helpful for simplifying `if-else` statements, especially when you're making a variable assignment or generating HTML code in response to the `if` condition. Here's the same "Love" radio button code rewritten to use the ternary operator:

```php
echo '<input type="radio" name="' . $response['response_id'] . '" value="1" ' .
($response['response'] == 1 ? 'checked="checked"' : '') . ' />Love ';
```

This true/false test controls the outcome of the ternary operator.

The checked attribute of the <input> tag is now generated using the ternary operator instead of an if-else statement.

If the response value stored in `$response['response']` is equal to 1, then the `checked` attribute will get generated as part of the `<input>` tag, resulting in the following **checked** "Love" radio button:

```
<input type="radio" name="279" value="1" checked="checked" />Love
```

This part of the <input> tag's code is controlled by the ternary operator.

Long hair: ⦿Love ○Hate

On the other hand, a response value of anything other than 1 will prevent the `checked` attribute from being generated, resulting in an `<input>` tag for the "Love" radio button that is unchecked.

Generate the Mismatch questionnaire form

We now have enough pieces of the Mismatch questionnaire form puzzle to use the response array ($responses) we created earlier to generate the entire HTML form. If you recall, this array was built by pulling out the current user's responses from the mismatch_response table. Let's go ahead and see the questionnaire generation code in the context of the full questionnaire.php script.

```php
<?php
  // Start the session
  require_once('startsession.php');

  // Insert the page header
  $page_title = 'Questionnaire';
  require_once('header.php');

  require_once('appvars.php');
  require_once('connectvars.php');

  // Make sure the user is logged in before going any further.
  if (!isset($_SESSION['user_id'])) {
    echo '<p class="login">Please <a href="login.php">log in</a> to access this page.</p>';
    exit();
  }

  // Show the navigation menu
  require_once('navmenu.php');

  // Connect to the database
  $dbc = mysqli_connect(DB_HOST, DB_USER, DB_PASSWORD, DB_NAME);

  // If this user has never answered the questionnaire, insert empty responses into the database
  $query = "SELECT * FROM mismatch_response WHERE user_id = '" . $_SESSION['user_id'] . "'";
  $data = mysqli_query($dbc, $query);
  if (mysqli_num_rows($data) == 0) {
    // First grab the list of topic IDs from the topic table
    $query = "SELECT topic_id FROM mismatch_topic ORDER BY category_id, topic_id";
    $data = mysqli_query($dbc, $query);
    $topicIDs = array();
    while ($row = mysqli_fetch_array($data)) {
      array_push($topicIDs, $row['topic_id']);
    }

    // Insert empty response rows into the response table, one per topic
    foreach ($topicIDs as $topic_id) {
      $query = "INSERT INTO mismatch_response (user_id, topic_id) VALUES ('" . $_SESSION['user_id'] .
        "', '$topic_id')";
      mysqli_query($dbc, $query);
    }
  }

  // If the questionnaire form has been submitted, write the form responses to the database
  if (isset($_POST['submit'])) {
    // Write the questionnaire response rows to the response table
    foreach ($_POST as $response_id => $response) {
      $query = "UPDATE mismatch_response SET response = '$response' " .
```

Include the template files that start the session and display the page header.

Restrict the page to users who are logged in.

questionnaire.php

1

2

```
        "WHERE response_id = '$response_id'";
      mysqli_query($dbc, $query);
    }
    echo '<p>Your responses have been saved.</p>';
  }
```

3
```
// Grab the response data from the database to generate the form
$query = "SELECT response_id, topic_id, response FROM mismatch_response WHERE user_id = '" .
  $_SESSION['user_id'] . "'";
$data = mysqli_query($dbc, $query);
$responses = array();
while ($row = mysqli_fetch_array($data)) {
  // Look up the topic name for the response from the topic table
  $query2 = "SELECT name, category FROM mismatch_topic WHERE topic_id = '" . $row['topic_id'] .
    "'";
  $data2 = mysqli_query($dbc, $query2);
  if (mysqli_num_rows($data2) == 1) {
    $row2 = mysqli_fetch_array($data2);
    $row['topic_name'] = $row2['name'];
    $row['category_name'] = $row2['category'];
    array_push($responses, $row);
  }
}

mysqli_close($dbc);
```

Grab the category of the first response to get started before entering the loop.

4
```
// Generate the questionnaire form by looping through the response array
echo '<form method="post" action="' . $_SERVER['PHP_SELF'] . '">';
echo '<p>How do you feel about each topic?</p>';
$category = $responses[0]['category_name'];
echo '<fieldset><legend>' . $responses[0]['category_name'] . '</legend>';
foreach ($responses as $response) {
  // Only start a new fieldset if the category has changed
  if ($category != $response['category_name']) {
    $category = $response['category_name'];
    echo '</fieldset><fieldset><legend>' . $response['category_name'] . '</legend>';
  }

  // Display the topic form field
  echo '<label ' . ($response['response'] == NULL ? 'class="error"' : '') . ' for="' .
    $response['response_id'] . '">' . $response['topic_name'] . ':</label>';
  echo '<input type="radio" id="' . $response['response_id'] . '" name="' .
    $response['response_id'] . '" value="1" ' .
    ($response['response'] == 1 ? 'checked="checked"' : '') . ' />Love ';
  echo '<input type="radio" id="' . $response['response_id'] . '" name="' .
    $response['response_id'] . '" value="2" ' .
    ($response['response'] == 2 ? 'checked="checked"' : '') . ' />Hate<br />';
}
echo '</fieldset>';
echo '<input type="submit" value="Save Questionnaire" name="submit" />';
echo '</form>';
```

Each category is created as a fieldset to help organize topics together.

Here the ternary operator is used to change the style of the label for unanswered topics.

Each topic is created as a label followed by "Love" and "Hate" radio buttons.

```
  // Insert the page footer
  require_once('footer.php');
?>
```

Each of these echo statements generates a radio button — one for "Love" and one for "Hate".

Remember, 1 = love, 2 = hate.

DONE

4 Generate the HTML questionnaire form from response data.

Test Drive

Try out the new Mismatch questionnaire.

Modify Mismatch to use the new Questionnaire script (or download the application from the Head First Labs site at www.headfirstlabs.com/books/hfphp). This requires creating a new questionnaire.php script, as well as adding a "Questionnaire" menu item to the navmenu.php script so that users can access the questionnaire.

Upload the scripts to your web server, and then open the main Mismatch page (index.php) in a web browser. Make sure you log in, and then click the "Questionnaire" menu item to access the questionnaire. Notice that none of the topics have answers since this is your first visit to the questionnaire. Answer the responses and submit the form. Return to the main page, and then go back to the questionnaire once more to make sure your responses are properly loaded from the database.

The Questionnaire script allows users to answer love/hate questions and store the results in the database.

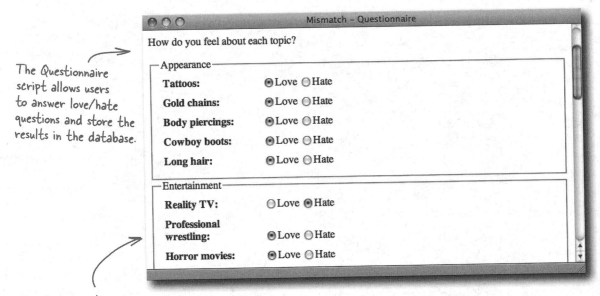

The topic questions in the form are dynamically generated from the database — if you add new topics, the form changes.

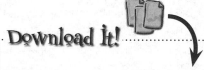

Download It!

The complete source code for the Mismatch application is available for download from the Head First Labs web site:

www.headfirstlabs.com/books/hfphp

there are no Dumb Questions

Q: How does the "Love" radio button code know that the ternary operator result is a string?

A: The ternary operator always evaluates to one of the two statements on each side of the colon based on the value (`true` or `false`) of the test expression. If these statements are strings, then the result of the ternary operator will be a string. That's what makes the operator so handy—you can insert it right into the middle of an assignment or concatenation.

Q: Does the ternary operator make my script run faster?

A: No, probably not. The ternary operator is more about adding stylistic efficiency to your code than performance efficiency, meaning that it literally requires less script code. Sometimes it's more concise to use the ternary operator rather than a full-blown `if-else` statement, even though the two are logically equivalent. Even so, don't get too carried away with the ternary operator because it can make some code more difficult to understand if you're attempting to recast a complex `if-else` statement. The idea is to use the ternary operator in places where eliminating an `if-else` can actually help simplify the code, as opposed to making it more complicated. This usually involves using the ternary operator to selectively control a value being assigned to a variable or inserted into an expression. In the case of the Mismatch radio buttons, the latter approach was used to selectively control the insertion of an HTML attribute (`checked`).

Q: How is it possible to generate the Mismatch questionnaire form from the `mismatch_response` table when the user has yet to respond to anything?

A: Excellent question. The questionnaire form has to deal with two possible scenarios: the user is answering the questionnaire for the first time or the user has already answered it and is revising answers. In the first scenario, no responses have been made, so the `mismatch_response` table has no data for this user yet. But we still need to dynamically generate the form. We could use the `mismatch_topic` table for this one-time form generation. This won't work for the second scenario, however, because this time the form must be generated based on the user's specific love/hate responses; remember, the radio buttons for "Love" and "Hate" are generated as part of the form. So we have a problem in that the code to generate the form is completely different depending on whether the users have answered the questionnaire. Not only that, but what if they only answered a few questions? This gets messy in a hurry. The solution taken by Mismatch is to pre-populate the `mismatch_response` table with unanswered responses the first time the user accesses the questionnaire. This allows us to always generate the questionnaire form from the `mismatch_response` table, and not worry about the complication of generating the form differently based on whether the users have responded before, or which specific topics they've responded to. Sure, the form generation code still isn't exactly trivial, but it's simpler than if we had not taken this approach.

Try this!

To simplify the code, Mismatch doesn't adjust to new topics automatically, at least not when it comes to users who've already answered the questionnaire. So you'll have to empty the mismatch_response table after adding a new topic.

① Add a new topic to your own mismatch_topic table with this SQL statement:

```
INSERT INTO mismatch_topic
   (name, category) VALUES
   ('Virtual guitars', 'Activities')
```

② Empty all the data from the mismatch_response table with this SQL statement:

```
DELETE FROM mismatch_response
```

③ View the questionnaire in the Mismatch application to see the new topic.

④ Respond to the new topic, submit the form, and check out your saved response.

The data is now driving the form

It took some doing, but the Mismatch application dynamically generates the questionnaire from responses stored in the database. This means that any changes made to the database will automatically be reflected in the form—that's the whole idea of driving the user interface of a web application from a database. But what happens when we have bad data?

> That form is, like, really confusing!

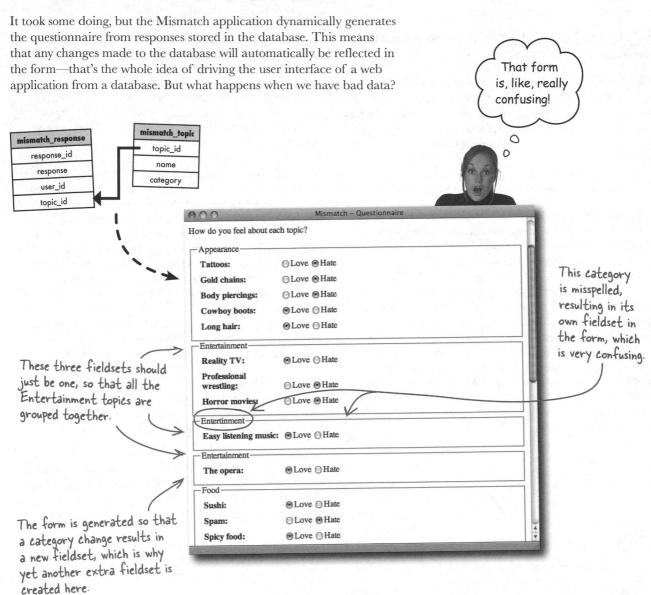

These three fieldsets should just be one, so that all the Entertainment topics are grouped together.

This category is misspelled, resulting in its own fieldset in the form, which is very confusing.

The form is generated so that a category change results in a new fieldset, which is why yet another extra fieldset is created here.

The data is driving the form's fine, but something's amiss. It appears that one of the categories has been misspelled in the database, causing the PHP code to generate a separate fieldset for it. This is a big problem because it ruins the effect of using fieldsets to help organize the form and make it easier to respond to topics.

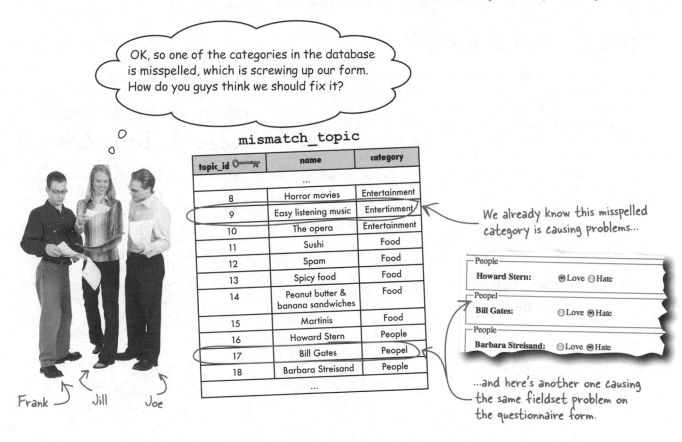

OK, so one of the categories in the database is misspelled, which is screwing up our form. How do you guys think we should fix it?

mismatch_topic

topic_id	name	category
...		
8	Horror movies	Entertainment
9	Easy listening music	Entertinment
10	The opera	Entertainment
11	Sushi	Food
12	Spam	Food
13	Spicy food	Food
14	Peanut butter & banana sandwiches	Food
15	Martinis	Food
16	Howard Stern	People
17	Bill Gates	Peopel
18	Barbara Streisand	People
...		

We already know this misspelled category is causing problems...

People
Howard Stern: ⊙Love ○Hate
Peopel
Bill Gates: ○Love ⊙Hate
People
Barbara Streisand: ○Love ⊙Hate

...and here's another one causing the same fieldset problem on the questionnaire form.

Frank ➞   Jill   Joe ➞

Frank: That's easy. Just change the name of the category in the `mismatch_topic` table to the correct spelling.

Joe: But there's more than one category misspelled. And now that I think about it, I'm not really understanding why the category names have to be stored more than once.

Jill: I agree. We went to the trouble of eliminating duplicate data in designing the database schema, yet here we are with a bunch of duplicate category names. Not only that, but we have a couple that aren't even correct.

Frank: OK, what about just getting rid of category names and maybe referring to categories by number? Then you wouldn't run the risk of typos.

Joe: True, but we still need the category names as headings in the questionnaire form.

Jill: Maybe we can refer to categories by number without throwing out the names. That's sort of what we're doing with topics already with the `mismatch_topic` table, right?

Joe: That's right! We didn't want to store a bunch of duplicate topic names in the `mismatch_response` table, so we put the topic names into the `mismatch_topic` table, and tied topics to responses with numeric keys.

Frank: Are you saying we could solve the duplicate category name problem by creating a new category table?

Jill: That's exactly what he's saying. We can create a new `mismatch_category` table where each category name is stored exactly one time. And then connect categories with topics using primary and foreign keys between `mismatch_topic` and `mismatch_category`. Brilliant!

Strive for a bit of normalcy

The process of redesigning the Mismatch database to eliminate duplicate data and break apart and connect tables in a logical and consistent manner is known as **normalization**. Normalization is a fairly deep database design topic that can be intimidating. But it doesn't have to be. There are enough simple database design techniques we can graft from the basics of normalization to make our MySQL databases much better than if we had just guessed at how data should be laid out.

Here are some very broad steps you can take to begin the database design process that will naturally lead to a more "normal" database:

> **Normalization means designing a database to reduce duplicate data and improve the relationships between data.**

1. **Pick your thing, the one thing you want a table to describe.**

   What's the main thing you want your table to be about?

2. **Make a list of the information you need to know about your one thing when you're using the table.**

   How will you use this table?

3. **Using the list, break down the information about your thing into pieces you can use for organizing the table.**

   How can you most easily query this table?

One fundamental concept in normalization is the idea of **atomic** data, which is data broken down into the smallest form that makes sense given the usage of a database. For example, the `first_name` and `last_name` columns in the Mismatch database are atomic in a sense that they break the user's name down further than a single `name` column would have. This is necessary in Mismatch because we want to be able to refer to a user by first name alone.

It might not always be necessary for an application to break a full name down into separate first and last columns, however, in which case `name` by itself might be atomic enough. So as you're breaking down the "one thing" of a table into pieces, think about **how** the data is going to be used, not just what it represents.

> **Atomic data is data that has been broken down into the smallest form <u>needed</u> for a given database.**

When normalizing, think in atoms

To help turn your database design brainstorms into actions, it's helpful to ask targeted questions of your data. This will help determine how the data fits into a table, and if it has truly been broken down into its appropriate atomic representation. No one ever said splitting the atom was easy, but this list of questions can help.

Making your data atomic is the first step in creating a normal table.

1. What is the one thing your table describes?

Does your table describe alien sightings, email list subscriptions, video game high scores, hopeless romantics?

2. How will you use the table to get at the one thing?

Design your table to be easy to query!

3. Do your columns contain atomic data to make your queries short and to the point?

Make sure data is only as small as it needs to be.

---

there are no Dumb Questions

Q: Should I try to break my data down into the tiniest pieces possible?

A: Not necessarily. Making your data atomic means breaking it down into the smallest pieces that you need to create an efficient table, not just the smallest possible pieces you can.

Don't break down your data any more than you have to. if you don't need extra columns, don't add them just for the sake of it.

Q: How does atomic data help me?

A: It helps you ensure that the data in your table is accurate. For example, if you have a column for the street address of an alien sighting, you might want to break the street address into two columns: the number and the street. Then you can make sure that only numbers end up in the number column.

Atomic data also lets you perform queries more efficiently because the queries are easier to write, and take a shorter amount of time to run, which adds up when you have a massive amount of data stored.

Why be normal, really?

If all this talk about nuclear data and normalcy seems a bit overkill for your modest database, consider what might happen if your web application explodes and becomes the next "big thing." What if your database grows in size by leaps and bounds in a very short period of time, stressing any weaknesses that might be present in the design? You'd rather be out shopping for your new dot-com trophy car than trying to come up with a retroactive Band-aid fix for your data, which is increasingly spiraling out of control. You yearn for some normalcy.

If you still aren't convinced, or if you're stuck daydreaming of that canary yellow McLaren, here are two proven reasons to normalize your databases:

Normalization has its benefits, namely improvements in database <u>size</u> and <u>speed</u>.

1. Normal tables won't have duplicate data, which will reduce the size of your database.

Huge bloated database bad...

Normalized databases tend to be much smaller than databases with inferior designs.

It's like they say, "size is money!"

...small, efficient database good!

2. With less data to search through, your queries will be faster.

Slow queries mired in duplicate data bad...

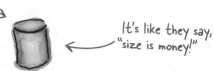

Uh, wait a minute, maybe it's "time is money!"

When it comes to databases, speed is always a good thing.

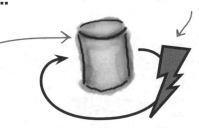

...speedy queries good!

Three steps to a normal database

You've pondered your data for a while and now have a keen appreciation for why it should be normalized, but general ideas only get you so far. What you really need is a concise list of rules that can be applied to any database to ensure normalcy... kinda like a checklist you can work through and use to make sure a database is sufficiently normal. Here goes:

Normalizing a database involves strictly adhering to a series of design steps.

❶ ❷ ❸

❶ Make sure your columns are atomic.

For a column to truly be atomic, there can't be several values of the same type of data in that column. Similarly, there can't be multiple columns with the same type of data.

love	hate
cowboy boots, long hair, reality TV, easy listening music, the opera	tattoos, gold chains, body piercings, professional wrestling, horror movies
...	
tattoos, gold chains, body piercings, cowboy boots, long hair, professional wrestling, horror movies	reality TV, easy listening music, the opera
...	

Several values of the same type of data are in the same column, and there are also multiple columns with the same data... big problem!

❷ Give each table its own primary key.

A primary key is critical for assuring that data in a table can be accessed uniquely. A primary key should be a single column, and ideally be a numeric data type so that queries are as efficient as possible.

username	password	...
dierdre	08447b...	...
baldpaul	230dcb...	...
jnettles	e511d7...	...
rubyr	062e4a...	...
theking	b4f283...	...

Without a primary key, there's no way to ensure uniqueness between the rows in this table.

❸ Make sure non-key columns aren't dependent on each other.

This is the most challenging requirement of normal databases, and one that isn't always worth adhering to strictly. It requires you to look a bit closer at how columns of data within a given table relate to each other. The idea is that changing the value of one column shouldn't necessitate a change in another column.

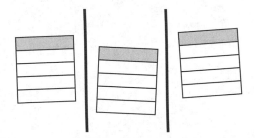

username	password	...	city	state	zip	picture
dierdre	08447b...	...	Cambridge	MA	02138	dierdrepic.jpg
baldpaul	230dcb...	...	Charleston	SC	29401	paulpic.jpg
jnettles	e511d7...	...	Athens	GA	30601	johanpic.jpg
rubyr	062e4a...	...	Conundrum	AZ	85399	rubypic.jpg
theking	b4f283...	...	Tupelo	MS	38801	elmerpic.jpg

The hypothetical ZIP code column is dependent on the city and state columns, meaning that changing one requires changing the others. To resolve the problem, we'll need to break out the user's location into its own table with the ZIP code as the primary key.

Exercise

The Mismatch database is in need of a normalization overhaul to solve the problem of duplicate category names. Given the existing database structure, sketch a modified design that solves the duplicate category problem, eliminating the risk of data entry errors. Make sure to annotate the design to explain how it works.

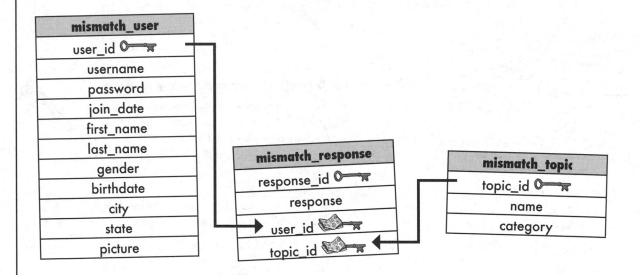

there are no
Dumb Questions

Q: How do I go about applying the third normalization step to Mismatch to fix the hypothetical city/state/ZIP problem?

A: The solution is to break out the location of a user into its own table, and then connect the `mismatch_user` table to the new table via a foreign key. So you might create a table called `mismatch_location` that has a primary key named `location_id`, along with columns to store the city and state for a user, for example. Then the `city` and `state` columns are removed from `mismatch_user` and replaced with a `location_id` foreign key. Problem solved! What makes this design work is that the `location_id` column actually uses the ZIP code as the primary key, alleviating the non-key dependency problem.

Q: Geez, that seems like a lot of work just to meet a picky database design requirement. Is that really necessary?

A: Yes and no. The first two normalization steps really are non-negotiable because atomic data and primary keys are critical to any good database design. It's the third step where you enter the realm of weighing the allure of an impeccable database design against the practical realities of what an application really needs. In the case of the Mismatch city/state/ZIP problem, it's probably worth accepting for the sake of simplicity. This isn't a decision that should be taken lightly, and many database purists would argue that you should rigidly adhere to all three normalization steps. The good news is that the ZIP code column is purely hypothetical, and not actually part of the `mismatch_user` table, so we don't really have to worry about it.

Q: Even without the ZIP code column, wouldn't city and state need to be moved into their own tables to meet the third normalization step?

A: Possibly. It's certainly true that you will end up with duplicate city/state data in the `mismatch_user` table. The problem with breaking out the city and state without a ZIP code is that you would have to somehow populate those tables with every city and state in existence. Otherwise users would no doubt misspell some cities and you'd still end up with problematic data. This is a good example of where you have to seriously weigh the benefits of strict normalization against the realities of a practical application.

An interesting possible solution that solves all of the problems is to use a ZIP code in the `mismatch_user` table instead of a city and state, and then look up the city and state from a static table or some other web service as needed. That's more complexity than we need at the moment, so let's just stick with the `city` and `state` columns.

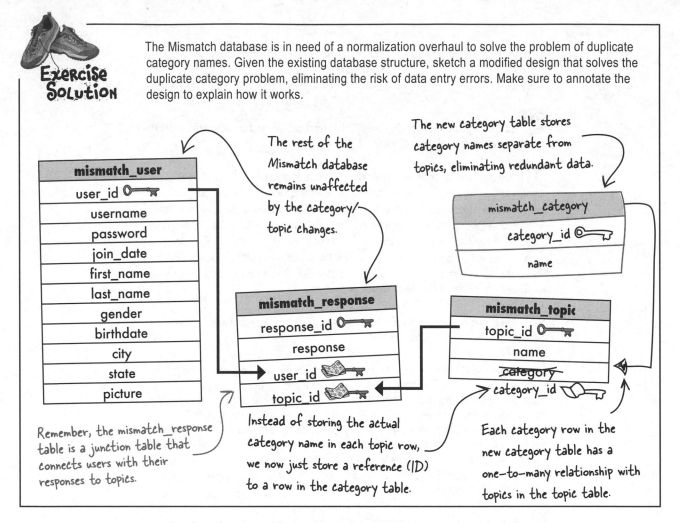

Exercise Solution

The Mismatch database is in need of a normalization overhaul to solve the problem of duplicate category names. Given the existing database structure, sketch a modified design that solves the duplicate category problem, eliminating the risk of data entry errors. Make sure to annotate the design to explain how it works.

The rest of the Mismatch database remains unaffected by the category/topic changes.

The new category table stores category names separate from topics, eliminating redundant data.

mismatch_user
- user_id
- username
- password
- join_date
- first_name
- last_name
- gender
- birthdate
- city
- state
- picture

mismatch_category
- category_id
- name

mismatch_response
- response_id
- response
- user_id
- topic_id

mismatch_topic
- topic_id
- name
- ~~category~~
- category_id

Remember, the mismatch_response table is a junction table that connects users with their responses to topics.

Instead of storing the actual category name in each topic row, we now just store a reference (ID) to a row in the category table.

Each category row in the new category table has a one-to-many relationship with topics in the topic table.

there are no
Dumb Questions

Q: How exactly does the new `mismatch_category` table solve the duplicate data problem?

A: The new table separates category names from the `mismatch_topic` table, allowing them to be stored by themselves. With categories stored in their own table, it's no longer necessary to duplicate their names—you just have a row for each category, and these rows are then referenced by rows in the `mismatch_topic` table. This means that category rows in the `mismatch_category` table have a one-to-many relationship with topic rows in the `mismatch_topic` table.

Q: So does that mean the `mismatch_category` table only has five rows, one for each category?

A: Indeed it does:

mismatch_category

category_id	name
1	Appearance
2	Entertainment
3	Food
4	People
5	Activities

Each category name is only stored once!

Altering the Mismatch database

In order to take advantage of the new schema, the Mismatch database requires some structural changes. More specifically, we need to create a new `mismatch_category` table, and then connect it to a new foreign key in the `mismatch_topic` table. And since the old `category` column in the `mismatch_topic` table with all the duplicate category data is no longer needed, we can drop it.

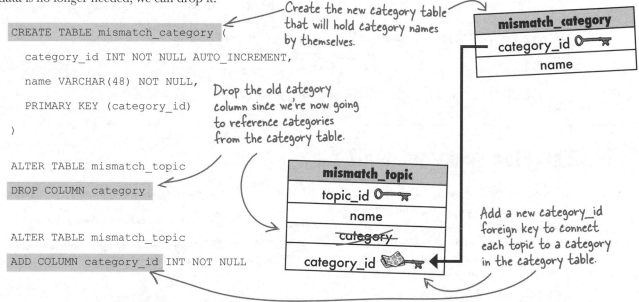

Create the new category table that will hold category names by themselves.

```
CREATE TABLE mismatch_category (

  category_id INT NOT NULL AUTO_INCREMENT,

  name VARCHAR(48) NOT NULL,

  PRIMARY KEY (category_id)

)
```

Drop the old category column since we're now going to reference categories from the category table.

```
ALTER TABLE mismatch_topic

DROP COLUMN category
```

```
ALTER TABLE mismatch_topic

ADD COLUMN category_id INT NOT NULL
```

Add a new category_id foreign key to connect each topic to a category in the category table.

mismatch_category

| category_id |
| name |

mismatch_topic

| topic_id |
| name |
| category |
| category_id |

The new `mismatch_category` table must be populated with category data, which is accomplished with a handful of `INSERT` statements.

```
INSERT INTO mismatch_category (name) VALUES ('Appearance')

INSERT INTO mismatch_category (name) VALUES ('Entertainment')

INSERT INTO mismatch_category (name) VALUES ('Food')

INSERT INTO mismatch_category (name) VALUES ('People')

INSERT INTO mismatch_category (name) VALUES ('Activities')
```

The new `category_id` column must then be populated with data to correctly wire the category of each topic to its appropriate category in the `mismatch_category` table.

```
UPDATE mismatch_topic SET category_id = 3

  WHERE name = 'Martinis'
```

This ID should match the auto-incremented ID for the category from the mismatch_category table.

mismatch_topic

topic_id	name	category_id
...		
8	Horror movies	2
9	Easy listening music	2
10	The opera	2
11	Sushi	3
12	Spam	3
13	Spicy food	3
14	Peanut butter & banana sandwiches	3
15	Martinis	3
16	Howard Stern	4
17	Bill Gates	4
18	Barbara Streisand	4
...		

Test Drive

Create and populate the new `mismatch_category` database table.

Using a MySQL tool, execute the CREATE TABLE SQL command on the previous page to add a new table named `mismatch_category` to the Mismatch database. Then issue the INSERT statements to populate the table with category data. Now run the two ALTER statements to modify the `mismatch_topic` table so that it has a `category_id` column. Finally, UPDATE each row in the `mismatch_topic` table so that its `category_id` column points to the correct category in the `mismatch_category` table.

Now run a SELECT on each of the tables just to make sure everything checks out.

So is Mismatch really normal?

Yes, it is. If you apply the three main rules of normalcy to each of the Mismatch tables, you'll find that it passes with flying colors. But even if it didn't, all would not be lost. Just like people, there are **degrees** of normalcy when it comes to databases. The important thing is to attempt to design databases that are completely normal, only accepting something less when there is a very good reason for skirting the rules.

① Make sure your columns are atomic.

② Give each table its own primary key.

③ Make sure non-key columns aren't dependent on each other.

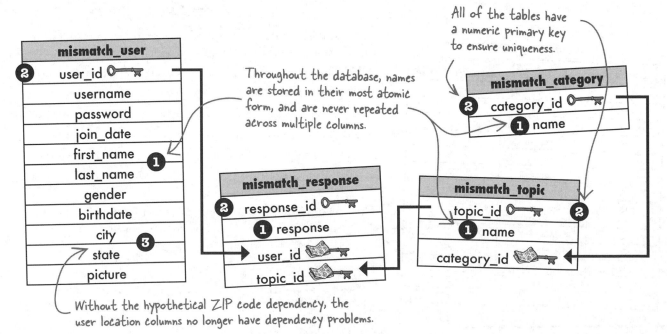

All of the tables have a numeric primary key to ensure uniqueness.

Throughout the database, names are stored in their most atomic form, and are never repeated across multiple columns.

Without the hypothetical ZIP code dependency, the user location columns no longer have dependency problems.

Doesn't the new Mismatch table design affect the queries that are being made in the questionnaire script code?

mismatch_category

category_id

name

```
...
// Grab the response data from the database to generate the form
$query = "SELECT response_id, topic_id, response FROM mismatch_response " .
  "WHERE user_id = '" . $_SESSION['user_id'] . "'";
$data = mysqli_query($dbc, $query);
$responses = array();
while ($row = mysqli_fetch_array($data)) {
  // Look up the topic name for the response from the topic table
  $query2 = "SELECT name, category FROM mismatch_topic " .
    "WHERE topic_id = '" . $row['topic_id'] . "'";
  $data2 = mysqli_query($dbc, $query2);
  if (mysqli_num_rows($data2) == 1) {
    $row2 = mysqli_fetch_array($data2);
    $row['topic_name'] = $row2['name'];
    $row['category_name'] = $row2['category'];
    array_push($responses, $row);
  }
}
...
```

questionnaire.php

Yes. In fact, most structural database changes require us to tweak any queries involving affected tables.

In this case, changing the database design to add the new `mismatch_category` table affects any query involving the `mismatch_topic` table. This is because the previous database design had categories stored directly in the `mismatch_topic` table. With categories broken out into their own table, which we now know is a great idea thanks to normalization, it becomes necessary to revisit the queries and code them to work with an additional table (`mismatch_category`).

A query within a query within a query...

One problem brought on by normalizing a database is that queries often require subqueries since you're having to reach for data in multiple tables. This can get messy. Consider the new version of the query that builds the response array to generate the Mismatch questionnaire form:

More tables usually lead to messier queries.

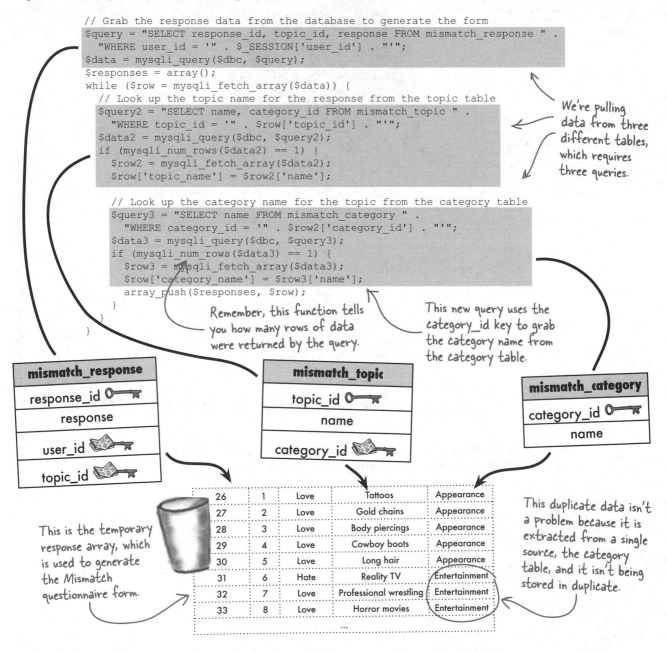

```php
// Grab the response data from the database to generate the form
$query = "SELECT response_id, topic_id, response FROM mismatch_response " .
  "WHERE user_id = '" . $_SESSION['user_id'] . "'";
$data = mysqli_query($dbc, $query);
$responses = array();
while ($row = mysqli_fetch_array($data)) {
  // Look up the topic name for the response from the topic table
  $query2 = "SELECT name, category_id FROM mismatch_topic " .
    "WHERE topic_id = '" . $row['topic_id'] . "'";
  $data2 = mysqli_query($dbc, $query2);
  if (mysqli_num_rows($data2) == 1) {
    $row2 = mysqli_fetch_array($data2);
    $row['topic_name'] = $row2['name'];

    // Look up the category name for the topic from the category table
    $query3 = "SELECT name FROM mismatch_category " .
      "WHERE category_id = '" . $row2['category_id'] . "'";
    $data3 = mysqli_query($dbc, $query3);
    if (mysqli_num_rows($data3) == 1) {
      $row3 = mysqli_fetch_array($data3);
      $row['category_name'] = $row3['name'];
      array_push($responses, $row);
    }
  }
}
```

We're pulling data from three different tables, which requires three queries.

Remember, this function tells you how many rows of data were returned by the query.

This new query uses the category_id key to grab the category name from the category table.

mismatch_response

| response_id 🔑 |
| response |
| user_id 🔑 |
| topic_id 🔑 |

mismatch_topic

| topic_id 🔑 |
| name |
| category_id 🔑 |

mismatch_category

| category_id 🔑 |
| name |

This is the temporary response array, which is used to generate the Mismatch questionnaire form.

26	1	Love	Tattoos	Appearance
27	2	Love	Gold chains	Appearance
28	3	Love	Body piercings	Appearance
29	4	Love	Cowboy boots	Appearance
30	5	Love	Long hair	Appearance
31	6	Hate	Reality TV	Entertainment
32	7	Love	Professional wrestling	Entertainment
33	8	Love	Horror movies	Entertainment
...

This duplicate data isn't a problem because it is extracted from a single source, the category table, and it isn't being stored in duplicate.

Let's all join ~~hands~~ tables

Yikes! Can anything be done about all those nested queries? The solution lies in an SQL feature known as a **join**, which lets us retrieve results from more than one table in a single query. There are lots of different kinds of joins, but the most popular join, an **inner join**, selects rows from two tables based on a condition. In an inner join, query results only include rows where this condition is matched.

> **A join grabs results from multiple tables in a single query.**

The topic ID and category name are selected by the query — these columns are in two different tables.

```
SELECT mismatch_topic.topic_id, mismatch_category.name

   FROM mismatch_topic

   INNER JOIN mismatch_category

   ON (mismatch_topic.category_id = mismatch_category.category_id)
```

The category table is joined to the topic table via an INNER JOIN.

The condition for the join is that the category ID must match for each row of data returned.

mismatch_topic

topic_id	name	category_id
1	Tattoos	1
2	Gold chains	1
3	Body piercings	1
4	Cowboy boots	1
5	Long hair	1
6	Reality TV	2
7	Professional wrestling	2
8	Horror movies	2
9	Easy listening music	2
10	The opera	2
11	Sushi	3
	...	

This column controls the join!

mismatch_category

category_id	name
1	Appearance
2	Entertainment
3	Food
4	People
5	Activities

1	Appearance
2	Appearance
3	Appearance
4	Appearance
5	Appearance
6	Entertainment
7	Entertainment
8	Entertainment
	...

The second column of the results holds category names from the category table that match up with each topic ID.

The first column of results consists of topic IDs from the topic table.

The resulting data contains columns from both tables!

This inner join successfully merges data from two tables that would've previously required two separate queries. The query results consist of columns of data from both tables.

Connect ~~the~~ with dots

Since joins involve more than one table, it's important to be clear about each column referenced in a join. More specifically, you must identify the table for each column so that there isn't any confusion—tables often have columns with the same names, especially when it comes to keys. Just preface the column name with the table name, and a dot. For example, here's the previous INNER JOIN query that builds a result set of topic IDs and category names:

> Dot notation allows you to reference the table a column belongs to within a join.

This is the name of the table.

The dot!

This is the name of the column within the table, separated from the table name by a dot (period).

```
SELECT mismatch_topic.topic_id, mismatch_category.name

   FROM mismatch_topic

   INNER JOIN mismatch_category

   ON (mismatch_topic.category_id = mismatch_category.category_id)
```

Here's another table/column reference that uses the dot notation.

This is where the dot really pays off – the column names are identical, resulting in total ambiguity without the table names.

Without the ability to specify the tables associated with the columns in this query, we'd have quite a bit of ambiguity. In fact, it would be impossible to understand the ON part of the query because it would be checking to see if the category_id column equals itself, presumably within the mismatch_topic table. For this reason, it's always a good idea to be very explicit about identifying the tables associated with columns when building JOIN queries.

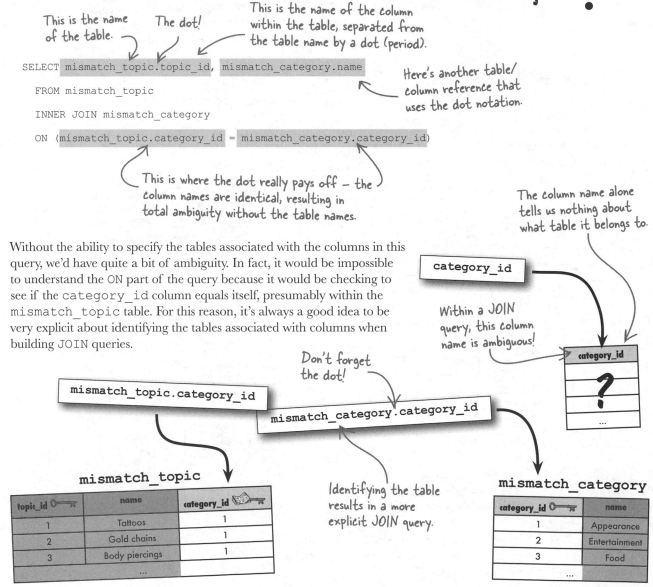

The column name alone tells us nothing about what table it belongs to.

category_id

Within a JOIN query, this column name is ambiguous!

category_id
?
...

Don't forget the dot!

mismatch_topic.category_id

mismatch_category.category_id

Identifying the table results in a more explicit JOIN query.

mismatch_topic

topic_id	name	category_id
1	Tattoos	1
2	Gold chains	1
3	Body piercings	1
...		

mismatch_category

category_id	name
1	Appearance
2	Entertainment
3	Food
...	

Surely we can do more with inner joins

Inner joins don't stop at just combining data from two tables. Since an inner join is ultimately just a query, you can still use normal query constructs to further control the results. For example, if you want to grab a specific row from the set of joined results, you can hang a WHERE statement on the INNER JOIN query to isolate just that row.

An **INNER JOIN** combines rows from two tables using comparison operators in a condition.

```
SELECT mismatch_topic.topic_id, mismatch_category.name

  FROM mismatch_topic

  INNER JOIN mismatch_category

  ON (mismatch_topic.category_id = mismatch_category.category_id)

  WHERE mismatch_topic.name = 'Horror movies'
```

So what exactly does this query return? First remember that the WHERE clause serves as a refinement of the previous query. In other words, it **further constrains** the rows returned by the original INNER JOIN query . As a recap, here are the results of the inner join **without** the WHERE clause:

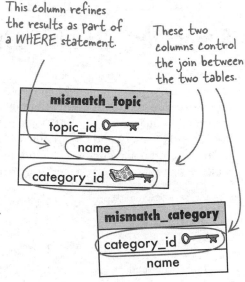

This column refines the results as part of a WHERE statement.

These two columns control the join between the two tables.

Topic IDs are extracted from the mismatch_topic table.

Category names are pulled from the mismatch_category table.

The WHERE clause has the effect of whittling down this result set to a single row, the row whose topic name equals 'Horror movies'. We have to look back at the mismatch_topic table to see which row this is.

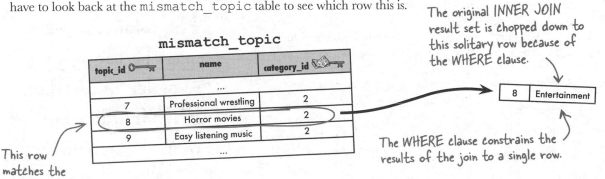

This row matches the WHERE clause.

The original INNER JOIN result set is chopped down to this solitary row because of the WHERE clause.

The WHERE clause constrains the results of the join to a single row.

there are no Dumb Questions

Q: So a WHERE clause lets you constrain the results of a JOIN query based on rows in one of the joined tables?

A: That's correct. Keep in mind that the actual comparison taking place inside a WHERE clause applies to the **original tables**, not the query results. So in the case of the Mismatch example, the query is retrieving data from two different tables that match on a certain column that appears in both tables (category_id), and then only selecting the row where the name column in mismatch_topic is a certain value ('Horror movies'). So the INNER JOIN takes place with respect to the category_id column in, **both tables** but the WHERE clause refines the results using only the name column in the mismatch_topic table.

Q: Could the WHERE clause in the Mismatch JOIN query be based on the mismatch_category table instead?

A: Absolutely. The WHERE clause can restrict query results based on either of the tables involved in the join. As an example, the WHERE clause could be changed to look only for a specific category, like this:

```
... WHERE mismatch_category.name = 'Entertainment'
```

This WHERE clause limits the result set to only include topics that fall under the Entertainment category. So the WHERE clause doesn't affect the manner in which the tables are joined, but it does affect the specific rows returned by the query.

Simplifying ON with USING

Remember that our goal is to simplify the messy Mismatch queries with INNER JOIN. When an inner join involves **matching columns with the same name**, we can further simplify the query with the help of the USING statement. The USING statement takes the place of ON in an INNER JOIN query, and requires the name of the column to be used in the match. Just make sure the column is named exactly the same in both tables. As an example, here's the Mismatch query again:

```
SELECT mismatch_topic.topic_id, mismatch_category.name

    FROM mismatch_topic

    INNER JOIN mismatch_category

    ON (mismatch_topic.category_id = mismatch_category.category_id)

    WHERE mismatch_topic.name = 'Horror movies'
```

The name of each of the columns is the same — only the tables are different.

> **Rewrite ON with USING for more concise inner join queries that match on a common column.**

Since the ON part of the query relies on columns with the same name (category_id), it can be simplified with a USING statement:

```
SELECT mismatch_topic.topic_id, mismatch_category.name

    FROM mismatch_topic

    INNER JOIN mismatch_category

    USING (category_id)

    WHERE mismatch_topic.name = 'Horror movies'
```

All that is required is the name of the column... no need to specify equality with =.

> **The column names must be the same in order to use the USING statement in an inner join.**

Nicknames for tables and columns

Our INNER JOIN query just keeps getting tighter! Let's take it one step further. When it comes to SQL queries, it's standard to refer to table and columns by their names as they appear in the database. But this can be cumbersome in larger queries that involve joins with multiple tables—the names can actually make a query tough to read. It's sometimes worthwhile to employ an **alias**, which is a temporary name used to refer to a table or column in a query. Let's rewrite the Mismatch query using aliases.

An alias allows you to <u>rename</u> a table or column within a query to help simplify the query in some way.

```
SELECT mt.topic_id, mc.name
  FROM mismatch_topic AS mt
  INNER JOIN mismatch_category AS mc
  USING (category_id)
  WHERE mt.name = 'Horror movies'
```

The code becomes a bit easier to read with the table names condensed into smaller aliases.

The AS keyword in SQL creates an alias, in this case for the mismatch_topic table.

The mismatch_category can now be referred to simply as "mc" thanks to this alias.

Any reference to the mismatch_topic table can now be shortened to "mt".

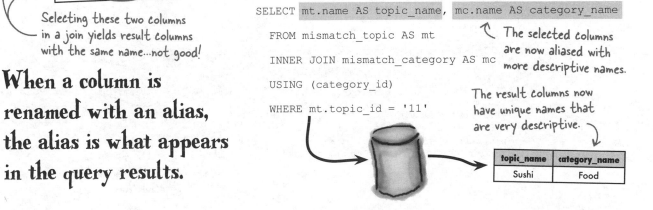

Selecting these two columns in a join yields result columns with the same name...not good!

When a column is renamed with an alias, the alias is what appears in the query results.

Are aliases only good for writing more compact queries? No, there are some situations where they're downright essential! A join that would be quite handy in the Mismatch application is retrieving both the topic name and category name for a given topic ID. But the `mismatch_topic` and `mismatch_category` tables use the same column name (`name`) for this data. This is a problem because the result of combining these two columns would leave us with ambiguous column names. But we can rename the result columns to be more descriptive with aliases.

```
SELECT mt.name AS topic_name, mc.name AS category_name
  FROM mismatch_topic AS mt
  INNER JOIN mismatch_category AS mc
  USING (category_id)
  WHERE mt.topic_id = '11'
```

The selected columns are now aliased with more descriptive names.

The result columns now have unique names that are very descriptive.

topic_name	category_name
Sushi	Food

Joins to the rescue

So joins make it possible to involve more than one table in a query, effectively pulling data from more than one place and sticking it in a single result table. The Mismatch query that builds a response array is a perfect candidate for joins since it contains no less than three nested queries for dealing with multiple tables. Let's start with the original code:

Joins are more efficient and require less code than nested queries.

```php
// Grab the response data from the database to generate the form
$query = "SELECT response_id, topic_id, response FROM mismatch_response " .
  "WHERE user_id = '" . $_SESSION['user_id'] . "'";
$data = mysqli_query($dbc, $query);
$responses = array();
while ($row = mysqli_fetch_array($data)) {
  // Look up the topic name for the response from the topic table
  $query2 = "SELECT name, category_id FROM mismatch_topic " .
    "WHERE topic_id = '" . $row['topic_id'] . "'";
  $data2 = mysqli_query($dbc, $query2);
  if (mysqli_num_rows($data2) == 1) {
    $row2 = mysqli_fetch_array($data2);
    $row['topic_name'] = $row2['name'];

    // Look up the category name for the topic from the category table
    $query3 = "SELECT name FROM mismatch_category " .
      "WHERE category_id = '" . $row2['category_id'] . "'";
    $data3 = mysqli_query($dbc, $query3);
    if (mysqli_num_rows($data3) == 1) {
      $row3 = mysqli_fetch_array($data3);
      $row['category_name'] = $row3['name'];
      array_push($responses, $row);
    }
  }
}
```

The last two queries in the code are responsible for obtaining the topic name and category name from their respective tables — one query per table.

And here's the new version of the code that uses a join:

```php
// Grab the response data from the database to generate the form
$query = "SELECT response_id, topic_id, response FROM mismatch_response " .
  "WHERE user_id = '" . $_SESSION['user_id'] . "'";
$data = mysqli_query($dbc, $query);
$responses = array();
while ($row = mysqli_fetch_array($data)) {
  // Look up the topic and category names for the response from the topic and category tables
  $query2 = "SELECT mt.name AS topic_name, mc.name AS category_name " .
    "FROM mismatch_topic AS mt " .
    "INNER JOIN mismatch_category AS mc USING (category_id) " .
    "WHERE mt.topic_id = '" . $row['topic_id'] . "'";
  $data2 = mysqli_query($dbc, $query2);
  if (mysqli_num_rows($data2) == 1) {
    $row2 = mysqli_fetch_array($data2);
    $row['topic_name'] = $row2['topic_name'];
    $row['category_name'] = $row2['category_name'];
    array_push($responses, $row);
  }
}
```

With a join, it's possible to grab both the topic name and category name in a single query.

Aliases are used to help simplify the code.

The topic ID is used as the basis for the main query, but the category ID controls the join itself.

I don't get it, you still have an extra query that looks up the category name. If joins are so great, why do you still need two queries?

We don't still need two queries, at least not if we use joins to their full potential.

It is possible to join more than two tables, which is what is truly required of the Mismatch response array code. We need a single query that accomplishes the following three things: retrieve all of the responses for the user, get the topic name for each response, and then get the category name for each response. The new and improved code on the facing page accomplishes the last two steps in a single query involving a join between the `mismatch_topic` and `mismatch_category` tables. Ideally, a single query with two joins would kill all three birds with one big join-shaped stone.

Exercise

Following is code that is capable of retrieving response data from the database with one query, thanks to the clever usage of joins. Be clever and write the SQL query that does the joining between the `mismatch_response`, `mismatch_topic`, and `mismatch_category` tables.

```
// Grab the response data from the database to generate the form
$query = ........................................................................
........................................................................
........................................................................
........................................................................
........................................................................
........................................................................
$data = mysqli_query($dbc, $query);
$responses = array();
while ($row = mysqli_fetch_array($data)) {
  array_push($responses, $row);
}
```

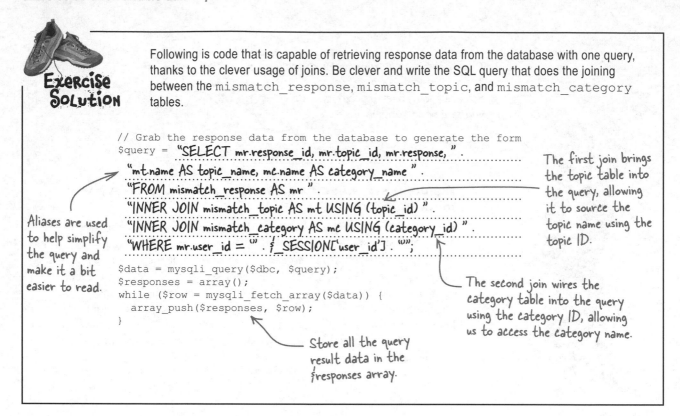

Following is code that is capable of retrieving response data from the database with one query, thanks to the clever usage of joins. Be clever and write the SQL query that does the joining between the `mismatch_response`, `mismatch_topic`, and `mismatch_category` tables.

Exercise Solution

```
// Grab the response data from the database to generate the form
$query = "SELECT mr.response_id, mr.topic_id, mr.response, " .
    "mt.name AS topic_name, mc.name AS category_name " .
    "FROM mismatch_response AS mr " .
    "INNER JOIN mismatch_topic AS mt USING (topic_id) " .
    "INNER JOIN mismatch_category AS mc USING (category_id) " .
    "WHERE mr.user_id = '" . $_SESSION['user_id'] . "'";
$data = mysqli_query($dbc, $query);
$responses = array();
while ($row = mysqli_fetch_array($data)) {
    array_push($responses, $row);
}
```

Aliases are used to help simplify the query and make it a bit easier to read.

The first join brings the topic table into the query, allowing it to source the topic name using the topic ID.

The second join wires the category table into the query using the category ID, allowing us to access the category name.

Store all the query result data in the $responses array.

there are no Dumb Questions

Q: **What other kinds of joins are there?**

A: Other types of inner joins include equijoins, non-equijoins, and natural joins. Equijoins and non-equijoins perform an inner join based on an equality or inequality comparison, respectively. You've already seen several examples of equijoins in the Mismatch queries that check for matching `topic_id` and `category_id` columns. Since the matching involves looking for "equal" columns (the same ID), these queries are considered equijoins.

Another kind of inner join is a natural join, which involves comparing all columns that have the same name between two tables. So a natural join is really just an equijoin, in which the columns used to determine the join are automatically chosen. This automatic aspect of natural joins makes them a little less desirable than normal inner joins because it isn't obvious by looking at them what is going on— you have to look at the database structure to know what columns are being used in the join.

Q: **So all SQL joins are really just variations of inner joins?**

A: No, there are lots of other joins at your disposal. The other major classification of joins is collectively called **outer joins**, but there are several different kinds of joins that are considered outer joins. There are **left** outer joins, **right** outer joins, **full** outer joins, and the seldom used but awe-inspiring triple helix ambidextrous join. OK, that last one isn't a real join, but it should be! The basic idea behind an outer join is that rows in the joined tables don't have to match in order to make it into the join. So it's possible to construct outer joins that always result in rows from a table being selected regardless of any matching conditions.

Outer joins can be just as handy as inner joins, depending on the specific needs of a database application. To learn more about the different kinds of joins and how they are used, take a look at *Head First SQL*.

TEST DRIVE

Revamp the Questionnaire script to grab the user's response data with a single query.

Modify the `questionnaire.php` script to use inner joins so that the queries that grab the user's response data are handled in a single query. Upload the new script to your web server, and then navigate to the questionnaire in a web browser. If all goes well, you shouldn't notice any difference... but deep down you know the script code is much better built!

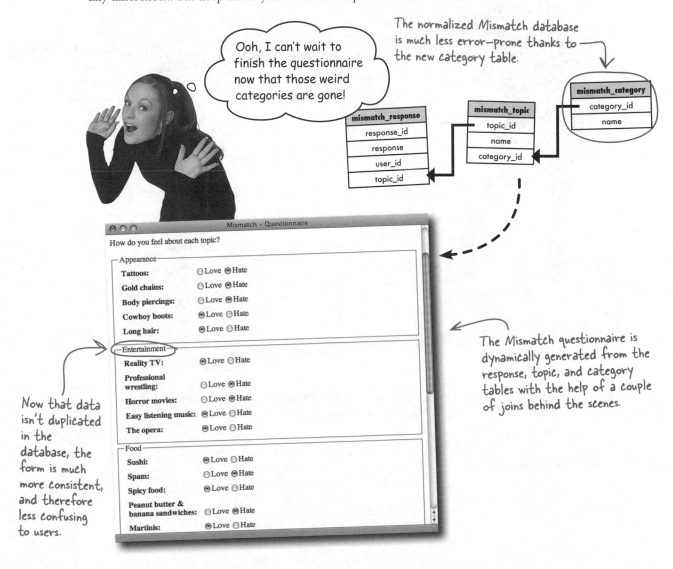

Ooh, I can't wait to finish the questionnaire now that those weird categories are gone!

The normalized Mismatch database is much less error-prone thanks to the new category table.

Now that data isn't duplicated in the database, the form is much more consistent, and therefore less confusing to users.

The Mismatch questionnaire is dynamically generated from the response, topic, and category tables with the help of a couple of joins behind the scenes.

Mismatch now remembers user responses but it doesn't yet do anything with them...like finding a mismatch!

The collection of user response data only gets us halfway to a successful mismatch. The Mismatch application is still missing a mechanism for firing Cupid's arrow into the database to find a love connection. This involves somehow examining the responses for all the users in the database to see who matches up as an ideal mismatch.

Figuring out an ideal mismatch sounds pretty complicated given all those categories, topics, and responses. Are you sure that's really doable?

It's definitely doable; we just need a consistent means of calculating how many mismatched topics any two users share.

If we come up with a reasonably simple way to calculate how many mismatched topics any two users share, then it becomes possible to loop through the user database comparing users. The person with the highest number of mismatches for any given user is that user's ideal mismatch!

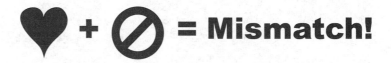

Write down how you would go about calculating the "mismatchability" of two users using data stored in the Mismatch database:

....

....

....

Love is a numbers game

If you recall, mismatch responses are stored in the `mismatch_response` table as numbers, with 0, 1, and 2 all having special meaning in regard to a specific response.

Unknown = 0   Love = 1   Hate = 2

This is the data used to calculate a mismatch between two users, and what we're looking for specifically is a love matching up with a hate or a hate matching up with a love. In other words, we're looking for response rows where `response` is either a 1 matched against a 2 or a 2 matched against a 1.

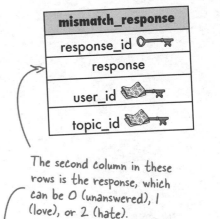

mismatch_response

response_id

response

user_id

topic_id

The second column in these rows is the response, which can be 0 (unanswered), 1 (love), or 2 (hate).

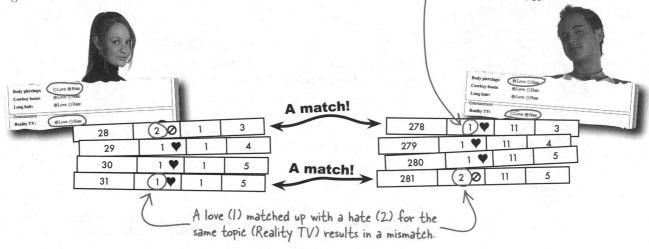

A match!

A match!

A love (1) matched up with a hate (2) for the same topic (Reality TV) results in a mismatch.

We're still missing a handy way in PHP code to determine when a mismatch takes place between two responses. Certainly a couple of `if-else` statements could be hacked together to check for a 1 and a 2, and then a 2 and a 1, but the solution can be more elegant than that. In either scenario, adding together the two responses results in a value of 3. So we can use a simple equation to detect a mismatch between two responses.

If ResponseA + ResponseB = 3, we have a mismatch!

So finding a love connection really does boil down to simple math. That solves the specifics of comparing individual matches, but it doesn't address the larger problem of how to actually build the My Mismatch script.

Five steps to a successful mismatch

Finding that perfectly mismatched someone isn't just a matter of comparing response rows. The My Mismatch script has to follow a set of carefully orchestrated steps in order to successfully make a mismatch. These steps hold the key to finally satisfying users and bringing meaning to their questionnaire responses.

1 Grab the user's responses from the `mismatch_response` table, making sure to join the topic names with the results.

2 Initialize the mismatch search results, including the variables that keep up with the "best mismatch."

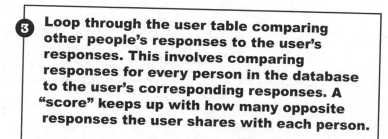

3 Loop through the user table comparing other people's responses to the user's responses. This involves comparing responses for every person in the database to the user's corresponding responses. A "score" keeps up with how many opposite responses the user shares with each person.

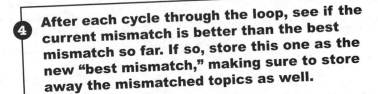

4 After each cycle through the loop, see if the current mismatch is better than the best mismatch so far. If so, store this one as the new "best mismatch," making sure to store away the mismatched topics as well.

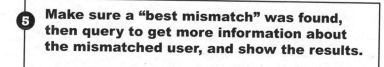

5 Make sure a "best mismatch" was found, then query to get more information about the mismatched user, and show the results.

Prepare for the mismatch search

Step 1 falls under familiar territory since we've already written some queries that perform a join like this. But we need to store away the user's responses so that we can compare them to the responses of other users later in the script (Step 3). The following code builds an array, $user_responses, that contains the responses for the logged in user.

This query uses a JOIN to select all of the responses for the user.

```
$query = "SELECT mr.response_id, mr.topic_id, mr.response, mt.name
AS topic_name " .

  "FROM mismatch_response AS mr " .

  "INNER JOIN mismatch_topic AS mt " .

  "USING (topic_id) " .

  "WHERE mr.user_id = '" . $_SESSION['user_id'] . "'";
$data = mysqli_query($dbc, $query);

$user_responses = array();

while ($row = mysqli_fetch_array($data)) {

  array_push($user_responses, $row);

}
```

A while loop is used to go through each row of the query results, building an array of user responses in the process.

When this loop finishes, the $user_responses array will hold all of the user's responses.

DONE

① Grab the user's responses from the `mismatch_response` table, making sure to join the topic names with the results.

Step 2 of the My Mismatch script construction process involves setting up some variables that will hold the results of the mismatch search. These variables will be used throughout the My Mismatch script as the search for the best mismatch is carried out:

```
$mismatch_score = 0;

$mismatch_user_id = -1;

$mismatch_topics = array();
```

This variable holds the mismatch score between two users — the highest score ultimately results in a mismatch.

This is the user ID of the person who is being checked as a potential mismatch... when the search is complete, this variable holds the ID of the best mismatch.

This array holds the topics that are mismatched between two users.

If this variable is still set to -1 after the search, we know there wasn't a mismatch — this can only happen when no other users have answered the questionnaire, which is very unlikely.

DONE

② Initialize the mismatch search results, including the variables that keep up with the "best mismatch."

Compare users for "mismatchiness"

The next mismatching step requires looping through every user, and comparing their responses to the responses of the logged in user. In other words, we're taking the logged in user, or **mismatcher** (Sidney, for example), and going through the entire user table comparing her responses to those of each **mismatchee**. We're looking for the mismatchee with the most responses that are opposite of the mismatcher.

Where to begin? How about a loop that steps through the $user_responses array (mismatcher responses)? Inside the loop we compare the value of each element with comparable elements in another array that holds the mismatchee responses. Let's call the second array $mismatch_responses.

This array holds responses from the logged in user, the mismatcher.

This array holds responses from another user in the database, the mismatchee.

This array changes as the mismatcher is compared to different mismatchees.

$user_responses

1	1	Hate	Tattoos
2	2	Hate	Gold chains
3	3	Hate	Body piercings
4	4	Love	Cowboy boots
5	5	Love	Long hair
6	6	Love	Reality TV
7	7	Hate	Professional wrestling
8	8	Hate	Horror movies
		...	

$mismatch_responses

76	1	Love	Tattoos
77	2	Love	Gold chains
78	3	Love	Body piercings
79	4	Love	Cowboy boots
80	5	Love	Long hair
81	6	Hate	Reality TV
82	7	Love	Professional wrestling
83	8	Love	Horror movies
		...	

We need to loop through these two arrays simultaneously, comparing responses to the same topics to see if they are the same or different.

The challenge here is that we need a loop that essentially loops through two arrays at the same time, comparing respective elements one-to-one. A foreach loop won't work because it can only loop through a single array, and we need to loop through two arrays **simultaneously**. A while loop could work, but we'd have to create a counter variable and manually increment it each time through the loop. Ideally, we need a loop that automatically takes care of managing a counter variable so that we can use it to access elements in each array.

~~foreach (...) {~~

Won't work!

while (...) {

Could work, but not exactly ideal.

All we need is a FOR loop

PHP offers another type of loop that offers exactly the functionality we need for the My Mismatch response comparisons. It's called a `for` loop, and it's great for repeating something a certain amount of **known** times. For example, `for` loops are great for counting tasks, such as counting down to zero or counting up to some value. Here's the structure of a `for` loop, which reveals how a loop can be structured to step through an array using a loop counter variable (`$i`).

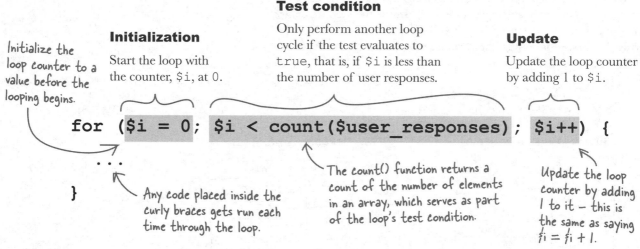

Initialize the loop counter to a value before the looping begins.

Initialization

Start the loop with the counter, `$i`, at 0.

Test condition

Only perform another loop cycle if the test evaluates to `true`, that is, if `$i` is less than the number of user responses.

Update

Update the loop counter by adding 1 to `$i`.

```
for ($i = 0; $i < count($user_responses); $i++) {

   ...

}
```

Any code placed inside the curly braces gets run each time through the loop.

The count() function returns a count of the number of elements in an array, which serves as part of the loop's test condition.

Update the loop counter by adding 1 to it — this is the same as saying $i = $i + 1.

Exercise

Step 3 of the My Mismatch script involves comparing two users by looping through each of their responses, and calculating a "score" based on how many responses are mismatched. Given the following pieces of data, finish writing the `for` loop that calculates this score.

`$user_responses`

The array of responses for the user.

`$mismatch_responses`

The array of responses for the potential mismatched user.

`$score`

The mismatch score to be calculated inside the loop.

```
for ($i = 0; $i < count($user_responses); $i++) {

  if ( ..........................................  + ...........................................  == ....... ) {

    ......................

    array_push($topics, $user_responses[$i]['topic_name']);

  }

}
```

Q: Why not just use a `foreach` loop to calculate the score instead of a `for` loop?

A: Although a `foreach` loop would work perfectly fine for looping through all of the different responses, it wouldn't provide you with an index (`$i`) at any given iteration through the loop. This index is important because the code is using it to access both the array of user responses and the array of mismatch responses. A `foreach` loop would eliminate the need for an index for one of the two arrays, but not both. So we need a regular `for` loop with an index that can be used to access similar elements of each array.

Q: What's the purpose of storing the mismatched responses in their own array?

A: The array of mismatched responses is important in letting the users know exactly how they compared topically with their ideal mismatch. It's not enough to just share the identity of the ideal mismatch person—what is even better is also sharing the specific topics the user mismatched against that person. This helps give the mismatch result a little more context, and lets the users know a bit more about why this particular person is truly such a great mismatch for them.

Q: In Step 5 of the Mismatch script, how would there ever not be a best mismatch for any given user?

A: Although unlikely, you have to consider the scenario where there is only one user in the entire system, in which case there would be no one else to mismatch that user against.

ExerCise SoLution

Step 3 of the My Mismatch script involves comparing two users by looping through each of their responses, and calculating a "score" based on how many responses are mismatched. Given the following pieces of data, finish writing the `for` loop that calculates this score.

$user_responses

1	1	Hate	Tattoos
2	2	Hate	Gold chains
3	3	Hate	Body piercings
4	4	Love	Cowboy boots
5	5	Love	Long hair
6	6	Love	Reality TV
7	7	Hate	Professional wrestling
8	8	Hate	Horror movies
...			

$mismatch_responses

76	1	Love	Tattoos
77	2	Love	Gold chains
78	3	Love	Body piercings
79	4	Love	Cowboy boots
80	5	Love	Long hair
81	6	Hate	Reality TV
82	7	Love	Professional wrestling
83	8	Love	Horror movies
...			

$score

The $score variable ends up being in the range 0 (no mismatches) to the total number of topics (complete mismatch).

Remember, the number of user responses is the same as the number of total topics since the responses come straight from the questionnaire.

The score is incremented for each mismatched response found.

```
for ($i = 0; $i < count($user_responses); $i++) {
    if ( $user_responses[$i]['response']  +  $mismatch_responses[$i]['response']  ==  3 ) {
        $score += 1;
        array_push($topics, $user_responses[$i]['topic_name']);
    }
}
```

The loop counter is used to step through each user response.

Each mismatched topic is added to an array so that it can be displayed to the user when revealing the mismatch.

A mismatch consists of a love (1) matched with a hate (2), so adding them together always results in a 3 if there is a mismatch.

DONE

③ **Loop through the user table comparing other people's responses to the user's responses.**

Finishing the mismatching

The shiny new loop that calculates a mismatch score is part of a larger script (`mymismatch.php`) that takes care of finding a user's ideal mismatch in the Mismatch database, and then displaying the information.

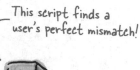

This script finds a user's perfect mismatch!

mymismatch.php

```
...

// Only look for a mismatch if the user has questionnaire responses stored

$query = "SELECT * FROM mismatch_response WHERE user_id = '" . $_SESSION['user_id'] . "'";

$data = mysqli_query($dbc, $query);

if (mysqli_num_rows($data) != 0) {
```

It's only possible to find a mismatch for a user who has responded to the questionnaire.

```
  // First grab the user's responses from the response table (JOIN to get the topic name)

  $query = "SELECT mr.response_id, mr.topic_id, mr.response, mt.name AS topic_name " .

    "FROM mismatch_response AS mr " .

❶  "INNER JOIN mismatch_topic AS mt " .

    "USING (topic_id) " .

    "WHERE mr.user_id = '" . $_SESSION['user_id'] . "'";

  $data = mysqli_query($dbc, $query);

  $user_responses = array();

  while ($row = mysqli_fetch_array($data)) {

    array_push($user_responses, $row);

  }
```

A familiar JOIN is used to retrieve the topic name when SELECTing the user's questionnaire responses.

The $user_responses array holds all of the responses for the user.

```
  // Initialize the mismatch search results

  $mismatch_score = 0;

❷  $mismatch_user_id = -1;

  $mismatch_topics = array();

...
```

These variables keep track of the mismatch search as it progresses.

Hang on, there's plenty more – turn the page!

```
// Loop through the user table comparing other people's responses to the user's responses
$query = "SELECT user_id FROM mismatch_user WHERE user_id != '" . $_SESSION['user_id'] . "'";
$data = mysqli_query($dbc, $query);
while ($row = mysqli_fetch_array($data)) {
  // Grab the response data for the user (a potential mismatch)
  $query2 = "SELECT response_id, topic_id, response FROM mismatch_response " .
    "WHERE user_id = '" . $row['user_id'] . "'";
  $data2 = mysqli_query($dbc, $query2);
  $mismatch_responses = array();
  while ($row2 = mysqli_fetch_array($data2)) {
    array_push($mismatch_responses, $row2);
  }

  // Compare each response and calculate a mismatch total
  $score = 0;
  $topics = array();
  for ($i = 0; $i < count($user_responses); $i++) {
    if (((int)$user_responses[$i]['response']) + ((int)$mismatch_responses[$i]['response']) == 3) {
      $score += 1;
      array_push($topics, $user_responses[$i]['topic_name']);
    }
  }

  // Check to see if this person is better than the best mismatch so far
  if ($score > $mismatch_score) {
    // We found a better mismatch, so update the mismatch search results
    $mismatch_score = $score;
    $mismatch_user_id = $row['user_id'];
    $mismatch_topics = array_slice($topics, 0);
  }
}
...
```

This query grabs all of the users except the user being mismatched.

3 For each user, this query grabs the questionnaire responses for comparing as a potential mismatch.

This curly brace marks the end of the main while loop.

Here's the for loop that calculates the mismatch score for a potential mismatch.

The text response ('2', for example) is cast to an integer (2) so that it can be added and compared

DONE

4 If this user is a better mismatch than the best mismatch so far, then set him as the best mismatch.

This function extracts a "slice" of an array. In this case we're just using it to copy the $topics array into $mismatch_topics.

We're still inside that first if statement from the previous page, and there's still more code...

```
// Make sure a mismatch was found
if ($mismatch_user_id != -1) {
```

Before displaying the mismatch results, make sure a "best mismatch" was actually found.

```
  $query = "SELECT username, first_name, last_name, city, state, picture FROM mismatch_user " .
    "WHERE user_id = '$mismatch_user_id'";
  $data = mysqli_query($dbc, $query);
```

Query for the mismatched user's information so we can display it.

```
  if (mysqli_num_rows($data) == 1) {
    // The user row for the mismatch was found, so display the user data
    $row = mysqli_fetch_array($data);
    echo '<table><tr><td class="label">';
```

Display the user's name.

```
    if (!empty($row['first_name']) && !empty($row['last_name'])) {
      echo $row['first_name'] . ' ' . $row['last_name'] . '<br />';
    }
    if (!empty($row['city']) && !empty($row['state'])) {
```

Show the user's city and state.

```
      echo $row['city'] . ', ' . $row['state'] . '<br />';
    }
```

DONE ⑤

```
    echo '</td><td>';
    if (!empty($row['picture'])) {
      echo '<img src="' . MM_UPLOADPATH . $row['picture'] . '" alt="Profile Picture" /><br />';
    }
    echo '</td></tr></table>';
```

Don't forget to generate an <img> tag with the user's picture!

```
    // Display the mismatched topics
    echo '<h4>You are mismatched on the following ' . count($mismatch_topics) . ' topics:</h4>';
    foreach ($mismatch_topics as $topic) {
      echo $topic . '<br />';
    }
```

It's important to show what topics actually resulted in the mismatch.

```
    // Display a link to the mismatch user's profile
    echo '<h4>View <a href=viewprofile.php?user_id=' . $mismatch_user_id . '>' .
      $row['first_name'] . '\'s profile</a>.</h4>';
  }
}
```

Finally, we provide a link to the mismatched user's profile so that the logged in user can find out more about him.

```
else {
  echo '<p>You must first <a href="questionnaire.php">answer the questionnaire</a> before you can ' .
    'be mismatched.</p>';
}
...
```

TEST DRIVE

Find your perfect Mismatch!

Modify Mismatch to use the new My Mismatch script (or download the application from the Head First Labs site at www.headfirstlabs.com/books/hfphp). This requires creating a new mymismatch.php script, as well as adding a "My Mismatch" menu item to the navmenu.php script so that users can access the script.

Upload the scripts to your web server, and then open the main Mismatch page (index.php) in a web browser. Make sure you log in and have filled out the questionnaire, and then click the "My Mismatch" menu item to view your mismatch.

Johan's My Mismatch page reveals Sidney as his perfect opposite.

We're so different in all the right ways... what a babe.

I had no clue I'd be so attracted, yet I can't resist the Johan!

When Sidney visits the My Mismatch page, she sees Johan, her ideal mismatch.

Database Schema Magnets

Remember the Guitar Wars application from eons ago? Your job is to study the Guitar Wars database, which could use some normalization help, and come up with a better schema. Use all of the magnets below to flesh out the table and column names, and also identify the primary and foreign keys.

The database drives the display of scores on the main Guitar Wars page.

Here's the original Guitar Wars database, which stores high scores that are submitted by users.

Here's the new and improved schema you need to build out with the magnets... good luck!

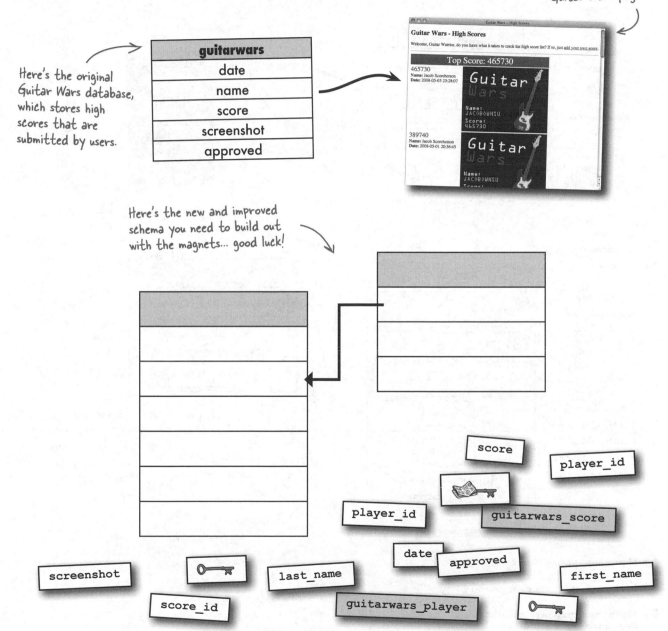

Database Schema Magnets Solution

Remember the Guitar Wars application from eons ago? Your job is to study the Guitar Wars database, which could use some normalization help, and come up with a better schema. Use all of the magnets below to flesh out the table and column names, and also identify the primary and foreign keys.

The database drives the display of scores on the main Guitar Wars page.

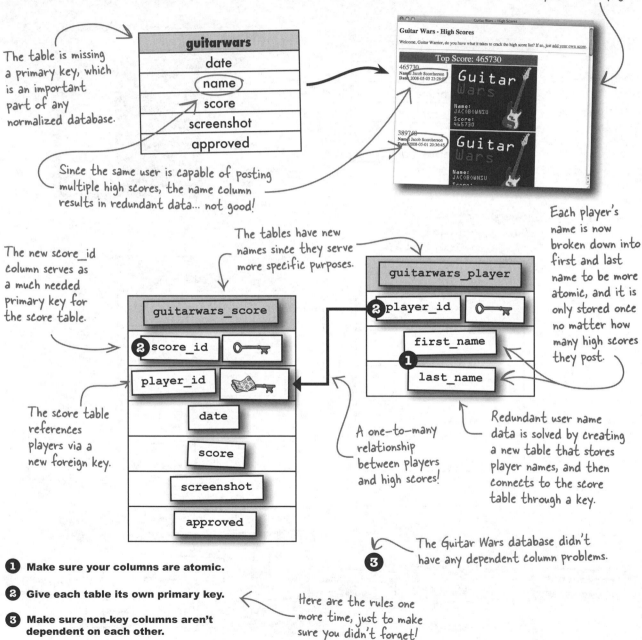

The table is missing a primary key, which is an important part of any normalized database.

Since the same user is capable of posting multiple high scores, the name column results in redundant data... not good!

The new score_id column serves as a much needed primary key for the score table.

The tables have new names since they serve more specific purposes.

Each player's name is now broken down into first and last name to be more atomic, and it is only stored once no matter how many high scores they post.

The score table references players via a new foreign key.

A one-to-many relationship between players and high scores!

Redundant user name data is solved by creating a new table that stores player names, and then connects to the score table through a key.

1 Make sure your columns are atomic.

2 Give each table its own primary key.

3 Make sure non-key columns aren't dependent on each other.

The Guitar Wars database didn't have any dependent column problems.

Here are the rules one more time, just to make sure you didn't forget!

PHP&MySQLcross

Concerned that your own perfect mismatch is still out there waiting to be found? Take your mind off it by completing this crossword puzzle.

Across

1. A representation of all the structures, such as tables and columns, in your database, along with how they connect.

4. This happens when multiple rows of a table are related to multiple rows of another table.

5. This allows you to convert between different PHP data types.

7. Use this to combine results from one table with the results of another table in a query.

10. The process of eliminating redundancies and other design problems in a database.

11. You can shorten some if-else statements with this handy little operator.

12. When one row of a table is related to multiple rows in another table.

Down

1. A join makes it possible to get rid of these.

2. A column in a table that references the primary key of another table.

3. When a form is generated from a database, it is considered ---- ------.

6. It's not nuclear, it's just data in the smallest size that makes sense for a given database.

8. Rows in two tables have this relationship when there is exactly one row in one table for every row in the other.

9. One of these can help greatly in figuring out the design of a table.

13. A temporary name used to reference a piece of information in a query.

PHP&MySQLcross Solution

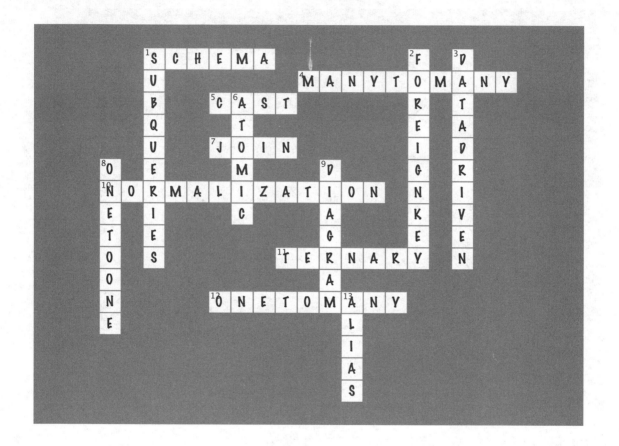

CHAPTER 8

Your PHP & MySQL Toolbox

Quite a few new MySQL database techniques were uncovered in this chapter, not to mention a few new PHP tricks. Let's do a quick recap!

Normalization

Normalization is the process of altering the design of a database to reduce duplicate data and improve the placement of and relationships between data. The goal is to produce a robust design that holds up well to growing data.

Schemas and Diagrams

A schema is a representation of all the structures (tables, columns, etc.) in your database, along with how they connect. A diagram is a visual depiction of your database, including details about the specific columns responsible for connecting tables.

Foreign Key

A column in a table that is used to link the table to another table. A foreign key in a child table typically connects to a primary key in a parent table, effectively linking rows between the two tables.

for (...)

A loop that is ideally suited to looping based on a specific number of iterations. Create a for loop by initializing a counter, establishing a test condition, and specifying how the counter is to be updated after each iteration.

? :

The ternary operator is a PHP construct that works like a really compact if-else statement. It is handy for performing simple choices based on a true/false expression.

INNER JOIN

This kind of join combines data from two tables that have matching rows. Unlike a normal query, a join allows you to grab data from more than one table, which is extremely helpful when a database consists of multiple tables.

AS *name*

This SQL statement establishes an alias, which is a name used to identify a piece of data within a query. Aliases are often used to simplify queries by shortening long table and column names. They can also be used to rename result data when the original table column isn't specific enough.

9 string and custom functions

Better living through functions

Now that I have this engineering degree, there's no stopping me. I'll find a lair, raise some laser sharks, and blow up the moon. Then maybe I'll get married and settle down.

Functions take your applications to a whole new level.

You've already been using PHP's built-in functions to accomplish things. Now it's time to take a look at a few more really useful **built-in functions**. And then you'll learn to build your very own **custom functions** to take you farther than you ever imagined it was possible to go. Well, maybe not to the point of raising laser sharks, but custom functions will streamline your code and make it reusable.

A good risky job is hard to find

The Internet startup, RiskyJobs.biz, is designed to help companies find the right people to fill their riskiest jobs. The business model is simple: for each risky job we can fill with the right candidate, we get a commission. The more successful matches, the bigger our profit.

Risky Jobs needs help improving its site's job-search functionality. Right now, there's a database full of risky jobs just waiting to be discovered by the right people. Let's take a look at the Risky Jobs search form and the underlying database of available jobs.

This simple search form calls a script that searches the riskyjobs table.

The Risky Jobs search form triggers a query on the riskyjobs table that searches for matching jobs.

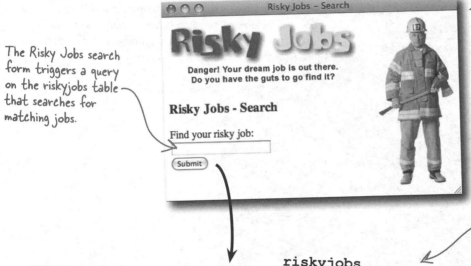

The riskyjobs table contains job titles and descriptions, along with location information and the posting date of each job.

riskyjobs

job_id	title	description	city	state	zip	company	date_posted
1	Matador	Bustling dairy farm...	Rutland	VT	05701	Mad About Milk Dairies	2008-03-11 10:51:24
2	Paparazzo	Top celebrity...	Beverly Hills	CA	90210	Diva Pursuit, LLC	2008-03-24 10:51:24
3	Shark Trainer	Training sharks to do...	Orlando	FL	32801	SharkBait, Inc.	2008-04-28 03:12:45
4	Firefighter	The City of Dataville...	Dataville	OH	45490	City of Dataville	2008-05-22 12:34:17
5	Voltage Checker	You'll be out in the...	Durham	NC	27701	Shock Systems, LLC	2008-06-28 11:16:30
6	Crocodile Dentist	Do you love animals...	Everglades City	FL	34139	Ravenous Reptiles	2008-07-14 10:51:24
7	Custard Walker	We need people...	Albuquerque	NM	87101	Pie Technologies	2008-07-24 10:54:05
8	Electric Bull Repairer	Hank's Honky Tonk...	Hoboken	NJ	07030	Hank's Honky Tonk	2008-07-27 11:22:28

...

Each job posting is uniquely identified by the job_id primary key.

Show the search results!

I'm ready to live my dream and become a matador...but my Risky Jobs search is coming up empty!

Ernesto, our fearless bullfighter, is seeing red because his job search isn't producing any results.

Sharpen your pencil

When the Risky Jobs form is submitted, the search string is stored in the variable $user_search, which is plugged into the following SQL query to do the actual searching. Write down how many rows in the riskyjobs database on the facing page will be found as a result of Ernesto's search.

```
$search_query = "SELECT job_id, title, state, description FROM riskyjobs " .
  "WHERE title = '$user_search'";

$result = mysqli_query($dbc, $search_query);
```

Write your answer here! ....

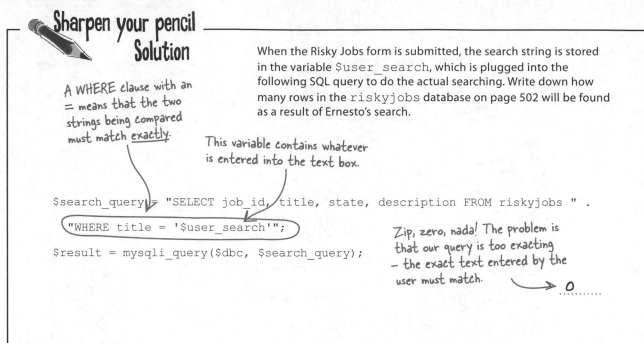

Sharpen your pencil
Solution

A WHERE clause with an = means that the two strings being compared must match <u>exactly</u>.

When the Risky Jobs form is submitted, the search string is stored in the variable `$user_search`, which is plugged into the following SQL query to do the actual searching. Write down how many rows in the `riskyjobs` database on page 502 will be found as a result of Ernesto's search.

This variable contains whatever is entered into the text box.

```
$search_query = "SELECT job_id, title, state, description FROM riskyjobs " .
    "WHERE title = '$user_search'";

$result = mysqli_query($dbc, $search_query);
```

Zip, zero, nada! The problem is that our query is too exacting – the exact text entered by the user must match.

0

The search leaves no margin for error

The SELECT query in the Risky Jobs script is very rigid, only resulting in a match if the two strings being compared are **identical**. This presents a problem for our job search because people need to be able to enter search terms that match job listings even if the job title isn't an exact match.

Let's go back to Ernesto's search, which results in a query that searches the `title` column of the `riskyjobs` table for the text "Bull Fighter Matador":

The case of the search term doesn't matter because the MySQL WHERE clause is case-insensitive by default.

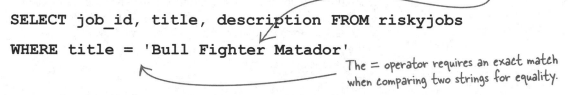

```
SELECT job_id, title, description FROM riskyjobs
WHERE title = 'Bull Fighter Matador'
```

The = operator requires an exact match when comparing two strings for equality.

See the problem? This query is only going to match rows in the table where the `title` column contains the exact text "Bull Fighter Matador". The job with the title "Matador" isn't matched, and neither are "Firefighter" or "Electric Bull Repairer". OK, maybe it's good those last two were missed, but the search still isn't working as intended. And it's not the mixed case that presents the problem (MySQL searches are by default **case-insensitive**), it's the fact that the entire search string must be an exact match due to the equality (=) operator in the WHERE clause.

SQL queries can be flexible with LIKE

What we really need is a way to search the database for a match on any portion of a search string. SQL lets us do just that with the LIKE keyword, which adds flexibility to the types of matches returned by a WHERE clause. You can think of LIKE as a more forgiving version of the = operator. Take a look at the following query, which uses LIKE to match rows where the word "fighter" appears **anywhere** in the title column:

```
SELECT job_id, title, description FROM riskyjobs
WHERE title LIKE '%fighter%'
```

The keyword LIKE lets you look for matches that aren't exactly the same as the word in quotes... and still case-insensitive.

The % signs are wildcards; they stand in for any other characters before or after the word.

LIKE makes it much easier to find matches, especially when you need to match the search string as part of a larger word or phrase. Check out these examples of strings that match up with the above query:

Firefighter**

Prize **Fighter**

FightErnesto**Please**

LIKE clauses typically work in conjunction with **wildcard characters**, which are stand-ins for characters in the data we're matching. In SQL, the percent sign (%) wildcard stands for any group of zero or more characters. Placing this wildcard in a query before and after a search term, as in the SELECT statement above, tells SQL to return results whenever the term appears somewhere in the data, no matter how many characters appear before or after it.

Geek Bits

SQL has another wildcard character that can be used with LIKE. It's the underscore (_), and it represents a single character. Consider the following LIKE clause:

```
LIKE '____fighter%'
```

It's saying: "Find the string "fighter" with any **four** characters in front of it, and any characters after it." This would match "bullfighter" and "firefighter" but not "streetfighter".

Time out! Take a moment to familiarize yourself with the Risky Jobs database... and try out a few searches.

Download the `riskyjobs.sql` file for the Risky Jobs application from the Head First Labs web site at `www.headfirstlabs.com/books/hfphp`. This file contains SQL statements that build and populate the `riskyjobs` table with sample data.

After you've executed the statements in `riskyjobs.sql` in a MySQL tool, try out a few queries to simulate job searches. Here are some to get you started.

```
SELECT * FROM riskyjobs
```
This query selects all columns for all jobs in the riskyjobs table.

```
SELECT job_id, title, description FROM riskyjobs
WHERE title = 'Bull Fighter Matador'
```
This query grabs the job ID, title, and description for jobs where the title is exactly "Bull Fighter Matador".

```
SELECT job_id, title, description FROM riskyjobs
WHERE description LIKE '%animals%'
```
This query uses LIKE to find jobs with the word "animals" anywhere in the job description.

Download It!

The complete source code for the Risky Jobs application is available for download from the Head First Labs web site:

www.headfirstlabs.com/books/hfphp

LIKE Clause Magnets

A bunch of LIKE clauses are all scrambled up on the fridge.
Can you match up the clauses with their appropriate results?
Which magnets won't be matched by any of the LIKE clauses?

⟵ Some may have multiple answers.

```
LIKE '%er'
```

```
LIKE '% T%'
```

```
LIKE 'c%'
```

```
LIKE '%test %'
```

```
LIKE '%Tipper Cow%'
```

```
LIKE '%do_'
```

```
LIKE '%ma%'
```

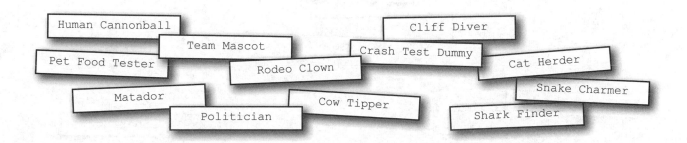

Human Cannonball

Team Mascot

Cliff Diver

Crash Test Dummy

Pet Food Tester

Rodeo Clown

Cat Herder

Matador

Cow Tipper

Snake Charmer

Politician

Shark Finder

LIKE Clause Magnets Solution

A bunch of LIKE clauses are all scrambled up on the fridge. Can you match up the clauses with their appropriate results? (Some may have multiple answers.) Which magnets won't be matched by any of the LIKE clauses?

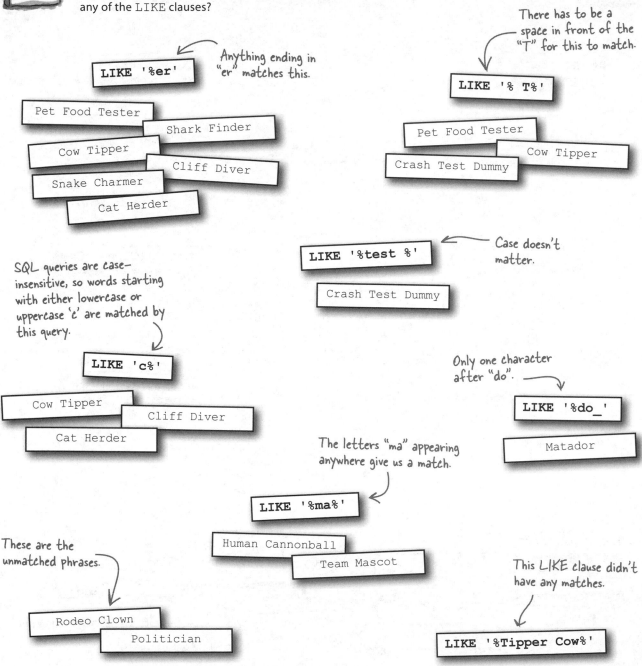

LIKE '%er'

Anything ending in "er" matches this.

Pet Food Tester

Shark Finder

Cow Tipper

Cliff Diver

Snake Charmer

Cat Herder

There has to be a space in front of the "T" for this to match.

LIKE '% T%'

Pet Food Tester

Cow Tipper

Crash Test Dummy

LIKE '%test %'

Case doesn't matter.

Crash Test Dummy

SQL queries are case-insensitive, so words starting with either lowercase or uppercase 'c' are matched by this query.

LIKE 'c%'

Cow Tipper

Cliff Diver

Cat Herder

Only one character after "do".

LIKE '%do_'

Matador

The letters "ma" appearing anywhere give us a match.

LIKE '%ma%'

Human Cannonball

Team Mascot

These are the unmatched phrases.

Rodeo Clown

Politician

This LIKE clause didn't have any matches.

LIKE '%Tipper Cow%'

That last LIKE clause, LIKE '%Tipper Cow%', doesn't match anything because "Tipper" and "Cow" don't show up together as a phrase. It sure would be handy to break up search phrases into individual keywords and then search on each of the keywords.

Our search would work much better if it looked for "Tipper" and "Cow" individually instead of "Tipper Cow" as one exact phrase.

Handy indeed! We just need to figure out how to match each of the individual keywords in the search phrase.

Taking what people type in the Risky Jobs search field and matching it exactly won't always work. The search would be much more effective if we searched on each search term entered, as opposed to searching on the entire search phrase. But how do you search on multiple terms? We could store each of the search terms in an array, and then tweak the SELECT query to search for each keyword individually.

Explode a string into individual words

To make Risky Jobs search functionality more effective, we need a way to break apart users' search strings when they enter multiple words in the form field. The data our risky job seekers enter into the search form is text, which means we can use any of the built-in PHP string functions to process it. One extremely powerful function is explode(), and it breaks apart a string into an array of separate strings. Here's an example:

The explode() function breaks a string into an array of substrings.

The explode() function chops a string into an array of substrings based on a common separator, also known as a delimiter.

This parameter is the text we want "exploded."

```
$search_words = explode(' ', 'Tipper Cow');
```

The $search_words variable now stores the array of search terms that we'll then feed into an SQL query.

This parameter tells explode() what separates the substrings within the string, in this case a space. You can specify one or more characters, which are called the delimiter.

The explode() function requires two parameters. The first is the **delimiter**, which is a character or characters that indicates **where** to break up the string. We're using a space character as our delimiter, which means the search string is broken everywhere a space appears. The delimiter itself is not included in the resulting substrings. The second parameter is the string to be exploded.

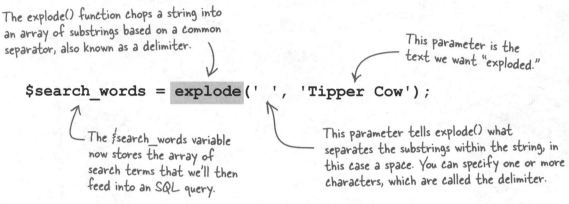

The space delimiter controls how the string is exploded.

explode()

Each substring is stored as a distinct array element.

$search_words

Incorporating the array of search terms into Risky Jobs involves adding a line of code before we run the query on the Risky Jobs database. Now, if someone enters "Tipper Cow" into the search field, this code breaks it into two words and stores each word in an array ($search_words).

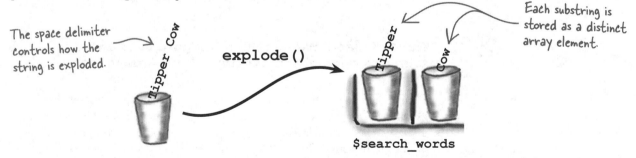

```
$user_search = $_GET['usersearch'];

$search_words = explode(' ', $user_search);
```

The explode() function stores each word in $user_search in an array called $search_words.

Exercise

In order to incorporate the exploded search terms into the Risky Jobs application, we have to plug each of the terms into an SQL `SELECT` query using `LIKE` and `OR`. For example, here's what a query would look like for Ernesto's earlier search on "Bull Fighter Matador":

We're now searching the job description instead of the title since the description has more information to match.

```
SELECT * FROM riskyjobs
  WHERE description LIKE '%Bull%' OR description LIKE '%Fighter%' OR
  description LIKE '%Matador%'
```

Now suppose we used the following PHP code to attempt to assemble this query from the search data entered by the user into the Risky Jobs search form:

```
$search_query = "SELECT * FROM riskyjobs";
$where_clause = '';
$user_search  = $_GET['usersearch'];
$search_words = explode(' ', $user_search);
foreach ($search_words as $word) {
  $where_clause .= " description LIKE '%$word%' OR ";
}


if (!empty($where_clause)) {
  $search_query .= " WHERE $where_clause";
}
```

Write down the SQL query generated by this code when Ernesto enters "Bull Fighter Matador" as his search, and then annotate any problems you think it might have.

....

....

....

Exercise Solution

In order to incorporate the exploded search terms into the Risky Jobs application, we have to plug each of the terms into an SQL `SELECT` query using `LIKE` and `OR`. For example, here's what a query would look like for Ernesto's earlier search on "Bull Fighter Matador":

We're now searching the job description instead of the title since the description has more information to match.

```
SELECT * FROM riskyjobs

  WHERE description LIKE '%Bull%' OR description LIKE '%Fighter%' OR

  description LIKE '%Matador%'
```

Now suppose we used the following PHP code to attempt to assemble this query from the search data entered by the user into the Risky Jobs search form:

```
$search_query = "SELECT * FROM riskyjobs";

$where_clause = '';

$user_search  = $_GET['usersearch'];

$search_words = explode(' ', $user_search);

foreach ($search_words as $word) {

  $where_clause .= " description LIKE '%$word%' OR ";

}
```

Each LIKE clause ends with an OR to link it with the next one, which works great except for the very last one.

Make sure the WHERE clause isn't empty before appending it to the search query.

```
if (!empty($where_clause)) {

  $search_query .= " WHERE $where_clause";

}
```

This operator concatenates one string onto the end of another string.

Write down the SQL query generated by this code when Ernesto enters "Bull Fighter Matador" as his search, and then annotate any problems you think it might have.

SELECT * FROM riskyjobs

WHERE description LIKE '%Bull%' OR description LIKE '%Fighter%' OR

description LIKE '%Matador%' (OR)   ← *There's an extra OR at the end of the query, which will make it fail!*

implode() builds a string from substrings

What we really need to do is only put OR between the LIKEs in our WHERE clause, **but not after the last one.** So how exactly can that be done? How about a special case inside the loop to see if we're on the last search term, and then not include OR for that one? That would work but it's a little messy. A much cleaner solution involves a function that does the reverse of the explode() function. The implode() function takes an array of strings and builds a single string out of them.

This is the delimiter that is wedged between each of the strings when they are stuck together as one.

```
$where_clause = implode(' OR ', $where_list);
```

The implode() function returns a single string.

This must be an array of strings that you want to join together.

But how does that help the dangling OR problem in our query? Well, implode() lets you specify a delimiter to stick between the strings when combining them together. If we use ' OR ' as the delimiter, we can construct a WHERE clause that only has OR **between** each LIKE clause.

Sharpen your pencil

Rewrite the PHP code that generates the Risky Jobs SELECT query so that it fixes the dangling OR problem by using the implode function.

....
....
....
....
....
....
....
....
....
....
....

Sharpen your pencil
Solution

Rewrite the PHP code that generates the Risky Jobs SELECT query so that it fixes the dangling OR problem by using the implode function.

```
$search_query = "SELECT * FROM riskyjobs";

$where_list = array();

$user_search = $_GET['usersearch'];

$search_words = explode(' ', $user_search);

foreach ($search_words as $word) {

  $where_list[] = "description LIKE '%$word%'";

}

$where_clause = implode(' OR ', $where_list);


if (!empty($where_clause)) {

  $search_query .= " WHERE $where_clause";

}
```

Since implode() accepts an array of strings to be joined together, we have to build an array of LIKE clauses.

When used like this, the [] operator acts the same as the array_push() function – it adds a new element onto the end of an array.

The delimiter passed to implode() is "OR" with a space on each side of it.

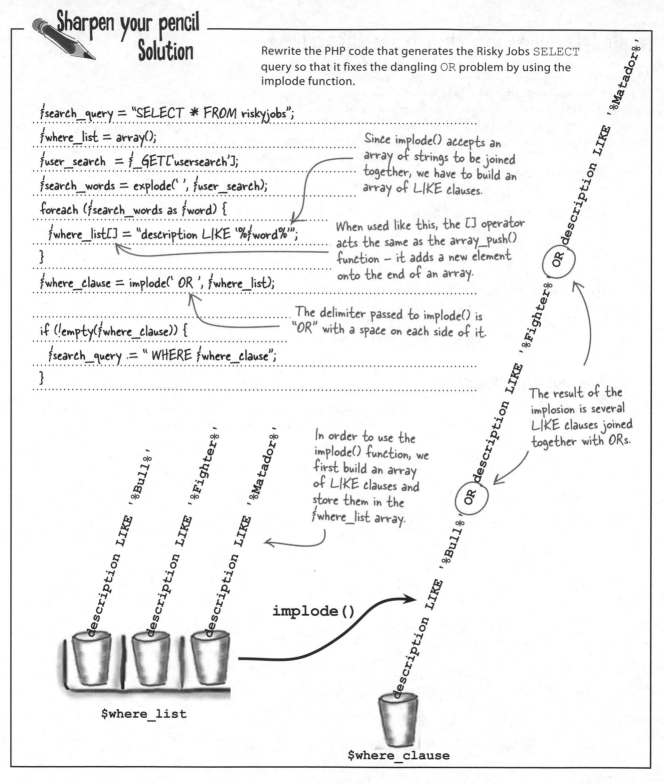

In order to use the implode() function, we first build an array of LIKE clauses and store them in the $where_list array.

$where_list

implode()

The result of the implosion is several LIKE clauses joined together with ORs.

$where_clause

Test Drive

Take the Risky Jobs search form for a spin.

Download the Risky Jobs application from the Head First Labs site at `www.headfirstlabs.com/books/hfphp`. The `search.php` script contains the query generation code you just worked through, and is used to process the search data entered into the form in the `search.html` page.

Upload the script and other Risky Jobs files to your web server, and then open the search form (`search.html`) in a web browser. Try a few different searches to see how your query generation code fares. Make sure to try Ernesto's "Bull Fighter Matador" search, which is a good test of the new `implode()` code.

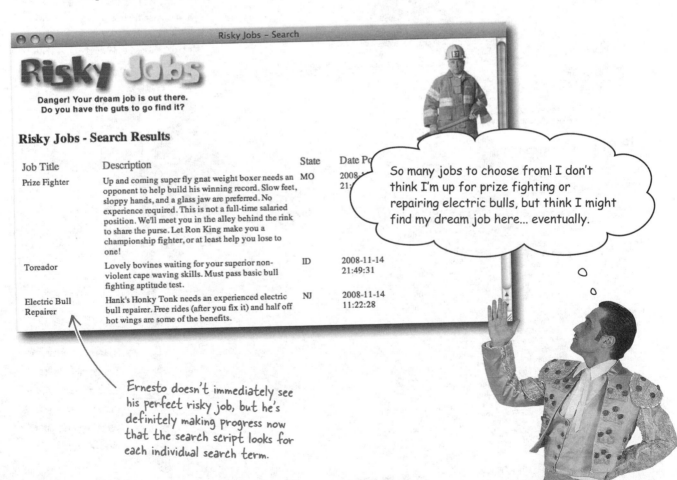

Ernesto doesn't immediately see his perfect risky job, but he's definitely making progress now that the search script looks for each individual search term.

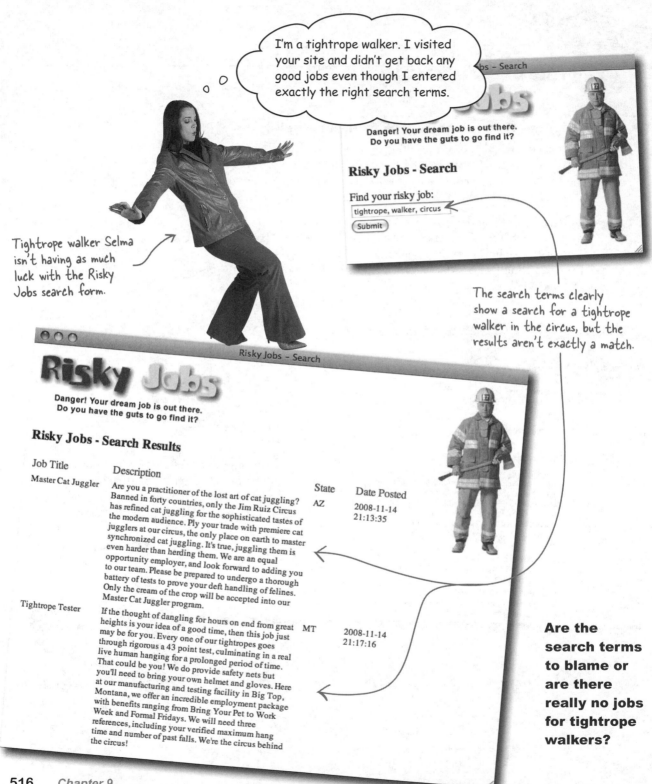

I'm a tightrope walker. I visited your site and didn't get back any good jobs even though I entered exactly the right search terms.

Risky Jobs - Search

Danger! Your dream job is out there.
Do you have the guts to go find it?

Risky Jobs - Search

Find your risky job:

tightrope, walker, circus

Submit

Tightrope walker Selma isn't having as much luck with the Risky Jobs search form.

The search terms clearly show a search for a tightrope walker in the circus, but the results aren't exactly a match.

Risky Jobs - Search

Danger! Your dream job is out there.
Do you have the guts to go find it?

Risky Jobs - Search Results

Job Title	Description	State	Date Posted
Master Cat Juggler	Are you a practitioner of the lost art of cat juggling? Banned in forty countries, only the Jim Ruiz Circus has refined cat juggling for the sophisticated tastes of the modern audience. Ply your trade with premiere cat jugglers at our circus, the only place on earth to master synchronized cat juggling. It's true, juggling them is even harder than herding them. We are an equal opportunity employer, and look forward to adding you to our team. Please be prepared to undergo a thorough battery of tests to prove your deft handling of felines. Only the cream of the crop will be accepted into our Master Cat Juggler program.	AZ	2008-11-14 21:13:35
Tightrope Tester	If the thought of dangling for hours on end from great heights is your idea of a good time, then this job just may be for you. Every one of our tightropes goes through rigorous a 43 point test, culminating in a real live human hanging for a prolonged period of time. That could be you! We do provide safety nets but you'll need to bring your own helmet and gloves. Here at our manufacturing and testing facility in Big Top, Montana, we offer an incredible employment package with benefits ranging from Bring Your Pet to Work Week and Formal Fridays. We will need three references, including your verified maximum hang time and number of past falls. We're the circus behind the circus!	MT	2008-11-14 21:17:16

Are the search terms to blame or are there really no jobs for tightrope walkers?

Sharpen your pencil

Write down the SQL query generated when Selma enters "tightrope, walker, circus" as her search, and then annotate any problems you think it might have.

....

....

....

Sharpen your pencil
Solution

Write down the SQL query generated when Selma enters "tightrope, walker, circus" as her search, and then annotate any problems you think it might have.

SELECT * FROM riskyjobs

WHERE description LIKE '%tightrope,%' OR description LIKE '%walker,%' OR

description LIKE '%circus%'

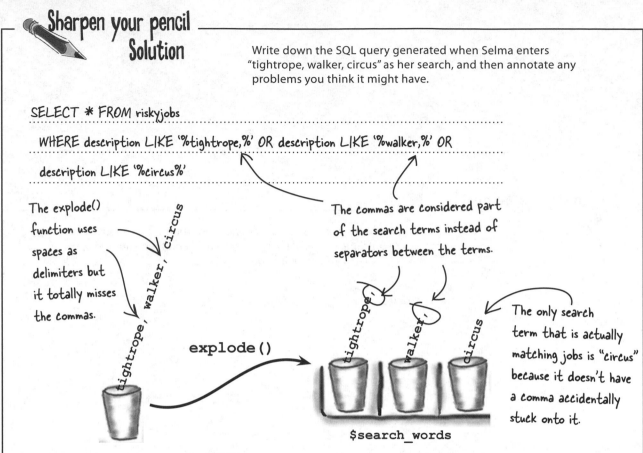

The explode() function uses spaces as delimiters but it totally misses the commas.

The commas are considered part of the search terms instead of separators between the terms.

explode()

The only search term that is actually matching jobs is "circus" because it doesn't have a comma accidentally stuck onto it.

$search_words

I don't see what the big deal is. Just call the explode() function twice - first to get rid of spaces and then to get rid of commas.

The `explode()` function lets you explode a single string into substrings, but in this case we already have substrings.

The first call to the `explode()` function leaves us with **multiple strings** stored in an array, so there's isn't a single string left to explode. And attempting to explode each string in the array would likely just create more problems. Instead of trying to solve the delimiter problem with multiple calls to `explode()`, we need to **preprocess** the search string to get it down to a **single delimiter** before we ever even call `explode()`. Then it can do what it does best—break apart the string using one delimiter.

Preprocess the search string

We want to hand the explode() function a string that it can break apart cleanly in one shot. How do we do that? By making sure that explode() only has to worry with a single delimiter, such as a space character. This means we need to **preprocess** the search string so that each search term is separated by a space, even if the user entered commas.

Preprocessing data allows us to remove unwanted characters and make the data easier to process.

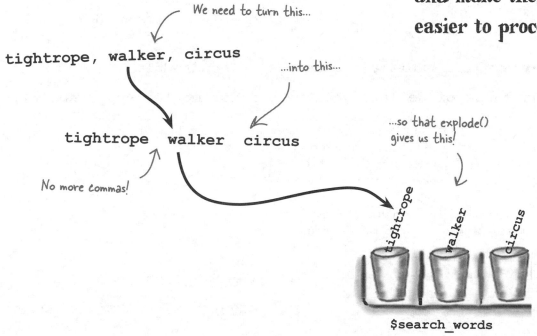

We need to turn this...

`tightrope, walker, circus`

...into this...

`tightrope  walker  circus`

No more commas!

...so that explode() gives us this!

tightrope   walker   circus

`$search_words`

---

there are no Dumb Questions

Q: Can we use more than one character as the delimiter when exploding the search string?

A: Yes, you can specify any number of characters to serve as your delimiter, but that's not the same as specifying **different** delimiters, and won't solve our problem here.

If we used explode(', ', $user_search) to break apart our string, it would use a combined comma and space as a delimiter, and would work if someone entered "tightrope, walker, circus". But it would fail if someone entered "tightrope walker circus". In that case, we'd be left with one long string—not good.

Q: Can we just delete the commas instead of turning them into spaces?

A: That will work only if users separate their search terms with both a comma and a space, which we can't count on. If we deleted commas, we'd run the risk of turning "tightrope,walker" into "tightropewalker", which probably wouldn't match anything in the Risky Jobs database.

Replace unwanted search characters

If you think about it, preprocessing the Risky Jobs search string is a lot like using find-and-replace in a word processor. In our case, we want to find commas and replace them with spaces. PHP's str_replace() lets you do just that by supplying it three parameters: the text you want to find, the text you want to replace it with, and the string you want to perform the find-and-replace on. Here's an example of str_replace() in action:

This is the substring you want to replace...

...and this is the string that gets inserted in its place.

```
$clean_search = str_replace('thousands', 'hundreds',
    'Make thousands of dollars your very first month. Apply now!');
```

The third parameter is the string that will be changed. We're adding a little truth to the advertising by replacing "thousands" with "hundreds".

But what about those commas in the search string? The str_replace() function works just as well at replacing individual characters:

Remember, this is the substring you're replacing...

...and this is the string you're replacing it with.

```
$clean_search = str_replace(',', ' ', 'tightrope, walker, circus');
```

Everywhere that a comma appears in this string, it will be replaced with a space.

After this code runs, the variable $clean_string will contain the string "tightrope walker circus".

Do you see anything suspicious about the results of the str_replace() function? Do you think replacing commas with spaces will work like we want?

Given the PHP code below, show what the output of the $search_words array will be for each of the following search strings. Make sure to write in data for the appropriate array elements, and scratch through elements if the $search_words array ends up being shorter.

```php
$clean_search = str_replace(',', ' ', $user_search);
$search_words = explode(' ', $clean_search);
```

bull,matador cape

$search_words

3 spaces!

bull matador   cape

$search_words

bull , matador cape

$search_words

2 spaces!

bull,matador, cape

$search_words

Exercise Solution

Given the PHP code below, show what the output of the $search_words array will be for each of the following search strings. Make sure to write in data for the appropriate array elements, and scratch through elements if the $search_words array ends up being shorter.

```
$clean_search = str_replace(',', ' ', $user_search);

$search_words = explode(' ', $clean_search);
```

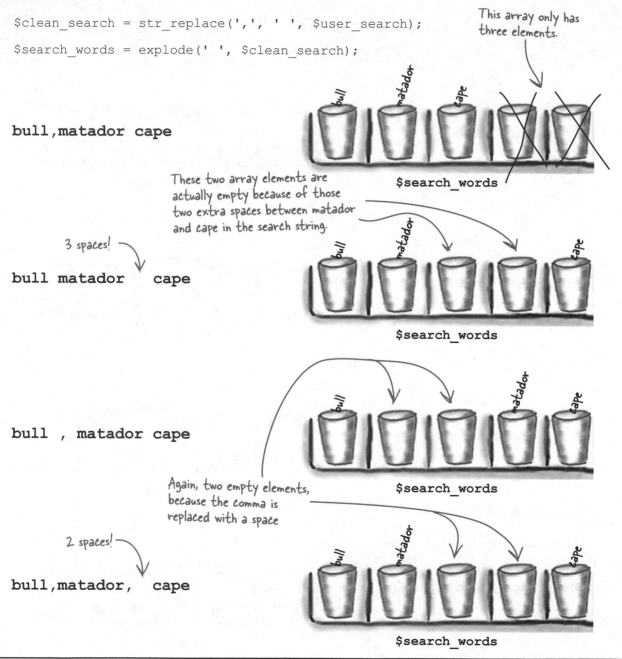

This array only has three elements.

bull,matador cape

These two array elements are actually empty because of those two extra spaces between matador and cape in the search string.

3 spaces!

bull matador   cape

$search_words

bull , matador cape

Again, two empty elements, because the comma is replaced with a space

$search_words

2 spaces!

bull,matador,   cape

$search_words

So we're all set now that we're preprocessing the search string, right?

Uh, no. Preprocessing gets rid of unwanted characters, but unfortunately, it doesn't result in an array containing all good search terms.

Remember, our goal is to end up with a string where each search term is separated by exactly the same delimiter, a space. Take another look at what happened in the last three examples on the facing page. Some of the elements in the $search_words array are empty. If we try to build our WHERE clause with the empty search elements, we might end up with something like this:

```
SELECT * FROM riskyjobs
    WHERE description LIKE '%bull%' OR
    description LIKE '%matador%' OR
    description LIKE '% %' OR
    description LIKE '% %' OR
    description LIKE '%cape%'
```

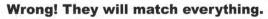

Those single spaces will match every single space in each job description. They are a real problem.

But those spaces won't match anything, right?

Wrong! They will match everything.

If there's a space anywhere in a job description (which is pretty much a given), this query will match it and return it as a result. So every job in the Risky Jobs database will be matched by this query. We need to get rid of those empty array elements before we construct the SQL query in order to make the search script useful again.

The query needs <u>legit</u> search terms

The good news it that it's not too difficult to clean up our search terms before using them in a query. We'll need to create a new array that only contains the real search terms. So we'll copy all the non-empty elements from our first array into the second array, and then use that array to construct the SELECT query.

To construct the new array, we can use a foreach loop to cycle through each element in the original array, and then use an if statement to find non-empty elements. When we find a non-empty element, we just add it to the new array. Here's what this process looks like:

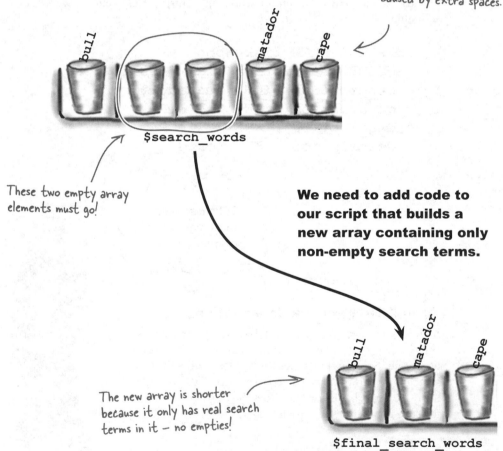

Here's the original array that contains the search terms and empty elements caused by extra spaces.

These two empty array elements must go!

We need to add code to our script that builds a new array containing only non-empty search terms.

The new array is shorter because it only has real search terms in it — no empties!

$search_words

$final_search_words

Copy non-empty elements to a new array

Now let's look at the code that will copy the non-empty elements from our `$search_words` array to the new `$final_search_words` array.

```
$search_query = "SELECT * FROM riskyjobs";

// Extract the search keywords into an array
$clean_search = str_replace(',', ' ', $user_search);
$search_words = explode(' ', $clean_search);
$final_search_words = array();
if (count($search_words) > 0) {
  foreach ($search_words as $word) {
    if (!empty($word)) {
      $final_search_words[] = $word;
    }
  }
}
```

This is nothing new — replace commas with spaces using str_replace().

Loop through each element of the $search_word array. If the element is not empty, put it in the array named $final_search_words.

After checking to make sure there is at least one search term in the `$search_words` array, the `foreach` loop cycles through the array looking for non-empty elements. When it finds a non-empty element, it uses the `[]` operator to add the element onto the end of the `$final_search_words` array. This is how the new array is assembled.

Then what? Well, then we generate the `SELECT` query just as before, except now we use the `$final_search_words` array instead of `$search_words`:

```
// Generate a WHERE clause using all of the search keywords
$where_list = array();
if (count($final_search_words) > 0) {
  foreach ($final_search_words as $word) {
    $where_list[] = "description LIKE '%$word%'";
  }
}
$where_clause = implode(' OR ', $where_list);

// Add the keyword WHERE clause to the search query
if (!empty($where_clause)) {
  $search_query .= " WHERE $where_clause";
}
```

This is the same code you've seen that builds the WHERE clause of the search query, but this time it uses the new $final_search_words array that contains no empty elements.

This code gives us a search query that no longer has empty elements. Here's the new query for the search "bull, matador, cape":

```
SELECT * FROM riskyjobs
  WHERE description LIKE '%bull%' OR
  description LIKE '%matador%' OR
  description LIKE '%cape%'
```

BRAIN POWER

Will this search give our users the results they're looking for?

Test Drive

Update the Search script to preprocess the user search string.

Update the `search.php` script to use the `explode()` and `implode()` functions to preprocess the user search string and generate a more robust `SELECT` query. Then upload the script to your web server and try out a few searches.

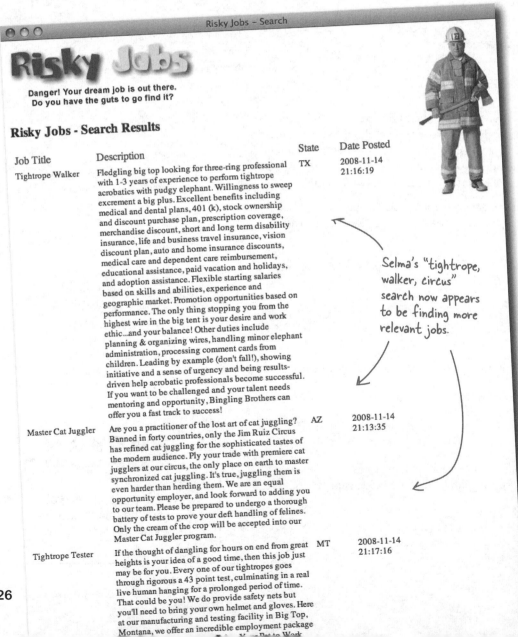

Selma's "tightrope, walker, circus" search now appears to be finding more relevant jobs.

I'm getting job listings, but I'm getting huge descriptions for each job. I don't need that much information. I may have to try hazardpays.com, where they show only part of the job, and I can see more listings per page.

Although Risky Jobs is doing much better at finding jobs, the huge job descriptions are a bit much.

What's really irking Selma is her inability to see more job listings in her browser without doing a bunch of scrolling. It isn't necessary to show the entire description of each job in the search results. Ideally, we really need to show part of the description of each job, maybe just the first few sentences.

Write down how you think we could trim the job descriptions so that they aren't quite so huge in the search results:

....

....

....

Sometimes you just need part of a string

Since the lengths of the job descriptions in the Risky Jobs database vary quite a bit and some are quite long, we could clean up the search results by chopping all the descriptions down to a smaller size. And to keep from confusing users, we can just stick an ellipsis (...) on the end of each one to make it clear that they're seeing only part of each description.

The PHP `substr()` function is perfect for extracting part of a string. You pass the "substring" function the original string and two integers. The first integer is the index of where you want the substring to start, and the second integer is its length, in characters. Here's the syntax:

> The PHP substr() function allows you to extract a portion of a string.

```
substr(string, start, length)
```

This is the original string we want to extract a substring from.

This specifies where to start the substring...

...and this is how many characters to return.

When it comes to the `substr()` function, you can think of a string as being like an array where each character is a different element. Consider the following string:

```
$job_desc = 'Are you a practioner of the lost art of cat juggling? ';
```

Similar to elements in an array, each character in this string has an index, starting at 0 and counting up until the end of the string.

Are you a practioner of the lost art of cat juggling?

0 1 2 3 4 5 6 7 8 9...   ... 50 51 52

We can use these character indexes with the `substr()` function to grab portions of the string:

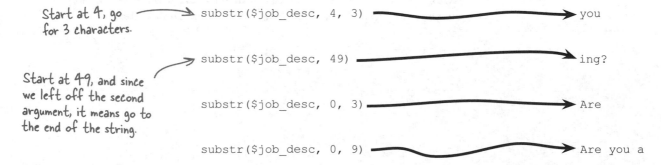

Start at 4, go for 3 characters. → `substr($job_desc, 4, 3)` → you

Start at 49, and since we left off the second argument, it means go to the end of the string. → `substr($job_desc, 49)` → ing?

`substr($job_desc, 0, 3)` → Are

`substr($job_desc, 0, 9)` → Are you a

Extract substrings from either end

The substr() function is not limited to grabbing substrings from the start of a string. You can also extract characters starting from the end of a string. The extraction still works left to right; you just use a negative index to identify the start of the substring.

Are you a practitioner of the lost art of cat juggling?

-53 -52 -51 -50 ...   ... -3 -2 -1

Here are a couple of examples:

Start at -53, then → substr($job_desc, -53, 7) ————————————→ Are you
grab 7 characters.

Start at -9 and take   substr($job_desc, -9) ————————————→ juggling?
the rest of the string.

Sharpen your pencil

Below is PHP code that generates an HTML table for the Risky Jobs search results. Finish the missing code, whose task is to limit the job description text to 100 characters, and also trim down the date posted text to only show the month, day, and year.

```
echo '<table border="0" cellpadding="2">';

echo '<td>Job Title</td><td>Description</td><td>State</td><td>Date Posted</td>';

while ($row = mysqli_fetch_array($result)) {

  echo '<tr class="results">';

  echo '<td valign="top" width="20%">' . $row['title'] . '</td>';

  echo '<td valign="top" width="50%">' . ................................................ . '...</td>';

  echo '<td valign="top" width="10%">' . $row['state'] . '</td>';

  echo '<td valign="top" width="20%">' . .............................. . '</td>';

  echo '</tr>';

}

echo '</table>';
```

Sharpen your pencil
Solution

Below is PHP code that generates an HTML table for the Risky Jobs search results. Finish the missing code, whose task is to limit the job description text to 100 characters, and also trim down the date posted text to only show the month, day, and year.

```php
echo '<table border="0" cellpadding="2">';

echo '<td>Job Title</td><td>Description</td><td>State</td><td>Date Posted</td>';

while ($row = mysqli_fetch_array($result)) {

  echo '<tr class="results">';

  echo '<td valign="top" width="20%">' . $row['title'] . '</td>';

  echo '<td valign="top" width="50%">' . substr($row['description'], 0, 100) . '...</td>';

  echo '<td valign="top" width="10%">' . $row['state'] . '</td>';

  echo '<td valign="top" width="20%">' . substr($row['date_posted'], 0, 10) . '</td>';

  echo '</tr>';

}

echo '</table>';
```

Stick an ellipsis on the end to indicate that this is only part of the description.

All of the date_posted data starts with MM-DD-YYYY, which takes up exactly 10 characters.

Geek Bits

It's possible to skip the PHP `substr()` function and limit the job description data in the SQL query itself. You use a very similar MySQL function called `SUBSTRING()` that accepts the same arguments as `substr()`. The only difference is that the starting index starts at 1 instead of 0. So grabbing the first 100 characters of the job description looks like this:

```sql
SELECT SUBSTRING(job_description, 1, 100)
  FROM riskyjobs;
```

The advantage of sticking with the PHP function is that we have both the partial job description and the full job description available to us. If we use MySQL, we only get the partial job description, and would have to make another query to get the full description.

there are no
Dumb Questions

Q: Does `substr()` work on numeric values?

A: No, it operates strictly on strings. However, If you have a number stored as a `CHAR`, `VARCHAR`, or `TEXT`, when you retrieve it via SQL, it's treated by PHP as a string, not a number, so you can use a `substr()` function on it.

Q: What if your length value is longer than the string? Will it return a string with spaces at the end to make it match the length value?

A: It will return the entire string. But it won't pad the end of the string with spaces to change the length. For example, the following code will return the string "dog":
```php
substr('dog', 0, 10)
```

TEST DRIVE

Tweak the Search script to limit the text displayed for job descriptions and dates posted.

Modify the `search.php` script so that it uses the PHP `substr()` function to trim down the job description and date posted text for the search results. Then upload the script to your web server and test it out with a few searches.

Selma is pleased now that she can see job search results without having to scroll through humongous job descriptions.

Risky Jobs – Search

Risky Jobs

**Danger! Your dream job is out there.
Do you have the guts to go find it?**

Risky Jobs - Search Results

Job Title	Description	State	Date Posted
Tightrope Walker	Fledgling big top looking for three-ring professional with 1-3 years of experience to perform tightr...	TX	2008-11-14
Master Cat Juggler	Are you a practitioner of the lost art of cat juggling? Banned in forty countries, only the Jim Ruiz...	AZ	2008-11-14
Tightrope Tester	If the thought of dangling for hours on end from great ...d time, then thi...	MT	2008-11-14

I'd really like to see the results sorted by date posted, or maybe by state. I really want to find a matador job in Vermont.

The posting date is also a bit easier to read now that it only shows the date and not the date and time.

⚛ **BRAIN POWER**

How can we change the page layout and query to allow us to sort by date posted, state, or job title?

Multiple queries can sort our results

In order to allow visitors to sort their search results, we need a way for them to identify how they want their results ordered. Maybe a form... or a button? It's actually way simpler than that. We can use HTML to turn each of the column headings in the search result table into links. Users can click a link to indicate which column they want to sort the results by.

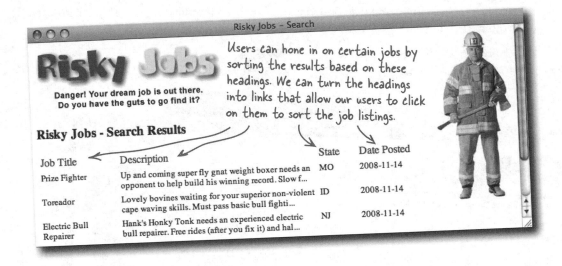

We can use these links to reload the same Search script but with a query that sorts the results according to the link clicked. We already know how to use ORDER BY to structure a query with sorted results. If we create different SQL queries to ORDER BY each individual column, we can allow the user to sort the search results alphabetically by job title, description, or state, or chronologically by date posted.

Here is the SQL query to sort results alphabetically by job description:

```
SELECT * FROM riskyjobs
   WHERE description LIKE '%Bull%' OR description LIKE '%Fighter%' OR
   description LIKE '%Matador%'
   ORDER BY description
```

This sorts the results of the query on job descriptions in ascending alphabetical order.

Sharpen your pencil

Write three different queries that sort the Risky Jobs results according to job title, state, and date posted. Assume the user has typed in the search string "window, washer, skyscraper".

....
....
....
....
....
....
....
....
....
....
....
....

How could we rewrite these queries if you wanted to see the job titles and states in reverse order? What about the newest jobs first?

....
....
....
....
....
....
....
....
....
....
....
....

Sharpen your pencil
Solution

Write three different queries that sort the Risky Jobs results according to job title, state, and date posted. Assume the user has typed in the search string "window, washer, skyscraper".

```
SELECT * FROM riskyjobs
    WHERE description LIKE '%window%' OR description LIKE '%washer%' OR
    description LIKE '%skyscraper%'
    ORDER BY job_title
```

The default for ORDER BY is ASCending order, which is the same as saying ORDER job_title ASC.

```
SELECT * FROM riskyjobs
    WHERE description LIKE '%window%' OR description LIKE '%washer%' OR
    description LIKE '%skyscraper%'
    ORDER BY state
```

```
SELECT * FROM riskyjobs
    WHERE description LIKE '%window%' OR description LIKE '%washer%' OR
    description LIKE '%skyscraper%'
    ORDER BY date_posted
```

How could we rewrite these queries if you wanted to see the job titles and states in reverse order? What about the newest jobs first?

```
SELECT * FROM riskyjobs
    WHERE description LIKE '%window%' OR description LIKE '%washer%' OR
    description LIKE '%skyscraper%'
    ORDER BY job_title DESC
```

We might want these if we've already ordered one of the columns and the user clicks on it again to reverse the order.

```
SELECT * FROM riskyjobs
    WHERE description LIKE '%window%' OR description LIKE '%washer%' OR
    description LIKE '%skyscraper%'
    ORDER BY state DESC
```

```
SELECT * FROM riskyjobs
    WHERE description LIKE '%window%' OR description LIKE '%washer%' OR
    description LIKE '%skyscraper%'
    ORDER BY date_posted DESC
```

> It seems like a lot of redundant code will be needed to generate all those queries. Can't we avoid having the same query generation code repeated three, or even six times?

Yes. While it's true that we'll need to run a different query when a user clicks a different link, it's possible to construct a single query based on the link clicked.

The first time the results are displayed, no links have been clicked so we don't have to worry about sorting. We can just take the keywords submitted into our form and build a query without an ORDER BY. The results are displayed with clickable headings, each of which links back to the script, but with a different sort order. So each link consists of a URL with the original keywords and a parameter named sort that indicates which order the results should be in.

What would really help in pulling this off is if we create our very own **custom function** that takes information about how to sort the job data, and returns a string with the WHERE clause and ORDER BY in place. Our new custom function takes a look at the sort parameter to figure out how to sort the search results. Here are the steps the function has to follow:

1 Preprocess the search keywords, and store them in an array.

2 Optionally take a sort parameter that tells the function what column to sort by.

3 Get rid of any empty search keywords.

4 Create a WHERE clause containing all of the search keywords.

5 Check to see if the sort parameter has a value. If it does, tack on an ORDER BY clause.

6 Return the newly formed query.

This might look like a lot of work, but we already have most of the code written. We just need to turn it into a function. But before we do that, let's take a look at how to put together custom functions...

Functions let you reuse code

A **function** is a block of code separate from the rest of your code that you can execute wherever you want in your script. Until now, you've used **built-in functions** that PHP has already created. `explode()`, `substr()`, and `mysqli_query()` are all functions that are predefined by PHP and can be used in any script.

But you can also write your own **custom functions** to provide features not supplied by the language. By creating a custom function, you can use your own code again and again without repeating it in your script. Instead, you just call the function by name when you want to run its code.

Following is an example of a custom function called `replace_commas()` that replaces commas with spaces in a string:

> **Custom functions allow you to organize a chunk of PHP code by name so that it can be easily reused.**

To create a custom function, you begin it with the word "function".

This is whatever you decide you want to name your function – make it as descriptive as possible.

A set of parentheses follow the function name. You can send one or more values into your function as arguments, each separated by a comma – in this case, there's just one value.

Curly braces indicate where the function code should go, just like in a loop or if statement.

```php
function replace_commas($str) {

    $new_str = str_replace(',', ' ', $str);

    return $new_str;

}
```

A function can return a value to the code that called it – in this case we return the altered string.

When you're ready to use a custom function, just call it by name and enter any values that it expects in parentheses. If the function is designed to return a value, you can assign it to a new variable, like this:

We pass in a string, "tightrope, walker, circus".

```php
$clean_search = replace_commas('tightrope, walker, circus');
```

The function returns a new string with the commas replaced by spaces.

Build a query with a custom function

We've already written much of the code we need to create the custom function that generates a Risky Jobs search query. All that's left is dropping the code into a PHP function skeleton. Here's the custom build_query() function:

We're passing into the function the $user_search array we created from the data entered into the search form.

```php
function build_query($user_search) {
  $search_query = "SELECT * FROM riskyjobs";

  // Extract the search keywords into an array
  $clean_search = str_replace(',', ' ', $user_search);
  $search_words = explode(' ', $clean_search);
  $final_search_words = array();
  if (count($search_words) > 0) {
    foreach ($search_words as $word) {
      if (!empty($word)) {
        $final_search_words[] = $word;
      }
    }
  }

  // Generate a WHERE clause using all of the search keywords
  $where_list = array();
  if (count($final_search_words) > 0) {
    foreach($final_search_words as $word) {
      $where_list[] = "description LIKE '%$word%'";
    }
  }
  $where_clause = implode(' OR ', $where_list);

  // Add the keyword WHERE clause to the search query
  if (!empty($where_clause)) {
    $search_query .= " WHERE $where_clause";
  }

  return $search_query;
}
```

Nothing new inside the function!

Actually, this is new. Here's where we return the new query so the code that called the function can use it.

The build_query() function returns a complete SQL query based on the search string passed into it via the $user_search argument. To use the function, we just pass along the search data entered by the user, and then store the result in a new string that we'll call $search_query:

```php
$search_query = build_query($user_search);
```

This lets us capture the value our function returns, in this case our new search query.

This is the value from the search form the user submitted.

Custom Functions Exposed

**This week's interview:
Custom functions: how custom are
they really?**

Head First: Look, we're all wondering one thing: what's so wrong with redundant code? I mean really, it's easy to create, you just copy and paste and boom. You're done.

Custom Function: Oh, don't get me started about redundant code. It's just plain ugly and makes your code more difficult to read. That's bad enough. But there is a much much more important reason to avoid redundant code.

Head First: Yes?

Custom Function: Well, what if something changes in your code? That happens pretty often.

Head First: So what? Things change all the time. You just go in and you fix it.

Custom Function: But what if the thing that changed was in your redundant code? And was in five, or maybe ten places throughout your application?

Head First: I don't see a problem. You'd just find them and change them all. Done.

Custom Function: Fine, okay. But what if you missed changing it in one place? You're only human, you programmers. If you missed it, you might have a very tough time tracking it down.

Head First: Sure, I guess that could happen. But how do you help?

Custom Function: Ah, but that's the beauty that is me. If that code had been in a function, you could have changed it once. Just once. Bim bam boom and done.

Head First: I have to admit, that's pretty compelling. But I still don't see why I should go out of my way to use you. I mean, you're pretty limited, right? You can only use strings.

Custom Function: Whoa! Wait a sec there, buckaroo! I can take any data type you care to send me. As long as the code inside me handles that data the way it should, I can use any data you want me to. Heck, I used an array in that last example. That's pretty darn sophisticated, I'd say.

Head First: But you returned a string.

Custom Function: I can return whatever you want. It's all about making the most of what I offer and using me correctly.

Head First: That's another thing. You're so demanding. You have to have data passed in.

Custom Function: Where are you getting these crazy ideas? You can call me with no variables if you want, and if I'm set up that way. If you don't want to send me data, don't write any variables in the parentheses next to my name when you create me. Although I can't think of many reasons why you wouldn't want to pass data to me. And get data back out again with a return statement.

Head First: We're all out of time. Thanks for the time.

Custom Function: Don't mention it. I live to serve. Or is that serve to live? Or serve liver? Something like that.

TEST DRIVE

Modify the Search script to use the `build_query()` function.

Create the new `build_query()` function in the `search.php` script, making sure to replace the original code with a call to the new function. Upload the script to your web server and try out a search in a web browser to make sure it works OK.

> That new custom build_query() function is cool, but it doesn't yet sort the search results. Could we add in another parameter that does that?

Absolutely. We can pass the `build_query()` function two parameters instead of just one.

We're already passing the function the `$user_search` argument, which contains the user's search terms. Now we need another argument, `$sort`, that indicates how to sort the data. The new `$sort` argument needs to control the order of data returned by the query in the six ways we came up with back on page 535: sorting by the `job_title`, `state`, and `date_posted` columns of the `riskyjobs` table in **both** ascending and descending order.

We could store the actual `ORDER BY` strings in `$sort` to indicate the sort order. Or we could use the numbers 1 through 6 to represent each of the sorts, like this:

`$sort == 1` ➡ `ORDER BY job_title`

`$sort == 2` ➡ `ORDER BY job_title DESC`

`$sort == 3` ➡ `ORDER BY state`

`$sort == 4` ➡ `ORDER BY state DESC`

`$sort == 5` ➡ `ORDER BY date_posted`

`$sort == 6` ➡ `ORDER BY date_posted DESC`

There's not much point in sorting by job description, as alphabetical order doesn't mean much there.

We just arbitrarily chose these numbers and the meaning that each one has. There are no special rules about it other than to use them consistently.

But aren't integers more cryptic when reading through your code? Without helpful comments, yes, but there's a more important reason to go with integers here. If we used `ORDER BY` strings, our data would show up in the URL of the script as part of each heading link. This would inadvertently reveal our table's column names, which you'd rather not make public for security reasons.

OK, I get how the new $sort argument works, but how do we know which value for $sort to pass into our function? Doesn't the user have to tell us that?

Yes, users must specify how to sort the search results, just as they specify the search terms themselves.

The good news is we already know how we want to implement this functionality: we're going to turn the column headings on our results page into hyperlinks. When a user clicks on a given heading, like "State," we'll pass the number for sorting by state into our build_query() function.

But we still have to get the sort order from the link to the script. We can do this when generating custom links for the headings by tacking on a sort parameter to the URL:

The search results are generated as part of an HTML table, which is why there's a <td> tag here.

We want to reload the page when users click a column heading to sort results, so we make this a self-referencing form.

```
$sort_links .= '<td><a href = "' . $_SERVER['PHP_SELF'] .
    '?usersearch=' . $user_search . '&sort=3">State</a></td>';
```

Our build_query() function needs the user's search keywords to display results, so we pass that in the URL.

We pass along sort data to indicate the desired sorting of the search. Since this is the state link, "sort" is equal to 3.

When the results page is generated, each heading link (except "Job Description") has its own customized URL, including a sort value for how the results should be sorted.

<a href="search.php?usersearch=bull fighter matador&sort=1">

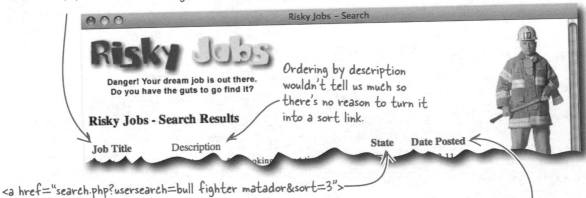

Ordering by description wouldn't tell us much so there's no reason to turn it into a sort link.

<a href="search.php?usersearch=bull fighter matador&sort=3">

<a href="search.php?usersearch=bull fighter matador&sort=5">

> Hmm. I see how those links work for the first three queries, but what about the other three ORDER BYs that sort in descending order? Where do they go?

Frank   Jill   Joe

Joe: Normally, the same heading would allow the user to sort in either ascending or descending order.

Jill: That's right. Each time they click a heading it just reverses the order.

Frank: Doesn't that mean we now have to somehow keep up with the state of the headings each time the user clicks them because they now have to link differently depending on what link they currently hold.

Joe: I don't see what you mean.

Frank: Well, the headings don't always do the same sort. For example, if you click the "Job Title" heading and it sorts the results by ascending job titles, then the link must change to now sort on descending job titles the next time it is clicked.

Jill: That's right. But keep in mind that each type of sort has a number in the link URL to let the script know what kind of sort to carry out. And since we're generating those links, we can control exactly what sort numbers get put in them.

Joe: I see. So the challenge for us is to somehow structure our code to be able to generate the correct link based on the current state of the sort, right?

Frank: Ah, I've got it! Isn't that something we can solve with a few `if` statements? I mean, that's the kind of decision making they're good for, right?

Joe: Yes, that would work but we're talking about several decisions involving the exact same piece of data, the sort type. It would really be nice if we could come up with a better way to make those decisions other than a bunch of nested `if-else` statements.

Jill: That's a great point, and it's a perfect opportunity to try out a new statement I heard about. The `switch` statement lets you make multiple decisions, way more than two, based solely on a single value.

Frank: That sounds great. Let's give it a try.

Joe: I agree. Anything to avoid complicated `if-else` statements. Those things give me a headache!

Jill: Yeah, me too. I think the `switch` statement might just be the ticket...

SWITCH makes far more decisions than IF

The switch statement offers an efficient way to check a value and execute one of several different blocks of code depending on that value. This is something that would require a small army of if-else statements, especially in situations involving quite a few options.

Instead of writing nested if-else statements to check for each possible value, you instead write a switch statement that has a case label corresponding to each possible value. At the end of each case label, you put the statement break;, which instructs PHP to drop out of the entire switch statement and not consider any other cases. This ensures that PHP will execute the code in no more than one case.

Let's take a look at an example that uses switch:

A SWITCH statement contains a series of CASE labels that execute different code blocks depending on the value of a variable.

```php
switch ($benefit_code) {

case 1:

  $benefits = 'Major medical, 10 sick days';

  break;

case 2:

  $benefits = 'Death and dismemberment only, one month paid leave';

  break;

case 3:

case 4:

  $benefits = 'Good luck!';

  break;

default:

  $benefits = 'None.';

}

echo 'We offer four comprehensive benefits packages';

echo 'The plan you have selected: ' . $benefits;
```

This is the value the switch statement is checking — it controls the entire switch.

This code is only executed when $benefit_code is 1.

The break statement tells PHP to drop out of the switch statement.

If you need to do the same thing for two or more values, just leave off the break statement until you reach the last value.

Any values stored in $benefit_code other than 1, 2, 3, or 4 will cause the default code to execute.

Not really. There are only three packages since 3 and 4 are both the same thanks to 3 not having a break.

542   Chapter 9

Risky Jobs has a new function called `generate_sort_links()` that allows users to sort search results by clicking on the result headings. Unfortunately, it's missing some important code. Finish the code for the function. And don't forget the numbers for each search type: 1 = ascending job title, 2 = descending job title, 3 = ascending state, 4 = descending state, 5 = ascending date posted, and 6 = descending date posted.

```php
.............. generate_sort_links($user_search, $sort) {
  $sort_links = '';

       ..............($sort) {
  case 1:
    $sort_links .= '<td><a href = "' . $_SERVER['PHP_SELF'] . '?usersearch=' . $user_search .
      '&sort=........">Job Title</a></td><td>Description</td>';
    $sort_links .= '<td><a href = "' . $_SERVER['PHP_SELF'] . '?usersearch=' . $user_search .
      '&sort=........">State</a></td>';
    $sort_links .= '<td><a href = "' . $_SERVER['PHP_SELF'] . '?usersearch=' . $user_search .
      '&sort=........">Date Posted</a></td>';
    ...............
  case 3:
    $sort_links .= '<td><a href = "' . $_SERVER['PHP_SELF'] . '?usersearch=' . $user_search .
      '&sort=........">Job Title</a></td><td>Description</td>';
    $sort_links .= '<td><a href = "' . $_SERVER['PHP_SELF'] . '?usersearch=' . $user_search .
      '&sort=........">State</a></td>';
    $sort_links .= '<td><a href = "' . $_SERVER['PHP_SELF'] . '?usersearch=' . $user_search .
      '&sort=........">Date Posted</a></td>';
    ...............
  case 5:
    $sort_links .= '<td><a href = "' . $_SERVER['PHP_SELF'] . '?usersearch=' . $user_search .
      '&sort=........">Job Title</a></td><td>Description</td>';
    $sort_links .= '<td><a href = "' . $_SERVER['PHP_SELF'] . '?usersearch=' . $user_search .
      '&sort=........">State</a></td>';
    $sort_links .= '<td><a href = "' . $_SERVER['PHP_SELF'] . '?usersearch=' . $user_search .
      '&sort=........">Date Posted</a></td>';
    ...............

  ...............
    $sort_links .= '<td><a href = "' . $_SERVER['PHP_SELF'] . '?usersearch=' . $user_search .
      '&sort=........">Job Title</a></td><td>Description</td>';
    $sort_links .= '<td><a href = "' . $_SERVER['PHP_SELF'] . '?usersearch=' . $user_search .
      '&sort=........">State</a></td>';
    $sort_links .= '<td><a href = "' . $_SERVER['PHP_SELF'] . '?usersearch=' . $user_search .
      '&sort=........">Date Posted</a></td>';
  }

  return ...................;
}
```

This is the default set of headings that should appear when the user hasn't chosen a sort method.

Risky Jobs has a new function called `generate_sort_links()` that allows users to sort search results by clicking on the result headings. Unfortunately, it's missing some important code. Finish the code for the function. And don't forget the numbers for each search type:
1 = ascending job title, 2 = descending job title, 3 = ascending state, 4 = descending state,
5 = ascending date posted, and 6 = descending date posted.

```php
function   generate_sort_links($user_search, $sort) {
  $sort_links = '';

  switch   ($sort) {
  case 1:
    $sort_links .= '<td><a href = "' . $_SERVER['PHP_SELF'] . '?usersearch=' . $user_search .
      '&sort= 2 ">Job Title</a></td><td>Description</td>';
    $sort_links .= '<td><a href = "' . $_SERVER['PHP_SELF'] . '?usersearch=' . $user_search .
      '&sort= 3 ">State</a></td>';
    $sort_links .= '<td><a href = "' . $_SERVER['PHP_SELF'] . '?usersearch=' . $user_search .
      '&sort= 5 ">Date Posted</a></td>';
    break;
  case 3:
    $sort_links .= '<td><a href = "' . $_SERVER['PHP_SELF'] . '?usersearch=' . $user_search .
      '&sort= 1 ">Job Title</a></td><td>Description</td>';
    $sort_links .= '<td><a href = "' . $_SERVER['PHP_SELF'] . '?usersearch=' . $user_search .
      '&sort= 4 ">State</a></td>';
    $sort_links .= '<td><a href = "' . $_SERVER['PHP_SELF'] . '?usersearch=' . $user_search .
      '&sort= 5 ">Date Posted</a></td>';
    break;
  case 5:
    $sort_links .= '<td><a href = "' . $_SERVER['PHP_SELF'] . '?usersearch=' . $user_search .
      '&sort= 1 ">Job Title</a></td><td>Description</td>';
    $sort_links .= '<td><a href = "' . $_SERVER['PHP_SELF'] . '?usersearch=' . $user_search .
      '&sort= 3 ">State</a></td>';
    $sort_links .= '<td><a href = "' . $_SERVER['PHP_SELF'] . '?usersearch=' . $user_search .
      '&sort= 6 ">Date Posted</a></td>';
    break;
  default:
    $sort_links .= '<td><a href = "' . $_SERVER['PHP_SELF'] . '?usersearch=' . $user_search .
      '&sort= 1 ">Job Title</a></td><td>Description</td>';
    $sort_links .= '<td><a href = "' . $_SERVER['PHP_SELF'] . '?usersearch=' . $user_search .
      '&sort= 3 ">State</a></td>';
    $sort_links .= '<td><a href = "' . $_SERVER['PHP_SELF'] . '?usersearch=' . $user_search .
      '&sort= 5 ">Date Posted</a></td>';
  }

  return   $sort_links  ;
}
```

If $sort is 1, it means we've already sorted by job title, so now we need to re-sort it in descending order.

If $sort hasn't been set yet or if it's 2, 4, or 6, we should display the original links that sort the data in ascending order.

Give build_query() the ability to sort

We now have two functions to handle Risky Jobs searches. build_query() constructs an SQL query based on search terms entered by the user, and generate_sort_links() generates hyperlinks for the search result headings that allow the user to sort the results. But build_query() isn't quite finished since the query it generates doesn't yet sort. The function needs to append an ORDER BY clause to the query. But it has to be the **correct** ORDER BY clause, as determined by a new $sort argument:

> We're now passing in the $sort argument to our function, in addition to $user_search.

```php
function build_query($user_search, $sort) {
  $search_query = "SELECT * FROM riskyjobs";

  ...

  // Add the keyword WHERE clause to the search query
  if (!empty($where_clause)) {
    $search_query .= " WHERE $where_clause";
  }

  // Sort the search query using the sort setting
  switch ($sort) {
  // Ascending by job title
  case 1:
    $search_query .= " ORDER BY title";
    break;
  // Descending by job title
  case 2:
    $search_query .= " ORDER BY title DESC";
    break;
  // Ascending by state
  case 3:
    $search_query .= " ORDER BY state";
    break;
  // Descending by state
  case 4:
    $search_query .= " ORDER BY state DESC";
    break;
  // Ascending by date posted (oldest first)
  case 5:
    $search_query .= " ORDER BY date_posted";
    break;
  // Descending by date posted (newest first)
  case 6:
    $search_query .= " ORDER BY date_posted DESC";
    break;
  default:
    // No sort setting provided, so don't sort the query
  }

  return $search_query;
}
```

> Here are the code additions to build_query(). This switch statement checks the value of $sort and adds the corresponding ORDER by statement to the end of the search query.

> When users load the results page without clicking a column heading, $sort will be empty, so as a default we won't sort the results at all.

> We return $search_query as before, only this time with an ORDER BY clause at the end.

Test Drive

Revamp the Search script to use the two new custom functions.

Create the new generate_sort_links() function in the search.php script, and then add the new code to the build_query() function so that it generates a query with sorted results. Don't forget to actually call the generate_sort_links() function in the script in place of the code that echoes the result headings.

Upload the script to your web server, open the search.html page in a browser, and try doing a search. Now click the headings above the search results to sort the jobs based on the different data. Make sure to click the same heading more than once to swap between ascending and descending order.

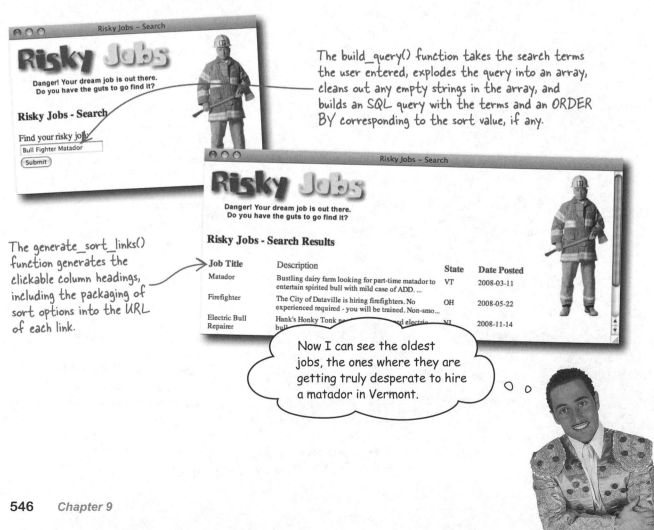

The build_query() function takes the search terms the user entered, explodes the query into an array, cleans out any empty strings in the array, and builds an SQL query with the terms and an ORDER BY corresponding to the sort value, if any.

The generate_sort_links() function generates the clickable column headings, including the packaging of sort options into the URL of each link.

Now I can see the oldest jobs, the ones where they are getting truly desperate to hire a matador in Vermont.

But sometimes I try a broader search and the results are overwhelming.

This is an awful lot of job listings to try and take in at once.

Risky Jobs

**Danger! Your dream job is out there.
Do you have the guts to go find it?**

Risky Jobs – Search

Risky Jobs - Search Results

Job Title	Description	State	Date Posted
Custard Walker	We need people willing to test the theory that you can walk on custard. We're going to fill a swi...	NM	2008-07-24
Shark Trainer	Training sharks to do cute tricks for the audiences at our new water theme park. You'll spend tim...	FL	2008-04-28
Voltage Checker	You'll be out in the field checking a.c. and d.c. voltages in the range of 3 to 250 or more volts. Y...	NC	2008-06-28
Antenna Installer	You'll be installing antennas and other metallic broadcast receiving equipment on the roofs of Miami...	FL	2008-09-04
Elephant Proctologist	Needed: experienced proctologist willing to work with large animals. Elephants at our zoo (in San Fr...	CA	2008-07-29
Airplane Engine Cleaner	Jet airplanes needing engines cleaned. In need of clean-minded individuals willing to handle rust an...	TX	2008-08-17
Matador	Bustling dairy farm looking for part-time matador to entertain spirited bull with mild case of ADD. ...	VT	2008-03-11
Paparazzo	Top celebrity photography firm looking for seasoned paparazzo to stalk temperamental lip-syncing pop...	CA	2008-03-24
Tightrope Walker	Fledgling big top looking for three-ring professional with 1-3 years of experience to perform tightr...	TX	2008-11-14
	Do you love animals and hate plaque? Well, then this ...ob for you! Our crocodile farm ...	FL	2008-07-14
	...fresh new faces. Full health insurance ...rovided. Must love kids....	NY	2008-11-02
	...elves on how good our pet food tastes. ...elp make our products even better. ...	MO	2008-11-09
	...s waiting for your superior non-violent ...kills. Must pass basic bull fighti...	ID	2008-11-14
	...Tonk needs an experienced electric bull ...ides (after you fix it) and hal...	NJ	2008-07-27
Firefighter	The City of Dataville is hiring firefighters. No experienced required - you will be trained. Non-smo...	OH	2008-05-22
Prize Fighter	Up and coming super fly gnat weight boxer needs an opponent to help build his winning record. Slow f...	MO	2008-11-14
Master Cat Juggler	Are you a practitioner of the lost art of cat juggling? Banned in forty countries, only the Jim Ruiz...	AZ	2008-11-14
		MT	2008-11-14

How do other sites avoid having lots of search results on a single page?

We can paginate our results

We're displaying all of our results on a single page right now, which is a problem when a search matches lots of jobs. Instead of forcing users to scroll up and down a huge page to see all the job matches, we can use a technique called **pagination** to display the search results. When you paginate results, you break the collection of job matches into groups, and then display each group on a separate web page, like this:

Each page shows five results, along with links to access the other pages of results. Users can easily click through each page and avoid having to scroll.

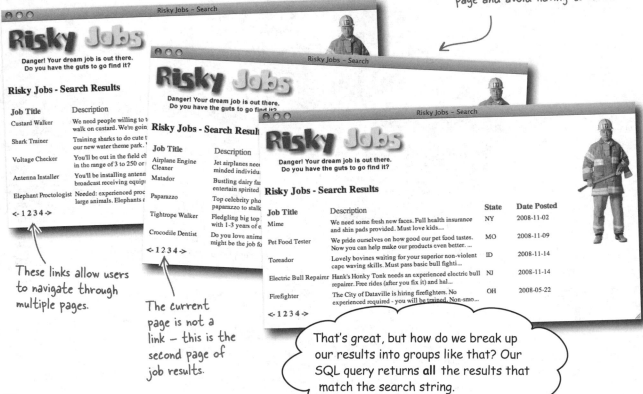

These links allow users to navigate through multiple pages.

The current page is not a link — this is the second page of job results.

> That's great, but how do we break up our results into groups like that? Our SQL query returns **all** the results that match the search string.

Pagination breaks query results into sets, and displays each set on its own web page.

We need a query that will return just a <u>subset</u> of the results, not all of them.

Luckily, SQL already gives us a way to do that: the LIMIT clause. Let's revisit LIMIT and see how we can use it to split our results up into groups of five...

Get only the rows you need with LIMIT

The key to controlling which rows we display on any given page is to add another clause to our search query, a LIMIT clause. To get a maximum of five rows, we add LIMIT 5 to the end of our query, like this:

```
SELECT * FROM riskyjobs
    ORDER BY job_title
    LIMIT 5
```

Without a WHERE clause, this query returns all the jobs in the database, which is equivalent to searching with no search terms.

Only return the first five matches no matter how many matches are actually found.

> **LIMIT controls what and how many rows are returned by an SQL query.**

If you recall, we use the custom build_query() function to create our Risky Jobs query. To force it to only display the first five matches, we just concatenate LIMIT 5 to the end of the query string after it's built:

```
$query = build_query($user_search, $sort);

$query =  $query . " LIMIT 5";
```

Adding a LIMIT clause to the end of a query limits the number of rows returned by the query, in this case to five rows.

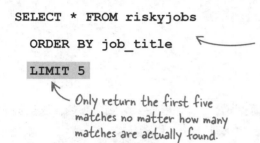

Custard Walker	...
Shark Trainer	...
Voltage Checker	...
Antenna Installer	...
Elephant Proctologist	...
Airplane Engine Cleaner	...
Matador	...
Paparazzo	...
Tightrope Walker	...
Crocodile Dentist	...
Mime	...
Pet Food Tester	...
Toreador	...
Electric Bull Repairer	...
Firefighter	...
...	

This works well for getting the first five rows of results, but what about the next five rows, and the five rows after that? To pull out rows deeper in the result set, we have to change our LIMIT up a bit. But how? LIMIT 10 would get the first 10 rows, so that wouldn't work. We need to get rows 6 through 10, and to do that we use LIMIT with different syntax. When you add two arguments to LIMIT, the first arguments controls how many rows you skip, and the second argument controls how many rows you get back. For example, here's how you get rows 11 through 25, which would be the third page of results:

```
$query = build_query($user_search, $sort);

$query =  $query . " LIMIT 10, 5";
```

The first argument tells LIMIT how many rows to skip – the first ten.

The second argument controls how many rows are returned – five, same as earlier.

Control page links with LIMIT

An important part of pagination is providing links that allow the user to move back and forth among the different pages of results. We can use the LIMIT clause to set up the naviagation links for the bottom of each page of results. For example, the "next" and "previous" links each have their own LIMIT. The same thing applies to the numeric links that allow the user to jump straight to a specific page of results.

Here are the LIMIT clauses for the first three pages of search results, along with LIMITs for some of the page links:

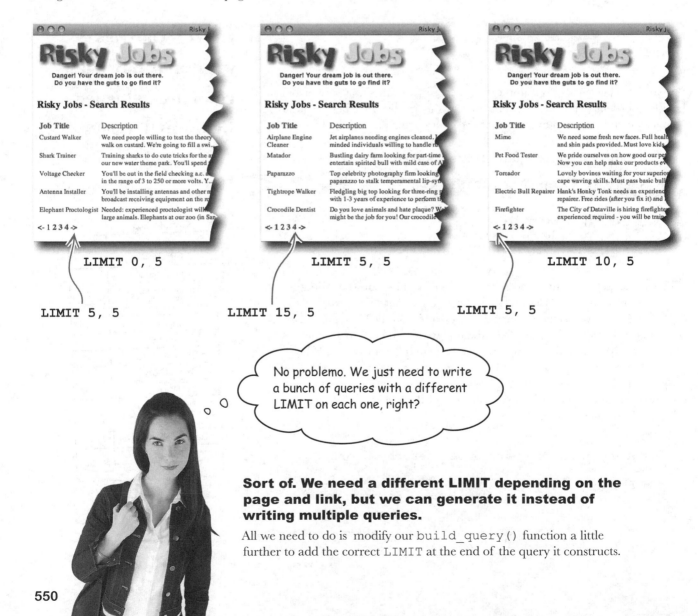

No problemo. We just need to write a bunch of queries with a different LIMIT on each one, right?

Sort of. We need a different LIMIT depending on the page and link, but we can generate it instead of writing multiple queries.

All we need to do is modify our build_query() function a little further to add the correct LIMIT at the end of the query it constructs.

Keep track of the pagination data

In order to add the new pagination functionality to `build_query()`, we need to set up and keep track of some variables that determine which search results to query and show on a given page. These variables are also important in determining how the navigation links at the bottom of the page are generated.

$cur_page

Get the current page, `$cur_page`, from the script URL via `$_GET`. If no current page is passed through the URL, set `$cur_page` to the first page (1).

$results_per_page

This is the number of results per page, which you choose based on the look and feel of the page, and how many search results fit nicely on the page with the layout. This is where the second argument to the `LIMIT` clause comes from.

$skip

Compute the number of rows to skip before the rows on the current page begin, `$skip`. This variable is what controls where each page begins in terms of results, providing the first argument to the `LIMIT` clause.

$total

Run a query that retrieves all the rows with no `LIMIT`, and then count the results and store it in `$total`. In other words, this is the total number of search results.

$num_pages

Compute the number of pages, `$num_pages`, using `$total` divided by `$results_per_page`. So for any given search, there is a total of `$total` matching rows, but they are displayed a page at a time, with each page containing `$results_per_page` matches. There are `$num_pages` pages, and the current page is identified by `$cur_page`.

Set up the pagination variables

Most of the pagination variables can be set up purely through information provided via the URL, which is accessible through the $_GET superglobal. For example, the $sort, $user_search, and $cur_page variables all flow directly from GET data. We can then use these variables to calculate how many rows to skip to get to the first row of data, $skip. The $results_per_page variable is a little different in that we just set it to however many search results we want to appear on each page, which is more of a personal preference given the layout of the results page.

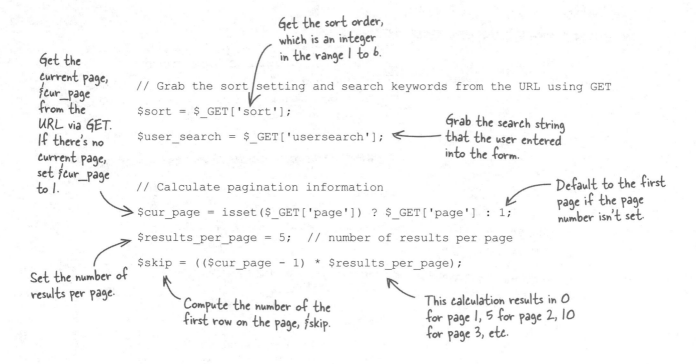

Get the sort order, which is an integer in the range 1 to 6.

Get the current page, $cur_page from the URL via GET. If there's no current page, set $cur_page to 1.

```
// Grab the sort setting and search keywords from the URL using GET
$sort = $_GET['sort'];

$user_search = $_GET['usersearch'];


// Calculate pagination information
$cur_page = isset($_GET['page']) ? $_GET['page'] : 1;

$results_per_page = 5;   // number of results per page

$skip = (($cur_page - 1) * $results_per_page);
```

Grab the search string that the user entered into the form.

Default to the first page if the page number isn't set.

Set the number of results per page.

Compute the number of the first row on the page, $skip.

This calculation results in 0 for page 1, 5 for page 2, 10 for page 3, etc.

We're still missing a couple of important variables: $total and $num_pages. These variables can only be set after performing an initial query to find out how many matches are found in the database. Once we know how many matches we have, it's possible to set these variables and then LIMIT the results...

Revise the query for paginated results

Now that we've got our variables set up, we need to revise the Search script so that instead of querying for all results, it queries for just the subset of results we need for the page the user is currently viewing. This involves first doing a query so that the $total variable can be set and the $num_pages variable can be calculated. Then we follow up with a second query that uses $skip and $results_per_page to generate a LIMIT clause that we add to the end of the query. Here's the revised section of the search.php script with these new additions highlighted:

> mysqli_num_rows() returns a count of how many total rows were returned by the query.

> This query retrieves all the rows with no LIMIT.

> Store away the total number of rows with a call to the mysqli_num_rows() function.

> Compute number of pages by dividing the total number of rows by the number of results per page, and then rounding up the result.

> The ceil() function rounds a number up to the nearest integer — the "ceiling".

> Skip this many rows...

> ...and return this many rows.

> Issue a second query, but this time LIMIT the results to the current page.

```php
// Query to get the total results
$query = build_query($user_search, $sort);

$result = mysqli_query($dbc, $query);

$total = mysqli_num_rows($result);

$num_pages = ceil($total / $results_per_page);


// Query again to get just the subset of results

$query = $query . " LIMIT $skip, $results_per_page";

$result = mysqli_query($dbc, $query);

while ($row = mysqli_fetch_array($result)) {

  echo '<tr class="results">';

  echo '<td valign="top" width="20%">' . $row['title'] . '</td>';

  echo '<td valign="top" width="50%">' . substr($row['description'], 0, 100) . '...</td>';

  echo '<td valign="top" width="10%">' . $row['state'] . '</td>';

  echo '<td valign="top" width="20%">' . substr($row['date_posted'], 0, 10) . '</td>';

  echo '</tr>';

}

echo '</table>';
```

Generate the page navigation links

So we've set up some variables and built a new SQL query that returns a subset of results for the page. All that's left to do is to generate the page navigation links for the bottom of the search results page: the "previous" link, numerical links for each page of results, and the "next" link. We already have all the information we need to put together the links. Let's go over it again to make sure it's clear how it will be used.

$user_search

Every page link still has to know what the user is actually searching for, so we have to pass along the search terms in each link URL.

$cur_page

The page navigation links are entirely dependent on the current page, so it's very important that it get packaged into every link URL.

$num_pages

We need to know how many pages there are in order to generate links for each of them.

$sort

The sort order also factors into the pagination links because the order has to be maintained or else the pagination wouldn't make any sense.

OK, we know what information we need in order to generate the page navigation links, so we're ready to crank out the PHP code to make it happen. This code could just be dropped into the `search.php` script, but what if we put it in its own custom function? That way the main script code that generates the search results can be much simpler, requiring only a single line of code to generate the page links—a call to to this new function, which we'll call `generate_page_links()`.

The only catch is that we don't want this function to get called if there is only one page of results. So we need to do a check on the number of pages before calling the new `generate_page_links()` function. Here's how we can perform the check and call the function, making sure to pass along the required information as function arguments:

```php
if ($num_pages > 1) {
  echo generate_page_links($user_search, $sort, $cur_page, $num_pages);
}
```

First check to make sure there is more than one page of search results; otherwise, don't generate the page links.

Pass along the search string, sort order, current page, and total number of pages to use in generating the page links.

PHP & MySQL Magnets

The generate_page_links() function is almost finished, but it's missing a few pieces of code. Use the magnets to plug in the missing code and give Risky Jobs the ability to generate page navigation links.

```php
function generate_page_links($user_search, $sort, $cur_page, $num_pages) {
  $page_links = '';

  // If this page is not the first page, generate the "previous" link

  if (                        ) {
       ...............................
    $page_links .= '<a href="' . $_SERVER['PHP_SELF'] .
      '?usersearch=' . $user_search .
      '&sort=' . $sort .

      '&page=' . (                        ) . '"><-</a> ';
                     ...............................
  }
  else {
    $page_links .= '<- ';
  }

  // Loop through the pages generating the page number links
  for ($i = 1; $i <= $num_pages; $i++) {

    if (                      ) {
         ...................................
      $page_links .= ' ' . $i;
    }
    else {
      $page_links .= ' <a href="' . $_SERVER['PHP_SELF'] .
        '?usersearch=' . $user_search .
        '&sort=' . $sort .
        '&page=' . $i . '"> ' . $i . '</a>';
    }
  }

  // If this page is not the last page, generate the "next" link

  if (                           ) {
       .........................................
    $page_links .= ' <a href="' . $_SERVER['PHP_SELF'] .
      '?usersearch=' . $user_search .
      '&sort=' . $sort .
      '&page=' . ($cur_page + 1) . '">-></a>';
  }
  else {
    $page_links .= ' ->';
  }

  return $page_links;
}
```

The "previous" link appears as a left arrow, as in "<-".

The "next" link appears as a right arrow, as in "->".

Magnets:

`$cur_page`
`$cur_page`
`$cur_page`
`$cur_page`

`<` `>`

`1`
`1`

`==`

`-` `$i`

`$num_pages`

PHP & MySQL Magnets Solution

The `generate_page_links()` function is almost finished, but it's missing a few pieces of code. Use the magnets to plug in the missing code and give Risky Jobs the ability to generate page navigation links.

```php
function generate_page_links($user_search, $sort, $cur_page, $num_pages) {
  $page_links = '';

  // If this page is not the first page, generate the "Previous" link
  if ( $cur_page > 1 ) {
    $page_links .= '<a href="' . $_SERVER['PHP_SELF'] .
      '?usersearch=' . $user_search .
      '&sort=' . $sort .

      '&page=' . ( $cur_page - 1 ) . '"><-</a> ';
  }
  else {
    $page_links .= '<- ';
  }

  // Loop through the pages generating the page number links
  for ($i = 1; $i <= $num_pages; $i++) {
    if ( $cur_page == $i ) {

      $page_links .= ' ' . $i;
    }
    else {
      $page_links .= ' <a href="' . $_SERVER['PHP_SELF'] .
        '?usersearch=' . $user_search .
        '&sort=' . $sort .
        '&page=' . $i . '"> ' . $i . '</a>';
    }
  }

  // If this page is not the last page, generate the "Next" link
  if ( $cur_page < $num_pages ) {
    $page_links .= ' <a href="' . $_SERVER['PHP_SELF'] .
      '?usersearch=' . $user_search .
      '&sort=' . $sort .
      '&page=' . ($cur_page + 1) . '">-></a>';
  }
  else {
    $page_links .= ' ->';
  }

  return $page_links;
}
```

We still have to pass along the user search data and the sort order in each link URL.

The "previous" link appears as a left arrow, as in "<-".

Make sure each page link points back to the same script — we're just passing a different page number with each link.

The link to a specific page is just the page number.

The "next" link appears as a right arrow, as in "->".

Putting together the complete Search script

And finally we arrive at a complete Risky Jobs Search script that displays the appropriate search results based on the user's search terms, generates clickable result heading links for sorting, paginates those results, and generates page navigation links along the bottom of the page.

```php
<?php
  // This function builds a search query from the search keywords and sort setting
  function build_query($user_search, $sort) {
    ...

    return $search_query;
  }

  // This function builds heading links based on the specified sort setting
  function generate_sort_links($user_search, $sort) {
    ...

    return $sort_links;
  }

  // This function builds navigational page links based on the current page and
  // the number of pages
  function generate_page_links($user_search, $sort, $cur_page, $num_pages) {
    ...

    return $page_links;
  }

  // Grab the sort setting and search keywords from the URL using GET
  $sort = $_GET['sort'];
  $user_search = $_GET['usersearch'];

  // Calculate pagination information
  $cur_page = isset($_GET['page']) ? $_GET['page'] : 1;
  $results_per_page = 5;   // number of results per page
  $skip = (($cur_page - 1) * $results_per_page);

  // Start generating the table of results
  echo '<table border="0" cellpadding="2">';

  // Generate the search result headings
  echo '<tr class="heading">';
  echo generate_sort_links($user_search, $sort);
  echo '</tr>';
```

We've already built these functions, so there's no need to rehash every line of their code here.

Grab the sort order and search string that were passed through the URL as GET data.

Initialize the pagination variables since we'll need them in a moment to LIMIT the query and build the pagination links.

Call the generate_sort_links() function to create the links for the result headings, and then echo them.

Hang on, there's more!

search.php

The complete Search script, continued...

```
// Connect to the database
require_once('connectvars.php');
$dbc = mysqli_connect(DB_HOST, DB_USER, DB_PASSWORD, DB_NAME);

// Query to get the total results
$query = build_query($user_search, $sort);
$result = mysqli_query($dbc, $query);
$total = mysqli_num_rows($result);
$num_pages = ceil($total / $results_per_page);

// Query again to get just the subset of results
$query =  $query . " LIMIT $skip, $results_per_page";
$result = mysqli_query($dbc, $query);
while ($row = mysqli_fetch_array($result)) {
  echo '<tr class="results">';
  echo '<td valign="top" width="20%">' . $row['title'] . '</td>';
  echo '<td valign="top" width="50%">' . substr($row['description'], 0, 100) . '...</td>';
  echo '<td valign="top" width="10%">' . $row['state'] . '</td>';
  echo '<td valign="top" width="20%">' . substr($row['date_posted'], 0, 10) . '</td>';
  echo '</tr>';
}
echo '</table>';

// Generate navigational page links if we have more than one page
if ($num_pages > 1) {
  echo generate_page_links($user_search, $sort, $cur_page, $num_pages);
}

mysqli_close($dbc);
?>
```

Call the build_query() to build the SQL job search query.

Here's the LIMIT clause we created to query only a subset of job results.

And here's the code we wrote that trims down the job description and date posted using the substr() function.

Call the generate_page_links() function to generate the page links, and then echo them.

Keep things tidy by closing the database connection.

there are no Dumb Questions

Q: Do we really have to pass the search, sort, and pagination information into `generate_page_links()`?

A: Yes. And the reason has to do with the fact that well-designed functions shouldn't manipulate data outside of their own code. So a function should only access data passed to it in an argument, and then only make changes to data that it returns.

Q: OK, so what about echoing data? Why doesn't `generate_page_links()` just echo the links?

A: Same problem. By echoing data to the browser, the function would be effectively reaching beyond itself to make a change somewhere else. It's much harder to debug and maintain functions when it isn't clear what data they change. The solution is to always return the data affected by a function, and then do whatever you want with the data returned by the function, **outside of the function**.

Test Drive

Finish the Risky Jobs Search script.

Add the new `generate_page_links()` function to the `search.php` script, making sure to also add the code that calls it after checking to see if there is more than one page of results. Also create and initialize the variables used as arguments to the function. And don't forget to update the query code so that it uses `LIMIT` to pull out the correct subset of results for each page.

When all that's done, upload the new `search.php` script to your web server, and then open the `search.html` page in a web browser. Try a few searches, making sure to search on some terms that will end up with lots of results so that the new pagination features kick in. For maximum result pages, do a search with an empty search form.

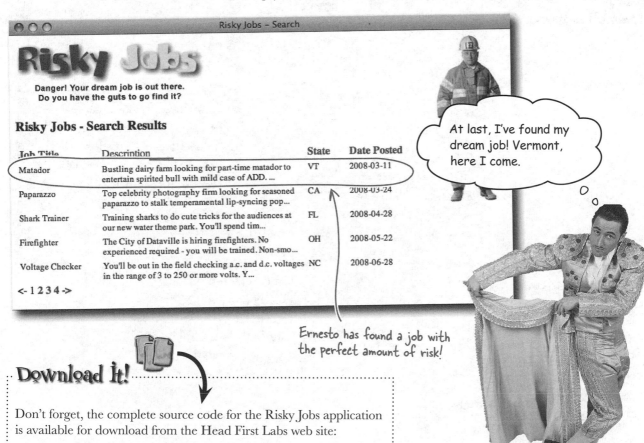

Ernesto has found a job with the perfect amount of risk!

Download It!

Don't forget, the complete source code for the Risky Jobs application is available for download from the Head First Labs web site:

www.headfirstlabs.com/books/hfphp

CHAPTER 9

Your PHP & MySQL Toolbox

The Risky Jobs Search script required quite a few new PHP and MySQL techniques. Let's recap some of the most important ones.

LIKE

Use LIKE to look for data within an SQL query without necessarily requiring an identical match. Put a % in front of and/or after a search term to let LIKE know that the term can have other characters surrounding it.

explode(), implode()

The PHP explode() function breaks a string apart into an array of substrings that are separated by a common delimiter, such as a space or comma. implode() does the opposite — it builds a single string from an array of strings, inserting a delimiter between them.

substr()

This PHP function extracts a portion of a string based on arguments you supply it. You can grab the beginning of a string, the end of a string, or some piece in between.

Custom function

A chunk of PHP code organized into a named, reusable package. The idea is to isolate code that performs a certain task so that it can be reused with minimal effort and code duplication.

str_replace()

Call this PHP function to do a find-and-replace on a string of text, replacing one character or sequence of characters with another.

switch-case

A PHP decision-making construct that allows you to execute one of many groups of code based on a single value. If you find yourself with a bunch of nested if-else statements, you may find that you can code it more efficiently as a switch statement.

LIMIT

The LIMIT clause lets you control exactly how many rows are returned by an SQL query. Not only that, but LIMIT can skip rows in the result set, allowing you to isolate a subset of results.

10 regular expressions

Rules for replacement

Mrs. Blatt replaced the class hamster! Did she think we wouldn't notice?

String functions are kind of lovable. But at the same time, they're limited. Sure, they can tell the length of your string, truncate it, and change certain characters to other certain characters. But sometimes you need to break free and tackle more complex text manipulations. This is where **regular expressions** can help. They can **precisely modify strings** based on a **set of rules** rather than a single criterion.

Risky Jobs lets users submit resumes

Riskyjobs.biz has grown. The company now lets job seekers enter their resumes and contact information into a web form so that our Risky Jobs employers can find them more easily. Here's what the form looks like:

In addition to normal contact information, a Risky Jobs candidate must also enter their desired job, as well as their resume.

The new Risky Jobs Registration form allows job candidates to enter information about themselves so that potential employers can find them.

Our job seeker information is stored in a table that can be searched by employers, recruiters, and headhunters to identify potential new employees. But there's a problem… the data entered into the form apparently can't be trusted!

First Name: Four Fingers
Last Name: McGraw
Email: four@gregs-listnet
Phone: 555-098
Desired Job: Knife Juggler

First, I couldn't get a ninja because his phone number is missing, and now my email to this knife juggler has bounced. I've pretty much had it with the bad data in the Risky Jobs resume bank.

First Name: Jimmy
Last Name: Swift
Email: JS@sim-u-duck.com
Phone: 636 4652
Desired Job: Ninja

Employers can search the Risky Jobs candidate database and then contact people to possibly hire them… assuming enough contact information has been entered!

Exercise

Below is some of the code for the `registration.php` script, which displays and processes the user data entered into the form to register a new job candidate. Annotate what you think is wrong with the code, and how it could be changed to resolve the bad data problem.

```php
<?php
  if (isset($_POST['submit'])) {
    $first_name = $_POST['firstname'];
    $last_name = $_POST['lastname'];
    $email = $_POST['email'];
    $phone = $_POST['phone'];
    $job = $_POST['job'];
    $resume = $_POST['resume'];
    $output_form = 'no';

    if (empty($first_name)) {
      // $first_name is blank
      echo '<p class="error">You forgot to enter your first name.</p>';
      $output_form = 'yes';
    }

    if (empty($last_name)) {
      // $last_name is blank
      echo '<p class="error">You forgot to enter your last name.</p>';
      $output_form = 'yes';
    }

    if (empty($email)) {
      // $email is blank
      echo '<p class="error">You forgot to enter your email address.</p>';
      $output_form = 'yes';
    }

    if (empty($phone)) {
      // $phone is blank
      echo '<p class="error">You forgot to enter your phone number.</p>';
      $output_form = 'yes';
    }

    ...          Continuing validating non-empty
  }              job and resume fields.
  else {
    $output_form = 'yes';
  }

  if ($output_form == 'yes') {
?>
...          Show the form.
```

Exercise Solution

Below is some of the code for the `registration.php` script, which displays and processes the user data entered into the form to register a new job candidate. Annotate what you think is wrong with the code, and how it could be changed to resolve the bad data problem.

```php
<?php
  if (isset($_POST['submit'])) {
    $first_name = $_POST['firstname'];
    $last_name = $_POST['lastname'];
    $email = $_POST['email'];
    $phone = $_POST['phone'];
    $job = $_POST['job'];
    $resume = $_POST['resume'];
    $output_form = 'no';

    if (empty($first_name)) {
      // $first_name is blank
      echo '<p class="error">You forgot to enter your first name.</p>';
      $output_form = 'yes';
    }

    if (empty($last_name)) {
      // $last_name is blank
      echo '<p class="error">You forgot to enter your last name.</p>';
      $output_form = 'yes';
    }

    if (empty($email)) {
      // $email is blank
      echo '<p class="error">You forgot to enter your email address.</p>';
      $output_form = 'yes';
    }

    if (empty($phone)) {
      // $phone is blank
      echo '<p class="error">You forgot to enter your phone number.</p>';
      $output_form = 'yes';
    }
      ...
  }
  else {
    $output_form = 'yes';
  }

  if ($output_form == 'yes') {
?>
      ...
```

The script checks for empty form fields, which is good, but some of the form fields have more specialized data that must adhere to a certain format.

There isn't much else we can check in regard to first and last names, so this code is fine.

An email address has a very specific format that we should enforce before accepting form data from the user.

Four Fingers McGraw left a dot out of his email address near the end – the form should catch those kind of errors!

Same thing with a phone number – the user's form submission shouldn't be allowed unless we can be certain that their phone number is in the correct format.

Continuing validating non-empty job and resume fields.

Jimmy Swift didn't provide an area code with his phone number, which the form should've demanded.

Show the form.

What we really need is a way to <u>verify</u> email addresses and phone numbers, the two fields in the form that have a specific format. For the other fields it's OK to just make sure they aren't empty.

> Why don't we use some string functions to fix the bad data? Can't we use str_replace() to add in the missing data?

You can fix some data with string functions but they don't help much when data must fit a very specific pattern.

String functions are well suited to simple find-and-replace operations. For example, if users submitted their phone numbers using dots to separate the blocks of digits instead of hyphens, we could easily write some str_ replace() code to substitute in hyphens in their place

But for anything that we can't possibly know, like the area code of Jimmy Swift's phone number, we need to ask the person who submitted the form to clarify. And the only way we can know that he's missing an area code is to understand the exact pattern of a phone number. What we really need is more advanced validation to ensure that things like phone numbers and email addresses are entered exactly right.

> OK, but can't we still use string functions to do this validation?

String functions really aren't useful for more than the most primitive of data validation.

Think about how you might attempt to validate an email address using string functions. PHP has a function called strlen() that will tell you how many characters are in a string. But there's no predefined character length for data like email addresses. Sure, this could potentially help with phone numbers because they often contain a consistent quantity of numbers, but you still have the potential dots, dashes, and parentheses to deal with.

Getting back to email addresses, their format is just too complex for string functions to be of much use. We're really looking for specific **patterns of data** here, which requires a validation strategy that can check user data against a pattern to see if it's legit. Modeling patterns for your form data is at the heart of this kind of validation.

Decide what your data should look like

Our challenge is to clearly specify exactly what a given piece of form data should look like, right down to every character. Consider Jimmy's phone number. It's pretty obvious to a human observer that his number is missing an area code. But form validation isn't carried out by humans; it's carried out by PHP code. This means we need to "teach" our code how to look at a string of data entered by the user and determine if it matches the pattern for a phone number.

Coming up with such a pattern can be a challenge, and it involves really thinking about the range of possibilities for a type of data. Phone numbers are fairly straightforward since they involve 10 digits with optional delimiters. Email addresses are a different story, but we'll worry about them a bit later in the chapter.

Why doesn't anyone call?

It's easy for a human to look and see that Jimmy forgot his area code, but not so trivial making the same "observation" from PHP code.

First Name: **Jimmy**
Last Name: **Swift**
Email: **JS@sim-u-duck.com**
Phone: **636 4652**
Desired Job: **Ninja**

there are no Dumb Questions

Q: I'm still not sure I see why I can't just stick with `isset()` and `empty()` for our form validation.

A: These two functions will tell you whether or not someone who submitted a form put data in a text field, but they won't tell you anything about the actual data they entered. As far as the `empty()` function is concerned, there's absolutely no difference between a user entering "(707) 827-700" or "4FG8SXY12" into the phone number field in our form. This would be a huge problem for sites like Risky Jobs, which depends on reliable data to get in touch with job candidates.

Q: If `isset()` and `empty()` won't work, can't we simply have someone check the data after it goes into the database?

A: You can, but by then it's often too late to fix the bad data. If a phone number is missing an area code, we need to ask the user to clarify things by resubmitting the data in that form field.
If you wait until later and check the data once it's already in the database, you may have no way of contacting the user to let them know that some of their data was invalid. And since the user probably won't realize they made a mistake, they won't know anything's wrong either.

So, the best plan of action is to validate the users form data immediately when they submit the form. That way you can display an error message and ask them to fill out the form again.

Q: So then how do you decide whether the data the user entered is valid or not?

A: That depends on what kind of data it is. Different types of information have different rules that they need to follow: what kind of characters they contain, how many characters they have, what order those characters are in. So you need to communicate those rules in your PHP code. Let's take a closer look at the rules governing phone numbers...

Sharpen your pencil

Write down all the different ways you can think of to represent a phone number.

....

....

....

....

....

....

....

....

....

....

What are some rules that are reasonable to expect your users to follow when filling out your form? For example, phone numbers should not contain letters.

Here's a rule to get you started.

We could insist on rules such as only digits and all 10 digits must be run together

....

....

....

....

....

....

Sharpen your pencil Solution

Write down all the different ways you can think of to represent a phone number.

555 636 4652

(555) 636-4652

(555)636-4652

(555) 6364652

555636-4652

555 636-4652

555.636.4652

5556364652

555-636-4652

555 ME NINJA

Spaces, dashes, right and left parentheses, and sometimes periods can show up in phone numbers.

It's even possible to include letters in a phone number, although this is stretching the limits of what we should consider a valid number.

What are some rules that are reasonable to expect your users to follow when filling out your form? For example, phone numbers should not contain letters.

Here's a rule to get you started.

We could insist on rules such as only digits and all 10 digits must be run together

We could break the number into three form fields, one for area code, one for the first three digits, and the final one for the last four digits.

Or we could tell the people filling out the form that their number must look like (555)636-4652. It's up to us to make the rules.

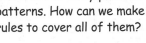

There are so many possible patterns. How can we make rules to cover all of them?

There are some things we know for sure about phone numbers, and we can use those things to make rules.

First, they can't begin with 1 (long distance) or 0 (operator). Second, there should be 10 digits. And even though some people might have clever ways to represent their phone numbers with letters, phone numbers are esentially numbers—10 digits when we include an area code.

Formulate a pattern for phone numbers

To go beyond basic validation, such as `empty()` and `isset()`, we need to decide on a pattern that we want our data to match. In the case of a phone number, this means we need to commit to a single format that we expect to receive from the phone field in our form. Once we decide on a phone number format/pattern, we can validate against it.

Following is what is likely the most common phone number format in use today, at least for domestic U.S. phone numbers. Committing to this format means that if the phone number data users submit doesn't match this, the PHP script will reject the form and display an error message.

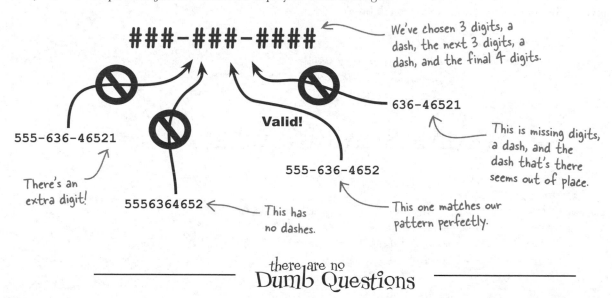

###-###-####

We've chosen 3 digits, a dash, the next 3 digits, a dash, and the final 4 digits.

555-636-46521

There's an extra digit!

5556364652 — This has no dashes.

Valid!

555-636-4652 — This one matches our pattern perfectly.

636-46521

This is missing digits, a dash, and the dash that's there seems out of place.

---

there are no Dumb Questions

Q: Do I have to use that pattern for matching phone numbers?

A: That's what we're using for Risky Jobs because it's pretty standard, but when you're designing your own forms you should pick one that makes sense to you. Just keep in mind that the more commonly accepted the pattern is, the more likely users will follow it.

Q: Couldn't I just tell users to enter a pattern like ########## and then use PHP's string functions to make sure the data contains 10 numeric characters?

A: You could, and that would be sufficient if that was the pattern your users expected. Unfortunately, it's not really a very good pattern because most people don't run their phone number together like that when filling out forms. It's a bit non-standard, which means users won't be used to it, and will be less likely to follow it.

Q: So? It's my pattern, I can do what I want, right?

A: Sure, but at the same time you want your users to have a good experience. Otherwise they'll quit visiting your site.

Q: OK, so couldn't I use three text fields for the phone number: one for area code, then three digits in the second, and then the last four digits in the third. Then I could use PHP's string functions.

A: Yes, you could, and some sites do that. But being able to match patterns gives you more flexibility. And matching patterns is useful for lots more things than just making sure your user enters the right pattern for a phone number, as you'll see later in this chapter.

Match patterns with regular expressions

PHP offers a powerful way to create and match patterns in text. You can create rules that let you look for patterns in strings of text. These rules are referred to as ***regular expressions,*** or ***regex*** for short. A regular expression represents a pattern of characters to match. With the help of regular expressions, you can describe in your code the rules you want your strings to conform to in order for a match to occur.

As an example, here's a regular expression that looks for 10-digits in a row. This pattern will only match a string that consists of a 10 digit number. If the string is longer or shorter than that, it won't match. If the string contains anything but numbers, it won't match. Let's break it down.

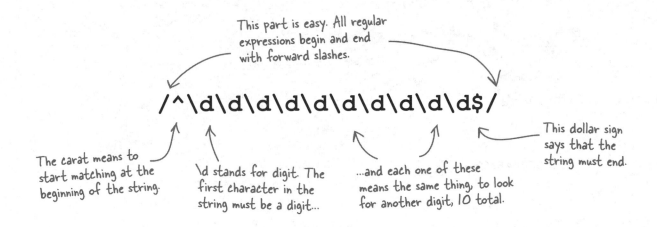

This part is easy. All regular expressions begin and end with forward slashes.

The carat means to start matching at the beginning of the string.

\d stands for digit. The first character in the string must be a digit...

...and each one of these means the same thing, to look for another digit, 10 total.

This dollar sign says that the string must end.

There's also a more concise way of writing this same regular expression, which makes use of curly braces. Curly braces are used to indicate repetition:

```
/^\d{10}$/
```

This means the same thing as the pattern above. {10} is a shorthand way to say 10 digits.

Regular expressions are rules used to match patterns in one or more strings.

Yeah, regular expressions are really clear. About as clear as mud.

It's true, regular expressions are cryptic and often difficult to read... but they are very powerful.

Power often comes at a cost, and in the case of regular expressions, that cost is learning the cryptic syntax that goes into them. You won't become a master of regular expressions overnight, but the good news is you don't have to. You can do some amazingly powerful and useful things with regular expressions, especially when it comes to form field validation, with a very basic knowledge of regular expressions. Besides, the more you work with them and get practice breaking them down and parsing them, the easier they'll be to understand.

Build patterns using metacharacters

Being able to match digits in a text string using \d is pretty cool, but if that's all the functionality that regular expressions provided, their use would be sorely limited. Just matching digits isn't even going to be enough for Risky Jobs phone number validation functionality, as we're going to want to be able to match characters like spaces, hyphens, and even letters.

Luckily, PHP's regex functionality lets you use a bunch more special expressions like \d to match these things. These expressions are called **metacharacters**. Let's take a look at some of the most frequently used regex metacharacters.

Metacharacters let us describe patterns of text within a regular expression.

\d

As you saw on the previous page, this metacharacter looks for a digit. It will match any number from 0 to 9. Keep in mind, on its own, \d matches just one digit, so if you wanted to match a two-digit number, you'd need to use either \d\d or \d{2}.

\w

Looks for any alphanumeric character—in other words, either a letter or a number. It will match one character from the following: a–z and A–z (both uppercase and lowercase letters), as well as 0–9 (just like \d) .

\s

Looks for whitespace. This doesn't mean just the space character you get on the screen when you hit the Space bar; \s also matches a tab character, or a newline or carriage return. Again, keep in mind that \s will only match one of these characters at a time. If you wanted to match exactly two space characters in a row, you'd need to use \s\s or \s{2}.

^

We saw the caret metacharacter on the previous page as well. It looks for the beginning of a string, so you can use it to indicate that a match must happen at the start of a text string, rather than anywhere in the string. For example, the regex /^\d{3}/ will match the string "300 applications", but not the string "We received 300 applications".

.

The period metacharacter, matches any one character, except a newline. It'll match a letter or digit, just like \w, as well as a space or tab, like \s.

$

Looks for the end of a string. You can use this metacharacter with ^ to bookend your match, specifying exactly where it will start and finish. For example, /^\w{5}\s\d{3}$/ will match "Nanny 411", but not "Nanny 411 is great" or "Call Nanny 411".

These metacharacters are cool, but what if you really want a specific character in your regex? Just use that character in the expression. For example, if you wanted to match the exact phone number "707-827-7000", you would use the regex /707-827-7000/.

Match each different phone number regular expression with the phone number that it matches.

Regex

String it matches

5556364652

`/^\d{3}\s\d{7}$/`

555 636 4652

`/^\d{3}\s\d{3}\s\d{4}$/`

555636-4652

`/^\d{3}\d{3}-\d{4}$/`

555 ME NINJA

`/^\d{3}-\d{3}-\d{4}$/`

555 6364652

`/^\d{3}\s\w\w\s\w{5}$/`

555-636-4652

`/^\d{10}$/`

WHO DOES WHAT? SOLUTION

Match each of the phone number regular expressions with the phone number that it matches.

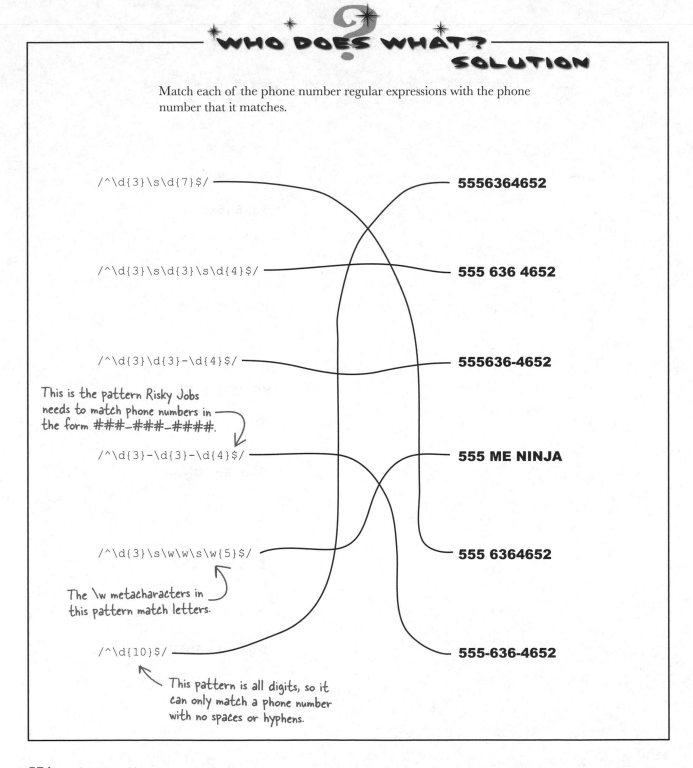

/^\d{3}\s\d{7}$/ ———————————— **5556364652**

/^\d{3}\s\d{3}\s\d{4}$/ ———————————— **555 636 4652**

/^\d{3}\d{3}-\d{4}$/ ———————————— **555636-4652**

This is the pattern Risky Jobs needs to match phone numbers in the form ###-###-####.

/^\d{3}-\d{3}-\d{4}$/ ———————————— **555 ME NINJA**

/^\d{3}\s\w\w\s\w{5}$/ ———————————— **555 6364652**

The \w metacharacters in this pattern match letters.

/^\d{10}$/ ———————————— **555-636-4652**

This pattern is all digits, so it can only match a phone number with no spaces or hyphens.

BE the Regular Expression

Your job is to play the role of regular expression, and either accept or reject phone numbers for Risky Jobs users. Check the box of phone numbers that you deem valid, and leave the others unchecked. Annotate why any invalid numbers are invalid.

This is the phone number regular expression – be it!

$$/^\d\{3\}-\d\{3\}-\d\{4\}\$/$$

☐ **(555) 935-2659**

☐ **(555)672-0953**

☐ **555-343-8263**

Surfing can be quite risky, especially when you work as professional shark bait!

☐ **555-441-9005**

☐ **555.903.6386**

☐ **555-612-8527-8724**

BE the Regular Expression Solution

Your job is to play the role of regular expression, and either accept or reject phone numbers for Risky Jobs users. Check the box of phone numbers that you deem valid, and leave the others unchecked. Annotate why any invalid numbers are invalid.

This is the phone number regular expression — be it!

$$/^\backslash d\{3\}-\backslash d\{3\}-\backslash d\{4\}\$/$$

☐ **(555) 935-2659**

Parentheses aren't allowed, and neither are spaces.

☐ **(555)672-0953**

No parentheses, please.

☑

☑ **555-441-9005**

Our regular expression requires dashes, not dots.

☐ **555.903.6386**

Whoa, there's an extra four numbers on this one. Is that an office extension?

☐ **555-612-8527-8724**

Sometimes people add additional digits to their telephone numbers, like a four-digit extension at the end. Is there any way we can match these patterns, too?

Yes, but the key is to specify such a pattern as optional in your regular expression.

If we changed our regex to `/^\d{3}-\d{3}-\d{4}-d{4}$/`, we'd be **requiring** our string to have a four-digit extension at the end, and we'd no longer match phone numbers like "555-636-4652". But we can use regular expressions to indicate that parts of the string are optional. Regexes support a feature called **quantifiers** that let you specify **how many times** characters or metacharacters should appear in a pattern. You've actually already seen quantifiers in action in regexes like this:

$$/^\backslash d\{10\}\$/$$

This says "a digit should show up 10 times in a row."

Here, curly braces act as a quantifier to say how many times the preceding digit should appear. Let's take a look at some other frequently used quantifiers.

{min,max}

When there are two numbers in the curly braces, separated by a comma, this indicates a range of possible times the preceding character or metacharacter should be repeated. Here we're saying it should appear 2, 3, or 4 times in a row.

+

The preceding character or metacharacter must appear **one or more times**.

?

The preceding character or metacharacter must appear **once or not at all**.

---

*

The character or metacharacter can appear **one or more times… or not at all**.

A quantifier specifies how many times a metacharacter should appear.

So, if we wanted to match those optional digits at the end of our phone number, we could use the following pattern:

$$/^\backslash d\{3\}-\backslash d\{3\}-\backslash d\{4\}(-\backslash d\{4\})?\$/$$

Surround the section the quantifier applies to in parentheses.

The question mark makes the hyphen and the last four digits optional.

You forgot one thing. U.S. phone numbers can't begin with 0 or 1.

You're absolutely right. 0 connects you to an operator, and 1 dials long distance.

We simply want the area code and number. We need to make sure the first digit is not 1 or 0. And to do that, we need a **character class**.

Character classes let you match characters from a specific set of values. You can look for a range of digits with a character class. You can also look for a set of values. And you can add a caret to look for everything that **isn't** in the set.

To indicate that a bunch of characters or metacharacters belongs to a character class, all you need to do is surround them by square brackets, **[ ]**. Let's take a look at a few examples of character classes in action:

[0-2]

This matches a range of numbers. It will match 0, 1, or 2.

[A-D]

This will match A, B, C, or D.

In a character class, the ^ means "don't match".

[^b-f]

This carat has a different meaning when it's used inside a character class. Instead of saying, "the string must start with...", the caret means "match everything except..."

This will match everything except b, c, d, e, or f.

A character class is a set of rules for matching a single character.

Write a regular expression that matches international phone numbers:

....

....

....

Fine-tune patterns with character classes

With the help of character classes, we can refine our regular expression for phone numbers so that it won't match invalid digit combinations. That way, if someone accidentally enters an area code that starts with 0 or 1, we can throw an error message. Here's what our new-and-improved regex looks like:

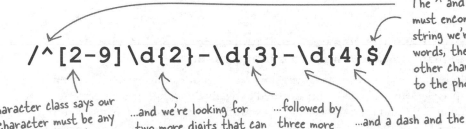

The ^ and $ specify that our regex must encompass the whole text string we're matching. In other words, the string can't contain any other characters that don't belong to the phone number.

The character class says our first character must be any digit from 2 to 9, inclusive.

...and we're looking for two more digits that can be any value from 0-9...

...followed by three more digits....

...and a dash and the last 4 digits.

there are no Dumb Questions

Q: So character classes let you specify a range of characters that will match the text string.

A: Yes, a character class lets you specify in your regular expression that any member of a specified set of characters will match the text string, instead of just one.
For example, the character class `[aeiou]` will match one instance of any lowercase vowel, and the class `[m-zM-Z]` will match one instance of any letter in the second half of the alphabet, lowercase or uppercase.
And the character class `[0-9]` is equivalent to the metacharacter `\d`, which is really just a shorthand way of saying the same thing.

Q: Don't I need to put spaces or commas in between the characters or ranges I specify in character classes?

A: No, if you do that, those extra characters will be interpreted as part of the set of characters that should match the text string.
For example, the character class

`[m-z, M-Z]`

would match not only uppercase and lowercase letters from m to z, but also a comma or space, which is probably not what you want.

Q: What if I want to match a character in a character class more than once? Like one or more vowels consecutively.

A: Just add a quantifier after the character class. The expression `/[aeiouAEIOU]+/` will match one or more vowels in a row.

Q: I thought quantifiers only applied to the character that immediately preceded them.

A: Usually that's the case, but if a quantifier directly follows a character class, it applies to the whole class.
And if you want to make a quantifier apply to a whole series of characters that aren't in a character class, you can surround these characters with parentheses to indicate that they should be grouped together. As an example, the regular expression `/(hello)+/` will match one or more consecutive instances of the word "hello" in a text string.

Q: What if I wanted to match two different spellings of a word, like "ketchup" or "catsup"?

A: You can use the vertical-pipe character (|) in your regular expressions to indicate a set of options to choose from.
So, the regular expression `/(ketchup|catsup|catchup)/` will match any one of the three most common spelling variants of the word.

What about putting characters like periods or question marks in a regular expression. If I type those in, won't PHP think they're metacharacters or quantifiers and screw up processing my regex?

If you want to use reserved characters in your regular expression, you need to escape them.

In regular expression syntax, there are a small set of characters that are given special meaning, because they are used to signify things like metacharacters, quantifiers, and character classes. These include the period (.), the question mark (?), the plus sign (+), the opening square bracket ([), opening and closing parentheses, the caret (^), the dollar sign ($), the vertical pipe character (|), the backslash (\), the forward slash (/), and the asterisk (*).

If you want to use these characters in your regular expression to signify their literal meaning instead of the metacharacters or quantifiers they usually represent, you need to "escape" them by preceding them with a backslash.

For example, if you wanted to match parentheses in a phone number, you couldn't just do this:

(555)636-4652 ✗   *These will simply be treated like a group.*

`/^(\d{3})\d{3}-\d{4}$/`

Instead, both the opening and closing parentheses need to be preceded by backslashes to indicate that they should be interpreted as actual parentheses:

Now PHP knows that these are literal parentheses.

(555)636-4652 ✓   `/^\(\d{3}\)\d{3}-\d{4}$/`

Exercise

Come up with a string that will match each pattern shown.

```
/^[3-6]{4}/
```

```
/^([A-Z]\d){2}$/
```

Suppose we want to expand the Risky Jobs validation scheme for phone numbers to allow users to submit their numbers in a few more formats. Write a single regular expression that will match ALL of the following text strings, and won't allow a 0 or 1 as the first digit. Your pattern should only allow digits, parentheses, spaces, and dashes.

555-636-4652   **555 636-4652**

(555)-636-4652   **(555) 636-4652**

Exercise Solution

Come up with a string that will match each pattern shown.

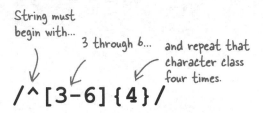

String must begin with...

3 through 6...

and repeat that character class four times.

/^[3-6]{4}/

Any string that starts with four digits in the range 3, 4, 5, or 6 will match. These will all match:

"5533", "3546 is a number.", "6533xyz"

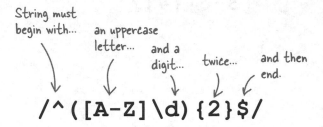

String must begin with...

an uppercase letter...

and a digit...

twice...

and then end.

/^([A-Z]\d){2}$/

Any string that starts with an uppercase letter and then a digit and then another uppercase letter and digit and then ends:

"B5C9", "R2D2"

Suppose we want to expand the Risky Jobs validation scheme for phone numbers to allow users to submit their numbers in a few more formats. Write a single regular expression that will match ALL of the following text strings, and won't allow a 0 or 1 as the first digit. Your pattern should only allow digits, parentheses, spaces, and dashes.

555-636-4652   555 636-4652
(555) 636-4652

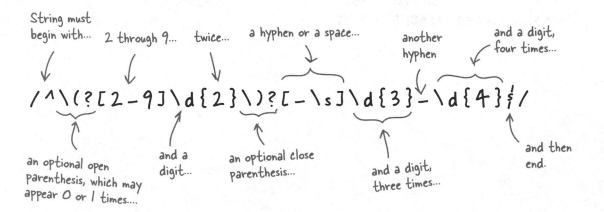

String must begin with...

2 through 9...

twice...

a hyphen or a space...

another hyphen

and a digit, four times...

/^\(?[2-9]\d{2}\)?[-\s]\d{3}-\d{4}$/

an optional open parenthesis, which may appear 0 or 1 times....

and a digit...

an optional close parenthesis...

and a digit, three times...

and then end.

I've pretty much had it with the bad data in the Risky Jobs resume bank. What good do these expressions do me if we don't use them in some way?

Risky Jobs needs to put regular expressions to work validating form data!

Check for patterns with preg_match()

We haven't been developing patterns just for the fun of it. You can use these patterns with the PHP function `preg_match()`. This function takes a regex pattern, just like those we've been building, and a text string. It returns `false` if there is no match, and `true` if there is.

preg_match($regex, $my_string)

Your regex goes here. The function expects a string, which means the regex should be surrounded by single quotes.

The string you are checking for a match goes here.

Here's an example of the `preg_match()` function in action, using a regex that searches a text string for a four-character pattern of alternating uppercase letters and digits:

When regexes are passed to preg_match(), they should be enclosed in quotes.

preg_match('/^\d{3}-\d{2}-\d{4}$/', '555-02-9983')

Returns an integer: 1 if the string matches the pattern, and 0 if it doesn't.

You can put the actual pattern in the function like this, but usually it's best to store it in a variable.

This string matches the regex, and the function will return 1.

We can take advantage of the `preg_match()` function to enable more sophisticated validation functionality in PHP scripts by building an `if` statement around the return value.

The preg_match() function is nested in the condition, so its result determines what code will run.

```
if (preg_match('/^\d{3}-\d{2}-\d{4}$/', '555-02-9983')) {
    echo 'Valid social security number.';
} else {
    echo 'That social security number is invalid!';
}
```

If the match is successful, preg_match() returns true, which signifies to PHP that the condition is true. So, this code is run.

If the match is not successful, preg_match() returns false, which makes the condition evaluate to false. So, this code is run.

Rewrite the highlighted portion of the Risky Jobs PHP script for checking the Registration form data below to validate the text entered into the phone field using `preg_match()` instead of `empty()`. Use the regex you created earlier in the `preg_match()` function.

```php
if (empty($phone)) {
  // $phone is blank
  echo '<p class="error">Your phone number is invalid.</p>';
  $output_form = 'yes';
}
```

....

....

....

....

....

Exercise Solution

Rewrite the highlighted portion of the Risky Jobs PHP script for checking the Registration form data below to validate the text entered into the phone field using `preg_match()` instead of `empty()`. Use the regex you created earlier in the `preg_match()` function.

```
if (empty($phone)) {

    // $phone is blank

    echo '<p class="error">Your phone number is invalid.</p>';

    $output_form = 'yes';

}
```

Instead of empty(), we use a preg_match to validate the phone number. We precede it with the not operator (!), because we want to throw an error whenever the data entered DOESN'T match the pattern.

Our phone number regular expression from before.

```
if (!preg_match('/^\(?[2-9]\d{2}\)?[-\s]\d{3}-\d{4}$/', $phone)) {

    // $phone is not valid

    echo '<p class="error">Your phone number is invalid.</p>';

    $output_form = 'yes';

}
```

The echo needs to be changed a bit, since we're not only checking to make sure data is entered, but that it matches a standard phone number pattern.

We set $output_form to 'yes', just as before.

> I got an error and then entered my entire phone number. And then I got a ninja job!

First Name: Jimmy
Last Name: Swift
Email: JS@sim-u-duck.com
Phone: (555) 636 4652
Desired Job: Ninja

Test Drive

Not just empty phone numbers!

Check for valid phone numbers in the Risky Jobs Registration script.

Download the `registration.php` script from the Head First Labs site at www. headfirstlabs.com/books/hfphp, along with the Risky Jobs style sheet (`style.css`) and images (`riskyjobs_title.gif` and `riskyjobs_fireman.png`). Then modify the `registration.php` script so that it uses the `preg_match()` function to validate phone numbers against the phone number regular expression. Make sure to tweak the error message so that users know the phone number is invalid, not just empty.

Upload the changed script to your web server, and then open it in a web browser. Try entering a few phone numbers with varying formats, and notice how the script catches the errors.

Now we can't accidentally enter bad phone numbers. That should keep us from missing job opportunities!

The script now displays an error message when a phone number is entered incorrectly, in this case with periods instead of hyphens.

Download It!

The complete source code for the Risky Jobs application is available for download from the Head First Labs web site:

www.headfirstlabs.com/books/hfphp

> Hmm. If our regex matches multiple patterns for the phone number, isn't the text going to be in all different formats in our database? That's not good. I think we need to standardize this stuff.

Just because you're permitting data to be *input* in all different formats doesn't necessarily mean you want your data *stored* in all those formats.

Luckily, there's another regex function that'll let us take the valid phone number data submitted by Risky Jobs's users and make all of it conform to just one consistent pattern, instead of four.

The `preg_replace()` function goes one step beyond the `preg_match()` function in performing pattern matching using regular expressions. In addition to determining whether a given pattern matches a given string of text, it allows you to supply a replacement pattern to substitute into the string in place of the matched text. It's a lot like the `str_replace()` function we've already used, except that it matches using a regular expression instead of a string.

preg_replace($pattern, $replacement, $my_string)

We need to find these unwanted characters.

When we find an unwanted character, we want to turn it into this.

The string we're doing the find-and-replace to.

Here's an example of the `preg_replace()` function in action:

$new_year = preg_replace('/200[0-9]/', '2010', 'The year is 2009.');

The result of the preg_replace() function, our revised text string after the find-and-replace is complete, is stored in $new_year.

This regex tells preg_replace to look for a match for 2000 through 2009.

When a match is found, it will be replaced with 2010.

Every time a year from 2000-2009 is found in our string, it will be replaced by 2010.

Standardize the phone number data entered into the Risky Jobs form by writing in each of the following numbers in the `phone` column of the database table below. Make sure to use a format that stores as little data as possible to represent a user's phone number.

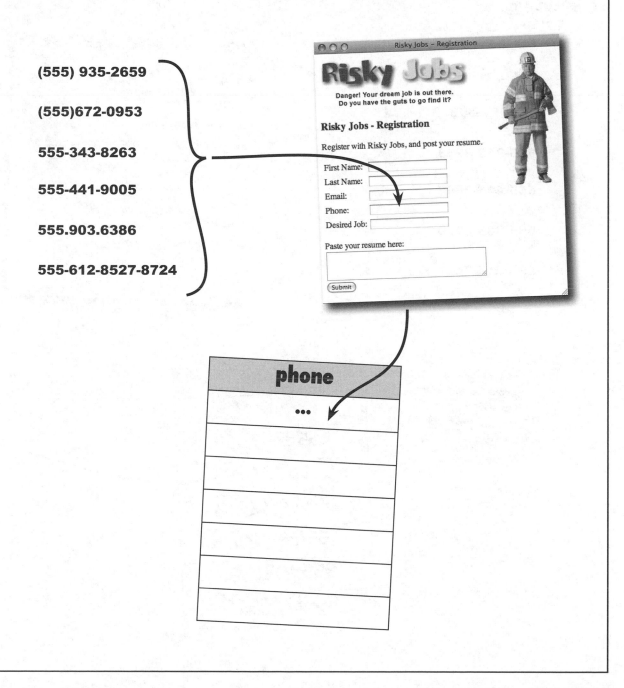

(555) 935-2659

(555)672-0953

555-343-8263

555-441-9005

555.903.6386

555-612-8527-8724

Exercise
Solution

Standardize the phone number data entered into the Risky Jobs form by writing in each of the following numbers in the `phone` column of the database table below. Make sure to use a format that stores as little data as possible to represent a user's phone number.

(555) 935-2659

(555)672-0953

555-343-8263

555-441-9005

555.903.6386

555-612-8527-8724

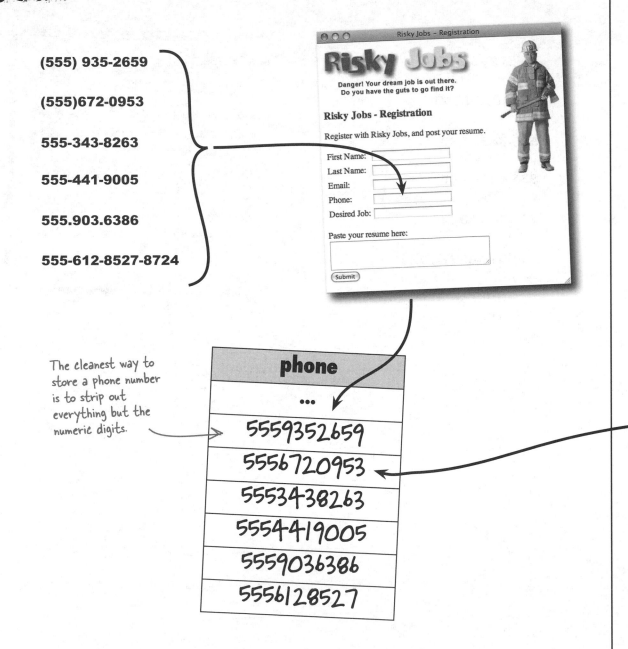

The cleanest way to store a phone number is to strip out everything but the numeric digits.

phone
...
5559352659
5556720953
5553438263
5554419005
5559036386
5556128527

Standardize the phone number data

Right now, Risky Jobs is using the following regular expression to validate the phone numbers users submit via their registration form:

```
/^\(?[2-9]\d{2}\)?[-\s]\d{3}-\d{4}$/
```

This will match phone numbers that fall into these four patterns:

✓
```
###-###-####

### ###-####

(###)-###-####

(###) ###-####
```

We want to reformat our data from this...

...to this.

While these formats are easily interpreted by people, they make it difficult for SQL queries to sort results the way we want. Those parentheses will most likely foil our attempts to group phone numbers by area code, for example, which might be important to Risky Jobs if we want to analyze how many of the site's users came from a specific geographical location.

To make these kinds of queries possible, we need to standardize phone numbers to one format using `preg_replace()` before we `INSERT` data into the database. Our best bet is to get rid of all characters except numeric digits. That way, we simply store 10 digits in our table with no other characters. We want our numbers to be stored like this in the table:

```
##########
```

This leaves us with four characters to find and replace. We want to find and **remove** open and closing parentheses, spaces, and dashes. And we want to find these characters no matter where in the string they are, so we don't need the starting carat (^) or ending dollar sign ($). We know we're looking for any one of a set, so we can use a character class. The order of the search doesn't matter. Here's the regex we can use:

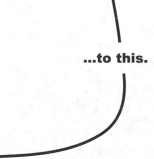

```
/[\(\)\-\s]/
```

open parenthesis

closing parenthesis   dash   space

Standardizing your data gives you better SQL query results.

Get rid of the unwanted characters

Now that we have our pattern that finds those unwanted characters, we can apply it to phone numbers to clean them up before storing them in the database. But how? This is where the preg_replace() function really pays off. The twist here is that we don't want to replace the unwanted characters, we just want them gone. So we simply pass an empty string into preg_replace() as the replacement value. Here's an example that finds unwanted phone number characters and replaces them with empty strings, effectively getting rid of them:

We store the results of our find-and-replace in this new phone number variable.

Perform this replacement on the text string in $phone.

```
$new_phone = preg_replace('/[\(\)\-\s]/', '', $phone);
```

Match these characters...

...and replace them with an empty string.

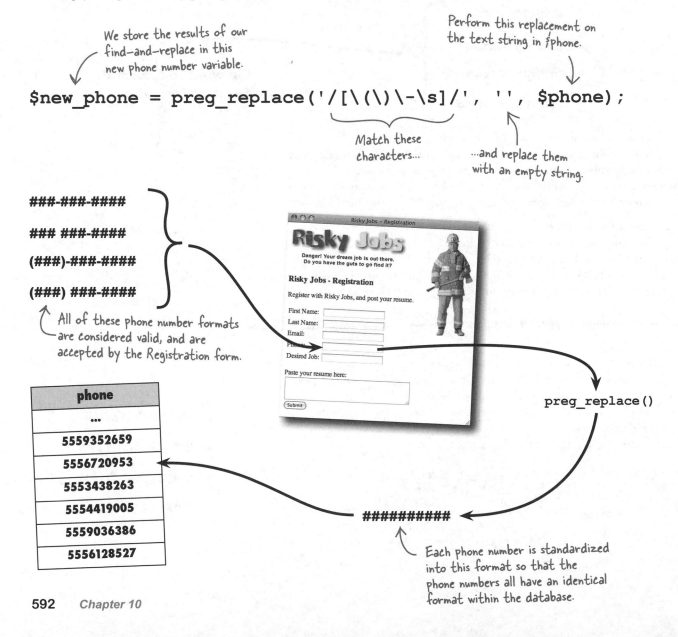

###-###-####

###-####

(###)-###-####

(###) ###-####

All of these phone number formats are considered valid, and are accepted by the Registration form.

Risky Jobs - Registration

Register with Risky Jobs, and post your resume.

First Name:
Last Name:
Email:
Phone:
Desired Job:

Paste your resume here:

Submit

preg_replace()

phone
...
5559352659
5556720953
5553438263
5554419005
5559036386
5556128527

##########

Each phone number is standardized into this format so that the phone numbers all have an identical format within the database.

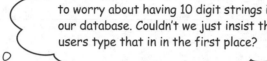

I don't know, it seems kinda like overkill to worry about having 10 digit strings in our database. Couldn't we just insist that users type that in in the first place?

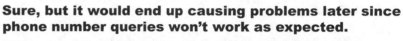

Sure, but it would end up causing problems later since phone number queries won't work as expected.

Most users are accustomed to entering phone numbers with some combination of dashes (hyphens), parentheses, and spaces, so attempting to enforce pure numeric phone numbers may not work as expected. It's much better to try and meet users halfway, giving them reasonably flexible input options, while at the same time making sure the data you store is as consistent as possible.

Besides, we're only talking about one call to `preg_replace()` to solve the problem, which just isn't a big deal. If we were talking about writing some kind of custom function with lots of code, it might be a different story. But improving the usability and data integrity with a single line of code is a no-brainer!

Test Drive

Clean up phone numbers in the Registration script.

Modify the `registration.php` script to clean up phone numbers by adding the following lines of code to the script, right after the line that thanks the user for registering with Risky Jobs:

```
$pattern = '/[\(\)\-\s]/';

$replacement = '';

$new_phone = preg_replace($pattern, $replacement, $phone);

echo 'Your phone number has been registered as ' . $new_phone . '.</p>';
```

Upload the script to your web server, and then open it in a web browser. Fill out the form, making sure to enter a phone number with extra characters, such as (707) 827-7000. Submit the form and check out the results.

The phone number is crunched down to just the numbers — no extra characters!

Try out a few other variations on the number, like these: 707-827-7000, (707)-827-7000, 707 827 7000. Notice how the regular expression and `preg_replace()` get rid of the extra characters.

My email to this knife juggler just bounced. I can't believe this stupid form lets people enter email addresses that don't even work!

First Name: Four Fingers
Last Name:McGraw
Email: four@gregs-listnet
Phone: 555-098
Desired Job: Knife Juggler

The email address is missing a period!

Similar to phone numbers, email addresses have enough of a format to them that we should be validating for more than just being empty.

Just like with validating phone numbers earlier, we first need to determine the rules that valid email addresses must follow. Then we can formalize them as a regular expression, and implement them in our PHP script. So let's first take a look at what exactly makes up an email address:

We know email addresses must contain these two characters.

$$LocalName@DomainPrefix.DomainSuffix$$

These will contain alphanumerics, where LocalName is at least one character and DomainPrefix is at least two characters.

This is usually 3 alphanumeric characters.

BRAIN POWER

See if you can come up with a regular expression that is flexible enough to match the email addresses to the right. Write it below:

aviator.howard@bannerocity.com

cube_lovers@youcube.ca

rocky@i-rock.biz

....

Matching email addresses can be tricky

It seems like it should be pretty simple to match email addresses, because at first glance, there don't appear to be as many restrictions on the characters you can use as there are with phone numbers.

For example, it doesn't seem like too big of a deal to match the *LocalName* portion of an email address (everything before the @ sign). Since that's just made up of alphanumeric characters, we should be able to use the following pattern:

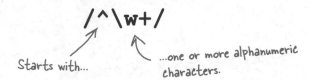

`/^\w+/`

Starts with...

...one or more alphanumeric characters.

This would allow any alphanumeric character in the local name, but unfortunately, it doesn't include characters that are also legal in email addresses.

Believe it or not, valid email addresses can contain any of these characters in the *LocalName* portion, although some of them can't be used to start an email address:

All these characters can appear in the LocalName part of an email address.

`! $ & * - = ^ ` | ~ # % ' + / ? _ { }`

If we want to allow users to register that have email addresses containing these characters, we really need a regex that looks something more like this:

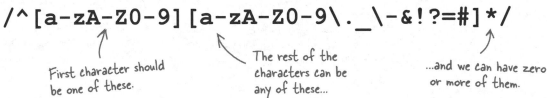

`/^[a-zA-Z0-9][a-zA-Z0-9\._\-&!?=#]*/`

First character should be one of these.

The rest of the characters can be any of these...

...and we can have zero or more of them.

This won't match every single valid *LocalName*, as we're still skipping some of the really obscure characters, but it's very practical to work with and should still match the email addresses of most of Risky Jobs users.

`!$&*-=^`|~#%'+/?_{}`

This email stuff is easy. We just use the same pattern we used for the local name to validate the domain name... no big deal!

That would work for part of the domain, the prefix, but it wouldn't account for the suffix.

While the domain prefix can contain pretty much any combination of alphanumerics and a few special characters, just like the *LocalName*, the restrictions on domain suffixes are much more stringent.

Most email addresses end in one of a few common domain suffixes: `.com`, `.edu`, `.org`, `.gov`, and so on. We'll need to make sure email addresses end in a valid domain suffix, too.

---

there are no Dumb Questions

Q: What if I want to allow every possible valid email address?

A: You can, and if it makes sense for your web site you certainly should. But sometimes it's best to take commonly accepted formats and not necessarily accept every possible variation. You need to decide what 99.9% of your users will have as their emails and be willing to not validate the remaining .1% simply for the sake of more streamlined code. Validation is really a trade-off between what's allowed and what is practical to accept.

If you do want to implement more robust email validation on your site, you can find some great open source (i.e., free) PHP code here: http://code.google.com/p/php-email-address-validation/.

Q: Won't people get angry at me if they have an email address I refuse to validate?

A: Possibly, but most people willl not have crazy email addresses. Most online email services have their own restrictive rules that keep users from creating crazy, although valid, email addresses like: `"_i'm crazy"@gregs-list.net`.

Validation is often a trade-off between what's allowed and what is practical to accept.

Domain suffixes are everywhere

In addition to super-common domain suffixes that you see quite frequently, like `.com` and `.org`, there are many, many other domain suffixes that are valid for use in email addresses. Other suffixes recognized as valid by the Domain Name System (DNS) that you may have seen before include `.biz` and `.info`. In addition, there's a list of suffixes that correspond to different countries, like `.ca` for Canada and `.tj` for Tajikistan.

Here is a list of just a few possible domain suffixes. This is not all of them.

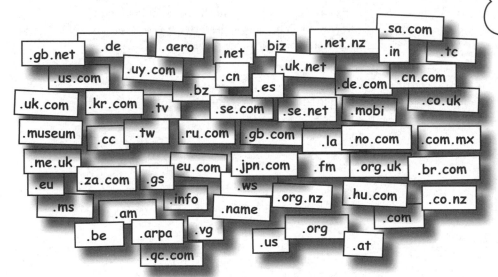

Even I wouldn't want to juggle all of those domains.

Some of those domains are only two letters long. Some have 2 or 3 letters, and a period and then two or three letters. Some are even 4 and 5 letters long. So do we need to keep a list of them and see if there's a match?

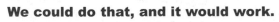

We could do that, and it would work.

But there's an easier way. Instead of keeping track of all the possible domains and having to change our code if a new one is added, we can check the domain portion of the email address using the PHP function `checkdnsrr()`. This function connects to the Domain Name System, or DNS, and checks the validity of domains.

Geek Bits

The **Domain Name System** is a distributed data service that provides a worldwide directory of domains and their IP addresses. It makes the use of domain names possible. Without DNS, we'd be typing 208.201.239.36 instead of oreilly.com.

Use PHP to check the domain

PHP provides the `checkdnsrr()` function for checking whether a domain is valid. This method is even better than using regular expressions to match the pattern of an email address, because instead of just checking if a string of text could possibly be a valid email domain, it actually checks the DNS records and finds out if the domain is actually registered. So, for example, while a regular expression could tell you that `lasdjlkdfsalkjaf.com` is valid, `checkdnsrr()` can go one step further and tell you that, in fact, this domain is not registered, and that we should probably reject `sdfhfdskl@lasdjlkdfsalkjaf.com` if it's entered on our registration form.

The syntax for `checkdnsrr()` is quite simple:

Returns 1 if it's a real domain or 0 if it's not.

checkdnsrr() expects a string containing a domain name. This is everything after the @ sign.

checkdnsrr('headfirstlabs.com')

If you're running PHP on a Windows <u>server</u>, this command won't work for you.

Watch it!

Instead, you can use this code:

```
function win_checkdnsrr($domain,$recType='') {
 if (!empty($domain)) {
  if ($recType=='') $recType="MX";
  exec("nslookup -type=$recType $domain",$output);
  foreach($output as $line) {
   if (preg_match("/^$domain/", $line)) {
    return true;
   }
  }
  return false;
 }
 return false;
}
```

This is only an issue if your web <u>server</u> is Windows. If you're using a Windows computer to build your web site, but you're actually posting it to a UNIX/Linux server, then this is not a problem.

This exec commands calls an external program running on the server to check the domain.

Just for fun, try echoing $line just after the foreach. You'll see something like this:

Server: 68.87.64.146Address: 68.87.64.146#53Non-authoritative answer: oreilly.com mail exchanger = 20 smtpl. oreilly.com.

Email validation: putting it all together

We now know how to validate both the *LocalName* portion of an email address using regular expressions, and the domain portion of an email address using checkdnsrr(). Let's look at the step-by-step of how we can put these two parts together to add full-fledged email address validation to Risky Jobs's registration form:

1   Use preg_match() to determine whether the *LocalName* portion of our email address contains a valid pattern of characters.

We can use the following regex to do so:

```
/^[a-zA-Z0-9][a-zA-Z0-9\._\-&!?=#]*@/
```

Note that there's no dollar sign at the end of this regex, as there will be characters following the @.

The email must start with an alphanumeric character, and then can contain any number of alphanumerics and certain special characters.

This time, we'll also search for an at symbol (@), to make sure our email address contains one before the domain.

2   If validation of the *LocalName* fails, echo an error to the user and reload the form.

3   If validation of the *LocalName* succeeds, pass the domain portion of the text string users submitted to checkdnsrr().

4   If checkdnsrr() returns 0, then the domain is not registered, so we echo an error to the user and reload the form.

5   If checkdnsrr() returns 1, then the domain is registered, and we can be fairly confident that we've got a valid email address. We can proceed with validating the rest of the fields in the form.

Exercise

Below is new PHP code to validate users' email addresses, but some pieces have disappeared. Fill in the blanks to get the code up and running.

```php
if (!preg_match('............................................................', $email)) {
  // $email is invalid because LocalName is bad
  echo 'Your email address is invalid.<br />';
  $output_form = 'yes';
}
else {
  // Strip out everything but the domain from the email
  $domain = preg_replace('..................................................', ....., ...........);
  // Now check if $domain is registered
  if (................................) {
    echo 'Your email address is invalid. <br />';
    $output_form = 'yes';
  }
}
```

Exercise Solution

Below is new PHP code to validate users' email addresses, but some pieces have disappeared. Fill in the blanks to get the code up and running.

Our regex for matching the LocalName portion of an email address, ending in an at symbol.

```
if (!preg_match(' [a-zA-Z0-9][a-zA-Z0-9\._-&!?=#]*@/ ', $email)) {

  // $email is invalid because LocalName is bad

  echo 'Your email address is invalid.<br />';

  $output_form = 'yes';

}

else {

  // Strip out everything but the domain from the email

  $domain = preg_replace(' /^[a-zA-Z0-9][a-zA-Z0-9\._-&!?=#]*@/ ', '' , $email );

  // Now check if $domain is registered

  if ( !checkdnsrr($domain) ) {

    echo 'Your email address is invalid. <br />';

    $output_form = 'yes';

  }

}
```

To strip out the LocalName and at symbol, specify the empty string ("") as the replacement string.

Perform the replacement on the $email value.

!checkdnsrr() returns true if the domain isn't registered.

If you're on a Windows server, don't forget to include the code for win_checkdnsrr(), and then call it here.

BULLET POINTS

- **preg_match()** locates matches for patterns in strings.

- **preg_replace()** changes matching strings.

- **Quantifiers** allow you to control how many times a character or set of characters can appear in a row.

- You can specify a set of characters to allow in your pattern using a **character class**.

- In your pattern, **\d**, **\w**, and **\s** are stand-ins for digits, alphanumeric characters, and whitespace, respectively.

- **checkdnsrr()** checks the validity of domain names.

TEST DRIVE

Add email validation to the Risky Jobs Registration script.

Use the code on the facing page to add email validation to the `registration.php` script. Then upload the script to your web server, and open it in a web browser. Try submitting an invalid email address, and notice how the new regular expression code rejects the form submission, and displays an error message to explain what happeened.

That's it, I filled my quota of risky jobs. Nothing to do now but add up all the money I just made.

An error message points out that the user's email address is invalid (it has a space instead of an @ symbol).

With the help of validation in the Risky Jobs Registration form, it's no longer a problem getting in touch with promising job candidates, and filling job openings in record time.

CHAPTER 10

Your PHP & MySQL Toolbox

Looking for patterns in text can be very handy when it comes to validating data entered by the user into web forms. Here are some of the PHP techniques used to validate data with the help of regular expressions:

\d, \w, \s, ^, $, ...

Regular expressions are created using metacharacters, which represent text expressions such as three numeric digits (\d\d\d) or whitespace (\w).

Regular expression

Rules that are used to match patterns of text in strings. PHP includes functions that allow you to use regular expressions to check a string for a certain pattern, as well as find-and-replace patterns of text within a string.

Character class

A set of rules for matching a single character within a regular expression. For example, [A-D] matches the characters A, B, C, or D.

preg_match()

This PHP function checks a string of text to see if it matches a regular expression. The function returns true if there was a match, or false if not.

preg_replace()

Use this PHP function to replace a substring within a string based on a regular expression. The function does a find-and-replace using a regular expression for the find, and replacing with a string you provide it.

checkdnserr()

This PHP function checks a domain name to see if it actually exists. This is handy when validating an email address because you want to make sure that the domain part of the email is real.

11 Visualizing your data... and more!

Drawing dynamic graphics

Hold still. Wait, stop moving. Now look directly at me and smile. No, not you, your data. OK, let's try crossing your columns and tilting your primary key just a bit to the left. Ah, perfect!

Sure, we all know the power of a good query and a bunch of juicy results. But query results don't always speak for themselves. Sometimes it's helpful to cast data in a different light, a more visual light. PHP makes it possible to provide a **graphical representation of database data**: *pie charts*, *bar charts*, *Venn diagrams*, *Rorschach art*, you name it. Anything to help users get a grip on the data flowing through your application is game. But not all worthwhile graphics in PHP applications originate in your database. For example, did you know it's possible to **thwart form-filling spam bots with dynamically generated images**?

Guitar Wars Reloaded: Rise of the Machines

The future is now. Robots have already been let loose in the virtual world and there isn't much to stop them other than some PHP coding vigilance. The robots are **spam bots**, which troll the Web for input forms that allow them to inject advertisements. These robots are chillingly efficient and care nothing about the intended usage of the forms they attack. Their one and only goal is to overrun your content with theirs in a bloodthirsty conquest of ad revenue for their masters. Sadly, the Guitar Wars high score application has fallen prey to the bots.

All web forms are at risk of attack from spam bots.

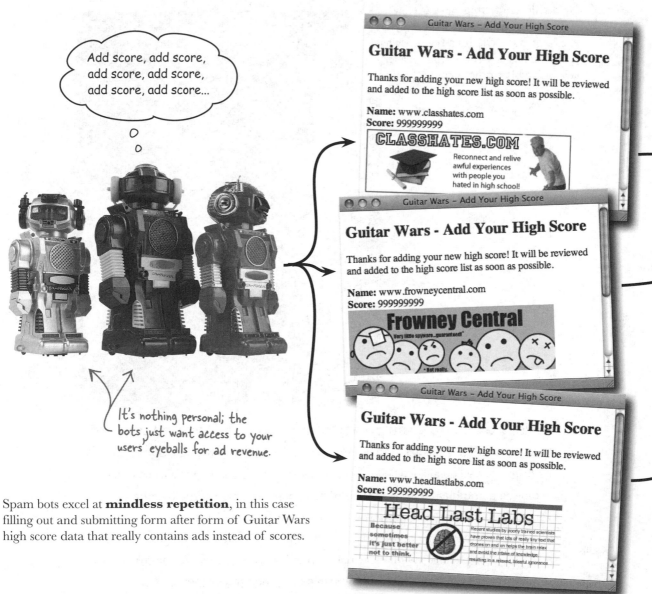

Add score, add score, add score, add score, add score, add score...

It's nothing personal; the bots just want access to your users' eyeballs for ad revenue.

Spam bots excel at **mindless repetition**, in this case filling out and submitting form after form of Guitar Wars high score data that really contains ads instead of scores.

No input form is safe

Fortunately for Guitar Wars, the spam bot attacks remain invisible to the end user thanks to the human moderation feature that was added back in Chapter 6. However, the human moderator is now being completely overwhelmed by the huge volume of spam bot posts, making it tough to sift through and approve legitimate high scores. Human moderation is a great feature, but humans are at a disadvantage when facing an automated adversary that never gets tired.

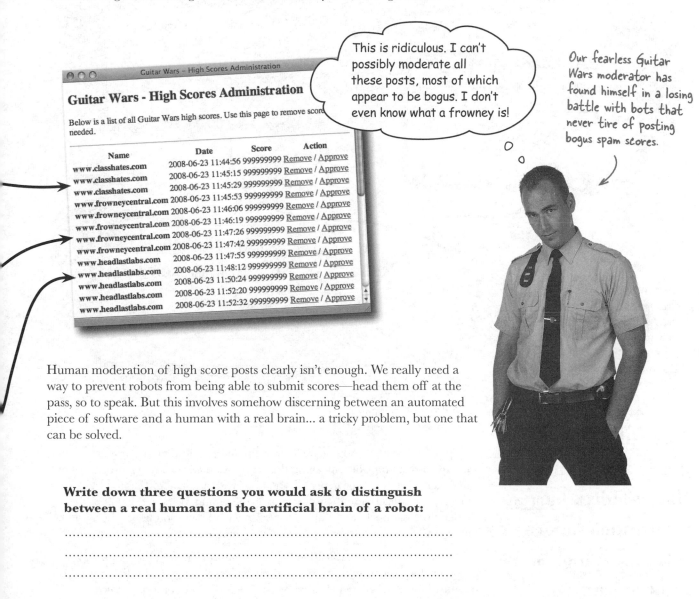

This is ridiculous. I can't possibly moderate all these posts, most of which appear to be bogus. I don't even know what a frowney is!

Our fearless Guitar Wars moderator has found himself in a losing battle with bots that never tire of posting bogus spam scores.

Guitar Wars - High Scores Administration

Below is a list of all Guitar Wars high scores. Use this page to remove score needed.

Name	Date	Score	Action
www.classhates.com	2008-06-23 11:44:56	999999999	Remove / Approve
www.classhates.com	2008-06-23 11:45:15	999999999	Remove / Approve
www.classhates.com	2008-06-23 11:45:29	999999999	Remove / Approve
www.frowneycentral.com	2008-06-23 11:45:53	999999999	Remove / Approve
www.frowneycentral.com	2008-06-23 11:46:06	999999999	Remove / Approve
www.frowneycentral.com	2008-06-23 11:46:19	999999999	Remove / Approve
www.frowneycentral.com	2008-06-23 11:47:26	999999999	Remove / Approve
www.frowneycentral.com	2008-06-23 11:47:42	999999999	Remove / Approve
www.headlastlabs.com	2008-06-23 11:47:55	999999999	Remove / Approve
www.headlastlabs.com	2008-06-23 11:48:12	999999999	Remove / Approve
www.headlastlabs.com	2008-06-23 11:50:24	999999999	Remove / Approve
www.headlastlabs.com	2008-06-23 11:52:20	999999999	Remove / Approve
www.headlastlabs.com	2008-06-23 11:52:32	999999999	Remove / Approve

Human moderation of high score posts clearly isn't enough. We really need a way to prevent robots from being able to submit scores—head them off at the pass, so to speak. But this involves somehow discerning between an automated piece of software and a human with a real brain... a tricky problem, but one that can be solved.

Write down three questions you would ask to distinguish between a real human and the artificial brain of a robot:

....

....

....

We need to separate man from machine

In order to figure out how to detect a real human on the other side of the Guitar Wars Add Score page, you have to first assess what exactly a spam bot is doing when filling out the form with bogus data.

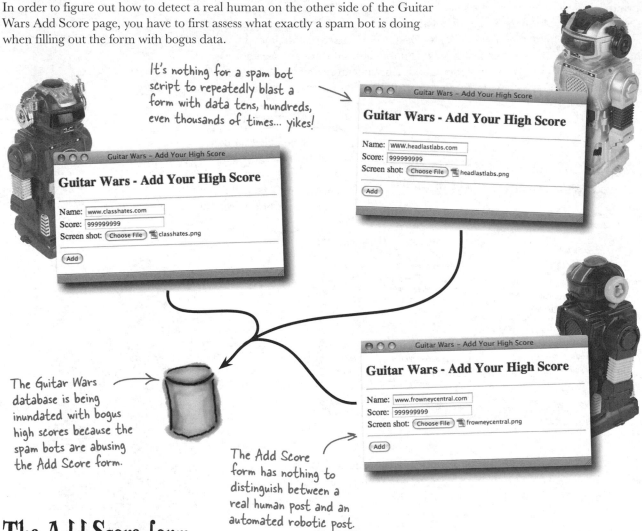

It's nothing for a spam bot script to repeatedly blast a form with data tens, hundreds, even thousands of times... yikes!

The Guitar Wars database is being inundated with bogus high scores because the spam bots are abusing the Add Score form.

The Add Score form has nothing to distinguish between a real human post and an automated robotic post.

The Add Score form needs a new field that requires <u>human</u> verification before allowing a high score to be submitted.

The problem with the Add Score form is that it does nothing to prevent **automated** submissions, meaning that any reasonably crafty bot programmer can create a bot that repeatedly fills the form with ad data and submits it. Sure, it never makes it to the front page of the Guitar Wars site thanks to the moderation feature, but it in many ways renders moderation useless because the human moderator is left manually removing hundreds of bogus ad posts.

The form needs a new verification field that must be entered successfully in order for the score to submit. And the specific verification of this field needs to be something that is easy for a real **human** but difficult for a **machine**.

Exercise

Following are some ideas for form fields that could potentially be used to prevent spam bots from submitting forms. Circle the form fields you think would **simply** and **successfully** allow only human form submissions, making sure to annotate why.

Are you a robot? ◯ Yes ◯ No

What was Elvis' favorite food? [ ]

Retinal scan: Look into your web cam and click

Enter the letters displayed: [ ] kdyqmc

What is the result of 7 + 5? [ ]

What kind of animal is this? [ ]

Enter the letters displayed: [ ] kdyqmc

Thumbprint scan: Press your thumb down and click

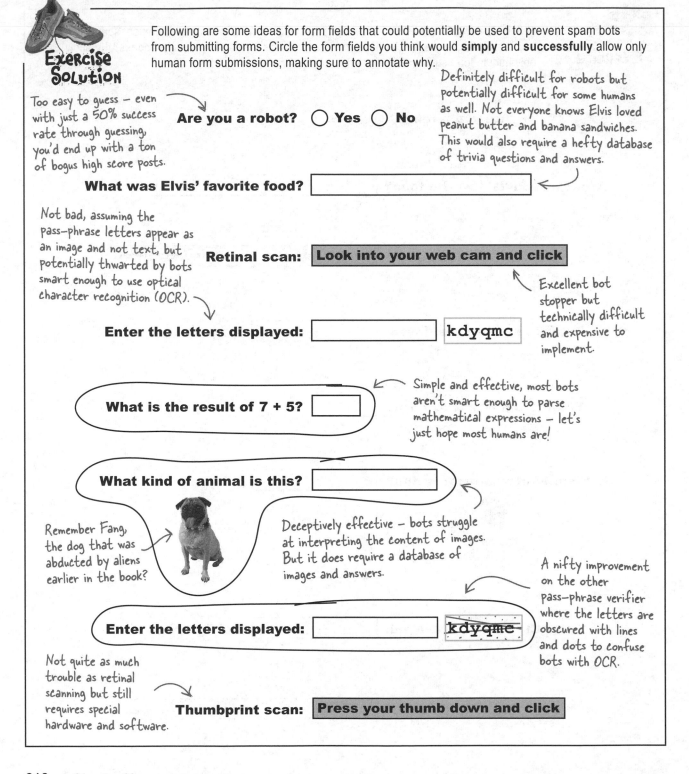

Exercise Solution

Following are some ideas for form fields that could potentially be used to prevent spam bots from submitting forms. Circle the form fields you think would **simply** and **successfully** allow only human form submissions, making sure to annotate why.

Too easy to guess — even with just a 50% success rate through guessing, you'd end up with a ton of bogus high score posts.

Are you a robot? ○ Yes ○ No

Definitely difficult for robots but potentially difficult for some humans as well. Not everyone knows Elvis loved peanut butter and banana sandwiches. This would also require a hefty database of trivia questions and answers.

What was Elvis' favorite food?

Not bad, assuming the pass-phrase letters appear as an image and not text, but potentially thwarted by bots smart enough to use optical character recognition (OCR).

Retinal scan: Look into your web cam and click

Enter the letters displayed: kdyqmc

Excellent bot stopper but technically difficult and expensive to implement.

What is the result of 7 + 5?

Simple and effective, most bots aren't smart enough to parse mathematical expressions — let's just hope most humans are!

What kind of animal is this?

Remember Fang, the dog that was abducted by aliens earlier in the book?

Deceptively effective — bots struggle at interpreting the content of images. But it does require a database of images and answers.

Enter the letters displayed: kdyqmc

A nifty improvement on the other pass-phrase verifier where the letters are obscured with lines and dots to confuse bots with OCR.

Not quite as much trouble as retinal scanning but still requires special hardware and software.

Thumbprint scan: Press your thumb down and click

We can defeat automation with <u>automation</u>

A test to verify that the entity on the other side of a form is a real person is known as ***CAPTCHA***, which stands for Completely Automated Public Turing Test to Tell Computers and Humans Apart. That's a long-winded way of referring to any "test" on a form that is ideally passable only by a human. Lots of interesting CAPTCHAs have been devised, but one of the most enduring involves generating a random pass-phrase that the user must enter. To help prevent craftier bots with optical character recognition (OCR) from beating the system, the pass-phrase letters are distorted or partially obscured with random lines and dots.

A CAPTCHA is a program that <u>protects</u> a web site from automated bots by using a test of some sort.

Since the letters in the pass-phrase are randomly generated, the phrase is different every time the form is displayed.

Enter the letters displayed: `dpmyta`

A normal text field is used to allow the user to enter the CAPTCHA pass-phrase.

Random lines and dots help to obscure the text just enough to thwart optical character recognition, while still allowing humans to discern it.

A CAPTCHA form field is just like any other form field except that its whole purpose is to prevent a form from being submitted unless the CAPTCHA test has been successfully completed. So unlike other form fields, which typically pass along data to the server upon submission, a CAPTCHA field is verified and used to control the submission process.

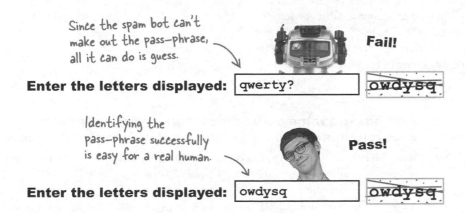

Since the spam bot can't make out the pass-phrase, all it can do is guess.

Fail!

Enter the letters displayed: `qwerty?` `owdysq`

Identifying the pass-phrase successfully is easy for a real human.

Pass!

Enter the letters displayed: `owdysq` `owdysq`

It's very important for the CAPTCHA pass-phrase to be displayed on the form as an image and not just text; otherwise bots would have a much easier time figuring out the text.

there are no

Dumb Questions

Q: **That image CAPTCHA with the dog is really cool. Could I use that instead of a pass-phrase CAPTCHA?**

A: Absolutely. Just keep in mind that you'll need to maintain a database of images and descriptions of what they are, because one of the keys to any successful CAPTCHA is variety. A good CAPTCHA should have a deep enough repository of content that a form rarely displays the same test twice. That's the benefit of pass-phrase CAPTCHA: since the pass-phrase is generated from random letters, it's very unlikely the exact same test will appear twice to any given user, even with lots of repeated attempts.

Q: **How does CAPTCHA impact the visually impaired? What if they can't pass a visual CAPTCHA test?**

A: Visual CAPTCHAs aren't the best answer for users who are visually impaired. An ideal CAPTCHA solution might involve an audio alternative to visual CAPTCHAs. For example, there is an audio CAPTCHA where a series of numbers are read aloud, after which the user must enter them to pass the test. But the same problem exists, where crafty bots use voice recognition to defeat such CAPTCHAs, which is why some of them use highly distorted audio that sounds a little creepy. Audio CAPTCHAs are similar technically to image

CAPTCHAs in that they require a database of audio clips and their respective answers. There are services that offer flexible CAPTCHAs that utilize both image and audio CAPTCHAs, such as *www.captcha.net*. Such services are excellent in terms of offering the latest in CAPTCHA technology, but they typically don't integrate quite as seamlessly as a custom CAPTCHA that is tailored specifically to your web application.

Q: **But there are also people who have poor eyesight and are also hearing impaired. What about them?**

A: Ultimately, CAPTCHA is all about weighing the reward of thwarting spam bots against the risk of alienating some users. Similar to viruses and anti-virus software, spam bots and CAPTCHAs will likely continue to play a cat and mouse game where bots are created to defeat a certain CAPTCHA, requiring a more sophisticated CAPTCHA, and on and on. Caught in the crossfire are users who may be left out due to the limited accessibility of some CAPTCHAs. It's up to the individual web developer to weigh the risks of a bot attack against the potential loss of users who may not be able to access parts of the site protected by CAPTCHA. If it's any consolation, keep in mind that the most sophisticated bots typically aim for large targets with huge ad revenue upside, meaning that you may not encounter a truly evil bot until your site grows to the point of being a big enough target for high-powered bots.

> OK, so a CAPTCHA pass-phrase has to be displayed as an image with random lines and dots. That's fine, but how in the world can that be created with PHP? PHP can only generate HTML code, right?

PHP has graphics capabilities that can dynamically generate images you can then display using HTML code.

With the help of a graphics library called GD (Graphics Draw), our PHP scripts can dynamically generate images in popular formats such as GIF, JPEG, and PNG, and either return them to a web browser for display or write them to a file on the server. This capability of PHP is extremely important because there is no notion of being able to "draw" on a web page purely through HTML. PHP allows you to "draw" on a portion of a page by performing graphics operations on an image, and then displaying that image on the page using the familiar `<img>` tag.

Generate the CAPTCHA pass-phrase text

Before we can even think about the graphical side of a pass-phrase CAPTCHA, we need to figure out how to generate the random pass-phrase itself, which begins as a sequence of text characters. A pass-phrase can be any number of characters, but somewhere in the range of six to eight characters is usually sufficient. We can use a constant for the pass-phrase length, which allows us to easily change the number of pass-phrase characters later if need be.

```
define('CAPTCHA_NUMCHARS', 6);
```

A CAPTCHA pass-phrase six characters long is probably sufficient to stop bots without annoying humans.

$pass_phrase

So how exactly do we go about generating a random string of text that is six characters long? This is where two built-in PHP functions enter the story: `rand()` and `chr()`. The `rand()` function returns a random number in the range specified by its two arguments, while `chr()` converts a numeric ASCII character code into an an actual character. ASCII (American Standard Code for Information Interchange) is a standard character encoding that represents characters as numbers. We only need ASCII character codes in the range 97-122, which map to the lowercase letters a-z. If we generate a code in this range six times, we'll get a random six-character pass-phrase of lowercase letters.

```
// Generate the random pass-phrase
$pass_phrase = "";
for ($i = 0; $i < CAPTCHA_NUMCHARS; $i++) {
  $pass_phrase .= chr(rand(97, 122));
}
```

Loop once for every character in the pass-phrase.

This code will eventually go into its own reusable script file, captcha.php.

The pass-phrase is constructed one random character at a time.

chr()

This built-in function converts a number to its ASCII character equivalent. As an example, the number 97 is the ASCII code for the lowercase letter `'a'`. So calling `chr(97)` returns the single character `'a'`.

rand()

This built-in function returns a random integer number, either within a specified range or between 0 and the built-in constant RAND_MAX (server dependent). To obtain a random number within a certain range, just pass the lower and upper limits of the range as two arguments to `rand()`.

The rand() function returns a random integer within a certain range.

Visualizing the CAPTCHA image

With the random pass-phrase nailed down, we can move on to generating an image consisting of the pass-phrase text along with random lines and dots to help obscure the text from bots. But where to start? The first thing to do is decide what size the CAPTCHA image should be. Knowing that this image will be displayed on a form next to an input field, it makes sense to keep it fairly small. Let's go with 100×25, and let's put these values in constants so that the image size is set in one place, and therefore easy to change later if necessary.

Drawing a dynamic image in PHP requires using GD library functions.

```php
define('CAPTCHA_WIDTH', 100);
define('CAPTCHA_HEIGHT', 25);
```

The size of the CAPTCHA image is stored in constants to make it easier to adjust the size later if desired.

Drawing the CAPTCHA image involves calling several functions in the GD library, all of which operate on an image in memory. In other words, you create an image in memory, then you draw on it, and then when you're all finished, you output it to the browser so that it can be displayed.

```php
// Create the image
$img = imagecreatetruecolor(CAPTCHA_WIDTH, CAPTCHA_HEIGHT);

// Set a white background with black text and gray graphics
$bg_color = imagecolorallocate($img, 255, 255, 255);      // white
$text_color = imagecolorallocate($img, 0, 0, 0);          // black
$graphic_color = imagecolorallocate($img, 64, 64, 64);    // dark gray

// Fill the background
imagefilledrectangle($img, 0, 0, CAPTCHA_WIDTH, CAPTCHA_HEIGHT, $bg_color);

// Draw some random lines
for ($i = 0; $i < 5; $i++) {
  imageline($img, 0, rand() % CAPTCHA_HEIGHT, CAPTCHA_WIDTH,
    rand() % CAPTCHA_HEIGHT, $graphic_color);
}

// Sprinkle in some random dots
for ($i = 0; $i < 50; $i++) {
  imagesetpixel($img, rand() % CAPTCHA_WIDTH,
    rand() % CAPTCHA_HEIGHT, $graphic_color);
}

// Draw the pass-phrase string
imagettftext($img, 18, 0, 5, CAPTCHA_HEIGHT - 5, $text_color,
  'Courier New Bold.ttf', $pass_phrase);

// Output the image as a PNG using a header
header("Content-type: image/png");
imagepng($img);
```

This code creates colors to be used by the other GD functions.

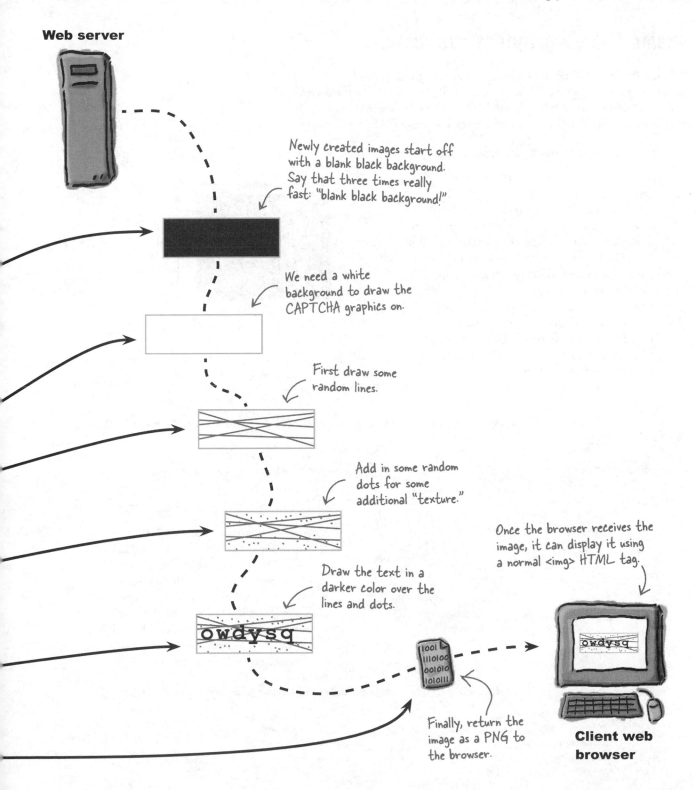

Web server

Newly created images start off with a blank black background. Say that three times really fast: "blank black background!"

We need a white background to draw the CAPTCHA graphics on.

First draw some random lines.

Add in some random dots for some additional "texture."

Once the browser receives the image, it can display it using a normal <img> HTML tag.

Draw the text in a darker color over the lines and dots.

owdysq

Finally, return the image as a PNG to the browser.

Client web browser

Inside the GD graphics functions

The magic behind CAPTCHA image creation is made possible by the GD graphics library, which you've already learned offers functions for dynamically drawing graphics to an image using PHP code. Let's examine some of these functions in more detail as they relate to generating a CAPTCHA image.

`imagecreatetruecolor()`

This function creates a blank image in memory ready to be drawn to with other GD functions. The two arguments to `imagecreatetruecolor()` are the width and height of the image. The image starts out solid black, so you'll typically want to fill it with a background color, such as white, before drawing anything. You can do this by calling the `imagefilledrectangle()` function. The return value of `imagecreatetruecolor()` is an **image identifier**, which is required as the first argument of most GD functions to identify the image being drawn.

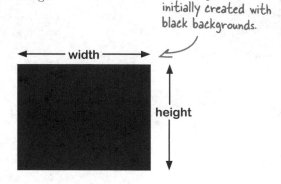

New images are initially created with black backgrounds.

width

height

The width of the new image, in pixels.

The height of the image.

```
$img = imagecreatetruecolor(CAPTCHA_WIDTH, CAPTCHA_HEIGHT);
```

The function returns an image identifier that is required by other drawing functions to actually draw on the image.

This code creates an image that is 100x25 in size thanks to our constants.

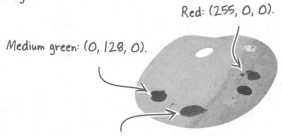

Red: (255, 0, 0).

Medium green: (0, 128, 0).

Blue: (0, 0, 255).

`imagecolorallocate()`

Use this function to allocate a color for use in other drawing functions. The first argument is the image resource identifier, followed by three arguments representing the three numeric components of the RGB (Red-Green-Blue) color value. Each of these values is in the range 0–255. The return value is a **color identifier** that can be used to specify a color in other drawing functions, often as the last argument.

```
$text_color = imagecolorallocate($img, 0, 0, 0);
```

The return value is a color identifier that you can use in other drawing functions to control the color being used, such as the color of CAPTCHA text.

The identifier of the image the color will be used with.

The red, green, and blue components of the color, in this case black.

imagesetpixel()

This function draws a single pixel at a specified coordinate within the image. Coordinates start at 0,0 in the upper left corner of the image, and increase to the right and down. Like most GD functions, the pixel is drawn using the color that is passed as the last argument to the function.

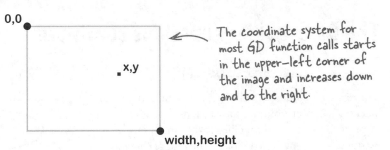

0,0

. x,y

width,height

The coordinate system for most GD function calls starts in the upper-left corner of the image and increases down and to the right.

```
imagesetpixel($img, rand() % CAPTCHA_WIDTH, rand() % CAPTCHA_HEIGHT, $graphic_color);
```

The image (identifier) the pixel is being drawn on.

The XY coordinate of the pixel, relative to the upper-left corner of the image, which in this case ends up being a random location within the CAPTCHA image.

The color (identifier) of the pixel.

imageline()

Call this function to draw a line between two coordinates (x1,y1 and x2,y2). The coordinates are specified relative to the upper-left corner of the image, and the line is drawn in the color passed as the last argument to the function.

x_1,y_1

x_2,y_2

The XY coordinate of the start of the line, in this case along the left edge of the CAPTCHA image.

```
imageline($img, 0, rand() % CAPTCHA_HEIGHT,
    CAPTCHA_WIDTH, rand() % CAPTCHA_HEIGHT, $graphic_color);
```

The XY end point of the line, which here lies on the right edge of the CAPTCHA image.

imagerectangle()

Draw a rectangle starting at one point (x_1,y_1) and ending at another point (x_2,y_2), in a certain specified color. The two points and the color are provided as the second through sixth arguments of the function, following the image identifier argument.

x_1,y_1

x_2,y_2

imagefilledrectangle()

Similar to imagerectangle(), this function draws a rectangle whose interior is filled with the specified color.

The imagerectangle() function takes the exact same arguments as imagefilledrectangle().

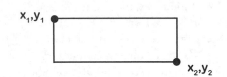

x_1,y_1

x_2,y_2

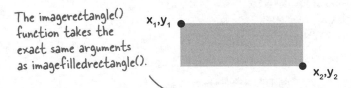

```
imagefilledrectangle($img, 0, 0, CAPTCHA_WIDTH, CAPTCHA_HEIGHT, $bg_color);
```

The XY coordinates of the start and end points – here it fills the entire CAPTCHA image.

The GD graphics functions continued...

imageellipse()

For drawing circles and ellipses, this function accepts a center point and a width and height. A perfect circle is just an ellipse with an equal width and height. The color of the ellipse/circle is passed as the last argument to the function.

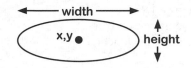

Ellipses aren't used in the CAPTCHA image but they're still quite handy!

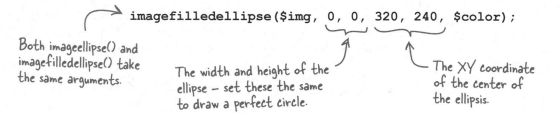

imagefilledellipse()

Need a filled ellipse instead? Just call `imagefilledellipse()`, which works the same as `imageellipse()` except the specified color is used to fill the ellipse instead of outline it.

imagefilledellipse($img, 0, 0, 320, 240, $color);

Both imageellipse() and imagefilledellipse() take the same arguments.

The width and height of the ellipse — set these the same to draw a perfect circle.

The XY coordinate of the center of the ellipsis.

imagepng()

When you're all finished drawing to an image, you can output it directly to the client web browser or to a file on the server by calling this function. Either way, the end result is an image that can be used with the HTML `<img>` tag for display on a web page. If you elect to generate a PNG image directly to memory (i.e., no filename), then you must also call the `header()` function to have it delivered to the browser via a header.

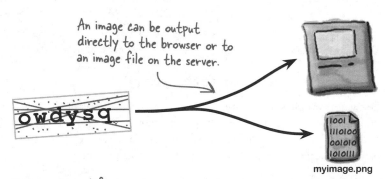

An image can be output directly to the browser or to an image file on the server.

myimage.png

The image identifier that you've been using in other draw functions.

imagepng($img);

The function returns true or false depending on whether the image was successfully created.

You can pass a filename as an optional second argument — without it, the function generates an image in memory that can be passed back to the browser in a header.

imagedestroy()

It takes system resources to work with images using the GD library, and this function takes care of cleaning up when you're finished working with an image. Just call it after you output the image with imagepng() to clean up.

Cleaning up after your images is a good idea to keep the server from wasting resources after you're finished with them.

Similar to imagepng(), this function returns true upon success, or false otherwise.

imagedestroy($img);

The identifier of the image you want to destroy.

Always free up images in memory with imagedestroy() once you've output them.

Always try to pair up a call to this function with each image that you create so that all images are destroyed.

imagestring()

This function draws a string of text using PHP's built-in font in the color specified. In addition to the image resource identifier, you pass the function the size of the font as a number (1–5), along with the coordinate of the upper left corner of the string, the string itself, and then the color.

A number in the range 1–5 sets the size of the font used to draw the string of text, with 5 being the largest size.

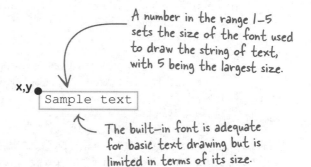

The built-in font is adequate for basic text drawing but is limited in terms of its size.

The font size of the string, in the range 1 to 5.

imagestring($img, 3, 75, 75, 'Sample text', $color);

The XY coordinate of the upper-left corner of the string.

This is the string of text to be drawn.

The color of the text.

imagestringup()

Text drawn with imagestringup() is rotated 90 degrees counter-clockwise so that it appears vertically.

Similar to imagestring(), this function draws a string of text using the built-in font, but it draws the text vertically, as if it were rotated 90 degrees counterclockwise. The function is called with the same arguments as imagestring().

Drawing text with a font

The `imagestring()` function is easy to use for drawing but it's fairly limited in terms of the control you have over the appearance of the text. To really get a specific look, you need to use a TrueType font of your own. The CAPTCHA pass-phrase image is a good example of this need, since the characters must be drawn fairly large and ideally in a bold font. To get such a custom look, you need the help of one last GD graphics function, which draws text using a TrueType font that you provide on the server.

imagettftext()

For drawing truly customized text, place a TrueType font file on your web server and then call this function. Not only do you get to use any font of your choosing, but you also get more flexibility in the size of the font and even the angle at which the text is drawn. Unlike `imagestring()`, the coordinate passed to this function specifies the "basepoint" of the first character in the text, which is roughly the lower-left corner of the first character.

This function does require you to place a TrueType font file on your server, and then specify this file as the last argument. TrueType font files typically have a file extension of `.ttf`.

Highly customized text drawing requires a TrueType font and the imagettftext() function.

x,y **Sample text**

Unlike imagestring(), the coordinate used to draw text with imagettftext() is at the lower-left corner of the text.

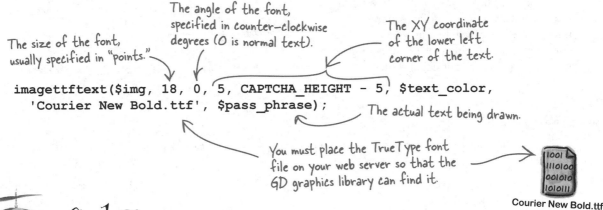

The size of the font, usually specified in "points."

The angle of the font, specified in counter-clockwise degrees (0 is normal text).

The XY coordinate of the lower left corner of the text.

```
imagettftext($img, 18, 0, 5, CAPTCHA_HEIGHT - 5, $text_color,
    'Courier New Bold.ttf', $pass_phrase);
```

The actual text being drawn.

You must place the TrueType font file on your web server so that the GD graphics library can find it.

Courier New Bold.ttf

Geek Bits

If you'd like to take a stab at creating your very own TrueType font to further customize your CAPTCHA, check out *www.fontstruct.com*. It's an online font-building community including a web-based tool for creating custom fonts.

Use the imagettftext() function to draw highly customized text with your own TrueType font.

WHO ~~DOES~~ DRAWS WHAT?

imagecolorallocate($img, 128, 128, 128);

Match each piece of PHP graphics drawing code to the graphical image that it generates. Assume the image ($img) and colors ($black_color, $white_color, and $gray_color) have already been created.

imagecolorallocate($img, 0, 0, 0);

imagecolorallocate($img, 255, 255, 255);

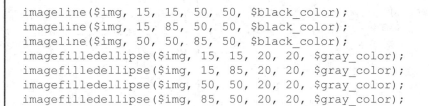

```php
imagefilledrectangle($img, 10, 10, 90, 90, $gray_color);
imagefilledellipse($img, 50, 50, 60, 60, $white_color);
imagefilledrectangle($img, 40, 40, 60, 60, $black_color);
```

```php
imageline($img, 15, 15, 50, 50, $black_color);
imageline($img, 15, 85, 50, 50, $black_color);
imageline($img, 50, 50, 85, 50, $black_color);
imagefilledellipse($img, 15, 15, 20, 20, $gray_color);
imagefilledellipse($img, 15, 85, 20, 20, $gray_color);
imagefilledellipse($img, 50, 50, 20, 20, $gray_color);
imagefilledellipse($img, 85, 50, 20, 20, $gray_color);
```

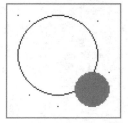

```php
imagefilledrectangle($img, 10, 10, 90, 60, $gray_color);
imagesetpixel($img, 30, 25, $black_color);
imagesetpixel($img, 70, 25, $black_color);
imageline($img, 35, 45, 65, 45, $black_color);
imagefilledrectangle($img, 45, 50, 55, 90, $gray_color);
```

```php
imageellipse($img, 45, 45, 70, 70, $black_color);
imagefilledellipse($img, 75, 75, 30, 30, $gray_color);
imagesetpixel($img, 10, 10, $black_color);
imagesetpixel($img, 80, 15, $black_color);
imagesetpixel($img, 20, 15, $black_color);
imagesetpixel($img, 90, 60, $black_color);
imagesetpixel($img, 20, 80, $black_color);
imagesetpixel($img, 45, 90, $black_color);
```

```php
imagefilledrectangle($img, 25, 35, 75, 90, $black_color);
imageline($img, 10, 50, 50, 10, $black_color);
imageline($img, 50, 10, 90, 50, $black_color);
imagefilledrectangle($img, 45, 65, 55, 90, $white_color);
imageline($img, 0, 90, 100, 90, $black_color);
```

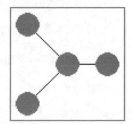

WHO ~~DOES~~ DRAWS WHAT? SOLUTION

Match each piece of PHP graphics drawing code to the graphical image that it generates. Assume the image ($img) and colors ($black_color, $white_color, and $gray_color) have already been created.

I'm an android, not a robot.

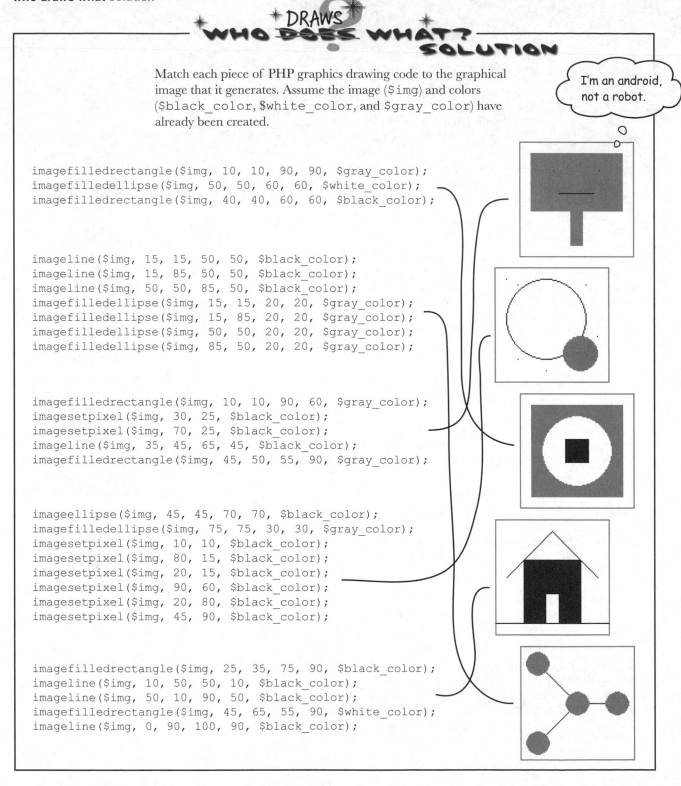

```
imagefilledrectangle($img, 10, 10, 90, 90, $gray_color);
imagefilledellipse($img, 50, 50, 60, 60, $white_color);
imagefilledrectangle($img, 40, 40, 60, 60, $black_color);
```

```
imageline($img, 15, 15, 50, 50, $black_color);
imageline($img, 15, 85, 50, 50, $black_color);
imageline($img, 50, 50, 85, 50, $black_color);
imagefilledellipse($img, 15, 15, 20, 20, $gray_color);
imagefilledellipse($img, 15, 85, 20, 20, $gray_color);
imagefilledellipse($img, 50, 50, 20, 20, $gray_color);
imagefilledellipse($img, 85, 50, 20, 20, $gray_color);
```

```
imagefilledrectangle($img, 10, 10, 90, 60, $gray_color);
imagesetpixel($img, 30, 25, $black_color);
imagesetpixel($img, 70, 25, $black_color);
imageline($img, 35, 45, 65, 45, $black_color);
imagefilledrectangle($img, 45, 50, 55, 90, $gray_color);
```

```
imageellipse($img, 45, 45, 70, 70, $black_color);
imagefilledellipse($img, 75, 75, 30, 30, $gray_color);
imagesetpixel($img, 10, 10, $black_color);
imagesetpixel($img, 80, 15, $black_color);
imagesetpixel($img, 20, 15, $black_color);
imagesetpixel($img, 90, 60, $black_color);
imagesetpixel($img, 20, 80, $black_color);
imagesetpixel($img, 45, 90, $black_color);
```

```
imagefilledrectangle($img, 25, 35, 75, 90, $black_color);
imageline($img, 10, 50, 50, 10, $black_color);
imageline($img, 50, 10, 90, 50, $black_color);
imagefilledrectangle($img, 45, 65, 55, 90, $white_color);
imageline($img, 0, 90, 100, 90, $black_color);
```

Generate a random CAPTCHA image

Putting all the CAPTCHA code together results in the brand-new `captcha.php` script, which takes care of generating a random pass-phrase and then returning a PNG image to the browser.

The captcha.php script is completely self-contained — you can open it in your browser and view the image that it generates.

```php
<?php
session_start();

// Set some important CAPTCHA constants
define('CAPTCHA_NUMCHARS', 6);   // number of characters in pass-phrase
define('CAPTCHA_WIDTH', 100);    // width of image
define('CAPTCHA_HEIGHT', 25);    // height of image

// Generate the random pass-phrase
$pass_phrase = "";
for ($i = 0; $i < CAPTCHA_NUMCHARS; $i++) {
  $pass_phrase .= chr(rand(97, 122));
}

// Store the encrypted pass-phrase in a session variable
$_SESSION['pass_phrase'] = sha1($pass_phrase);

// Create the image
$img = imagecreatetruecolor(CAPTCHA_WIDTH, CAPTCHA_HEIGHT);

// Set a white background with black text and gray graphics
$bg_color = imagecolorallocate($img, 255, 255, 255);   // white
$text_color = imagecolorallocate($img, 0, 0, 0);       // black
$graphic_color = imagecolorallocate($img, 64, 64, 64); // dark gray

// Fill the background
imagefilledrectangle($img, 0, 0, CAPTCHA_WIDTH, CAPTCHA_HEIGHT, $bg_color);

// Draw some random lines
for ($i = 0; $i < 5; $i++) {
  imageline($img, 0, rand() % CAPTCHA_HEIGHT, CAPTCHA_WIDTH, rand() % CAPTCHA_HEIGHT, $graphic_color);
}

// Sprinkle in some random dots
for ($i = 0; $i < 50; $i++) {
  imagesetpixel($img, rand() % CAPTCHA_WIDTH, rand() % CAPTCHA_HEIGHT, $graphic_color);
}

// Draw the pass-phrase string
imagettftext($img, 18, 0, 5, CAPTCHA_HEIGHT - 5, $text_color, "Courier New Bold.ttf", $pass_phrase);
// Output the image as a PNG using a header
header("Content-type: image/png");
imagepng($img);

// Clean up
imagedestroy($img);
?>
```

Create constants to hold the number of characters in the CAPTCHA and the width and height of the CAPTCHA image.

Although you could store the encrypted pass-phrase in the database, it's simpler to just stick it in a session variable — we have to store it so the Add Score script can access it.

Some versions of the GD graphics library require a relative path to the font file, such as "./Courier New Bold.ttf".

The PNG image is actually delivered to the browser through a header.

Generate a PNG image based on everything that has been drawn.

Finish up by destroying the image from memory (it still gets sent to the browser via the header).

captcha.php

Test Drive

Create the CAPTCHA script and try it out.

Create a new text file named captcha.php, and enter the code for the CAPTCHA script from the previous page (or download the script from the Head First Labs site at www.headfirstlabs.com/books/hfphp).

Upload the script to your web server, and then open it in a web browser. You'll immediately see the CAPTCHA image with the random pass-phrase in the browser. To generate a new random pass-phrase, refresh the browser.

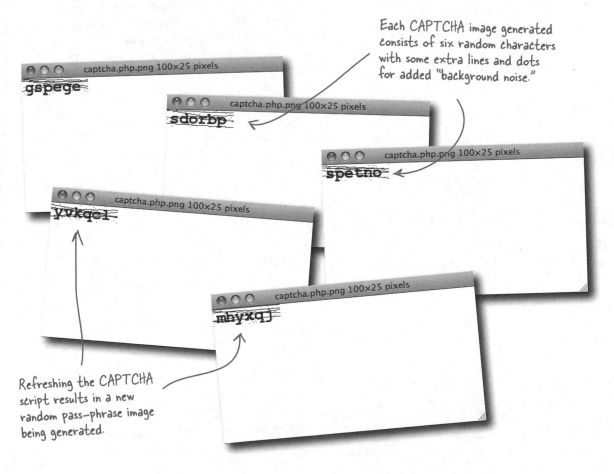

Each CAPTCHA image generated consists of six random characters with some extra lines and dots for added "background noise."

Refreshing the CAPTCHA script results in a new random pass-phrase image being generated.

These robots are making me crazy! I need help stopping them now!

Returning sanity to Guitar Wars

Now that we've conjured up your inner PHP artist with some GD functions and a CAPTCHA image, it's time to use the CAPTCHA image to rescue the Guitar Wars moderator from the spam bot assault. There are actually a few steps involved in solving the bot problem with a pass-phrase CAPTCHA. The good news is we've already knocked out two of them: generating the random pass-phrase and drawing the CAPTCHA image. Let's knock out the remaining steps to make Guitar Wars officially bot-free!

The Guitar Wars moderator is so frazzled that he's lashing out at imaginary robots — he needs a solution now!

Already done!

1 ~~Generate a random pass-phrase.~~

Drawing complete!

2 ~~Draw a CAPTCHA image using the pass-phrase.~~

3 Display the CAPTCHA image on the Guitar Wars Add Score form and prompt the user to enter the pass-phrase.

4 Verify the pass-phrase against the user input.

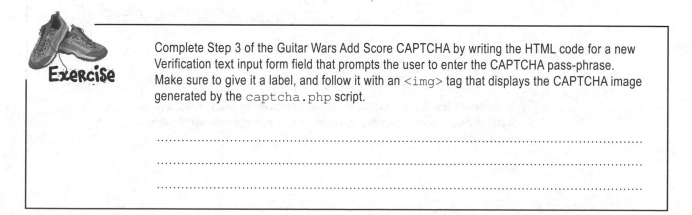

Exercise

Complete Step 3 of the Guitar Wars Add Score CAPTCHA by writing the HTML code for a new Verification text input form field that prompts the user to enter the CAPTCHA pass-phrase. Make sure to give it a label, and follow it with an `<img>` tag that displays the CAPTCHA image generated by the `captcha.php` script.

....

....

....

Exercise Solution

Complete Step 3 of the Guitar Wars Add Score CAPTCHA by writing the HTML code for a new Verification text input form field that prompts the user to enter the CAPTCHA pass-phrase. Make sure to give it a label, and follow it with an `<img>` tag that displays the CAPTCHA image generated by the `captcha.php` script.

A <label> tag is used to label the new Verification text field.

This text field is where the user will enter the pass-phrase revealed in the CAPTCHA image.

```
<label for="verify">Verification: </label>
<input type="text" id="verify" name="verify" value="Enter the pass-phrase." />
<img src="captcha.php" alt="Verification pass-phrase" />
```

The CAPTCHA image is displayed on the form next to a verification text input field.

The "source" of the image is the name of the PHP script that dynamically generates the CAPTCHA image. This works because the captcha.php script returns an image directly to the browser via imagepng() and a header.

Guitar Wars – Add Your High Score

Guitar Wars - Add Your High Score

Name:
Score:
Screen shot: (Choose File) no file selected

Verification: [Enter the pass-phrase.] ~~wgkeib~~

(Add)

Finished! One more step to go.

3 ~~Display the CAPTCHA image on the Guitar Wars Add Score form and prompt the user to enter the pass-phrase.~~

Add CAPTCHA to the Add Score script

On the client side of the equation, the addscore.php script contains the new Verification text field with the CAPTCHA image beside it. The most important change, however, is the new if statement in the Add Score script (Step 4) that checks to make sure the user-entered pass-phrase matches the CAPTCHA pass-phrase.

~~**④ Check to make sure the user entered the correct CAPTCHA pass-phrase.**~~

We're all done!

```php
<?php
 session_start();
?>

<html>
<head>
 <title>Guitar Wars - Add Your High Score</title>
 <link rel="stylesheet" type="text/css" href="style.css" />
</head>
<body>
 <h2>Guitar Wars - Add Your High Score</h2>

<?php
 require_once('appvars.php');
 require_once('connectvars.php');

 if (isset($_POST['submit'])) {
  // Connect to the database
  $dbc = mysqli_connect(DB_HOST, DB_USER, DB_PASSWORD, DB_NAME);

  // Grab the score data from the POST
  $name = mysqli_real_escape_string($dbc, trim($_POST['name']));
  $score = mysqli_real_escape_string($dbc, trim($_POST['score']));
  $screenshot = mysqli_real_escape_string($dbc, trim($_FILES['screenshot']['name']));
  $screenshot_type = $_FILES['screenshot']['type'];
  $screenshot_size = $_FILES['screenshot']['size'];

  // Check the CAPTCHA pass-phrase for verification
  $user_pass_phrase = sha1($_POST['verify']);
  if ($_SESSION['pass_phrase'] == $user_pass_phrase) {
   ...
  else {
   echo '<p class="error">Please enter the verification pass-phrase exactly as shown.</p>';
  }
  }
?>

  <hr />
  <form enctype="multipart/form-data" method="post" action="<?php echo $_SERVER['PHP_SELF']; ?>">
   <input type="hidden" name="MAX_FILE_SIZE" value="<?php echo GW_MAXFILESIZE; ?>" />
   <label for="name">Name: </label>
   <input type="text" id="name" name="name" value="<?php if (!empty($name)) echo $name; ?>" /><br />
   <label for="score">Score: </label>
   <input type="text" id="score" name="score" value="<?php if (!empty($score)) echo $score; ?>" /><br />
   <label for="screenshot">Screen shot: </label>
   <input type="file" id="screenshot" name="screenshot" /><br />
   <label for="verify">Verification: </label>
   <input type="text" id="verify" name="verify" value="Enter the pass-phrase." />
   <img src="captcha.php" alt="Verification pass-phrase" />
   <hr />
   <input type="submit" value="Add" name="submit" />
  </form>
</body>
</html>
```

This is where the encrypted pass-phrase is read from a session variable and checked to see if the user entered it correctly.

This is where the CAPTCHA script was "wired" to the Add Score script in Step 3, resulting in the CAPTCHA image being displayed on the page.

addscore.php

Test Drive

Modify the Add Score script to support CAPTCHA.

Change the `addscore.php` script so that it has a new Verification form field, as well as using the `captcha.php` script to display a CAPTCHA image. Also add the code to check and make sure the user entered the correct pass-phrase before adding a score.

Upload both scripts to your web server, and then open `addscore.php` in a web browser. Try to add a new score without entering a CAPTCHA pass-phrase. Now try again after entering the pass-phrase displayed in the CAPTCHA image.

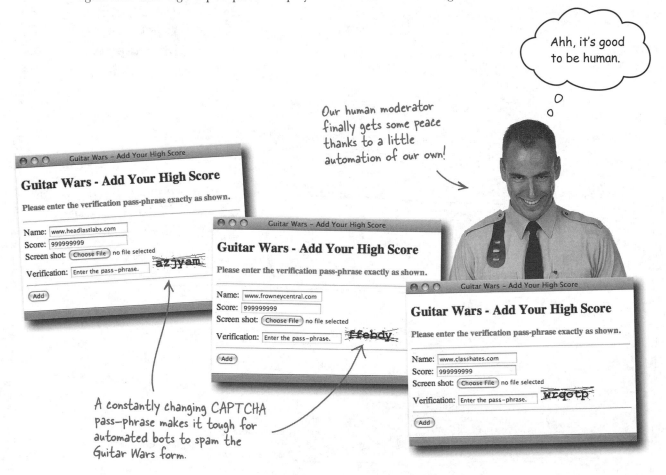

Ahh, it's good to be human.

Our human moderator finally gets some peace thanks to a little automation of our own!

A constantly changing CAPTCHA pass-phrase makes it tough for automated bots to spam the Guitar Wars form.

there are no
Dumb Questions

Q: Can I use the GD functions to create images in formats other than PNG?

A: Yes. The `imagegif()` and `imagejpeg()` functions work very similarly to `imagepng()` but create GIF and JPEG images, respectively.

Q: Can the image creation functions create images with transparency?

A: Yes! There is a function called `imagecolortransparent()` that sets a color as a transparent color within an image. This must be a color that you've already created using the `imagecolorallocate()` function. After setting the color as transparent, anything drawn with that color in the image will be considered transparent. To generate the image with transparency, just call `imagegif()` or `imagepng()`; you can't use `imagejpeg()` because JPEG images don't support transparency.

Q: When using `imagepng()` to output a PNG image directly to the client browser, where is the .png file for the image stored, and what is its name?

A: There is no .png file for the image, and the reason is because the image isn't stored in a file. Instead, the `imagepng()` function generates a binary PNG image in memory on the server and then delivers it directly to the browser via a header. Since the image data is created and sent directly to the browser, there's no need to store it in an image file.

Q: Is that why I'm able to put the name of the CAPTCHA script directly in the `src` attribute of an `<img>` tag?

A: That's correct. Referencing a PHP script in the `src` attribute of an `<img>` tag, as was done with the captcha.php script in Guitar Wars, results in the image being delivered directly by the script. This is in contrast to the normal way the `<img>` tag works, where the name of an image file is specified in the `src` attribute. Since the script is sourcing the image directly to the browser through a header (by way of the `imagepng()` function), no file is involved. And the browser knows to connect the image from the header to the `<img>` tag because the script is specified in the `src` attribute.

BULLET POINTS

- All web forms are at risk of attack from spam bots, but all spam bots are at risk from clever PHP programmers who use techniques such as CAPTCHA to thwart them.

- GD is a standard PHP graphics library that allows you to dynamically create images and then draw all kinds of different graphics and text on them.

- The `createtruecolorimage()` GD function is used to create a blank image for drawing.

- To output a PNG image to the browser or to a file on the server, call the `imagepng()` GD function.

- When you're finished working with an image, call `imagedestroy()` to clean up after it.

Five degrees of opposability

Since Mismatch is a community of registered (human!) users, spam bots haven't been a problem. However, users want a little more out of the mismatch feature of the site, primarily the "five degrees of opposability" that they've been hearing about. Mismatch users want more than just a list of topics for their ideal mismatch—they want some visual context of how those topics break down for each major category of "mismatchiness."

Mismatch's "five degrees of opposability" involves measuring mismatched topics by __category__.

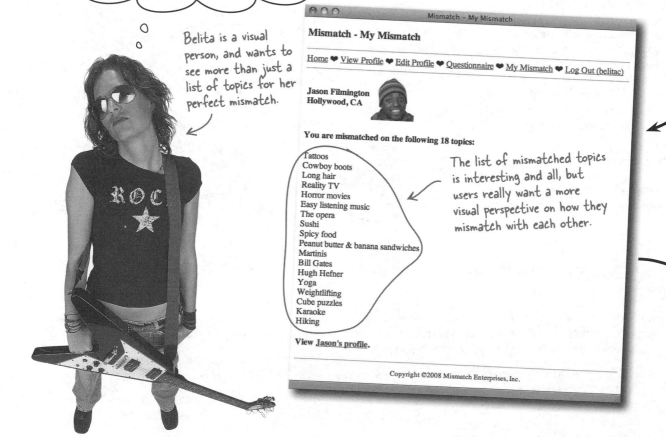

I see a bunch of topics, but I don't really know how we mismatch in different categories. I was sold on the "five degrees of opposability," but I can't even see how they relate to my mismatch. What gives?

Belita is a visual person, and wants to see more than just a list of topics for her perfect mismatch.

Mismatch – My Mismatch

Mismatch - My Mismatch

Home ❤ View Profile ❤ Edit Profile ❤ Questionnaire ❤ My Mismatch ❤ Log Out (belitac)

Jason Filmington
Hollywood, CA

You are mismatched on the following 18 topics:

Tattoos
Cowboy boots
Long hair
Reality TV
Horror movies
Easy listening music
The opera
Sushi
Spicy food
Peanut butter & banana sandwiches
Martinis
Bill Gates
Hugh Hefner
Yoga
Weightlifting
Cube puzzles
Karaoke
Hiking

The list of mismatched topics is interesting and all, but users really want a more visual perspective on how they mismatch with each other.

View Jason's profile.

Copyright ©2008 Mismatch Enterprises, Inc.

Charting mismatchiness

If you recall, Mismatch includes a categorized questionnaire where users selcet Love or Hate for a variety of topics. These responses are what determine the topics for an ideal mismatch. When presenting a user's ideal mismatch, the My Mismatch script displays a list of mismatched topics that it builds as an array from the Mismatch database. But users now want more than a list of topics... they want a visual categorized breakdown of their "mismatchiness," perhaps in the form of a bar graph?

Exercise

Draw a bar graph for the Mismatch data that visually shows the "five degrees of opposability" for Belita and Jason. Annotate what the information in the bar graph means.

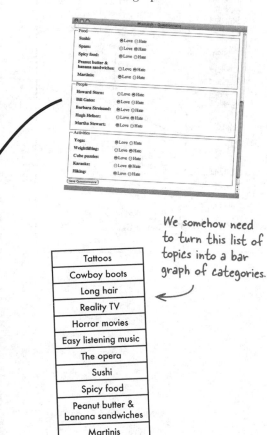

We somehow need to turn this list of topics into a bar graph of categories.

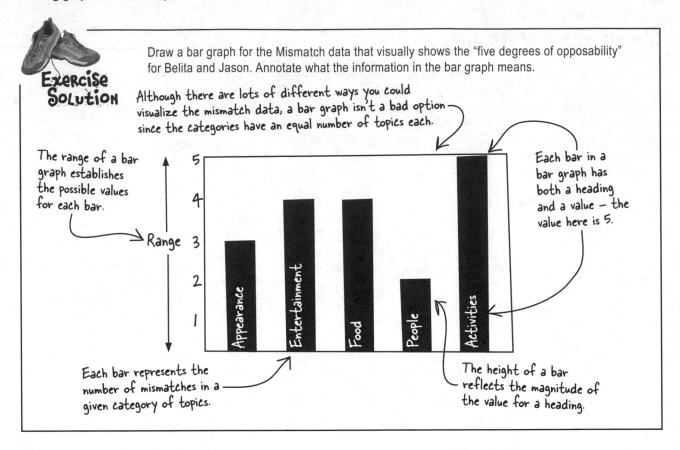

Draw a bar graph for the Mismatch data that visually shows the "five degrees of opposability" for Belita and Jason. Annotate what the information in the bar graph means.

Although there are lots of different ways you could visualize the mismatch data, a bar graph isn't a bad option since the categories have an equal number of topics each.

The range of a bar graph establishes the possible values for each bar.

Each bar in a bar graph has both a heading and a value — the value here is 5.

Each bar represents the number of mismatches in a given category of topics.

The height of a bar reflects the magnitude of the value for a heading.

Storing bar graph data

When it comes down to it, the data behind a bar graph is perhaps even more important than the graphics. Knowing that a bar graph is really just a collection of headings and values, we can view the data for a bar graph as a two-dimensional array where the main array stores the bars, while each sub-array stores the heading/value pair for each bar.

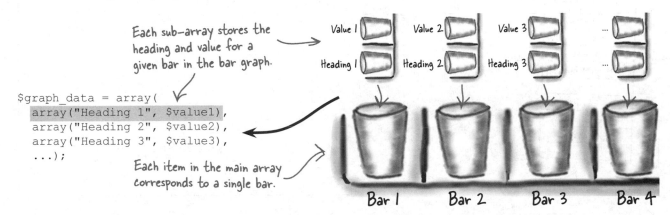

Each sub-array stores the heading and value for a given bar in the bar graph.

```
$graph_data = array(
  array("Heading 1", $value1),
  array("Heading 2", $value2),
  array("Heading 3", $value3),
  ...);
```

Each item in the main array corresponds to a single bar.

there are no
Dumb Questions

Q: **Does a bar graph have to be fed with a two-dimensional array of data?**

A: No, not at all. But keep in mind that each bar in a bar graph typically involves two pieces of information: a heading and a value. And each bar graph consists of multiple bars, so a two-dimensional array is a logical and efficient way to store data for use in populating a bar graph. As the old saying goes, "If you only see one solution, you really don't understand the problem." In this case, the problem is how to best store the data that is injected into a bar graph, and one particular solution that works out pretty well is a two-dimensional array. Of course, the challenge still remaining is how exactly to build this two-dimensional array of Mismatch category totals. The first step is to isolate what data in the database factors into the solution.

Exercise

The database schema for the Mismatch application is shown below. Circle all of the pieces of data that factor into the dynamic generation of the "five degrees of opposability" bar graph, making sure to annotate how they are used to create the graph.

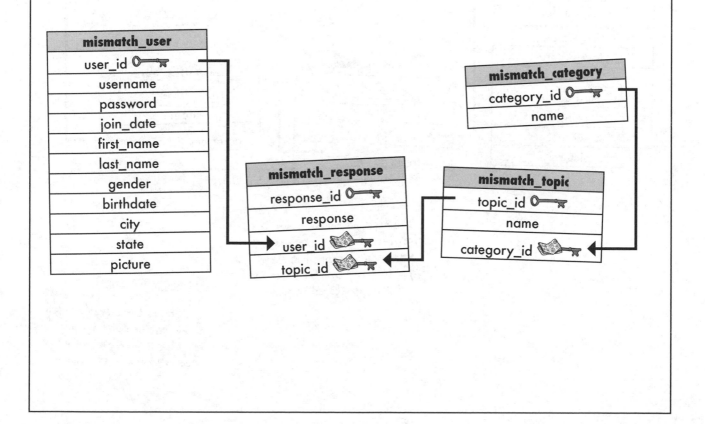

The database schema for the Mismatch application is shown below. Circle all of the pieces of data that factor into the dynamic generation of the "five degrees of opposability" bar graph, making sure to annotate how they are used to create the graph.

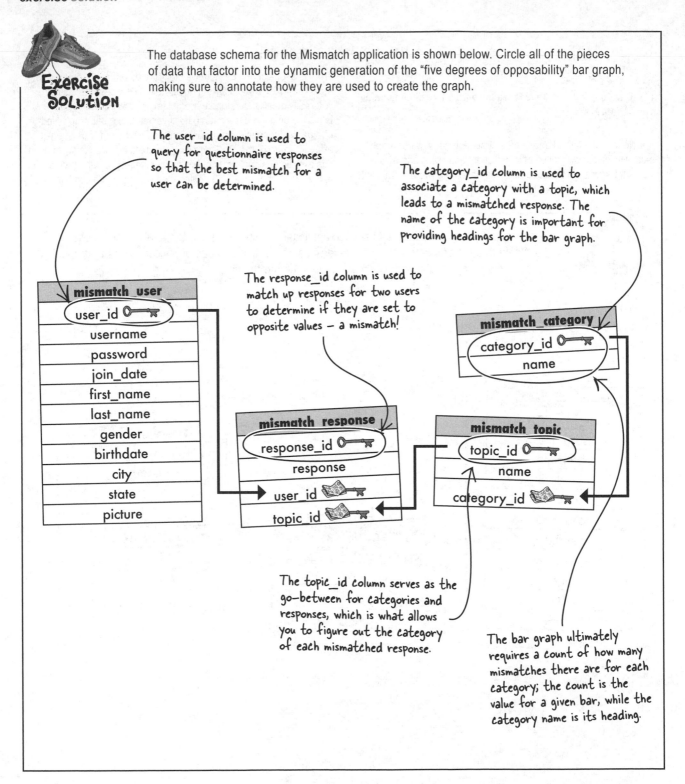

The user_id column is used to query for questionnaire responses so that the best mismatch for a user can be determined.

The category_id column is used to associate a category with a topic, which leads to a mismatched response. The name of the category is important for providing headings for the bar graph.

The response_id column is used to match up responses for two users to determine if they are set to opposite values — a mismatch!

The topic_id column serves as the go-between for categories and responses, which is what allows you to figure out the category of each mismatched response.

The bar graph ultimately requires a count of how many mismatches there are for each category; the count is the value for a given bar, while the category name is its heading.

Bar Graph Exposed

This week's interview:
Reading between the lines with the
master of charts

Head First: So you're the guy people call when they need a visual representation of some data. Is that right?

Bar Graph: Oh yeah. I'm adept at all facets of data visualization, especially the rectangular variety.

Head First: So your drawing capabilities are limited mostly to rectangles?

Bar Graph: I'd say "limited" is a strong word in this case. It's one of those deals where simpler is better—people just seem to relate to the bars, maybe because they're used to seeing things measured that way. You know, like the little meter on mobile phones that tells you how good your signal is. "Can you hear me now?" I love that.

Head First: Right. But I've also seen some pretty effective graphs that are round. Makes me think comforting thoughts... like apple pie, know what I mean?

Bar Graph: I know where you're headed, and I'm fully aware of Pie Chart. Look, it's two different ways of thinking about the same thing. Pie Chart sees the world in curves; I see it a bit straighter, that's all.

Head First: But don't people inherently relate better to pie than a bunch of bars?

Bar Graph: No, they don't. At least people who aren't hungry don't. You see, Pie Chart is really good at revealing parts of a whole, where the data being represented adds up to something that matters, like 100%, 32 teams, or 50 states. There are 50 states, right?

Head First: Yes. Well, assuming you count Washington, D.C. as a "capital district" and places like Puerto Rico and Guam as "territories." But anyway, I see what you're saying about Pie Chart being more about revealing parts of a whole, but don't you do the same thing?

Bar Graph: Yes, but keep in mind that I'm much more flexible than Pie Chart. You can add as many bars to me as you want and I have no problem at all showing them.

The more you add to Pie Chart, the smaller the slices have to get. At some point the parts get hard to visualize because of the whole. All that matters with me is that the bars all have values that can show up on the same scale.

Head First: What does that mean?

Bar Graph: Well, it's difficult for me to graph things that have wildly different values, unless of course, you don't mind the bars being dramatically different. Where I really excel is at showing the difference between values that are within the same range. For example, maybe you want to use me to show the price of gasoline over a one-year period, in which case all the values would be within a reasonably constrained range, like within a few dollars of each other.

Head First: You sure about that?

Bar Graph: I know, the price of gasoline seems like a wildly varying value, but not really within the realm of what I deal with.

Head First: So you've seen some wild stuff, eh?

Bar Graph: You wouldn't believe some of it. I once had a guy who built a web application that kept up with how many miles he dragged his mouse in a given month. He blogged about it constantly, and used me to chart his "travels." Pretty crazy but people loved it.

Head First: So is that where you fit into the web picture—providing visual glimpses into people's data?

Bar Graph: Yeah, I guess so. Anytime I can drop into a page and provide some eye appeal to data that might otherwise be a little dull and hard to grasp, I consider it a good day.

Head First: Glad to hear it. Hey, I appreciate you sharing your thoughts, and I hope we can do this again.

Bar Graph: It was my pleasure. And don't worry, you'll be seeing me around.

From one array to another

When we last left off at Mismatch, we had a list of topics that corresponded to mismatches between two users. More specifically, we really have an **array** of topics. Problem is, the bar graph we're trying to draw isn't about topics per se—it's about the **categories** that are associated with the topics. So we're one level removed from the data we actually need. It appears that some additional SQL querying is in order. Not only do we need the array of mismatched topics, but we also need a similar, parallel array of mismatched categories.

An alias is used to eliminate confusion when referring to the name column of the mismatch_category table.

A multiple join connects the category table to the response table so that the category name can be extracted.

```
$query = "SELECT mr.response_id, mr.topic_id, mr.response,
    mt.name AS topic_name, mc.name AS category_name " .
    "FROM mismatch_response AS mr " .
    "INNER JOIN mismatch_topic AS mt USING (topic_id) " .
    "INNER JOIN mismatch_category AS mc USING (category_id) " .
    "WHERE mr.user_id = '" . $_SESSION['user_id'] . "'";
```

The additional join in this query causes the category name corresponding to each response topic to be tacked on to the result data, ultimately making its way into the `$user_responses` array. But remember, we need only the **mismatched** categories, not all of the categories. We need to build another array containing just the mismatched categories for the responses.

We still need a new array holding <u>only</u> the mismatched response categories for this pair of users.

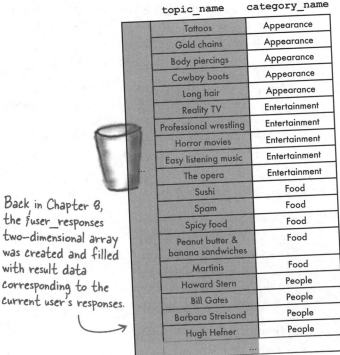

The new "column" of mismatch result data holds the category name of <u>every</u> response.

We need to extract only the category names of mismatched responses into an array.

Back in Chapter 8, the `$user_responses` two-dimensional array was created and filled with result data corresponding to the current user's responses.

topic_name	category_name
Tattoos	Appearance
Gold chains	Appearance
Body piercings	Appearance
Cowboy boots	Appearance
Long hair	Appearance
Reality TV	Entertainment
Professional wrestling	Entertainment
Horror movies	Entertainment
Easy listening music	Entertainment
The opera	Entertainment
Sushi	Food
Spam	Food
Spicy food	Food
Peanut butter & banana sandwiches	Food
Martinis	Food
Howard Stern	People
Bill Gates	People
Barbara Streisand	People
Hugh Hefner	People
...	

`$user_responses`

Appearance
Appearance
Appearance
Entertainment
Entertainment
Entertainment
Entertainment
Food
Food
Food
Food
People
People
Activities
Activities
Activities
Activities
Activities

But we're still falling short of our goal of building an array of mismatched categories. To do that, we need to revisit the code that builds the array of mismatched topics...

Test Drive

Try out the new query to grab mismatched topics and categories.

Using a MySQL tool, issue the following query to SELECT mismatched topics and categories
for a specific user. Make sure to specify a user ID for a user who not only exists in the database,
but who also has filled out the Mismatch questionnaire form:

```
SELECT mr.response_id, mr.topic_id, mr.response,
  mt.name AS topic_name, mc.name AS category_name
  FROM mismatch_response AS mr
  INNER JOIN mismatch_topic AS mt USING (topic_id)
  INNER JOIN mismatch_category AS mc USING (category_id)
  WHERE mr.user_id = 3;
```

The user ID must be for a
valid user who has answered
the Mismatch questionnaire.

```
File Edit Window Help Oppose
mysql> SELECT mr.response_id, mr.topic_id, mr.response,
  mt.name AS topic_name, mc.name AS category_name
  FROM mismatch_response AS mr
  INNER JOIN mismatch_topic AS mt USING (topic_id)
  INNER JOIN mismatch_category AS mc USING (category_id)
  WHERE mr.user_id = 3;

+-------------+----------+----------+--------------------------+----------------+
| response_id | topic_id | response | topic_name               | category_name  |
+-------------+----------+----------+--------------------------+----------------+
| 26          | 1        | 1        | Tattoos                  | Appearance     |
| 27          | 2        | 2        | Gold chains              | Appearance     |
| 28          | 3        | 1        | Body piercings           | Appearance     |
| 29          | 4        | 2        | Cowboy boots             | Appearance     |
| 30          | 5        | 1        | Long hair                | Appearance     |
| 31          | 6        | 2        | Reality TV               | Entertainment  |
| 32          | 7        | 1        | Professional wrestling   | Entertainment  |
| 33          | 8        | 1        | Horror movies            | Entertainment  |
| 34          | 9        | 2        | Easy listening music     | Entertainment  |
```

Notice that the results of this query
match up with the $user_responses array
on the facing page, which is what we want.

It's always a good idea to test
out a query in a MySQL tool
before sticking it in PHP code.

Build an array of mismatched topics

We now have a query that performs a multiple join to grab the **category** of each response in addition to the topic, which is then extracted into the `$user_responses` array. Remember that another similar query also grabs data for each other user in the database so that mismatch comparisons can be made. So `$user_responses` holds the response data for the user logged in to Mismatch, while `$mismatch_responses` holds one of the other users in the system. This allows us to loop through all of the users and update `$mismatch_responses` for each mismatch user comparison.

We're already using these two arrays to score mismatches and build an array of mismatched topics. We can now add a new line of code to also construct an array of mismatched categories—**this array contains the category of each mismatched topic between two users**.

This is the same code from the earlier version of Mismatch, except now it builds an array of mismatched categories in addition to the array of topics.

```php
$categories = array();
for ($i = 0; $i < count($user_responses); $i++) {
  if ($user_responses[$i]['response'] + $mismatch_responses[$i]['response'] == 3) {
    $score += 1;
    array_push($topics, $user_responses[$i]['topic_name']);
    array_push($categories, $user_responses[$i]['category_name']);
  }
}
```

This code results in an array containing only the mismatched categories.

When all is said and done, the $categories array contains one category for each and every mismatch.

An array of mismatched categories is built by storing away the category associated with each mismatched response.

there are no Dumb Questions

Q: I'm a little confused. What's the difference between a MySQL result set and a PHP array?

A: One big difference is access. A result set is only made available a row of data at a time, while an array can hold multiple "rows" of data thanks to multiple dimensions. Extracting a result set into a two-dimensional array lets us move through rows of data efficiently without having to constantly go back to the database server to fetch and re-fetch rows. This doesn't work with huge sets of data, as you'd be creating huge arrays, but in the case of Mismatch responses, the arrays are never larger than the total number of topics in the system.

Q: Don't we still need to count how many times a category was mismatched in order to generate the bar graph?

A: Yes. An array of mismatched categories is not enough. Remember that the idea behind the Mismatch bar graph is that each bar represents a mismatched category, and the height of the bar represents how many times the category was mismatched. So we need to come up with a count of how many times each category was mismatched. But it's probably worth taking a step back to formulate a general plan of attack...

Formulating a bar graphing plan

With an array of mismatched categories and a bunch of big ideas about how to use it to generate a bar graph image for the My Mismatch page, we're still missing a plan. As it turns out, there are only three steps required to dynamically generate the bar graph, and we've already knocked out one of them.

This step provides us with the list of mismatched categories.

1 ~~Query the Mismatch database for mismatched category names.~~

The list of categories needs to be converted into a list of category totals.

2 **Calculate the mismatch totals for each category.**

3 **Draw the bar graph using the categorized mismatch totals.**

With the category totals in hand, we can get down to the fun part of drawing the bar graph with GD functions.

To complete Step 2 of our plan, we somehow need to take the array of mismatched categories and turn it into a set of category totals, meaning a count of how many times each category appears in the mismatched category array. If you recall, this is precisely the kind of data required to drive a bar graph, where the categories are the headings and the count for each category is the value of each bar. A two-dimensional array can be used to combine categories and totals into a single data structure.

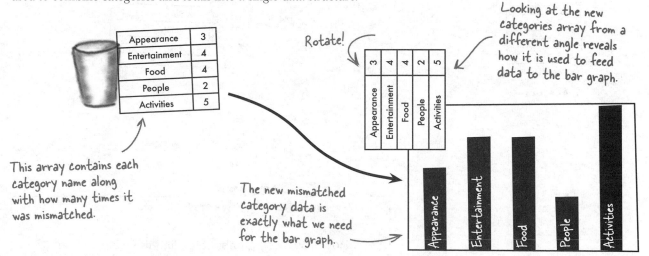

Appearance	3
Entertainment	4
Food	4
People	2
Activities	5

This array contains each category name along with how many times it was mismatched.

Rotate!

Looking at the new categories array from a different angle reveals how it is used to feed data to the bar graph.

The new mismatched category data is exactly what we need for the bar graph.

Once this array of category totals is built, we'll be ready to move on to Step 3 and actually use some GD functions to crank out the bar graph visuals.

Crunching categories

The challenge now is to get the array of categories totaled up and put into a two-dimensional array of headings and values. We have an array of mismatched categories stored in the $categories array. We need to build a new array called $category_totals that contains one entry for each category, along with the number of mismatches for each.

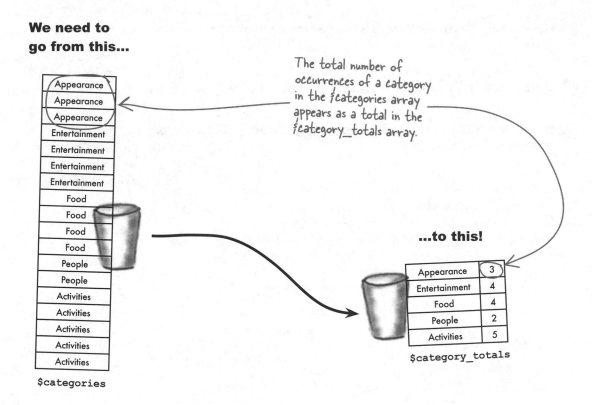

We need to go from this...

The total number of occurrences of a category in the $categories array appears as a total in the $category_totals array.

...to this!

$categories

$category_totals

BRAIN POWER

How would you go about totaling the mismatched categories in the $categories array to build the two-dimensional $category_totals array?

Doing the category math

Moving from a one-dimensional array of mismatched categories to a two-dimensional array of category totals is a bit trickier than you might think at first glance. For this reason, it's helpful to work through the solution in **pseudocode** before actually cranking out any PHP. Pseudocode frees you from syntactical details and allows you to focus on the core ideas involved in a particular coding solution.

> **Create a new two-dimensional array to store the category totals, making sure to initialize the first element with the first mismatched category and a count of 0.**
>
> **Loop through the array of mismatched categories. For each category in the array...**
>
> > **Is the last element in the category totals array a different category than the current mismatched category?**
> >
> > ◆ **Yes! This is a new category so add it to the category totals array and initialize its count to 0.**
> >
> > ◆ **No. This is another instance of the current category, so increment the count of the last element in the category totals array.**

The product of this code is a two-dimensional array of category totals where the main array holds a single category, while each sub-array contains the category name and its value.

Exercise

Translate the pseudocode to finish the real PHP code that builds a two-dimensional array of Mismatch category data called `$category_totals`.

```
$category_totals = array(array($mismatch_categories[0], 0));
foreach ($mismatch_categories as $category) {

......................................................................................

......................................................................................

......................................................................................

......................................................................................

......................................................................................

......................................................................................

}
```

EXERCISE SOLUTION

Translate the pseudocode to finish the real PHP code that builds a two-dimensional array of Mismatch category data called `$category_totals`.

Arrays are zero–indexed, so the last element in an array is always count() minus one.

```
$category_totals = array(array($mismatch_categories[0], 0));
foreach ($mismatch_categories as $category) {
    if ($category_totals[count($category_totals) - 1][0] != $category) {
        array_push($category_totals, array($category, 1));
    }
    else {
        $category_totals[count($category_totals) - 1][1]++;
    }
}
```

This is a new category, so add it to the array of category totals as a new sub–array consisting of the category name and an initial count of 1.

The increment operator (++) is applied to the second element in the sub–array, which is the category count.

$category_totals

The $category_totals variable now holds precisely the data needed to generate a bar graph for the mismatched categories.

Appearance	3
Entertainment	4
Food	4
People	2
Activities	5

This is the end result of this code.

We can now safely scratch this step off the list, leaving us only with the drawing of the bar graph.

~~2 Calculate the mismatch totals for each category.~~

3 Appearance 4 Entertainment 4 Food 2 People 5 Activities

there are no
Dumb Questions

Q: What happens to the category total code if the categories in the **$mismatch_categories** array aren't in order?

A: Big problems. The code is entirely dependent upon the categories in the $mismatch_categories array being in order. This is revealed in how the code assumes that any change in the category is the start of a new category, which works as long as categories are grouped together. Fortunately, the query in the Questionnaire script that originally selects topics for insertion into the mismatch_response table is smart enough to order the responses by category.

```
SELECT topic_id FROM mismatch_topic ORDER BY category_id, topic_id
```

This query is the one that first grabs topics from the database and then inserts them as empty responses for a given user. This ensures that user responses are stored in the database ordered by category, which allows the category total code to work properly.

Q: But isn't it risky writing code that is dependent upon the order of data stored in a database table?

A: Yes and no. Remember that this database is entirely controlled by script code that you write, so the order of the data really only changes if you write script code that changes it. Even so, an argument could certainly be made for ordering the join query in the My Mismatch script by category to make absolutely sure that the mismatched category list is in order.

Bar graphing basics

With a shiny new two-dimensional array of mismatched category data burning a hole in your pocket, it's time to get down to the business of drawing a bar graph. But rather than focus on the specifics of drawing the Mismatch bar graph, why not take a more generic approach? If you design and create an all-purpose bar graph function, it's possible to use it for Mismatch **and** have it at your disposal for any future bar graphing needs. In other words, it's **reusable**. This new function must perform a series of steps to successfully render a bar graph from a two-dimensional array of data.

1. Create the image.
2. Create the colors you'll be using to draw the graphics and text.
3. Fill the background with a background color.
4. Draw the bars and headings.
5. Draw a rectangle around the entire bar graph.
6. Draw the range up the left side of the graph.
7. Write the bar graph to an image file.
8. Clean up by destroying the image.

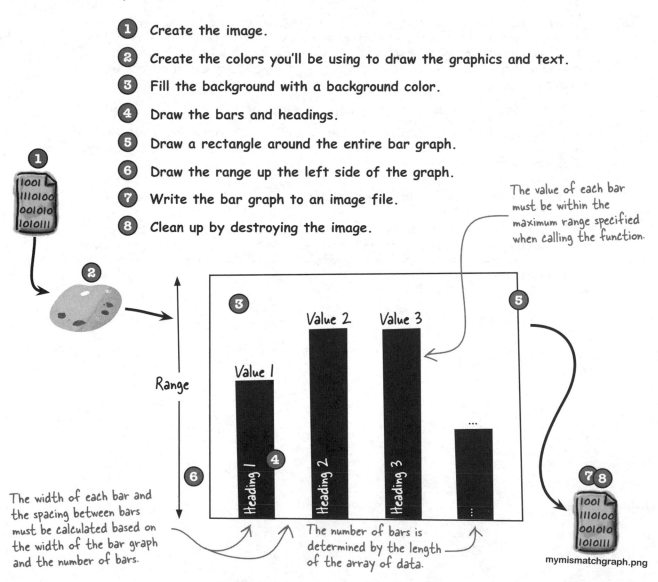

The value of each bar must be within the maximum range specified when calling the function.

Range

The width of each bar and the spacing between bars must be calculated based on the width of the bar graph and the number of bars.

The number of bars is determined by the length of the array of data.

mymismatchgraph.png

PHP Magnets

The My Mismatch script contains a new `draw_bar_graph()` function that takes care of drawing a bar graph given a width, height, a two-dimensional array of graph data, a maximum value for the range, and a filename for the resulting PNG image. Use the magnets to add the missing GD drawing function calls.

```php
function draw_bar_graph($width, $height, $data, $max_value, $filename) {
  // Create the empty graph image
  $img =.............................. ($width, $height);
  // Set a white background with black text and gray graphics
  $bg_color =.............................. ($img, 255, 255, 255);     // white
  $text_color =.............................. ($img, 255, 255, 255);   // white
  $bar_color =.............................. ($img, 0, 0, 0);          // black
  $border_color =.............................. ($img, 192, 192, 192); // light gray

  // Fill the background
  .............................. ($img, 0, 0, $width, $height, $bg_color);

  // Draw the bars
  $bar_width = $width / ((count($data) * 2) + 1);
  for ($i = 0; $i < count($data); $i++) {
    ..............................($img, ($i * $bar_width * 2) + $bar_width, $height,
      ($i * $bar_width * 2) + ($bar_width * 2), $height - (($height / $max_value) * $data[$i][1]), $bar_color);
    .............................. ($img, 5, ($i * $bar_width * 2) + ($bar_width), $height - 5, $data[$i][0],
      $text_color);
  }
  // Draw a rectangle around the whole thing
  .............................. ($img, 0, 0, $width - 1, $height - 1, $border_color);
  // Draw the range up the left side of the graph
  for ($i = 1; $i <= $max_value; $i++) {
    .............................. ($img, 5, 0, $height - ($i * ($height / $max_value))), $i, $bar_color);
  }
  // Write the graph image to a file
  .............................. ($img, $filename, 5);
  .............................. ($img);
}
```

imagedestroy

imagestringup imagerectangle

imagecreatetruecolor imagecolorallocate

imagecolorallocate imagepng imagestring imagefilledrectangle

imagefilledrectangle imagecolorallocate imagecolorallocate

PHP Magnets Solution

The My Mismatch script contains a new `draw_bar_graph()` function that takes care of drawing a bar graph given a width, height, a two-dimensional array of graph data, a maximum value for the range, and a filename for the resulting PNG image. Use the magnets to add the missing GD drawing function calls.

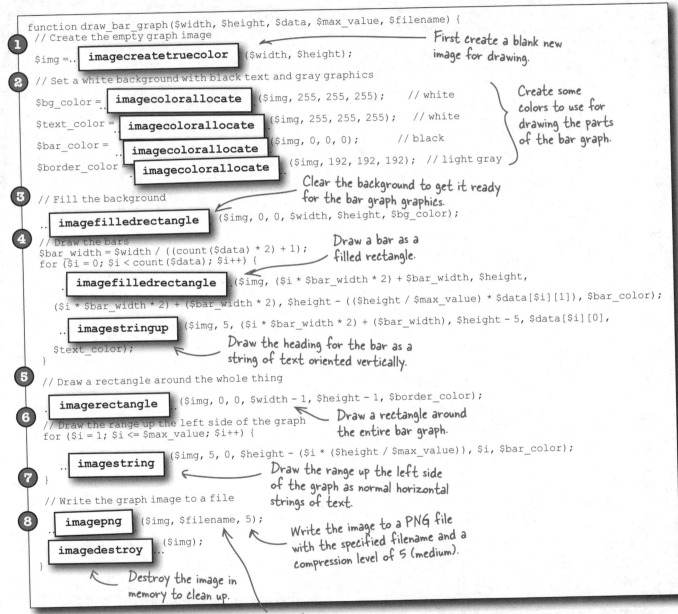

```
function draw_bar_graph($width, $height, $data, $max_value, $filename) {
  // Create the empty graph image
```
①   `$img = ..` **imagecreatetruecolor** `($width, $height);` ← First create a blank new image for drawing.

②   `// Set a white background with black text and gray graphics`

`$bg_color = ..` **imagecolorallocate** `($img, 255, 255, 255);    // white`

`$text_color = ..` **imagecolorallocate** `($img, 255, 255, 255);    // white`

`$bar_color = ..` **imagecolorallocate** `($img, 0, 0, 0);          // black`

`$border_color = ..` **imagecolorallocate** `($img, 192, 192, 192);  // light gray`

⟩ Create some colors to use for drawing the parts of the bar graph.

③   `// Fill the background`

Clear the background to get it ready for the bar graph graphics.

`..` **imagefilledrectangle** `($img, 0, 0, $width, $height, $bg_color);`

④   `// Draw the bars`

`$bar_width = $width / ((count($data) * 2) + 1);`
`for ($i = 0; $i < count($data); $i++) {`

Draw a bar as a filled rectangle.

`..` **imagefilledrectangle** `..($img, ($i * $bar_width * 2) + $bar_width, $height,`
`  ($i * $bar_width * 2) + ($bar_width * 2), $height - (($height / $max_value) * $data[$i][1]), $bar_color);`

`..` **imagestringup** `($img, 5, ($i * $bar_width * 2) + ($bar_width), $height - 5, $data[$i][0],`
`  $text_color);`

Draw the heading for the bar as a string of text oriented vertically.

`}`

⑤   `// Draw a rectangle around the whole thing`

`..` **imagerectangle** `($img, 0, 0, $width - 1, $height - 1, $border_color);`

⑥   `// Draw the range up the left side of the graph`

Draw a rectangle around the entire bar graph.

`for ($i = 1; $i <= $max_value; $i++) {`

`..` **imagestring** `($img, 5, 0, $height - ($i * ($height / $max_value)), $i, $bar_color);`

⑦   `}`

Draw the range up the left side of the graph as normal horizontal strings of text.

`// Write the graph image to a file`

⑧   **imagepng** `($img, $filename, 5);`

`..` **imagedestroy** `..($img);`

Write the image to a PNG file with the specified filename and a compression level of 5 (medium).

`}`

Destroy the image in memory to clean up.

The folder on the server where the file is to be written must be writeable in order for this function to work.

there are no
Dumb Questions

Q: Why does the `draw_bar_graph()` function write the bar graph image to a file instead of just returning it directly to the browser?

A: Because the function isn't contained within its own script that can return an image through a header to the browser. Remember, the only way to return a dynamically generated image directly to the browser is for a script to use a header, meaning that the entire purpose of the script has to be the generation of the image.

Q: So then why isn't the `draw_bar_graph()` function placed in its own script so that it can return the bar graph image directly to the browser using a header?

A: While it is a good idea to place the function in its own script for the purposes of making it more reusable, there is still a problem when it comes to returning an image via a header. The problem has to do with how you reuse code. When code is included in a script using `include`, `include_once`, `require`, or `require_once`, the code is dropped into the script as if it had

originally existed there. This works great for code that doesn't do anything that manipulates the browser. But sending a header impacts the output of a script, which can be problematic for included code. It's not that you can't send a header from included code; you've actually done so in earlier examples. The problem is that you have to be extremely careful, and in some cases it isn't safe to assume that headers haven't already been sent. The My Mismatch script, for example, can't **return** an image to the browser because its job is to output HTML code containing mismatch results. Including script code that dynamically generates and returns an image would cause a header conflict.

Q: OK, so can I just reference the bar graph code like the `captcha.php` script from Guitar Wars. That seemed to work fine without an include, right?

A: Yes, it did, and it referenced the `captcha.php` script directly from the `src` attribute of an `<img>` tag. The problem here is that we have a lot of data that needs to be passed to the bar graph code, and this would be very cumbersome to try and pass via GET or POST.

Draw and display the bar graph image

The `draw_bar_graph()` function makes it possible to dynamically generate a bar graph image, provided you give it the proper information. In the case of the Mismatch bar graph, this involves sending along a suitable width and height that works on the My Mismatch page (480×240), the two-dimensional array of mismatched category data, 5 as the maximum range value (maximum number of mismatch topics per category), and a suitable upload path and filename for the resulting bar graph image. After calling the function, the image is generated and suitable for display using an HTML `<img>` tag.

The image file generated by this function call is named mymismatchgraph.png, and is stored on the web server in the path identified by MM_UPLOADPATH.

```
echo '<h4>Mismatched category breakdown:</h4>';

draw_bar_graph(480, 240, $category_totals, 5, MM_UPLOADPATH . 'mymismatchgraph.png');

echo '<img src="' . MM_UPLOADPATH . 'mymismatchgraph.png" alt="Mismatch category graph" /><br />';
```

With the help of a reusable function, it's possible to go from database data to a bar graph stored in an image file.

The same path and image filename are specified in the src attribute of the <img> tag.

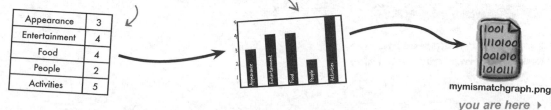

Appearance	3
Entertainment	4
Food	4
People	2
Activities	5

mymismatchgraph.png

TEST DRIVE

Create the My Mismatch script and try it out.

Create a new text file named `mymismatch.php`, and enter the code for the My Mismatch script (or download the script from the Head First Labs site at `www.headfirstlabs.com/books/hfphp`). Also add a new menu item for My Mismatch to the `navmenu.php` script.

Upload the scripts to your web server, and then open the main Mismatch page (`index.php`) in a web browser. Log in if you aren't already logged in, and the click "My Mismatch" on the main navigation menu. Congratulations, this is your ideal mismatch!

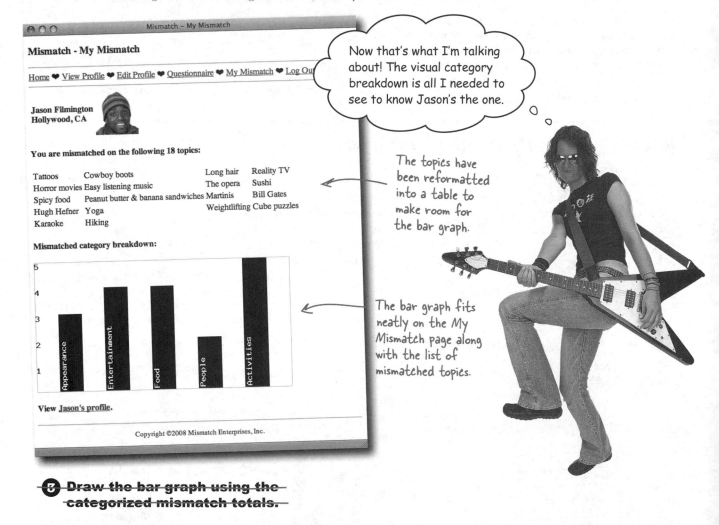

Now that's what I'm talking about! The visual category breakdown is all I needed to see to know Jason's the one.

The topics have been reformatted into a table to make room for the bar graph.

The bar graph fits neatly on the My Mismatch page along with the list of mismatched topics.

~~③ Draw the bar graph using the categorized mismatch totals.~~

So I'm curious, how are we able to store the My Mismatch bar graph image in a single file when a unique image is generated for every different user?

A bit of luck, as it turns out.

It's true, there is only one bar graph image at any given time, no matter how many users there are. This could present a problem if two users ever happen to view the My Mismatch page at the exact same moment. We run the risk of generating separate images for the two people and then trying to write them to a single image file.

This problem is probably fairly isolated in reality, but as Mismatch grows in popularity and expands to thousands and thousands of users, it could become significant. The fact that each one of the users thinks of the bar graph image as **their own** is a clue that there's a weakness in the single image bar graph design.

Here we clearly have three different bar graph images in view, but we know only one image file is used to store them.

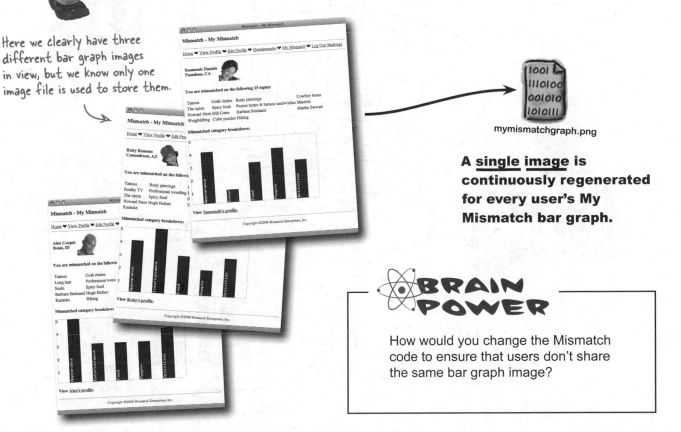

mymismatchgraph.png

A <u>single</u> <u>image</u> is continuously regenerated for every user's My Mismatch bar graph.

BRAIN POWER

How would you change the Mismatch code to ensure that users don't share the same bar graph image?

Individual bar graph images for all

The solution to the shared bar graph image problem lies in generating multiple images, one for every user, in fact. But we still need to ensure that each of these images is tied to exactly one user and no more. That's where a familiar database design element comes into play... the primary key! The primary key for the `mismatch_user` table, `user_id`, uniquely identifies each user, and therefore provides an excellent way to uniquely name each bar graph image and also associate it with a user. All we have to do is prepend the users' IDs to the filename of their bar graph image.

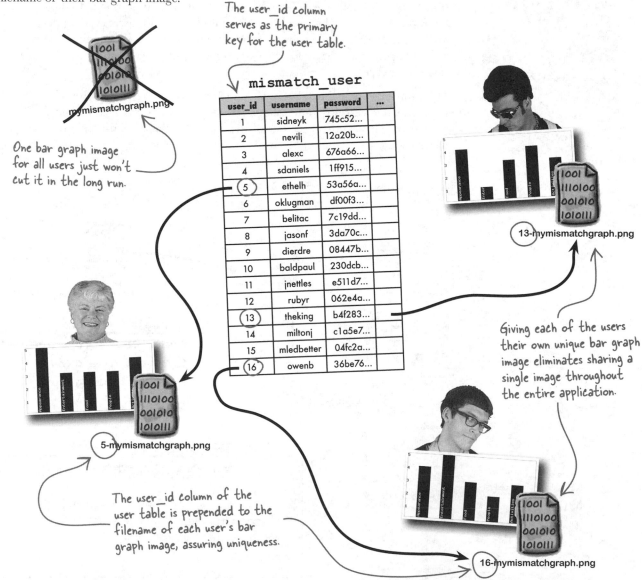

The user_id column serves as the primary key for the user table.

mismatch_user

user_id	username	password	...
1	sidneyk	745c52...	
2	nevilj	12a20b...	
3	alexc	676a66...	
4	sdaniels	1ff915...	
5	ethelh	53a56a...	
6	oklugman	df00f3...	
7	belitac	7c19dd...	
8	jasonf	3da70c...	
9	dierdre	08447b...	
10	baldpaul	230dcb...	
11	jnettles	e511d7...	
12	rubyr	062e4a...	
13	theking	b4f283...	
14	miltonj	c1a5e7...	
15	mledbetter	04fc2a...	
16	owenb	36be76...	

One bar graph image for all users just won't cut it in the long run.

mymismatchgraph.png

13-mymismatchgraph.png

5-mymismatchgraph.png

16-mymismatchgraph.png

Giving each of the users their own unique bar graph image eliminates sharing a single image throughout the entire application.

The user_id column of the user table is prepended to the filename of each user's bar graph image, assuring uniqueness.

there are no
Dumb Questions

Q: Is there any advantage to outputting dynamically generated images as PNG images versus GIFs or JPEGs?

A: No, none beyond the reasons you would choose one image format over another for static images. For example, GIFs and PNGs are better for vector-type graphics, whereas JPEGs are better for photorealistic graphics. In the case of Mismatch, we're dealing with vector graphics, so either PNG or GIF would work fine. PNG happens to be a more modern image standard, which is why it was used, but GIF would've worked too. To output a GD image to a GIF and JPEG, respectively, call the `imagegif()` and `imagejpeg()` functions.

Q: How do I know what compression level to use when outputting PNG images to a file?

A: The compression level settings for the `imagepng()` function enter the picture when outputting a PNG image to a file, and they range from 0 (no compression) to 9 (maximum compression). There are no hard rules about how much compression to use when, so you may want to experiment with different settings. Mismatch uses 5 as the compression level for the bar graphs, which appears to be a decent tradeoff between quality and efficiency.

Q: Are there file storage issues introduced by generating a bar graph image for each user?

A: No, not really. This question relates back to the compression level question to some degree, but it's unlikely that you'll overwhelm your server with too many or too huge files unless you really go crazy generating thousands of large image files. As an example, consider that the Mismatch bar graph images average about 2 KB each, so even if the site blows up and has 50,000 users, you're talking about a grand total of 100 MB in bar graph images. Granted, that's a decent little chunk of web hosting space, but a site with 50,000 users should be generating plenty of cash to offset that kind of storage.

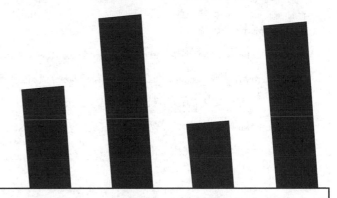

Exercise

Below is the Mismatch code that dynamically generates a bar graph image and then displays it on the page. Rewrite the code so that it generates a unique image for each user. Hint: use `$_SESSION['user_id']` to build a unique image filename for each user.

```
echo '<h4>Mismatched category breakdown:</h4>';

draw_bar_graph(480, 240, $category_totals, 5, MM_UPLOADPATH . 'mymismatchgraph.png');

echo '<img src="' . MM_UPLOADPATH . 'mymismatchgraph.png" alt="Mismatch category graph" /><br />';
```

....

....

....

....

....

Below is the Mismatch code that dynamically generates a bar graph image and then displays it on the page. Rewrite the code so that it generates a unique image for each user. Hint: use $_SESSION['user_id'] to build a unique image filename for each user.

```
echo '<h4>Mismatched category breakdown:</h4>';

draw_bar_graph(480, 240, $category_totals, 5, MM_UPLOADPATH . 'mymismatchgraph.png');

echo '<img src="' . MM_UPLOADPATH . 'mymismatchgraph.png" alt="Mismatch category graph" /><br />';
```

The standard file upload path is still used to ensure that the image is stored in the desired place on the server.

Make sure this folder on the server is writeable so that the image file can be written.

The unique image filename follows the form X-mymismatchgraph.png, where X is the ID of the user.

```
echo '<h4>Mismatched category breakdown:</h4>';
draw_bar_graph(480, 240, $category_totals, 5,
MM_UPLOADPATH . $_SESSION['user_id'] . '-mymismatchgraph.png');
echo '<img src="' . MM_UPLOADPATH . $_SESSION['user_id'] . '-mymismatchgraph.png" .
'alt="Mismatch category graph" /><br />';
```

We can use the user ID that we already have stored away in a session variable.

The same image filename is used when setting the src attribute of the <img> tag for the bar graph image in HTML code.

Test Drive

Change the My Mismatch script to generate unique bar graph images.

Modify the My Mismatch script so that it generates a unique bar graph image for each user. Upload the `mymismatch.php` script to your web server, and then open it in a web browser. The page won't look any different, but you can view source on it to see that the bar graph image now has a unique filename.

Mismatch users are digging the bar graphs

With the shared bar graph image problem solved, you've helped eliminate a potential long-term performance bottleneck as more and more users join Mismatch and take advantage of the "five degrees of opposability" graph. Each user now generates their own unique bar graph image when viewing their ideal mismatch. Fortunately, this fix took place behind the scenes, unbeknownst to users, who are really taking advantage of the mismatch data in the hopes of making a love connection.

Elmer is perfecting a few new dance moves to share with his ideal mismatch.

13-mymismatchgraph.png

Each user's mismatch bar graph image is now stored in its own file.

5-mymismatchgraph.png

Ethel has some minor doubts about all this "opposites attract" business, but she's willing to give it a go.

16-mymismatchgraph.png

Owen has already lined up a date with his mismatch, and is gearing up for a night on the town.

CHAPTER 11

Your PHP & MySQL Toolbox

Dynamic graphics open up all kinds of interesting possibilities in terms of building PHP scripts that generate custom images on the fly. Let's recap what makes it all possible.

CAPTCHA

A program that protects a web site from automated spam bots by using a test of some sort. For example, a CAPTCHA test might involve discerning letters within a distorted pass-phrase, identifying the content of an image, or analyzing an equation to perform a simple mathematical computation.

GD library

A set of PHP functions that are used to draw graphics onto an image. The GD library allows you to dynamically create and draw on images, and then either return them directly to the browser or write them to image files on the server.

imagecreatetruecolor()

This function is part of the GD graphics library, and is used to create a new image for drawing. The image is initially created in memory, and isn't output for display purposes until calling another function, such as imagepng().

imagestring(), imagestringup(), imagettftext()

The GD graphics library also allows you to draw text, either with a built-in font or with a TrueType font of your own choosing.

imageline(), imagerectangle(), ...

The GD graphics library offers lots of functions for drawing graphics primitives, such as lines, rectangles, ellipses, and even individual pixels. Each function operates on an existing image that has already been created with imagecreatetruecolor().

imagepng()

When you're finished drawing to an image using GD graphics functions, this function outputs the image so that it can be displayed. You can choose to output the image directly to the web browser or to an image file on the server.

After drawing to an image and outputting it as desired, it's a good idea to destroy the resources associated with it by calling this function.

PHP&MySQLcross

When you could actually use a robot, they're nowhere to be found. Oh well, your analog brain is up to the challenge of solving this little puzzle.

Across

1. This PHP graphics function draws a line.

6. The visual used to show how mismatched users compare on a categorized basis.

7. To generate custom bar graph images for each user in Mismatch, this piece of information is used as part of the image filename.

8. Mismatch uses this kind of array to store bar graph data.

10. Give it two points and this graphics function will draw a rectangle.

11. If you want to draw text in a certain font, call the image...text () function.

13. Always clean up after working with an image in PHP by calling this function.

14. Call this graphics function to create a new image.

Down

2. The name of PHP's graphics library.

3. Call this function to output an image as a PNG.

4. Owen's ideal mismatch.

5. Mismatch uses a bar graph to compare users based upon "five degrees of ....".

9. A test used to distinguish between people and automated spam bots.

12. When PHP outputs an image, the image is either sent directly to the client browser or stored in a .....

PHP&MySQLcross Solution

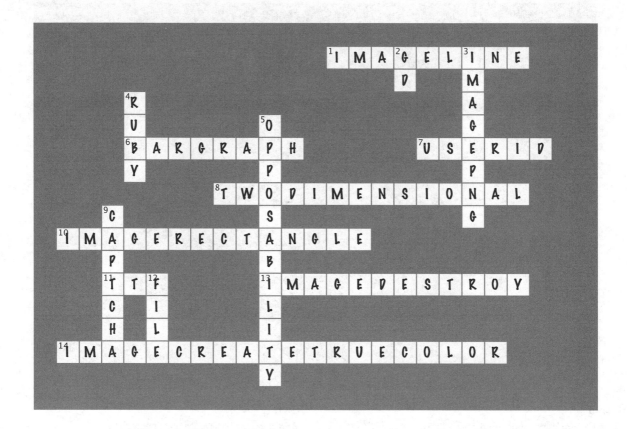

12 syndication and web services

Interfacing to the world

This is amazing. Instead of having to travel around asking people what's going on, we can get news delivered to us...brilliant!

Indeed. Technology brings the world to our ink-smudged fingertips!

It's a big world out there, and one that your web application can't afford to ignore. Perhaps more importantly, you'd rather the world not ignore your web application. One excellent way to tune the world in to your web application is to make its data available for syndication, which means users can subscribe to your site's content instead of having to visit your web site directly to find new info. Not only that, your application can interface to other applications through web services and take advantage of other people's data to provide a richer experience.

Owen needs to get the word out about Fang

One of the big problems facing any web site is keeping people coming back. It's one thing to snare a visitor, but quite another to get them to come back again. Even sites with the most engaging content can fall off a person's radar simply because it's hard to remember to go visit a web site regularly. Knowing this, Owen wants to offer an alternative means of viewing alien abduction reports—he wants to "push" the reports to people, as opposed to them having to visit his site on a regular basis.

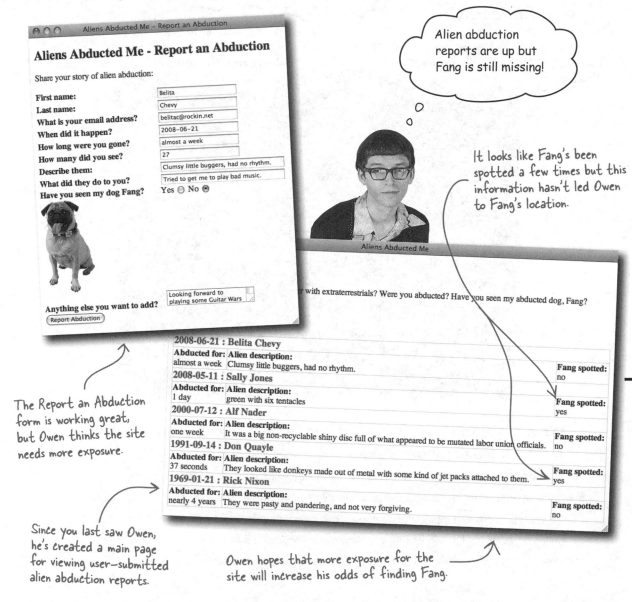

Alien abduction reports are up but Fang is still missing!

It looks like Fang's been spotted a few times but this information hasn't led Owen to Fang's location.

The Report an Abduction form is working great, but Owen thinks the site needs more exposure.

Since you last saw Owen, he's created a main page for viewing user-submitted alien abduction reports.

Owen hopes that more exposure for the site will increase his odds of finding Fang.

Push alien abduction data to the people

By pushing alien abduction content to users, Owen effectively creates
a virtual team of people who can help him monitor abduction reports.
With more people on the case, the odds of identifying more Fang
sightings and hopefully homing in on Fang's location increase.

Pushing web content to users is a great way to help gain more exposure for a web site.

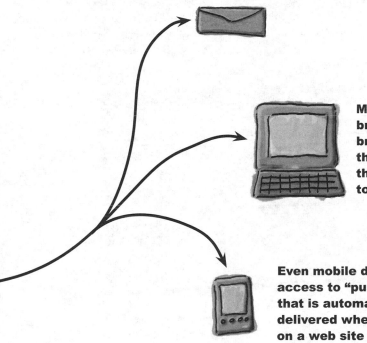

Some email clients support "push" content, allowing you to receive web site updates the same way you receive email messages.

Many regular web browsers also let you browse "push" content that quickly reveals the latest news posted to a web site.

Even mobile devices provide access to "push" content that is automatically delivered when something on a web site changes.

Owen isn't exactly sure how to push content to users but he really likes the idea.

Owen's virtual team of alien abduction content viewers will hopefully increase the chances of him finding Fang.

RSS pushes web content to the people

The idea behind posting HTML content to the Web is that it will be viewed by people who visit a web site. But what if we want users to receive our web content without having to ask for it? This is possible with RSS, a data format that allows users to find out about web content without actually having to visit a site.

RSS is kinda like the web equivalent of a digital video recorder (DVR). DVRs allow you to "subscribe" to certain television shows, automatically recording every episode as it airs. Why flip channels looking for your favorite show when you can just let the shows come to you by virtue of the DVR? While RSS doesn't actually record anything, it is similar to a DVR in that it brings web content to you instead of you having to go in search of it.

By creating an RSS feed for his alien abduction data, Owen wants to notify users when new reports are posted. This will help ensure that people stay interested, resulting in more people combing through the data. The cool thing is that the **same database** can drive both the web page and the RSS feed.

HTML is for <u>viewing</u>; RSS is for <u>syndicating</u>.

A newsreader allows you to subscribe to newsfeeds, which contain news items that are derived from web site content.

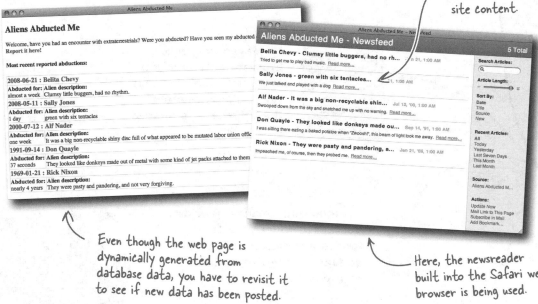

Even though the web page is dynamically generated from database data, you have to revisit it to see if new data has been posted.

Here, the newsreader built into the Safari web browser is being used.

RSS offers a view on web data that is delivered to users automatically as new content is made available. An RSS view on a particular set of data is called an **RSS feed**, or **newsfeed**. Users subscribe to the feed and receive new content as it is posted to the web site—no need to visit the site and keep tabs.

To view an RSS feed, all a person needs is an RSS **newsreader**. Most popular web browsers and email clients can subscribe to RSS feeds. You just provide the newsreader with the URL of the feed, and it does all the rest.

RSS is really XML

RSS is like HTML in that it is a plain text **markup language** that uses tags and attributes to describe content. RSS is based on XML, which is a general markup language that can be used to describe any kind of data. XML's power comes from its flexibility—it doesn't define any specific tags or attributes; it just sets the rules for how tags and attributes are created and used. It's up to specific languages such as HTML and RSS to establish the details regarding what tags and attributes can be used, and how.

In order to be proficient with RSS, you must first understand the ground rules of XML. These rules apply to all XML-based languages, including RSS and the modern version of HTML known as XHTML. These rules are simple but important—your XML (RSS) code won't work if you violate them! Here goes:

RSS is a markup language used to describe web content for syndication.

☑ **Tags that contain content must appear as matching pairs.**

Incorrect! There's no matching end-tag.

`<p>Phone home!`

`<p>Phone home!</p>`

Correct.

☑ **Empty tags that have no content must be coded with a space and a forward slash at the end before the closing brace.**

Incorrect! The empty tag needs a space and a forward slash before the >.

`<br>`

`<br />`

Correct.

Incorrect! The attribute must be enclosed in double quotes.

`<img src=alien.gif />`

`<img src="alien.gif" />`

Correct.

☑ **All attribute values must be enclosed in double quotes.**

Unlike PHP, which allows you to use double or single quotes in most situations, XML is rigid in only allowing double quotes for attribute values.

XML is a markup language used to describe <u>any</u> kind of data.

there are no
Dumb Questions

Q: Why is RSS so much better than someone just coming to my web site?

A: If people regularly visited your web site to seek out the latest content, then RSS wouldn't be any better than simply displaying content on your web site. But most people forget about web sites, even ones they like. So RSS provides an effective means of taking your web content directly to people, as opposed to requiring them to seek it out.

Q: What does RSS stand for?

A: Nowadays RSS stands for Really Simple Syndication. Throughout its storied history there have been several different versions, but the latest incarnation of RSS (version 2.0) stands for Really Simple Syndication, which is all you need to worry about.

Q: So what does RSS consist of?

A: RSS is a data format. So just as HTML is a data format that allows you to describe web content for viewing in a web browser, RSS is a data format that describes web content that is accessible as a news feed. Similar to HTML, the RSS data format is pure text, and consists of tags and attributes that are used to describe the content in a newsfeed.

Q: Where do I get an RSS reader?

A: Most web browsers have a built-in RSS reader. Some email clients even include RSS readers, in which case RSS news items appear as email messages in a special news feed folder. There are also stand-alone RSS readers available.

Below is RSS code for an Aliens Abducted Me news feed. Annotate the highlighted code to explain what you think each tag is doing.

```xml
<?xml version="1.0" encoding="utf-8"?>
<rss version="2.0">
  <channel>
    <title>Aliens Abducted Me - Newsfeed</title>
    <link>http://aliensabductedme.com/</link>
    <description>Alien abduction reports from around the world courtesy of Owen and his
      abducted dog Fang.</description>
    <language>en-us</language>

    <item>
      <title>Belita Chevy - Clumsy little buggers, had no rh...</title>
      <link>http://www.aliensabductedme.com/index.php?abduction_id=7</link>
      <pubDate>Sat, 21 Jun 2008 00:00:00 EST</pubDate>
      <description>Tried to get me to play bad music.</description>
    </item>

    <item>
      <title>Sally Jones - green with six tentacles...</title>
      <link>http://www.aliensabductedme.com/index.php?abduction_id=8</link>
      <pubDate>Sun, 11 May 2008 00:00:00 EST</pubDate>
      <description>We just talked and played with a dog</description>
    </item>

    ...

  </channel>
</rss>
```

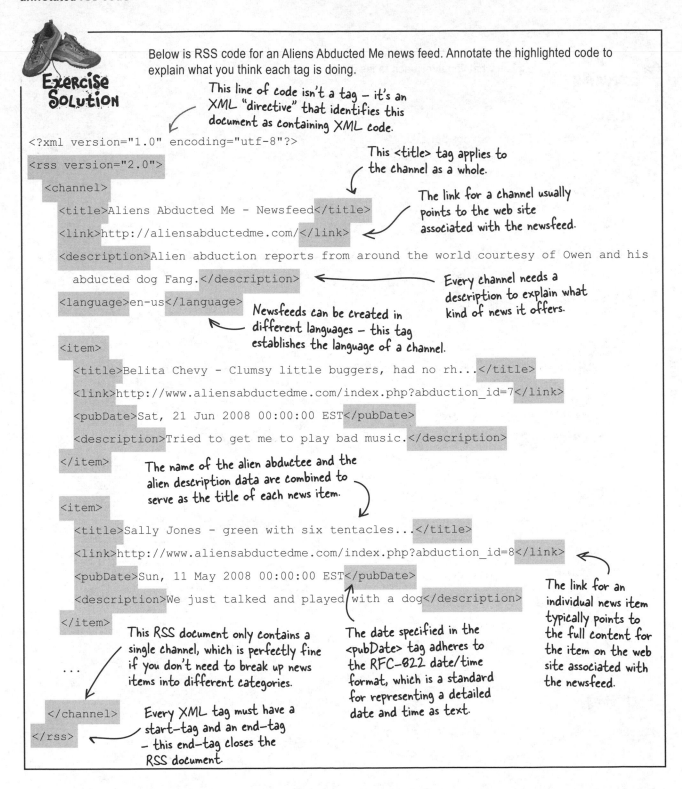

Exercise Solution

Below is RSS code for an Aliens Abducted Me news feed. Annotate the highlighted code to explain what you think each tag is doing.

This line of code isn't a tag – it's an XML "directive" that identifies this document as containing XML code.

```
<?xml version="1.0" encoding="utf-8"?>

<rss version="2.0">

  <channel>

    <title>Aliens Abducted Me - Newsfeed</title>

    <link>http://aliensabductedme.com/</link>

    <description>Alien abduction reports from around the world courtesy of Owen and his

      abducted dog Fang.</description>

    <language>en-us</language>

    <item>

      <title>Belita Chevy - Clumsy little buggers, had no rh...</title>

      <link>http://www.aliensabductedme.com/index.php?abduction_id=7</link>

      <pubDate>Sat, 21 Jun 2008 00:00:00 EST</pubDate>

      <description>Tried to get me to play bad music.</description>

    </item>

    <item>

      <title>Sally Jones - green with six tentacles...</title>

      <link>http://www.aliensabductedme.com/index.php?abduction_id=8</link>

      <pubDate>Sun, 11 May 2008 00:00:00 EST</pubDate>

      <description>We just talked and played with a dog</description>

    </item>

    ...

  </channel>

</rss>
```

This <title> tag applies to the channel as a whole.

The link for a channel usually points to the web site associated with the newsfeed.

Every channel needs a description to explain what kind of news it offers.

Newsfeeds can be created in different languages – this tag establishes the language of a channel.

The name of the alien abductee and the alien description data are combined to serve as the title of each news item.

The link for an individual news item typically points to the full content for the item on the web site associated with the newsfeed.

This RSS document only contains a single channel, which is perfectly fine if you don't need to break up news items into different categories.

The date specified in the <pubDate> tag adheres to the RFC-822 date/time format, which is a standard for representing a detailed date and time as text.

Every XML tag must have a start-tag and an end-tag – this end-tag closes the RSS document.

OK, so RSS is really XML, which means it's just a bunch of tags. That seems easy enough. So all we have to do to create a newsfeed is just create an XML file, right?

Yes, sort of. But you don't typically create XML code by hand, and it often doesn't get stored in files.

It's true that XML can and often does get stored in files. But with RSS we're talking about dynamic data that is constantly changing, so it doesn't make sense to store it in files—it would quickly get outdated and we'd have to continually rewrite the file. Instead, we want XML code that is generated on-the-fly from a database, which is how the HTML version of the main Aliens Abducted Me page already works. So we want to use PHP to dynamically generate RSS (XML) code and return it directly to an RSS newsreader upon request.

From database to newsreader

In order to provide a newsfeed for alien abduction data, Owen needs to dynamically generate RSS code from his MySQL database. This RSS code forms a complete RSS **document** that is ready for consumption by RSS newsreaders. So PHP is used to format raw alien abduction data into the RSS format, which is then capable of being processed by newsreaders and made available to users. The really cool part of this process is that once the newsfeed is made available in RSS form, everything else is automatic—it's up to newsreaders to show updated news items as they appear.

> **An RSS newsreader is designed to <u>consume</u> the data made available by an RSS newsfeed.**

aliens_abduction

abduction_id	first_name	last_name	when_it_happened	how_long	how_many	alien_description	what_they_did	...
1	Alf	Nader	200-07-12	one week	at least 12	It was a big non-recyclable shiny disc full of...	Swooped down from the sky and...	...
2	Don	Quayle	1991-09-14	37 seconds	dunno	They looked like donkeys made out of metal...	I was sitting there eating a baked...	
3	Rick	Nixon	1969-01-21	nearly 4 years	just one	They were pasty and pandering, and not very...	Impeached me, of course, then they probed...	
4	Belita	Chevy	2008-06-21	almost a week	27	Clumsy little buggers, had no rhythm.	Tried to get me to play bad music.	
5	Sally	Jones	2008-05-11					

PHP is used to generate an RSS newsfeed document from a MySQL database.

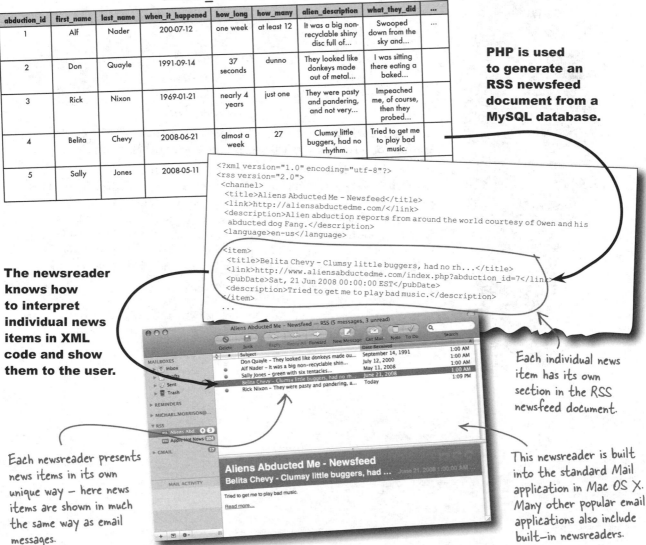

```xml
<?xml version="1.0" encoding="utf-8"?>
<rss version="2.0">
 <channel>
  <title>Aliens Abducted Me - Newsfeed</title>
  <link>http://aliensabductedme.com/</link>
  <description>Alien abduction reports from around the world courtesy of Owen and his
   abducted dog Fang.</description>
  <language>en-us</language>

  <item>
   <title>Belita Chevy - Clumsy little buggers, had no rh...</title>
   <link>http://www.aliensabductedme.com/index.php?abduction_id=7</link>
   <pubDate>Sat, 21 Jun 2008 00:00:00 EST</pubDate>
   <description>Tried to get me to play bad music.</description>
  </item>
  ...
```

The newsreader knows how to interpret individual news items in XML code and show them to the user.

Each individual news item has its own section in the RSS newsfeed document.

Each newsreader presents news items in its own unique way — here news items are shown in much the same way as email messages.

This newsreader is built into the standard Mail application in Mac OS X. Many other popular email applications also include built-in newsreaders.

WHO DOES WHAT?

Creating RSS feeds is all about understanding the RSS language, which means getting to know the tags that are used to describe news items. Match each RSS tag to its description.

<rss>

    This tag has nothing to do with RSS. But it sure sounds like a cool name for a piece of news data!

<channel>

    The publication date is an important piece of information for any news item, and this tag is used to specify it.

<cronkite>

    This tag represents a single channel in an RSS feed, and acts as a container for descriptive data and individual news items.

<title>

    Represents an individual news item, or story, which is further described by child elements.

<language>

    This tag always contains a URL that serves as the link for a channel or news item.

<link>

    Encloses an entire RSS feed—all other tags must appear inside of this tag.

<description>

    This tag stores the title of a channel or news item, and is typically used within the <channel> and <item> tags.

<pubDate>

    Used to provide a brief description of a channel or news item, appearing within either the <channel> and <item> tags.

<item>

    This tag applies to a channel, and specifies the language used by the channel, such as en-us (U.S. English).

WHO DOES WHAT? SOLUTION

Every RSS feed consists of at least one channel, which is basically a group of related news items.

Creating RSS feeds is all about understanding the RSS language, which means getting to know the tags that are used to describe news items. Match each RSS tag to its description.

The <rss> tag is the "root" tag for an RSS document – all other tags must appear inside of it.

<rss>

This tag has nothing to do with RSS. But it sure sounds like a cool name for a piece of news data!

<channel>

The publication date is an important piece of information for any news item, and this tag is used to specify it.

<cronkite>

This tag represents a single channel in an RSS feed, and acts as a container for descriptive data and individual news items.

<title>

Represents an individual news item, or story, which is further described by child elements.

This tag is only used in channels.

<language>

This tag always contains a URL that serves as the link for a channel or news item.

<link>

Encloses an entire RSS feed—all other tags must appear inside of this tag.

<description>

This tag stores the title of a channel or news item, and is typically used within the `<channel>` and `<item>` tags.

This tag only applies to news items.

<pubDate>

Used to provide a brief description of a channel or news item, appearing within either the `<channel>` and `<item>` tags.

<item>

This tag applies to a channel, and specifies the language used by the channel, such as `en-us` (U.S. English).

The <title>, <link>, <pubDate>, and <description> tags are used within <item> to describe a news item.

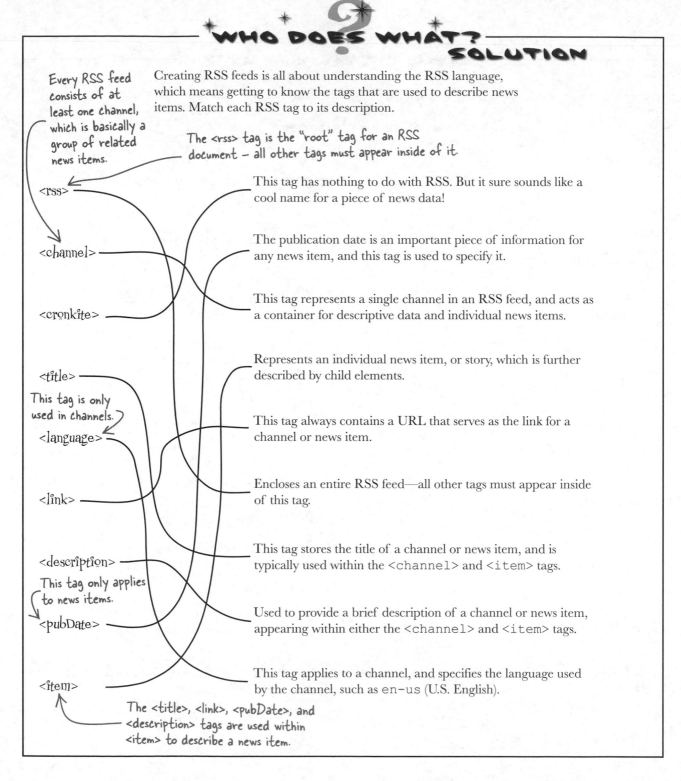

Visualizing ~~XML~~ RSS

You already learned that XML code consists of tags, which are also sometimes referred to as **elements**, that form **parent-child relationships** within the context of a complete XML document. It is very helpful to be able to visualize this parent-child relationship as you work with XML code. As an example, the RSS document on the facing page can be visualized as a hierarchy of elements, kind of like a family tree for newsfeed data, with parent elements at the top fanning out to child elements as you work your way down.

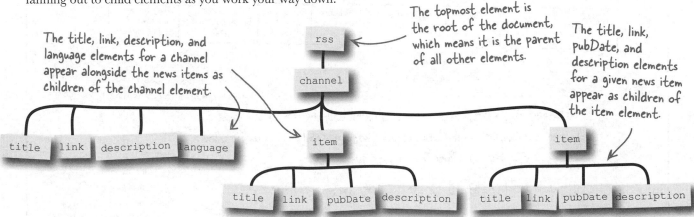

The title, link, description, and language elements for a channel appear alongside the news items as children of the channel element.

The topmost element is the root of the document, which means it is the parent of all other elements.

The title, link, pubDate, and description elements for a given news item appear as children of the item element.

Exercise

Below is a brand-new alien abduction report that has been added to the `aliens_abduction` database. Write the XML code for an RSS `<item>` tag for this abduction report, making sure to adhere to the RSS format for newsfeeds.

aliens_abduction

abduction_id	first_name	last_name	when_it_happened	how_long	how_many	alien_description	what_they_did	...
			...					
14	Shill	Watner	2008-07-05	2 hours	don't know	There was a bright light in the sky...	They beamed me toward a gas station...	...

....

....

....

....

....

....

Exercise Solution

Below is a brand-new alien abduction report that has been added to the `aliens_abduction` database. Write the XML code for an RSS `<item>` tag for this abduction report, making sure to adhere to the RSS format for newsfeeds.

aliens_abduction

abduction_id	first_name	last_name	when_it_happened	how_long	how_many	alien_description	what_they_did	...
			...					
14	Shill	Watner	2008-07-05	2 hours	don't know	There was a bright light in the sky...	They beamed me toward a gas station...	...

The `<item>` tag encloses the news item.

The `<title>`, `<link>`, `<pubDate>`, and `<description>` tags spell out the details of the news item.

```
<item>
    <title>Shill Watner – There was a bright light in the sky...</title>
    <link>http://www.aliensabductedme.com/index.php?abduction_id=14</link>
    <pubDate>Sat, 05 Jul 2008 00:00:00 EST</pubDate>
    <description>They beamed me toward a gas station...</description>
</item>
```

The `<pubDate>` tag <u>must</u> be in mixed case with the capital D, so it can't be `<pubdate>` or `<PUBDATE>`.

there are no Dumb Questions

Q: Is XML case-sensitive?

A: Yes, the XML language is case-sensitive, so it matters whether text is uppercase or lowercase when specifying XML tags and attributes. A good example is the RSS `<pubDate>` tag, which must appear in mixed case with the capital D. Most XML tags are either all lowercase or mixed-case.

Q: What about whitespace? How does it fit into XML?

A: First of all, whitespace in XML consists of carriage returns (`\r`), newlines (`\n`), tabs (`\t`), and spaces (`' '`). The majority of whitespace in most XML documents is purely for aesthetic formatting purposes, such as indenting child tags. This "insignificant" whitespace is typically ignored by applications that process XML data, such as RSS news readers. However, whitespace that appears inside of a tag is considered "significant," and is usually rendered exactly as it appears. This is what allows things like poems that have meaningful spacing to be accurately represented in XML.

Q: Can an RSS feed contain images?

A: Yes. Just keep in mind that not every news reader is able to display images. Also, in RSS 2.0 you can only add an image to a channel, not individual news items. You add an image to a channel using the `<image>` tag, which must appear inside the `<channel>` tag. Here's an example:

```
<image>
 <url>http://www.aliensabductedme.com/fang.jpg</url>
 <title>My dog Fang</title>
 <link>http://www.aliensabductedme.com</link>
</image>
```

It is technically possible to include an image in a news item in RSS 2.0; the trick is to use the HTML `<img>` tag within the description of the item. While this is possible, it requires you to encode the HTML tag using XML entities, and in many ways, it goes against the premise of an RSS item being pure text content.

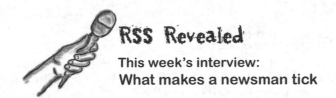

RSS Revealed

This week's interview:
What makes a newsman tick

Head First: So I hear that when people are looking for news on the Web, they turn to you. Is that true?

RSS: I suppose it depends on what you consider "news." I'm mainly about packaging up information into a format that is readily accessible to newsreaders. Now whether that content is really news or not... that's something I can't control. That's for people to decide.

Head First: Ah, so by "newsreaders," you mean individual people, right?

RSS: No, I mean software tools that understand what I am and how I represent data. For example, a lot of email programs support me, which means that you can subscribe to a newsfeed and receive updates almost like receiving email messages.

Head First: Interesting. So then how are you different than email?

RSS: Oh, I'm a lot different than email. For one thing, email messages are sent from one person to another, and are usually part of a two-way dialog. So you can respond to an email message, get a response back, etc. I only communicate one way, from a web site to an individual.

Head First: How does that make it a one-way communication?

RSS: Well, when a person elects to receive a newsfeed by subscribing to it in their newsreader software, they're basically saying they want to know about new content that is posted on a given web site. When new content actually gets posted, I make sure it gets represented in such a way that the news reader software knows about it and shows it to the person. But they aren't given an opportunity to reply to a news item, which is why it's a one-way communication from a web site to an individual.

Head First: I see. So what are you exactly?

RSS: I'm really just a data format, an agreed-upon way to store content so that it can be recognized and consumed by news readers. Use me to store data, and newsreaders will be able to access it as a newsfeed.

Head First: OK, so how are you different than HTML?

RSS: Well, we're both text data formats that are ultimately based on XML, which means we both use tags and attributes in describing data. But whereas HTML is designed specifically to be processed and rendered by web browsers, I'm designed to be processed and rendered by newsreaders. You could say that we provide different views on the same data.

Head First: But I've seen where some web browsers can display newsfeeds. How does that work?

RSS: Good question. As it turns out, some web browsers include built-in newsreaders, so they are really two tools in one. But when you view a newsfeed in a web browser, you're looking at something completely different than an HTML web page.

Head First: But most newsfeeds link to HTML web pages, correct?

RSS: That's right. So I work hand in hand with HTML to provide better access to web content. The idea is that you use me to learn about new content without having to go visit a web site directly. Then if you see something you want to find out more about, you click through to the actual page. That's why each news item has a link.

Head First: So you're sort of a preview for web pages.

RSS: Yeah, kinda like that. But remember that I come to you, you don't have to come to me. That's what people really like about me—I keep them from having to revisit web sites to keep tabs on new content.

Head First: I see. That is indeed convenient. Thanks for clarifying your role on the Web.

RSS: Hey, glad to do it. Stay classy.

Dynamically generate an RSS feed

Understanding the RSS data format is all fine and good, but Owen still needs a newsfeed to take alien abduction reports to the people. It's time to break out PHP and dynamically generate a newsfeed full of alien abduction data that has been plucked from Owen's MySQL database. Fortunately, this can be accomplished by following a series of steps:

The resulting newsfeed isn't stored in a file but it is an XML <u>document</u>.

❶ Set the content type of the document to XML.

We have to set the content type of the RSS document to XML by using a header.

```php
<?php header('Content-Type: text/xml'); ?>
```

❷ Generate the XML directive to indicate that this is an XML document.

```php
<?php echo '<?xml version="1.0" encoding="utf-8"?>'; ?>
```

❸ Generate the static RSS code that doesn't come from the database, such as the <rss> tag and the channel information.

```xml
<rss version="2.0">
  <channel>
    <title>...
    <link>...
    <description>...
    <language>...
```

This code isn't affected by the database — it's always the same for this newsfeed.

❹ Query the aliens_abduction database for alien abduction data.

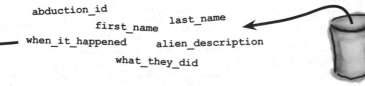

abduction_id

first_name   last_name

when_it_happened   alien_description

what_they_did

Before generating the RSS code for news items, we must query the MySQL database for alien abduction data.

❺ Loop through the data generating RSS code for each news item.

```xml
<item>
  <title>...
  <link>...
  <pubDate>...
  <description>...
</item>
```

This code contains data extracted from the database, and therefore must be carefully generated.

❻ Generate the static RSS code required to finish up the document, including closing </channel> and </rss> tags.

```xml
    </channel>
  </rss>
```

& XML!
PHP & MySQL Magnets

Owen's Aliens Abducted Me RSS newsfeed script (`newsfeed.php`) is missing some important code. Carefully choose the appropriate magnets to finish the code and dynamically generate the newsfeed.

1
2

```php
<?php header('Content-Type: text/xml'); ?>
<?php echo '<?xml version="1.0" encoding="utf-8"?>'; ?>
<rss version="2.0">

   ....................

   <title>Aliens Abducted Me - Newsfeed</title>
                http://aliensabductedme.com/ .................
   ................
   <description>Alien abduction reports from around the world courtesy of Owen
     and his abducted dog Fang.</description>

           .................en-us.........................

<?php
   require_once('connectvars.php');

   // Connect to the database
   $dbc = mysqli_connect(DB_HOST, DB_USER, DB_PASSWORD, DB_NAME);

   // Retrieve the alien sighting data from MySQL
   $query = "SELECT abduction_id, first_name, last_name, " .
     "DATE_FORMAT(when_it_happened,'%a, %d %b %Y %T') AS when_it_happened_rfc, " .
     "alien_description, what_they_did " .
     "FROM aliens_abduction " .
     "ORDER BY when_it_happened ..............";

   $data = mysqli_query($dbc, $query);

   // Loop through the array of alien sighting data, formatting it as RSS
   while ($row = mysqli_fetch_array($data)) {
     // Display each row as an RSS item

     echo '            ';
               .................
     echo ' <title>' . $row['first_name'] . ' ' . $row['last_name'] . ' - ' .
       substr($row['alien_description'], 0, 32) . '...</title>';
     echo ' <link>http://www.aliensabductedme.com/index.php?abduction_id=' .
       $row['            '] . '</link>';
               .................
     echo '            ' . $row['when_it_happened_rfc'] . ' ' . date('T') . '            ';
           .................                                                     .................
     echo ' <description>' . $row['what_they_did'] . '</description>';
     echo '</item>';
   }
?>

   </channel>
```

3

4

5

6

   ....

Magnets:

`</pubDate>` `DESC` `<item>` `</channel>` `abduction_id` `<rss>` `<language>`

`first_name` `</link>` `last_name` `</language>` `<channel>` `</item>` `<link>`

`<pubDate>` `</rss>` `ASC`

& XML!
PHP & MySQL Magnets Solution

Owen's Aliens Abducted Me RSS newsfeed script (`newsfeed.php`) is missing some important code. Carefully choose the appropriate magnets to finish the code and dynamically generate the newsfeed.

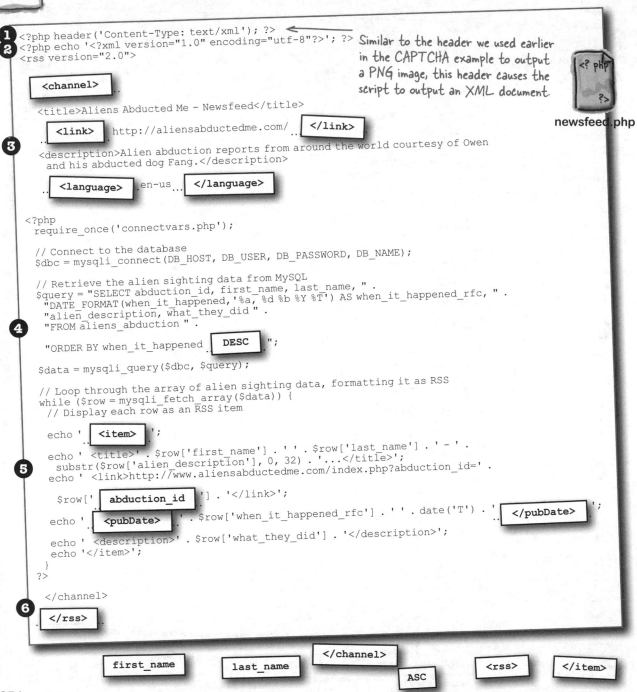

```php
❶ <?php header('Content-Type: text/xml'); ?>
❷ <?php echo '<?xml version="1.0" encoding="utf-8"?>'; ?>
   <rss version="2.0">

      <channel>

      <title>Aliens Abducted Me - Newsfeed</title>
         <link> http://aliensabductedme.com/ </link>
❸     <description>Alien abduction reports from around the world courtesy of Owen
      and his abducted dog Fang.</description>

         <language> en-us </language>

   <?php
      require_once('connectvars.php');

      // Connect to the database
      $dbc = mysqli_connect(DB_HOST, DB_USER, DB_PASSWORD, DB_NAME);

      // Retrieve the alien sighting data from MySQL
      $query = "SELECT abduction_id, first_name, last_name, " .
         "DATE_FORMAT(when_it_happened,'%a, %d %b %Y %T') AS when_it_happened_rfc, " .
         "alien_description, what_they_did " .
         "FROM aliens_abduction " .
❹        "ORDER BY when_it_happened . DESC . ";

      $data = mysqli_query($dbc, $query);

      // Loop through the array of alien sighting data, formatting it as RSS
      while ($row = mysqli_fetch_array($data)) {
         // Display each row as an RSS item

         echo ' <item> ';
         echo ' <title>' . $row['first_name'] . ' ' . $row['last_name'] . ' - ' .
            substr($row['alien_description'], 0, 32) . '...</title>';
❺        echo ' <link>http://www.aliensabductedme.com/index.php?abduction_id=' .
            $row[' abduction_id '] . '</link>';
         echo ' . <pubDate> . $row['when_it_happened_rfc'] . ' ' . date('T') . ' . </pubDate> ';
         echo ' <description>' . $row['what_they_did'] . '</description>';
         echo '</item>';
      }
   ?>

      </channel>
❻  </rss>
```

Similar to the header we used earlier in the CAPTCHA example to output a PNG image, this header causes the script to output an XML document.

newsfeed.php

first_name   last_name   </channel>   ASC   <rss>   </item>

Test Drive

Add the RSS Newsfeed script to Aliens Abducted Me.

Create a new text file named `newsfeed.php`, and enter the code for Owen's RSS Newsfeed script from the Magnets exercise a few pages back (or download the script from the Head First Labs site at `www.headfirstlabs.com/books/hfphp`).

Upload the script to your web server, and then open it in a newsreader. Most web browsers and some email clients allow you to view newsfeeds, so you can try those first if you don't have a stand-alone newsreader application. The Newsfeed script should display the latest alien abductions pulled straight from the Aliens Abducted Me database.

If your browser has trouble viewing the newsfeed, try using feed:// in the URL instead of http://.

Aliens Abducted Me ~ Newsfeed

Aliens Abducted Me - Newsfeed	8 Total

Meinhold Ressner - They were in a ship the size of ...   Aug 10, 1:00 AM
Carried me to the top of a mountain and dropped me off. Read more...

Mickey Mikens - Huge heads, skinny arms and legs...   Jul 11, 1:00 AM
Read my mind, Read more...

Shill Watner - There was a bright light in the ...   Jul 5, 1:00 AM
They beamed me toward a gas station in the desert. Read more...

Belita Chevy - Clumsy little buggers, had no rh...   Jun 21, 1:00 AM
Tried to get me to play bad music. Read more...

Sally Jones - green with six tentacles...   May 11, 1:00 AM
We just talked and played with a dog Read more...

...er - It was a big non-recyclable shin...   Jul 12, '00, 1:00 AM
...om the sky and snatched me up with no warning. Read more...

...They looked like donkeys made ou...   Sep 14, '91, 1:00 AM
...ting a baked potatoe when "Zwoosh!", this beam of light took me away. Read more...

...hey were pasty and pandering, a...   Jan 21, '69, 1:00 AM
...of course, then they probed me. Read more...

Search Articles:

Article Length:

Sort By:
Date
Title
Source
New

Recent Articles:
All
Today
Yesterday
Last Seven Days
This Month
Last Month

Source:
Aliens Abducted M...

Actions:
Update Now
Mail Link to This Page
Subscribe in Mail
Add Bookmark...

The newsfeed.php script generates an RSS newsfeed document that can be viewed by any RSS newsreader.

The newsfeed looks great, but how do site visitors find out about it?

Just provide a link to it from the home page.

Don't forget that `newsfeed.php` is nothing more than a PHP script. The only difference between it and most of the other PHP scripts you've seen throughout the book is that it generates an RSS document instead of an HTML document. But you still access it just as you would any other PHP script—just specify the name of the script in a URL. What Owen is missing is a way to share this URL with people who visit his site. This is accomplished with very little effort by **providing a syndication link**, which is just a link to the `newsfeed.php` script on Owen's server.

Link to the RSS feed

It's important to provide a prominent link to the newsfeed for a web site because a lot of users will appreciate that you offer such a service. To help aid users in quickly finding an RSS feed for a given site, there is a standard icon you can use to visually call out the feed. We can use this icon to build a newsfeed link at the bottom of Owen's home page (`index.php`).

A standard RSS 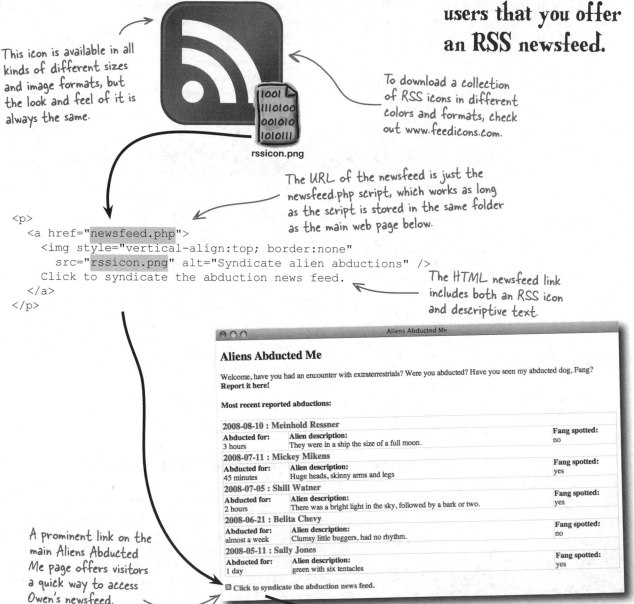 icon is available to make it clear to users that you offer an RSS newsfeed.

This icon is available in all kinds of different sizes and image formats, but the look and feel of it is always the same.

To download a collection of RSS icons in different colors and formats, check out www.feedicons.com.

rssicon.png

The URL of the newsfeed is just the newsfeed.php script, which works as long as the script is stored in the same folder as the main web page below.

```
<p>
  <a href="newsfeed.php">
    <img style="vertical-align:top; border:none"
      src="rssicon.png" alt="Syndicate alien abductions" />
    Click to syndicate the abduction news feed.
  </a>
</p>
```

The HTML newsfeed link includes both an RSS icon and descriptive text.

A prominent link on the main Aliens Abducted Me page offers visitors a quick way to access Owen's newsfeed.

Aliens Abducted Me

Welcome, have you had an encounter with extraterrestrials? Were you abducted? Have you seen my abducted dog, Fang? **Report it here!**

Most recent reported abductions:

2008-08-10 : Meinhold Ressner		Fang spotted: no
Abducted for: 3 hours	**Alien description:** They were in a ship the size of a full moon.	
2008-07-11 : Mickey Mikens		Fang spotted: yes
Abducted for: 45 minutes	**Alien description:** Huge heads, skinny arms and legs	
2008-07-05 : Shill Watner		Fang spotted: yes
Abducted for: 2 hours	**Alien description:** There was a bright light in the sky, followed by a bark or two.	
2008-06-21 : Belita Chevy		Fang spotted: no
Abducted for: almost a week	**Alien description:** Clumsy little buggers, had no rhythm.	
2008-05-11 : Sally Jones		Fang spotted: yes
Abducted for: 1 day	**Alien description:** green with six tentacles	

Click to syndicate the abduction news feed.

TEST DRIVE

Add the newsfeed link to the Aliens Abducted Me home page.

Modify the index.php script for Aliens Abducted Me to display the newsfeed link near the bottom of the page. Also download the rssicon.png image as part of the code from this chapter from the Head First Labs site at www.headfirstlabs.com/books/hfphp.

Upload the index.php script and rssicon.php image to your web server, and then open the script in a web browser. Click the new link to view the RSS newsfeed.

With all these abductions going on, I'm always on the lookout for aliens.

I haven't seen Fang, but these reports are amazing.

Thanks to RSS, new alien abduction reports are "pushed" to subscribers without them having to visit the Aliens Abducted Me web site directly.

I wonder if that's the same dog I saw on that YouTube video...

Chloe, an avid Aliens Abducted Me newsfeed reader, thinks she might have seen Fang in a YouTube video.

A ~~picture~~ video is worth a ~~thousand~~ million words

After a newsfeed subscriber alerted Owen to a YouTube video with a dog in it that resembles Fang, Owen realized that he's going to have to use additional technology to expand his search for Fang. But how? If Owen could incorporate YouTube videos into Aliens Abducted Me, his users could all be on the lookout for Fang. Not only that, but he really needs to come up with a way to avoid constantly doing manual video searches on YouTube.

> YouTube is an amazing tool for gathering alien abduction evidence in my search for Fang... but it's a drag having to painstakingly search for new alien abduction videos.

Although YouTube holds a lot of promise for helping Owen in his quest to find Fang, he currently has to do an awful lot of manual video searching.

Owen thinks video may hold the final answer to finding Fang.

Could this be Fang?

Try this!

1. Visit Owen's YouTube videos at www.youtube.com/user/aliensabductedme.

2. Watch a few of the alien abduction videos that Owen has found. Do you think the dog in the videos is Fang?

Wouldn't it be dreamy if I could see videos directly on Aliens Abducted Me rather than having to search on YouTube? If only there was a way I could just go to a web page and have the search already done for me. But that's nothing but a dream...

Pulling web content from others

The idea behind an RSS newsfeed is that it **pushes your content** to others so that they don't have to constantly visit your web site for new content. This is a great way to make it more convenient for people to keep tabs on your site, as Owen has found out. But there's another side to the web syndication coin, and it involves **pulling content from another site** to place on your site. So you become the consumer, and someone else acts as the content provider. In Owen's case of showing YouTube videos on his site, YouTube becomes the provider.

YouTube is the <u>provider</u> of videos.

Aliens Abducted Me is the <u>consumer</u> of videos.

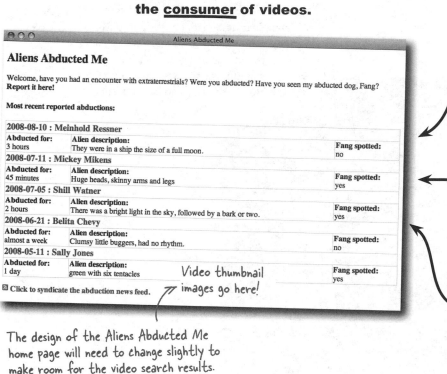

Video thumbnail images go here!

The design of the Aliens Abducted Me home page will need to change slightly to make room for the video search results.

Videos that are the result of a YouTube alien abduction search are returned by YouTube and fed into Owen's main page.

It's important to understand that Owen doesn't just want to embed a specific YouTube video or a link to a video. That's easy enough to accomplish by simply cutting and pasting HTML code from YouTube. He wants to actually **perform a search** on YouTube videos and display the results of that search. So Aliens Abducted Me needs to perform a real-time query on YouTube data, and then dynamically display the results. This allows Owen and his legion of helpful Fang searchers to keep up-to-the-minute tabs on alien abduction videos that have been posted to YouTube.

Syndicating YouTube videos

In order to source videos from YouTube, we must learn exactly how YouTube makes videos available for syndication. YouTube offers videos for syndication through a **request/response communication process** where you make a request for certain videos and then receive information about those videos in a response from YouTube's servers. You are responsible for both issuing a request in the format expected by YouTube and handling the response, which includes sifting through response data to get at the specific video data you need (video title, thumbnail image, link, etc.).

Following are the steps required to pull videos from YouTube and display them:

> **Syndicating videos from YouTube involves issuing <u>requests</u> and handling <u>responses</u>.**

① Build a request for YouTube videos.

This request is often in the form of a URL.

② Issue the video request to YouTube.

③ Receive YouTube's response data containing information about the videos.

YouTube uses XML to respond to video requests.

④ Process the response data and format it as HTML code.

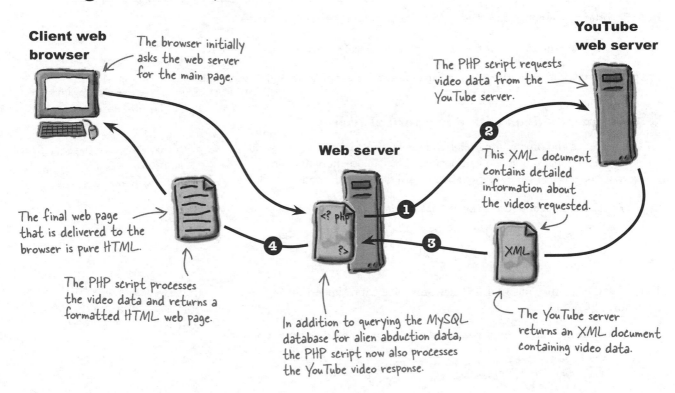

Client web browser

The browser initially asks the web server for the main page.

YouTube web server

The PHP script requests video data from the YouTube server.

Web server

The final web page that is delivered to the browser is pure HTML.

This XML document contains detailed information about the videos requested.

The PHP script processes the video data and returns a formatted HTML web page.

In addition to querying the MySQL database for alien abduction data, the PHP script now also processes the YouTube video response.

The YouTube server returns an XML document containing video data.

Make a YouTube video request

Pulling videos from YouTube and incorporating them into your own web pages begins with a request. YouTube expects videos to be queried through the use of a **REST request**, which is a custom URL that leads to specific resources, such as YouTube video data. You construct a URL identifying the videos you want, and then YouTube returns information about them via an XML document.

The details of the URL for a YouTube request are determined by what videos you want to access. For example, you can request the favorite videos of a particular user. In Owen's case, the best approach is probably to perform a keyword search on all YouTube videos. The URL required for each of these types of video REST requests varies slightly, but the base of the URL always starts like this:

```
http://gdata.youtube.com/feeds/api/
```
This base URL is used for all YouTube REST requests.

Request videos by user

Requesting the favorite videos for a particular YouTube user involves adding onto the base URL, and also providing the user's name on YouTube.

The user name of a YouTube user provides access to that user's favorite videos.

```
http://gdata.youtube.com/feeds/api/users/username/favorites
```

To request the favorite videos for the user `elmerpriestley`, use the following URL:

```
http://gdata.youtube.com/feeds/api/users/elmerpriestley/favorites
```

The result of this REST request are the favorite videos for the YouTube user elmerpriestley.

Request videos with a keyword search

A more powerful and often more useful YouTube video request is to carry out a keyword search that is independent of users. You can use more than one keyword as long as you separate them by forward slashes at the end of the URL.

Multiple keywords can be used in a video search by separating them with forward slashes.

```
http://gdata.youtube.com/feeds/api/videos/-/keyword1/keyword2/...
```

The URL starts the same as requesting by user but here you use "videos" instead of "users".

Don't forget the slashes and the hyphen!

To request the favorite videos for the keywords "elvis" and "impersonator," use the following URL:

Here the search keywords "elvis" and "impersonator" are used to search for videos.

```
http://gdata.youtube.com/feeds/api/videos/-/elvis/impersonator
```

The keywords are case-insensitive, so "elvis", "Elvis", and "eLvIs" all give you the same result.

BE the YouTube REST Request

Your job is to get inside the mind of YouTube and become a video REST request. Use the magnets below to assemble video REST requests for the following YouTube videos, and then try them out in your web browser.

All videos that match the keyword "Roswell":

....

All videos that match the keywords "alien" and "abduction":

....

All videos tagged as favorites for the user headfirstmork:

....

All videos that match the keywords "ufo", "sighting", and "dog":

....

All videos tagged as favorites for the user aliensabductedme:

....

`alien`

`http://gdata.youtube.com/feeds/api/`

`ufo`

You may need to use some of the magnets more than once.

`abduction`

`Roswell`

`sighting`

`-`

`/`

`videos`

`dog`

`headfirstmork`

`aliensabductedme`

`users`

`favorites`

`Area 51`

BE the YouTube REST Request Solution

Your job is to get inside the mind of YouTube and become a video REST request. Use the magnets below to assemble video REST requests for the following YouTube videos, and then try them out in your web browser.

You may have used some of the magnets more than once.

The same base YouTube URL is used for all of the REST requests.

The single keyword appears last in the URL.

All videos that match the keyword "Roswell":

| http://gdata.youtube.com/feeds/api/ | videos | / | - | / | Roswell |

Each of the search keywords appear at the end of the URL, and are separated by forward slashes.

All videos that match the keywords "alien" and "abduction":

| http://gdata.youtube.com/feeds/api/ | videos | / | - | / | alien | / | abduction |

All videos tagged as favorites for the user headfirstmork:

| http://gdata.youtube.com/feeds/api/ | users | / | headfirstmork | / | favorites |

The URL for a user's favorites requires the word "users" here instead of "videos".

All videos that match the keywords "ufo", "sighting", and "dog":

| http://gdata.youtube.com/feeds/api/ | videos | / | - | / | ufo | / | sighting | / | dog |

The URL ends with the word "favorites".

All videos tagged as favorites for the user aliensabductedme:

| http://gdata.youtube.com/feeds/api/ | users | / | aliensabductedme | / | favorites |

| Area 51 |

This magnet wasn't used... it's a conspiracy!

This is the name of the user whose favorite videos you want to access.

there are no
Dumb Questions

Q: How is REST different than, say, a GET request?

A: It's not. Any time you've used a **GET** request, such as simply requesting a web page, you're using **REST**. You can think of a normal web page as a **REST** resource in that it can be accessed via a URL, and **GET** is the **REST** "action" used to access the resource. Where **REST** gets more interesting is when it is used to build queries, such as YouTube video requests. In this case you're still dealing with **REST** requests but they are querying a database for data instead of simply requesting a static web page.

Q: Does the order of arguments matter when performing a YouTube keyword search?

A: Yes. The first keywords are given a higher precedence than later keywords, so make sure to list them in order of decreasing importance.

Q: When there are multiple matches for a video search, how does YouTube determine what videos to return?

A: YouTube keyword video requests return videos based on search relevance, meaning that you will get the videos that best match the keywords, regardless of when the videos were posted to YouTube.

I'm ready to see some video results...

Owen is ready to build a REST request

Since Owen's goal is to scour YouTube for alien abduction videos that might have Fang in them, a keyword search makes the most sense as the type of REST request to submit to YouTube. There are lots of different keyword combinations that could be used to search for possible Fang videos, but one in particular will help home in on videos related specifically to Fang:

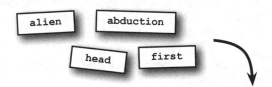

`http://gdata.youtube.com/feeds/api/videos/-/alien/abduction/head/first`

While you probably wouldn't reference the title of a book series when carrying out a normal YouTube video search, it just so happens to be a good idea in this particular case. Let's just say it's a coincidence that a lot of alien abduction videos have been made by Head First fans! With a REST request URL in hand, Owen can scratch off Step 1 of the YouTube video syndication process.

The last two keywords help to make sure you find the alien abduction videos related to Owen and Fang!

The first step is knocked out thanks to the YouTube request URL.

① ~~Build a request for YouTube videos.~~

② Issue the video request to YouTube.

③ Receive YouTube's response data containing information about the videos.

④ Process the response data and format it as HTML code.

Test Drive

Try out Owen's YouTube request URL.

Enter Owen's YouTube request URL in a web browser:

```
http://gdata.youtube.com/feeds/api/videos/-/alien/abduction/head/first
```

What does the browser show? Try viewing the source of the page to take a look at the
actual code returned by YouTube.

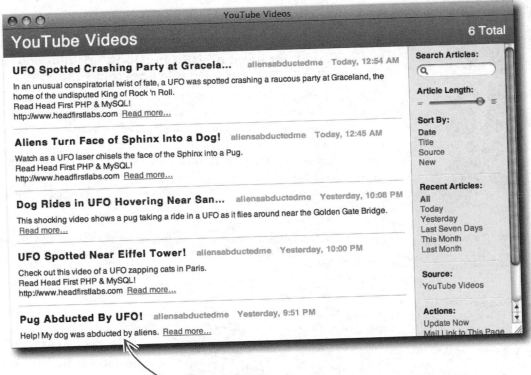

The web browser views the XML
data returned by the YouTube
response as a newsfeed, except in
this case each item is actually a video.

Requesting videos from YouTube by typing a URL into a web browser is neat and all, but what does that have to do with PHP? Why can't we access the video results from a script?

The SimpleXML extension to PHP, which offers the simplexml_load_file() function, was added to PHP in version 5. So prior versions of PHP don't have built-in support for XML processing.

We can, we just need a PHP function that allows us to submit a REST request and receive a response.

The built-in PHP function `simplexml_load_file()` lets us submit REST requests that result in XML responses, such as YouTube requests/responses. The function actually loads an XML document into a PHP object, which we can then use to drill down into the XML data and extract whatever specific information is needed. So how does that impact Owen's YouTube video request? Check out this code, which creates a constant to hold a YouTube URL, and then issues a REST request using the `simplexml_load_file()` function:

```
define('YOUTUBE_URL', 'http://gdata.youtube.com/feeds/api/videos/-/alien/abduction/head/first');

$xml = simplexml_load_file(YOUTUBE_URL);
```

Although not strictly necessary, it's generally a good idea to store static URLs in constants so that you know where to change them if the need ever arises.

~~❶ Build a request for YouTube videos.~~

~~❷ Issue the video request to YouTube.~~

~~❸ Receive YouTube's response data containing information about the videos.~~

❹ Process the response data and format it as HTML code.

These two steps are now done!

Don't sweat it if you don't know what an object is, especially in the context of PHP.

A ***PHP object*** is a special data type that allows data to be packaged together with functions in a single construct. All you need to know for now is that it's much easier to process XML data in PHP by using objects. You'll learn more about how this is possible in just a bit.

```
<?xml version='1.0' encoding='UTF-8'?>
<feed xmlns='http://www.w3.org/2005/Atom'
  xmlns:openSearch='http://a9.com/-/spec/opensearchrss/1.0/'
  xmlns:gml='http://www.opengis.net/gml'
  xmlns:georss='http://www.georss.org/georss'
  xmlns:media='http://search.yahoo.com/mrss/'
  xmlns:batch='http://schemas.google.com/gdata/batch'
  xmlns:yt='http://gdata.youtube.com/schemas/2007'
  xmlns:gd='http://schemas.google.com/g/2005'>
  <id>http://gdata.youtube.com/feeds/api/users/aliensabductedme/favorites</id>
  <updated>2008-08-01T20:37:48.798Z</updated>
  <category scheme='http://schemas.google.com/g/2005#kind' term='http://gdata.youtube.com/schemas/2007#video'/>
  <title type='text'>Favorites of aliensabductedme</title>
  <logo>http://www.youtube.com/img/pic_youtubelogo_123x63.gif</logo>
  <link rel='related' type='application/atom+xml' href='http://gdata.youtube.com/feeds/api/users/aliensabductedme/'/>
  <link rel='alternate' type='text/html' href='http://www.youtube.com/profile_favorites?user=aliensabductedme'/>
  <link rel='http://schemas.google.com/g/2005#feed' type='application/atom+xml' href='http://gdata.youtube.com/feeds/api/users/aliensabductedme/favorites'/>
  <link rel='http://schemas.google.com/g/2005#batch' type='application/atom+xml' href='http://gdata.youtube.com/feeds/api/users/aliensabductedme/favorites/batch'/>
  <link rel='self' type='application/atom+xml' href='http://gdata.youtube.com/feeds/api/users/aliensabductedme/favorites?start-index=1&amp;max-results=25'/>
  <author>
    <name>aliensabductedme</name>
    <uri>http://gdata.youtube.com/feeds/api/users/aliensabductedme</uri>
  </author>
  <generator version='2.0' uri='http://gdata.youtube.com/'>YouTube data API</generator>
  <openSearch:totalResults>9</openSearch:totalResults>
  <openSearch:startIndex>1</openSearch:startIndex>
  <openSearch:itemsPerPage>25</openSearch:itemsPerPage>
  <entry>
    <id>http://gdata.youtube.com/feeds/api/videos/_6Uibqf0vtA</id>
    <published>2006-06-20T07:49:05.000-07:00</published>
    <updated>2008-08-01T09:19:58.000-07:00</updated>
    <category scheme='http://gdata.youtube.com/schemas/2007/keywords.cat' term='sightings'/>
    <category scheme='http://gdata.youtube.com/schemas/2007/keywords.cat' term='ca'/>
    <category scheme='http://gdata.youtube.com/schemas/2007/keywords.cat' term='51'/>
    <category scheme='http://schemas.google.com/g/2005#kind' term='http://gdata.youtube.com/schemas/2007#video'/>
    <category scheme='http://gdata.youtube.com/schemas/2007/keywords.cat' term='area'/>
    <category scheme='http://gdata.youtube.com/schemas/2007/keywords.cat' term='aliens'/>
    <category scheme='http://gdata.youtube.com/schemas/2007/keywords.cat' term='alien'/>
    <category scheme='http://gdata.youtube.com/schemas/2007/categories.cat' term='Travel' label='Travel &amp; Events'/>
    <category scheme='http://gdata.youtube.com/schemas/2007/keywords.cat' term='california'/>
    <category scheme='http://gdata.youtube.com/schemas/2007/keywords.cat' term='nevada'/>
    <category scheme='http://gdata.youtube.com/schemas/2007/keywords.cat' term='ufo'/>
    <category scheme='http://gdata.youtube.com/schemas/2007/keywords.cat' term='sighting'/>
    <title type='text'>UFO Sighting in Yosemite Park near Area 51</title>
    <content type='text'>I went on a trip to Yosemite Park in 2002. Yosemite Park is very close to the border between California and N
evening, on my way out of the park, I was driving down a winding road, when I saw a small ball of light high up in the sky, w
and a video twirled trail behind it. I video taped it for a few seconds, and then I grapped my camera to take some photos a
it well enough. Unfortunately it was too dark for the photo camera, so the pictures didn't come out. All I have is the vi

The ball of light with the huge halo moved across the sky, leaving a trail. After about 2 minutes the ball of light disa
was illuminated and still brightly visible even when the surrounding sky was already pitch black.

A few minutes later several Air Force jets appeared and circled in the sky where the light had disappeared.</content>
    <link rel='alternate' type='text/html' href='http://www.youtube.com/watch?v=_6Uibqf0vtA'/>
    <link rel='related' type='application/atom+xml' href='http://gdata.y
    <link rel='http://gdata.youtube.com/schemas/2007#video.responses' type='application/atom+xml' href='http://gdata.yout
    <link rel='http://gdata.youtube.com/schemas/2007#video.related' type='application/atom+xml' href='http://gdata.yout
    <link rel='self' type='application/atom+xml' href='http://gdata.youtube.com/feeds/api/users/aliensabductedme/favorite
    <author>
      <name>gaspirtz</name>
      <uri>http://gdata.youtube.com/feeds/api/users/gaspirtz</uri>
    </author>
    <media:group>
      <media:title type='plain'>UFO Sighting in Yosemite Park near Area 51</media:title>
      <media:description type='plain'>I went on a trip to Yosemite Park in 2002. Yosemite Park is very close to the border between California and Nevada, and close to
Area 51. In the evening, on my way out of the park, I was driving down a winding road, when I saw a small ball of light high up in the sky, with a large halo of light
surrounding it, and a long twirled trail behind it. I video taped it for a few seconds, and then I grapped my camera to take some photos as well, in case the video
camera didn't capture it well enough. Unfortunately it was too dark for the photo camera, so the pictures didn't come out. All I have is the video I took before and
after I took the photos.

The ball of light with the huge halo moved across the sky, leaving a trail. After about 2 minutes the ball of light disappeared, and only the trail remained. The trail
was illuminated and still brightly visible even when the surrounding sky was already pitch black.

A few minutes later several Air Force jets appeared and circled in the sky where the light had disappeared.</media:description>
      <media:keywords>51, alien, aliens, area, ca, california, nevada, sighting, sightings, ufo</media:keywords>
      <yt:duration seconds='50'/>
      <media:category label='Travel &amp; Events' scheme='http://gdata.youtube.com/schemas/2007/categories.cat'>Travel</media:category>
      <media:content url='http://www.youtube.com/v/_6Uibqf0vtA' type='application/x-shockwave-flash' medium='video' isDefault='true' expression='full' duration='50'
yt:format='5'/>
      <media:content url='rtsp://rtsp2.youtube.com/ChoLENy73wIaEQnQvvSnbiKl_xMYDSANFEgGDA==/0/0/0/video.3gp' type='video/3gpp' medium='video' expression='full'
duration='50' yt:format='1'/>
      <media:content url='rtsp://rtsp2.youtube.com/ChoLENy73wIaEQnQvvSnbiKl_xMYESARFEgGDA==/0/0/0/video.3gp' type='video/3gpp' medium='video' expression='full'
duration='50' yt:format='6'/>
      <media:player url='http://www.youtube.com/watch?v=_6Uibqf0vtA'/>
      <media:thumbnail url='http://img.youtube.com/vi/_6Uibqf0vtA/2.jpg' height='97' width='130' time='00:00:25'/>
      <media:thumbnail url='http://img.youtube.com/vi/_6Uibqf0vtA/1.jpg' height='97' width='130' time='00:00:12.500'/>
      <media:thumbnail url='http://img.youtube.com/vi/_6Uibqf0vtA/3.jpg' height='97' width='130' time='00:00:37.500'/>
      <media:thumbnail url='http://img.youtube.com/vi/_6Uibqf0vtA/0.jpg' height='240' width='320' time='00:00:25'/>
    </media:group>
    <yt:statistics viewCount='2528356' favoriteCount='1931'/>
    <gd:rating min='1' max='5' numRaters='1648' average='4.17'/>
    <gd:comments>
    ...
```

This is the XML file returned by the simplexml_load_file() function, which consists of YouTube XML data for the videos requested.

Awesome... an even bigger problem! What on earth do we do with all that messy XML data? There's no way a PHP script can make sense of all that.

Oh, but there is! The XML code returned by YouTube isn't really as messy as it looks... you just have to know where to look.

YouTube speaks XML

The video response from YouTube isn't exactly a DVD packaged up in a shiny box and delivered to your front door. No, it's an XML document containing detailed information about the videos you requested, not the videos themselves.

YouTube responds to video requests with XML data that describes the videos.

```
<?xml version='1.0' encoding='UTF-8'?>
<feed xmlns='http://www.w3.org/2005/Atom'
 xmlns:openSearch='http://a9.com/-/spec/opensearchrss/1.0/'
 xmlns:gml='http://www.opengis.net/gml'
 xmlns:georss='http://www.georss.org/georss'
 xmlns:media='http://search.yahoo.com/mrss/'
 xmlns:batch='http://schemas.google.com/gdata/batch'
 xmlns:yt='http://gdata.youtube.com/schemas/2007'
 xmlns:gd='http://schemas.google.com/g/2005'>
<id>http://gdata.youtube.com/feeds/api/users/aliensabductedme/favorites</id>
<updated>2008-07-25T03:22:37.001Z</updated>
<category scheme='http://schemas.google.com/g/2005#kind'
 term='http://gdata.youtube.com/schemas/2007#video'/>
<title type='text'>Favorites of aliensabductedme</title>
...
```

Although there's a lot going on in this XML code, one thing to home in on is that each individual video appears inside of an <entry> tag.

```
<entry>
 <id>http://gdata.youtube.com/feeds/api/videos/_6Uibqf0vtA</id>
 <published>2006-06-20T07:49:05.000-07:00</published>
 ...
 <media:group>
  <media:title type='plain'>UFO Sighting in Yosemite Park near Area 51</media:title>
  <media:description type='plain'>I went on a trip to Yosemite Park in 2002. Yosemite Park is very
   close to the border between California and Nevada, and close to Area 51...</media:description>
  <media:keywords>51, alien, aliens, area, ca, california, nevada, sighting, sightings,
   ufo</media:keywords>
  <yt:duration seconds='50'/>
  <media:category label='Travel &amp; Events'
   scheme='http://gdata.youtube.com/schemas/2007/categories.cat'>Travel</media:category>
  <media:content url='http://www.youtube.com/v/_6Uibqf0vtA' type='application/x-shockwave-flash'
   medium='video' isDefault='true' expression='full' duration='50' yt:format='5'/>
  <media:content url='rtsp://rtsp2.youtube.com/ChoLENy73wIaEQnQvvSnbiKl_xMYDSANFEgGDA==/0/0/0/video.3gp'
   type='video/3gpp' medium='video' expression='full' duration='50' yt:format='1'/>
  <media:content url='rtsp://rtsp2.youtube.com/ChoLENy73wIaEQnQvvSnbiKl_xMYESARFEgGDA==/0/0/0/video.3gp'
   type='video/3gpp' medium='video' expression='full' duration='50' yt:format='6'/>
  <media:player url='http://www.youtube.com/watch?v=_6Uibqf0vtA'/>
  <media:thumbnail url='http://img.youtube.com/vi/_6Uibqf0vtA/2.jpg' height='97' width='130'
   time='00:00:25'/>
  <media:thumbnail url='http://img.youtube.com/vi/_6Uibqf0vtA/1.jpg' height='97' width='130'
   time='00:00:12.500'/>
  <media:thumbnail url='http://img.youtube.com/vi/_6Uibqf0vtA/3.jpg' height='97' width='130'
   time='00:00:37.500'/>
  <media:thumbnail url='http://img.youtube.com/vi/_6Uibqf0vtA/0.jpg' height='240' width='320'
   time='00:00:25'/>
 </media:group>
 <yt:statistics viewCount='2478159' favoriteCount='1897'/>
 <gd:rating min='1' max='5' numRaters='1602' average='4.17'/>
 <gd:comments>
  <gd:feedLink href='http://gdata.youtube.com/feeds/api/videos/_6Uibqf0vtA/comments'
   countHint='4426'/>
 </gd:comments>
</entry>
<entry>
 <id>http://gdata.youtube.com/feeds/api/videos/XpNd-Dg6_zQ</id>
 <published>2006-11-19T16:44:43.000-08:00</published>
 ...
</entry>
</feed>
```

This <entry> tag starts another video within the XML response data.

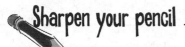

Sharpen your pencil

Study the highlighted XML code for the YouTube response on the facing page and answer the following questions. You might just know more about YouTube's video XML format than you thought at first glance!

1. What is the title of the video? ....

2. What are three keywords associated with the video? ....

3. How long is the video, in seconds? ....

4. To what YouTube video category does the video belong? ....

5. How many times has the video been viewed? ....

6. What average rating have users given the video? ....

Sharpen your pencil
Solution

Study the highlighted XML code for the YouTube response on page 690 and answer the following questions. You might just know more about YouTube's video XML format than you thought at first glance!

```
<media:title type='plain'>UFO Sighting in Yosemite Park near Area 51</media:title>
```

1. What is the title of the video?   UFO Sighting in Yosemite Park near Area 51

```
<media:keywords>51, alien, aliens, area, ca, california, nevada, sighting, sightings,
    ufo</media:keywords>
```

2. What are three keywords associated with the video?   51, aliens, nevada

3. How long is the video, in seconds?   50

```
<yt:duration seconds=50/>
```

XML encodes some characters using special codes, such as &, which represents an ampersand (&).

```
<media:category label='Travel &amp; Events'
    scheme='http://gdata.youtube.com/schemas/2007/categories.cat'>Travel</media:category>
```

4. To what YouTube video category does the video belong?   Travel & Events

```
<yt:statistics viewCount='2478159' favoriteCount='1897'/>
```

Wow, that's a lot of views... nearly 2.5 million!

5. How many times has the video been viewed?   2478159

```
<gd:rating min='1' max='5' numRaters='1602' average='4.17'/>
```

6. What average rating have users given the video?   4.17

Hmm, I'm a little confused with those XML tags that have two names separated by a colon. Is that somehow a way to organize tags? And what about the weird & code in the video category?

The unusual XML code uses namespaces and entities, which help organize tags and encode special characters.

When you see an XML tag that has two names separated by a colon, you're looking at a ***namespace***, which is a way of organizing a set of tags into a logical group. The purpose of namespaces is to keep tags with the same name from clashing when multiple XML vocabularies are used in the same document. As an example, consider the following two XML tags:

```
<title type='text'>Favorites of aliensabductedme</title>
```

```
<media:title type='plain'>UFO Sighting in Yosemite Park near Area 51</media:title>
```

Namespaces are named groups of XML tags, while **entities** are used to encode special characters within XML documents.

Without the `media` namespace in the second `<title>` tag, it would be impossible to tell the two tags apart if they appeared in the same XML code. So you can think of a namespace as a surname for tags—it helps keep an XML document full of "first names" from clashing by hanging a "last name" on related tags. The YouTube response code uses several different namespaces, which means it is using several different XML languages at once—namespaces allow us to clearly tell them apart.

To ensure uniqueness, an XML namespace is always associated with a URL. For example, the `media` namespace used in YouTube XML data is established within the `<feed>` tag like this:

This URL isn't actually a web page — it's just a unique identifier for a namespace.

```
xmlns:media='http://search.yahoo.com/mrss/'
```

It may seem odd that a Yahoo! namespace appears in YouTube XML code — it just means that YouTube relies partly on an XML data format created by Yahoo!.

The other strange thing in the YouTube XML code is `&amp;`, which is XML's way of representing the ampersand character (&). This is an XML **entity**, a symbolic way of referencing a special character, such as &, <, or >, all of which have special meaning within XML code. Following are the five predefined XML entities that you will likely encounter as you delve deeper into XML code:

 `&amp;` = `&`   `&lt;` = `<`   `&gt;` = `>`    `&quot;` = `"`    `&apos;` = `'`

Deconstruct a YouTube XML response

Once you get to know the structure of a YouTube response, extracting the video data you need is pretty straightforward. In addition to understanding what tags and attributes store what data, it's also important to understand how the tags relate to one another. If you recall from earlier in the chapter when analyzing an RSS feed, an XML document can be viewed as a hierarchy of elements. The same is true for the XML data returned in a YouTube video response.

```xml
<entry>
  <id>http://gdata.youtube.com/feeds/api/videos/_6Uibqf0vtA</id>
  <published>2006-06-20T07:49:05.000-07:00</published>
  ...
  <media:group>
    <media:title type='plain'>UFO Sighting in Yosemite Park near Area 51</media:title>
    <media:description type='plain'>I went on a trip to Yosemite Park in 2002. Yosemite Park is very
     close to the border between California and Nevada, and close to Area 51...</media:description>
    <media:keywords>51, alien, aliens, area, ca, california, nevada, sighting, sightings,
     ufo</media:keywords>
    <yt:duration seconds='50'/>
    <media:category label='Travel &amp; Events'
     scheme='http://gdata.youtube.com/schemas/2007/categories.cat'>Travel</media:category>
    <media:content url='http://www.youtube.com/v/_6Uibqf0vtA' type='application/x-shockwave-flash'
     medium='video' isDefault='true' expression='full' duration='50' yt:format='5'/>
    <media:content url='rtsp://rtsp2.youtube.com/ChoLENy73wIaEQnQvvSnbiKl_xMYDSANFEgGDA==/0/0/0/video.3gp'
     type='video/3gpp' medium='video' expression='full' duration='50' yt:format='1'/>
    <media:content url='rtsp://rtsp2.youtube.com/ChoLENy73wIaEQnQvvSnbiKl_xMYESARFEgGDA==/0/0/0/video.3gp'
     type='video/3gpp' medium='video' expression='full' duration='50' yt:format='6'/>
    <media:player url='http://www.youtube.com/watch?v=_6Uibqf0vtA'/>
    <media:thumbnail url='http://img.youtube.com/vi/_6Uibqf0vtA/2.jpg' height='97' width='130'
     time='00:00:25'/>
    <media:thumbnail url='http://img.youtube.com/vi/_6Uibqf0vtA/1.jpg' height='97' width='130'
     time='00:00:12.500'/>
    <media:thumbnail url='http://img.youtube.com/vi/_6Uibqf0vtA/3.jpg' height='97' width='130'
     time='00:00:37.500'/>
    <media:thumbnail url='http://img.youtube.com/vi/_6Uibqf0vtA/0.jpg' height='240' width='320'
     time='00:00:25'/>
  </media:group>
  <yt:statistics viewCount='2478159' favoriteCount='1897'/>
  <gd:rating min='1' max='5' numRaters='1602' average='4.17'/>
  <gd:comments>
   <gd:feedLink href='http://gdata.youtube.com/feeds/api/videos/_6Uibqf0vtA/comments'
    countHint='4426'/>
  </gd:comments>
</entry>
```

The <title> tag contains the title of the video.

In this code, the tag is named "title" and the namespace is "media".

The keywords for the video.

The length of the video, in seconds.

The YouTube category for the video.

The link to the video on YouTube.

A thumbnail image of the video, for previewing.

The "gd" namespace stands for Google Data, and includes tags defined by Google for representing various kinds of data – YouTube is part of Google.

The average user rating of the video.

The number of times the video has been viewed.

One important clue toward understanding the video data buried in this XML code is the different namespaces being used. The `media` namespace accompanies most of the tags specifically related to video data, while the `yt` namespace is used solely with the `<statistics>` tag. Finally, comments are enclosed within the `<comments>` tag, which falls under the `gd` namespace. These namespaces will matter a great deal when you begin writing PHP code to find specific tags and their data.

Visualize the XML video data

Earlier in the chapter when working with RSS code, it was revealed that an XML document can be visualized as a hierarchy of elements (tags) that have a parent-child relationship. This relationship becomes increasingly important as you begin to process XML code and access data stored within it. In fact, it can be an invaluable skill to be able to look at an XML document and immediately visualize the relationship between the elements. Just remember that any element enclosed within another element is a child, and the enclosing element is its parent. Working through the XML code for the YouTube video on the facing page results in the following visualization.

> An element is just an abstract way of thinking of an XML tag and the data it contains.

The XML data is organized into a hierarchy of elements (tags).

The entry element is the topmost element in this particular chunk of XML code.

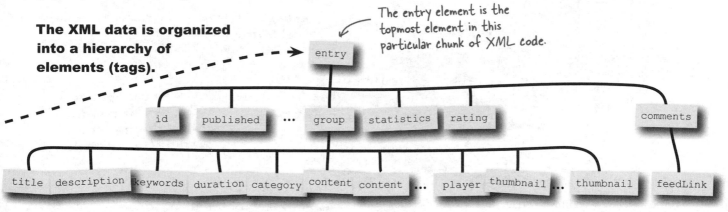

The significance of this hierarchy of elements is that you can navigate from any element to another by tracing its path from the top of the hierarchy. So, for example, if you wanted to obtain the title of the video, you could trace its path like this:

Navigating to an element in an XML document involves following the path from parent to child.

there are no Dumb Questions

Q: Why do I even need to worry about namespaces?

A: Because XML code generated by others often involves namespaces, which affects how you access XML elements programmatically. As you're about to find out, the namespace associated with an element directly affects how you find the element when writing PHP code that processes XML data. So the namespace must be factored into code that is attempting to grab the data for a given element.

Q: How do I know if a tag is part of a namespace?

A: Although it's possible to have a default namespace that doesn't explicitly appear in the code for a tag, in most cases you'll see the namespace right there in the tag name, so the tag is coded as `<media:title>` instead of just `<title>`. The name to the left of the colon is always the namespace.

Access XML data with objects

There are lots of different ways to work with XML data with PHP, and one of the best involves objects. An **object** is a special PHP data type that combines data and functions into a single construct. But what does that have to do with XML? The entire hierarchy of elements in an XML document is contained within a single variable, an object. You can then use the object to drill down into the data and access individual elements. Objects also have **methods**, which are functions that are tied to an object, and let us further manipulate the object's data. For an object that contains XML data, methods let us access the collection of child elements for an element, as well as its attributes.

Objects are a special PHP data type that combine data and functions together.

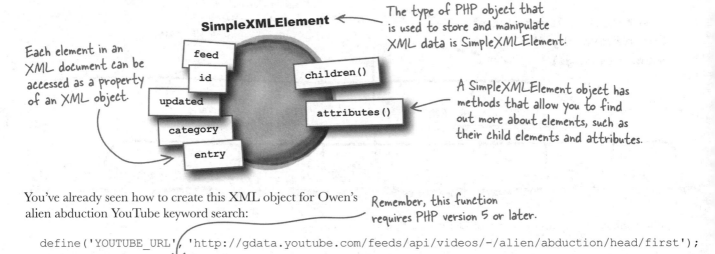

Each element in an XML document can be accessed as a property of an XML object.

SimpleXMLElement

The type of PHP object that is used to store and manipulate XML data is SimpleXMLElement.

feed
id
updated
category
entry

children()
attributes()

A SimpleXMLElement object has methods that allow you to find out more about elements, such as their child elements and attributes.

You've already seen how to create this XML object for Owen's alien abduction YouTube keyword search:

Remember, this function requires PHP version 5 or later.

```
define('YOUTUBE_URL', 'http://gdata.youtube.com/feeds/api/videos/-/alien/abduction/head/first');

$xml = simplexml_load_file(YOUTUBE_URL);
```

This function creates a PHP object of type SimpleXMLElement containing all of the XML data in the YouTube video response.

This code results in a variable named $xml that contains all of the XML YouTube video data packaged into a PHP object. To access the data you use object **properties**, which are individual pieces of data stored within an object. Each property corresponds to an XML element. Take a look at the following example, which accesses all of the entry elements in the document:

```
$entries = $xml->entry;
```

By specifying the name of the element (entry), you can grab all of the elements that are in the XML data.

The -> operator lets you access a property within an object.

This code accesses all the entry elements in the XML data using a property. Since there are multiple entry elements in the data, the $entries variable stores an array of objects that you can use to access individual video entries. And since we're now dealing with an array, each video <entry> tag can be accessed by indexing the array. For example, the first <entry> tag in the document is the first item in the array, the second tag is the second item, etc.

All of the video entries are stored in the $entries array.

$entries

From XML elements to PHP objects

When it comes to XML data and PHP objects, you're really dealing with a **collection** of objects. Remember that stuff about visualizing an XML document as a hierarchy of elements? Well, that same hierarchy is realized as a **collection of objects** in PHP. Take a look:

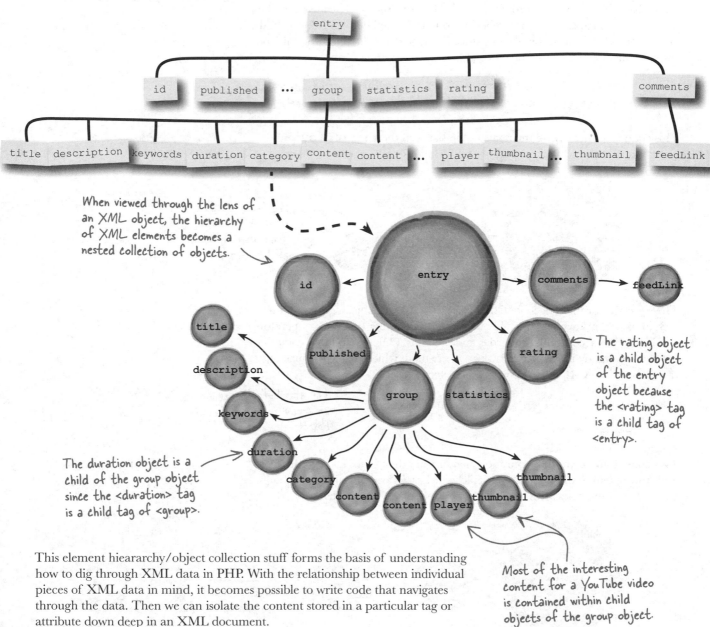

When viewed through the lens of an XML object, the hierarchy of XML elements becomes a nested collection of objects.

The rating object is a child object of the entry object because the <rating> tag is a child tag of <entry>.

The duration object is a child of the group object since the <duration> tag is a child tag of <group>.

Most of the interesting content for a YouTube video is contained within child objects of the group object.

This element hieararchy/object collection stuff forms the basis of understanding how to dig through XML data in PHP. With the relationship between individual pieces of XML data in mind, it becomes possible to write code that navigates through the data. Then we can isolate the content stored in a particular tag or attribute down deep in an XML document.

Drill into XML data with objects

Getting back to Owen, our goal is to pull out a few pieces of information for videos that are returned as part of the XML YouTube response. We know how to retrieve the XML data into a PHP object using the `simplexml_load_file()` function, but most of the interesting data is found down deeper in this data. How do we navigate through the collection of objects? The answer is the `->` operator, which is used to reference a property or method of an object. In the case of an XML object, the `->` operator accesses each child object. So this code displays the title of a video entry stored in a variable named `$entry`:

```
echo $entry->group->title;
```

Here the -> operator is used to drill down through nested child objects to access the title object.

This code relies heavily on the relationship between the `title`, `group`, and `entry` objects, which form a parent-child relationship from one to the next.

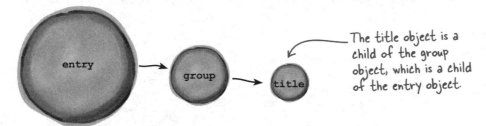

The title object is a child of the group object, which is a child of the entry object.

The `->` operator references a child object from a parent object. So `title` is a child of `group`, which is a child of `entry`. Remember that the `->` operator can be used to access both properties and methods. One method that comes in particularly handy is the `attributes()` method, which is able to pluck out the value of an XML attribute for a given element.

```
$attrs = $entry->group->duration->attributes();

echo $attrs['seconds'];
```

The attributes() method obtains an array of attributes for an object (element).

This code drills down to the duration element and then grabs all of its attributes and stores them in the `$attrs` variable, which is an array of all the attributes. The value of the `seconds` attribute is then retrieved from the array.

A specific attribute value can be retrieved by using the name of the attribute as the array key.

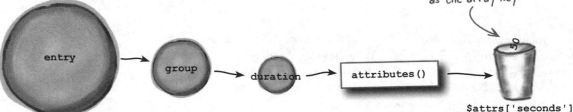

$attrs['seconds']

Not without a namespace!

There's a small problem with the code on the facing page that accesses XML data using objects, and it has to do with namespaces. If you recall, namespaces act as surnames for tags by organizing them into meaningful collections. So in a YouTube response, the `<duration>` tag is actually coded as `<yt:duration>`, and the title for a video is coded as `<media:title>`, not `<title>`. When an element is associated with a namespace, you can't just reference it by tag name in PHP code. Instead, you have to first isolate it by namespace by calling the `children()` method on the parent object.

Namespaces make it a bit trickier to access elements within XML data.

```php
$media = $entry->children('http://search.yahoo.com/mrss/');
```

The children() method returns an array containing all of the child elements that are within the specified namespace.

This code retrieves all the child objects of the video entry whose namespace is `http://search.yahoo.com/mrss/`. But that's the URL for a namespace, not the namespace itself. This URL is located in the `<feed>` tag at the start of the XML document. This is where you'll find all the namespaces being used.

```
<feed xmlns='http://www.w3.org/2005/Atom'
  xmlns:openSearch='http://a9.com/-/spec/opensearchrss/1.0/'
  xmlns:gml='http://www.opengis.net/gml'
  xmlns:georss='http://www.georss.org/georss'
  xmlns:media='http://search.yahoo.com/mrss/'
  xmlns:batch='http://schemas.google.com/gdata/batch'
  xmlns:yt='http://gdata.youtube.com/schemas/2007'
  xmlns:gd='http://schemas.google.com/g/2005'>
```

All tags starting with "<media:" belong to this namespace.

This namespace is for tags starting in "<yt:".

This code reveals how each namespace is associated with a URL. More specifically, it shows how the `media` and `yt` namespaces are specified for use in the document. This is all you need to find tags related to these two namespaces.

Once you've isolated the child elements for a particular namespace by calling the `children()` method on the parent element, you can then resume accessing child objects with the `->` operator. For example, this code obtains the video title from the `<media:group>` tag:

Use the children() method to isolate all elements associated with a namespace.

```php
$title = $media->group->title;
```

The <title> tag is a child of the <media:group> tag.

Sharpen your pencil

Using the namespace information and PHP code above, finish the PHP code that gets the duration (in seconds) of a video clip.

```php
$yt = $media->children('.......................................................');

$attrs = ...........................................;

echo $attrs['.............'];
```

Sharpen your pencil
Solution

Using the namespace information and PHP code above, finish the PHP code that gets the duration (in seconds) of a video clip.

```php
$yt = $media->children(' http://gdata.youtube.com/schemas/2007 ');
$attrs = $yt->duration->attributes() ;
echo $attrs[' seconds '];
```

This is the URL for the namespace as listed in the <feed> tag at the beginning of the document.

Grab all of the attributes for the <yt:duration> tag.

The name of the attribute is used as the key for accessing the attribute array.

there are no
Dumb Questions

Q: How is an object different than an array? Don't arrays also store collections of data?

A: Yes. Arrays and objects are actually a lot alike. But one huge difference is that objects can have executable code attached to them in the form of methods. Methods are pretty much the same as functions except that they are tied to an object, and are usually designed to work specifically with the data stored in an object. Arrays are purely about storing a set of related data, and have no notion of methods. Additionally, array elements are accessed by specifying the index or key of an element inside square brackets ([ ]), while object properties and methods are accessed by name using the -> operator.

Q: What exactly is an object? Is it like a normal variable?

A: Yes. An object is exactly like any other variable in PHP; it's just that it is able to store more complex data. So instead of just storing a string of text or a number, an object is able to store a combination of strings, numbers, etc. The idea is that by combining related data together with functions that act on them, the overall design and coding of applications becomes more logical.

Q: So how do objects help in processing XML data?

A: Objects help in regard to XML data processing because they are able to model the element hierarchy of an XML document in nested child objects. The benefit to this approach is that you can navigate through child objects using the -> operator and access whatever data you need.

Q: I thought the -> operator was for accessing object properties. How does it allow me to access a child object?

A: The reason is that when dealing with XML objects in PHP, child objects are actually stored as properties. So when you use the -> operator to access a child object, you really are just accessing a property. The `SimpleXMLElement` object is what makes this possible.

Q: Hang on, what's the `SimpleXMLElement` object?

A: Every object in PHP has a specific data type, meaning that "object" is really a generic term. So when you create an object, you're creating an object of a specific type that is designed to accomplish a specific task. In the case of XML, the object type is `SimpleXMLElement`, and it is automatically returned by the `simplexml_load_file()` function. In other words, calling the `simplexml_load_file()` function results in the creation of an object of type `SimpleXMLElement`.

Q: What do I need to know about `SimpleXMLElement`?

A: Surprisingly, not a whole lot. The main thing to know is that it exposes the elements in an XML document as properties, and that these properties lead to child objects that themselves are instances of the `SimpleXMLElement` object, and so on. The `SimpleXMLElement` object also has methods that allow you to access data within an element, such as `children()` and `attributes()`.

Fang sightings are on the rise

While Owen has been busy brushing up on XML and figuring out how to communicate with YouTube, Fang has been busy. Numerous video sightings have turned up with the little guy apparently serving as a tour guide for his alien abductors. Owen is ready to finish up the YouTube script, get some videos showing on the Aliens Abducted Me home page, and find his lost dog.

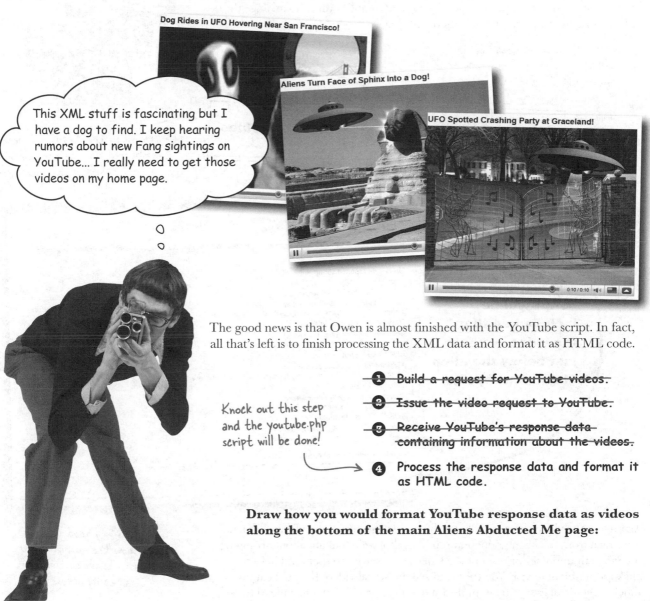

> This XML stuff is fascinating but I have a dog to find. I keep hearing rumors about new Fang sightings on YouTube... I really need to get those videos on my home page.

The good news is that Owen is almost finished with the YouTube script. In fact, all that's left is to finish processing the XML data and format it as HTML code.

Knock out this step and the youtube.php script will be done!

1. ~~Build a request for YouTube videos.~~
2. ~~Issue the video request to YouTube.~~
3. ~~Receive YouTube's response data containing information about the videos.~~
4. Process the response data and format it as HTML code.

Draw how you would format YouTube response data as videos along the bottom of the main Aliens Abducted Me page:

Lay out videos for viewing

The idea behind the `youtube.php` script is that it will be included in the main `index.php` script for Aliens Abducted Me. This means that the `youtube.php` script needs to take care of submitting a video request, processing the XML response, and formatting the individual videos so that they are displayed via HTML in such a way that they can coexist with the alien abduction reports that are already on the main page. A good way to accomplish this is to arrange the videos horizontally along the bottom of the page.

These are the videos dynamically accessed from YouTube as XML data.

This row of video thumbnail images is what the youtube.php script is responsible for generating.

Video	Video	Video	Video	Video

Five video thumbnails is a decent number to arrange horizontally without taking up too much room.

The `youtube.php` script will be included so that the videos appear just below the alien abduction reports.

```
                              Aliens Abducted Me
```

Aliens Abducted Me

Welcome, have you had an encounter with extraterrestrials? Were you abducted? Have you seen my abducted dog, Fang? **Report it here!**

Most recent reported abductions:

2008-08-10 : Meinhold Ressner		
Abducted for: 3 hours	**Alien description:** They were in a ship the size of a full moon.	**Fang spotted:** no
2008-07-11 : Mickey Mikens		
Abducted for: 45 minutes	**Alien description:** Huge heads, skinny arms and legs	**Fang spotted:** yes
2008-07-05 : Shill Watner		
Abducted for: 2 hours	**Alien description:** There was a bright light in the sky, followed by a bark or two.	**Fang spotted:** yes
2008-06-21 : Belita Chevy		
Abducted for: almost a week	**Alien description:** Clumsy little buggers, had no rhythm.	**Fang spotted:** no
2008-05-11 : Sally Jones		
Abducted for: 1 day	**Alien description:** green with six tentacles	**Fang spotted:** yes

▧ Click to syndicate the abduction news feed.

This is a good spot to show the row of video thumbnails so that visitors can easily access them.

Arranging the videos horizontally on the main page keeps them from detracting too much from the alien abduction reports. Also, we're talking about arranging the video thumbnail images, not the videos themselves, so users will have to click a thumbnail to visit YouTube and see the actual video. It would eat up too much screen real estate to attempt to show multiple videos large enough to be embedded directly on the Aliens Abducted Me page.

Format video data for display

Although a video thumbnail image is certainly one of the most important pieces of information when assessing whether or not a video is worth watching, it isn't the only data useful for Owen's YouTube script. For example, the title of a video could hold some important information about the nature of the video—like whether it might include a dog. The length of the video could also be helpful. And of course, we need the URL of the video link to YouTube so that the user can click on a video thumbnail to actually view a video. So the following information is what we need to extract from the XML data in the YouTube response:

Title   **Length**   **Thumbnail**   **Link**

Several pieces of video data are required in order to place YouTube videos on a web page.

This data forms the basis for the HTML code that displays a horizontal row of videos. In fact, each video in the row ends up looking like this:

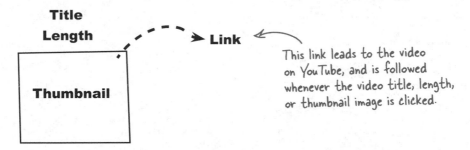

Title
Length   **→ Link**

Thumbnail

This link leads to the video on YouTube, and is followed whenever the video title, length, or thumbnail image is clicked.

In the YouTube response data, the length of a video is specified in the seconds attribute of the `<yt:duration>` tag. Unfortunately, most people don't think in terms of total seconds because we're accustomed to times being specified in minutes and seconds. For example, it isn't immediately obvious that 330 seconds is a five-and-a-half-minute video—you have to do the math for the value to make sense as a length of time. Knowing this, it's a good idea to go ahead and do the math for users when displaying the length of a video, converting seconds into minutes and seconds.

That is, unless you're part of the YouTube Director program, in which case you can post videos longer than 10 minutes.

Length → ~~330 seconds~~

5 minutes, 30 seconds

More intuitive and easier for users to understand.

Geek Bits

It isn't necessary to factor in hours in the video length calculation because YouTube doesn't currently allow videos longer than 10 minutes to be posted.

Exercise

The `youtube.php` script uses PHP code to grab the top five matches for an alien abduction YouTube video search. It then displays thumbnail images for those videos in a horizontal row, with links to the actual videos on YouTube. Fill the missing code for the script, using the example YouTube XML video response data on the facing page as a guide.

```php
<?php
  define('YOUTUBE_URL', 'http://gdata.youtube.com/feeds/api/videos/-/alien/abduction/head/first');
  define('NUM_VIDEOS', 5);


  // Read the XML data into an object
  $xml = ........................... (YOUTUBE_URL);


  $num_videos_found = count( .................... );
  if ($num_videos_found > 0) {
   echo '<table><tr>';
   for ($i = 0; $i < min($num_videos_found, NUM_VIDEOS); $i++) {
    // Get the title
    $entry = $xml->entry[$i];
    $media = $entry->children('http://search.yahoo.com/mrss/');
    $title = $media->group-> ......... ;


    // Get the duration in minutes and seconds, and then format it
    $yt = $media->children('http://gdata.youtube.com/schemas/2007');
    $attrs = $yt->duration->attributes();
    $length_min = floor($attrs[' ............ '] / 60);
    $length_sec = $attrs[' ............ '] % 60;
    $length_formatted = $length_min . (($length_min != 1) ? ' minutes, ':' minute, ') .
     $length_sec . (($length_sec != 1) ? ' seconds':' second');


    // Get the video URL
    $attrs = $media->group->player-> ................ ();
    $video_url = $attrs['url'];
```

```
            // Get the thumbnail image URL

            $attrs = $media->          ->thumbnail[0]->attributes();

            $thumbnail_url = $attrs['url'];



            // Display the results for this entry

            echo '<td style="vertical-align:bottom; text-align:center" width="' . (100 / NUM_VIDEOS) .

             '%"><a href="' . $video_url . '">' .          . '<br /><span style="font-size:smaller">' .

             $length_formatted . '</span><br /><img src="' .                    . '" /></a></td>';

          }

         echo '</tr></table>';

        }

        else {

         echo '<p>Sorry, no videos were found.</p>';

        }

      ?>
```

Feel free to reference this example XML code while writing the missing PHP code.

```
...
<entry>
 <id>http://gdata.youtube.com/feeds/api/videos/_6Uibqf0vtA</id>
 <published>2006-06-20T07:49:05.000-07:00</published>
 ...
 <media:group>
  <media:title type='plain'>UFO Sighting in Yosemite Park near Area 51</media:title>
  <media:description type='plain'>I went on a trip to Yosemite Park in 2002. Yosemite Park is very
   close to the border between California and Nevada, and close to Area 51...</media:description>
  <media:keywords>51, alien, aliens, area, ca, california, nevada, sighting, sightings,
  ufo</media:keywords>
  <yt:duration seconds='50'/>
  <media:category label='Travel &amp; Events'
   scheme='http://gdata.youtube.com/schemas/2007/categories.cat'>Travel</media:category>
  <media:content url='http://www.youtube.com/v/_6Uibqf0vtA' type='application/x-shockwave-flash'
   medium='video' isDefault='true' expression='full' duration='50' yt:format='5'/>
  <media:content url='rtsp://rtsp2.youtube.com/ChoLENy73wIaEQnQvvSnbiKl_xMYDSANFEgGDA==/0/0/0/video.3gp'
   type='video/3gpp' medium='video' expression='full' duration='50' yt:format='1'/>
  <media:content url='rtsp://rtsp2.youtube.com/ChoLENy73wIaEQnQvvSnbiKl_xMYESARFEgGDA==/0/0/0/video.3gp'
   type='video/3gpp' medium='video' expression='full' duration='50' yt:format='6'/>
  <media:player url='http://www.youtube.com/watch?v=_6Uibqf0vtA'/>
  <media:thumbnail url='http://img.youtube.com/vi/_6Uibqf0vtA/2.jpg' height='97' width='130'
   time='00:00:25'/>
  <media:thumbnail url='http://img.youtube.com/vi/_6Uibqf0vtA/1.jpg' height='97' width='130'
   time='00:00:12.500'/>
  <media:thumbnail url='http://img.youtube.com/vi/_6Uibqf0vtA/3.jpg' height='97' width='130'
   time='00:00:37.500'/>
  <media:thumbnail url='http://img.youtube.com/vi/_6Uibqf0vtA/0.jpg' height='240' width='320'
   time='00:00:25'/>
 </media:group>
 <yt:statistics viewCount='2478159' favoriteCount='1897'/>
 <gd:rating min='1' max='5' numRaters='1602' average='4.17'/>
 <gd:comments>
  <gd:feedLink href='http://gdata.youtube.com/feeds/api/videos/_6Uibqf0vtA/comments'
   countHint='4426'/>
 </gd:comments>
</entry>
<entry>
 ...
</entry>
...
```

The title of the video.

The duration (length) of the video, in seconds.

The URL of the video link on YouTube.

The URL of a thumbnail image (preview) of the video.

Exercise Solution

The `youtube.php` script uses PHP code to grab the top five matches for an alien abduction YouTube video search. It then displays thumbnail images for those videos in a horizontal row, with links to the actual videos on YouTube. Fill in the missing code for the script, using the example YouTube XML video response data on the facing page as a guide.

```php
<?php

  define('YOUTUBE_URL', 'http://gdata.youtube.com/feeds/api/videos/-/alien/abduction/head/first');
```
↖ Owen's YouTube keyword search URL.

```php
  define('NUM_VIDEOS', 5);
```
The number of videos to be displayed is stored as a constant.

```php
  // Read the XML data into an object
  $xml = simplexml_load_file(YOUTUBE_URL);
```
The simplexml_load_file() function is used to request the XML data from YouTube.

```php
  $num_videos_found = count($xml->entry);

  if ($num_videos_found > 0) {
    echo '<table><tr>';

    for ($i = 0; $i < min($num_videos_found, NUM_VIDEOS); $i++) {
```
Check to see how many videos were actually returned by YouTube by counting the number of <entry> tags.

Loop through the video data one entry at a time.

```php
      // Get the title
      $entry = $xml->entry[$i];
      $media = $entry->children('http://search.yahoo.com/mrss/');
      $title = $media->group->title;
```
Extract the title of the video entry, which is stored in the <media:title> tag.

Grab all of the children for this entry that are in the Yahoo! media namespace, media.

```php
      // Get the duration in minutes and seconds, and then format it
      $yt = $media->children('http://gdata.youtube.com/schemas/2007');

      $attrs = $yt->duration->attributes();

      $length_min = floor($attrs['seconds'] / 60);

      $length_sec = $attrs['seconds'] % 60;
```
Grab all of the children for this entry that are in the YouTube namespace, yt.

Get the duration of the video in seconds from the <yt:duration> tag, and then convert it to minutes.

```php
      $length_formatted = $length_min . (($length_min != 1) ? ' minutes, ':' minute, ') .
        $length_sec . (($length_sec != 1) ? ' seconds':' second');


      // Get the video URL
      $attrs = $media->group->player->attributes();

      $video_url = $attrs['url'];
```
Grab the video link (URL) from the url attribute of the <media:player> tag.

```php
    // Get the thumbnail image URL
    $attrs = $media-> group ->thumbnail[0]->attributes();
    $thumbnail_url = $attrs['url'];
```

Extract the first thumbnail image URL from the url attribute of the `<media:thumbnail>` tag.

```php
    // Display the results for this entry
    echo '<td style="vertical-align:bottom; text-align:center" width="' . (100 / NUM_VIDEOS) .
      '%"><a href="' . $video_url . '">' . $title . '<br /><span style="font-size:smaller">' .
      $length_formatted . '</span><br /><img src="' . $thumbnail_url . '" /></a></td>';
  }
  echo '</tr></table>';
  }
  else {
    echo '<p>Sorry, no videos were found.</p>';
  }
?>
```

Format the video results as a table cell with the video title, length, and thumbnail image.

❶ ~~Build a request for YouTube videos.~~

❷ ~~Issue the video request to YouTube.~~

❸ ~~Receive YouTube's response data containing information about the videos.~~

❹ ~~Process the response data and format it as HTML code.~~

Finished!

```xml
...
<entry>
<id>http://gdata.youtube.com/feeds/api/videos/_6Uibqf0vtA</id>
<published>2006-06-20T07:49:05.000-07:00</published>
...
 <media:group>
 <media:title type='plain'>UFO Sighting in Yosemite Park near Area 51</media:title>
 <media:description type='plain'>I went on a trip to Yosemite Park in 2002. Yosemite Park is very
  close to the border between California and Nevada, and close to Area 51...</media:description>
 <media:keywords>51, alien, aliens, area, ca, california, nevada, sighting, sightings,
  ufo</media:keywords>
 <yt:duration seconds='50'/>
 <media:category label='Travel &amp; Events'
  scheme='http://gdata.youtube.com/schemas/2007/categories.cat'>Travel</media:category>
 <media:content url='http://www.youtube.com/v/_6Uibqf0vtA' type='application/x-shockwave-flash'
  medium='video' isDefault='true' expression='full' duration='50' yt:format='5'/>
 <media:content url='rtsp://rtsp2.youtube.com/ChoLENy73wIaEQnQvvSnbiKl_xMYDSANFEgGDA==/0/0/0/video.3gp'
  type='video/3gpp' medium='video' expression='full' duration='50' yt:format='1'/>
 <media:content url='rtsp://rtsp2.youtube.com/ChoLENy73wIaEQnQvvSnbiKl_xMYESARFEgGDA==/0/0/0/video.3gp'
  type='video/3gpp' medium='video' expression='full' duration='50' yt:format='6'/>
 <media:player url='http://www.youtube.com/watch?v=_6Uibqf0vtA'/>
 <media:thumbnail url='http://img.youtube.com/vi/_6Uibqf0vtA/2.jpg' height='97' width='130'
  time='00:00:25'/>
 <media:thumbnail url='http://img.youtube.com/vi/_6Uibqf0vtA/1.jpg' height='97' width='130'
  time='00:00:12.500'/>
 <media:thumbnail url='http://img.youtube.com/vi/_6Uibqf0vtA/3.jpg' height='97' width='130'
  time='00:00:37.500'/>
 <media:thumbnail url='http://img.youtube.com/vi/_6Uibqf0vtA/0.jpg' height='240' width='320'
  time='00:00:25'/>
 </media:group>
 <yt:statistics viewCount='2478159' favoriteCount='1897'/>
 <gd:rating min='1' max='5' numRaters='1602' average='4.17'/>
 <gd:comments>
  <gd:feedLink href='http://gdata.youtube.com/feeds/api/videos/_6Uibqf0vtA/comments'
   countHint='4426'/>
 </gd:comments>
</entry>
<entry>
 ...
</entry>
...
```

The title of the video.

The duration (length) of the video, in seconds.

The URL of the video link on YouTube.

The URL of a thumbnail image (preview) of the video.

Test Drive

Add the YouTube script to Aliens Abducted Me.

Create a new text file named `youtube.php`, and enter the code for Owen's YouTube script from the previous two pages (or download the script from the Head First Labs site at `www.headfirstlabs.com/books/hfphp`). You still need to plug the script into the `index.php` script to turn YouTube videos loose on the main Aliens Abducted Me page. Here are the two lines of PHP code to do it:

```
echo '<h4>Most recent abduction videos:</h4>';

require_once('youtube.php');
```

Upload the scripts to your web server, and then open `index.php` in a web browser. The bottom of the page should show a dynamically generated row of YouTube video links that are related to alien abductions.

I think I know where Fang is...

Including the youtube.php script in the main page is all it takes to add the row of alien abduction videos.

Aliens Abducted Me

Welcome, have you had an encounter with extraterrestrials? Were you abducted? Have you seen my abducted dog, Fang? Report it here!

Most recent reported abductions:

2008-08-10 : Meinhold Ressner		Fang spotted:
Abducted for: 3 hours	**Alien description:** they were in a ship the size of a full moon	no
2008-07-11 : Mickey Mikens		Fang spotted:
Abducted for: 45 minutes...and counting	**Alien description:** huge heads, skinny arms and legs	yes
2008-07-05 : Shill Watner		Fang spotted:
Abducted for: 2 hours	**Alien description:** there was a bright light in the sky, followed by a bark or two	yes
2008-06-21 : Belita Chevy		Fang spotted:
Abducted for: almost a week	**Alien description:** clumsy little buggers, had no rhythm	no
2008-05-11 : Sally Jones		Fang spotted:
Abducted for: 1 day	**Alien description:** green with six tentacles	yes

🔊 Click to syndicate the abduction news feed.

Most recent abduction videos:

UFO Spotted Crashing Party at Graceland! 0 minutes, 10 seconds	Aliens Turn Face of Sphinx Into a Dog! 0 minutes, 10 seconds	Dog Rides in UFO Hovering Near San Francisco! 0 minutes, 11 seconds	UFO Spotted Near Eiffel Tower! 0 minutes, 13 seconds	Pug Abducted By UFO! 0 minutes, 18 seconds

YouTube videos have helped Owen narrow Fang's location.

Sharpen your pencil

Please help me find Fang.

Start here!

Sharpen your pencil
Solution

Thank you PHP and MySQL!

CHAPTER 12

Your PHP & MySQL Toolbox

With Fang now accounted for, it's possible to reflect a little on what all it took to track him down. As it turns out, PHP and MySQL required some help from a few other technologies.

REST

A means of accessing information on the web purely through URLs. REST allows you to make powerful data requests simply by creating a URL. Such requests are often referred to as "RESTful" requests.

XML

A generic markup language used to provide a predictable structure to data. There are many different markup languages built from XML, such as XHTML and RSS. The idea is that you create a set of tags specific to whatever data you're storing as XML.

RSS

An XML-based language used to store syndicated content, such as news stories. RSS allows web sites to make their data available to other applications and web sites for syndication, and allows you to take advantage of data made available by other sites.

simplexml_load_file()

This built-in PHP function loads an XML file from a URL, and then makes the resulting XML data accessible through an object.

SimpleXMLElement

A built-in PHP object that is used to access XML data. This object is returned by the simplexml_load_file() function, and contains the entire document hierarchy of an XML document.

Namespace

A way of organizing a set of XML tags into a logical group, sort of like how your last name organizes your family into a named group. A namespace is always associated with a URL, which ensures uniqueness among all other namespaces.

The End.

appendix i: leftovers

The Top Ten Topics
(we didn't cover)

Even after all that, there's a bit more. There are just a few more things we think you need to know. We wouldn't feel right about ignoring them, even though they only need a brief mention. So before you put the book down, take a read through these short but important PHP and MySQL tidbits. Besides, once you're done here, all that's left are a couple short appendices... and the index... and maybe some ads... and then you're really done. We promise!

#1. Retrofit this book for PHP4 and mysql functions

With the exception of XML functions in Chapter 12, most of the code in this book will run on PHP 4 servers with only a little modification. We've used the mysqli family of functions in this book, which are only available in PHP 4.1 and later, and since the library has to be manually installed, some servers won't support mysqli.

Mysqli functions are generally faster, but this really only begins to matter when your database becomes huge. Small or average databases won't be perceptibly slower with the older mysql functions. This section is designed to tell you how to retrofit your mysqli functions to work as mysql functions with older versions of PHP.

If you see:

```
$dbc = mysqli_connect(localhost, 'mork', 'fromork');

mysqli_select_db($dbc, 'alien_database');
```

you'll use:

```
$dbc = mysql_connect(localhost, 'mork', 'fromork');

mysql_select_db('alien_database', $dbc);
```

The database connection variable is not the first argument here, as it is with mysqli_select_db().

In general, you just remove the i from `mysqli`, making it `mysql`, and then swap the order of the arguments so that the database connection variable (`$dbc` in this example) appears last.

But it gets a little trickier when the `mysqli_connect()` function sidesteps `mysqli_select_db()` and uses a database name. There's nothing quite like that in the mysql family of functions. For the single `mysqli_connect()` function that uses a database name, you'll need two mysql functions.

If you see:

```
$dbc = mysqli_connect(localhost, 'mork', 'fromork', 'alien_database');
```

Here the database is selected as part of making the connection — something that isn't possible in one step with mysql functions.

you'll need to use two commands:

```
$dbc = mysql_connect(localhost, 'mork', 'fromork');

mysql_select_db('alien_database', $dbc);
```

This connection variable is also known as a database connection "link."

With mysql functions, it always takes two function calls to establish a connection with a specific database.

Here's how mysql and mysqli functions match up.

Close MySQL connection	`mysqli_close(conn)`	`mysqli_close(conn)`
Open a connection to a MySQL server	`mysql_connect(host, username, password)` You must use `mysql_select_db()` to select a database.	`mysqli_connect(host, username, password, database)` You don't need `mysqli_select_db()` to select a database.
Return the text of the error message from previous MySQL operation	`mysql_error(conn)`	`mysqli_error(conn)`
Escape a string	`mysql_escape_string(string, conn)` The order of arguments is opposite, expects the string, then the connection (link).	`mysqli_escape_string(conn, string)` Expects the connection (link) followed by the string.
Fetch a result row as an associative array, a numeric array, or both	`mysql_fetch_row(result)`	`mysqli_fetch_row(result)`
Get number of rows in result	`mysql_num_rows(result)`	`mysqli_num_rows(result)`
Execute a MySQL query	`mysql_query(query, conn)`	`mysqli_query(conn, query)`
Escape special characters in a string	`mysql_real_escape_string(string, conn)` The order of arguments is opposite, expects the string, then the connection (link).	`mysqli_real_escape_string(conn, string)` Expects the connection (link) followed by the string.
Select a MySQL database	`mysql_select_db(dbname, conn)` The order of arguments is opposite, expects the string, then the connection (link).	`mysqli_select_db(conn, dbname)` Expects the connection (link) followed by the string.

#2. User permissions in MySQL

Suppose you've created a web application that only allows visitors to SELECT data from your table. You perform queries on your data using a specific database, and MySQL gives you power over your data.

But consider this: the login and password you use in your mysqli connection string would, if connected directly to the database via the MySQL terminal or GUI, allow the user to INSERT, UPDATE, and DELETE data.

If your application doesn't need to do those things, there's no reason why the user/password you are using to connect with needs to be able to. With MySQL, you can limit the access to your database. You can tell MySQL to only allow the user to SELECT. Or SELECT and INSERT. Or any combination you need.

And what's even more impressive, you can control access to specific tables. For example, if your application only works with a table called alien_info and doesn't need access to the cyborg_info table, you can limit it.

First, you may want to create an entirely new user/password to be used for your application. You can do this in the MySQL terminal:

```
File Edit Window Help  Aliens!
mysql> CREATE USER alienguy IDENTIFIED BY 'aliensRsc4ry';
Query OK, 0 rows affected (0.07 sec)
```

Then you can use the MySQL GRANT command to control what alienguy can do to your database. If he only needed to SELECT and INSERT data into your database, this would work:

```
File Edit Window Help  TheyLive
mysql> USE alien_database;
Database changed
mysql> GRANT SELECT, INSERT ON alien_info TO alienguy;
Query OK, 0 rows affected (0.03 sec)
```

If you don't like using the MySQL terminal to create users and set privileges, you can download and install a handy program caled MySQLAdministrator. Get it here: http://dev.mysql.com/downloads/gui-tools/5.0.html.

You can set very specific user privileges, even control what your user can do to a specific column. To learn more, check out Head First SQL.

The MySQL Administrator lets you control your user accounts and what each user account can access in your database. It even allows you to specify which kind of queries that user can perform on each table in your database. To control the access every user has to each table and each query, open the MySQL Administrator application, and click on the **Accounts** tab.

Here's the interface and an overview of how to control what each user can do. First, create an account:

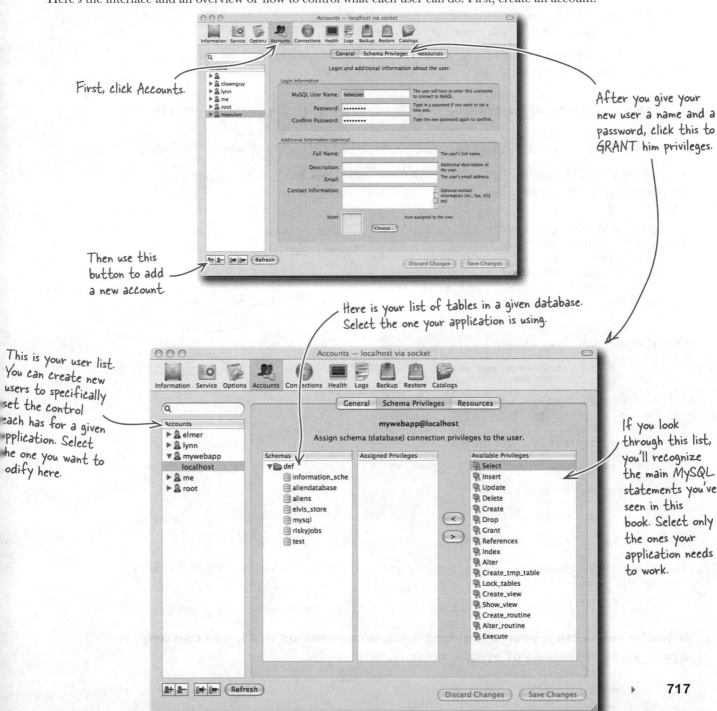

First, click Accounts.

Then use this button to add a new account.

After you give your new user a name and a password, click this to GRANT him privileges.

Here is your list of tables in a given database. Select the one your application is using.

This is your user list. You can create new users to specifically set the control each has for a given application. Select the one you want to modify here.

If you look through this list, you'll recognize the main MySQL statements you've seen in this book. Select only the ones your application needs to work.

#3. Error reporting for MySQL

In many of our code examples, you'll see lines like this:

```
mysqli_connect(localhost, 'mork', 'fromork') or die ('Could not connect.')
```

When this command fails, the words "Could not connect." are displayed on the web page. It tells us that something went wrong, but it doesn't give us information beyond that.

Fortunately, PHP offers a function, **mysql_error()**, that will give us a clue as to exactly what went wrong. Consider this code where we are trying to connect to a MySQL server that doesn't exist:

```php
<?php
  mysqli_connect('badhostname', 'mork', 'fromork') or die (mysqli_error());
?>

Unknown MySQL server host 'badhostname' (1)
```

Here's the error message you'll see.

This will return clear information as to what actually went wrong when the `mysqli_connect()` function fails. You can also use `mysqli_error()` with other mysqli functions:

```php
<?php
  $dbc = mysqli_connect('localhost', 'mork', 'fromork');
  mysqli_select_db($dbc, 'alien_database');
  echo mysqli_error($dbc) . '<br />';
  mysqli_select_db($dbc, 'alien_database');
  mysqli_query($dbc, "SELECT * FROM alien_info");
  echo mysqli_error($dbc);
?>
```

We try to connect to a database that doesn't exist.

We try to SELECT from a table that doesn't exist.

Here's the output:

```
Unknown database 'alien_database'
Table 'alien_info' doesn't exist
```

Here are some other error messages you might see:

```
Table 'test.no_such_table' doesn't exist

Can't create table

Can't create database 'yourdatabase'; database exists

Can't drop database 'yourdatabase(; database doesn't exist
```

There are dozens more, and it would be a waste of paper to list them here. Browse on over to this site to get more information:

```
http://dev.mysql.com/doc/refman/5.0/en/error-messages-server.html
```

If you're retrofitting your mysql functions, as mentioned in #1, you can use `mysql_error()` **instead of** `mysqli_error()`.

#4. Exception handling PHP errors

Exception handling allows you to change the normal flow of your code and execute a special block of code when a specific exception occurs. PHP 5 and 6 offer exception handling. Here's a brief introduction.

Let's say you want to withdraw $200 bucks from an ATM.

But maybe you're required to have a minimum balance of $1000, and this withdrawal will put you under $1000. That isn't allowed.

Transaction failed!

Here's how this scenario might play out in PHP code with the help of exception handling to catch the failure.

```php
<?php

    function checkBalance($balance) {

        if($balance < 1000) {

            throw new Exception("Balance is less than $1000.");

        }

        return true;

    }

    try {

        checkBalance(999);

        echo 'Balance is above $1000.';

    }

    catch(Exception $e) {

        echo 'Error: ' . $e->getMessage();

    }

?>
```

Here's the feedback we'll send out if our balance is less than 1000.

The "try" block is used to test our value without ending the code flow.

We check our balance here.

If our exception occurs, we execute the code in this block. In this case, we echo our message.

When the code runs, you'll see this:

```
Error: Balance less than $1000.
```

#4. Exception handling PHP errors (cont.)

Exception handling consists of three blocks of code:

1. **Try** - This block is where you check to see if your value is what you expect it to be.

If it is, everything is great, and your code continues on its way. If not, an exception has ocurred. In programmerese, an exception is "thrown."

And when something is thrown, there needs to be something to catch it. If there is an exception, the "catch" block code is executed. If not, the code will continue as normal.

2. **Throw** - The "throw" commands the "catch" block and sends it an error message. Each "throw" has at least one "catch."

3. **Catch** - An **object** is created with the exception information. More information on objects, on the facing page.

```php
<?php

  function checkBalance($balance) {

    if($balance < 1000) {

      throw new Exception("Balance is less than $1000.");

    }

    return true;

  }

  try {

    checkBalance(999);

    echo 'Balance is above $1000.';

  }

  catch(Exception $e) {

    echo 'Error: ' . $e->getMessage();

  }

?>
```

#5. Object-oriented PHP

Object-oriented languages use a very different progamming model than their procedural counterparts. You've been using PHP procedurally, but it also has an object-oriented side. Instead of a chronological step-by-step set of instructions, particular structures become objects. **Objects include not only a definition of your data, but also all the operations that can be performed on it.** When you use object-oriented PHP, you create and work with **objects**.

Before we discuss why you might want to use OO PHP, let's write some:

① Write your class.

This is our Song class that defines our object.

Song
title, lyrics
sing()

```
class Song
{
  var $title;          These are instance
  var $lyrics;         variables.

  function Song($title, $lyrics) {        This sets the title
    $this->title = $title;                and lyrics of a song
    $this->lyrics = $lyrics;              when we create one.
  }
                          This is a method that uses the
  function sing() {       instance variables of the object.
   echo 'This is called ' . $this->title . '.<br />';
   echo 'One, two, three...' . $this->lyrics;
  }
}
```

② Create a new object.

Our new song has the value "Blue Suede Shoes" for its name.

```
$shoes_song = new Song('Blue Suede Shoes', 'Well it\'s one for the money...');
$shoes_song->sing();
```

Here's where we call the sing() method for our object.

③ Your song can sing itself!

When you run this code, you get this:

This is called Blue Suede Shoes.
One, two, three...Well it's one for the money...

But if you can just write the echo code without all the object stuff, why use OO PHP?

There are some great reasons...

#5. Object-oriented PHP (cont.)

Instead of a chronological step-by-step set of instructions, your data structures become objects. **Objects include not only a definition of your data, but also all the operations that can be performed on it.** In our `Song` example, we set the title and lyrics of the song inside the class, and we create the `sing()` method inside the class. If we needed to add more functionality to our `Song` object, we'd add new methods and variables to our `Song` class. For example, if we wanted the songwriter for each song to be associated with each song object, we could add that as a variable in our class.

The power of OO really shines as an application grows. Suppose we decided to use the `Song` class as part of a karaoke application with hundreds or even thousands of individual song objects, all with their own unique titles, lyrics, and songwriters. Now let's say someone wants to choose from only songs that were written by Elvis. All we'd have to do is look at the songwriter instance variable of each object.

And to actually feed the lyrics to the karaoke application? We could just call the `sing()` method on each song object when it is being performed. Even though we're calling the exact same method on each object, it is accessing data unique to each of the objects.

So two big advantages of using Object Oriented PHP are:

Objects can be easily reused. They are designed to be independent of the code where they are used and can be reused as needed.

The code is easier to understand and maintain. If a data type needs to change, the change occurs only in the object, nowhere else in the code.

A big disadvantage is that, in general, OO code can be longer and take more time to write. If you simply need to display the lyrics from one song, then writing a small procedural program might be your best bet. But if you think you might want to build that online karaoke app, consider diving further into object-oriented PHP.

#6. Securing your PHP application

There are some simple steps you can follow to protect your PHP scripts from those nefarious hackers that are crouched over their keyboards waiting for you to slip up.

1 Remove `phpinfo()` references. When you first start building PHP applications on new web servers, you'll probably create a script that contains the `phpinfo()` function, so you can see what version of PHP you are using and if it has MySQL support, along with a list of other installed libraries. It's fine to check with `phpinfo()`, but you should remove that function after you've taken a look. If you don't, any hacker out there who discovers a new PHP vulnerability will be able to see if your site is susceptible to it.

2 If you aren't using a web hosting service and have access to the `php.ini` file, there are a few changes you can make to it to further secure your PHP applications. Ironically, the location of your `php.ini` file can be found by using `phpinfo()`:

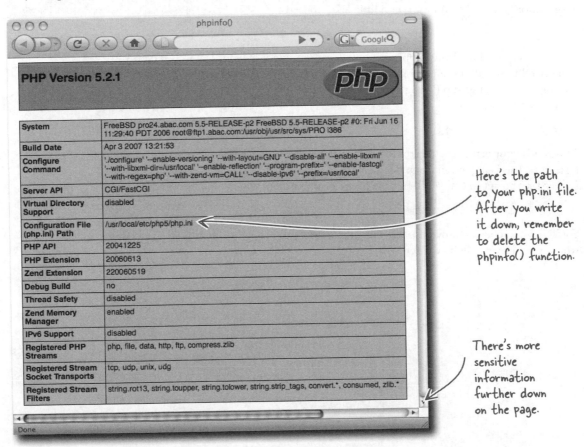

Here's the path to your php.ini file. After you write it down, remember to delete the phpinfo() function.

There's more sensitive information further down on the page.

#6. Securing your PHP application (cont.)

Here are some specific settings you should consider changing in the `php.ini` file. Open the file in a text editor, make the changes, save them, and then restart your web server.

```
safe_mode = On
```

When you turn on `safe_mode`, no PHP scripts can be called by another script with a different owner on the same web server. Obviously, if you need to allow scripts from other owners to call yours, you can't use this setting.

```
open_basedir = directory[:...]
```

This restricts the scripts and files that PHP will be able to execute or access to this directory and subdirectories beneath it.

```
expose_php = Off
```

With this set to On, every web browser that visits your site will be sent header information that reveals information about you PHP server. Turning it off hides that information and makes your server a little less exposed.

```
display_errors = Off
```

Once you've developed your application and are running it on your live web server, you don't need to see all those error messages. Hopefully, you've already addressed errors, but sometimes things slip through the cracks. To hide the error messages from site visitors, set this to Off.

```
log_errors = On
```

This sends your errors to an error log. When you want to check your application for errors, this is a good place to begin. With `display_errors` set to Off and `log_errors` set to On, you'll be able to see problems, but your site's visitors won't.

```
error_log = filename
```

You'll have to check with your particular web server software to locate this file. This is where your errors will be written when `log_errors` is set to On.

#7. Protect your app from cross-site scripting

You may have heard of cross-site scripting sometimes referred to as XSS. Cross-site scripting is an attack against a web app where script code is passed to your form processing script and hijacks your output. It's a big security problem in PHP web apps. Let's take a look at precisely what it is and how to defend against it.

Cross-site scripting usually takes advantage of sites that display user-submitted data. Any data you get from your users and display could potentially be corrupt and cause visitors to your site to be vulnerable to a hacker.

Using an XSS attack, a hacker can do any number of things. One of the worse is to redirect your results page to a page on a site under their control that might ask the user for further information. Your user might not notice that he's no longer on your site, and since he trusts your site, he might willingly submit sensitive information directly on the attackers server.

Here's how it might happen on the Guitar Wars site:

Ethel, instead of submitting her name in the Name field on the form, types in some JavaScript code. In the example, she's using the `window.location` function to redirect the browser to her own site. And since she controls her own site, she can show the visitor anything she wants, including a site that looks just like Guitar Wars. She could do something even more nefarious with sites that expect people to submit more important information than high scores, such as financial information.

There are other, even more insidious things that she could do, including stealing cookies or presenting the user with a screen that appeared to be a login screen. As soon as the user logs in, she has his username and password and can pretend to be him back on the original site.

So how do you avoid cross-site scripting attacks on your web applications?

Guitar Wars - Add Your High Score

Name: Ethel Heckel
Score: 1000000', 'ethelsscore2.gi
Screen shot: [Choose File] ethelsscore2.gif
[Add]

If Ethel can't cheat, she'll redirect the scores page to her own site with cross-site scripting.

You thought you foiled me. I'm going to hijack your site, and you're going down!

```
<script language="javascript">window.location="http://ethelrulz.com";</script>
```

All she has to do is submit this code in the name field on the form. When someone views the score, their browser will be redirected to her web site with this JavaScript code.

#7. Protect your app from cross-site scripting (cont.)

Fortunately, if you are validating your data, you are already on the road to protecting your application. You've already learned how to do just that in Guitar Wars. Here are three guidelines that will keep your applications safe:

Validate everything

Any data that you receive, such as form input, needs to be validated so that hacker code is detected before it can harm your application. If you assume the data is bad until you prove that it's not through validation, you'll be much safer.

Built-in PHP functions can help

Use built-in PHP functions such as `strip_tags()` to help you sanitize external data. `strip_tags()` is a great function that removes any html tags from a string. So if you use `strip_tags()` on Ethel's `$_POST['name']`, you'll end up with this:

```
window.location='http://ethelrulz.com'
```

While this is still not a name, it won't actually redirect the browser because the important JavaScript tags have been removed.

Data is guilty until proven innocent

Start with the most restrictive validation you can, and then only ease up if you have to. For example, if you begin by accepting only numbers in a phone number field, then start allowing dashes or parentheses, you'll be much safer than if you allowed any alphanumeric characters in the first place. Or in the case of Guitar Wars, if we don't allow anything except letters in the name field, we'll never even get the less than sign (<) that opens Ethel's evil JavaScript code. Regular expressions (Chapter 10) can go a long way toward making sure only the exact data you want is allowed.

#8. Operator precedence

Consider this line of code.

```
$marbles = 4 / 2 - 1;  ←——————— It will be 1.
```

The value stored by `$marbles` could be either 1 or 4. We can't tell from the code, but we can assume certain rules of **precedence**. By precedence, we mean the **order** in which they are executed. Operators in PHP are carried out in a certain order. In the example above, the division will take place before the subtraction does, so `$marbles` will equal 1.

Depending on what we need our code to output, we could have written it two different ways

```
$marbles = (4 / 2) - 1;
$marbles = 4 / (2 - 1);
```

In the first expression, we divide 4 by 2 and then subtract 1. In the second case, we subtract 1 from 2 and then divide 4 by the resulting 1. Using parentheses allow you to precisely control the order of operations. But knowing the precedence of operators in PHP can help you figure out what's going on in a complex expression. And, trust us, it will help you debug your code when you've forgotten to use parentheses.

Before we get to the PHP operator precedence list, here's another reason why you should use parentheses. Consider this:

```
$marbles = 4 - 3 - 2;  ←——————— It will be -1.
```

No precedence rules apply here. The result could be either 3 or -1. This is pretty confusing when you're writing code. Instead, it's better to code with parentheses, like in these two lines:

```
$marbles = 4 - (3 - 2);
$marbles = (4 - 3) - 2;
```

Now the list, from highest precedence (evaluated first) to lowest (evaluated last).

Operator	Operator Type
++ --	increment/decrement
*/ %	arithmetic
+ - .	arithmetic and string
< <= > >= <>	comparison
== != === !==	comparison
&&	logical
| |	logical
= += -= *= /= .= %= &= |= ^= <<= >>=	assignment
and	logical
xor	logical
or	logical

Comparison operators, like those you use in IF statements, also have a precedence.

#9. What's the difference between PHP 5 and PHP 6

As of the writing of this book, PHP 5 is the latest production version of PHP. But PHP 6 is being worked on and is available for developers here: `http://snaps.php.net/`.

The differences between PHP 4 and 5 are much greater than between 5 and 6. In many ways, 6 offers a refinement of the object-oriented features introduced in 5. Other changes include more support for XML and Unicode.

More Unicode support

Suppose your application needed to output text in Greek.

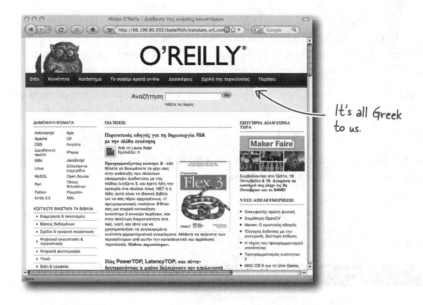

It's all Greek to us.

Consider the kinds of things you sometimes have to do with strings, such as needing to know the length of them or sorting them. It's straightforward in English, but when you are working with characters in other languages, string operations become more complicated.

Unicode is a set of characters and technologies to encode them. In Unicode, the Greek character that looks like a triangle has a specific numeric value assigned to it, along with other characters in other languages. Unicode is a standard, which means it receives wide support from major technology providers. In Unicode, every character has a unique number, no matter what language, program, or platform is used. Before the advent of PHP 5, PHP had no real support for Unicode. PHP 6 has enhanced support for Unicode strings in its functions and functions built specifically for creating and decoding Unicode.

#9. What's the difference between PHP 5 and PHP 6 (cont.)

OO refinements, XML support, and other changes

PHP 5 offers an object-oriented programming model but still allows for the mingling of procedural style. PHP 6 moves farther into the object-oriented realm. One of the biggest changes here is that dynamic functions will no longer be permitted to be called with static syntax. There are any number of small, but important, changes to the way PHP handles its OO code that make it more consistent with other OO languages such as C++ and Java.

None of the code in this book uses dynamic functions, so you don't have to worry about any of the code not working in PHP 6.

A few other changes are:

- Both XML Reader and XML Writer will be extensions in PHP 6, making it easier to work with XML files.

- The `register_globals`, `magic_quotes`, and `safe_mode` options in the `php.ini` file will no longer be available.

- The ereg extension, which provided another way to build regular expressions, is removed. Fortunately, the same `preg_match()` code covered in this book will be the main way to build regular expressions in PHP 6.

- A 64-bit integer type will be added.

- Multi-dimensional arrays will be able to use `foreach`.

- Version 6 of PHP is, more than anything, a version that cleans up and refines the language.

#10. Reusing other people's PHP

It's not always necessary to write your own PHP code from scratch. Sometimes it's best to reuse someone else's. The following are several popular and highly successful PHP-based software packages that you should consider using if you have a need and would prefer not reinventing the PHP wheel. Oh, and they're all free!

Drupal

One of the most impressive PHP projects to date, Drupal is a powerful content management system that can be used to build just about any kind of content-driven web site. NASA, The Onion, the Electronic Frontier Foundation, and Popular Science all use Drupal for their web sites. It's flexible enough to build just about anything that is heavy on content. Check it out at `http://drupal.org/`.

phpBB

A category killer in the realm of online message boards (forums), phpBB is easy-does-it when it comes to building your own forum. It is extremely flexible and hard to beat at the one thing it does so well—managing threaded discussions. Find out more at `http://www.phpbb.com/`.

Coppermine Gallery

If image hosting is what you have in mind, Coppermine Gallery is the PHP application to check out. In an era of Flickr, Photobucket, Shutterfly, and Snapfish, hosting your own photo library sounds downright quaint. But with control comes power, and if you want complete control over your photos, take a look at Coppermine Gallery at `http://coppermine-gallery.net/`.

WordPress

One of the heavy hitters in the blogosphere, WordPress is PHP-based blogging software that lets you build and maintain a blog with minimal hassle. There's lots of competition out there, so you might want to do some exploring, but you could do worse than to pick WordPress if you're launching a blog. Download it at `http://wordpress.org/`.

Another really nice PHP-based content management system is Joomla!, which you can learn about at http://www.joomla.org/.

Hold it right there! Why bother learning PHP if you're just going to reuse other people's code?

Because reusing code isn't always as simple as it sounds—sometimes it requires PHP skills.

Many PHP software packages still require customization, and that often requires some strong PHP development skills. Not only that, but you may elect to only reuse a small component of someone else's code, or not reuse it at all. Either way, by having PHP knowledge, you have options, and options are always a good thing!

A place to play

He thinks I'm a great cook, but I hide all my mistakes before he sees them.

You need a place to practice your newfound PHP and MySQL skills without making your data vulnerable on the web. It's always a good idea to have a safe place to develop your PHP application before unleashing it on the world (wide web). This appendix contains instructions for installing a web server, MySQL, and PHP to give you a safe place to work and practice.

Create a PHP development environment

Before you can put your finished application on the web, you need to develop it. And it's never a good idea to develop your web application on the Web where everyone can see it. You can **install software locally that lets you build and test your application before you put it online.**

There are three pieces of software you'll need on your local computer to build and test PHP applications:

1. A web server

2. PHP

3. A MySQL database server

PHP isn't a server; it's a set of rules that your web server understands that allow it to interpret PHP code. Both the web server and the MySQL server are executable programs that run on a computer.

Keep in mind that we're talking about setting up your **local computer** as a web server for PHP development. You'll ultimately still need an **online web server** to upload your finished application to so that other people can access and use it.

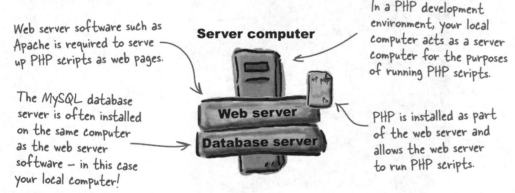

Web server software such as Apache is required to serve up PHP scripts as web pages.

The MySQL database server is often installed on the same computer as the web server software — in this case your local computer!

Server computer

Web server

Database server

In a PHP development environment, your local computer acts as a server computer for the purposes of running PHP scripts.

PHP is installed as part of the web server and allows the web server to run PHP scripts.

Find out what you have

Before trying to install any of the pieces of the PHP development puzzle, your best bet is to first evaluate what you already have installed. Let's take a look at the three pieces and how you can tell what's already on your system.

The platform of your local computer makes a big difference when it comes to what's already installed. For example, Mac OS X has a web server installed by default, while most Windows computers do not.

NOTE: This appendix covers Windows 2000, XP, Vista, Windows Server 2003/2008, or other 32-bit Windows operating system. For Mac, it applies to Mac OS X 10.3.x or newer.

Do you have a web server?

You probably already have a web server if you are using a newer PC or
Mac. To find out quickly on either system, open a browser window and
type `http://localhost` in the address bar. If you get an introductory
page, that means your web browser is alive and well on your local machine.

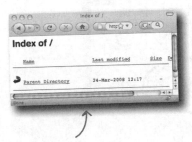

If you have a Mac or Windows
machine with the Apache web
server installed, you might see
something like this.

If you have a Windows
machine with IIS, you might
see something like this.

Do you have PHP? Which version?

If you have a web server, you can check to see if you have PHP installed very easily, as well
as which version you have. Create a new script named `info.php` and type this in it:

```php
<?php phpinfo(); ?>
```

Save this file to the directory your web server uses. On Windows it's typically:

```
C: inetpub/wwwroot/
```

On the Mac, it's usually something like:

```
/Users/yourname/sites/
```

If you try to open this file in your browser by typing `http://localhost/info.php`,
you'll see something like this if you have PHP installed:

Here's the version of
PHP you have installed.

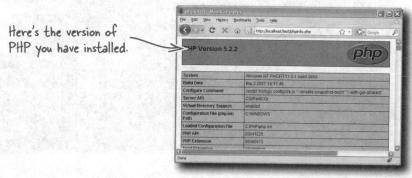

Do you have MySQL? Which version?

On Windows, you can tell by opening the **Control Panel** --> **Administrative Tools** --> **Services**:

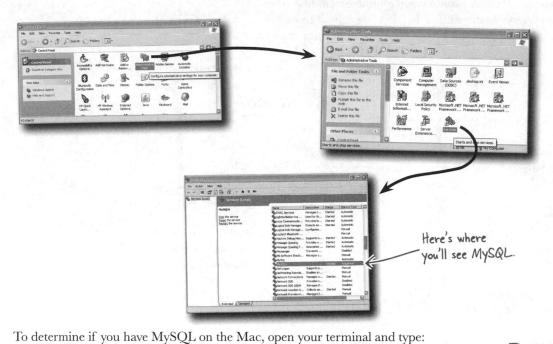

Here's where you'll see MySQL.

To determine if you have MySQL on the Mac, open your terminal and type:

```
cd /user/local/mysql
```

If the command works, you have MySQL installed. To check the version, type:

```
mysql
```

The MySQL Terminal is also known as the MySQL "monitor."

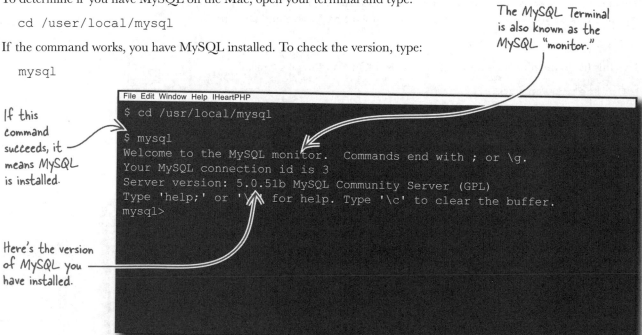

If this command succeeds, it means MySQL is installed.

```
File Edit Window Help IHeartPHP
$ cd /usr/local/mysql

$ mysql
Welcome to the MySQL monitor.  Commands end with ; or \g.
Your MySQL connection id is 3
Server version: 5.0.51b MySQL Community Server (GPL)
Type 'help;' or '\h' for help. Type '\c' to clear the buffer.
mysql>
```

Here's the version of MySQL you have installed.

Start with the Web Server

Depending on the version of Windows you have, you can download Microsoft's Internet Information Server (IIS), or the open source Apache web server. If you need a server on the Mac, you should probably go with Apache since it's already installed.

Here's a brief overview of installing Apache on Windows:

Head over to `http://httpd.apache.org/download.cgi`

If you're using Windows, we suggest you download the `apache_2.2.9-win32-x86-no_ssl-r2.msi` file. This will automatically install Apache for you after you download and double click it.

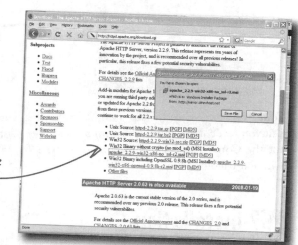

Grab this version and double click on it after you've downloaded it.

Next you'll see the Installation Wizard. Most of the instructions are straightforward, and you can accept the default choices.

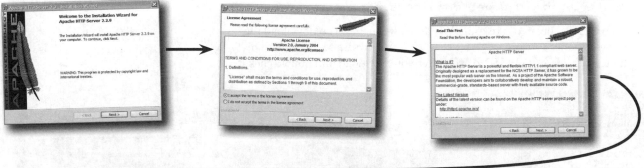

Choose the domain your computer is on. If you don't have one, you can enter `localhost`.

Your best bet is to choose the typical installation option.

You can usually choose the default directory for installation of the software.

Apache installation... concluded

You're nearly finished. Click ***Install*** and wait a minute or so for the installation to complete. That's it!

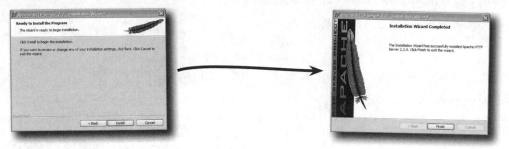

Your web server is set to start automatically when you start up your computer. But you can control it using the ***Services*** panel by stopping and starting it in the the ***Control Panel*** --> ***Administrative Tools*** --> ***Services*** dialogue where it will now show up.

PHP installation

Go to `http://www.php.net/downloads.php`.

Just as with Apache, if you're using Windows, we suggest you download the Windows installer version, `php-5.2.6-win32-installer.msi`. This will automatically install PHP for you after you download and double click it.

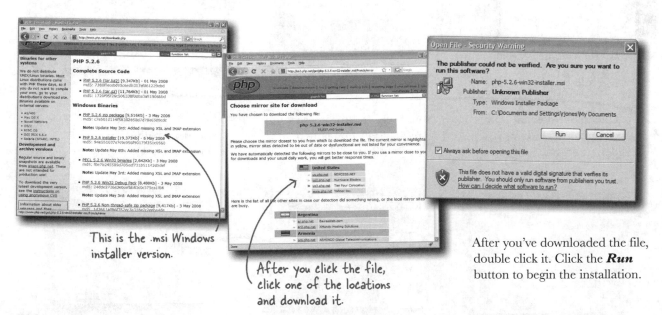

This is the .msi Windows installer version.

After you click the file, click one of the locations and download it.

After you've downloaded the file, double click it. Click the ***Run*** button to begin the installation.

PHP installation steps

It starts with a basic Setup.

Accept the License Agreement to continue.

Selecting the default installation folder is usually a good idea.

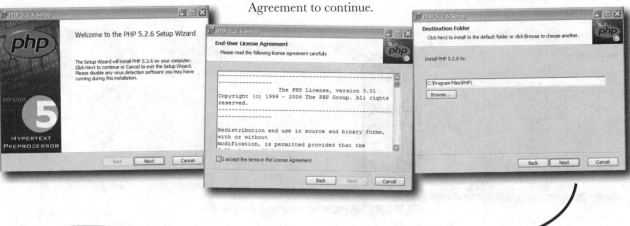

Careful on this screen. If you're using Apache, select the right version. If you're using IIS, you will probably select the IISAPI module. Check with your particular software to determine exactly what you need.

This next screen is also tricky. You need to scroll down under **Extensions** and choose **MySQLi**. This will enable you to use the built in PHP mysqli functions that we use throughout this book!

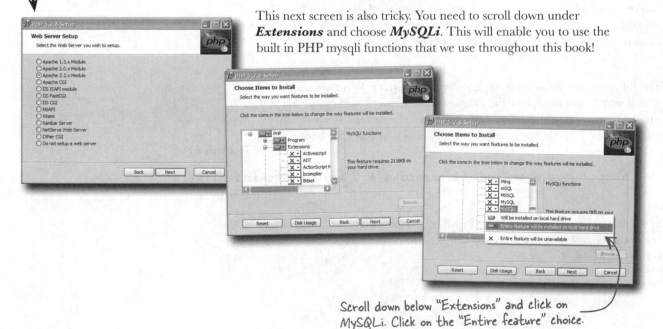

Scroll down below "Extensions" and click on MySQLi. Click on the "Entire feature" choice.

PHP installation steps... concluded

That's it. Click on **Install**, then **Done** to close the installer.

Now try looking at your `http://localhost/info.php` file in your web browser and see what version is showing up.

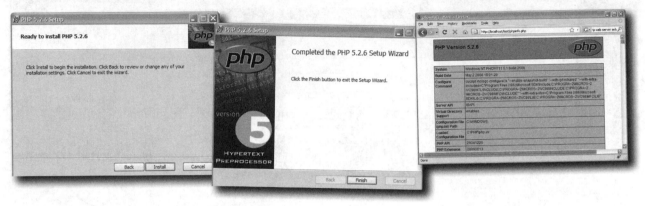

Installing MySQL

Instructions and Troubleshooting

You still need MySQL, so let's work through the downloading and installing of MySQL. The official name for the free version of the MySQL RDBMS server these days is **MySQL Community Server**.

The following is a list of steps for installing MySQL on Windows and Mac OS X. This is **not** meant to replace the excellent instructions found on the MySQL web site, and **we strongly encourage you to go there and read them!** For much more detailed directions, as well as a troubleshooting guide, go here:

Get version 6.0 or newer.

        http://dev.mysql.com/doc/refman/6.0/en/windows-installation.html

You'll also like the MySQL Query Browser we talked about. There, you can type your queries and see the results inside the software interface, rather than in a console window.

Steps to Install MySQL on Windows

1 Go to:

`http://dev.mysql.com/downloads/mysql/6.0.html`

and click on the **MySQL Community Server** download button.

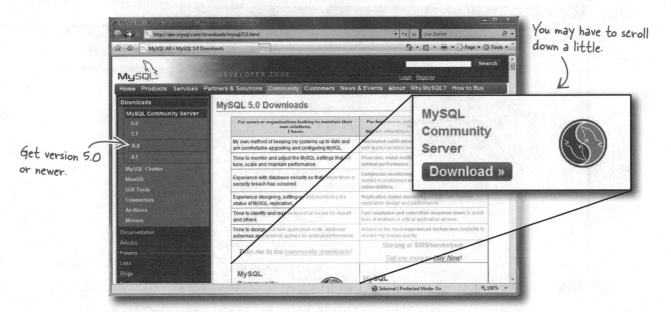

You may have to scroll down a little.

Get version 5.0 or newer.

2 Choose **Windows** from the list.

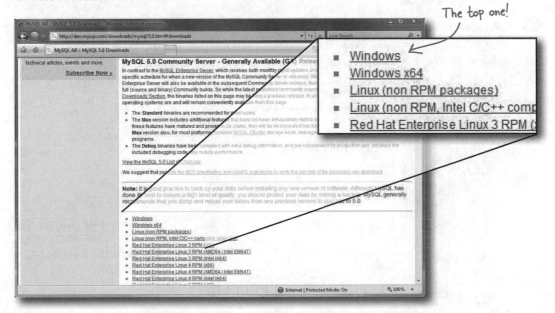

The top one!

Download your installer

❸ Under ***Windows downloads***, we recommend that you choose the `Windows ZIP/Setup.EXE` option because it includes an installer that greatly simplifies the installation. Click on ***Pick a Mirror***.

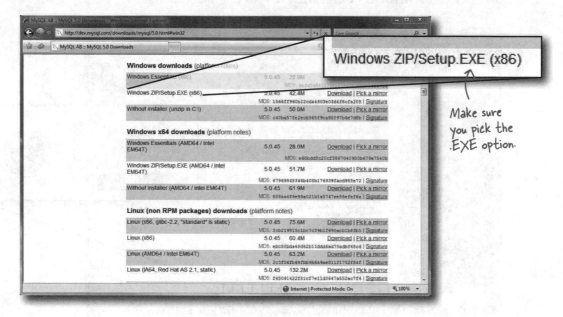

Make sure you pick the .EXE option.

❹ You'll see a list of locations that have a copy you can download; choose the one closest to you.

❺ When the file has finished downloading, double-click to launch it. At this point, you will be walked through the installation with the ***Setup Wizard***. Click the ***Next*** button.

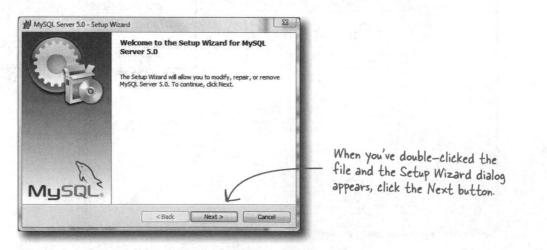

When you've double-clicked the file and the Setup Wizard dialog appears, click the Next button.

Pick a destination folder

6 You'll be asked to choose ***Typical***, ***Complete***, or ***Custom***. For our purposes in this book, choose ***Typical***.

You can change the location on your computer where MySQL will be installed, but we recommend that you stay with the default location:

`C:\Program Files\MySQL\MySQL Server 6.0`

Click the ***Next*** button.

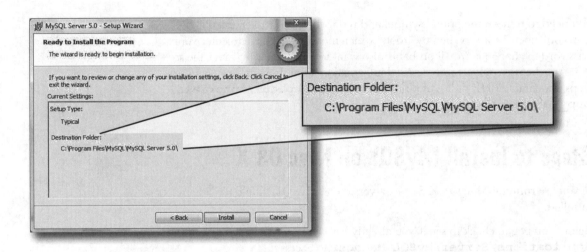

Click "Install" and you're done!

7 You'll see the ***Ready to Install*** dialog with the ***Destination Folder*** listed. If you're happy with the destination directory, click ***Install***. Otherwise, go ***Back***, ***Change*** the directory, and return here.

Click ***Install***.

Enabling PHP on Mac OS X

PHP is included on Macs with OS X version 10.5+ (Leopard), but it's not enabled by default. You have to access the main Apache configuration file and comment out a line of code in order to get PHP going. This file is called `http.conf`, and is a hidden file located down inside the Apache install folder.

You're looking for the following line of code, which has a pound symbol (#) in front of it to comment it out:

```
#LoadModule php5_module          libexec/apache2/libphp5.so
```

You need to remove the pound symbol and restart the server to enable PHP. The http.conf document is owned by "root," which means you'll have to enter your password to change it. You'll probably also want to tweak the `php.ini` file so that Apache uses it. For more detailed information about how to carry out these steps and enable PHP, visit **http://foundationphp.com/tutorials/ php_leopard.php**.

Steps to Install MySQL on Mac OS X

If you are running Mac OS X Server, a version of MySQL should already be installed.

Before you begin, check to see if you already have a version installed. Go to **Applications/Server/MySQL Manager** to access it.

1 Go to:

> **http://dev.mysql.com/downloads/mysql/6.0.html**

and click on the MySQL Community Server **Download** button.

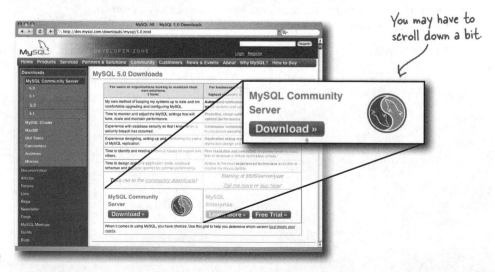

You may have to scroll down a bit.

2 Choose **Mac OS X (package format)** from the list.

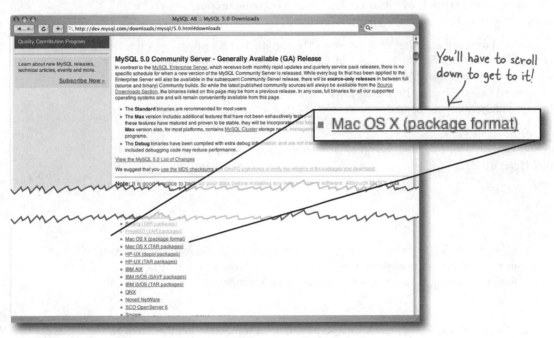

You'll have to scroll down to get to it!

3 Choose the appropriate package for your Mac OS X version.
Click on **Pick a Mirror**.

4 You'll see a list of locations that have a copy you can download; choose the one closest to you.

5 When the file has finished downloading, double-click to launch it. You can now open a Terminal window on your Mac and type:

```
shell> cd /usr/local/mysql
shell> sudo ./bin/mysqld_safe
```

(Enter your password, if necessary)

(Press Control-Z)

```
shell> bg
```

(Press **Control-D** or enter **exit** to exit the shell)

If you're using a GUI tool such as phpMyAdmin, check its documentation for how to access it once MySQL is successfully installed.

Moving from production to a live site

You've spent days or weeks working on your site, and you feel it's ready to go live. To move your PHP and MySQL site from your local computer to the web requires a little planning and a few specific techniques.

First, you need to make sure that the place your site is going has the same versions of PHP and MySQL you expect. If not, you may need to make your code to match what is available. Most of the code in this book is portable, but you may need to retrofit your PHP code back to the mysql functions, as opposed to the mysqli functions we use in this book. If that's the problem, check out #1 of The Top Ten Topics (we didn't cover) for more information.

If the software on your live site is compatible, then moving your site over is simple. Here are the steps:

Your PHP files need to be FTP'ed to the web directory of your live site.

1. Upload the PHP files from your production server to the web directory on your live server. Keep the file structure intact, and make sure you don't lose any folders you might have created to contain your included files.

You need to get at the structure of your tables and the data stored in them. Here's how:

2. Do a database dump (which we'll show you in a moment) to get the MySQL statements you need to create your tables and the INSERT statements you need to move your data from the table on the production server to the live server.

Your SQL dump will give you the exact syntax of your CREATE TABLE statements and INSERT statements.

3. Log in to your live database where you can run the CREATE and INSERT MySQL statements to move your data from your local site to the live site.

4. Modify any database connection code in your PHP files to point at the live database server. If you don't change this, your live code will try to connect to your production site and won't be able to connect.

Change those mysqli_connect() statements to point at your MySQL server associated with your live site, along with the correct username and password to get you connected.

Dump your data (and your tables)

You've FTP'ed your PHP files to the live server, but your data is still not on the live site's MySQL server. When your table is full of data, the idea of moving it to another MySQL server can be daunting. Fortunately, bundled with MySQL is the **MySQLdump** program, which gives you an easy way to recreate the CREATE TABLE statement that can recreate your table and all the INSERT statements with the data in your table. You simply need to use the MySQLdump program. To make a copy of your data that you can move to another MySQL server, type this in your terminal:

```
File Edit Window Help DumpYourData
$ mysqldump
Usage: mysqldump [OPTIONS] database [tables]
OR     mysqldump [OPTIONS] --databases [OPTIONS] DB1 [DB2 DB3...]
OR     mysqldump [OPTIONS] --all-databases [OPTIONS]
For more options, use mysqldump --help

$mysqldump riskyjobs jobs > riskyjobstable.sql
```

This sends the CREATE TABLE statement for the jobs table to a text file we just created named riskyjobsttable.sql. If you leave off the >riskyjobstable.sql part, then the CREATE TABLE and INSERT statements will simply scroll by you on the screen in your terminal. Try it to see what we mean. It's not very useful, but you'll see all your data fly by, nicely formatted in INSERT statements.

Once you've sent all that data to your new file using the greater than sign, you can grab that file and use the contents as MySQL queries at your hosting site to move your tables and your data.

Prepare to use your dumped data

Get ready to move your data by running a CREATE DATABASE statement on your live MySQL statement. Then run a USE DATABASE on your new database. Now you are ready to move your data from your production server to your live server.

Move dumped data to the live server

You've created a file called `riskyjobstable.sql` that contains
MySQL statements that create your table and insert data into it. The
file `riskyjobstable.sql` probably looks a bit like this:

riskyjobstable.sql

These are
all comments,
you can
ignore them.

```
-- MySQL dump 10.11
--
-- Host: localhost     Database: riskyjobs
-- -------------------------------------------------------
-- Server version      5.0.51b

/*!40101 SET @OLD_CHARACTER_SET_CLIENT=@@CHARACTER_SET_CLIENT
*/;
--
-- Table structure for table `jobs`
--
```

If you know there isn't a table
named "jobs" where you are creating
this one, you can ignore this command.

The
mysqldump
always writes
a DROP
statement to
start with
a clean slate
before doing
a CREATE
and INSERT.

```
DROP TABLE IF EXISTS `jobs`;
CREATE TABLE `jobs` (
  `job_id` int(11) NOT NULL auto_increment,
  `title` varchar(200) default NULL,
  `description` blob,
  `city` varchar(30) default NULL,
  `state` char(2) default NULL,
  `zip` char(5) default NULL,
  `co_id` int(11) default NULL,
  PRIMARY KEY  (`job_id`)
) ENGINE=MyISAM AUTO_INCREMENT=14 DEFAULT CHARSET=utf8;
```

Here's the
CREATE
TABLE
statement.

```
--
-- Dumping data for table `jobs`
--
```

You can ignore this LOCK
statement and copy and
paste starting at the
INSERT statement.

Mysqldump
makes
a single
INSERT
statement
that
inserts
every row
in the
table.

```
LOCK TABLES `riskyjobs` WRITE;
/*!40000 ALTER TABLE `riskyjobs` DISABLE KEYS */;
INSERT INTO `riskyjobs` VALUES (8,'Custard Walker','We need
people willing to test the theory that you can walk on
custard.\r\n\r\nWe\'re going to fill a swimming pool with
custard, and you\'ll walk on it. \r\n\r\nCustard and other
kinds of starchy fluids are known as non-Newtonian fluids.
They become solid under high pressure (your feet while you
walk) while remaining in their liquid form otherwise.\r\n\r\
nTowel provided, own bathing suit, a must.\r\n\r\nNote: if
you stand on for too long on the custard\'s surface, you will
slowly sink. We are not liable for any custard sinkages;
```

Take the entire text of the .sql file and paste it into your MySQL terminal or the query window of your MySQL graphical client (like phpMyAdmin).

This performs the queries in the file. In the case of the example on this page, the dumped file contains a CREATE TABLE statement and an INSERT statement. Along the way, the dumped file tells your MySQL server to drop any existing table and to LOCK (or keep anyone from using) the table while you INSERT the new data.

Connect to the live server

You've moved your PHP files to your live site. You've taken your table structures as CREATE TABLE statements and your data as a massive INSERT statement from the mysqldump and executed them on your live web server, so your data has been moved.

There's a small step left. The PHP code you FTP'ed to your live web site isn't connecting to your live MySQL server.

You need to change the connection string in your mysqli_connect() function to point to your live MySQL server. Anywhere in your PHP code where you call the mysqli_connect() function, you'll need to change it.

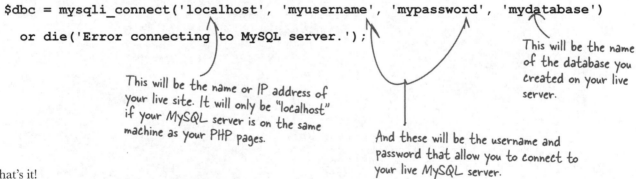

```
$dbc = mysqli_connect('localhost', 'myusername', 'mypassword', 'mydatabase')
    or die('Error connecting to MySQL server.');
```

This will be the name or IP address of your live site. It will only be "localhost" if your MySQL server is on the same machine as your PHP pages.

And these will be the username and password that allow you to connect to your live MySQL server.

This will be the name of the database you created on your live server.

That's it!

- You've copied your FTP files to your web server,
- you've dumped your tables and data into a .sql file,
- you've run the queries in the .sql file on your live MySQL server,
- and you've changed your PHP file to call your live MySQL server database.

Your site should now be live!

Get even more

I know I have everything any run-of-the-mill, heartbreakingly beautiful, fiendishly clever femme fatale needs, but it's not enough.

Yes, you can program with PHP and MySQL and create great web applications. But you know there must be more to it. And there is. This short appendix will show you how to install the mysqli extension and GD graphics library extension. Then we'll mention a few more extensions to PHP you might want to get. Because sometimes it's okay to want more.

Extending your PHP

This book discusses installing both the mysqli and GD modules on Windows. In this section, we'll show you how to see what modules you have, how to get GD or mysqli if you are missing them, and how to install them in Windows. Unfortunately, installing these modules on a Mac or Linux system is kinda tricky. More on that at the end of this appendix.

> **NOTE: This appendix covers Windows 2000, XP, Vista, Windows Server 2003/2008, or other 32-bit Windows operating system.**

If you're using Windows, you're in luck

You probably already have both the mysqli and GD modules on your computer. And even if you don't, adding them is relatively easy. We'll show you how to check to see what you have, if you're missing one of them, how to get it, and how to activate one or both modules.

It starts with checking to see what you have.

1 First, figure out if GD or mysqli is on your system. To do that, begin by navigating to the directory where the PHP extensions are installed. They are typically in the `C:/PHP/ext` directory, although the path may be different on your machine. Open the `ext` directory and look for `php_gd2.dll` and `php_mysqli.dll`. In general, these are installed with PHP 5 and later, and simply need to be activated. If you have them, great, move on to step 3. If not, go to step 2.

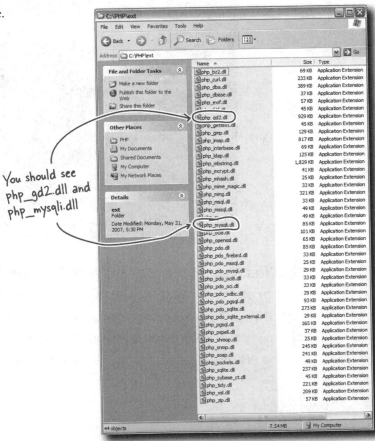

You should see php_gd2.dll and php_mysqli.dll

2 If you're missing either `php_mysqli.dll` or `php_gd2.dll`, you'll have to get it. Chances are you already have both DLLs on your machine, but if you don't, you can find `php_gd2.dll` at: `http://www.libgd.org/Downloads`. Download it and copy it to the folder `ext` under your PHP install. In our examples, it's located at `C:/PHP/ext`.

You can get the mysqli extension from MySQL.com. First, browse to `http://www.mysql.com`. Click on ***Downloads*** (along the top) --> ***Connectors*** (it's in the left menu) --> ***MySQL native driver for PHP*** --> ***Download*** `php_mysqli.dll` for PHP 5.2.1 (Windows) (Make sure this is your version).

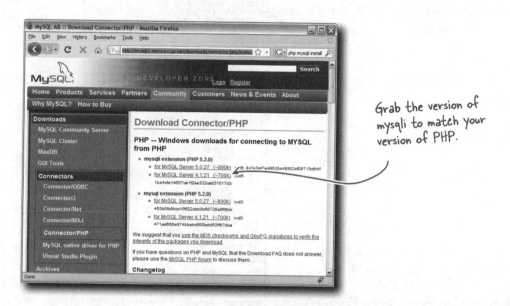

Grab the version of mysqli to match your version of PHP.

3 By now you should have `php_mysqli.dll` and `php_gd2.dll` copied to your `/PHP/ext` folder. We need to tell our `php.ini` file to use these DLLs. To do that, browse to the directory it's in, and open the file in a text editor.

Sometimes your PHP install ends up in the Program Files\PHP directory. Find your php.ini file and open it for the next step.

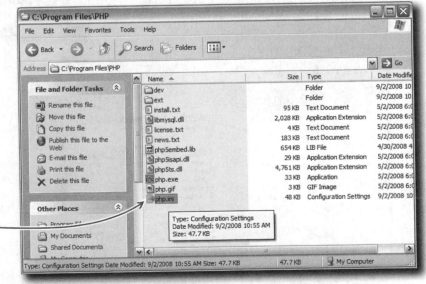

4 Dig through your `php.ini` file and locate the lines:

    extension=php_gd2.dll

and

    extension=php_mysqli.dll

If either of these have semicolons (**;**) or pound signs (#) in front of them, that means they are commented out. Remove them and save your file.

Delete the semicolons from in front of these two lines if they have them. Then save your file.

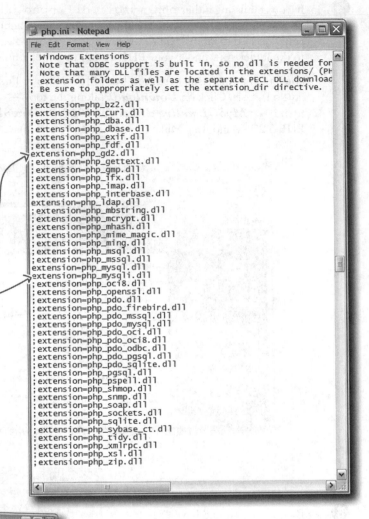

5 The last step is to restart your Apache web server so that the changes you made to your `php.ini` file will take effect. To do this, go to your Windows Control Panel, double-click on ***Administrative Tools***, then click ***Services***. You should see this:

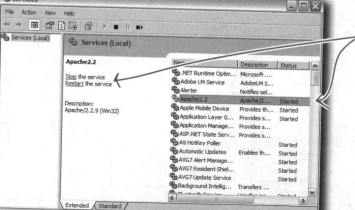

Select Apache and then click the Restart link.

Click the ***Apache*** service, then click on ***Restart*** from the menu on the left. The next time you try to use the GD or mysqli functions, they should work correctly.

And on the Mac...

Unfortunately, it's quite a bit more difficult. Adding modules on the Mac means recompiling the PHP source code and passing in arguments to add in the modules you want. There are simply too many possible combinations of Mac operating systems and PHP versions to include in this short appendix. There is a terrific guide that may help you install the GD module located here:

`http://macoshelp.blogspot.com/2008/02/adding-gd-library-for-mac-os-x-leopard.html`

It will only work if you have the right OS X version (Leopard), and the right PHP version (5). If you don't, or the instructions don't work for you, you may want to dig through the comments on that site and on the original GD website, `http://www.libgd.org/`, for more detailed and specific installation instructions for your flavor of OS X and PHP.

For help in adding mysqli to your Mac version of PHP, which also means recompiling PHP, we recommend the instructions here:

`http://dev.mysql.com/downloads/connector/php-mysqlnd/`

Keep in mind that this complication of installing the GD and mysqli extensions only applies if you're trying to run a web server on a Mac, such as a local development server. But if you're just using a Mac to write PHP code that is being uploaded and tested on some other server, it's not an issue.

Index

Symbols

! (NOT operator) 174, 221

$ (dollar sign) 25, 26

$_COOKIE variable 376, 382, 414

$_FILES variable 239, 252, 293
   upload errors 269

$_GET 276

$_POST 32–36, 55–56, 134, 276
   array 34
   providing form data to MySQL database 91–94
   seeing if form has been submitted 202
   superglobal 33

$_SERVER['PHP_SELF'] 200, 289

$_SERVER variable 342
   securing applications 300

$_SESSION variable 391, 395–396, 414

$i counting variable 264

$ metacharacter 572

$result variable 135

% (percent sign) wildcard 505

&& (AND operator) 179, 221

* (asterisk) 70, 130

-> operator 698, 700

-> prompt 119

. (period) 40, 41

/* and */ 335

; (semicolon) 125
   MySQL 64, 67
   PHP 25
   SQL statements 111

< (less than) 168, 221

<> (not equal) 168, 221

== (equal signs) 167

> (greater than) 168, 221

>= (greater than or equal to) 168, 221

<?php> tag 16, 24, 55–56
   spaces inside 305

<? tag 27

@ PHP error suppression 269, 288

\ (backslash) 46

\d metacharacter 572

\n (newline characters) 47

\s metacharacter 572

\w metacharacter 572

^ metacharacter 572

_ (underscore) 26

_ (underscore) wildcard 505

|| (OR operator) 179, 221

A

accidental deletions 149

action attribute 14

ADD COLUMN statement 232, 293

addemail.php script 126–131

Add Score Form Up Close 237

admin pages 272–278
   protecting 300
   score removal links 275
   securing application, authenticating Admin page
     with headers 306

alias 477, 499

B

F

H

I

N

O

object-oriented PHP 721–722

objects 688, 696–700
    accessing XML with 696
    collection of 697
    drilling into XML data with objects 698
    versus arrays 700

One-to-Many relationship 438–439

One-to-One relationship 438–439

ON keyword 476

open_basedir 724

operator precedence 727

ORDER BY clause 258, 293, 532–534, 545–546

OR operator (| |) 179

outer joins 480

overwriting files 252

P

pagination 548–554
    LIMIT clause 549–550
    page navigation links 554
    revising results 553
    tracking pagination data 551
    variables 552

parent table 438

passwords 348
    comparing 355
    encryption 352
        SHA( ) function 354–356
    HTTP authentication
        password encryption 360
    visual security 353

percent sign (%) wildcard 505

period (.) 40, 41

period metacharacter 572

persistence
    sessions plus cookies 409
    short-term versus long-term 410
    temporary 375
    user 383

personalized web apps 345–416
    community web sites 347
        security 372
    cookies (see cookies)
    logging out users 385–387
    signing up new users 365–371
    storing user data on server (see sessions)
    user log-ins (see user log-ins)
    (see also Mismatch application)

phone number pattern 568–569, 573–577
    getting rid of unwanted characters 592
    standardizing 591

PHP 55–56
    browsers 42
    building and testing applications 732
    checking if installed on server 19
    database connection strings 81–82
    difference between versions 5 and 6 728
    exception handling PHP errors 719–720
    extending 749–753
    identifying version 733
    installing 736–738
    mixing PHP and HTML in same file 27
    object-oriented 721–722
    rules 25
    securing applications 723–724
    sending form data as email 9–14
    servers 11
    switching between HTML and 193
    what PHP stands for 15
    working with HTML 3

PHP&MySQLcross 155–156, 291–292, 497–498, 655–656

PHP & MySQL Toolbox
    ! (NOT operator) 221
    $_COOKIE 414